John M. Striker and Andrew O. Shapiro

SIMON AND SCHUSTER

New York

How You Can Sue Without Hiring a Lawyer

A Guide to Winning in Small Claims Court

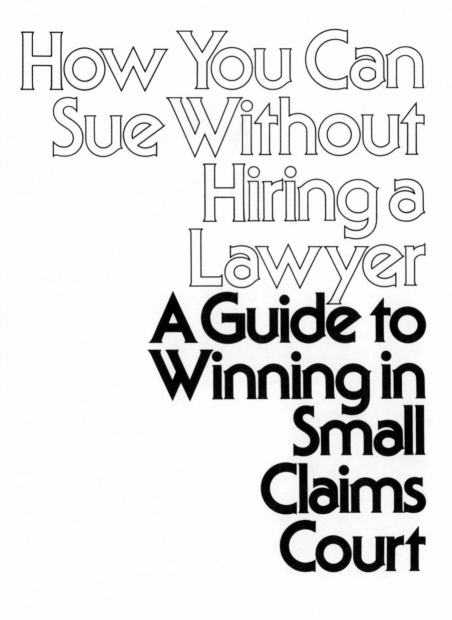

Published by Simon and Schuster
A Division of Gulf & Western Corporation
Simon & Schuster Building
Rockefeller Center
1230 Avenue of the Americas
New York, New York, 10020

SIMON and SCHUSTER and colophon are trademarks of
Simon & Schuster.
Designed by Irving Perkins and Associates
Manufactured in the United States of America

10 9 8 7 6 5 4 3 2

Library of Congress Cataloging in Publication Data

Striker, John M
   How you can sue without hiring a lawyer.

   1.   Small claims courts—United States—Popular works.
I.   Shapiro, Andrew O.   II.   Title.
KF8769.Z9S75   347.73'28   81-744
                                     AACR2
ISBN 0-671-25366-2

FOR MY SISTER SUSAN GLAZIER
WITH WARM AFFECTION
ANDREW O. SHAPIRO

FOR MY FRIEND OTHMAR REDLICH
WITH A SECOND GENERATION OF LOVE
JOHN M. STRIKER

Acknowledgments

Peter Schwed, our editor, worked closely with us on developing the idea for this book, as well as the final form it took. His encouragement and creative suggestions were most helpful.

Fred Hills of Simon & Schuster also deserves our thanks for listening to our plans, offering constructive criticism, and lending his editorial support during this project.

This is the third book of ours that Don Congdon, our literary agent, has ably directed through the New York publishing scene. We are grateful to him for his sound editorial sense and business judgment.

Diane Ungar, a bright graduate of Fordham University School of Law, assisted us greatly with the extensive legal research that went into this book.

For the seventh time since our graduation from New York University School of Law in 1968, we express our continuing appreciation to the staff of the school's law library: Margaret Aycock, Gerome Leone, Julius Marke, Michael Matthew, and Diana Vincent-Daviss. They filled our every research need fully, promptly, and thoughtfully.

Contents

A Word of Caution

This is our sixth book about the law. Like the others, it attempts to demystify the law—to make it more accessible to nonlawyers. Unlike the other five books, however, this one is more about *people and the law* than just the law itself.

You are going to meet some great people in the pages that follow. People like yourself: home owners, tenants, shoppers, taxpayers, car buyers, pet owners, bus riders, restaurant patrons, to name a few. They are not great because of wealth or status or even mighty achievement, but because they have exhibited one rare characteristic: gumption.

The people in this book thought highly enough of themselves and the rule of law under which they live to stand up for their rights—often against stiff odds and in the sometimes intimidating arena of the courtroom. You'll meet people like:

—Adele Ellis, who won back her $220 membership fee after the health club she had joined deteriorated into a massage parlor;

—Robert Weaver, who won $100 from J. C. Penney after traveling to the department store in vain to buy an advertised item that was out of stock;

—Dorothy Johnson, who won $500 from the Moonglow Club, because the coat-check room had carelessly lost her Persian lamb coat;

—Estelle Brown, who won $100.30 from the Fifth Avenue Coach Lines, because a rude bus driver mistakenly missed her stop;

—Herbert Harwood, who won $101.65 from his landlord after the building's central air conditioning broke down, forcing Herbert to rent an individual room air conditioner.

These are but a few of the dozens of determined citizens whose legal success stories are told in this book. Each one went to court rather than allow himself or herself to be taken advantage of. We think you will not only learn from the example set by these litigants, but also be inspired to vindicate your own rights, if necessary.

The cases recounted here are not one-in-a-million flukes. They are real court cases. More importantly, as we explain in each chapter, the decisions in these cases are based on broad legal principles or uniform statutes that apply to citizens throughout the country. Therefore, you too can invoke these principles if you have been wronged.

This book is not intended as a substitute for professional legal counsel. Should you conclude, after reading these chapters, that you have a substantial legal problem—either in terms of money or principle—you should consult a lawyer rather than representing yourself in small claims court. Only by retaining counsel can you receive the kind of personalized professional attention to your individual needs that no self-help book can possibly provide.

We have done much painstaking research and careful writing in order to explain your legal rights accurately. But the law is not black-and-white in every case: slight variations in facts can lead to different results; and one judge may interpret the law differently from another. Although it is unlikely that the key statutes and court cases reported in this book will undergo major revision, it is possible that some of the legal principles recited may, from time to time, grow outmoded. And the procedural rules governing your local small claims court may change (as you can readily discover by consulting the court clerk).

Therefore, we cannot predict results, nor guarantee a favorable outcome, to readers who use this book. We can only express our conviction that whether you win or lose in small claims court, you will gain something valuable from the experience: namely, the satisfaction of having stood up for yourself whereas, formerly, you might have swallowed your pride and let yourself be taken.

J. M. S.
A. O. S.

PART I

You and the Court

CHAPTER 1

When to Be Your Own Lawyer (and When Not To)

When is the right time to think about being your own lawyer? Any time you have a gripe that is too big to ignore but too small to justify the expense of legal counsel. For example:

—the dry cleaner returns your leather overcoat badly shrunken and claims that the material was to blame, not his chemical treatment; or

—you vacate an apartment in tidy shape, but the landlord won't return your $325 security deposit; or

—the bank, despite your recent stop-payment order, pays out on a $130 check you wrote; or

—a car dealer promises delivery of your new car within six weeks but refuses to refund your $500 deposit when, after ten weeks, the car still has not been delivered; or

—the neighborhood bully tackles your son in a *touch* football game, and you get stuck with a $110 doctor's bill for your son's sprained ankle; or

—six months before your bon voyage party, you're forced to cancel your contract with the caterer, who then refuses to refund your $450 down payment.

Had enough? These are but six of the hundred little headaches that afflict us all at one time or another. You can shrug

17

them off and absorb the toll they take—both financial and psychological—as a "cost of daily living." You can hire a lawyer and wind up spending more for professional help than your claim is ultimately worth. Or you can act out some of that pent-up anger you feel through constructive and profitable legal channels: become your own lawyer and sue your adversary in the local small-claims court.

Every state devotes at least one branch of its court system to folks like you who appear *pro se*, i.e., on their own behalf. It's usually known as small-claims court, although in some states, it's called "justice of the peace court," "magistrate's court," "county court," "municipal court," and so on. A small-claims court is ideally suited for the little-headache kinds of cases, where real wrongs have been committed, but the regular court system is too costly and time-consuming to use. Procedures are informal and fast in small-claims court, as we will soon see, and costs are surprisingly low.

Best of all, the watchword of small-claims court judges is to dispense *substantial justice*. Substantial justice does not mean nit-picking over legal technicalities; it means settling disputes expeditiously, according to the law, but with a constant eye toward basic fairness. "Substantial justice," confessed one judge recently in New York City Small-Claims Court, "means where you don't know what to do, you do something!"

So you don't have to be a legal eagle to fare well in small-claims court. It helps, nonetheless, to have some idea about the rules of the game—i.e., how the court works and what your fundamental rights are—before you start to play. Part I of this book ("You and the Court") explains how small-claims courts generally work. Each of the fifty states prescribes different rules for its small-claims courts, so no two states' systems are alike. We have, therefore, emphasized the characteristics common to most small-claims courts and pointed out, wherever possible, those questions you ought to get answered before using the small-claims court in your state.

Fortunately, there is a local expert ready, willing, and able to answer your questions. He is the *clerk* of your small-claims court. The clerk knows all the ins and outs. He can tell you, for example, the cost of various court fees, how to file a complaint, when and where to appear for your trial, and so on. Whenever you need up-to-the-minute local information on something we've alerted you to in the pages to come, by all means call or visit the clerk of your local small-claims court. Part of his job is to inform you and guide you in this unique "people's court." (To telephone the clerk, look in your directory under listings for local or county government. There you should find a listing for the lowest-level trial court—it may even be listed as "Small-Claims Court." Call and ask for the small-claims court clerk.)

In Part II ("You and the Law"), we turn from procedure to substance. There you will learn about your basic rights when confronted by a wide variety of legal problems: breach of contract, assault and battery, bothersome neighbors, stubborn insurance companies, defective products, liars, and just plain SOBs, to name but a few. Our discussion is down-to-earth, as is the court where you will be representing yourself. Instead of lecturing you on legal theory, we try in each chapter to get down to cases—to relate the actual case histories of other lawyers-for-a-day, just like you, who chose to vindicate their rights in court. These cases are not flukes; they rest on well-established legal principles, which we show you how to take advantage of. We hope that you will find these legal success stories inspiring as well as instructive. (Who knows, some day your case history might appear in a revised edition of this book!)

Before proceeding further, a friendly caution is in order. As much as you might want to sue someone on your own, don't overestimate your abilities or underestimate the size of your case. Some cases are simply too big for you to handle or for small-claims court to accommodate. In such a case you would be well advised to consult a lawyer. For example, you will learn about personal injury lawsuits in chapter 17. While minor personal injuries belong in small-claims court, major cases can easily involve tens or even hundreds of thousands of dollars. If so, you'll need professional legal counsel, and you'll no doubt be heading for a much higher branch of the court system than small-claims court. We trust that you will learn enough about the law in Part II to realize not only when you can be your own lawyer, but also when, if you represent yourself, you will wind up with a fool for a client.

CHAPTER

Do You Have a Case?

There is no point in suing someone if you have no case. You'll only waste your time—not to mention the defendant's and the court's—and in the end, your case will be dismissed. Some cases, no matter how clear an injury is involved, are simply losers; not even a lawyer in a three-piece suit could win them. Why? Because the law doesn't right all wrongs—only those for which the person (or business) you're suing is legally responsible.

Take a case in point. Let's say that during a particularly strong thunderstorm, a tree growing on your next-door neighbor's property is blown over. It falls on your garage, causing $880 damage to the roof. Clearly, you have suffered a loss, and visions of a lawsuit against your neighbor dance in your head.

But if you sue your neighbor for $880, you will most likely be able to prove only two things:

1. A tree grew on your neighbor's property near the border line with yours.

2. That tree was blown over during a storm, causing $880 worth of damage to your garage roof.

Unfortunately, proving (1) and (2) will get you nowhere. These two factors alone do not amount to a sustainable legal case. Why not? Because you have failed to connect your neighbor with the damaged roof in a way that makes him legally responsible for it. As lawyers would say, you haven't established your neighbor's *liability*—i.e., his obligation to compensate you for the loss you have suffered. You have merely succeeded in proving that an unavoidable accident occurred, and your neighbor cannot be made to answer for such a mishap.

Suppose we vary the case slightly. That tree on your neighbor's property was old and decayed. You had complained to him about the potential danger it created, as it was located so near the boundary line and your garage. Still, your neighbor did nothing to lessen the hazard. Then one day the ailing tree simply toppled onto your garage roof, causing $880 in damage.

Now you have a case, and you can establish your neighbor's liability for your $880 loss. If you sue him, you will establish in court:

1. A weak old tree grew on your neighbor's property near the border line with yours.

2. Your neighbor knew about this unsound tree and the risk it posed to your nearby garage, because you had warned him about it.

3. Even though he was aware of the risk, your neighbor took no reasonable preventive steps against it.

4. As a result of his carelessness, the dangerous tree finally fell, causing $880 worth of damage to your garage roof.

These four factors are what lawyers would call the *elements of your case*. Think of them as the legal legs on which it stands. If you establish all of them, a judgment for so-called *money damages* ($880 in this instance) will be granted in your favor; you have proven that your neighbor is liable to pay you that amount, based on the consequences of his misconduct.

Why are the elements of your case so vital to a courtroom victory? Because they are an abbreviated way of stating often complex legal theories. On the basis of these theories, judges reason their way to holding someone liable or letting him off scot-free. The theory behind winning the tree case derives from the law of *negligence* (see chapter 17); it would be summed up by a lawyer this way: If a landowner knows, or should have known, about conditions on his property that pose an unreasonable risk of harm to neighbors, and he fails to take any reasonable precautions to contain those conditions, despite his having had ample opportunity to do so, and, as a result of his lack of care, the dangerous conditions cause damage to a neighbor, then the landowner will be held liable to the neighbor for the damage caused.

Whew! Who but lawyers could spout off legal theories that ponderous? It's much easier, and far more practical, for you to concentrate on the elements of your case; these elements tell you exactly what you need to prove in court *in order to bring your case within the right legal theory* and thereby win. Throughout this book, therefore, we keep legal theory to a minimum (it really has no place in the down-to-earth atmosphere of small-claims court) and focus, instead, on the essential supports for a successful lawsuit: namely, the elements of your case.

You must be able to prove *all* the elements of your case if you expect to win. If one of them is missing or even weak, your case will be as wobbly as a three-legged chair, likely to collapse at any moment. For example, in our second tree case, suppose it came out in court that your neighbor *did* take certain reasonable precautions after you had warned him about the dangerous tree (say he trimmed several rotten branches and bolstered the trunk with heavy iron rods). Nonetheless, the tree was blown against your garage during a storm. Under those circumstances, you'll have a tough time proving element (3) of your case— namely, your neighbor's failure to take reasonable preventive steps. As a result, your chances of winning become extremely iffy: your neighbor is not, after all, the absolute insurer of your safety; he's bound only to act reasonably; and if he appears to have done so, the judge is likely to conclude that you were the unfortunate victim of an unavoidable accident.

Your legally defective three-legged case will be thrown out of court—*dismissed,* as judges say. So you can see how critical it is not to overlook a single element in your case. Each chapter in Part II of this book examines a different kind of legal wrong that may befall you: e.g., assault and battery, buying a defective product. The chapter then goes on to list (in a handy checklist format) the elements of your case, should you become the victim of that particular wrong. Your initial task will be to compare the circumstances of the mishap you have suffered with the legal elements outlined in the chapter. Ask yourself: Does my situation fall within all the elements listed? Given the facts as I know them, will I be able to prove that all the necessary elements exist in my case? In essence, what you will be asking yourself is: do I have a case?

When going through this screening process, be honest with yourself. If certain elements necessary to establish liability are missing, you probably shouldn't waste time suing; your case will only be dismissed as legally insufficient. Never assume that the judge will smile on you in your plight and supply from somewhere in the folds of his black robe the missing element in your case. Justice may be blind, but not toward the elements of your case!

CHAPTER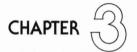

How Much Is Your Case Worth?

Suppose you have followed the process outlined in the last chapter: you have stacked up the facts in your situation against the so-called elements of your case. Your conclusion is that you do, indeed, have a case. Should you rush off to the nearest small-claims court and file suit? Not quite yet. You must first give careful thought to how much you can realistically expect to win in court.

To begin with, the only kind of legal relief generally offered by small-claims courts is *money damages*—that is, money awarded by the judge to compensate for your losses. Small-claims courts don't have the broad authority that higher courts do to grant other kinds of legal relief: e.g., divorces, divisions of property, injunctions against illegal conduct. So, unless your claim translates into dollars and cents, small-claims court is probably not the answer to your problem; you should consider consulting a lawyer to see whether suing in a higher court is worthwhile.

Assuming money damages are what you seek, how much can you hope to win? Initially, that depends on the so-called *jurisdictional limit* of the small-claims court you're suing in. "Jurisdictional limit" is legalese for the maximum amount of money damages you will be allowed to sue for. All states place a jurisdictional limit on their small-claims courts. These limits vary widely. For example, you can sue for up to $500 in New Jersey, $1,000 in Iowa, and $2,000 in Alaska (see below). Jurisdictional limits are constantly changing, so you should always check with your local small-claims clerk to make certain you know the current limit.

SMALL-CLAIMS COURT JURISDICTIONAL LIMITS
State-by-State Review

Alabama	$ 500	Montana	
Alaska	$2,000	(Justice's Court)	$ 750
Arizona	$1,000	(District Court)	$1,500
Arkansas	$ 300	Nebraska	$1,000
California	$ 750	Nevada	$ 750
Colorado	$ 500	New Hampshire	$ 500
Connecticut	$ 750	New Jersey	$ 500
Delaware	$1,500	New Mexico	$2,000
District of Columbia	$ 750	New York	$1,500
Florida	$1,500	North Carolina	$ 800
Georgia	$ 300	North Dakota	
Hawaii	$ 600	(County Justice Court)	$ 500
Idaho	$1,000	(County Court with Increased	
Illinois	$1,000	Jurisdiction)	$1,000
(Cook County		Ohio	$ 500
Pro Se)	$ 500	Oklahoma	$ 600
Indiana	$1,500	Oregon	$ 700
Iowa	$1,000	Pennsylvania	$2,000
Kansas	$ 500	(In Philadelphia)	$1,000
Kentucky	$ 500	Puerto Rico	$ 500
Louisiana		Rhode Island	$ 500
(Rural Justice		South Carolina	$1,000
of the Peace Court)	$ 750	South Dakota	$1,000
(Urban City Court—		Tennessee	$5,000
Small-Claims Division)	$3,000	Texas	$ 500
Maine	$ 800	Utah	$ 400
Maryland	$1,000	Vermont	$ 500
Massachusetts	$ 750	Virginia	$5,000
(on consumer		Washington	$ 500
deception claims—		(In some smaller counties	
see chapter 30)	$2,250	operating under older	
Michigan	$ 600	rules)	$ 200
Minnesota	$1,000	West Virginia	$1,500
Mississippi	$ 500	Wisconsin	$1,000
Missouri	$ 500	Wyoming	$1,000

What if the amount of money damages you want to sue for exceeds the jurisdictional limit of your small-claims court? You can still sue, but you will have to forgo the excess amount of your claim. Let's say you intend to sue a restaurant in Connecticut for losing your raccoon coat, valued at $1,000. The jurisdictional limit in Connecticut small-claims court is only $750, so your claim is $250 too high. You can sue the restaurant in small-claims court, but only for $750. You must then say good-bye to the other $250 part of your claim, which will be lost forever. (Don't expect to win a $750 judgment against the restaurant and then come back a week later to sue it again over the same lost coat, this time for the remaining $250. That's called *splitting your claim*, i.e., dividing up one lawsuit into multiple lawsuits so as to sneak each one in under the jurisdictional limit. The court won't let you get around the jurisdictional limit this way.)

Of course, you don't have to squeeze your case under the small-claims court limit if you don't want to. You can sue for the full amount in a higher court where the jurisdictional limit is greater. If you do, however, you'll probably have to pay for an attorney's services, because you may be unable to cope with the technical procedures typical of higher courts. You will have to ask yourself, therefore, whether the attorney's fee will wind up costing you more than the portion of your claim that you would have given up by suing in small-claims court. In the case of the lost raccoon coat, an attorney might easily charge $500 to try the $1,000 claim; if so, it would probably make more sense to lop $250 off the claim and sue on your own in small-claims court.

Aside from the ceiling set by the jurisdictional limit, how do you decide what amount of money damages you will sue for? There are certain rules for calculating the proper measure of damages in different kinds of lawsuits. In a *breach of contract* case, for example, the plaintiff is entitled to be put in as good a position—so far as the award of money damages can do so—as he would have occupied had the defendant performed his contractual obligations, instead of breaching the contract.

Say that a cabaret owner agrees to pay a professional musician $500 to perform at his club; he pays the musician $200 down, the remainder to be paid after the performance. Just one week before the scheduled performance, however, the owner cancels the engagement. As a result of this breach of contract, the musician could sue for $300—the amount that would put him in as good a position as if the cabaret owner had kept his promise.

Of course, the breach-of-contract victim is not entitled to wind up in a *better* position than he would have been in had the contract been honored. Suppose that after the cabaret appearance had been canceled, the musician lined up another job for the same night and earned $200. Then his true measure of damages would be only $100, and that's how much he should sue for. (Beside being unwarranted, it's embarrassing to sue for more than you deserve, only to have that fact exposed in court.)

There's one further catch to breach-of-contract damages: a legal doctrine known as *mitigation of damages*. When a contract is breached, the plaintiff is obliged to make a reasonable effort to mitigate, i.e., lessen the amount of, his losses. Our musician friend might be expected, therefore, to make some reasonable efforts to get substitute work. If he failed to do so, and this laxity was brought out in court, the judge might very well reduce the amount of damages awarded to the musician. The reasonable expenses incurred by the musician in trying to mitigate his damages (e.g., an ad in an entertainment newspaper) should be added to the amount of money damages that he sues for.

Besides breach-of-contract actions, perhaps the most common kind of small-claims lawsuit arises over damage to property. For example, someone carelessly rams his motor boat into your sailboat, or the moving company drops your TV set. In such situations you will be suing on the grounds of so-called *negligence* (see chapter 17). How much should you sue for?

Generally speaking, your measure of damages is the amount of money it would take to restore your property to the condition it was in just before the accident occurred. Suppose someone sideswipes your car, badly denting the doors on one side. A body shop tells you that it will charge $650 to repair the damage. You would, therefore, sue for that amount.

There's a twist here, though, similar to the breach-of-contract situation (where you can't wind up in a better position than you would have been in had the contract been kept). In a property damage case, you can't recover more than the *fair market value* of the property immediately before the accident. If the cost of restoring the property exceeds its fair market value, you'll unfortunately have to settle for the latter amount.

For example, your car that was sideswiped happened to be a gas-guzzling, ten-year-old, purple Cadillac sedan, with a fair market value of maybe $250. You're in no position, therefore, to sue for $650 to repair the dented doors, because that amount is $400 more than the car's fair market value. You'll be limited to suing for $250.

To drive this point home, let's assume that your Caddy was not merely sideswiped, but totally demolished. You know that to replace it, a good used car will cost you at least $1000. Can you sue for that amount on the theory that $1000 is how much it will cost to replace what you've lost? No, because the *replacement value* of what you've been deprived of is more than its fair market value. So once again, you'll have to content yourself with suing for $250, even though you know how well-tuned and spiffy you kept that old Caddy and how impossible it will be for you to replace it with any vehicle (short of a ten-speed bike) for a measly $250.

Of course, don't gyp yourself by suing for some bargain-basement figure as the fair market value. You're entitled to claim that the Caddy really had a market value of maybe $400 or $500, especially if you can present witnesses who will attest to its mint condition. Maybe you had the car repainted recently and a new transmission installed. Such expenditures probably upgraded the car's value, which should be reflected in the amount you sue for.

There are many other kinds of injuries for which you can seek money damages in small-claims court. Take personal injury cases, for instance, where someone negligently injures you (see chapter 17). As a result, you have to go to the doctor, buy prescription medicines, rent crutches, and so on. Include the cost of each such item in the amount you sue for. And don't overlook the fact that you were forced to miss time from work; if you lost pay as a direct result of having to recuperate, add the lost pay onto the money damages you seek.

There's also the matter of what the law calls *pain and suffering*. Every personal injury involves a certain amount of pain. Legally, you can put a price tag on this pain, or at least try to. Although you shouldn't blow this item out of all proportion to the injury involved—as lawyers routinely do—don't be afraid to add a reasonable sum to your money damages as compensation for your pain and suffering. To the extent that you've incurred substantial medical costs, your claim of damages for pain and suffering is likelier to receive a sympathetic hearing from the judge. Your claim will lose credibility, though, if it's based solely on your subjective testimony as to how much you have suffered.

What other kinds of harm can you place a price tag on in small-claims court? One you might not think of is *mental distress*. If someone willfully causes you to feel extreme humiliation or anxiety—for example, a bill collector, landlord, or insurance adjuster—you can place a reasonable dollar value on the distress he has caused (see chapters 20, 24, and 33).

Another item you can collect money damages for is *injury to your reputation*. If someone exposes you to scorn and ostracism by telling lies about you, you can uphold your good name in court by suing the culprit for libel or slander (see chapter 34).

As a general rule, any injury or harm that is the direct result of the defendant's misconduct is a potential source of additional money damages when you sue. For example, if a bank wrongfully dishonors one of your checks (when, in fact, you had a sufficient balance in your account), and as a result you're denied credit somewhere, this loss may be compensated in court (see chapter 35). If you buy a defective product, and while it's being repaired you're forced to rent a substitute, you can recover your rental costs in court (see chapter 29).

In certain instances you can even sue for *more* than you've actually lost. How can this be? Because as we'll see in Part II of this book, there are laws that allow you to collect so-called *statutory penalties*—that is, amounts of money over and above your true losses (see chapters 26, 30, and 32). The general rationale behind such laws is to encourage consumers to vindicate their rights (when only small sums are at stake) and to deter certain kinds of misconduct.

One kind of damages that you generally *cannot* recover in small-claims court are so-called *punitive damages*, which lawyers sometimes call "sting money." Such damages may be awarded in higher courts, at the judge's discretion, when the defendant has engaged in some extremely malicious form of misconduct. The object of awarding punitive damages, when it is done, is to teach the defendant a lesson and to warn others who might be tempted to imitate him.

A final piece of advice is in order on the whole subject of how much to sue for: don't shortchange yourself by being too conservative in calculating your money damages. There's a good reason for erring a bit on the high side, if you must err at all: no judge can award you more than you sued for; he can award you less, but more, never. So don't cut your own throat. If you're not really sure about your true measure of damages (and often there is no hard-and-fast rule), sue for a bit more, rather than less.

CHAPTER

Who and Where to Sue

One of the biggest hangups in using small-claims court is knowing *whom* to sue. The problem is not so acute when you're suing a person, but if you're suing a business, it's often tricky to determine the defendant's true legal name. The importance of knowing that name can't be overemphasized: if you sue a defendant under the wrong name, any judgment you win will probably be worthless; it can only be enforced against the *named* defendant, and he doesn't exist. So extreme care must be taken to discover the defendant's proper name before you go to court and file your complaint.

Let's start with the easiest situation. When you sue a person, proceed against him under his full name, that is, the one he uses regularly to identify himself (e.g., Martin Granger, G. Kent Donovan). If you're suing more than one person, use the full name of each defendant.

Suppose the person who caused you harm was, at the time, acting as an employee of a certain business. For example, Mike, the parking attendant at Midtown Garage, smashed up your car as he was bringing it down the ramp. Your best bet is to sue the business that employs Mike, rather than Mike himself: assuming you win a money judgment, who knows whether Mike would have enough money to pay it off; chances are much better that Mike's employer will pay.

In general, whenever your loss is caused by an employee, it

makes more sense to sue his employer. Under a legal doctrine known as *respondeat superior* (that's Latin for "let the master answer"), an employer is ordinarily liable for legal wrongs committed by his employees as long as they were acting within the scope of their employment (as was Mike when driving your car down the garage ramp).

The most important thing to be aware of when you're suing a business is that the business name printed on a sign or a bill or letterhead is not necessarily the correct legal name of the person or entity that you intend to sue.

First let's take the case of a business that is owned by an individual (as opposed to one that's incorporated). In such a situation, you have to be sure to sue the owner in his own name, as well as in the name he uses to do business. For example, your friendly neighborhood dry cleaner loses the pants to your silk suit. Whom do you sue? Well, the name over the door proclaims "Ace Dry Cleaners." In reality, though, Ace is a sole proprietorship, owned and operated by one David L. Gonzales. Therefore, you should bring your case against "David L. Gonzales, doing business as Ace Dry Cleaners." (Just suing David L. Gonzales or Ace Dry Cleaners alone would not be good enough.)

If the business you're suing is a corporation, the situation is a bit different. You don't sue the person(s) behind the corporation as you do in the case of a sole proprietorship. How come? Because the folks who own or operate a corporation are shielded from personal liability. This immunity is one of the privileges that the law confers on people who choose to incorporate themselves as a way of doing business.

So whom do you sue when you're up against a corporation? The corporation itself under its correct legal name. (A corporation *can* be held liable to you, even though the persons behind it cannot.) Here again, don't be misled by signs or letterheads; the business names that they proclaim may not be the ones you should use when suing. It is entirely possible, for example, that Green Thumb Landscaping Enterprises is really owned by a corporation named Plant World, Inc. In that case, don't sue Green Thumb, sue Plant World, Inc.

Some of you may be thinking that all this advice may be fine, but how in the world will you discover the correct name of a business? By doing a little detective work. Understand that businesses can't just spring into existence without leaving a trail of official paperwork behind them, often in several different local and state governmental offices. (Of course, fly-by-night businesses may ignore all the official steps for going into business in your locale; if you're up against such an irresponsible operation, you'll probably have trouble trying to locate the real owners, let alone collecting on any judgment you win against them.)

Your task, therefore, is to track down the true legal owner or correct business name of the prospective defendant at the proper governmental office. Generally, you'll have several different offices to choose from. For example, persons or corporations operating under an assumed name usually must file a certificate of their true identity in the county clerk's office where they do business; a similar certificate often has to be filed at the municipal clerk's office where the business operates. Another governmental layer of offices that can be a good source of information are the business tax offices, local and state, where businesses must register and file their tax returns (e.g., sales tax, corporate tax, unincorporated tax, occupancy tax).

A third category of governmental offices to consult is that which handles licensing. In many cities and states, a wide variety of businesses cannot operate without first having obtained a license to do business and paid a license fee. Such licensed businesses and occupations run the gamut from auto repair shops, food markets, and parking lots, to therapists, building contractors, and chauffeurs. Finally, a special state office, usually that of the secretary of state, keeps track of all corporations doing business in the state, and all corporations must register, with that office.

With all these leads at your fingertips, pull out your telephone directory; turn to the listings under city, county, or state government; and locate the right tax, licensing, or clerk's office. A few phone calls, letters, or visits should yield the true legal identity of the defendant you intend to sue.

In 1979, New Yorkers got a significant legal break with regard to suing business defendants. The law was amended so as to aid New Yorkers who did not know the true legal name of a business person, partnership, or corporation. Now such a defendant can be sued under its true name or under *the name it uses to conduct business*—e.g., the name used on business signs, vehicles, sales slips, advertisements. Any judgment won against a business under its business name is fully as enforceable as if the business had been sued under its true legal name (see p. 61).

Where to Sue

Now that you've discovered whom to sue, the next question is *where?* It's not always a matter of simply marching down to the nearest small-claims court and filing suit. To avoid wasting time, you must make sure that you go to the right small-claims court. The best way to pinpoint this court is to seek the assistance of a small-claims court clerk (a piece of advice we imparted at the beginning of this book that bears constant repetition, especially at this point when things can get a bit dicey). Rules regarding where to sue a given defendant vary widely from state to state, so it makes sense to contact the clerk of the nearest small-claims court, describe whom you intend to sue, and ask where you must go in order to file suit.

The question of where to sue arises because the small-claims courts in your state serve different and distinct geographic areas. These areas vary in size. A given area may encompass an entire county, or, perhaps, just a municipality, or maybe only part of a municipality. (Exactly which geographic area the court serves can best be discovered from the clerk.) Because of prevailing court rules, there may be only one geographic area—and hence one small-claims court—where you can legally file suit against the defendant. On the other hand, depending on the nature of your case, it may be possible for you to sue the defendant in more than one area, in which case you will be able to choose the court location that is most convenient for you.

In general, the rules about where to sue can be summed up

thus: First, you can always sue a defendant in the county where he resides or where he is maintaining a place of business at the start of your lawsuit.

Second, in most states you can also sue a defendant in the county where the injury or harm you are suing over arose. For example, you rented an apartment in county X; that's where you would sue the landlord if he refused to refund your security deposit (see chapter 26); or you were assaulted in county Y; you'd sue the ruffian there. (Of course, you could also sue the landlord—or the ruffian—in the county where he resides; it's just that you have the option, if you wish, to sue in the county where the harm took place. The choice is yours.)

Third, in most states you can also sue a defendant wherever he was supposed to have carried out some agreement with you. For example, you sign an agreement with a landscaper, who agrees to build a small patio at your summer house in county Z. You make a down payment, but the landscaper never shows up to do the work. For this breach of contract, you could sue the landscaper in county Z where he was obligated to perform the services agreed on.

Given these general guidelines, you can see what basic factors determine where you can sue the defendant. When you contact the small-claims court clerk, just explain the relevant factors in your case and ask what your options are in terms of which court(s) you can file suit in.

CHAPTER

The "Settle-or-Else" Letter

At this point, you have a pretty fair idea of how good your case is, how much you can sue for, whom to sue, and where to sue him. So you're all set to file suit, right? Wrong! Although this may sound odd, now is the right time to avoid a lawsuit, if possible, rather than start one.

In general, it always makes sense to attempt settlement of your dispute without going to court. Who knows, your adversary may prove more accommodating than you ever imagined. Maybe he'll see your side and agree to some form of compensation that you'll find acceptable. You'll never find out if you don't ask. Even if you do discover that your adversary is a bit stubborn, perhaps you can still pressure him into a favorable settlement, given what you already know about his potential liability.

Seeking a settlement makes sense for other reasons as well. Just because you feel wronged and believe you have a good case does not necessarily dictate filing a lawsuit. Understand that a lawsuit is not a picnic: as speedy as small-claims proceedings are supposed to be, they're still time-consuming; as eager as you may be to vindicate yourself in court, don't discount the often taxing experience of being your own lawyer. Nor is the outcome of a lawsuit ever entirely predictable: solid though your case seems now, it may not stand up in court quite as well as you had expected, and regardless of what you think your case is worth, it may fetch only a fraction of that amount when the court renders judgment.

It is not our intention here to paint a gloomy picture—merely to disabuse you of any notion that suing is better than settling. It isn't—at least not always. Smart lawyers spend half their time trying to resolve disputes outside of court; so should you.

How, then, do you go about settling a dispute? First, at the risk of sounding elementary, get in touch with your adversary. He may not even realize that he *is* your adversary. For example, your next-door neighbor mounts spotlights on his garage roof, which shine right into your bedroom and deprive you of sleep. Potentially, you could sue him for creating what the law terms a *nuisance* (see chapter 13). But before you come anywhere near taking such a drastic step, begin by simply talking to your neighbor. Chances are, he doesn't even know that he's disturbing you. Explain the problem, and show a willingness to work out a mutually acceptable solution (one that lets him fulfill his need, i.e., burglar protection, while not interfering with yours, i.e., peace of mind.)

Second, if you've suffered some loss that translates into dollars and cents fairly readily, see if you can convince your adversary that he's responsible for making you "whole" again by compensating you. For example, you bought a food blender for $69 that is supposed to perform six functions: stir, mix, chop, puree, whip, and blend. But from day one, it has not worked in either the whip or blend position; clearly you're stuck with a defective product. If it's possible to repair the blender, see if the dealer is willing to do so, or at least pay for your repair expenses; or else shoot for a complete refund or an exchange.

Third, if your adversary appears to be uncooperative, write him a "settle-or-else" letter stating your grievance, demanding compensation, and threatening to sue for money damages if you don't receive satisfaction. For example, you were bitten in the left calf by your neighbor's German shepherd dog as you were walking past his house on the public sidewalk. The dog had bitten others before you, and your neighbor had been warned about his pet's vicious streak. Nevertheless, your neighbor took no reasonable precautions to restrain his beast. As a result of your injury, you incurred $84 in medical expenses and lost two days' pay ($124) when you were home from work recuperating. (There's also your pain and suffering to consider.) You complained to your neighbor and asked him to reimburse you for your losses, but he rebuffed you completely, charging that you had incited the dog's attack (a total fabrication).

Now's the time to send your neighbor a "settle-or-else" letter that may stir him into more of a negotiating mood. (Beside being of practical value, the letter also serves a specific legal function in some states, where you must at least make a demand on your adversary for payment before filing a small-claims case against him.) Here's a sample of the sort of letter you should send to your neighbor:

February 1, 1981

Your name
Your mailing address
City, state, zip code

John Q. Neighbor
Mailing address
City, state, zip code

Re: Dog Bite

Dear Mr. Neighbor:

As you know, on January 1, 1981, I was attacked without provocation by your 100-pound German shepherd dog and bitten on the left calf, while walking peaceably along the public sidewalk in front of your house.

At the time, your dog was not tied up or restrained in any way, although the dog had bitten other passersby on two previous occasions: namely, on August 1, 1980, and November 30, 1980. Following each of those incidents, you were warned by the victims about your dog's vicious propensities.

As a direct result of the injury inflicted by your dog, I have incurred medical expenses of $84, lost two days' pay totaling $124, and suffered great pain, for which, I believe, I am entitled to recover the additional sum of $400. I do not intend to bear these losses for which you should be held responsible. If you and I are unable to settle this matter by your compensating me for my monetary losses and my pain and suffering, I will be forced to take legal action by suing you for money damages in small-claims court.

Unless I hear from you on this matter no later than February 21, 1981, I will take appropriate legal action to enforce my rights.

Sincerely,
Your signature

After reading this letter, some of you may be thinking that it takes too long to get to the point: namely, pay up or else! You're right. The first two paragraphs merely recount things that John Q. Neighbor is undoubtedly well aware of: e.g., his dog is a German shepherd; it weighs 100 pounds; it was not tied up on January 1. So why belabor the obvious?

Because you're not writing the letter for Mr. Neighbor's sake alone. You're writing this letter with a different ultimate reader in mind: the small-claims court judge who will hear your case if you have to carry out your threat and sue. Put bluntly, you are engaged in what lawyers call *manufacturing evidence.*

Your letter to John Q. Neighbor will be admissible as evidence in small-claims court. There, it will serve as a cogent summary of your side of the case (a sort of minibrief), which the judge can refer to as a convenient way of tying together whatever other evidence, testimony, and witnesses you may have presented.

Bearing in mind that you are writing (potentially) for the judge as well as for your adversary, here are some basic pointers on writing an effective "settle-or-else" letter:

1. Type it. Don't write in longhand. Business is business, and this is business!

2. Keep it short and to the point. As a rule of thumb, bend every effort to make your letter no longer than one page. Remember the judge is a busy person; he's trying to get to the heart of dozens of different cases. Help out by not taxing his patience with a long letter. (Your letter doesn't have to cover every little detail; you'll have time to raise these in court.)

3. Review the background for your complaint. Briefly state the facts as to how the dispute arose and what resolution you

are seeking. Granted, your adversary may yawn, because you're just repeating things you've already told him on the phone. Let him yawn; he'll be more attentive when he sees the judge reading your letter in court. Never forget that the judge, unlike your adversary, knows zero about your problem. So take this opportunity to fill him in on the basics.

4. Be civil. Don't indulge in any name-calling or sarcasm; it'll only serve to antagonize your adversary (hardly a mood conducive to settling out of court) and undermine your credibility with the judge.

5. Set a deadline. Notice that the letter to John Q. Neighbor gives a specific date by which he must respond. Such a deadline is essential in a letter of this sort so that things don't drag on indefinitely. Of course, make sure that your deadline is a reasonable one (that way the judge won't get the impression that you acted precipitously).

6. Keep copies of the letter. Obviously, you're going to need a copy of the letter to bring to court with you and present in evidence. You should also keep a copy for yourself.

7. Obtain proof that the letter was mailed to your adversary and received by him. The best way to do this is to send the letter via registered mail, return receipt requested. That way you will have a post office slip attesting to the date on which you made a mailing to your adversary; you will also get a return postcard proving receipt of the envelope by your adversary. It will therefore be hard for him to wriggle out of the fact that you wrote him, stated your case, and sought resolution.

CHAPTER

How to Negotiate a Settlement

Okay, so you've sent a "settle-or-else" letter to your adversary. Now what? Wait for his response. Chances are he will respond —assuming he is halfway rational—because you've written him a blunt letter that poses the threat of legal entanglement if no response is forthcoming. (Of course, if you've made the unfortunate mistake of dealing with a total fly-by-night business or someone who laughs at the law, don't expect your letter to produce any miracles.) Should there be no response by the deadline set in your letter, then you should initiate contact.

Before there is any contact, however, make sure that you know exactly what you're willing to settle for. In some instances—when you've suffered a clearly ascertainable loss, and you believe you have a strong case—you may not be willing to settle for much less than was stated in your letter. You're prepared to discount that amount by a little—say, 10 percent—to save yourself the time and aggravation of a lawsuit; beyond that, however, you won't budge.

The "won't-budge" situation is generally the exception, rather than the rule. Usually, the amount of your loss is not clear-cut. You will recall from chapter 3, for instance, that establishing the fair market value of damaged property is not always a straightforward task. So there may well be doubt about the amount of money damages that you can prove in court. What's more, you may not be completely confident of your ability to establish in court all the necessary elements of your case. Some cases, where the basic facts are hotly disputed and there is much contradictory evidence, boil down to a question of credibility: Whom does the judge believe—you or your adversary? The outcome in such cases is often hard to predict.

When such doubts exist, you should realistically be prepared to settle for less than you might otherwise sue for. How much less? A quarter, a half, maybe as much as two-thirds less—it all depends on how shaky you feel about your case and how much you want to avoid the hassle of a lawsuit. Whatever figure is your bottom line—the amount below which you'll sue rather than settle—make sure it's fixed in your mind when you mail that "settle-or-else" letter, because it's entirely likely that you'll be hearing from your adversary soon after he receives your letter. You don't want to be caught hemming and hawing when he calls; you want to be clear in your own mind about how far you're prepared to go toward settlement, and where you will absolutely draw the line.

There is no pat formula for handling settlement talks with your adversary. Each case varies with the facts involved, as well as the parties and their goals. Nevertheless, we can offer ten tips to bear in mind when working toward a settlement:

1. Keep cool. It is often exasperating to talk with someone you intend to sue. Passions can run high on both sides. Don't let that happen to you, because ranting and raving is a sign of weakness, which is incompatible with your firm resolve to commence a lawsuit.

2. Beware of bulldozing. If your adversary is at all a tough guy, he'll try from the word go to overwhelm you with the weakness of your case: "You've got the facts all wrong," he'll bluster; or "You know you can't prove that"; or "You don't seriously expect to sue for that kind of money over this little incident, do you?" Hold your ground, not by getting into a shouting match, but by sticking to the facts as you know them. If there seems to be total disagreement over the merits of your case, calmly remind your adversary of the ultimate test: "Well, we seem to be pretty far apart," you might volunteer, "and if

you and I can't bridge the gap on our own, we'll have to let a court referee this thing for us; personally, I feel confident of the outcome."

3. Invoke some legal authority. Don't be afraid to display some of the legal knowledge you've gained by reading up on the elements of your case in Part II of this book. It's not necessary for you to start throwing out the names of cases and laws; that's a bit too highfalutin. Just show enough of an acquaintance with the basic legal principles affecting your case to impress your adversary with the logic and authoritativeness of your position. Bringing a familiarity with law into your negotiations keeps them on a businesslike level and, incidentally, intimidates your adversary.

4. Wait for a settlement offer. Don't jump the gun by bringing up the possibility of a settlement. It's always preferable if your adversary raises that issue first. By doing so, he clues you in to his interest in avoiding litigation (maybe he thinks you have a sound case or he just wants to save himself the time and expense of going to court).

Only if your negotiations seem to be going nowhere and there has been no talk of settling matters, should you broach the subject. This is not a sign of weakness as long as you don't betray eagerness to settle rather than sue. Therefore, raise the idea of settlement casually, as just another topic that ought to be looked into, *perhaps*, before negotiations are abandoned and courtroom formalities take over. "It seems to me," you might volunteer, "that we're not getting any closer to resolving this matter. Is there any point to our exploring the possibility of an out-of-court settlement or should we just let things take their course in court." This is enough of a hint for your adversary to pick up on, that is, if he has any interest at all in settling, rather than defending a lawsuit.

5. Reject initial settlement offers without hesitation. Sounds like a wooden sort of rule, doesn't it? Why reject an initial settlement offer if it's a good one? Because the next offer will be *better*. It's extremely rare that someone interested in settling opens with his best offer. He may *say* it's the best he can do, but almost invariably, he can top it, and will, if you push. So be prepared to jump right in after an initial offer (any hesitation

will show that you're tempted) with something like, "Oh I couldn't possibly settle for *that* little. That's just not a realistic figure in view of what I've lost." Don't sound uppity; just be firm and somber. You're trying to show your adversary that he'll have to do better if he expects you to abandon your claim. (Of course, you shouldn't follow this advice in that rare instance when your adversary turns out to be no adversary at all but an amazingly decent fellow, who readily assumes responsibility for what's occurred and makes you an offer that's too good to refuse. Lucky you, if you encounter such an upright citizen!)

6. Make a stiff counteroffer. After rejecting your adversary's initial offer, don't leave things hanging. Shoot back with a counteroffer that's somewhat on the high side. Never counteroffer with what you would realistically be willing to settle for. Because your adversary will always assume, if he has any savvy at all, that your counteroffer is not a firm figure (his initial offer wasn't, so why should your counteroffer be?). Therefore, you must build enough of a cushion into your counteroffer to leave room for further negotiations (these matters are rarely settled in one or two steps). Essentially, the function of your counteroffer is to signal two things: first, your willingness to settle; and second, your determination to hold out for what your claim is really worth or you will sue.

7. Defend your counteroffer. Predictably, your adversary will have the same nothing-doing attitude toward your counteroffer that you exhibited toward his initial offer. You can't realistically expect to persuade him to accept your figure, but you should nevertheless go through the motions. Emphasize the amount of damages that you have incurred; tick off any actual out-of-pocket expenses; even recount your pain and suffering, mental distress, and so on. Not that any of this woeful tale is likely to make your adversary agree to your counteroffer. Understand, though, that in this part of the negotiation game, you're not really arguing about your counteroffer, or for that matter his initial offer. What's truly at stake here is an as yet unknown figure that lies somewhere between his and yours— preferably closer to yours than his. By staunchly defending your counteroffer, you're signaling that he will have to come very close to it if he expects you to settle rather than sue.

8. Ask for the best possible offer. If your adversary seems to be hesitating about making any improved offer, back off and give him some breathing space. It's never smart to push for too much in one conversation; people tend to get defensive about making too great a concession. So if things seem stalled, try this approach. Suggest to your adversary that both of you "think things over" for a day (never allow more than a day; that's enough time to weigh matters, but not long enough to brush them aside). "Why don't you consider what would be the best possible offer you can make; let me know what it is tomorrow; I assure you that whatever it is, I'll consider it." Without committing yourself to anything (other than merely considering a better offer), you've invited your adversary to up his offer, but you haven't pressured him unduly.

9. Squeeze for the last dollars. Suppose your adversary comes back with what he calls his best offer. It's higher than his initial offer but not as high as your counteroffer. What should you do? There's no hard-and-fast answer. Your inclination may be to grab what's offered before it's withdrawn, and that may well be an accurate reading of the situation. But not necessarily. There is one last maneuver you can try if you feel that your adversary has come this far down the road toward settlement and is likely to take one more step to avoid a lawsuit. Explain to your adversary that while his offer is in the ballpark, it still doesn't adequately cover the losses you've incurred. "Rather than drag this out unduly, though," you would continue, "I'd be prepared to settle with you this instant for X dollars." Obviously, X dollars must lie somewhere between your adversary's latest offer and your original counteroffer. The X-dollar figure can't be more than a small percentage above your adversary's latest offer, because you're only trying to prod him into taking one more small step—not a giant leap. If he says okay, then *that's it;* you must be prepared to settle for that sum without any further haggling.

10. Get it in writing. Never settle for an oral agreement. Put it in writing immediately for both you and your adversary to sign. Once the settlement agreement is signed, you have a binding contract, which can itself be enforced in court if your adversary reneges.

Here is a simple model for written settlements, which you can adapt to suit your needs:

SETTLEMENT OF CLAIM

John Q. Neighbor and [insert your name] agree as follows:

1. On January 1, 1981, [your name] was bitten on the left calf by John Q. Neighbor's German shepherd dog, while walking on the public sidewalk in front of John Q. Neighbor's home.

2. As a direct result of the injury, [your name] incurred medical expenses of $84; lost two days' pay in the amount of $124 while recuperating at home; and experienced considerable pain and suffering.

3. In consideration of the losses suffered by [your name], it is hereby agreed that John Q. Neighbor will pay to [your name] the sum of $400.

4. This sum will be payable to [your name] in four equal installments, the first one to be made on the date of this agreement, and the remaining three to be made on or before the following dates: [supply exact dates].

5. It is understood that payment of the $400 under the terms of this agreement shall satisfy all claims that [your name] may have against John Q. Neighbor, arising out of the dog bite incident described above.

Your signature	Date of signature
John Q. Neighbor	Date of signature

This discussion on settlements has proceeded on the assumption that your adversary will be willing to negotiate with you immediately after reading your "settle-or-else" letter. Alas, that's not always the case. An adversary with a particularly tough skin may gamble that you're just bluffing—that you'll never carry out on your threat to sue. In that case, negotiations are not apt to progress very far, if they get started at all.

Faced with such a stalemate, as soon as the deadline in your letter passes, you should make good on your threat and file suit (see chapter 7). Following this step, your adversary may all of a sudden become more accommodating. What has happened to change his mind? Very simple. In the interim, a stranger knocked on his door, inquired as to his identity, and handed him a scary-looking court summons—the processs server cometh! After this sobering brush with the long arm of the law, things tend to even out between you and your once-haughty adversary. No longer are you pleading for favors; you've enlisted the state on your side. The recalcitrant adversary finds himself the defendant in a real-life dollars-and-cents lawsuit. Visions of court appearances, testimony under oath, and possible attorney's fees begin to shake his gruff confidence: You really did it; you weren't bluffing, after all!

The virtue of a formal court summons is that you now have something more immediate to bargain over with your adversary —namely, *forebearance*. You are in a position to forebear from dragging him into court on a fixed date. Obviously, you won't do so—and your adversary knows it—unless you receive something valuable in return. Don't be surprised if, two weeks before the date set for trial, your adversary calls, offering to settle with you out of court.

In that eventuality, you should still pay heed to the ten negotiating tips given above. In addition, if you do wind up signing a settlement agreement, notify the court clerk of this fact, and let him know that you won't be appearing on the date scheduled for your trial.

CHAPTER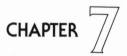

Filing Your Case

The deadline in your "settle-or-else" letter has come and gone. Yet, no out-of-court settlement seems in sight. It's time to carry out on the threat in your letter. Get ready for a trip to small-claims court, where you will file the necessary court papers to start a lawsuit against your adversary. Don't be intimidated by the prospect of a lot of legal gobbledygook and fine print. The legal papers involved in a small-claims court action are extremely simple.

If you're visiting the court for the first time, double-check to make sure you know where you're going. Call the court where you intend to file suit and ask directions. When you get to the court, locate the clerk's office. The clerk is there to assist you in filing your claim and handling other formalities.

To begin with, the clerk will supply you with a form to fill out. It's generally entitled something like "Plaintiff's Claim." (In case you didn't know, you are the *plaintiff*, the complaining party, and your adversary is about to become the *defendant*, the defending party.) The form calls for such straightforward information as your name and address, the name and address of the defendant, how much you are suing for, and the reason why you're suing. This last item does not call for a prize-winning essay; in fact, you'll have only two or three lines to state the nature of your claim. So don't go off on some highfalutin legal theory; stick to the bare-bones facts of your case.

For example:

"The Third National Bank failed to credit my account with a $185 deposit I made."

"The defendant landlord failed to supply heat during December, forcing me to rent a space heater for $100."

"Ace Contractors reshingled my roof in a careless manner, causing many new leaks."

If you have any doubts at all about how to summarize the gist of your lawsuit, ask the clerk for assistance.

When you've completed the form, return it to the clerk, who will then type it on an official complaint form. You'll then be asked to sign that form and pay a filing fee. Such fees vary from state to state, but all are relatively low (generally about $10). (Also, as you will learn in chapter 9, you can recoup your filing fee from the defendant if you win your case.)

After filing your claim, arrange with the clerk for a hearing date—i.e., the time when you will actually appear in court to try your case.

Your day in court will not be years or even months down the road, as is so often the case in our typically congested courts. Small-claims courts offer much speedier justice. Rarely will you have to wait more than a few weeks for a hearing date. As you will learn from the clerk, the small-claims court schedule is generally held during regular business hours, which will unfortunately require you to take time off from work. (New York City sensibly holds its small-claims court sessions during evening hours, starting at 6:30 P.M.) Select a hearing date that is most convenient for you.

The final thing you must arrange for is *service of process;* that's legalese for delivering to the defendant a copy of your formal complaint. This step is essential to your lawsuit. Unless the defendant has been served, the court will not gain jurisdiction (i.e., legal power) over him. As a result, no judgment can be entered against him. Service of process also satisfies certain basic notions of legal fair play; obviously, the defendant is entitled to be notified who is suing him, why, and for how much, as well as where and when he must appear to defend himself.

There are different ways in which service of process can be accomplished. Ask the clerk about the options available and which one is preferable in your situation. Perhaps the most common method of service is via certified or registered mail; a copy of your complaint is mailed to the defendant. This simple step can be handled by the clerk, usually for a fee of no more than a few dollars. Another common alternative is so-called personal service; a copy of your complaint is personally delivered to the defendant by a sheriff or other law officer. This form of personal service can cost as much as $20. (Incidentally, the cost of service, like your filing fees, can be recouped from the defendant if you win your case.)

CHAPTER

Preparing for the Trial

As any lawyer will tell you, there is nothing worse than going into court unprepared. It can be embarrassing to stand before the judge shuffling through disorganized papers or completely losing the string of your argument; worse than embarrassment, lack of preparation may spell defeat. You won't have to worry about such fatal lapses, though, if you get everything organized in advance.

Spend some time objectively analyzing the strengths and weaknesses of your case as if you were the judge. You have essentially performed this analysis already when deciding whether you really had a case (see chapter 2). To repeat the analysis always helps, because it redirects your attention to the critical *elements of your case*. Remember, they are the legs on which it stands. (Think of your upcoming trial as a courtroom demonstration in which you are going to show the judge how to set up a folding bridge table. You will show him one leg at a time, which is pretty much how you will present the elements of your case.)

Ask yourself, "What is the best evidence I can present to convince the judge about the elements of my case?" In Part II, we help you answer this question. Each chapter there contains a section entitled "Proving your side." That section suggests the kinds of evidence, as well as testimony, that are best calculated to establish the elements of your case.

After completing your mental review, collect all of the physical evidence that you will be bringing to court: for example, sales slips, insurance policies, bills, leases, agreements—in short, every relevant document that helps to establish the nature of a disputed transaction or to clarify your relationship with someone else. (Note that we refer only to *revelant* documents.) There is no sense ransacking the house for every little scrap of paper that is vaguely related to your case. If you present all that to the judge, he'll be distracted by insignificant details, while missing the gist of your claim. Don't forget that important piece of evidence that you "manufactured"—the "settle-or-else" letter—which summarizes all the salient features in your case.

Of course, not all evidence is in the form of a document. Sometimes the best evidence may be an object (e.g., a defective product like a broken clock radio) or a picture of an object (e.g., a photograph of a wrecked car). In this regard, think creatively: what sort of evidence would demonstrate a disputed point most convincingly? In chapter 11, we will meet a man who successfully sued a dry cleaner for ruining his draperies. To prove the degree of damage, the plaintiff brought into court not only the ruined draperies, but also a piece of the fabric from which they had originally been made. This dramatic before-and-after evidence won the day.

In deciding what sort of evidence to present, you may conclude that certain witnesses will lend support to your case. Sometimes a witness may be critical to the establishment of one of the elements of your case. Say you were suing for slander (see chapter 34). One of the elements of your case would be "publication": the fact that the defendant communicated a damaging falsehood about you to some third party. Obviously, one of the best ways to prove publication is to present that third party as a witness who will testify that he heard the defendant utter the falsehood.

While a witness can, thus, be essential to your case, don't make the mistake of assuming that the more witnesses you present, the stronger your case will be. A judge won't be impressed —indeed, he may balk at the waste of time—if your witness does nothing more than parrot what you've already said. When a witness is sworn in, it's not uncommon for the judge to inquire of the witness: "Do you have anything *new* or *different* to add to the testimony that's already been given?" The judge is simply trying to keep the case moving along without unnecessary repetition.

Throughout the chapters in Part II, under the heading "proving your side," we offer specific suggestions as to when a witness can help your case. At this point, some general guidelines are in order: First, select as witnesses people who truly *witnessed* something, for example, an accident or an assault. Don't call on people who have heard about the incident secondhand.

Second, use witnesses to bolster the reasonableness of your reaction to an event, if that reaction might be called into question by the defendant. Suppose you were suing your neighbor for creating a nuisance (see chapter 13). He could counter by claiming that you are overly sensitive and that the average person would not be offended by the conditions you're complaining about. Well, show him—and the judge—that other normal people share your reaction. Present a witness who experienced the nuisance and had a reaction similar to yours.

Third, a witness may be an expert whose opinion strengthens your case. In chapter 27, we'll meet a man who successfully sued a parking garage for damaging his car. The garage maintained that the cause of the accident was not the garage attendant, but defective brakes in the plaintiff's car. To counter this argument, the car owner called as a witness the mechanic who had serviced the car; this expert testified that the car's brakes were perfectly adjusted just ten days before the accident.

Fourth, don't ask someone to be your witness if you harbor any fears that he is unfriendly to you, your position in the case, or the very idea of having to go to court and testify. There are few things that can sabotage a case more effectively than a witness who turns against you in the courtroom (what lawyers call a *hostile witness*).

Fifth, review your case thoroughly with the witness. Make sure he knows exactly what you plan to prove in court and where you think his testimony fits in. Go over the testimony that he is prepared to give so that there will be no surprises in court; you don't want to be caught offguard with a witness who all of a sudden begins testifying to things you never expected.

Sixth, tell your witness the date and time when you are supposed to appear for the trial. Give the witness directions on getting to the courthouse and arrange to meet him there at least a half-hour early, so there will be no last minute slip-ups.

CHAPTER

Your Day in Court

Sooner than you think, your day in court will arrive. You're all prepared except, perhaps, for one nagging detail: what should you wear? Whatever you feel comfortable in is probably the best answer. By all means try to look neat and presentable—not outlandish or sloppy. Remember the judge has never met you before, and you will be trying to impress him with your credibility and your reasonableness.

Don't get the wrong idea about creating a favorable impression and show up in a three-piece charcoal suit, looking like a well-established banker or lawyer—unless of course, you *are* a well-established banker or lawyer! Such formal attire is by no means required in small-claims court, and if you're not accustomed to wearing it, chances are you'll wind up looking as if you're pretending to be somebody or something that you really aren't. Obviously, that sort of an impression will do nothing to enhance your credibility in the eyes of the judge.

Arrange your schedule so that you arrive at the courthouse well in advance of the time set for your trial. Your prior visit to the courthouse may not have prepared you for the hubbub that commonly precedes a small-claims court session. The hallway outside the courtroom often resembles nothing so much as a political convention, with little knots of people caucusing here and there, arguing, pleading, gesticulating.

One face in the crowd that is likely to stand out will be the defendant's. There is no reason to avoid him. On the contrary, you might want to seek him out and attempt a last-minute settlement—something that had eluded you in prior discussions. (A surprisingly large proportion of small-claims cases are settled in the hallway outside the courtroom.) If ever the defendant thought you were bluffing about suing him, he now knows that you're for real. Rather than take his chances before the judge, he may now be more willing than before to compromise with you.

Suppose you do hammer out a settlement in the hallway. Don't just shake hands with the defendant and stroll out of the courthouse. Both of you must still appear before the judge when your case is called—not to conduct a trial, but to inform the judge of the settlement that you have reached. Ask the judge to enter judgment in your favor for the amount that you agreed on in the hallway. (If the defendant is prepared to pay you right there in court, the judge can simply dismiss the case.)

Let's move from the hallway into the courtroom. If you've never been in a courtroom before, here's what to expect: About three-quarters of the room will be filled with rows of benches facing toward the front. The litigants waiting to try their cases, as well as the spectators, sit on these benches. The front quarter of the room is separated from the rest by a waist-high railing with a swinging gate. Trials are conducted on the other side of the railing. This area is dominated by an elevated dais, where the judge sits. (The dais is referred to in legal parlance as "the bench," so if the judge should ever ask you to "approach the bench," you will know which way to walk—straight toward the dais.) Before the dais are two long tables with chairs facing toward the judge. You and your witnesses, if any, will sit at one of these tables, while the defendant will occupy the other one.

Before the judge enters the courtroom—usually through a private door located at the rear of the dais—you will probably become aware of two court officials busying themselves with details in the front part of the room. One is the bailiff, who generally calls the court into session and maintains order; the other is the clerk who calls the various cases on the calendar and assists the judge in making each trial run smoothly.

Soon enough the clerk will call your case. That's your cue to walk up to the railing (with your witnesses) and pass through the gate. The clerk will tell you at which table to sit. He will swear you in by administering an oath, and the trial will be ready to begin.

In New York, there's an alternative to a full-dress trial; it's called *arbitration*. Basically, arbitration is an informal hearing conducted by a lawyer instead of a judge. Both you and the defendant get the opportunity to tell your sides of the story; then the lawyer-arbitrator renders a decision, which is as binding on both parties as a judge's decision would have been. (In one sense, the arbitrator's decision is more binding than a judge's, because there is no appeal from an arbitrator's decision, whereas an appeal can be taken from a judge's ruling.) At the start of each courtroom session in New York, the presiding judge will announce that you can opt to have your case go immediately to arbitration, and the vast majority of New Yorkers take this option. (Arbitration is being tried outside of New York and soon may be adopted in a growing number of states.)

Whether you go to trial or arbitration, there are several general pointers we wish to offer on how you should conduct yourself:

1. Don't play Philadelphia lawyer. Small-claims court is a people's court. It is not meant for lawyers—or, even worse, would-be lawyers—who get their kicks from striding around a courtroom, poking holes in the air with their forefingers. So don't pretend you're Melvin Belli; just be yourself; act naturally.

Maybe this caveat sounds ironic in a book about being your own lawyer. But our aim is not to initiate you into a lot of courtroom theatrics and legalistic nit-picking. Leave that to the $100-an-hour professionals. True, we will teach you a variety of legal principles in Part II, but not with the idea of allowing you to strut your stuff before the judge. Every chapter in Part II distills technical principles into the simple, everyday elements of your case. Stick to those elements when you're in court and you can't go too far wrong. Start behaving like a lawyer, however, and the judge is apt to treat you like one, parrying legal wits with you in a contest that is bound to end disastrously— for you!

2. Be respectful. In general, treat the judge with respect. (If you'd spent years sitting elevated above the rest of the world, wearing a flowing black robe, you'd want respect, too, regardless of whether you deserved it!) Always address the judge as "Your Honor" or simply "Judge."

3. Don't interrupt. Unless you have the patience of Job, you will be sorely tempted during the trial to interrupt someone else—be it the defendant or a witness—usually with cries of "That's a lie!" or "I never said that!" Keep cool. Jot down the point you disagree with. Your turn will come to counter what's been said. Above all, *never interrupt the judge;* that's a sure way of alienating him.

4. Be civil. Whatever vindictiveness you may feel toward the defendant, leave it in the hallway outside the courtroom. Name-calling, snide cracks, even disparaging gestures (e.g., shaking your head in disbelief, grimacing) have no place in the courtroom. The judge will draw his own conclusions as to whom he should believe. Your histrionics won't help; in fact, they may hurt by convincing the judge that you're engaged in a personal vendetta or, worse, you're just a plain nut.

5. Get to the point. When the judge asks you to begin your presentation, start with a concise summary of the case. This introductory step is vital, because the judge knows nothing about your dispute. You must, therefore, orient him quickly to the gist of your case before raising a lot of details that might otherwise overwhelm him.

Say you're suing a bill collector who has been hounding you mercilessly for months (see chapter 33). You might make the following opening remarks: "Your Honor, this case centers on a pattern of extreme harassment by the defendant, a bill collector. He has been dunning me for the past six months over a debt that I have assured him, time and time again, I do not owe." In just two short sentences, you have succeeded in putting the judge in the picture.

How confused the judge might have been had you begun with a long and seemingly pointless tale, such as: "Your Honor, this all began about six months ago when I was home one night watching TV. It must have been around midnight, because I remember I was watching the "Tonight Show." Anyway, all of a sudden the phone rings, and it's the defendant who starts right in telling me about some bill I owe some department store. Well, I was real annoyed and hung up, but who should call again the very next morning while I was shaving. . . ." Et cetera, et cetera. Steer clear of such rambling time-consuming tales of woe.

6. Stick to the elements of your case. They are, you will recall, the legs on which your case stands. It may help you, therefore, to jot down the elements of your case on a file card. Under each listed element, you might note any piece of evidence (or witness) you will present to help prove that element. When reviewing the elements for the judge, don't wander off into legal theory (you will be learning a good deal in Part II, but that's just for background). Instead, emphasize the facts that tend to support each element.

7. Present supporting evidence. If you have pieces of evidence that you wish to present (e.g., photographs, sales receipts, warranty cards), have them handily arranged (e.g., individually labeled in a folder) when you sit down at the start of the trial. There's nothing more disconcerting than having to hunt through a pile of papers for some elusive document, while keeping the judge and everyone else waiting.

When you present a piece of evidence, simply identify it for the judge and hand it to the clerk, who will then pass it up to the judge. For example, in an apartment security deposit case (see chapter 26), you might say: "Your honor, here is the canceled check, dated April 1, 1980, with which I paid the defendant landlord $375 for a security deposit." Then give the check to the clerk.

Don't forget to present a copy of the "settle-or-else" letter that you sent to the defendant (see chapter 5). Remember, it will provide the judge with a forceful summary of your side of the case. You can introduce the letter simply by telling the judge: "Your Honor, I wrote this letter to the defendant in an attempt to settle this matter, but we were unable to reach an agreement." Hand a copy of the letter to the clerk.

8. Call witnesses. Any witnesses you may wish to call will sit next to you at the table. Let the judge know that you have witnesses who will be testifying on certain points. The judge

will indicate when it is time for them to testify. Don't be nervous about having to interrogate your witnesses. This process —often the stuff of high courtroom drama on TV—is straightforward in small-claims court. Frequently, the judge takes over and simply asks the witness to "tell what you know personally about this case." Then the witness just offers his perspective on the facts. Usually, all of this is accomplished without the witness ever having to leave his or her seat at your table.

9. Ask questions. There will probably be several points during the trial when you'll want to ask a question or make a comment. Wait until whoever is speaking finishes and then politely ask the judge for permission to speak. For example, the defendant presents his case after you've finished with yours. He says things—or his witnesses may—that you disagree with. When he finishes, simply say politely: "Your Honor, there are two questions I would like to put to the defendant"; or "Your Honor, May I add one key detail omitted from the defendant's account of the accident?"

10. Ask for court costs. Don't forget that you have incurred certain costs in having to file a lawsuit—most notably, a filing fee and the expense of service of process (see chapter 7). You are entitled to recover these costs from the defendant if you win your case. So when you conclude your presentation, be sure to call the judge's attention to your court costs. Request that these costs be added to any judgment that may be awarded in your favor.

After both sides have finished their presentations, the judge will usually announce that he "reserves" decision in the case. That means he hasn't made up his mind, or if he has, he chooses not to reveal his decision yet—perhaps out of concern for any outburst by the loser. When will you learn about the outcome of your case? Probably in a few days. The clerk will send you a postcard—nothing more elaborate—stating which side won and how much, if anything, was awarded in money damages.

Assuming you win, how and when do you get the money that his been awarded to you? With any luck, the defendant will pay you within a few weeks. He, too, receives a postcard from the clerk, informing him of the judgment entered against him. If the defendant is halfway responsible, he will pay up without prodding (this is especially true of established businesses).

If you have not received a check within three or four weeks, write the defendant a brief note. In it, remind him of the date and amount of the money judgment that was entered against him. Close with the following polite warning: "Please pay this judgment promptly so that I will not have to involve you in further legal procedures now available to me as your judgment creditor." (Your status is that of a judgment creditor because of the judgment in your favor; the defendant is known technically as a judgment debtor.)

Your reminder note should pressure the defendant into paying. If it doesn't, you'll have to get tougher by returning to small-claims court and obtaining a court order that will allow you to reach the defendant's assets. (Of course, you have to know *where* those assets are—i.e., where the defendant works or banks or runs a business or owns property.) The court order is known as a *writ of execution.* You can find out all about it and obtain one (for a small fee) through the small-claims court clerk. He will instruct you on how to deliver the writ to the local sheriff, who will then use it to reach the defendant's wages, bank account, or other assets to satisfy the judgment you have won.

New Yorkers enjoy some special legal ammunition when it comes to collecting judgments from slow-paying businesses. You will recall that a New York business may be sued under any name it uses to conduct business, instead of just its true legal name (see pp. 33–34). A judgment obtained in such a lawsuit is fully as enforceable as if the business had been sued under its true legal name. Indeed, the judgment must be paid within thirty-five days after the business has been notified by the court. If no payment has been made by that deadline, the plaintiff will be entitled to sue the business all over again in small-claims court—this time for the amount of the original unpaid judgment, plus any court costs, plus reasonable attorney's fees, plus a statutory penalty of $100.

New York law also provides for *treble-damage awards* against businesses that have a record of not paying at least three small-claims court judgments. If you win a judgment against such a business and it doesn't pay you within thirty days after having been notified by the court, you can sue the business once more in small-claims court—this time for three times the amount of the original unpaid judgment, plus any court costs, plus reasonable attorney's fees.

PART II

You
and the
Law

CHAPTER 10

Broken Contracts

The Case of the Sexy Health Club

Most contracts are built on faith. Not, we suspect, because people have great faith in each other. But rather because contracts are boring. It's easier to shake hands and hope that the other guy will hold up his end of the bargain than to spell out every last detail in a written contract. And if the other guy hands you a printed contract, it's easier to sign on the dotted line, rather than read through the fine print. No wonder so many people end up in small-claims court arguing that the other side breached a contract.

Broken contract cases come in all shapes and sizes. But they all have one thing in common: the other guy didn't give you what you bargained for. The 1973 New York Small-Claims Court case of *Ellis* v. *Tower Health Club, Inc.* is a good example.

Adele Ellis's doctor advised her to take up swimming, so she went looking for a health club. She found one in the very building where she lived. It was the Tower Health Club, and it had a swimming pool, a gymnasium, and separate saunas and showers for men and women. She joined the club, signed a one-year membership contract, and paid a membership fee of $220.

Adele's problems with the Tower Health Club began right away.

She got inklings that the club was not living up to its contract when she entered the women's sauna one day and discovered a man—*nude*. She sought refuge in the women's shower only to discover another man—also nude—nonchalantly washing himself. Adele quit the Tower Health Club right away.

A few months later the club was raided by the police. Fourteen young women and two men were arrested. Adele learned that flyers for the club were being distributed that read: "Now you can sneak away at lunch or right after work to New York's most unique and beautiful private club. Experience the ultimate in total relaxation. A trained team of lovely masseuses are waiting to rub your weary body back to life in one of our many private massage rooms. Massage is just one of the many services available to you at no extra charge."

Adele had signed a health-club contract in order to go swimming, not to get a massage by "lovely masseuses" or to take co-ed showers and saunas with strange and disreputable men. She demanded her $220 back from the club. Tower refused, so Adele took the club to small-claims court on the grounds that Tower had broken the health-club contract.

Judge Irving Younger analyzed the contractual relationship between the parties thus: "The contract reflects a bargain between Adele Ellis and Tower Health Club whereby Ms. Ellis paid $220 and Tower was to make available to her for a period of one year the facilities of the health club. Implicit in Tower's promise was the further promise that a health club it would be; not a bordello, not a dance hall, and not, as it became, a massage parlor. When Tower changed the nature of the enterprise, they breached their implied promise to Ms. Ellis. Since the breach was substantial, Ms. Ellis in turn had the right to rescind [i.e., cancel the agreement]."

Judge Younger awarded Adele $220, the amount she had paid to join a health club, not a massage parlor.

Courtroom Pointers

The *Ellis* case is typical of the kind of broken contract case which comes to small-claims court. Any time you have a problem with someone who doesn't give you what you bargained for, suing him in small-claims court for a breach of contract may be the answer.

Elements of your case. There are four basic elements in every breach of contract case:

1. You and another person or business entered into an agreement that you both intended to be a binding contract.

2. As part of this contract, each side promised to do something for the other (e.g., pay money in return for delivery of merchandise or performance of services).

3. The other person didn't perform his part of the bargain as prescribed by the contract.

4. As a result of this breach of contract, you suffered a loss.

Proving your side. The first element of your case is to prove that a contract existed. The contract may be oral or written. Whatever form it is in, you must prove that you and the other person intended to create a binding contract according to certain agreed-upon terms.

If there is a written contract, you'll have no problem proving this element of your case. However, if the contract was informal, you must present evidence showing that the other side intended to be legally bound by the agreement you had with him. If there were any witnesses when the contract was made, bring them along. If you performed your part of the bargain, be sure to bring this to the judge's attention. For example, you hired a painter to paint your house and gave him a down payment of $300. Bring in a copy of the canceled check or payment receipt. The fact that the other side accepted money from you is good evidence that a contract existed.

The second element of your case is what the law calls *consideration* for the contract. In order to have a legally enforceable contract, there must be an exchange of mutually binding promises. A court won't enforce a gratuitous promise. If your neighbor says he'll drive you to a ball game and then never shows up so you miss the game, odds are you can't sue him for the cost of your ticket to the game. Since you didn't promise to give him anything in return for the ride, there was no legally binding contract between the two of you.

When you prove the second element of your case, explain

exactly what the mutual promises in your contract were. Be prepared to explain that you performed your part of the bargain, or at least that you were ready and willing to perform it.

The third element of your case requires you to prove that the person with whom you had a contract didn't do what he agreed to do. As a result, you will argue, the contract was breached. If you have properly presented the first two elements of your case, the third element should not be much of a problem. Explain what the defendant was supposed to do, and give any facts you have showing that he didn't do it.

In a 1979 New York Small-Claims Court case, *Hoffman* v. *Ryan*, Harold Hoffman consulted an apartment referral agency, which had advertised an apartment in the *New York Times*. The ad described the apartment as containing three rooms and being located in a brownstone building. When Harold visited the agency, he was required to pay a $100 fee before the agency would give him the keys to the apartment and allow him to inspect it. On inspection, the apartment turned out not to be as advertised; it was only a one-room studio, and it wasn't in a brownstone. Of course, Harold complained, but the agency informed him that his fee was nonrefundable.

Unfazed, Harold sought a refund in small-claims court. Clearly, there was a contract. The newspaper ad established precisely what service the agency had offered to provide for anyone who responded. Harold did respond and paid $100 (his receipt from the agency proved that much). That the agency had breached the contract was clear to the judge: "Inasmuch as the apartment referral agency represented to Mr. Hoffman that for $100 he could see an apartment with specific characteristics and Mr. Hoffman paid the fee, the referral to an apartment which was not as described amounts to breach of contract." The court awarded Harold a full refund of his $100 fee.

As the fourth and final element in your case, you must justify the amount of money damages that you seek as compensation for the breach of contract. In general, you are entitled to recover enough money to put you in the same position that you would have been in had the defendant properly performed the contract (see chapter 3). Assume you buy an air conditioner when it's on sale for $200. But the store neither delivers the unit as it promised to, nor does it refund your purchase price. So you go to another store and buy the same air conditioner, but this time for $350 (it's not on sale). The loss you have suffered is $350—$200 for the undelivered sale item, plus $150 additional expense incurred to purchase the air conditioner at its regular price. When you receive $350, you will be in the same position that you would have been in had the store originally delivered the air conditioner for $200.

Countering the other side. The most likely argument you will face is a claim that the contract was not actually breached. The other side will say, in effect: "Show me where in the contract I made you the promise that you now say I didn't perform!" This argument is especially likely if the contract was informal and didn't clearly spell out all the obligations of the parties.

You can generally counter this argument by explaining that although the contract may not have specifically set forth a particular promise, that promise was, nonetheless, clearly *implied* in the contract. In the health-club case, Adele Ellis's membership contract didn't state specifically that the club she was joining would remain a bona fide health club instead of turning into a massage parlor. Nevertheless, the judge decided that just such a promise was implicit in the contract and had been breached.

Another good illustration of how a judge may "fill in the blanks" in a contract is the case of *Johnson* v. *Colonial Buick, Inc.* On October 3, 1976, Robert Johnson put down a $500 deposit with Colonial Buick for a Buick Riviera sport coupe, costing $8,272.05. He signed a purchase order, but the clause in the contract specifying when the car would be delivered was left blank. The dealer, however, told Robert that delivery would take about eight weeks.

Fourteen weeks later the car had still not arrived, so Robert decided to cancel the contract. He notified Colonial Buick and asked for a refund of his $500 deposit. Colonial refused and one week later told him his car had arrived. Robert decided to stick with his cancellation decision, and when Colonial Buick again refused to return his deposit, he went to court.

The judge had to decide whether a fourteen-week delay in delivery amounted to a breach of the purchase contract. The contract itself said nothing about a delivery date; the judge decided that "since no time was agreed upon a reasonable time for delivery was implied." According to the judge, "The determination of reasonableness requires a consideration of what the parties intended when the agreement was made." The evidence showed that neither party anticipated a fourteen-week delay when the contract was signed. The judge decided, therefore, that the delay amounted to a breach of the contract entitling Robert Johnson to recover his $500 deposit.

In the *Ellis* and *Johnson* cases, both judges interpreted the contract by determining what the intentions of the parties to the contract were. The judges applied a standard of reasonableness: what would a reasonable person have expected when entering into the contract?

If the person you are suing challenges you to show where the contract requires him to do what you claim he didn't do, don't be fooled. Just respond that the conduct required of him was an implied term of the contract. As a reasonable person, you naturally assumed that he, too, would act reasonably in order not to render the contract meaningless. The judge will then be free to fill in the blanks of your contract according to what reasonable people would have expected had they entered into a contract like yours.

CHAPTER

Dry Cleaners

The Case of the Dye That Died

How many times have you been taken to the cleaners by your dry cleaner? Remember that $100 silk blouse of yours that came back from the cleaners looking as if it had been boiled rather than cleaned; or your sleek new leather slacks that returned two sizes too small; or the suit you left to be altered that was butchered instead; or worst of all, the rugs you delivered that *never* came back at all!

Of course, you complained. But the cleaner (or tailor) proved to be a master at holding up your now pathetic garment (or the remnants thereof) and explaining innocently, "This is just the way you brought it in." Or else he hid behind some fine print on the back of your ticket: "Not responsible for shrinkage, running of dyes, or other damage to fabrics."

What can you do? If push comes to shove, you can sue that cleaner for not taking good care of your property. The legal theory you will rely on goes under the rubric *bailments*. A bailment arises when you entrust your property to another for safekeeping or the performance of some service—e.g., cleaning, tailoring. If that person negligently harms your property or loses it altogether, he will be liable to you for the damage that he's caused.

A typical dry cleaner bailment occurred in the 1974 Louisiana case of *Axelrod* v. *Wardrobe Cleaners, Inc.* (This is a good case to look at because it's a microcosm of many issues that generally arise in a dry-cleaning dispute.) Dr. Arthur Axelrod wished to have a set of dining room draperies dry-cleaned. He called Wardrobe Cleaners, which sent over a representative to inspect the drapes. After examining the draperies closely for thirty minutes, the man from Wardrobe accepted them for dry-cleaning. (Legally speaking, he entered into a *bailment:* he was the *bailee;* Dr. Axelrod, the *bailor.*)

When the draperies returned from Wardrobe, they were, alas, ruined. The fabric, formerly a gold floral design on an eggshell white background, was now a blotchy gold throughout and unfit for use. Since no settlement could be worked out with Wardrobe over the disaster, Dr. Axelrod sued.

The most important piece of evidence was, of course, the draperies themselves, which Dr. Alexrod brought right into court. Cleverly, he also produced a piece of the fabric from which the draperies had been made. According to the judge, a comparison between this piece, which had not been dry-cleaned, and the draperies "visibly demonstrates the damage caused by the cleaning process."

The ball was now in Wardrobe's court. Dr. Axelrod had established the existence of a bailment: that is, acceptance of the draperies by Wardrobe for the purpose of dry-cleaning. He had further shown that damage to the draperies occurred while they were in Wardrobe's custody. As a result, he had made out what is known in the law of bailments as a *prima facie case of negligence.* Without any rebuttal to this prima facie case, Wardrobe would clearly be held liable. The effect of Dr. Axelrod's establishing a prima facie case was to shift the *burden of proof* to Wardrobe, the bailee. Wardrobe now had to come forward and exonerate itself by proving it had acted with the care ordinarily required of a prudent dry cleaner. Otherwise, Dr. Axelrod's prima facie case would win the day.

What did Wardrobe have to say on its behalf? First, Wardrobe's owner, Pete Kissgen, Jr., testified. He raised a defense often heard in dry-cleaning cases: *it was the fabric's fault not ours!*

According to Kissgen, it is difficult to predict how the dyes in imported fabric (like that in Axelrod's draperies) will react to dry-cleaning. He claimed that there was no way of safely pretesting Dr. Axelrod's draperies for colorfastness, because if the draperies failed the test, their dye would run in the test area.

The court gave little weight to these excuses. To begin with, Kissgen's representative had inspected the draperies for thirty minutes at the Axelrod home. His purpose had been to determine precisely whether the draperies were for any reason (age, fading, etc.) unsuitable for cleaning. The inspector's unqualified acceptance of the draperies was an implied assurance to Dr. Axelrod that the draperies could withstand the cleaning process. "If any doubt existed in Wardrobe's mind," said the judge, "as to the advisability of dry-cleaning these drapes, as a prudent bailee it should have either subjected them to additional tests or refused to accept them."

The next witness for Wardrobe was Joe Watson, an alleged fabric expert. He expressed the opinion that the color ran because of an inferior dyeing process in the fabrication of the drapery material (another variation on the theme, it's the fabric's fault not ours). His testimony was seriously discounted, however, when it came to light that he was hardly a disinterested witness; he had been doing business with Wardrobe for several years, selling it chemical additives. So his credibility was highly questionable.

The court decided Wardrobe had failed to prove that its actions were those of a reasonably prudent dry cleaner. (Technically speaking, therefore, Dr. Axelrod's prima facie case still stood— unrebutted.) Wardrobe had clearly been negligent in its handling of the draperies, and it was liable for the resulting harm. The final hurdle for Dr. Axelrod was the question of money damages: how much money would compensate him for the ruined draperies? Here, his case was a bit weak. He was unable to present certain important facts: namely the original cost of the draperies, their expected useful life, and their age when sent to Wardrobe. (The problem was that the draperies had originally belonged to the former owner of the Axelrod home and had been hanging there when the Axelrods moved in.) Consequently, the court could not make any precise calculations regarding: (1) the fair market value of the draperies when they went in for cleaning; and (2) their even lower value when they returned. (Ordinarily, the difference between these two sums would determine the amount of money damages.)

But Dr. Axelrod was resourceful enough to fill the evidentiary vacuum with certain telling facts: First, Wardrobe's inspector had spent fully thirty minutes carefully looking over the draperies—hardly the sort of attention one would pay to a cheap pair of chintz curtains. Second, Axelrod's wife had intended to coordinate her entire redecoration of the dining room around these draperies—suggesting that they were of superior quality and still in prime condition.

In assessing damages, the court had to exercise its discretion. Dr. Axelrod won an award of $1,000 from Wardrobe Cleaners.

Courtroom Pointers

Just as Dr. Axelrod took Wardrobe to the cleaners, you too can win in court, whether you're up against a careless cleaner, a sloppy seamstress, or a turkey of a tailor.

Elements of your case. Your basic aim is to establish, as Dr. Axelrod did, a prima facie case of negligence. There are three elements to such a case:

1. You entered into a bailment with the dry cleaner. In other words you (the bailor) delivered your property (e.g., suit, scarf, carpet) to the dry cleaner (the bailee) for the purpose of having certain work performed on it.

2. When you entered into the bailment, your property was in satisfactory condition—except, of course, for needing a cleaning or alterations.

3. When you sought return of your property, it was in a damaged state—or the dry cleaner was unable to return it.

Establish these three elements, and you will succeed in shifting the burden of proof to the dry cleaner. He must come up with some explanation as to why the judge should not find him negligent and, therefore, liable to you for money damages.

Proving your side. Begin your case by simply testifying to the fact that you delivered your property to—or it was picked up by—the dry cleaner. You aren't likely to have the claim check to present as evidence of delivery, unless, of course, the property was never returned to you. In the latter case, bring the check with you to court.

As far as proving element (2) goes, you can testify to the condition of your property when you delivered it to the dry cleaner. For example, "This was a new trench coat, Your Honor. I bought it only one month before having it cleaned, and I had only worn it three or four times." (Present your sales receipt for the coat, if you have it, to prove the date of purchase.)

Of course, you may be able to pull off a graphic before-and-after demonstration as Dr. Axelrod did with his draperies. Do you have a sample of the material that shows its color and texture before cleaning? Or maybe a photograph that gives a clear impression of what the material was like? If so, present that evidence to prove the "before" element.

Element (3), the "after" element, is usually the easiest to prove. If your property was lost by the dry cleaner, you simply testify that you presented your claim check, but the cleaner was unable to produce your property. If your property was damaged, rather than lost, then by all means bring in the *corpus delicti*—the damaged goods. No evidence of damage can be more convincing, for instance, than the sight of you trying to wriggle into your favorite leather coat, now sadly shrunken by the cleaner's mistreatment.

Countering the other side. Watch out for curves the other side may throw at you. Some of them we've already seen in Dr. Axelrod's case. Perhaps the most common one is the excuse that the material or the manufacturer was the culprit, not the dry cleaner. For example, a substandard fabric or an inferior dyeing process was used in the manufacture of your garment.

Don't be unnerved by testimony to this effect. There are ways to counter it. Recall two techniques Dr. Axelrod used. First, question the credibility of the witness who gives the testimony. If he's a so-called fabric expert, feel free to cross-examine him regarding his relationship with the dry cleaner. Is the dry cleaner, for instance, a regular client of his? Does he make a practice of testifying on behalf of dry cleaners—and this dry cleaner in particular?

Second, point out, when appropriate, that the dry cleaner inspected your property—perhaps at your request—before accepting it for dry-cleaning. "Once he accepted it, Your Honor, I felt assured that the garment could be successfully dry-cleaned—or, at least, that no harm would come to it. After all, he looked the thing over and decided he could do the job. As a consumer, I have to rely on the judgment of professionals, which I did here." (Of course, if the cleaner specifically told you that he could safely clean your garment, tell the judge exactly what he said.)

One of the trickiest curves you may be thrown is called the *disclaimer of liability.* The dry cleaner argues that even if he *is* responsible for your loss, his liability to you is severely limited or completely wiped out. How so? Because of a disclaimer of liability in the fine print on your claim check or on some sign in the dry cleaner's store. The disclaimer states that the dry cleaner is not liable for loss or damage, or is liable only up to a maximum of, say, $10.

You won't strike out here as long as you can honestly say you did not know about this disclaimer. For instance, you didn't bother to read the claim check, because you thought it was merely a receipt, not an important notification about liability; or you did not see the sign in the store; or the dry cleaner did not call your attention to the disclaimer. Whatever the reason for your ignorance, it should get you off the hook (unless the disclaimer was so conspicuous that you couldn't possibly have overlooked it). Legally speaking, a disclaimer can't bind you unless you *agree* to it; and you couldn't have agreed to it if you weren't even *aware* of it! (Besides, most judges are highly reluctant to let anyone escape from the consequences of his own negligence merely by using a clever disclaimer.)

The final biggest obstacle you're likely to run up against occurs at the end of the rainbow, just before the pot of gold. You've proven the dry cleaner was negligent; he's clearly liable to you; but for *how much?* Ideally, you'd like to win enough money so that you could go out and buy new clothing (draperies, etc.) to replace what was ruined by the dry cleaner. But he's going to claim you're not entitled to that much, because at the time the clothing was damaged, it had already depreciated considerably from its original purchase price.

Technically speaking, the dry cleaner is correct. You don't have a right to recover the *replacement value* of the clothing— only its *fair market value* (see chapter 3). For example, you bought a three-piece suit for $450, but one month later, when it was dry-cleaned and ruined, it had a fair market value (as used clothing) of only $250!

Obviously this rule of valuation leaves you with the short end of the stick, and judges are often sympathetic. They will lean toward setting as high a fair market value on your clothing as is reasonable under all the circumstances. So make sure you bring all those circumstances to the judge's attention. Show him the sales receipt on the garment (if you still have it), or a canceled check for its purchase, or a store catalog advertising the original price. Emphasize how recently you bought the garment, how little you had worn it, and what good condition it was in. The more convincing your evidence is, the likelier the judge is to set a fair market value that approximates what the clothing was worth to *you*—not to a second-hand clothes buyer.

In one Connecticut small-claims court case, a woman won $150 for severe damage done to her raincoat, which had originally been purchased for around $200. Strictly speaking, the fair market value of this used garment was probably under $100. But the woman emphasized that the coat still had at least 75 percent of its useful life ahead of it before the fatal dry-cleaning. Apparently, the judge sympathized with her when he set a highly favorable market value.

CHAPTER

Shoddy Workmanship

The Waterproofing System That Was All Wet

Why should you pay for something you don't get? There's no good reason. Yet each year thousands of consumers do exactly that. They hire a plumber or carpenter or painter or other so-called professional only to discover that he is a rank amateur. Too often he does more harm than good, and you're stuck with a rotten job and a bill. If you're the victim of shoddy workmanship, take heart in the 1973 Ohio case, *Nosse* v. *Vulcan Basement Waterproofing, Inc.*

Mrs. Nosse saw an advertisement in the newspaper for a basement waterproofing service provided by Vulcan. She contacted Vulcan, signed an agreement to have her basement waterproofed, and made a $200 down payment. When the crack team from Vulcan showed up, they simply squirted a mysterious substance into the ground around Mrs. Nosse's house and promptly left. The result of this so-called waterproofing job was that the basement began to leak even more.

Mrs. Nosse complained, and Vulcan said it would fix the problem if she signed another contract, which she did. This time Vulcan's version of waterproofing was a little ditch dug in the basement floor, which did nothing to stop the leaks, but merely funneled water from them into a drain. This ditch Vulcan glorified with the title of "floor system."

Mrs. Nosse finally realized that Vulcan was not doing the job she had hired them to do. She told them to stop working and demanded back her $200 down payment. Vulcan refused to make a refund and, instead, demanded payment of the full contract price. Mrs. Nosse went to court where she sued Vulcan for $200.

The judge decided that Mrs. Nosse had "paid two hundred dollars down to Vulcan for which she has received nothing but additional damage to her property." Since Vulcan failed to do a workmanlike job, Mrs. Nosse was entitled to a full refund of her down payment of $200.

Courtroom Pointers

The principle underlying Mrs. Nosse's victory is very straight-forward. The law generally implies in every contract for work or services a duty to perform the job skillfully, carefully, diligently, and in a *workmanlike manner*. If the service, whatever it may be, is not so performed, a consumer need not pay for it and may sue for money damages based on any injury that resulted from the shoddy workmanship.

Elements of your case. There are three elements to your case:

1. You hired a craftsman or business to perform a service for you.

2. The service was not performed skillfully, carefully, diligently, or in a workmanlike manner.

3. As a result of the shoddy workmanship, you suffered a loss or simply failed to get your money's worth.

Proving your case. You are not likely to have much trouble proving the first element of your case: that you hired an individual or business to perform a service for you. Bring along a copy of any contract you signed. If you had only an oral agreement with the workman, you will have to testify regarding just what services he agreed to perform.

A bigger obstacle may lie in proving shoddy workmanship. If you hire a bricklayer to build a wall and the wall falls down, you'll have no problem proving this element of your case. A picture of the fallen wall is all that you're likely to need. But what if the shoddy workmanship can't be shown so easily: e.g., a poor job of house painting. How do you show the judge that the work performed was not up to the standard that a reasonable consumer would expect when hiring a professional painter? You can't bring the house to court with you, and pictures may not fully expose the low quality of the work. In these situations you must bring the best available evidence.

Assume the painter changed paints while doing your house, resulting in a bright white in one room and an off-white in another. You ordered bright white for both rooms. Pictures won't show the difference between the paints. But perhaps chips of paint from both rooms or a color chart from the paint store would help you to make the point. If the painter threw away different paint cans, you could use the cans as evidence of the different paints and, therefore, different colors in the rooms. Even though this kind of evidence may not absolutely prove shoddy workmanship, the fact that you are presenting the *best available* evidence will undoubtedly impress the judge.

The final element of your case is the payoff: the damages you are claiming. Since you are suing for breach of contract, the general rule is that you should claim an amount of money damages that will put you in the position you would have been in had the person you hired done a proper job (see chapter 3).

For example, you hire an air-conditioner installer and pay him $50 to install one air conditioner. On the very next day, that air conditioner falls out of the window damaging itself and the floor. Repairs to the air conditioner cost $75 and to the floor, $45.

Had the installer done a proper job you would have had a working air conditioner and no damage to your floor. To put yourself in that position, you will have to pay $50 to have someone reinstall the air conditioner, $75 to have someone repair it, and $45 to have your floor repaired. Your damages would be $170, which you should seek in any lawsuit against the slipshod installer.

Sometimes damages cannot be measured so neatly. Consider the case of *Grather* v. *Tipery Studios, Inc.* Before Mr. and Mrs. Grather got married, they hired the Tipery Studios to send a photographer to take pictures at their wedding. After the wedding, when the pictures arrived, they made a depressing discovery. The pictures were terrible. The backgrounds in all the pictures showed either exit signs, a kitchen in disarray, or glasses and paper cups left on tables.

The Grathers went to court arguing that the poor wedding pictures caused them damages. Tipery Studios didn't put up much of a fight. Instead, they argued that all the Grathers were entitled to was their money back if they returned the wedding pictures.

The court had no problem establishing the first two elements of the Grathers' case: Clearly, the Grathers had hired the studio to take professional photographs. Equally clearly, the photographs were not made with the skill one would ordinarily expect from a professional photographer.

The problem was in the third element: damages. How could the judge put the Grathers in the same position they would have been in had the photographer done a proper job? There was no way to restage the wedding for a second round of photographs.

The answer was to compensate the Grathers in another way: "a bride and groom who desire non-amateur photographs are seeking the gratification of some intellectual enjoyment. . . . When the photographs are of less than professional quality, the bride and groom are deprived of the full enjoyment, which they can rightfully expect, of pictures commemorating their wedding and reception. The Grathers are entitled to compensation in damages for this loss of enjoyment."

The judge ordered Tipery Studios to pay the Grathers $125 to compensate them for their lost enjoyment. The enjoyment of receiving the money would, presumably, blot out the grief caused by the bad pictures.

Countering the other side. The sneakiest way for the defendant to upset your case is by claiming that you signed away any right to complain about the quality of the service you received. For example, when Mrs. Nosse hired Vulcan to waterproof her basement, they asked her to sign a contract including the following clause: "No action may be maintained against Vulcan." This is a typical *disclaimer of liability*. When Mrs. Nosse went to court, Vulcan argued that the disclaimer precluded her bringing a lawsuit.

The judge, however, was not about to let Vulcan get away with this ploy. Mrs. Nosse had, indeed, signed a contract, but it was up to the judge to decide whether to *enforce* the contract. He decided not to, because the contract was so one-sided, so unfair, that to enforce it would simply be wrong. In legalese, the contract was *unconscionable* and against public policy. In such a situation, the law gives the judge the authority simply to ignore the unconscionable parts of the contract. And that is exactly what the judge in Mrs. Nosse's case did.

If the defendant you sue argues that you signed away your right to a workmanlike job, respond that it would be "unconscionable" to make you pay for something you didn't get. The word "unconscionable" will clue the judge into exactly what you want him to do.

CHAPTER

Inconsiderate Neighbors

The Case of the Noisy Air Conditioner

A man's home is his castle, goes the ancient legal dictum. So the occupant can presumably do whatever he wants there. However valid such a notion may have been in days of yore, contemporary castles are set much closer together. Indeed, they are piled on top of one another in today's apartment buildings. With each lord of the castle bent on enjoying his home to the fullest, clashes are inevitable. When one man's enjoyment seriously impinges on his neighbor's, the result may be what the law calls a *nuisance* (you probably use a sharper term), and the victim is entitled to relief.

Such was the case in *Nair* v. *Thaw,* a 1968 Connecticut lawsuit. The Nairs lived across the street from the Thaws in a choice residential area of West Hartford. The Thaw home, which had cost over $300,000, was fully air-conditioned. Therein lay the problem. While the Thaws were keeping cool, the Nairs were heating up because of the noise emanating from the central air-conditioning system that serviced the Thaw home. At the cost of over $2,500, Mr. Thaw had baffles installed to lessen the noise, but it still bothered his neighbors across the street.

So Mrs. Nair sued Mr. Thaw on the grounds that his noisy air-conditioning system created a nuisance. The court found that although the system was reasonably suited for cooling the Thaw home and did not violate any local zoning ordinances, nevertheless, operation of the system invaded the peace and quiet of the Nairs' home. Not that the Nairs were overly sensitive. The noise would have been "annoying and irritating to persons of average sensibilities," reasoned the court.

Had the noise from the Thaw air conditioner resulted in a legal nuisance? Yes, concluded the court: "It is the duty of every person to make a reasonable use of his own property so as to occasion no unnecessary damage or annoyance to his neighbor. If the use is unreasonable, the law will hold him responsible. . . ." When Mr. Thaw's interest in cooling his home was weighed against the Nairs' interest in peace and quiet, the former came up wanting.

For the results of this imbalance, was Mrs. Nair entitled to recover money damages from Mr. Thaw? Yes ruled the court: "The plaintiff was entitled to recover for the physical discomfort and annoyance caused by the defendant's unreasonable use of his air-conditioning equipment so far as it materially affected the comfortable enjoyment and occupancy of her home and interfered with her use and enjoyment of her property. . . . In the nature of things such damages are not susceptible of exact pecuniary computation and must be left largely to the sound discretion of the judge."

The judge awarded Mrs. Nair $3,500. He also enjoined Mr. Thaw from operating his air-conditioning system between the hours of 10:00 P.M. and 8:00 A.M., until the noise had been further reduced to an acceptable level. (If you decide to go to small-claims court with a nuisance lawsuit like *Nair* v. *Thaw,* you will probably have to content yourself with suing for money damages; small-claims courts do not generally grant injunctive relief, only money damages—see pages 21–22.)

Courtroom Pointers

A nuisance lawsuit is the typical sort of case that you ought to try to resolve outside of court. But if you can't settle matters with your neighbor on reasonable, live-and-let-live terms, there is legal relief.

Elements of your case. There are three principal elements to your case:

1. Your neighbor is using his property (or apartment) in a way that interferes substantially with your ability to use and enjoy your property (or apartment).

2. This interference is, considering all the circumstances, unreasonable.

3. As a result of this interference, you have suffered serious inconvenience, distress, or property damage.

Proving your side. Nuisance cases invariably turn on questions of degree. Almost any condition, if carried too far by your neighbor, may result in a legal nuisance. As one judge has remarked: "A musical instrument played loud enough and long enough has been held to be a nuisance comparable to the water torture of the Chinese." Therefore, it's your job to convince the judge of how substantially your neighbor has encroached upon your happiness, health, or safety.

Don't expect to prove a nuisance if there has been only a trifling interference with your home life: e.g., occasional smoke from a chimney, a temporary odor. The law won't afford you relief from the petty irritations of daily living.

In a Pennsylvania case, *Marzacco* v. *Crossley,* the plaintiff complained that limbs from seven large pine trees on his neighbor's property were overhanging his house. In and of itself, that fact might not have amounted to much; overhanging limbs that do no particular harm are just the sort of trifling invasion of property rights that ordinarily don't amount to a nuisance. But the plaintiff went on to detail just how substantially these limbs interfered with his property: the limbs brushed against the roof of the plaintiff's house making disturbing noises; during the winter, limbs dropped on to the plaintiff's roof resulting in a continuing dampness; pine cones and needle from the branches clogged the gutters and spouts on the plaintiff's roof, causing water to gush over his house and leak in through the ceiling. Given such persuasive proof, the court easily concluded that the defendant's allowing his pine trees to extend over the plaintiff's property created a nuisance.

Photographs can often be worth a thousand words when introduced as evidence of a nuisance. In the overhanging-limb situation, for instance, photos of the limbs, clogged gutters, and water-stained ceilings inside would be highly convincing. It's also advisable to present any witnesses who can confirm your side of the story. The fact that witnesses have experienced an adverse reaction similar to yours tends to prove that you're not overly squeamish. (The law measures a nuisance according to average sensibilities, not one person's extreme sensitivity.)

Countering the other side. The defendant may very likely try to characterize his activities differently from the way you do. His aim will be to prove a perfectly lawful and unobjectionable use of his property. Be ready to rebut this, if necessary, with any evidence of the excessiveness of the defendant's conduct.

For example, you sue the defendant because of the smoke coming regularly from his backyard into yours. He claims you're exaggerating, because he is operating only an outdoor barbecue, which burns charcoal that is virtually smokeless. If the defendant convinces the judge, no nuisance is likely to be found, because outdoor cooking, which is usually attended by relatively pleasant fumes, if any, is a normal and rightful aspect of owning a home.

But suppose you respond with proof that the defendant has repeatedly used his otherwise tolerable barbecue as a trash incinerator. Every few days he burns garbage, causing acrid smoke and soot to pour onto your property and even into your house. (If you're really sharp, you'll have photographs of thick black smoke billowing from the defendant's barbecue-turned-furnace into your backyard.) Now you've gone a long way toward overcoming the defendant's protestations of innocence and establishing an obnoxious nuisance.

Always bear in mind that the judge will be balancing your interests against your neighbor's. That's how he decides whether your neighbor's conduct was reasonable or not. If you can persuade the judge that the utility of your neighbor's conduct (e.g., getting rid of his trash by incinerating it) is outweighed by the harm to which you've been subjected (e.g., smoke stains, eye and nose irritation), then the judge will conclude that your neighbor has acted unreasonably and created a nuisance.

Don't let a wily defendant get away with minimizing the adverse effects of his conduct. If he succeeds, no nuisance may be found, or else any money damages you win will be greatly reduced. Be prepared with hard evidence of the annoyance you've suffered and the expense to which you've been put: for example, ill health, doctor's visits, time lost from work, fees paid to various contractors to restore your property after the ill effects of the defendant's activity.

CHAPTER 14

Nasty Neighbors

Trench Warfare Comes to the Suburbs

There are bad neighbors, and there are *bad* neighbors. The first kind are merely inconsiderate: they sometimes throw raucous parties or let their trees hang dangerously over your house (see chapter 13). But the second kind are not just thoughtless; they are nasty wretches, intent on making your life miserable. You can teach a nasty neighbor a legal lesson he won't soon forget. Sue him for what the law calls *nuisance* (a fitting legal term), and you can win money damages to compensate you for the aggravation he has caused.

The California case of *Griffin* v. *Northridge* shows how you can make a nasty neighbor pay. The Griffins lived next door to the Northridges, who set out to harass the Griffins in ways that may seem petty, but which took their collective toll. For example:
 • Mrs. Northridge deliberately walked over Mrs. Griffin's geranium-filled flower beds and ground her heels into the flowers. (She even removed Mrs. Griffin's only blooming hibiscus plant from an outdoor flower pot.)
 • Along the common boundary line with the Griffins' property, the Northridges embarked on what seemed to be the suburban equivalent of trench warfare. First, they moved their garbage can almost directly underneath the Griffins' adjacent dining room win-

dow. Then they raised a long string hung with many tin-can tops that clanged constantly, annoying the Griffins during the day and keeping them awake at night. Finally, they erected a hideous board fence that deprived the poor Griffins of light and view.

• To add insult to injury, Mrs. Northridge constantly chided Mrs. Griffin with cracks like: "Why don't you do something with your figure?" and "Why don't you spend a little of your dirty money to have your car washed?"

Eventually, enough was enough. The Griffins decided to put some sort of a price tag on the grief that the Northridges had caused them. They sued for money damages on the grounds that the Northridges were liable for creating a legal nuisance. Both Mr. and Mrs. Griffin testified to the indignities they had suffered; friends of theirs also testified to malicious acts that they had observed while visiting the Griffins.

"That the acts of the defendants created a nuisance," declared the court, "is established by the proof that the acts committed were of such a nature as to harass and annoy plaintiffs continuously and to interfere with their comfortable enjoyment of life and of their home." The court gave little weight to the Northridges' arguments that, strictly speaking, none of their various acts was prohibited by law: "If the contention were established that defendants did no unlawful acts and therefore created no nuisance, the maintenance of a comfortable home in a city would be imperiled by the presence of a neighbor who would wilfully frustrate the peace and comfort of another without just cause."

So the Northridges were guilty of creating a nuisance. That's fine in principle, but what's the bottom line? Did the defendants have to pay for their wrongdoing? Not surprisingly, the Northridges argued that it was impossible to assess money damages for the acts that had been proven—especially when each relatively innocuous act (e.g., making insulting remarks, picking Mrs. Griffin's flowers) was viewed individually.

But the court took a far different approach; it weighed the cumulative impact of the Northridges' misdeeds: "The financial value of . . . the plants or flowers destroyed . . . of peace and quiet disturbed, of cruel epithets spoken, of unsightly fences that precluded view and darkened the home . . . the detriment caused by any one of these factors measured by its money value alone is of little importance in appraising the sum total of them all as a nuisance to those who occupy the adjoining home." In assessing money damages against nasty neighbors, the court said it was proper to consider "the sentimental and aesthetic values of things destroyed, the owner's affection for his possessions, as well as his peace, comfort and quiet which have been scorned by his neighbor." Considering all these factors, the court awarded the Griffins a judgment of $1,000 against the Northridges.

Courtroom Pointers

If you find yourself locked in a reenactment of the Griffin-Northridge war, you, too, may want to hang a legal price tag on your neighbor's nastiness by suing him for creating a nuisance.

Elements of your case. There are four basic elements to such a lawsuit:

1. Your neighbor has deliberately or recklessly engaged in certain malicious acts, intended to harass you.

2. These dirty tricks have interfered substantially with your enjoyment of your property (or apartment).

3. This interference by your nasty neighbor has been wholly unreasonable.

4. As a result of this interference, you have suffered extreme nervousness, distress, or damage to your property.

Proving your side. You are your own best witness in a nasty-neighbor case. You're the victim. So tell the judge exactly what you have suffered. A good way to do this is to tick off a diary of the defendant's misdeeds: For example, on May 3, 11, 15, and 21, he maliciously incited his dog to bark right under your bedroom window. On June 6, 10, and 14, he directed his children to rampage through your childrens' tree house, resulting in damage to the tree. On June 9, 15, and 20, he deliberately backed his car into your garden while turning in his driveway. Et cetera, et cetera.

Don't go overboard and dredge up trivialities. Remember that the interference with your enjoyment of your property

must have been *substantial.* A certain amount of petty annoyance simply has to be tolerated, although as we saw in the
Griffin case, the cumulative impact of many seeming trifles can
be substantial. The more specific outrages that you can catalog
(giving dates and details), the likelier it is that the judge will
conclude that you have been the victim of relentless psychological warfare.

Bring to court any revealing photographs—e.g., a picture of
an ugly tall fence that your nasty neighbor built to spite you.
Witnesses, too, can help to corroborate your testimony. In a
Maryland case, *Gorman* v. *Sabo,* the vindictive neighbors
beamed a radio full-blast at the house next door. Witnesses for
the beleaguered victim of this sound-and-spite show testified
that during many different visits, the radio made such a racket
that it was impossible to carry on a conversation. (Incidentally,
the nasty neighbor got stung with a $3,500 judgment in that
case.)

You must convince the judge that the interference with your
property has been *unreasonable.* The judge will use a balancing test—weighing the utility of your neighbor's conduct
against the harm caused to you; if the latter outweighs the former, the interference will be branded unreasonable. Be sure to
emphasize, therefore, that your nasty neighbor's conduct had
little or no utility to him—other than, perhaps, gratifying his
base instincts. Given such proof, the balancing test is likely to
tip in your favor.

Countering the other side. Don't be surprised if your nasty
neighbor tells the judge that you're overly sensitive. That's one
way for him to escape liability. By definition, a nuisance of-
fends everyone of ordinary sensibilities—not just those
who are peculiarly susceptible. Here again, witnesses will
strengthen your case; their testimony can indicate that they,
too, were disturbed while visiting you, so you're not the only
one who was offended.

The nasty neighbor may claim that he never intended you
any harm. Malice, although common in nasty-neighbor cases, is
not absolutely essential, because a nuisance is the end result of
your neighbor's conduct, regardless of his motivation. At any

rate, you can usually establish your neighbor's maliciousness by testifying to snide remarks he made, or to the fact that his misconduct served no conceivable purpose other than harassment.

In one Florida case, the nasty neighbor actually tried to excuse his acts of harassment (e.g. deliberately operating a noisy lawn mower early in the morning right under the neighbor's bedroom) by claiming he was not mentally well. But the court held him liable in the sum of $500: "Persons are responsible for their wrongful acts where they possess sufficient capacity to distinguish between right and wrong and comprehend the nature and effect of their action."

Finally, the nasty neighbor may argue that even if he did cause a nuisance, nevertheless, you suffered no real loss. Essentially, that contention was raised and rejected in the *Griffin* case. You must be ready to catalog exactly what you have suffered: for instance, constant nervousness, lack of sleep, days lost from work, humiliation before your friends. To whatever extent possible, bolster this evidence with proof of visits to a physician or medication prescribed. (Bring in any relevant bills from the doctor or pharmacist). Remember, you are trying to put a price tag on damage to your peace of mind, so make your suffering as tangible and convincing as possible.

CHAPTER 15

Bothersome Business Neighbors

The Home That Went to the Cleaners

You say the Fandango Disco next door keeps you up all night to the beat of the latest Johnny Raucous records. And that nice little muffler shop across the street has just expanded into auto painting *outdoors*, sending noxious fumes your way. And a new drive-in food stand on the corner has cars backed up the street, blocking your driveway and honking their horns. Is that what's making your temples throb?

Take heart. You've got a law on your side that even the biggest business can't flout with impunity. It's called the law of *nuisance*. If you tell it to the judge, you can make bothersome business neighbors start paying more than rent—namely, money damages to you for interfering with your health, safety, or peace of mind.

In the Massachusetts case of *Proulx* v. *Basbanes,* Lionel and Rita Proulx bought a house located next door to a dry-cleaning plant, operated by John Basbanes. Shortly after moving in, the Proulxes noticed vibrations and rumbling noises emanating from Basbane's plant. These disturbances were caused by machines

93

known as washer extractors, equipped with drums that revolved 650 times per minute.

The vibration and noise began as early as 4:00 A.M. and lasted as late as 9:00 P.M., with devastating results: Mortar began to fall from the cellar foundation of the Proulx home; cracks appeared in walls; door frames were forced out of line; cabinets pulled away from the walls; grout fell from bathroom tiling; windows loosened; and in many corners, the house literally started coming apart.

When it was clear that Basbanes' business could no longer mix with the Proulxes' pleasure, they sued him on the grounds of nuisance. By means of a parade of witnesses, the Proulxes proved that their house vibrated constantly. There was even testimony about such details as that the dishes always rattled; coffee spilled from cups onto the table; and milk in glasses always had "waves" in it.

Lionel Proulx testified that the vibrations caused a deafening sound that interfered with his hearing and made him nervous and upset. Rita Proulx testified that the noise and vibrations caused her to lose sleep and weight; she was compelled to take constant medication to relieve her nervous tension and allow her to sleep.

The Proulxes were found by the court to be persons with ordinary sensibilities—i.e., not overly sensitive—who had clearly grown sick and nervous as a result of the noise and vibration.

The constant disturbance emanating from Basbanes' plant constituted a nuisance from which the Proulxes were entitled to relief. For the suffering they had endured, the judge awarded $1,200 to Lionel Proulx and $2,400 to Rita Proulx—plus $4,000 for damage to the Proulxes' house (that sum being sufficient to cover the cost of repairs). The judge also granted an injunction, prohibiting John Basbanes from continuing to operate his plant in such a way as to subject the Proulxes to more vibrations and noise. (While such injunctive relief is not generally available in small-claims court, money damages certainly are.)

Courtroom Pointers

The *Proulx* case demonstrates how a little guy can stand up to a big business and win. Before you go to court, however, you may want to check with local authorities regarding any zoning requirements that the business may be violating. Find out if the business is located on property where zoning restricts its activities. Sometimes zoning limitations on business activities are exceeded when a legitimate business changes or expands its operations (e.g., from light industrial to heavy industrial). If there seems to be a zoning violation, file a complaint with your local zoning board.

Elements of your case. If you have to take a bothersome business neighbor to court, there are essentially three things you must prove:

1. The business is being operated near your residence in a way that interferes substantially with your normal living patterns.

2. The business's encroachment on your life-style is unreasonable.

3. As a result of this encroachment, you have suffered serious inconvenience, distress, or property damage.

Proving your side. Almost any business activity, when carried to excess, can create a nuisance for neighbors. In the *Proulx* case, vibrations were the culprit. Flashing headlights pulling into a parking lot created a nuisance in a Pennsylvania case. Dust from a concrete plant was the nuisance in a New York case. Other typical nuisance conditions include foul industrial odors, excessive noise, traffic congestion, litter, and pollution.

Your job in court is to show how a bothersome business neighbor's activities are at extreme odds with residential living. As one judge has explained: "The use of property for other than residential purposes may be, and at times is, an annoyance to dwellers in the vicinity, but the mere fact of annoyance does not establish the existence of a nuisance. . . . On the other hand, the law does not allow anyone, whatever his circumstances or conditions may be, to be driven from his home or compelled to live in it in discomfort, although by a lawful and useful business carried on in his vicinity."

Present any tangible evidence of the business's encroachment on residential living. Is the garage next door burning old tires? Photograph the billows of dark smoke, and bring the pictures to court. Is there horn-honking or blaring music emanating from a neighboring drive-in restaurant? Tape record it and offer to play the tapes in court. Do chemical effluents discharged from a factory overflow your property? As evidence, bring in a bottle containing a sample of these effluents. In effect, *show* it to the judge, rather than just telling it to him.

To prove the extent of a business's interference with residential living, be prepared to tick off all the normal pursuits you can engage in only with difficulty, if at all: for example, sleep, meals, use of the backyard, children's outdoor play, hanging clothes out to dry. Testify to any physical ills you have suffered as a result of the business nuisance; for example, nervous tension, eye irritation, headaches.

It always helps to present witnesses who can confirm the adverse effect on your domestic living habits. For example, guests of yours might testify that an outdoor barbecue you gave was ruined because of foul odors from the exhaust fan of the company next door.

Remember, even if a bothersome business does interfere with your home life, the interference must be unreasonable, or there will be no nuisance. Reasonableness, or the lack of it, is determined through a judicial balancing process. On one side of the scale go the utility and value of the business's activities; on the other side, goes the harm you're being subjected to. Emphasize the gravity of the harm, so the judge will see the unreasonableness of permitting the defendant to continue business as usual at your expense.

Countering the other side. Since you're suing a business rather than just another homeowner, you can expect somewhat different defenses to pop up than usually do in a nuisance lawsuit between neighbors. Two typical lines of defense that a business may raise can be summarized thus:

1. "I'm a big important business, and you're just a little homeowner; you can't stop progress by branding my business a nuisance."

2. "Don't blame me for any nuisance, because it's my *customers* who are the cause; and they're beyond my control."

There are ways to counter both of these defenses. The first one was overcome by homeowners in the Indiana case of *Cox v. Schlachter*. The Schlachters sued a scientific firm that was in the business of breeding white mice for biological testing. Vile "mousey" odors were expelled from the business's exhaust fans. The "mouse house" argued that the smell was a minor inconvenience, which had to be borne by the Schlachters, especially in light of the importance of the company's work in the field of biological testing.

But the court sided with the plaintiffs. "We find it difficult to agree with the company that the 'mousey' odor is but an occasional personal annoyance. . . . A putrid smell which brings tears to the eyes of nearby residents, drives them from their yards to the protection of their homes and robs them of their sleep, constitutes a nuisance. . . . We agree with the company that its business is of vital utility to all people, but the lax and negligent manner in which the company has conducted sanitation procedures in relation to surrounding residents of its property has nothing to do with the social import of its business." In short, even big, important companies don't have a license to interfere unreasonably with their neighbors.

The second typical line of defense was raised—unsuccessfully—in the Utah case of *Wade* v. *Fuller*. Neighbors sued Polar King, a drive-in café. They complained of a nuisance created by teenagers patronizing Polar King, who were constantly gunning the engines in their hot rods, playing their car radios, and blowing their horns. Polar King claimed it wasn't responsible for the conduct of customers, who were beyond its control.

"This contention is without merit," ruled the court. "Until the establishment of the café in the area, the offensive noise and conduct had been practically nonexistent. It was the establishment of the business that attracted the teenagers and their 'hot rods,' whose conduct disturbed the peace and quiet of the neighborhood. Under such circumstances it may reasonably be found that the defendants, as owners of the business, may be held responsible for the creation of a nuisance."

You too can counter the "Polar King"-kind of defense with a "but-for" line of argument" "But for the establishment of this business," you might tell the judge, "this nuisance never would have arisen in the first place. So the defendant shouldn't be allowed to escape responsibility now by claiming that some outside force created the nuisance."

A third kind of defense, common to all nuisance cases (not just those involving businesses), consists of the defendant trying to characterize you as an overly sensitive person. Be ready to fire back that any person of ordinary sensibilities (like one of the witnesses you brought with you, for example) would have been offended by the business conditions next door. Emphasize that the harm you've suffered—e.g., physical ills, property damage—are not imagined but very real and substantial.

CHAPTER

Scoundrels, Smart Alecks & SOBs

The Hospital that Turned a Poodle into a Cat

Have you ever been hurt by a real SOB—not hurt in a physical sense, like from a shove or a kick (for assault problems, see chapter 22), but hurt emotionally or mentally. Emotional hurt is as real as the physical kind and often more painful. Fortunately, the law provides a remedy for victims of sheer anguish. If some troublemaker or just a thoughtless individual seriously hurts your feelings, you can sue him for what the law calls the *infliction of mental distress.*

Consider the heart-rending saga of a misplaced dog in the 1979 New York case, *Corso* v. *Crawford Dog and Cat Hospital, Inc.* Kay Corso brought her fifteen-year-old poodle into the Crawford Hospital for treatment, but after an examination, it was decided, alas, that the dog had to be put to sleep. Corso and the hospital agreed that the dog's body was not to be destroyed, but would instead be given a decent burial.

Kay Corso arranged an elaborate funeral for her dearly departed pet, including a headstone, an epitaph, and attendance by herself, two sisters, and a friend. A casket was delivered to the funeral site at the appointed time. But on opening the casket, Corso found—a dead *cat!*

Anguished by this macabre mixup, Corso sued the hospital for the emotional pain it had caused her. The issue before the court was whether Corso could collect money damages *based solely on her mental distress*—unaccompanied by any physical injury or monetary loss. The judge decided yes: "I find that plaintiff Ms. Corso did suffer shock, mental anguish and despondency due to the wrongful destruction and loss of the dog's body.

"She had an elaborate funeral scheduled and planned to visit the grave in the years to come. She was deprived of this right."

Given this victory in principle, what price tag was to be put on Kay Corso's suffering? The court rejected the idea that her recovery should be limited to the mere dollar value of the dog's body, which would, of course, have been negligible. "In ruling that a pet such as a dog is not just a thing I believe the plaintiff is entitled to damages beyond the market value of the dog. A pet is not an inanimate thing that just receives affection; it also returns it."

In calculating the degree of emotional attachment between Ms. Corso and her poodle and, therefore, the intensity of her sense of loss, the judge distinguished other situations where people should not ordinarily expect to be compensated for their hurt feelings: "This decision is not to be construed to include an award for the loss of a family heirloom which would also cause great mental anguish. An heirloom while it might be the source of good feelings is merely an inanimate object and is not capable of returning love and affection. It does not respond to human stimulation; it has no brain capable of displaying emotion which in turn causes a human response. Losing the right to memorialize a pet rock or a pet tree or losing a family picture album is not actionable. But a dog—that is something else. To say it is a piece of personal property and no more is a repudiation of our humaneness. This I cannot accept."

To compensate Kay Corso for the hurt feelings inflicted on her by the hospital's mistake, the judge awarded her $700.

Courtroom pointers

If your feelings are abused as Kay Corso's were, you, too, can sue, based on *infliction of mental distress*.

Elements of your case. There are basically three elements to your case:

1. The defendant engaged in misconduct that exceeded all bounds of decency.

2. The defendant acted intentionally or with wanton disregard for the likelihood that your feelings would be hurt.

3. As a result of the defendant's misconduct, you suffered severe mental distress.

Proving your side. Getting the facts across in all their gory detail is especially important in this kind of lawsuit. The facts you recite must be such that any decent member of the community (including, presumably, the judge), upon hearing them, would be aroused to exclaim, "Outrageous!"

What sorts of affronts are apt to arouse such righteous indignation? A survey of recent cases reveals these examples of extreme misconduct that courts will not condone:

• In a Maryland case, a grocery clerk played a practical joke by packing a dead rat into the customer's groceries.

• In a Utah case, a man hounded a woman for months, asking her to have sex with him and, at one point, even exposing himself.

• In a New York case, a real cad jilted his girlfriend, married another, and then sent a taunting letter to his ex, entitled "Ode to Vicky," which derided her for her unsuccessful efforts to marry him and prophesied that she would be the source of great amusement in his happily married household for years to come!

Generally, you must establish that the defendant *intended* to make you suffer. Often, the very facts you recite—such as those in the jilted-girlfriend case—will be so extreme that the judge will easily infer the necessary intent on the part of the defendant. In other instances, it may appear that the defendant was simply *reckless*—that is, oblivious to the probable consequences of his misconduct (e.g., the Utah wolf whose sole concern was his animal pleasures).

Sometimes it may be difficult to prove the element of intent (or recklessness). Maybe the defendant was merely negligent. That certainly appeared to be so in Kay Corso's case. The hospital did not deliberately set out to cause her anguish; instead, there was simply a careless mixup. Ordinarily, this lack of intent (or recklessness) might have torpedoed Ms. Corso's case, because proof of mere negligence (i.e., carelessness) on the defendant's part is not good enough when you're suing for infliction of mental distress.

What probably salvaged Ms. Corso's case was the fact that she stood in a *special relationship* with the defendant. The hospital obviously knew (or should have known) that any slip-up in funeral preparations would be likely to touch a highly sensitive nerve—which, in fact, it did. Therefore, the hospital had a special duty not to subject Ms. Corso to any painful stimuli. If, like Ms. Corso, you too feel that you stood in such a special relationship to the defendant (where he had reason to know of your vulnerability and a duty not to exploit it), by all means bring that fact to the judge's attention. It could save your case if you're unable to prove that the defendant acted intentionally.

The most important point you must prove is that your mental distress was *real* and *extreme*. For a long time, courts would not allow recovery for mental distress unless it was accompanied by some measurable *physical injury*. Courts wanted tangible proof that the plaintiff was not just making the whole thing up. While proof of physical harm is no longer absolutely necessary, it will certainly strengthen your case. Therefore, bring to the judge's attention any evidence of how gravely you have suffered: e.g., nausea, headaches, sleepless nights, consultation with a doctor because of nervous fright. It should go without saying that the more outrageous the affront that you were subjected to, the likelier the judge will be to infer that you have experienced great anguish, even if there were no physical symptoms.

Countering the other side. You can almost count on the defendant's trying to belittle your claim of mental distress. He'll argue that you're exaggerating both his misconduct and your reaction. It's then up to you to convince the court that you're not making a mountain out of a molehill.

In a 1968 New York case, *Flamm* v. *Van Nierop*, the plaintiff complained that the defendant was harassing him in a weird but persistent manner by: (1) dashing at the plaintiff in various public places with "threatening gestures, grimaces, leers, distorted faces and malign looks" accompanied by "ridiculous utterances and laughs"; (2) walking closely behind plaintiff on sidewalk; (3) driving behind the plaintiff's car at a dangerously close distance; and (4) constantly telephoning the plaintiff at home and at work and either hanging up or saying nothing!

The defendant pooh-poohed this bizarre litany. After all, it's not against the law to make faces at somebody, he reminded the judge. On this elementary point, the judge agreed: "Offenses of a minor nature, such as name-calling or angry looks, are not actionable though they may wound the feelings of the victim and cause some degree of emotional upset. This is because the law has no cure for trifles."

Ah, but were the defendant's misdeeds simply trifles? No said the court: "If a man finds himself perpetually haunted by an enemy; if he is greeted at every turn by baleful looks, sudden sorties which fall short of physical contact, and derisive laughter; if he cannot drive his car without the imminent threat of a collision from the rear; and if he is troubled at all hours by telephone calls followed only by silence, then it can hardly be doubted that he is being subjected to the extreme and outrageous conduct" for which money damages will be awarded.

The moral of *Flamm* v. *Van Nierop* is: a dividing line exists between trivial affronts that we must all learn to bear—no matter how annoying—and truly aggravated harassment, which none of us need tolerate. In *Van Nierop* the defendant had crossed that line, because his behavior was so outrageous. It's your job to show the judge that the defendant you're suing also crossed that line and now must pay for the suffering that he has inflicted on you.

CHAPTER 17

Personal Injury and Property Damage

The Lady Who Slipped on a Mouse

There are an almost infinite number of ways to be careless. The kid next door belts a home run through your picture window. The delivery man backs his truck into your new car. The fast-food stand mops its floor without warning customers, and you slip and fall. Whenever such carelessness is present, a negligence lawsuit can't be far behind. Put simply, you can sue a person or business for negligence, if they have acted without reasonable care under all the given circumstances and, as a result, have caused you to suffer personal injury or property damage.

Rarely are the circumstances of a negligence case simple. So don't worry if you think your case could be in Ripley's "Believe It or Not." Many negligence cases could be.

Consider the 1975 Louisiana case of *Thomas* v. *Hanover Insurance Company*. The facts were recounted succinctly by the court: "The injuries occurred on March 6, 1973, at about 8:30 P.M. Mrs. Agnes Thomas, a schoolteacher, had gone to a laundromat to dry a bedspread. After placing the spread in the dryer, she seated herself in one of a row of chairs provided for customers' use and began grading school papers. Shortly after she sat down, she felt something on her foot. She looked down and saw a mouse. She screamed and jumped from her seat. It is not clear from the evidence whether she jumped once or twice. The testimony shows she did not intend to jump on the mouse. Nevertheless, her foot came down on the mouse, mashing it on the floor. This caused her foot to slip. She fell and injured her hip and back."

Agnes Thomas sued the laundromat, claiming that the owner had been negligent in not preventing mice from running around his business establishment and endangering his patrons. In the eyes of the judge, the lawsuit raised three basic questions (they are common to all negligence cases, so it's worth looking at them in detail): (1) Did the defendant owe the plaintiff some duty of care? (2) Did the defendant breach this duty—i.e., was he negligent? (3) Was that negligence a substantial cause of the plaintiff's injury?

On the question of duty, the judge noted the general rule that shopkeepers are not absolute insurers of their patrons' safety. But they do owe patrons a duty to maintain business premises in reasonably safe condition. Keeping a laundromat free from mice was, in the judge's estimation, part of the owner's duty toward his patrons: "In a business establishment such as a laundromat, where the customers are principally women, whose fear of mice is well known, a reasonably foreseeable hazard is that if a woman sees a mouse on or near her person, she will jump or run and, in so doing, may suffer injury."

So the laundromat owner was obliged to take reasonable precautions to keep his business premises free from mice. Had he violated that duty (put another way, was he negligent)? Yes, ruled the judge. Why? Because the owner had carelessly allowed litter (potato chips, soda bottles, candy wrappers, and so on) to accumulate regularly on the laundromat floor and had done nothing to get rid of the mice that were inevitably lured into the laundromat.

"We find," said the court, "that the operator of the laundromat knew or should have known that the food particles would attract mice. Yet he failed to take reasonable precautions to keep those rodents from the premises. He allowed the premises to remain in a filthy condition most of the time, and he failed to employ a pest control service on a regular basis prior to the accident."

Hence, the owner had been negligent. That conclusion led to the final question: Did the owner's negligence cause Agnes Thomas's injury? The judge concluded that the owner's negligence had contributed substantially to the injury: after all, the litter attracted mice; Agnes saw a mouse; she jumped, landed on the mouse, slipped, and was injured. So the chain of causation was clear, although a bit like something out of a Rube Goldberg cartoon.

The laundromat owner protested, however, that his negligence could not be considered the cause of Agnes's injury, because no one could have reasonably foreseen that such a freak accident as this one—i.e., stepping on a mouse and then slipping—would ever occur. But the court pointed out that it is not essential to holding someone liable for negligence that the *exact manner of injury* be foreseeable; it's sufficient that *the general risk of harm* was foreseeable:

"In the present case," explained the judge, "the duty breached was to take reasonable precautions to keep mice out of the premises. A purpose of this duty was to protect against the risk that a woman might become frightened by a mouse and, in attempting to flee, suffer injury. This is precisely the risk and harm suffered by Mrs. Thomas. Although we have here the unusual fact that Mrs. Thomas stepped on the mouse, and this caused her foot to slip, the result would be the same had she not stepped on the mouse but, instead, had fallen from the chair or had attempted to run and fell over some other object."

The court held the laundromat owner liable for negligence and awarded Agnes Thomas $1,875 to cover her medical expenses, plus $1,000 for pain and suffering.

Courtroom Pointers

The *Thomas* case, although a bit unusual, illustrates how the law of negligence generally works. Negligence may be thought of as a legal chain; each link must be forged and attached to the next one or you have no case. The main links are *duty* (the defendant owed you some duty of care), *negligence* (the defendant carelessly violated his duty), and *causation* (the defendant's negligence caused you harm).

Elements of your case. There are four elements that must be proven in a lawsuit based on negligence:

1. The defendant had a duty not to create an unreasonable risk of harm to you or your property.

2. He violated this duty by acting in careless disregard for your well-being (in legal parlance, he was *negligent*).

3. The defendant's negligence was a substantial cause of the harm that befell you.

4. You suffered a loss (e.g., personal injury or property damage).

Proving your side. The one recurring standard in all negligence lawsuits is *reasonableness*. The law of negligence demands that everyone act reasonably. If someone doesn't, and as a result, causes harm to others, then he must pay for the consequences. So if all else fails you in court, keep hammering away at the fact that the defendant simply did not act as a reasonable man would have under similar circumstances.

The first element in your case requires that the defendant must have had some duty not to create an unreasonable risk of harm to you. Exactly what duty the defendant may have had will vary with the nature of his activities and other circumstances. Most businesses, for example, have a duty to keep their premises reasonably safe for patrons. A driver has a duty to operate his car with reasonable care, observing the rules of the road and not endangering other drivers or pedestrians. A doctor has a duty to live up to those standards of professional competence that prevail among his colleagues; otherwise he may be liable for malpractice (a form of negligence).

Some people, because of the nature of their activities, have a higher duty of care than others. For example, the operator of a nursing home has a higher duty to avoid dangerous conditions than, say, the operator of a warehouse. What is reasonable in a warehouse may not be reasonable in a nursing home. When you present your case, be sure to point out any facts that would indicate the particularly high responsibility owed to you by the defendant. The higher the duty, the easier it will be for you to prove that the defendant acted negligently, which is the second element of your case.

Proving negligence is largely a matter of laying out convincing facts before the judge; it's then up to him to decide whether the defendant has acted negligently. For example, Agnes Thomas established that the laundromat owner allowed food to litter the floor, thereby attracting mice; under the circumstances, that sloppiness was negligent. In another situation, it might be negligent for, say, a bank to mop a floor and not post a sign warning patrons about possible slipperiness. Or it might be negligent for someone to put a flower pot out on a window sill when there is a danger that it will fall off. In general, let the facts speak for themselves; rest assured, the judge will hear them loud and clear.

If you're aware of any laws or ordinances that the defendant has violated, by all means bring them to the judge's attention. For example, a town ordinance may prohibit burning leaves. Raking a pile of leaves and setting it on fire will, therefore, almost certainly be viewed as negligence. Similarly, driving the wrong way up a one-way street is negligent.

Negligence does not always involve misconduct; sometimes a person *fails to act* when he was obligated to do something. (As lawyers say, negligence includes acts of *omission* as well as *commission*.) Suppose your lease requires the landlord to keep your apartment in "good repair." You complain to him about a leak under your sink, but he fails to make an inspection or any repairs. Two weeks later that leaking pipe bursts, flooding your apartment and ruining your rug. Here, the landlord had a duty to act but didn't; any reasonably prudent landlord would at least have inspected the pipe. Therefore, it's likely that the landlord's inaction was negligent, and he may be held liable for the damage to your rug.

Note two key factors in our last example: (1) the landlord knew about the potentially risky condition; and (2) he had a reasonable opportunity (i.e., two weeks) to do something about it. In any negligence case—whether it involves a landlord, storekeeper, next-door neighbor, or anyone else—it is always important to emphasize these two factors. Make certain that the judge realizes that the defendant was aware of the condition that ultimately caused you grief. Point out how much time elapsed between the moment when the defendant first became aware of the risk and the moment when you were finally harmed. It is the very essence of negligence for a defendant to do nothing in the face of a known danger—or to do too little too late.

In chapter 5, we offered the example of the dog owner who knows that his German shepherd has bitten people. Given this awareness, any reasonably prudent dog owner would take precautions against future mishaps (e.g., by muzzling the dog or tying it up). However, the owner in our example does nothing, and sure enough, a few months later the dog gives a repeat performance, biting the next-door neighbor. When the neighbor sues for negligence, he will have a strong case. He can prove that the owner knew his dog had bitten other people and had a few months in which to do something. If, however, the dog had never attacked anyone, and the owner had no reason to suspect that the dog was vicious, the neighbor would have a difficult time proving negligence.

The third element of your case requires you to prove that the negligent acts of the defendant caused damage to you or your property. The key word here is "caused." The law doesn't hold a person responsible for every consequence of his careless acts; we are not all walking insurance companies. A person is liable only for the *reasonably foreseeable* consequences of his carelessness.

Assume that your upstairs neighbor lets his bathtub overflow, resulting in water damage to your apartment. You could sue the neighbor, claiming that he was negligent and should be held liable for the water damage, which was a reasonably foreseeable consequence of letting the bathtub overflow.

But let's add a twist to the case. Suppose the water caused a short circuit in your television set, which caused the picture tube to explode, which, in turn, injured your cat. Is the upstairs neighbor responsible for your cat's veterinarian bills?

The answer will depend on whether the judge believes that injury to your cat was a reasonably foreseeable consequence of your neighbor's letting his bathtub overflow. We won't presume to second-guess the judge. (We would venture, however, that the damage to the television set was certainly reasonably foreseeable.)

When you present your case, emphasize any facts that show how the loss you suffered was a reasonably foreseeable consequence of the defendant's negligence. Don't worry if the exact manner in which you were injured was not foreseeable. Remember from the laundromat case that causation is established as long as the general risk of harm was reasonably foreseeable.

The final element of your case is proving the amount of damages you suffered. Present whatever documentation you have to back up your claim. If you suffered property damage, bring a repair bill to court or get a written estimate of what repairs would cost. If you suffered personal injuries, bring along any medical bills. Don't forget to put a price tag on your *pain and suffering* (see chapter 3).

Countering the other side. Be on the lookout for three defenses that are commonly raised in negligence cases. First, the defendant may say that he did not know about the potential risk; therefore, he can't be considered negligent for having done nothing about it. One obvious way to overcome this defense is to point out that you—or someone else—specifically notified the defendant about the risk. (Maybe you even have a copy of a warning letter that you sent to the defendant shortly before the mishap occurred.) Even if the defendant was not so notified, you can argue that any reasonable person standing in the defendant's shoes would have or should have discovered the risk on his own; that's often good enough evidence to make the defendant responsible.

Second, the defendant may argue that you were well aware of the potential risk and, nevertheless, chose to ignore it when you engaged in the activity that led to your injury. Therefore, you can't now legitimately complain. Lawyers call this defense, *assumption of the risk*—in other words, you voluntarily stuck your neck out.

To counter this defense, tell the judge that you did not assume the *particular* risk that caused you harm. The case of *Bourque* v. *Duplechin* dramatizes this countering technique. In the summer of 1974, two amateur softball teams met: the team from Boo Boo's Lounge versus the boys from Murray's Steak House. Jerome Bourque was playing second base for Boo Boo's. Adrien Duplechin was at bat for Murray's and he hit a single. Steve Pressler was next up and he hit a ground ball to the shortstop. The shortstop threw the ball to Bourque at second in hopes of getting a double play. Bourque caught the ball, touched the bag, and threw to first.

Meanwhile, Duplechin, who had been on first, was bearing down on second base. He collided with Bourque about four or five feet *outside the base path* leading from first to second base. Duplechin had deliberately run outside of the base path in order to knock Bourque down and break up the double play.

Bourque sued Duplechin for the injuries he suffered in the collision. He claimed Duplechin had been negligent when he caused the collision. Duplechin defended his base-running tactics by saying that baseball is a rough sport, and base runners often collide with other players. Stopping a double play is just part of the game, and players assume the risk of possible injury.

Bourque countered this defense by saying that he never assumed the risk that Duplechin would run four or five feet outside the base path. It is, after all, against the rules of the game for a runner to run outside the base path.

The judge agreed with Bourque: "A participant in a game or sport assumes all the risks incidental to that particular activity which are obvious and foreseeable. A participant does not assume the risk of injury from fellow players acting in an unexpected or unsportsmanlike way with a reckless lack of concern for others." As a result, the judge concluded that Bourque "did not assume the risk of Duplechin's negligent act."

The best way to counter an assumption-of-the-risk argument is to say that you never assumed the *particular* risk which caused injury to you or your property. To back up this argument, point out that it was not obvious or foreseeable that a person doing what you were doing would be injured.

The third and final defense to beware of is the tricky *disclaimer of liability*. In effect, the defendant concedes that he was negligent and caused you injury, but claims that he still can't be held liable. Why not? Because you signed a piece of paper that contained a clause absolving him of all liability for negligence (in other words, he can be careless and not have to pay for the consequences).

For instance, you rent a floor sander, and the rental contract contains a disclaimer of liability for negligence. Because of the rental agency's lack of careful maintenance, the sander, which is defective, goes out of control and damages your apartment.

Can the rental company escape liability for its own negligence? Probably not. Judges will generally strain for any possible way not to enforce a disclaimer of liability for negligence. Such disclaimers are considered grossly unfair; no one should be able to confer upon himself what amounts to a license to be careless. If you can give the judge any legitimate grounds for overlooking the disclaimer, he will probably do so. For example, you may never actually have read the disclaimer (it was probably buried deep in the fine print). If so, tell the judge you were unaware that the defendant was insulating himself from liability; had you known this, you would never have signed the paper. The judge will be extremely reluctant to enforce a provision against you that you had not consciously agreed to.

CHAPTER 18

Coat Checking

A Persian Lamb Coat Goes on the Lam

Sometimes checking your coat can mean losing your shirt. After a candlelit dinner in some charming bistro, you're shocked to discover that the checkroom has "misplaced" your cashmere overcoat. Or maybe you left your belongings in a store's dressing room, and somehow they departed before you did. In situations like these, the proprietor is usually liable to you for the value of your coat or belongings. That's so because you entered into a so-called *bailment* relationship with the proprietor when you entrusted your belongings to him for safekeeping (technically speaking, he is known as the *bailee;* you are the *bailor*). The proprietor can be held liable to you as a negligent bailee for failing to guard your belongings adequately.

Dorothy Johnson was up against a negligent bailee in the 1959 Pennsylvania case of *Johnson v. B & N, Inc.* One night she visited the Moonglo Club to have dinner and see a fashion show. The club was packed, and when Dorothy went to check her Persian lamb coat, she learned that the checkroom was full; there were no more checks left.

Not to worry. Patty, the checkroom attendant, who knew Dorothy, agreed to take her coat anyway, despite the lack of checks, and return it to her whenever she claimed and identified it.

Alas, when Dorothy revisited the checkroom following the show, Patty wasn't there, nor was the Persian lamb coat. There was just an unattended checkroom, open to passersby, save for a little half-gate across the doorway. Although Patty was later found, the coat wasn't, and no one seemed to have any explanation.

Dorothy sought one in court; she sued the Moonglo Club for the value of her lost coat. Dorothy testified to Patty's acceptance of the coat without giving a receipt. The judge ruled that a bailment had resulted: "Checkroom service was an incident of the club's business and was necessary for the accommodation of its patrons. And the authority of Patty, the checkroom attendant, to accept Dorothy Johnson's coat, without giving her a check, must be implied from the circumstances." (Incidentally, witnesses from Moonglo claimed the coat had never been delivered to the checkroom—i.e., there was no bailment—but Dorothy was simply a more credible witness, and the judge chose to believe her story, rather than the club's.)

Since a bailment existed, the next issue was whether the bailee (Moonglo Club) had been negligent and, therefore, should be held liable. Dorothy testified that during dinner she saw Patty moving about the restaurant seating guests. It was thus established that Patty, beside being the sole checkroom attendant, doubled as a hostess in the restaurant. While Patty played hostess, the patrons' coats were left all alone.

A case of clear-cut negligence, concluded the court: "The evidence was clear and precise that the cloakroom attendant was absent therefrom at times, leaving it and its contents unguarded and an easy prey to the covetous eyes of a purloiner, an early departing patron, perhaps, or one entering, taking the coat, and leaving unseen."

The judge awarded Dorothy a judgment against Moonglo Club in the amount of $500. That was the value of her coat according to a reputable furrier whom she had called as a witness.

Courtroom Pointers

Dorothy Johnson's victory demonstrates that you don't have to settle for any more feeble excuses when some restaurant (or other business) treats your belongings as though they were part of a rummage sale. Before examining the elements of your case against such a bailee, let's get acquainted with some of the finer points of bailment law.

There are two kinds of bailments: *actual* and *constructive.* The first kind arose in the Moonglo Club: Dorothy Johnson handed her coat directly to a club employee; she conferred exclusive possession over the garment to the club for the duration of her stay. When such a clear transfer of control over your personal property occurs, the legal result is an actual bailment.

Quite a different legal situation arises, however, when you don't actually give physical custody over your property to the restaurant's personnel (or other business employees). Suppose the restaurant (hotel, lounge) maintains a free unattended room where patrons themselves may hang up their coats and later retrieve them on their own. In all likelihood, no bailment results if you leave your coat in such an unprotected environment. Certainly, this is so when no restaurant employee assists you or encourages you or even takes notice of what you're doing. (Your only hope in such a situation is to prove that the establishment was negligent in maintaining the unattended room in the first place—not an easy thing to do.)

Take this example one step farther into an even less classy eaterie, such as a cafeteria or fast-food outlet. Far from offering checkroom accommodations or unattended cloakrooms, the establishment may provide nothing more than wall hooks or coat trees. When you hang up your coat and umbrella here, you're not playing bailor to the eaterie's bailee. No way!

Why not? Because it's pretty clear that you did not deliver exclusive possession of your belongings to the eating establishment. At any time during your meal, had you wished to get something from the coat's pockets or take it back to keep you warm, you were entirely free to do so, without having to ask an employee of the establishment. (Indeed, a sign on the wall may have warned you pointedly: "Watch your hat and coat.")

Is the rule, then, that bailments arise only if a restaurant (or other public place) has a checkroom with an attendant? Not necessarily. While circumstances may dictate that there was no *actual* bailment, there may have been a *constructive* one. In a constructive bailment, there is no clear transfer of possession over property, as there must always be in an actual bailment. Generally speaking, a constructive bailment occurs when (1) circumstances make it necessary for you to lay aside your belongings in some business establishment; (2) the business proprietor (or his employees) knows about this necessity; and (3) the proprietor (or his employees) know that you, in particular, have laid aside your belongings.

Dressing rooms in clothing stores are typical places where constructive bailments may easily arise. After all, you have to remove your coat (or whatever) in order to try another one on. Recognizing this necessity, stores provide dressing rooms. (How else could they get you to buy from them?) If they don't accommodate your needs, you're forced to leave your coat or hat (or whatever) on the counter while you try things on; and here, too, a constructive bailment can arise.

Elements of your case. The name of the game is establishing that a bailment (actual or constructive) was created when you left your coat or personal belongings in someone else's establishment. Of course, the elements of your case will vary a bit, depending on whether you seek to establish an actual or a constructive bailment:

For an actual bailment, there are two key elements:

1. You delivered your belongings directly into the physical custody of a checkroom attendant (or similar person), giving him or her exclusive possession of your things until you demanded their return.

2. When you asked the attendant to return your property, he could not or would not comply with your request.

For a constructive bailment, there are four basic elements:

1. You were in an establishment where surrounding circumstances made it necessary for you to put your belongings aside somewhere.

2. The proprietor of the establishment (or his employees) recognized the need for patrons like you to put things aside— usually as an inducement to do business in the establishment.

3. The proprietor (or his employees) knew, or should have known, that you did, in fact, put your belongings aside for a while.

4. When you sought to retrieve your belongings, they were nowhere to be found.

If you establish these four elements—two in the case of an actual bailment—a presumption will arise that the bailee was negligent in safeguarding your property. The burden is then on him to come forward with some plausible explanation as to how he did, in fact, exercise reasonable care and why he therefore should not be held liable for your loss.

Proving your side. To prove an actual bailment, testify to the manner in which you handed your property over to another person for safekeeping. If you happen to have any tangible evidence (e.g., a coat check), present that to the judge. Witnesses can be helpful here (e.g., the friend you dined with) to corroborate your story, especially if you suspect the proprietor may deny that you ever gave him your property. The witness may also confirm your testimony as to the failure of the proprietor to return your belongings.

Proving a constructive bailment is a bit trickier; it's not as black and white as handing your things over to another person. Be sure to impress upon the judge the necessity for laying aside your belongings in the first place. For example, you visited a doctor and left your coat in his waiting room (e.g., in a closet or on a coat tree), but when you emerged from your appointment, the coat was gone. To establish a constructive bailment, emphasize the fact that it was necessary for you to put your coat somewhere before you went in for medical treatment. (As one judge recently observed: "It is not the custom for a patient to lie on the couch or sit in the chair in a psychiatrist's office wrapped in a fur coat.") Because of this obvious necessity, the doctor provided facilities in his waiting room where patients like you would be expected to leave their coats before entering his office. Courts have routinely held that dentists, psychiatrists, and other doctors are liable as negligent bailees (just like restaurateurs) when patients lose coats left in the waiting room.

It never hurts to point out to the judge that being able to lay aside your belongings was for the mutual benefit of you and the proprietor. He must have expected—indeed, wanted—to cater to your needs; otherwise, how could he expect you to patronize his establishment?

In the New York case of *Morrow* v. *Cuisine de Coeur,* Sally Morrow and some friends dined at Cuisine de Coeur one night. When they entered, the maitre d' directed them to hang up their coats on a metal coatrack, which was located in a recessed alcove at the rear of the restaurant. (The restaurant had no other facilities for coats.) The members of the dinner party followed this suggestion; no fee was asked or paid, and no check or receipt was given. The party was then seated at a table that had only an obstructed view of the coat rack. After dinner, when Sally returned to the coat rack, her mink coat was missing.

Sally Morrow sued the restaurant. Of course, there was no *actual* bailment, because the diners had not delivered their coats into the possession of restaurant employees. But applying the general principles we've already learned about, the court found that a *constructive* bailment had been created. Why? For three reasons: First, it was necessary for Sally Morrow to lay aside her mink, because the coat was bulky and heavy; the restaurant was small, crowded, and of the kind conducive to leisurely dining; and there were no coat hooks or other facilities within the reach and view of patrons. Second, Cuisine de Coeur recognized the necessity for laying aside coats and responded to it by maintaining a coat alcove for the convenience of its patrons. Third, the restaurant's employees knew that Sally Morrow had, in fact, laid aside her mink; indeed, the maitre d' had specifically invited her to do so. (These employees also must have realized that Sally Morrow's view of the alcove was obstructed so that her personal continuous surveillance was impossible.)

Given these circumstances, Cuisine de Coeur became the constructive bailee of Sally Morrow's coat, bound to return that coat as any other bailee would have been. The failure to return the coat created a presumption that Cuisine de Coeur had been a negligent bailee. It could not overcome the presumption and was thus held liable to Sally Morrow for the value of her coat ($3,550).

Countering the other side. Don't get thrown if the bailee tries to overcome the presumption that he was negligent. He may testify that his employees are vigilant, and there's no way your coat could have been taken because of their carelessness. Feel free to respond honestly: "All I know, Your Honor, is that they weren't able to return my coat when I asked for it. Regardless of what he says, the facts speak for themselves. They had custody over my coat; somehow, through oversight or a mixup, they lost my coat or let it be taken." Of course, you'll be in much better shape if, like Dorothy Johnson, you can testify about actual instances of negligence (e.g., a temporarily unattended coatroom) that you observed.

A much more serious obstacle is the ubiquitous *disclaimer of liability*. The bailee testifies that a sign, prominently posted in his establishment, warned you: "Not responsible for hats, coats, and umbrellas" or "Not responsible for personal property unless checked with the management." Or perhaps you did check your property, and the bailee points out that a warning was printed on your check: e.g., "Loss or damage—No claim shall be made in excess of $25 for loss or damage to any piece checked."

Now what do you do? If you never saw the sign or read the check, say so. For example: "Your Honor, I thought that stub was just a way to identify my coat. Quite frankly, I was paying attention to my dinner date, and I stuffed the tickets in my pocket without thinking I had to read them. Certainly, no one pointed out any disclaimer to me."

In effect you're saying, I shouldn't be bound by some hidden conditions I didn't know about—let alone agreed to; if they were that important, they should have been called to my attention by the folks who made them up! Basically, the law agrees with you. One judge expressed the point well in regard to a stub given out by a parcel checkroom at a train station: "In the mind of the bailor the little piece of cardboard, which was undoubtedly hurriedly handed to him, and which he doubtless as hurriedly slipped into his pocket, without any reasonable opportunity to read it, and hastened away without any suggestion having been made upon the part of the parcel room clerk as to the statements in fine print thereon, did not rise to the dignity of a contract by which he agreed that in the event of the loss of the parcel, even through the negligence of the bailee itself, he would accept therefore a sum which, perhaps, would be but a small fraction of its value."

While the law backs you up in principle, there may be a

genuine factual dispute as to whether you were actually on notice of the disclaimer. For example, in the *Cuisine de Coeur* case, the restaurant produced three witnesses who testified that over the coatrack was a sign stating: "Not responsible for items left here. Guard valuables, thank you, management." Sally Morrow countered with five witnesses who testified that either there was no such sign or else they didn't see it. The judge believed Sally's story, concluding that "either there was no sign or that it was so poorly posted or illuminated that it could not be readily seen."

Finally, the bailee may dispute the value of your lost belongings. Technically, you're entitled to collect only the *fair market value* of your property at the time of its loss (see chapter 3). Unfortunately, market value may be far lower than cost, even on an overcoat you bought yesterday; secondhand clothing and personal effects depreciate rapidly. What you must emphasize to the judge is the relative newness of the property and how little you had used it. In effect, you are appealing to the judge's sense of fairness, rather than his adherence to the strict letter of the law. If you can substantiate a higher value for your property by using an expert witness—the way Dorothy Johnson called on a furrier to testify on her behalf—by all means do so; it will impress the judge and give him a peg to hang his decision on.

CHAPTER

Insurance Coverage Disputes

Of Stolen TV Sets, Yacht Insurance, and Blue Cross

One of the least comprehensible things known to man is an insurance policy. Reading a policy is hard enough; collecting on it can be even tougher. The words you always assumed meant one thing are twisted to mean another. Suddenly, when you need your policy's protection most, it turns out to be legal Swiss cheese. Needless to say, a good insurance lawyer can assist you greatly at this juncture if you can afford his expertise. On fairly straightforward insurance disputes, involving modest sums, however, you may choose to handle your own case in court—using common sense and some basic principles of insurance law that will help you to win.

Consider the 1966 Brooklyn Small-Claims Court case, *Breslerman v. Newark Insurance Company*. Eva Breslerman was going on a trip to Europe. She had some of her belongings, including a small battery-operated Panasonic television, delivered to her son's apartment for safekeeping during her absence. Unfortunately, the television was stolen from her son's apartment. Eva filed a claim with the Newark Insurance Company, which had sold her a "Personal Effects Floater Policy." Newark maintained, however, that

121

theft of the television was not covered by the policy. Eva disagreed, and to prove her point she sued Newark for $135.15—the purchase price of the set.

The meaning and applicability of three basic provisions from Eva's policy were in dispute. First, the policy specifically covered "personal effects such as are usually carried by tourists and travelers, belonging to and used or worn by the insured." According to Eva, the Panasonic television qualified as a "personal effect," but the insurance company argued to the contrary; depending on which interpretation was correct, the policy either did or did not cover the television.

Second, the policy specifically *excluded* from its coverage over thirty named articles—such as automobiles, bicycles, boats, artificial teeth, plus a broad category labeled "household furniture." Was the Panasonic television set a piece of household furniture excluded from coverage? No, contended Eva; yes, maintained Newark Insurance Company.

Third, the policy stated that it did not insure any personal effects while they were "in storage." Did this limitation apply after Eva had given the television to her son for safekeeping in his apartment? Predictably, Eva and the insurance company argued on opposite sides of this question.

On the fundamental question of whether a portable television set was a "personal effect" covered by the policy, Judge Joseph Heller pointed out that the term "personal effects" has no settled technical meaning; generally it denotes property having a more or less intimate relation to the person of the possessor. "The words, 'usually carried by tourists and travelers,'" reasoned Judge Heller, "do not necessarily apply only to such articles as most tourists and travelers carry, but mean merely that the personal effects are to be of the kind usually carried by such tourists and travelers *as own them*." Judge Heller concluded that a portable television was precisely the kind of personal effect that might well be carried by a traveler who owned one.

So the television set seemed to be covered by Eva's policy—unless it was specifically *excluded*. But it was not. Judge Heller decided that the set did not constitute "household furniture"; that term was simply too general to be applied to something as narrow and describable as a portable television set. Judge Heller observed: "The policy in question enumerates more than 30 items of personal property which are not covered by the policy. Household furniture is one of the many enumerated articles not covered. It would seem the insurance company had a duty to spell out in plainest terms any exclusionary or delimiting policy provisions. It could have defined household furniture." But it chose not to, and Judge Heller was not about to rewrite the insurer's policy for it— at the expense of the insured.

The final hurdle to recovery under the policy was posed by Eva Breslerman's transfer of the television to her son's apartment. Did that act mean that the television had been placed "in storage" and, therefore, outside of the policy's coverage. No, answered Judge Heller: "Storage denotes a certain degree of permanency. Specifically it may be said storage is the safekeeping of goods in a warehouse or other depository. Storage is not synonymous with possession or custody. . . . Breslerman's son kept the article in his apartment, which was not a warehouse, storehouse or store-room, during his parent's travels."

Judge Heller ruled that under the policy Eva Breslerman was entitled to a judgment against her insurance company in the amount of $120—representing the purchase price of the Panasonic, less $10.15 in depreciation.

Courtroom Pointers

Three cheers for Eva Breslerman, you're probably thinking. You must admit, though, that the arguments raised by Newark Insurance Company were not entirely groundless. They made almost as much sense as Eva Breslerman's arguments, because the language in the policy was ambiguous, admitting of different interpretations. This ambiguity, so common to many insurance policies, is one reason why Eva Breslerman won (it's also why you may win a lawsuit against your insurer).

Traditionally, judges interpret ambiguous insurance policies in favor of the insured person. There are three basic guidelines that judges generally follow when interpreting such policies (Judge Heller followed these guidelines):

First, an insurance policy will be interpreted most favorably toward the insured, because he had no say in the policy's wording, which was determined solely by the insurance company.

Second, where reasonable and intelligent men, on reading the policy, could honestly differ as to its meaning (as in the *Breslerman* case), any doubt should be resolved against the insurance company.

Third, if the insurance company desires to exclude something from the policy's coverage, it has the responsibility of expressing the exclusion in clear and unmistakable language that will not mislead the average person.

Bear these guidelines in mind whenever you dispute the meaning of your policy with the insurer. Don't settle for any strained interpretation of your policy that jeopardizes your interests. It won't hurt to remind the insurer's representative that *in a courtroom* ambiguous insurance policies are usually interpreted in favor of the insured.

Elements of your case. If you're forced to sue the insurance company over a disputed policy, there are five basic elements you'll have to establish:

1. You were insured against a specific kind of risk by the insurance company.

2. The risk insured against occurred on a given date.

3. At that time, the policy was in full force and effect, all premiums then due having been paid punctually.

4. You gave the insurance company timely notification that the risk insured against had occurred (notification requirements are spelled out in your policy and should be followed closely).

5. The insurance company refused to honor your claim because of a dispute about coverage under your policy.

Proving your side. There are three pieces of evidence that you will want to bring to court:

• the insurance policy;

• any canceled check(s) that shows that the policy was paid up and in force at the time the risk occurred; and

• a copy of whatever notification you sent to the insurance company informing it that the risk had occurred and claiming the right to payment.

Explain the nature of the risk, how it occurred, and why you think it is covered under the terms of your policy.

Countering the other side. The main obstacle you must anticipate is the one that confronted Eva Breslerman: the insurance company will maintain that your policy does not cover the risk that befell you. The wording of your policy—both its coverage sections and its exclusionary sections—will then come under close scrutiny by the judge. When interpreting your policy, the judge will rely on the three general guidelines discussed earlier.

Consider another small-claims court case, *Tuchman* v. *Public Service Mutual Insurance Company,* decided in 1976. Sam Tuchman insured his 17-foot pleasure boat under a "Yacht Policy (all risks)." An 85-horsepower outboard motor was stolen from the boat, and Sam Tuchman filed a claim with Public Service. The insurer denied that Sam's policy covered any losses due to theft. So Sam was forced to sue Public Service for the value of the motor—$1,000.

Admittedly, theft was not specifically mentioned in the policy as one of the risks insured against. But then it was not specifically excluded either. All that the policy specified under "Perils Insured" was: "All risks of physical loss or damage to the property covered from any external cause." Certainly, this broad language could be interpreted to include physical losses caused by theft; had Public Service wanted to exclude theft, it could have inserted an appropriate provision in the policy. Following general guidelines for interpreting an insurance policy, Judge Felice Shea resolved doubt over the policy in favor of Sam Tuchman, rather than Public Service: "It is clear . . . that a small boat owner who takes out an 'all risk' policy which does not exclude theft has a right to assume he has purchased coverage for loss by theft."

Health insurance frequently turns out to be the most difficult sort of policy to collect on. "It has become an increasingly widespread practice among insurance companies," said a judge in a 1978 New York case, "to deny coverage for major medical expenses for reasons amounting more to creative thought than to legitimate defense." The New York case arose when Blue

Cross-Blue Shield refused to pay one of its policy holders for anticancer laetrile treatment. This treatment had been prescribed by the policyholder's physician. But Blue Cross took a hard line: its policy covered only "medically necessary" treatment; according to Blue Cross's medical experts, laetrile treatment, being of largely unproven effectiveness, could not be considered "medically necessary" (despite the opinion of the policyholder's physician) and, therefore, lay outside the policy's coverage.

The court, however, sided with the cancer victim, because of the general guidelines for interpreting insurance policies: "Defendants [Blue Cross-Blue Shield] contend that the claims in the contract containing the term necessary treatment allows them to present expert testimony to show that the treatment plaintiff [the policyholder] received was not necessary or effective. Defendants are attempting to construe their contract most harshly against plaintiff. This they cannot do. It is a general rule of construction that policies of insurance are construed liberally in favor of the insured and strictly against the insurance company." In other words, Blue Cross would not be allowed to second-guess the policyholder's physician as to what sort of treatment was medically necessary under the policy.

Nasty Insurance Adjusters

The Insurance Company that Contested the Incontestable

You never really know how good (or bad) your insurance company is until you file a claim. With luck, your insurer will prove to be understanding and cooperative. Don't be surprised, though, if your claim meets with stiff resistance: The insurer may flatly refuse to pay out on your claim, even though your right to collect appears to be beyond dispute. Or the company may drive a hard bargain solely to wear you out and make you settle for less. Or a claims adjuster may be particularly nasty to you.

There's legal relief for this sort of sharp dealing and abuse. You can sue the insurer for willfully and wantonly breaching its contract with you and, as a result, causing you to suffer extreme mental distress (that's a bit of a mouthful, but it can spell dollars and cents when you tell it to the judge).

Consider the hard time Rex Insurance Company gave to Myrtle Baldwin in the 1975 Indiana case, *Baldwin* v. *Rex Insurance Company*. Myrtle's husband, Rufus, purchased a $1,000 life insurance policy from Rex on July 20, 1970; Myrtle was named as the beneficiary. Exactly two years later, the policy, under its own terms, became "incontestable"—that is, Rex could not refuse to pay off on the policy except on one ground, nonpayment of premiums. Just about four months after the policy had become incontestable, Rufus Baldwin died; on that day the policy was in full force and effect, because all premiums had been paid on it.

Myrtle Baldwin filed a claim with Rex for the $1,000 benefit due on her husband's death. A more straightforward and valid claim is hard to imagine. But Rex flatly refused to pay off. Even though the policy was legally incontestable, Rex chose to contest it! Rex charged that Rufus Baldwin had failed to report a prior illness when he had applied for life insurance. When Myrtle Baldwin pressed her claim, Rex merely offered to refund the premiums on the policy ($332.80); if Myrtle wanted the $1,000 benefit, Rex told her to go to court.

Which is just what she did. In court, Myrtle testified to the worry and anguish she had been subjected to by Rex's unjustified refusal to pay benefits that were clearly due her. She had been put to unnecessary bother and expense to collect on her husband's policy.

The court concluded that Rex's refusal to pay had been not only unfounded, but also malicious, causing Myrtle extreme mental distress. Based on Rex's wrongful breach of contract, Myrtle was awarded the $1,000 that was rightfully hers under the policy. In addition, Myrtle was awarded $2,500 in *punitive damages,* to punish Rex for its maliciousness. (Myrtle did not sue in small-claims court. Had she done so, she would not have been awarded the extra $2,500, because punitive damages are not generally recoverable in small-claims court (see page 30). As we will shortly see, however, money damages can be awarded against an insurance company in small-claims court based on the *infliction of mental distress.* Such damages may not be as high as punitive damages, but the award helps to compensate you for the ordeal you have suffered.)

Courtroom Pointers

You can see that no insurance company may jerk you around with impunity. So if the company or its agents start giving you a rough time without any justification, remind them that they may have to pay not only on their policy, but also for their misconduct. Before going to court, you may also want to complain to the commissioner of insurance in your state; he is responsible for licensing insurance companies and investigating complaints against them.

Elements of your case. There are six basic elements to your case against an obtuse insurer:

1. You were insured against a specific kind of risk by the insurance company.

2. That risk occurred on a given date.

3. On that date, your policy was in full force and effect, all premiums then due having been paid on time.

4. You gave the insurance company timely notification that the risk had occurred (according to the notification requirements spelled out in your policy) and filed a claim for payment under your policy.

5. Without any reasonable justification, the insurance company or its agents strenuously resisted paying off on your claim and subjected you to abuse or painfully sharp bargaining.

6. As a result of this intentional misconduct on the insurer's part, you suffered extreme mental distress.

Proving your side. In the eyes of the law, insurers have a special obligation toward policyholders, because insurance plays such a vital role in our society. At a minimum, policyholders are entitled to fair treatment. Therefore, courts frown on abusive, hard-driving, short-changing tactics on the part of insurers. Your task is to convince the judge that your insurance company violated its trust by willfully and unreasonably disparaging your claim and, perhaps, harassing you in the process.

Be sure to bring with you to court three vital pieces of evidence:

• the insurance policy;

• the canceled check(s) establishing that the policy was fully paid up and effective at the time the risk occurred; and

• a copy of the notice and claim that you filed with the company.

You will have to testify about the circumstances surrounding the filing of your claim. The most important part of your testimony will concern the way in which your claim was treated by the insurance company. For example, the company "stonewalled" by putting you off with endless excuses, despite your repeated requests for payment. Or the company drove an unreasonably hard bargain with you, knowing that you were desperate for money and would eventually settle for a pittance. Whatever attitude the company manifested through its words, correspondence, and conduct, bring this evidence to the judge's attention.

In a 1970 Ohio case, the insured filed a claim under his homeowner's policy. His house had been burglarized, and he had carefully documented the value of the stolen furniture at over $4,000. Despite this documentation, the insurance company sent a nasty letter to the insured, offering him $1,000 on a take-it-or-leave-it basis. He left it and went to court where the judge concluded that the insurance company never had any intention of honoring the claim filed with it; instead, the company had willfully violated its contract. The court awarded the insured $4,450 to compensate him for the value of the stolen furniture.

Be sure to emphasize to the judge any outrageous abuse that you have been subjected to by the insurance company or its agents. An insurance company—just like a bill collection agency, or a hotel, or even a private individual—can be held liable for the *intentional infliction of mental distress* (see chapters 16, 28, and 33). In a Mississippi case, a policyholder filed a health insurance claim. A few days later, a claims adjuster visited the policyholder at home where he was convalescing in bed. Without any provocation, the adjuster began browbeating the policyholder: "You are a liar," the adjuster charged. "If I paid this claim I would be sent down the road. A few days ago I caught a woman in bed with her shoes on stealing from the company, playing sick, and I am getting tired of people stealing from the company like that." This whole outrageous scene caused the policyholder great anguish. When he recovered he sued the insurance company, based on the adjuster's outburst, and won $250.

CHAPTER

Collision Insurance Hangups

The Case of the Fourteen-Month Repair Job

There's one thing worse than being stalled in traffic; it's being stalled by your automobile insurance company following a collision. Instead of paying you for the loss you've incurred, the insurer opts for an easier and cheaper way out—namely, having your wreck towed to a garage and repaired. (Under most collision policies, the option to repair, rather than to pay cash for the decrease in the car's value, is open to the insurance company.)

If your insurer takes this option, brace yourself. Like many other disgruntled policyholders, you may soon find yourself facing long delays and endless excuses while your car sits in a garage somewhere; or you may get caught in the middle of a dispute between your insurer and the garage over the extent and cost of the repairs; or the long awaited repair job may turn out to be unsatisfactory, necessitating still more work and delay. To add insult to injury, all the while you're enduring this ordeal, you are also, of course, being deprived of the use of your car. Take some solace, though, in the fact that you can make the insurance company pay for all the inconvenience and aggravation you've put up with.

131

Fourteen months was the exasperating delay in a 1974 Florida case, *Travelers Indemnity Company* v. *Parkman*. Kenneth Parkman had purchased a comprehensive automobile insurance policy from the Travelers Indemnity Company, which included collision protection. When Parkman's car was damaged in an accident, he notified Travelers immediately. Rather than pay Parkman for the loss caused by the accident, Travelers opted to get the car repaired.

When the repairs were completed, however, Travelers refused to pay for them! Why? Because the insurer suddenly claimed that Parkman's policy had not been in effect at the time of the accident. As a result of the insurer's failure to pay for repairs, the garage refused to release the car to Parkman. For fourteen months, Parkman went without a car until at last the dispute with Travelers was settled in Parkman's favor. Thereupon, Travelers paid for the repairs, and the garage released Parkman's car.

Travelers refused, however, to pay Parkman anything by way of compensation for the fourteen months he had gone carless. Determined not to bear this loss alone, Parkman sued Travelers. The insurance policy did not require Travelers to compensate Parkman for the loss of the use of his car. But the court decided, nonetheless, that Travelers was liable.

How could the court possibly rule in Parkman's favor, given the strict terms of his policy? By applying some basic insurance law that may prove useful to any policyholder involved in a collision: You see, when Travelers opted to repair Parkman's car—rather than pay him outright for the damage—a new "contract" was formed between Travelers and Parkman—a contract wholly independent of Parkman's insurance policy. This new contract obligated Travelers to see to it that Parkman's car was adequately repaired and restored to him *within a reasonable period of time.*

The fourteen-month delay in restoring Parkman's car to him was entirely unreasonable. The court decided, therefore, that Travelers had breached its contract to repair. What loss had Parkman suffered as a direct result of this breach of contract? He had been deprived of the use of his car for fourteen months. To compensate him for this loss, the court ordered Travelers to pay Parkman $1,700 in money damages.

Courtroom Pointers

The *Travelers Indemnity* case states a basic rule of insurance law that you can use to good advantage: Say your car is involved in an accident and your insurer opts, under the terms of your collision insurance, to get your auto repaired. You now know that the insurer, by taking this option, is entering into a *new contract* with you. That contract obligates it to repair your car within a reasonable time or risk being held liable for the time you were deprived of the use of your car. Therefore, if the repair is starting to take too long, you have some leverage to use against your insurer. Remind the insurer that if it takes an unreasonable time to restore your repaired car to you, you intend to hold it responsible for all the time during which you've been deprived of the use of your car. If necessary, you may just have to sue as Kenneth Parkman did.

Elements of your case. There are seven basic elements to your case against the insurance company:

1. You had an automobile insurance policy with the company that covered collision liability.

2. Your car was involved in a collision.

3. At the time of the collision, your automobile insurance policy was in full force and effect, all premiums then due having been paid on time.

4. You gave the insurance company timely notification of the collision.

5. Exercising its option under the policy, the insurance company chose to get your car repaired.

6. Through no fault of yours, repair of the car was delayed beyond a reasonable time (or the car was repaired inadequately).

7. As a direct result of the delay or inadequate repairs, you were deprived of the use of your car and thereby suffered a financial loss.

Proving your side. Bring with you to court three basic pieces of evidence:

- the insurance policy;
- the canceled check(s) that shows the policy was paid up and in force when the collision took place; and
- a copy of the notification you sent to your insurance company, informing it about the collision.

Testify to the circumstances under which the insurer opted to get your car repaired. Recount the nature of the delays, excuses, or shoddy workmanship you have had to cope with. Offer the court an estimate of what would have been a reasonable time for the insurer to repair your car. (Here, the testimony of a mechanic may be persuasive.)

Finally, you must give the judge some basis for determining how much of a loss you have suffered as a result of the insurer's mishandling of your car and your collision claim. In a 1973 Arizona case, *Home Indemnity Company* v. *Bush*, the policy holder, Walter Bush, was deprived of the use of his damaged Ford camper for sixteen months. In court, Bush proved that, as a result, he was unable to use the camper during this period for over 200 days (to take hunting trips); Bush would have driven about 10,000 miles during 200 days of hunting. He established that the reasonable rental value of a comparable vehicle would have been $12 per day, plus 6 cents per mile. This detailed evidence was accepted by the court as a sound basis for awarding Walter Bush several thousand dollars in money damages.

Countering the other side. The insurance company may try to shift the blame to you. It will claim that the repairs took a long time or were never completed because your standards were unrealistic; you arbitrarily refused to accept the quality of the work done (or attempted) at the company's behest. Your best response to this defense is that, contrary to what the company says, any reasonable person would have concluded, as you did, that the repair work on your car was sorely inadequate; therefore, you were under no obligation to accept it.

In a 1975 Ohio case, *Sweet* v. *Grange Mutual Casualty Company*, Jerry Sweet's 1972 Dodge was totaled in a collision. Rather than pay Sweet the value of his wrecked car (about $3,000), Grange insisted on trying to have the heap repaired. But the repairs that Grange proposed were enough to make any driver balk. Basically, Grange wanted to have a repair shop perform a "clip" job: the ruined Dodge would have been cut in half and the front half welded onto the back half of *another* car. Understandably, Sweet refused to settle for a clip job, so his wreck just sat around; he incurred storage charges on it; and he also had to pay for alternate transportation.

Finally, Sweet sued Grange. The court held that the clip job fell far short of Grange's obligation to repair, which entailed restoring the Dodge to its former condition: "We find the nature of the 'clipping' operation to be so inconsonant with the plain meaning of the word repair as to compel the conclusion that the offer to comply with the insurance policy by the offer to 'clip' was made in bad faith." The court awarded Sweet $3,500.

CHAPTER 22

Assault and Battery

The Case of the $1,000 Football Punch

Street justice demands an eye for an eye and a tooth for a tooth. No wonder so many people who abide by street justice have so few teeth left. But there is an alternative to street justice. If somebody punches you, instead of punching back (which benefits only the dentist), try hitting him where it really hurts: in his wallet.

Assault and battery, in addition to being a crime, is also a civil wrong (what the law calls a *tort*). If someone assaults you, you can sue him for money damages. Perhaps because assault and battery is a crime, many people think it occurs only when the victim suffers serious injury. Nothing could be further from the truth, as the 1974 Louisiana case of *Earle* v. *Wilhite* demonstrates.

Robert Earle was the football coach at Sterlington High School in the fall of 1973. He was also a respected school teacher. At least one person, though, did not respect his coaching ability.

On November 3, Sterlington High played a football game against another school. During the game Coach Earle made substitutions from time to time. One player didn't see much action that day, which incensed his father, John Wilhite. The angry father thought his son should have played for a longer period.

Many fathers have undoubtedly shared John Wilhite's sense of wounded pride at some time or other during their sons' school days. Most fathers don't, however, do what Wilhite did. After the game he walked up to Coach Earle and punched him in the face. Coach Earle suffered no appreciable physical injury, just some soreness in his jaw and a slight swelling that subsided over the weekend.

Coach Earle sued John Wilhite for assault and battery. He claimed that the unprovoked assault had embarrassed him and caused him pain and suffering. Wilhite countered that the assault was, to some extent, justified, because of Coach Earle's failure to put Wilhite's son in the game more often. The judge decided that not putting a boy into a football game does not justify the boy's father's punching the coach (good news for high school coaches across the country!). The judge went on to decide that although the coach had suffered only minor physical injuries, he certainly had been embarrassed. As compensation for these injuries, the judge awarded Coach Earle $1,000.

Courtroom Pointers

Before you go to court on an assault and battery case, you should understand the technical difference between "assault" and "battery." An assault occurs when someone puts you in fear of any unjustified contact. If someone points a gun at you, you've been assaulted, even though you haven't been touched. A battery occurs when someone unjustifiably comes in contact with you. For example, he hits you with his fist. Thus, if someone winds up to hit you (an assault) and then follows through by hitting you (a battery), what has occurred is an assault and battery. As a practical matter, the distinction between assault and battery is frequently overlooked by judges, perhaps because most cases involve both an assault and a battery.

Elements of your case. The basic elements of an assault and battery case are:

1. The defendant intended to make some sort of physical contact with your body or with something closely attached to it

(e.g., clothing). His intent need not necessarily have been hostile; he may have intended only a practical joke or, conceivably, even a complimentary kiss.

2. The defendant made physical contact with you in some way to which you did not consent. Your consent will be presumed only to innocuous contacts, which would ordinarily offend no reasonable person (e.g., a slight tap on the shoulder).

3. As a result of the contact, you were offended or, even worse, physically hurt. Mere personal indignity (or mental distress) is a sufficient offense to justify the award of money damages; actual physical harm is not essential to an assault and battery, although its presence will almost certainly increase any money damages awarded.

The beauty of an assault and battery case lies in its simplicity. Basically, all that's required is an unjustified contact. There's no requirement that severe injury result. In fact, judges tend to be very responsive to sincerely initiated assault and battery cases. They like to believe, quite properly, that people should resolve their disputes in court, not on the street. A person who retaliates by going to court is likely to get a sympathetic hearing.

Judges also recognize that the harm caused by a contact is not necessarily measured by the size of a bruise. In the Arizona case of *Skousen* v. *Nidy,* the assaulter had amorous intentions. Miriam Nidy was a sixty-five-year-old woman who was the victim of sexual harassment. According to the court, her employer at various times placed his hand on her private parts and attempted to seduce her. On one occasion, he pushed her. Ms. Nidy resisted these assaults, and eventually she was fired.

At the time this case arose, in 1961, there was no federal law prohibiting sexual harassment on the job. But Ms. Nidy was not without a case. She went to court and accused her former employer of assault and battery. The court acknowledged that no physical injury was caused by the assault and battery, but according to the court, "Mental suffering, including shame for the indignities of the acts, is usually considered an injury for which damages may be given." To compensate Ms. Nidy for her shame and suffering, the court awarded $5,000.

Here are some other examples of court cases involving an assault and battery:

• A client of an apartment referral agency in New York City complained about the service he had received. An agency employee "bounced" the client off the wall and threw him out of the office. There was no serious physical injury. But the indignant client sued in small-claims court, where that "bounce" cost the referral agency $100.

• A teenager involved in a brawl after a school dance slapped another teenager across the face with the back of his hand. There was no physical injury. However, the victim suffered embarrassment and humiliation. Award: $100.

• A black man attending a luncheon buffet in Houston had his plate snatched from his hand by another man, who shouted that Negroes could not eat in the restaurant. The Texas court found that snatching the plate was an unauthorized contact and, hence, an assault and battery. Award: $900

Proving your side. Evidence of an assault and battery can come from eye witnesses or medical documentation. (Bear in mind that if the injury was severe enough to require a doctor's care, you should probably consult a lawyer.) If there was a police report of the altercation, get a copy to see if it contains any information helpful to your case.

If no physical injury was inflicted, you'll probably be depending on a claim that you suffered humiliation, embarrassment, and mental anguish. Your credibility will determine how much, if any, damages you will be awarded. So a word of caution is in order. Sometimes when an assault and battery case is brought to small-claims court, the assault and battery continues in the hallway or courtroom. If you give the judge the impression that you're a fighter, your credibility will be hurt. The judge may suspect that you provoked the altercation. While provocation does not justify the assault and battery, it may go toward reducing any award of money damages.

Countering the other side. A frequent defense in an assault and battery case is the claim that it was all an accident. This excuse allows the scoundrel to admit that he did it but claim he didn't mean to. The facts are no longer an issue; instead, the intent of the assaulter becomes the focal point, and who knows that intent better than the assaulter himself?

There are two ways to counter this defense. First, you could be prepared to present evidence that the assaulter *did* intend to come into contact with you. If you've had previous run-ins with him, for example, recount them in court. If he said anything before the altercation that would tend to show a malicious intent, testify as to what he said.

Second, point out that you are not involved in a *criminal* prosecution where the intent of the defendant to inflict serious injury is crucial. You are involved in a *civil* case, where the standard to be applied is whether, under the circumstances, the contact was justified, not whether the defendant intended to injure you. Therefore, the defendant who caused the "accident" should be held responsible for the consequences.

CHAPTER

Common Carriers

The Bus Driver Who Ignored a Passenger's Stop

Did you ever get the impression that bus drivers, train conductors, cabbies, and the like all attended a special school for meanness? Required courses probably included, "How to pull away from the curb just as the bus passenger arrives," "How not to make change," and "Seventy-six snappy insults." Nowadays, when you board a bus or train, you're lucky if your ticket is the only thing that gets punched.

You don't have to put up with this sort of abuse, though. What you may not realize is that every time you take a ride on public transportation, you enter into a *contract* with the bus, train, or taxi. That contract entitles you to respect and a safe trip. If you don't get it, you can sue for breach of contract.

That's what Estelle Brown did in a 1959 small-claims case from New York City, *Brown* v. *Fifth Avenue Coach Lines, Inc.* Estelle boarded a bus at Fifth Avenue and Thirty-fourth Street; the bus was headed up Fifth Avenue to Fifty-ninth Street, then east on Fifty-ninth, and over the Fifty-ninth Street bridge into Queens. When the bus passed Fifty-ninth Street and Third Avenue heading toward the bridge, Estelle signaled twice to the driver, because she was getting off at the next stop—Fifty-ninth and Second Avenue. But the driver failed to stop and carried Estelle all the way across the bridge into darkest Queens.

Needless to say, Estelle was upset. She had been carried far out of her way (she lived on East Fifty-eighth Street in Manhattan), and she had out-of-town guests staying at her home, who were waiting for dinner. As soon as the driver missed her stop, Estelle complained, but he responded, with a devil-may-care attitude, that it was too late to stop. When Estelle asked to have her fare refunded, the driver refused and went into a "tirade of senseless and unprovoked wrath."

Estelle managed to get back to Manhattan, exhausted, humiliated, and late, but she refused to forget about the affront. "Actuated by the thought that the way to promote and inflict further indignities upon a long-suffering public is to submit to them," Estelle went to court (probably by limousine), where she sued the bus driver's employer, Fifth Avenue Coach Lines.

In court, Estelle testified to the vexation, indignity, and delay she had suffered because of the driver's failure to honor her signal and because of his rudeness. The court had little trouble deciding that the bus driver had breached the contract for safe and courteous passage that Estelle Brown had entered into at the moment she boarded the bus. The seriousness of this breach was only accentuated by the indignities that were heaped on Estelle by the driver. The court awarded Estelle 30 cents for the two fares she had to pay (to Queens and back), plus $100 in damages (to compensate her for the mental distress she had suffered, as well as the delay and inconvenience).

Courtroom Pointers

Like Estelle Brown, you too are protected against outrages when you travel on what the law calls a *common carrier* (e.g., a public conveyance such as a bus, train, taxi). As a passenger, you have a contract of passage, which obligates the carrier to treat you with respect, convey you safely to your destination, and protect you from other passengers who may threaten you. If the carrier breaches this contract, you can sue for any damages you suffer.

Elements of your case. There are three elements to your case against a common carrier:

1. You were a passenger aboard one of the vehicles operated by the common carrier in question.

2. An employee of the carrier (e.g., the driver, conductor) acted in disregard of your comfort or safety.

3. As a result of this misconduct, you were harmed or greatly inconvenienced or humiliated.

Proving your case. Begin by describing how you came to be a passenger on the common carrier that you're suing. Recite the circumstances under which the carrier's employee shirked his legal responsibility to take proper care of you during your trip. Be sure to make it clear that the employee was aware of the position you were in—e.g., being carried beyond the stop you'd signaled for or being menaced by another passenger. You can do this by testifying how you, for example, or other passengers complained to the employee, but he refused to take any action or he responded haphazardly or abusively.

Finally, you must establish that the employee's misconduct caused you some damage. One element of this damage may be added expense in getting to your destination (e.g., the extra fare Estelle Brown paid), or inconvenience. Perhaps, the major element will be mental distress (embarrassment, fear, vexation).

The range of abusive conduct for which common carriers have been held liable to their passengers is varied. For example:

• The $500 kiss. In a Missouri case, a bus driver was aware of an unruly drunk who was harassing other passengers. But the driver made no effort to control the drunk, even though passengers had complained. Indeed, the driver seemed to be amused by the drunk's antics. Things ceased to be funny when the drunk fell on a woman passenger and deliberately kissed her—legally speaking, an assault and battery. The woman sued the driver's employer and won $500 for that kiss!

• The $250 wisecrack. In a Louisiana case, a rather stout woman was just getting off a street car (her contract with the common carrier had, therefore, not yet terminated) when the driver remarked: "You had no business sitting in the front of the car—a big fat woman like you. Why didn't you sit in the back?" Needless to say, this gratuitous reprimand hurt the lady's feelings. "The personal appearance of a patron of a street car," ruled the court, "is not a proper subject of comment by the employees of the defendant company. Neither should the conductor undertake to dictate to a passenger as to where she should sit in a car which has no reserved seats." The court awarded the insulted lady $250 to soothe her hurt pride.

• A Greyhound in heat. In a Georgia case, a Greyhound bus driver objected to a passenger's opening a bus window, even though the bus was frightfully hot. When the passenger coolly replied that he would file a complaint with Greyhound, if necessary, the driver flew off the handle and yelled: "You goddamned bald-headed son of a bitch, step over here and I'll settle the whole business with you." Suffice it to say, Greyhound was liable for the mortification suffered by the passenger —who turned out to be an ordained Baptist minister!

Countering the other side. There are several defenses that the common carrier may try to hide behind. First, the carrier will disown the misconduct of its employee: Why hold us liable, the carrier will argue, for acts over which we had no control? Your answer lies in the legal doctrine of *respondeat superior* ("Let the master answer"). Under this doctrine, a common carrier— indeed, any employer—can be held liable for the negligence and misdeeds of its employee, as long as the employee was acting within the ordinary scope of his employment (e.g., while driving a bus, loading luggage).

Second, the carrier will object to being made the absolute guarantor of your well-being. It is true that the carrier cannot insure that your trip will be perfect. Under your contract with the carrier, however, the carrier's employees are bound to use every reasonable precaution that prudent foresight allows—not to guard against every conceivable mishap, but to keep you reasonably secure from danger, discomfort, and indignity.

Finally, if the carrier thinks it's going to lose, it may try this ploy: you're not entitled to recover more than the amount of the fare. That's just what the Fifth Avenue Coach Lines tried to do —limit Estelle Brown's recovery to a piddling 30 cents. But the court followed the general rule that although the passenger's injury arises technically from breach of a contract, the passenger is, nevertheless, entitled to collect more than the mere price of that contract (i.e., the fare). The passenger can collect for other damages caused by the breach—for instance, mental distress, lost time, extra travel expenses, discomfort—and that amounted to $100 for Estelle.

CHAPTER

Landlord Harassment

The Seventeen-Day Landlord Sit-in

The second most passionate relationship is that between landlord and tenant. Rarely do they see eye to eye—how could it
be otherwise when one man's home is another man's business?
Too often, the animosity felt on both sides breaks out into open
warfare. The landlord, who generally occupies the dominant
position, harasses the tenant or cuts back on building services
(e.g., heat, water) or wrongfully evicts the tenant (e.g., by lock-
ing him out of his apartment). If you are being victimized by
your landlord, you don't have to suffer in silence; you can take
legal action and make the landlord pay for all the grief he's
caused you.

Consider the outrageous 1952 Montana case, *Welsh* v. *Pritchard.*
John and Katherine Welsh were renting a house from Griff Pritchard. The Welshes' rent was paid up, and their continued tenancy was assured under a governmental "rent control" program.
Legalities aside, Griff Pritchard decided he wanted the Welshes
out, and he told them so. But John Welsh stood on his right to
remain a lawful tenant in possession.

To overcome this resistance, Griff Pritchard showed up at the
Welsh home on June 25. When Mrs. Welsh let him in through the
kitchen door, Pritchard blithely walked right into the living room

and took a seat—just as though he lived there. Minutes later, Pritchard's wife Dora—a paralytic who used both a crutch and a cane—entered through the front door, which Pritchard had opened for her. Dora also took a seat in the Welshes' living room. In a short while, these two uninvited visitors were followed by certain of their belongings: namely, a bed, rocking chair, radio, and magazines. When Mrs. Welsh, understandably miffed, asked Pritchard what was going on, he calmly replied, "We came over to stay."

John Welsh's reaction on arriving home that night was later described by a Montana court: "If Welsh had any idea that his home was his castle, or that he and his family alone would enjoy the privacy and quiet of his domicile, such idea was rudely shattered and took wing when he reached home and found the Pritchards and their belongings cluttering up the living room. Things looked bad and they were to become worse before becoming better. He was in for days and nights that would try any man's soul."

Seventeen days and nights, to be precise—that's how long the Pritchards camped in the Welshes' living room! During that time, Welsh and Pritchard had one knock-down drag-out fight, and Pritchard was served with an arrest warrant but never actually taken into custody. Dora Pritchard, being a paralytic, was regrettably unable to control her bowel movements and repeatedly befouled the living room. Throughout this ordeal, the Welshes refused to move out, knowing that, once they left, they would be locked out by Pritchard. "It was just a cold war," John Welsh later testified in court. Finally, after a seventeen-day occupation, the Pritchards gave up the cause and left.

John Welsh seized this opportunity to leave also, but just long enough to file suit against the landlord. Later on in court, Welsh testified to the constant strain that he and his wife had been subjected to by the Pritchards' intrusion: "You can imagine having probably the worst enemy in the world living under the same roof with you. . . . The first two nights he was in there I didn't sleep a wink. . . . He boasted outright he was never going to move out. . . . It was his house and we were the trespassers."

The court had little trouble concluding that the Pritchards had grievously and unjustifiably invaded the Welshes' privacy. "Such invasion, trespass, entry and stay were intentional, wrongful and malicious. . . . The law presumes that the usurpation by strangers . . . of a man's home, and their continued intrusion for 17 days and nights into the very heart and privacy of his family life, resulted in detriment and damage." To compensate the Welshes for their distress, the court awarded them $500. (Probably, the award would have been higher had Welsh not assaulted Pritchard during the encampment.)

Courtroom Pointers

As outlandish as *Welsh* v. *Pritchard* may seem, it underlines a basic legal principle: A tenant's home (or apartment) is his castle. No one may trespass there—*not even the landlord!* Indeed, a tenant's right to exclusive use of his apartment is generally set forth in the lease itself, although in legalese that often makes little sense. Check your lease for a clause that reads something like this: "The landlord covenants that the tenant, on paying the rent and performing the covenants herein, shall peaceably and quietly have, hold, and enjoy the demised premises for the term mentioned herein." This legalese is known technically as the *covenant of quiet enjoyment;* it means that a tenant who pays his rent and abides by the terms of his lease is entitled to enjoy his apartment in peace, without any intrusions or disturbance from the landlord.

Even if a tenant does *not* pay his rent or abide by his lease, the landlord can't just throw him out or change the lock on his apartment door (a so-called *lockout*). Almost every state bars the landlord from thus taking the law into his own hands. Instead, the landlord must follow state laws, which assure an orderly judicial process for determining whether the tenant shall be evicted (the tenant is entitled to be served with proper advance notification and to have a day in court). The bottom line is: landlords can't evict tenants; only judges can.

If a landlord locks you out (or otherwise illegally evicts you), he violates the covenant of quiet enjoyment and probably commits a trespass. You can immediately summon the police and file a complaint for criminal trespass. You can also seek a court order that reinstates you in the apartment, although you'll need to hire a lawyer to pull this off.

Taking a cue from *Welsh* v. *Pritchard*, there is another effective legal remedy at your disposal—one you can pursue on your own in small-claims court. Sue the landlord for what the law calls *intentional infliction of mental distress.* Just as John Welsh did, you too can make the landlord pay for harassing you.

Elements of your case. There are four elements to your case against the landlord:

1. You were the rightful tenant in your apartment.

2. The landlord deliberately harassed you or locked you out or otherwise wrongfully evicted you.

3. The landlord intended to make you suffer or wantonly disregarded the probable consequences of his actions.

4. As a result of the landlord's misconduct, you were deprived of the right to enjoy your apartment and were forced to suffer or vacate instead.

Proving your side. To prove that you are the rightful tenant, the best evidence is your lease. If you don't have a written lease, testify to any oral agreement that you have with the landlord— or simply that you have been renting from the landlord on a month-to-month basis.

Next recite exactly what the landlord did that caused you distress. Don't succumb to the constant temptation to relate every little hallway squabble that you've had with the landlord. Instead, catalogue as coolly and succinctly as possible whatever significant wrongs the landlord has committed. (For instance, he removed personal belongings from your apartment; he cut off your water supply; he changed the lock on your door.) Your testimony about the landlord's misconduct should go far toward establishing (in the judge's mind) the malicious intentions behind the landlord's actions.

Be prepared to describe in court how severely the landlord disrupted your home life, disturbed your peace of mind, deprived you of sleep, and, perhaps, cost you money (e.g., to rent a space heater when the landlord deliberately cut off heat to your apartment). Here are some recent examples of tenants who won money damages to compensate for what they had suffered at the hands of their landlords:

• Electricity cutoff. A Virginia landlord cut off electricity to the apartment of a 79-year-old stroke victim, aggravating her condition. For deliberately threatening her well-being, the landlord had to pay $750 in court (covering the tenant's pain and suffering, medical expenses, spoiled food, and so on).

• Computer foulup. A New York City tenant was mistakenly evicted (and not restored to occupancy in his apartment for a week), because of a computer error on the landlord's part. The tenant sued and won $260 for personal property damaged during the eviction, $130 in lost earnings, $18 in food spoilage, $55 for eating out, plus $1,000 for mental distress.

• Removal of door. In a 1977 Georgia case, the landlord tried to hasten a tenant's departure by removing the tenant's front door ("there goes your door; what's your hurry?"). The tenant was awarded $600 for this willful interference with his right to quiet enjoyment.

• Premature paint job. One Louisiana landlord was so anxious to get an apartment ready for new tenants that he sent in a crew of painters to refurbish the place *before* the old tenants had moved out. Not surprisingly, the old tenants objected to this invasion; they were humiliated because their neighbors suspected that they were being evicted. They sued and were awarded $150 to assuage their hurt pride.

• Lockout. In a 1976 Washington case, the tenant was wrongfully locked out and her personal belongings dumped on the sidewalk. She sued the landlord and won $1,000 to cover her mental distress and the cost of having her property picked up and warehoused.

• Sic 'em! In a 1977 case, a Texas landlord was pressuring the tenant to vacate. One of his dirty tricks was to let the tenant's dog (which was ordinarily kept on the patio) into her apartment while no one was there to supervise. Left to its own incisors, the dog did substantial damage to the tenant's belongings. She sued the landlord for this trespass and won $1,735.

Countering the other side. Watch out for two arguments that the landlord is likely to raise. First, the landlord will claim that you're blowing things out of proportion. After all, you were only deprived of heat for a day or two, so what's the big deal?

The landlord may well be right if you've testified to only an isolated incident or some minor annoyance (e.g., an exchange of insults in the elevator). But not if you're complaining about a *pattern of misconduct.* Then it's up to you to emphasize the cumulative impact of all the little wrongs and the obvious single-minded intent behind them. That's exactly what Janet Tooke did in the California case, *Tooke* v. *Allen.* There the landlord had, at different times, threatened Ms. Tooke, broken the lock on her door, entered her apartment and scattered her personal belongings, reduced the hot water supply, cut off the gas several times, and disconnected switchboard service. When Tooke sued the landlord, he pooh-poohed the "minor inconveniences" she had suffered as "too inconsequential to engage the time of the court." But the court refused to lose sight of the underlying justification for the tenant's lawsuit—namely, the landlord's "pursuit of a purpose of unrelenting persecution by petty annoyances, the cumulative effect of which would be to render plaintiff emotionally disturbed to the point where further occupancy of the apartment would be intolerable." Considering the distress Tooke had suffered because of the indignities continuously heaped upon her, the court awarded her $2,500.

The second argument that may be thrown at you is that you are basically a bad tenant who provoked the landlord into doing what he did. If this charge is false, deny it; even if there may be some truth to it, provocation is no excuse for the landlord to harass you or take the law into his own hands. The 1973 New York Case, *Yates* v. *Kaplan,* dramatizes this point well.

Mrs. Yates moved in with a tenant named Mr. Surlack to serve as his housekeeper, which she did for several years. "On August 1, 1973," as Judge Irving Younger later reconstructed events, "Mrs. Yates entered Mr. Surlack's bedroom to serve breakfast. She found him dead. Unable to decide what to do, she did nothing. The next day passed, and the morning of the next. By then the body had reached the state of ripeness foretold by Hamlet of the murdered Polonious (Act IV, Scene 3):

'But indeed, if you find him not within this month, you shall nose him as you go up the stairs into the lobby.'

"The police were called. Mrs. Yates refused to let them in. They asked whether Mr. Surlack was all right. 'Yes,' she said. 'I take good care of him.'

" 'Then why can't we go in to see him?'

" 'Well, I guess he's not all right. He needs an undertaker.'

"The body was removed that day. Mrs. Yates stayed elsewhere until the apartment could be fumigated. When she returned, a padlock was on the door."

It's hard to imagine a less desirable tenant than one who keeps dead bodies lying around. Still, Mrs. Yates was entitled not to be locked out vigilante-style, but to have the fate of her tenancy decided in court (which it soon was, not surprisingly, adversely!). Because of the landlord's unlawful lockout, Mrs. Yates was awarded $225 in court.

CHAPTER

Apartment Repairs

The Case of the Central Air-conditioning Breakdown

Today's consumers insist on getting what they pay for. The same sort of toughness ought to be displayed by tenants. If you rent an apartment that the landlord fails to maintain or heat or supply with other required services, you're being gypped; each month you pay your rent, but you don't get your money's worth in return. Fed up with such a one-sided bargain, some tenants have taken it upon themselves to do the landlord's work for him —e.g., by performing do-it-yourself repairs—and have then turned around and sued the landlord for their expenses.

That's just what three tenants from New York City's Lincoln Square Apartments did in the 1973 small-claims court case, *Harwood* v. *Lincoln Square Apartments.* The building had central air conditioning. Under the standard form lease used by the landlord, he was obligated to maintain this air-conditioning service, the cost of which was included in the rent: "As long as there shall be no breach or default by tenant," said the lease, "landlord shall furnish . . . (a) automatic elevator service; (b) hot and cold water . . . (c) heat . . . (d) gas . . . (e) a master television antenna; (f) refrigeration for food . . . (g) air conditioning by installation of one air conditioning unit in the living room of the apartment and in each room of the apartment designated by landlord as a bedroom, and (h) electricity."

New York City had a long hot summer in 1973, and right in the middle of it, what should go on the fritz but the central air conditioning at Lincoln Towers. Three tenants there—Herbert Harwood, Wendy Evans, and Millie Shogan—went on dutifully paying their rent despite the interruption in services. But they also acted to help themselves; they rented their own individual room air conditioners to supply what the landlord could not. This do-it-yourself spirit turned out to be well advised, because the Lincoln Towers' central air conditioning was out for *six weeks* that summer!

Having weathered the heat wave with no thanks to the landlord, our three stalwarts were obviously disgruntled with having had to pay twice for air conditioning: once to the landlord (as part of the monthly rent check) and once to the air conditioner rental company. So they all went to New York City Small-Claims Court, where they sued the landlord to recover their air conditioner rental expenses for the six-week period.

Judge Stanley Danzig held in favor of the three tenants. The lease between the landlord and each of the three tenants was a binding contract that obligated the landlord to provide air conditioning, among other services, in return for the monthly payment of rent: "The inclusion of air conditioning," reasoned Judge Danzig, "among such other services as hot and cold water, heat and refrigeration, indicates that air conditioning is deemed by the landlord, as well as by the plaintiff tenants, to be a basic necessity. It is clear that the landlord's promise to provide air conditioning formed an inherent part of [the quid pro quo] in return for which plaintiffs paid rent."

In plain English, the landlord and the tenants had struck a bargain: in consideration for the tenants' promise to pay their rent, the landlord had promised to supply, among other things, air conditioning. These two promises were mutually binding: the tenants had performed their end of the bargain; by not performing his, the landlord had breached the contract.

To what extent had the tenants incurred damages as a result of this breach? Here the tenants had clear proof: the rental bills for their individual air conditioners during the six-week hiatus. On the basis of this evidence, Judge Danzig awarded judgments to Wendy Evans and Millie Shogan each in the amount of $197.95, and to Herbert Harwood in the amount of $101.65 (their respective rental expenses).

Courtroom Pointers

The *Harwood* case demonstrates that a lease is a two-way street. If you do all the giving and don't get back what you're entitled to, then you may want to follow the example set by Herbert Harwood and the other two tenants.

Before you resort to do-it-yourself tactics, however, make sure you've exhausted all other reasonable alternatives. To begin with, contact the landlord whenever you feel he's not performing essential services that he owes to you. Write him a dated letter specifically requesting the steps you want taken: e.g., replaster cracked and crumbling ceiling; repair leak under sink; replace nonfunctioning gas range. (Keep a copy of this letter, which you may need later as evidence.)

If the landlord doesn't respond, file a complaint with your local department of housing, emphasizing any threat to your life, health, or safety that may be posed by the landlord's inaction. Any administrative inspection or sanction that results from such a complaint may prod the landlord into doing his duty.

When all else fails, you're ready to do it yourself. That may involve steps such as those taken in the *Harwood* case. Or you may have to hire the skilled services of a plumber, electrician, or carpenter. You will then sue the landlord for the expenses he forced you to incur.

Elements in your case. You will have to prove five basic elements in your case:

1. In return for your payment of rent, the landlord was obligated to perform an essential service—e.g., make repairs, supply a working refrigerator.

2. You paid all your rent and abided by any other obligations that were yours under the lease.

3. But the landlord failed, despite your complaints, to perform an essential service.

4. That service was a vital part of your bargain with the land-

lord, and the lack of it seriously and substantially affected your tenancy in an adverse way.

5. After exhausting all other alternatives, you supplied the essential service at your own expense, which you now seek to recoup from the landlord.

Proving your side. Documentary evidence is usually important in do-it-yourself cases. Be sure to bring a copy of your lease in order to establish what your landlord's obligations were. Also bring a copy of the letter(s) you sent him, complaining about the lack of services and demanding his assistance.

If the service you provided involved repair work, bring in any "before-and-after" photographs: for example, photos showing the hole in your ceiling where plaster had fallen and then showing the same area after replastering.

To prove the amount of money damages you're entitled to, bring in any bills or receipts you may have, say, for a plumber's services or for some product, such as a new toilet bowl. If, for instance, the landlord failed to supply heat, and you had to buy a space heater, present the receipt for that purchase as well as your electricity bills to show any additional charges for running the heater.

Countering the other side. There are three ploys your landlord may resort to. First, he may argue that the condition you remedied on your own was not really a substantial one. (In effect, he's arguing that you failed to established element (4) in your case.) He may have a point. Generally speaking, a do-it-yourself case is not likely to succeed unless the condition you fixed was one that you clearly had a right to regard as an essential part of your bargain with the landlord (as in the *Harwood* case). Thus, trifles like the failure to supply a shower curtain or to paint the kitchen with enamel rather than flat paint may not convince the court that there has been a serious breach of contract.

To the extent that you can, counter the landlord's argument with any evidence that the condition involved was adversely affecting your life, health, or safety. If the situation you remedied was an *emergency*, you'll be in an especially strong position to maintain that you were forced to act.

In a 1970 small-claims court case in New York, *Garcia* v. *Freeland Realty, Inc.*, the tenant's apartment was painted with dangerous lead-based paint. It was peeling off the walls, and his infant children were eating the poisonous flakes. When the landlord refused to correct this perilous situation, the tenant bought his own plaster and paint and did the job on his own. He then sued the landlord. The court awarded the tenant $29.53 for materials, plus $16 for his labor (computed by multiplying the 10 hours he had worked by the then minimum wage of $1.60 per hour).

Second, the landlord may argue that you acted precipitously, without giving him a chance to do the job. Here's where your complaint letter to the landlord comes in handy. It establishes that as of a certain date you put the landlord on notice of the need for certain essential services. If, within a reasonable time thereafter, the landlord did not respond, then you were justified in helping yourself. But you must have allowed the landlord a reasonable time in which to act. (Of course, reasonableness will vary with the circumstances; two to four weeks might be reasonable in a run-of-the-mill situation, but not in an emergency, where as little as twenty-four hours might be reasonable.)

Third, the landlord may try to escape through some tricky *disclaimer of liability* in your lease. That's what the landlord in *Harwood* v. *Lincoln Square Apartments* tried to do. He pointed to a disclaimer clause in the lease that said: "Interruption or curtailment of any service . . . shall not . . . entitle tenant to any compensation . . . nor subject landlord to any liability for damages. . . ." Sounds pretty devastating, doesn't it?

But Judge Danzig decided it would be grossly unfair to enforce this disclaimer. Perhaps it might have been enforceable if the breakdown of air conditioning had lasted for no more than a day or so. But a six-week hiatus could hardly have been in the minds of the parties to the lease. Given such an unforeseen contingency, Judge Danzig settled upon what would have been the reasonable and honorable intentions of the parties had their attention been called to the possibility of a six-week breakdown in an essential service: "I think that honest and fair-minded people expect to get what they pay for and to return that for which they have given nothing. The tenants paid for six weeks of air conditioning and the landlord did not furnish six weeks of air conditioning." Therefore, it would have been unconscionable to let the landlord off scot-free just because of a loophole in the lease.

Another reason why Judge Danzig found this disclaimer to be unconscionable and unenforceable had to do with the nature of the lease. It was a typical printed form lease. The tenants had no choice but to sign it, if they expected to get an apartment in New York's tight housing market. There was no room for negotiation—as is true in so many American cities today. Thus, the tenants suffered from a gross inequality in bargaining position, and Judge Danzig refused to force them to abide by a particularly one-sided clause, which they had had no choice but to accept.

Apartment Security Deposits

The $125 Deposit That Led to a $525 Victory

It's tough enough to get heat and hot water from your landlord. But just try to get your money's worth after you've vacated. That's precisely the difficult position you'll usually be in when you ask for return of your security deposit.

The deposit is that lump sum you paid to the landlord (usually one or two months' rent) when you first moved into the apartment. While the purpose of a security deposit is to secure the landlord against damage to the apartment, some landlords act as though the deposit were a substitute for social security; they just pocket your deposit or claim all sorts of phony deductions from it. When you're up against a greedy landlord, you may have to take him to court.

In the 1977 Louisiana case, *Curtis* v. *Katz,* Frances Curtis rented a one-room efficiency apartment from Alice Katz. At the beginning of the lease, Frances gave the landlady a security deposit of $125. Under the lease, the deposit was refundable at the termination of the lease "provided that the premises are in the same clean condition as when lessee moved in." The lease terminated on March 15, 1976.

About two weeks before the lease was to terminate, Frances began moving her possessions to her new apartment (she wished to complete the move in stages). Mrs. Katz reminded Frances of her obligation to clean the apartment, and Frances assured her that she planned to do so herself before March 15.

On March 9, however, a week before Frances moved out, Mrs. Katz jumped the gun and brought in her own crew to clean the apartment. Mrs. Katz did not offer to refund any of the last month's rent because of her premature entry into the apartment. And on March 14, when Frances requested the return of her $125 security deposit, Mrs. Katz summarily handed her a $150 cleaning bill and told her that the entire security deposit had been applied against it.

After over a month of fruitless negotiations for return of the deposit, Frances finally sued Mrs. Katz for $125. In court, Frances testified that she had fully intended to clean the apartment before vacating on March 15. Coming a week before that date, Mrs. Katz's cleanup was, therefore, unjustified. Not only was it premature, but also, according to Frances's testimony, it was excessive. The crew had gone far beyond a routine cleaning and had proceeded to clean the outside windows, the shutters, air conditioner vents, and the floors and walls.

The court concluded that Mrs. Katz had no right to take it upon herself to clean the apartment one week before the end of the lease. What's more, the cleanup performed at Frances's expense "far exceeded the cleaning required to restore the premises to 'the same clean condition as when the lessee moved in.' " The court awarded Frances Curtis a judgment against Mrs. Katz in the amount, not of $125, but $525.

Courtroom Pointers

Why $525? You're no doubt wondering. How come Frances Curtis won $400 more than she had lost? The answer is that Louisiana has a special law, as do the majority of other states, that penalizes landlords for wrongfully witholding a tenant's security deposit. The Louisiana law is fairly representative of many other states' laws. First, it requires a landlord to refund a tenant's security deposit within one month after the lease terminates. Second, it allows the landlord to make deductions from the deposit only for unpaid rent or damage to the apartment. Third, if the landlord does make such deductions, he must account for them in a written itemized statement submitted to the tenant within one month after the lease terminates. Fourth, if the landlord willfully fails to comply with the law, he may be held liable to the tenant for a *penalty* of up to $200. Fifth, the tenant can also recover his attorney's fees from the landlord. (In *Curtis* v. *Katz,* Frances Curtis's recovery of $525 consisted of the $125 security deposit, plus a $200 penalty based on Mrs. Katz's willful refusal to refund the security deposit within one month, plus $200 for the attorney Frances had retained.)

At last count, thirty-six states, plus the District of Columbia, had enacted laws governing the use and refund of security deposits. These states are Alaska, Arizona, California, Colorado, Connecticut, Delaware, Florida, Georgia, Hawaii, Idaho, Illinois, Iowa, Kansas, Kentucky, Louisiana, Maine, Maryland, Massachusetts, Michigan, Minnesota, Missouri, Montana, Nevada, New Jersey, New Mexico, New York, North Carolina, North Dakota, Ohio, Oklahoma, Oregon, Pennsylvania, South Dakota, Tennessee, Texas, and Washington. (To check on the particulars of the security deposit law in your state—or to find out whether your state has very recently adopted such a law— contact a representative on the legal staff of your local housing department or consumer affairs department.)

Generally speaking, the state security deposit laws provide:

1. Misuse of a security deposit. It's illegal for a landlord to keep your security deposit without just cause. Basically, there are only two legal uses to which a security deposit may be applied: making up for unpaid rent and paying for necessary repairs and cleaning.

What are necessary repairs and cleaning? Well, if you left your kitchen appliances caked with grease and dirt which the landlord had to clean off, or if you wallpapered the living room without permission and the landlord had to steam it off the walls, then the work performed by the landlord probably constitutes necessary repairs and cleaning. He can, therefore, legitimately deduct his expenses from your security deposit.

One item he can't make deductions for is so-called *ordinary wear and tear.* "No security deposit shall be retained," provides the Georgia security deposit law in fairly typical fashion, "to cover ordinary wear and tear which occurred as a result of the use of the premises for the purposes for which the premises were intended, without negligence, carelessness, accident, or abuse of the premises by the tenant or members of his household, or their invitees or guests." What such legalese boils down to is: all things eventually wear out on their own, and when they do, the tenant can't be charged for their refurbishment. For instance, floor boards will at some point break under the constant passage of tenants; that's to be expected. But if you repeatedly throw wild crowded parties with lots of dancing and jumping, you or your guests may have been careless—in which case, damage to the floor will not be considered ordinary wear and tear, and a deduction for repairs might be legitimately made from your security deposit.

2. Written accounting by landlord. Most security deposit laws require a landlord who makes deductions from a security deposit to give the tenant a written itemized accounting of these deductions. This accounting must generally be rendered no later than from 14 to 30 days after the lease terminates.

3. Refund by landlord. By the same 14-to-30-day deadline, the landlord must refund the tenant's security deposit—or what is left of it—following any legitimate deductions.

4. Penalty for violation. Like the Louisiana law under which Frances Curtis won a $200 bonus, most state security deposit laws provide for penalties in the case of a landlord's willful violation. California and Iowa, for instance, authorize the same $200 penalty as Louisiana does. In a dozen states, the tenant can win a penalty of twice the amount of money wrongfully withheld by the landlord: Alaska, Connecticut, Delaware, Kansas (2½ times the amount withheld), Maine, Massachusetts, Michigan, Minnesota (plus an additional penalty of up to $200), Montana, New Jersey, Oregon, and Pennsylvania. In a half-dozen states, the tenant can win a penalty of three times the amount of money wrongfully withheld by the landlord: Arizona, Colorado, Georgia, Maryland, North Dakota, and Texas (plus an additional penalty of $100). In one state, Hawaii, a tenant is entitled to recover *four times* the amount of money wrongfully withheld by the landlord.

5. Attorney's fees. Fifteen states authorize a judge to award attorney's fees to a tenant: Colorado, Florida, Georgia, Illinois, Iowa, Louisiana, Maine, Maryland, Montana, New Jersey, New Mexico, North Carolina, Ohio, Texas, and Washington.

As you can see, tenants are nowhere near as helpless as you might have imagined when it comes to getting a security deposit back. Before resorting to the legal leverage provided by state security deposit laws, a tenant should first take some preliminary steps:

Contact the landlord before the lease terminates. Give him your new address to where the security deposit refund can be sent. Before you vacate, clean the apartment, if that is your duty under the lease. Then try to go over the apartment with the landlord, compiling a list of what items, if any, need repair, and which of them deteriorated because of ordinary wear and tear. (Ideally, you'll be in a position to double-check such a list against one that you drew up on first moving into the apartment; then you'll know which defects "came with" the apartment.)

If you haven't heard from the landlord, say, within two weeks after the end of your lease, write him a letter requesting either a full refund of your security deposit or an itemized accounting of any deductions he has made. (Keep a copy of this letter, because you may have to present it in court later on.) If more than a month goes by, and the landlord still refuses to refund your security deposit, or claims deductions that you think are phony, then, like Frances Curtis, you'll probably have to go to court to get your money back.

Elements of your case. There are basically six elements to the typical security deposit case:

1. You rented an apartment from the landlord for a specified period of time at a particular rent.

2. You paid the landlord a specified sum of money as a security deposit, which was to be refunded at the end of your lease.

3. You vacated the apartment at the end of your lease, having paid all the rent then due.

4. You left the apartment in clean condition, with little or no damage except for ordinary wear and tear.

5. You made a demand on the landlord for refund of your security deposit.

6. The landlord has failed to refund your security deposit (or he has made illegitimate deductions from it).

Proving your side. There are several important pieces of evidence that you should bring with you to court.
- a copy of the lease on the apartment for which you are seeking a refund;
- a receipt or canceled check evidencing your payment of the security deposit to the landlord;
- a copy of the letter you sent the landlord requesting return of your security deposit;
- any list you may have made of defects in the apartment when you moved in and when you vacated (ideally, the landlord will have confirmed the accuracy of this list by signing it);
- any "before-and-after" photographs you may have taken of the apartment, revealing its condition when you moved in, as well as when you vacated.

Your main task will be to convince the judge that you left the apartment ship-shape. To bolster your testimony about the cleanup that you performed, present in evidence any receipts for such things as cleaning supplies or the services of a maid. Were there any witnesses (e.g., next-door neighbors) to the condition in which you left the apartment? If so, bring them to testify on your behalf.

Countering the other side. Predictably, the landlord will dispute the condition in which you left the apartment. He'll claim that the place was filthy or in serious disrepair; therefore, he had to expend all or most of your security deposit. Be prepared to defend yourself against such accusations. If, for example, the landlord exaggerates and says that you left gaping holes in the walls, you might explain that what the landlord is referring to were, in truth, nothing more than a few minor nail holes necessary for the hanging of some pictures.

Don't let your landlord get away with what Alice Katz attempted in our Louisiana case, namely, using the termination of your lease as an occasion to perform a major overhaul or a remodeling job—all at your expense. There are certain tasks that the landlord may have to perform for the incoming tenant *regardless of the condition in which you left the apartment:* e.g., repainting, sanding the floors. Be sure to object stren-uously if he tries to deduct the cost of these jobs from your security deposit.

CHAPTER

Parking Garages

The Broken Brakes Brouhaha

It seems that many parking-garage attendants are frustrated race car drivers. You leave your car with them, and it's ten-to-one they'll be off to a jack-rabbit start, which may leave a good portion of your tires streaked across the garage floor. When you return to pick up your trusty steed, you'll *hear* it long before you *see* it—screeching around each garage ramp. With all these amateur Mario Andrettis wheeling your car—and others—around local garages, parking lots, and service stations, it's no wonder that scrapes and dents start to show up.

Fortunately, you don't have to foot the bill for this demolition derby. A parking lot or garage that accepts your car is legally bound to return it to you safe and sound. That duty is imposed because you've entered into a legal relationship, known as a *bailment,* with the parking proprietor (he is known technically as the *bailee;* you are the *bailor*). If your car is damaged or lost, the proprietor will be liable to you as a negligent bailee, unless he comes up with a convincing explanation of why he's not to blame.

Take the Illinois case of *Black* v. *Downtown Parking Stations, Inc.* Shortly after 8:00 A.M. one morning, Sidney Black left his Buick at the Downtown Parking Station in Chicago. When Sidney called for his car at noon, he was told there'd been a slight mishap. In bringing the Buick down from the second floor of the garage, the parking attendant had collided with two other parked cars. According to the attendant, the accident wasn't his fault; he told Sidney that the Buick's brakes had failed completely. The Buick was towed to a repair shop, where Sidney paid for $188.91 worth of body work.

The next car that the Downtown manager parked was his own —in front of the Municipal Court of Chicago. Stanley had sued the garage for damages. He established a *prima facie case of negligence* by testifying that (1) he had left the Buick in good condition at Downtown, but (2) it was returned to him in damaged condition.

By way of defense, the garage called as a witness Albert Zaremba, the attendant who had smashed up the Buick. Predictably, Zaremba testified about brake failure during his fateful trip down the ramp: "I put my foot on the brake to slow up in case anybody was coming up and there was no brakes. My foot went clear down to the floor board." At that moment, Zaremba was about fifteen feet away from another parked car. "There is an emergency foot brake on the left-hand side," Zaremba admitted: "I couldn't reach it at all," he continued, "and tried to put the car in reverse but the gears meshed a little bit and I didn't get it in reverse at all. The Buick glided against two cars."

Sidney was not caught offguard by Zaremba's story, which he'd heard back at the garage. To offset it, Sidney testified that he had had no trouble at all with the Buick's brakes on the morning of the accident, when he drove the car twelve miles from his home to the garage.

Then, to be on the safe side, Sidney called as a witness, Henry Sadorf, the mechanic who regularly serviced the Buick and did the body work after the accident. Sadorf testified that he had completely serviced the Buick just ten days before the accident, and at that time, "the brakes were in perfect condition." On inspecting the car immediately following the accident, Sadorf did not test out the brake pedal (unfortunately), but he did check the brake system and found it to be intact: "There were no leaks in the brake system."

As it turned out, Sidney had presented an even stronger case than was necessary. The court did not have to reach the question of whether the brakes really failed. Even assuming they had, the garage was still negligent because Zaremba neglected to use the emergency foot brake. "We think Zaremba was not excused," said the court, "by his endeavor to put the car in reverse. . . . Since Zaremba testified that he was an expert and had been engaged in hiking cars up and down in garages for a number of years, and that he was familiar with the mechanics of the car in question, we think that before Downtown Parking Station could be relieved of the prima facie case of negligence made by Sidney Black, Zaremba should have used the foot emergency brake. And his testimony that he could not reach it (for which he gave no reason) does not excuse him."

The court ordered Downtown Parking Station to pay Sidney Black the amount of damage caused by the collision: namely, $188.91.

Courtroom Pointers

Sidney Black's victory presents a working outline for winning a typical bailment case, whether you're up against a parking garage, parking lot, or, perhaps, a garage that is servicing your car.

Elements of your case. Like Sidney, you must first establish a prima facie case of negligence, which consists of two basic elements:

1. You delivered your car over to the care and custody of a parking attendant (auto mechanic, etc.), who took possession and control of it.

2. When you demanded that the attendant return your car, he either could not (e.g., because the car had been stolen) or he returned your car in a damaged condition.

Assuming you can make out a prima facie case as Sidney did, the law will presume that the garage (parking lot, etc.) was negligent in not taking proper care of your car. It's then up to the garage to explain how it exercised due care, or else it will be held liable to you.

Proving your side. The easiest kind of car bailment to prove arises in the so-called valet parking situation: you leave your car with the key in it for an attendant to park. At all times your car is under the control of the garage or lot. They park it wherever they please and move it whenever necessary to accommodate other cars.

The valet-parking type bailment is the easiest to prove, because it's generally clear that the garage took actual physical custody of your car. You relinquished all control over it—symbolized by your handing over the key.

You'll have an increasingly hard time proving a bailment as the parking operation becomes more impersonal, and it's less clear that the business actually took control over your car. In a 1966 Missouri case, an automobile owner paid $10.50 per month for a "Parkard," which could be inserted into a slot at the front gate of a "self-park garage." After the gate opened automatically, the owner would find his own parking place, park his car, lock it, and take the keys; there were no attendants. The Parkard itself contained the following warning: "This card licenses the holder to park one automobile in this area at the holder's risk. Only a license is created hereby, and no bailment is created." The court held there was *no* bailment here, because the owner did not deliver the automobile into the garage's custody; the owner maintained control over the car, because he kept the key and could take the car out whenever he wanted to, or empower anyone else to do so simply by giving them the key.

This Missouri case is typical of a line of "park-and-lock" cases involving self-park lots and garages, where owners park their own cars, lock them, and keep the keys. About the best you can do in such a situation is to point out to the judge any signs of control over your car manifested by the parking operator. For example, was there an attendant who directed you where to park your car? Were you given a ticket that had to be shown to a cashier before the lot would release your car? Were there security guards (or devices) that gave you the justifiable impression your car would be protected? Did an attendant say anything to you to assure you that your car would be well cared for? Any testimony you can give in this regard may persuade the judge that a sufficient degree of control over your car was transferred to the parking establishment to create a bailment.

If you can't prove the existence of a bailment, you're not out in the cold; you just have a harder case to win. Without a bail-ment, no *presumption* of negligence will arise; instead, you will have to *prove* that the parking establishment was negli-gent. Assuming you can do so, the establishment will be held liable to you.

Consider two recent park-and-lock cases, where negligence was proven by the car owners. In a New York case, the garage kept duplicate sets of keys for all cars on a pegboard in its office. The office was unlocked, and the pegboard was in plain view to any intruder. Just such an intruder entered the office when the attendant was out, took a set of keys, and stole a car. The car's owner presented evidence of how the self-park garage had left keys unprotected and thereby proved its negligence.

In a District of Columbia case, the attendant at a park-and-lock lot was negligent in allowing a theft to occur right before his eyes. A stranger walked into the lot, claimed he was the brother of the owner of a car parked in the lot, and blithely proceeded to remove the transmission from that car! When the owner returned, the attendant told him that his "brother" had dropped by to remove the transmission. Merely by testifying to this idiotic lack of vigilance on the attendant's part, the car owner established the parking lot's negligence.

Countering the other side. If you make out a prima facie case of negligence, the parking garage will often try to rebut the pre-sumption that it was negligent. For example, the Downtown Parking Station cried "faulty brakes" (an oft-heard refrain) to excuse itself for smashing up Sidney Black's Buick. Such a re-buttal will rarely catch you offguard, because nine out of ten times you will already have heard it—at the scene of the crime! Inevitably the parking attendant gave you some sort of excuse for the three-foot gash down your right fender. You can expect to hear that tale again in court.

Be prepared to counter it with the best evidence you can muster. Remember Sidney Black's response. He testified that his brakes were in good condition both before and after the accident. (As it turned out this evidence turned out to be extra icing on the cake, because the garage was negligent regardless of whether the brakes had failed).

In the Pennsylvania case of *Mervine* v. *Sley System Garages, Inc.*, the car owner, Jean Mervine, skillfully countered testimony given by the parking attendants. He had left his car to be parked by attendants in an outdoor lot. It was winter and the lot was covered with snow. When Jean returned to pick up his car, he had to pick up pieces instead. Parts of the transmission were lying in the snow underneath the car. It cost Jean $349.45 to have the transmission repaired, and he sued the parking lot for his expenses.

Jean easily established a bailment. So the parking lot was presumed to have acted negligently. But the parking lot attendant testified that it wasn't his fault. He explained that as he started to back Jean's car into a vacant spot, the transmission lever jumped out of reverse into drive on its own accord. "Something popped!" testified the attendant innocently.

Then Jean took the stand again. He testified that he had observed deep cavities dug into the snow both in front of and behind the rear wheels of his car, suggesting that the car had been rocked violently back and forth after getting stuck in the snow.

Next Jean called to the stand Anderson Winters, the transmission expert who had fixed Jean's car. Winters testified that the extreme damage to the transmission was not brought about by ordinary wear and tear. Instead, an unusually heavy load had been exerted on the transmission—the kind of load, in Winters's expert opinion, that results when a car's rear wheels are spun violently back and forth on a slippery surface.

Jean Mervine won. The parking lot had managed only momentarily to neutralize his prima facie case of negligence. But Jean had come back swinging with evidence that allowed the judge to infer that the parking lot attendant must have acted negligently, despite his testimony to the contrary.

The other important hurdle you may have to overcome in a car bailment case is the *disclaimer of liability*. The parking garage will take the position that even if it was negligent, you have no recourse, because the garage is insulated from liability. How so? Because on the claim check you were given (or on a sign in the garage) there was a notice to the effect: "Not responsible for loss by fire, theft, or accident."

Sounds like they've really got you stymied, doesn't it? Well, don't worry. Most courts hold that such disclaimers by professional parking bailees are contrary to public policy and will not be enforced against car owners. This is emphatically so if you had not read the disclaimer, and no one called it to your attention. If you were completely ignorant of the disclaimer, you can't be said to have agreed to it; therefore, it could not become a legally binding part of your bailment arrangement.

Assuming you did not read the disclaimer, be sure to point this out to the judge. If the disclaimer was particularly obscure —e.g., in fine print or on a dirty, hidden sign—say so. And stick to the justifiable position that it's unfair to victimize trusting car owners by letting parking garages escape the consequences of their own negligence.

CHAPTER

Hostile Hotel-keepers, Wiseacre Waiters, and Uppity Ushers

The Case of the $2500 "Fisherman's Platter"

When you patronize a hotel, restaurant, or theater, you expect to be treated like a guest. After all, you are entrusting your comfort and well-being, however temporarily, to another. The least that person or business can do is treat you with common courtesy. In many cases the law requires nothing less—especially when you enter into a special legal relationship, such as that between innkeeper and guest. If, instead of being shown consideration, you are grossly mistreated, your rude host may have to pay for his abusiveness in court.

Consider the case of the $2,500 "fisherman's platter," *Wiggs* v. *Courshon,* decided in Florida in 1973. Joe Wiggs and his family were guests at the Twelve Caesars Motel in Miami. After a day of sightseeing, they returned to the motel and entered its restaurant for dinner. Knowing his family's fondness for seafood, Wiggs ordered the fisherman's platter. Ordinarily, this dish included shrimps, scallops, and fish fillets, and the waitress had confirmed that all the ingredients were available. When the fisherman's platter was served, however, it contained no scallops.

Disappointed at being deprived of scallops, Wiggs summoned the waitress and inquired why there were none. A dispute developed. Wiggs reminded the waitress that she had assured him of the availability of the seafood platter; had she not done so, Wiggs maintained, he would have ordered something else. At this point, the waitress lost her temper and blew up at Wiggs: "You can't talk to me like that, you black son-of-a-bitch," she exclaimed. "I will kill you."

Not about to risk death over some missing scallops, Wiggs and his family walked out of the restaurant. They were so upset by the incident that they checked out of the motel and cut their vacation short by two days. They also decided to cut their losses by suing the motel for the indignity they had suffered.

In court, Wiggs testified as to exactly what the waitress had said to him. He also pointed out that when he complained to the manager about the waitress's racial slur, the manager tried to placate him by explaining merely, "You shouldn't feel so bad. She is prejudiced against Catholics, Jews, and all other kinds of minorities."

There was no evidence that Joe Wiggs and his family had incurred any out-of-pocket loss because of the incident. In fact, the motel had not charged them for the meal or for their rooms. However, Joe Wiggs did point out that the family had suffered such emotional distress and humiliation that they cut their vacation short two days early.

For inflicting distress on one of its guests, the motel was held liable to Joe Wiggs for $2,500. (Actually, the jury brought in a whopping verdict of $25,000, but the court reduced it as being excessive. "It is certain," the judge observed, "a line would quickly form by members of any ethnic group to receive $25,000 as balm for an ethnic or racial epithet.")

Courtroom Pointers

The *Wiggs* case dramatizes the special obligations owed to guests by hotels. For centuries, a special *inkeeper-guest relationship* has been recognized by the common law. (This relationship began in medieval England, where inns were the only safe refuge from the dangers and toils of travel by horse or coach.) In the eyes of the law, a contract arises between hotel and guest that entitles the latter to certain fundamental courtesies: "One of the things which a guest . . . at a public inn has the right to insist upon," explained a New York court in the early 1900s, "is respectful and decent treatment at the hands of the innkeeper and his servants. That is an essential part of the contract . . . The right of the guest necessarily implies an obligation on the part of the innkeeper that neither he nor his servants will abuse or insult the guest, or indulge in any conduct or speech that may unnecessarily bring upon him physical discomfort or distress of mind." If a hotel or its employees breaches this implied contract—as the waitress did when she crudely insulted Joe Wiggs—the hotel will be held liable for the suffering inflicted on the guest.

The special innkeeper-guest relationship does not specifically cover other similar relationships, like that between theater and ticketholder, store and customer, or restaurant and diner (remember, the restaurant in the *Wiggs* case was *part of the motel* where Joe Wiggs was a registered guest, so the innkeeper-guest relationship existed there). Nevertheless, courts have held nonhotels (e.g., theaters) liable for rudely demeaning their patrons. Basically, any nonhotel establishment can be held liable—as any private individual can—for the intentional *infliction of mental distress.*

Elements of your case. There are three elements that you must prove in any case against a hotel or similar establishment:

1. You patronized a business establishment, such as a hotel, restaurant, or theater, that holds itself out as a place where members of the public can come to be taken care of (e.g., fed, housed, entertained).

2. One of the employees there rudely mistreated you in a manner that would have outraged any decent-minded person.

3. This mistreatment caused you to feel humiliation, extreme anxiety, or mental distress.

Proving your side. Describe the kind of establishment you patronized (e.g., motel, restaurant). Explain what the employee there did or said that offended you. Be graphic; remember, you're trying to convince the judge that you suffered a serious affront.

You won't win your case if you're merely complaining about some petty insult or dirty look. To be the basis for an award of money damages, the affront must have been truly nasty and degrading—the kind that any reasonable judge would consider intolerable. Here are some examples of indignities on account of which victims have sued successfully:

• Hotel mishaps. In numerous cases, hotels have been held liable for an employee's crudely insisting on entering a guest's room—usually because of some mistaken notion that the guest was not supposed to be staying at the hotel. In a Mississippi case, a hotel was held liable for $500 because the manager had shaken his fist at a guest and called him a "damn liar."

• Rude usher. The Barnum & Bailey circus wound up in a three-ring lawsuit because of the misconduct of its ushers. In the Tennessee case of *Boswell* v. *Barnum & Bailey*, J. M. Boswell purchased reserved-seat tickets for himself, his wife, and sister. When the eager threesome were ushered to their seats, other people were already sitting there. Instead of moving these interlopers, the usher asked the Boswells whether they would mind sitting in some nearby seats. It was okay with them, and they sat down.

A short while later, who should show up but the folks who had tickets for the seats that the Boswells were then occupying. At the request of the usher, the Boswells shifted once more to seats a little farther away.

No sooner had they settled into their new seats than the usher showed up again with—you guessed it—the ticketholders for those seats! This time the only seats that the usher could offer the poor uprooted Boswells were way up at the back of the tent. Tired of being treated like a refugee, Mr. Boswell refused to relocate a third time; he insisted that his party be returned to the original seats for which they held tickets. Boswell made this perfectly understandable request in a courteous manner, but the usher responded angrily, cursing Boswell, his wife, and sister. Soon other ushers joined in the fray, insulting Boswell and addressing profanity to the Boswell women. All of this occurred in the presence of a crowd of onlookers.

Outraged by the abuse, J. M. Boswell forced Barnum & Bailey to walk the legal high wire in court—without a net. The Tennessee court held: "The patrons of places of amusement are required by law to demean themselves in an orderly and civil manner. It seems to us the law necessarily imposes a like duty upon those conducting places of amusement. Those lawfully assembled are entitled to demand that order be preserved in such gatherings, and conspicuously rude and unseemly treatment of their patrons by the owners of theaters, circuses, and such enterprises, or their employees, is an invasion of the legal right of such patrons to participate in lawful gatherings free from disturbance." To compensate for the affront they had suffered, each of the three Boswells was awarded $500.

• Mean ticket-taker. In a Mississippi case, the manager of a movie theater received complaints that a certain fourteen-year-old girl giggled during movie showings. So one Saturday, after the girl had bought a ticket, the ticket-taker refused to let her in. In a fit of thoughtless anger, he accused the girl of "indecent and low-down conduct," which sent her running away in shame and tears. She sued the theater and was awarded $1,000 for the mental distress inflicted on her.

Countering the other side. If you're suing anything but a hotel, the defendant may protest that only innkeepers are charged, under the law, with the duty to treat their guests politely. While this is technically correct, other types of establishments have been held liable for humiliating their patrons—as we have just seen. No business can, with impunity, inflict mental distress on another person.

Another excuse the defendant may raise is that he's not responsible for the misbehavior of his employees (e.g., waiters, bellhops, ushers). The easy answer to this argument lies in the legal doctrine of *respondeat superior.* An employer can be held liable for the abuses of his employee, as long as the employee was, at the time of the abuse, acting within the general scope of his employment (as the Barnum & Bailey usher was).

CHAPTER 29

Product Warranties

The Case of the Thrice-Squeezed Lemon

When consumers buy a product, they want a written warranty to come with it. They believe the warranty is their assurance that the product will measure up to their expectations. Few people realize, however, that written warranties are often designed to protect primarily the manufacturer, not the consumer; the big print giveth and the little print taketh away.

Surprisingly enough, in many cases a consumer would be better off with *no* written warranty. Even then, the consumer would have warranty protection because of a uniform state law known as the Uniform Commercial Code (UCC), which applies in all fifty states. This law forces every seller to give a so-called *implied warranty* with every product he sells. This implied warranty isn't in writing (it doesn't have to be). Most likely, the seller won't tell you about it, but we will, because we think it's one of the most potent and overlooked weapons in the consumer's arsenal.

The 1973 New York case of *Mintz* v. *Daimler-Benz of North America, Inc.* shows how the UCC implied warranty works. Morris Mintz bought a Mercedes-Benz automobile for $13,500. As standard equipment, the car came with an AM-FM radio. Shortly after the car was delivered, its radio malfunctioned. The dealer replaced the radio, but the replacement, too, broke down. Still another new radio was installed, and incredibly it broke down also. Morris Mintz figured it was time to give up, and he demanded that the cost of the radio, $450, be returned to him.

The dealer, however, had a surprise for Morris. He pointed out that the car warranty specifically said that the radio came without any warranty at all; the car, yes, but the radio, no. The dealer claimed that since the radio had no warranty, he wasn't obligated to make sure that it worked.

Morris Mintz went to court on his own, claiming he was entitled to a refund of $450 from the dealer. The judge looked at the evidence and found that the radio had, indeed, come with no written warranty promising that it would work. The judge, however, had a surprise for the dealer. He pointed to sections 2–314 and 2–315 of the Uniform Commercial Code, which require that the radio, like any other product, come with an implied warranty. This implied warranty guarantees that the product will measure up to the consumer's reasonable expectations. The judge decided that a radio that doesn't work and can't be repaired clearly violates the implied warranty. He ordered the dealer to pay Morris Mintz $450 for breach of the implied warranty.

Courtroom Pointers

The implied warranty exists because a specific law, the Uniform Commercial Code, created it. You must be sure, therefore, that each element of your case required by the law has been met.

Elements of your case. There are three elements to a case based on the implied warranty contained in sections 2–314 and 2–315 of the Uniform Commercial Code.

1. A merchant sold you certain goods.

2. These goods were not of the quality you reasonably expected.

3. As a result of the defective condition of the goods, you suffered a loss.

Let's look at these elements in a bit more detail. First, you must have made your purchase from a "merchant." The UCC defines a merchant as a person or business that regularly deals in the type of goods you purchased. For example, if you bought a lawn mower from the local hardware store, the lawn mower would come with an implied warranty. However, if you bought your neighbor's lawn mower and it didn't work, you couldn't claim that the implied warranty had been violated. Your neighbor is not a merchant, because he doesn't regularly sell lawn mowers.

A merchant need not be a store. In the case of *Goldberg* v. *Ziskin,* an interior decorator delivered lumpy pillows to a client. The client argued that the lumpy condition violated the implied warranty. He wanted the cost of the pillows, $452, returned to him.

But the interior decorator argued that the pillows did not come with an implied warranty, because she was not a "purveyor of pillows or of fabric," i.e., she was not a merchant. The court decided, however, that she was a pillow merchant. While she didn't make the pillows herself, she had done the ordering for them, and the client had paid her (she, in turn, paid the actual pillow-maker). The interior decorator was ordered to pay the client $452 for having violated the implied warranty that the pillows would be fit for ordinary use, i.e., not lumpy.

Assuming you bought your defective product from a merchant, the next element of your case is that the goods were not of the quality that a reasonable person would expect, what the law calls "not merchantable." Good common sense should tell you whether the goods you bought are merchantable. If you don't think they're fit for ordinary use, or that they don't measure up to what you reasonably expected, odds are they are not merchantable.

The third and final element of your case requires that you must have suffered some loss as a result of having received defective goods. In most cases, the loss will be the difference in value between what you bought and what you actually received. (In Morris Mintz's case, the loss was total, because the car radio was worthless.)

Suppose you bought an air conditioner for $300, which turned out to be defective. The dealer you bought it from was unable to make it work properly, so you hired a repairman to fix it. He charged $75. You could claim that the implied warranty had been violated, causing you damages of $75.

You may also suffer another kind of loss. Assume that while your air conditioner was broken, you were forced to rent a substitute air conditioner. This rental cost could be claimed as a loss that resulted from the dealer having sold you a defective air conditioner. The law calls this kind of loss *consequential damages*, i.e., the loss results as a consequence of the defective goods.

A typical case in which a consumer claimed consequential damages is *Williams* v. *College Dodge, Inc.* Williams bought a defective used car from College Dodge. The car kept breaking down and required repairs that ultimately cost a total of $105.60. While the car was being repaired, Williams was required to use alternate transportation, which cost $60.

Williams sued College Dodge claiming a breach of the implied warranty. He claimed consequential damages of $165.60 ($105.60 for repairs and $60 for alternate transportation). He argued that these damages resulted directly from the fact that the used car was defective. The court agreed and awarded him $165.60.

There was no mention under the elements of your case of any *written warranty* that might come with the goods you bought. Whether there is a written warranty will *not* affect your right to an implied warranty. If you have a written warranty, you still have the implied warranty.

There is also no specific requirement that you give the seller a chance to repair or replace the defective goods before you go to court. However, we recommend that you give the seller a fair chance to give you what you bargained for before you incur expenses repairing the goods and going to court. Give the seller a chance. If he doesn't take it, then you'll have to help yourself.

Proving your case. Before you go to court, make sure you have all the evidence you will need. Be sure to bring along any receipt showing that you bought the defective goods from the person or company you are suing. It's always possible the defendant will say he never saw you before. The burden will then be on you to prove that he sold you the defective goods.

Since the heart of your case is your claim that the goods were defective, you must present enough evidence to convince the judge that what you received did not conform to what you reasonably expected to receive. The best evidence, of course, is the product itself. If it isn't too big, bring it to court with you. A lumpy pillow, a watch that won't run, a hair dryer that won't heat up, a toaster that's scratched; all such items can be demonstrated easily in court.

If the product is too large to bring to court, think of what other evidence you might submit. Photographs can be very useful. For example, if a dinner table you bought was delivered scratched, try to get a picture of the scratched surface to bring to court.

The most important part of your case will be proving damages. Give the judge as much specific information as you can on which he can decide the amount of damages to award. Say you buy a washing machine that requires repairs. The dealer you bought it from is unwilling or unable to get the machine to work properly. You hire your own repairman who charges you $75. You could claim damages of $75. But be sure to bring a copy of your repairman's bill to court.

If you decide not to have a defective product repaired, get a written estimate, nonetheless, as to what repairs would cost. Bring the estimate to court with you as evidence of the damages you have suffered.

Countering the other side. The defendant's only way to counter your case is to convince the judge that the goods you bought from him did not come with an implied warranty. To support his claim he may point to the receipt or written warranty you have, which says: "This product comes with no implied warranty of merchantability." Nothing could be clearer, he will argue; you don't have an implied warranty because it has been excluded.

You can counter this argument by using a little-known federal law called the Magnuson-Moss Warranty Act. (Since it's a federal law, it applies in all states.) Quite simply, the law says that if a product costing $15 or more comes with *any* warranty at all, then the implied warranty comes with it also: *it can't be taken away regardless of what is printed on the package or warranty card.*

Check to see if the product you bought comes with any warranty. Don't just look for a warranty card. Any promise made by the seller or manufacturer relating to the quality, ability, or appearance of what you bought is a warranty. Perhaps a warranty is written on the package. For example, the packaging on a coffee maker may promise that it brews ten cups of coffee. If you have that promise, you have a warranty.

Don't worry if the promise is unrelated to the problem you are having with the product. For example, you buy a television set that comes with the promise that you will receive clear, sharp pictures. The set also comes with a statement saying there are no implied warranties on the set. Your problem has nothing to do with the quality of the picture; you don't get any sound. The fact that the promise you received (a clear picture) has nothing to do with your problem (no sound) does not affect the operation of the Magnuson-Moss Warranty Law. The fact that the television dealer made a promise—any promise—when he sold you the set immediately eliminated any possibility that he could take away your implied warranty.

(Note: because the Magnuson-Moss Warranty Law is relatively new, some judges may not be familiar with it. Just in case your judge wants to know where this law is, here is where he can find it: volume 15 of the United States Code at section 2308.)

Caveat: There is only one situation in which you don't have any implied warranty—if the goods you bought come with no written warranty of any kind, and the goods are sold "as is" or with a statement saying you have no implied warranty. If there is no warranty of any kind on the goods, the Magnuson-Moss Warranty Law does not apply. That leaves the seller free to take away the implied warranty on the goods. He can do that by using terms such as "as is" or "This product comes with no implied warranties of merchantability." If what you bought comes with no promises other than that it is sold "as is," or with no warranties, then you are likely to lose your case.

CHAPTER

Deception in the Marketplace

The $100 Bonus on a $9.99 Waffle Baker

Shopping for goods and services you can afford is hard enough nowadays without having to beware of deception too. Yet we are constantly discovering that the marketplace is filled with slick salesmen, cheating car dealers, and rip-off repairmen. They suck us in with a come-on and then mislead us into parting with our hard-earned cash. We are not entirely helpless, though. Victims of marketplace trickery can use the law to strike back.

Robert Weaver did just that in the 1977 Ohio small-claims court case, *Weaver* v. *J. C. Penney Company.* The J. C. Penney Company's store in Cleveland advertised a closeout sale on waffle bakers for $9.99 apiece. No doubt with visions of maple syrup and butter melting through his mind, Weaver rushed down to J. C. Penney's. But the waffle bakers were sold out, and the store refused to give him a raincheck.

What to do? Most consumers would probably trudge home, cursing their bad luck—but not Weaver; he refused to waffle. He dragged the giant department store into small-claims court over its failure to supply the item advertised. He presented a copy of

J. C. Penney's ad in evidence and testified about what had happened when he arrived at the store, ready, willing, and able to make a purchase.

The court decided that J. C. Penney had engaged in what the law calls a *deceptive trade practice*. It had lured Weaver into the store through an ad that failed to disclose the limited number of sales items available. To make matters worse, once Weaver had traveled all the way to the store, he was refused any sort of raincheck on the out-of-stock sale item.

For subjecting Weaver to this deception, J. C. Penney was ordered to pay him $100 in money damages.

Courtroom Pointers

How could Robert Weaver win $100, you may well ask, when the waffle baker cost only $9.99—and he didn't spend a cent on it anyway? The answer lies in an Ohio law that allows a *minimum statutory award* of $100 to a consumer who has been tricked—that is, the consumer can sue for his actual damages or $100, whichever sum is greater. So Robert Weaver, who had lost no money, wound up winning $100 for his time and trouble.

Nice work if you can get it! And you can, because laws similar to Ohio's—known generally as *deceptive trade practice statutes*—are on the books of most other states. At last count, the following forty-three states, plus the District of Columbia, had enacted deceptive trade laws: Alaska, Arizona, California, Colorado, Connecticut, Florida, Georgia, Hawaii, Idaho, Illinois, Indiana, Kansas, Kentucky, Louisiana, Maine, Maryland, Massachusetts, Michigan, Minnesota, Mississippi, Missouri, Montana, Nebraska, New Hampshire, New Jersey, New Mexico, New York, North Carolina, Ohio, Oregon, Pennsylvania, Rhode Island, South Carolina, South Dakota, Tennessee, Texas, Utah, Vermont, Virginia, Washington, West Virginia, Wisconsin, and Wyoming.

Basically, these laws outlaw deceptive practices in a variety of consumer transactions, including not only the *sale of goods*, but also *leasing* (e.g., you rent a typewriter) and providing *services* (e.g., repairs, plumbing). Not all laws define what a deceptive practice is, leaving that task to judges on a case-by-case basis. In general, though, deceptive practices would include such tricks as:

• advertising goods or services with the intent not to sell them as advertised (i.e., the old "bait-and-switch" game, in which the salesman pressures you into buying an item priced higher than the one in the ad);

• advertising goods or services with the intent not to supply reasonably expectable public demand, unless the ad discloses a limited quantity;

• making false or misleading statements concerning the existence of, reasons for, or amounts of, price reductions;

• representing that a service, replacement, or repair is needed when it is not (e.g., the TV repairman lies to you when he tells you your set needs a new picture tube);

• falsely passing off goods or services as those of another (e.g., selling phony Cartier "tank" watches on Fifth Avenue in Manhattan);

• using deceptive designations of geographic origin in connection with goods and services;

• representing that goods are original or new if they are, in fact, used or reconditioned;

• disparaging the goods, services, or business of another by means of false or misleading statements;

• representing that a consumer transaction confers certain rights or duties on a consumer when it does not.

If you are the victim of some commercial "dirty trick," you can sue the business under your state's deceptive trade practice statute. You may even be able to sue for *more than you lost,* as Robert Weaver did. Many states, like Ohio, provide minimum statutory damages (i.e., you can win your actual money damages or the minimum statutory amount, *whichever is greater*). For example, the minimum statutory award is $50 in New York (if a business violates the New York statute intentionally, you can win three times the amount of your actual damages, up to a maximum of $1,000); $100 in at least five states (New Mexico, Ohio, Pennsylvania, Utah, and Virginia); $200 in another five states (Kansas, Montana, Oregon, Rhode Island, and West Virginia); $250 in one state (Michigan); and $500 in another (Idaho). A few states allow you to win a penalty in addition to your actual damages (e.g., $100 in New Hampshire, $1,000 in Vermont).

You can win double the amount of your actual damages in Wisconsin and triple the amount (what lawyers call *treble damages*) in ten states (Alaska, Delaware, Hawaii, Massachusetts, New Jersey, North Carolina, South Carolina, Tennessee, Texas, and Washington—plus the District of Columbia).

(It should also be pointed out that in almost every state with a deceptive trade practice statute, a consumer who wins his case can be awarded *attorney's fees* by the judge. So if you're considering hiring a lawyer, instead of representing yourself, there's a good chance that your adversary may wind up having to pay your legal fees.)

Why do these deceptive trade laws allow such windfalls to victorious consumers? To encourage you to take the law into your own hands if you've been wronged, to teach con artists an expensive lesson; to muster a citizen force of *private attorney generals*, who will help clean up the marketplace. So get out there and join the ranks of the Robert Weavers!

Elements of your case. If you sue under a deceptive trade practice statute, you will have to prove three basic elements:

1. You entered into some sort of a consumer transaction—whether for goods, services, or leasing.

2. The business you dealt with deceived or misled you—i.e., engaged in a deceptive trade practice.

3. As a result of this deception, you suffered a loss.

Proving your side. You can testify to the nature of the consumer transaction and the circumstances under which you entered into it. Be sure to present any documentary evidence that substantiates the details of the transaction: e.g., receipts, bills, canceled checks.

Documentary evidence can also be useful in proving element 2. For example, bring in copies of any advertisements and explain how they misled you. Or repeat whatever statements the defendant made and show how they deceived you; a witness who also heard these statements can help to confirm your story. Often, it's a good idea to bring the defective product (or a picture of it) into court as a way of dramatizing how badly you were duped (don't let pride stand between you and a money judgment).

Of course, deception in the marketplace can take many different forms. Here are just a few recent examples of how businesses violated the deceptive trade laws in their states:

• Sorry, no refunds. In another Ohio case, Jacqueline Riley entered into a contract with Levey's Interiors for the purchase of some furniture. She put down a deposit of $52. Unfortunately, the store later refused her request for financing, so she requested return of her deposit. Levey's then sprung an unwanted surprise on Jacqueline: it was store policy not to allow refunds!

Jacqueline sued Levey's in municipal court. The store pointed to a rubber-stamped clause on Jacqueline's contract, which read: "Deposits are not refundable." But Jacqueline was able to convince the court that the clause had, in fact, been added to her contract *after* she had already signed! For engaging in this deception, Levey's was ordered to pay Jacqueline $100 in money damages. (Like her fellow Ohioan, Robert Weaver, Jacqueline cashed in on the law that awards $100 if that sum exceeds the amount of actual damages.)

• Tent falsely labeled. An Oregon outdoorsman, Floyd Scott, went shopping for a tent at the Eugene Surplus Sales Store. He found a tent that appeared to fit the bill. It was sealed in a plastic container, which described the tent as being equipped with a zippered rear window and extending eaves—two features Floyd needed for winter camping. He paid $38.86 for the tent, but when he opened it up at home, he discovered that the tent lacked both special features described on its packaging.

When Floyd returned to the store, they offered him only credit, which he did not want. Floyd sued Eugene Surplus, and the court held that the store had engaged in a deceptive practice by misrepresenting the true characteristics of the tent.

Floyd had suffered actual damages of $38.86, but he was awarded $200 (the minimum statutory damages in Oregon).

• Price hike on new car. In a 1975 Texas case, Marvin Mc-Larty, Jr., ordered a new Chevrolet Blazer from Crawford Chevrolet. The purchase contract specified that the delivery price on the vehicle would be $4,000. There was a seven-month delay in delivery. When the Blazer finally arrived, Crawford demanded $4,234.76, which Marvin paid under protest, because he was desperate for the vehicle.

Perturbed by the $234.76 price hike, Marvin sued Crawford Chevrolet for that amount. The court held that coercing extra payment was a deceptive trade practice. Crawford Chevrolet was ordered to pay Marvin $704.28 (treble damages).

As you can see, almost any kind of commercial chicanery may violate your state's deceptive trade law. Invariably, some form of misrepresentation is involved. So be sure to emphasize to the judge the discrepancy between what you were told—or not told—and what you ultimately got—or failed to get.

When it comes to element 3, remember that the amount of your damages may well exceed your actual losses (because of minimum statutory awards, treble damages, and so on). Before you even file your case, therefore, check with your local department of consumer affairs or state attorney general's office to confirm exactly how much you can sue for under your state's deceptive trade law. Be sure to sue for the maximum possible amount when you file your complaint, because you can never win more than the amount of damages you claim (see p. 30).

Countering the other side. The defense you're most apt to encounter is *good faith:* the business will argue that its heart was in the right place; even though a deception may have occurred, it was purely unintentional. Absent any proof of its intent to deceive, the business will contend, it should not be held liable for an innocent mistake.

Respond with this argument: Proof of intent is unnecessary under a deceptive trade law. The law outlaws acts, not intentions. If there is proof that one of these acts has been committed by a business, that proof alone should suffice to hold the business liable. Liability is based solely on commission of the act, regardless of what intentions—good, bad, or indifferent—the business may have had. Most judges agree with this line of reasoning, because otherwise it would be very difficult for consumers to prove a case under the deceptive trade laws.

CHAPTER

Buying Things from Friends or Strangers

The Secret Warranty on a Used $150 Frigidaire

It's pretty much pot luck, most of us figure, when we buy things from our friends, neighbors, or some stranger across town. For example, the guy down the street sells you his lawn mower, which he claims is in "A-1 condition" and "runs like a top." When you get it home, however, the mower won't even start—let alone run like a top. Naturally, you complain that the mower is hardly in "A-1" condition (it's not even in Z-12 condition!). But the guy just responds that he was only expressing his honest opinion, and if there's now something wrong with *your* lawn mower, well, that's your problem, not his!

So what are you to do? Sue for breach of warranty! But the guy down the street never gave me a warranty, you're probably moaning. Oh yes he did, even though you didn't realize it, nor did he. By stating flatly that the lawn mower was in "A-1 condition" and "runs like a top," the guy down the street was providing you—unwittingly, no doubt—with what the law calls an *express warranty*. Because the lawn mower didn't live up to that warranty, you're entitled to sue for breach of warranty— just as you might sue a retail merchant.

Amos Eddington won such a lawsuit in *Eddington* v. *Dick,* a 1976 small-claims court case from upstate New York. Eddington saw a classified ad in the *Geneva Times,* which read: "Large Frigidaire refrigerator. Good condition. $150.00." Responding to the ad, Eddington visited the seller, a woman named Joanne Dick, and purchased the refrigerator for the advertised price. But when the refrigerator was delivered to his home, it did not work. Eddington requested a full refund, but Ms. Dick refused, so he sued her for breach of warranty in the City Court of Geneva.

Eddington testified regarding the facts surrounding his purchase of the refrigerator. He presented a copy of the classified ad as evidence that Ms. Dick had represented the refrigerator to be in "good condition." Then Eddington submitted a written estimate from a service repairman, who had inspected the refrigerator just six days after its delivery. That estimate read: "The compressor cycles off on overload, compressor burning off, needs new compressor and drier. Estimate of repair: $175.00."

The judge decided that by advertising a refrigerator to be in "good condition," Joanne Dick had, legally speaking, extended an express warranty to Amos Eddington. And that warranty had been breached, because the refrigerator was not, in fact, in good condition: "The term 'good condition,'" reasoned the judge, "under these circumstances legally requires the goods sold be in reasonable working order. Where the item was sold for a fair price but required additional expenditure of more than one hundred percent of the purchase price to put it in working order, the item did not comply with such warranty."

Joanne Dick tried unsuccessfully to escape liability by arguing that whatever defects there may have been in the refrigerator were not her fault but Eddington's, because the unit had been okay when she sold it. No way, ruled the court, relying heavily on the repair estimate submitted by Eddington: "It is apparent from the nature of the repairs required [and the fact that they were diagnosed just six days after delivery] that they were inherent at the time of purchase, and not the result of damage upon delivery or use by the Plaintiff."

As a result of the breach of warranty, Eddington had been stuck with a worthless lemon. The judge therefore awarded him money damages in the amount of $180—representing the original purchase price of $150, plus $30 for the cost of delivery and the repairman's service call. (Incidentally, Joanne Dick was entitled to recover the refrigerator at her own expense.)

Courtroom Pointers

The *Eddington* case is not just a fluke from some little court in upstate New York. You, too, can take advantage of express warranties, because they are created under the Uniform Commercial Code (UCC), a law that applies in all fifty states. Specifically, section 2–313 of the UCC governs the creation of express warranties.

Section 2–313 is unique, because it applies not only to regular merchants, but also to *ordinary individuals,* like Joanne Dick or the guy who sold you that bum lawn mower. Anyone who sells you something, whether he is a merchant or your next-door neighbor, can wind up extending the protection of an express warranty to you.

Basically, UCC section 2–313 holds a seller to his word by transforming that word into a legally binding warranty. Joanne Dick may have thought that she was merely expressing her opinion when she advertised the refrigerator as being in "good condition." But the UCC and the judge took a different view of her representations; under the law, the words "in good condition" amounted to an express warranty, which Amos Eddington had a right to enforce—and did!

Elements of your case. If you sue for breach of an express warranty, you will have to prove five basic elements in your case:

1. In the course of your sales transaction, the seller made some promise to you or affirmed certain facts about the goods.

2. The natural tendency of the seller's promise or affirmation was to induce you to buy the goods.

3. You did, in fact, buy the goods in reliance on the seller's promise or affirmation.

4. The goods did not live up to the factual representations or

standard of quality set by the seller's promise or affirmation (in short, there was a breach of warranty).

5. Because of the breach of warranty, you suffered a loss.

Proving your side. Element 1 requires proof that the seller truly made an express warranty. Such a warranty may be created in a variety of ways: e.g., a classified newspaper advertisement, a hand-lettered sign, even a photograph of goods to be sold. There is no necessity, though, for the seller's promise or affirmation to be written down; it may have been *spoken* during the course of your negotiations. (In this sense, the UCC express warranty is much more informal than, but equally as valid as, the typical gilt-edged certificate you're accustomed to receiving in a department store.) If the promise or affirmation was spoken, however, it's a good idea to bring a witness to court who can testify as to what the seller said.

Basically, an express warranty consists of any promise or affirmation of fact about the goods that you are considering purchasing. For example, the seller might boast that his transoceanic radio "will receive any station in Rome loud and clear." His statement would constitute an express warranty as to the performance capabilities of the radio. Or another seller might write on the windshield of his car: "1977 Ford for sale." Such a sign is an express warranty that the car is a Ford—not a Chevy—and a 1977 model. (If, in fact, the radio won't pick up stations from Rome, or the Ford is a 1975 model, there has been a breach of express warranty.)

The best way to prove elements 2 and 3 is through testimony about your state of mind at the time of the sale. No doubt the seller's statements (amounting to an express warranty) were a key part of the bargain that you believed you were striking with him. But for these statements, you probably would not have gone through with the deal. Therefore, be sure to impress upon the judge the extent to which the seller's statements clinched the sale from your point of view.

When it comes to element 4, you can pick up pointers from Amos Eddington. Bring in any documentary evidence (e.g., written appraisals or estimates of repair) that reveals how far your purchase fell short of the quality standard set by the seller's express warranty. Sometimes the discrepancy will be evident, as in the case of the Ford that is two years older than the seller said it was.

The same documentary evidence that substantiates a breach of warranty may also tend to prove how great a loss you have suffered because of the seller's breach. That was so in Eddington's case, where the repairman's estimate proved that the cost of repairs would exceed the purchase price.

Countering the other side. Watch out for six defensive ploys, all of which you can counter handily. First, the seller may claim it was never his *intention* to give you any sort of warranty, so he shouldn't be held to one now. The easy answer to this argument lies in UCC section 2–313: "It is not necessary to the creation of an express warranty that the seller . . . have a specific intention to make a warranty." Thus, even though the seller may have harbored contrary intentions or no intentions at all, he can still be held to have created an express warranty.

Second, the seller may point out that in nothing he said to you (or wrote down) did he ever use the words *guarantee* or *warranty*. Nice try, but no cigar. Under section 2–313, an express warranty arises despite the complete absence of any magic words like "guarantee" or "warranty."

Third, the seller may contend that he was only expressing his *opinion* ("puffing," salesmen call it), which should not be transformed into a binding warranty. Here, the seller may have a legal leg to stand on. Section 2–313 does provide that "an affirmation merely of the value of the goods or a statement purporting to be merely the seller's opinion or commendation of the goods does not create a warranty." If, for example, the seller had boasted that the patio furniture you were buying would "last forever," he was most likely giving you his personal commendation only, not an affirmation of fact. And unlike an express warranty, a mere commendation or opinion can't be enforced against the seller.

Does the unenforceability of puffing create a big loophole? Not really. Judges will carefully examine the circumstances surrounding a sales transaction; they will ask which of the seller's statements, when viewed objectively, became an integral part of his bargain with the buyer? Ordinarily, any factual representations made by the seller during his dealings with you are regarded as part of his basic description of the goods, which entered into the bargain struck. To take these representations out of the bargain (as mere puffing) requires clear proof from the seller.

Joanne Dick was unable to muster such proof in the *Eddington* case. Describing a refrigerator as being in "good condition" was not just an expression of opinion: "The Court finds that the printed advertisement goes beyond mere affirmation of value, opinion or commendation but definitely relates inherently to the condition of the goods and thus creates an express warranty."

Fourth, the seller may protest that he was acting in *good faith*. "I had no idea that what I was saying might be false," he'll tell the judge. Tough luck! In order to win your case, you don't have to prove that the seller *knew* his representations were false; that they were, in fact, false is enough.

Fifth, the seller may complain that everything is your fault, because you should have carefully inspected the goods, instead of just relying on his word. That's not true. Legally speaking, you had a right to rely on the express warranty and were under no duty to investigate. (Of course, you can't deliberately overlook open and obvious defects.)

Sixth, as his final ploy, the seller may seek refuge in some tricky *disclaimer of liability*. Suppose he sold you a Tiffany-style lamp "as is" but also stated that it was in "original mint condition." You later discover that, in fact, the lamp was not in its original condition, having undergone substantial repairs and replacement of parts, thereby lessening its value considerably. Can the seller now hide behind his "as is" disclaimer? No way. Under the UCC, an express warranty (e.g., "original mint condition") is almost impossible to disclaim. To the extent that some attempted disclaimer (e.g., "sold as is," "no guarantees") tends to limit or negate the warranty, the disclaimer is, in the UCC's blunt terminology, "inoperative." So don't let the seller wriggle off the hook of liability.

CHAPTER

Used Cars

A $1,500 Windfall for Odometer Turnback Victims

When most people shop for a used car, they do two things: kick the tires and look at the odometer. The first move tells you how tough your shoes are. The second move yields a bit more information, namely, how many miles the car has been driven. You can't always rely on the odometer's recorded mileage, however. One of the most common scams in used-car sales is turning back the odometer—or disconnecting it for a period of time— so that the car appears to have an attractively low mileage. Eventually, the truth comes out when, for example, the used-car buyer has to service the car, and a savvy mechanic discovers that the odometer has been tampered with. Fortunately for the victim, there is powerful legal relief available, which allows him to win *more* than he has lost.

Consider the 1979 New York case, *Schuierer* v. *Pascu.* Frank Schuierer was in the market for a used car. He read a classified ad in the newspaper for a 1971 Cadillac and called the owners, Mr. and Mrs. Pascu, who told him that the Caddy was a "low mileage automobile." When Schuierer inspected the car, its odometer read 47,000 miles. Pleased with this relatively low mileage, Schuierer bought the car from the Pascus for $2,150.
    Several days later, Schuierer found some old vehicle registra-

tion papers in the Caddy, which led him to the discovery that the car's prior owner had put 84,000 miles on the car before selling it to the Pascus. So Schuierer had been taken for a ride—about a 40,000-mile ride.

He sued the Pascus for tricking him into paying more for the Caddy than it was really worth. The prior owner testified on Schuierer's behalf, establishing that the odometer had been turned back after sale of the car to the Pascus. Mrs. Pascu admitted allowing the odometer to be turned back by an auto mechanic, who had assured her that such a practice would not be illegal.

The mechanic was dead wrong. It is illegal to turn back a car's odometer. What's more, it's illegal for a seller to hide the car's true mileage from a buyer. (We'll learn more about these rules shortly.) So the judge decided that the Pascus had violated the law.

How much was Frank Schuierer entitled to recover in money damages? He had paid $2,150 for the Cadillac, but the car, despite extensive repairs by the Pascus, was worth only $1,820 at the time of sale. So Schuierer had incurred actual damages in the amount of the overcharge: $330. But he won much more than that; the judge awarded him $1,500!

Courtroom Pointers

Why was the judge so generous? Because an important federal law authorizes awarding a windfall to the victim of an odometer turnback. (Presumably, by rewarding victims at the expense of their deceivers, the fraud of turning back an odometer will be discouraged.) The law is known as the Motor Vehicle Information and Cost Savings Act (MVICS Act). It is a little-known 1972 federal statute, which can be found in the United States Code (the basic compilation of federal laws) at title 15, sections 1901–1991. Because the MVICS Act is a federal law, it applies equally in all fifty states. If you sue under the MVICS Act, you don't have to make a "federal" case out of it; you can bring your suit in any appropriate state court—e.g., your local small-claims court.

Basically, the MVICS Act provides used-car shoppers with

two important safeguards: First, it outlaws odometer turnbacks. "No person," says section 1984, "shall disconnect, reset, or alter or cause to be disconnected, reset, or altered, the odometer of any motor vehicle with intent to change the number of miles indicated thereon." Mrs. Pascu ran afoul of this prohibition when she allowed a mechanic to reset the Caddy's odometer.

Second, the MVICS Act requires the seller of a used car to give the buyer a *written and signed statement*, containing the following information:

- the date of the sale;
- the odometer reading at the time of the sale;
- the name and address of the seller, as well as those of the buyer; and
- the identity of the vehicle, including its make, model, year, and body type, and its vehicle identification number.

In addition, the statement must contain *one* of the following certifications by the seller:

[ ] I hereby certify that, to the best of my knowledge, the odometer reading as stated above reflects the actual mileage of the vehicle.

[ ] I hereby certify that, to the best of my knowledge, the odometer reading as stated reflects the amount of mileage in excess of the designed mechanical odometer limit of 99,999 miles/kilometers of the vehicle. [Obviously, this certification must be made when the vehicle's odometer is on its second—or maybe even third—time around.]

[ ] I hereby certify that, to the best of my knowledge, the odometer reading as stated is *not* the actual mileage of the vehicle and should not be relied on. [This certification would be appropriate if the seller had reason to know that the odometer reading was not correct, but at the same time, did not know the correct reading.]

Finally, the seller must also include in his statement *one* of the following certifications:

[ ] I hereby certify that the odometer of the vehicle was not altered, set back, or disconnected while in my possession, and I have no knowledge of anyone else doing so.

[ ] I hereby certify that the odometer was altered for repair

or replacement purposes while in my possession, and that the mileage registered on the repaired or replacement odometer was identical to that before such service.

[ ] I hereby certify that the repaired or replacement odometer was incapable of registering the same mileage, that it was reset to zero, and that the mileage on the original odometer or the odometer before repair was —— miles.

The failure to make any of these required disclosures—or the making of false disclosures—violates the MVICS Act, just as surely as does the act of turning back an odometer.

Now we come to the payoff. Suppose somebody who sells you a used car violates the MVICS Act's prohibitions or disclosure requirements. You can sue them for three times the amount of your actual damages or $1,500, *whichever sum is greater.* For example, Frank Schuierer's actual damages were $330—the difference between the amount he paid ($2,150) and the fair market retail value of the vehicle with its true mileage ($1,820). Three times the amount of actual damages (a so-called treble-damage award) would have been $990. Since this amount was less than the *minimum statutory damages* ($1,500), the judge automatically awarded $1,500.

Elements of your case. If you sue someone for violation of the MVICS Act, you will have to prove four basic elements:

1. You purchased a specific vehicle (make, model, year, etc.) from the defendant at a particular time and place.

2. At the time of the sale, the mileage on the car was represented to be a certain figure.

3. This mileage figure was false.

4. As a result of this misrepresentation, you incurred damages.

Proving your side. Begin by testifying to the basic facts surrounding the sale: e.g., when it occurred; what kind of car you bought; how much you paid. Present any supporting documentation, such as copies of classified ads for the car, a bill of sale, your canceled check.

Did the defendant give you the written signed statement required by the MVICS Act? If not, tell that to the judge. Describe how the car's mileage was represented to you: e.g., through statements made by the defendant, in an ad, or merely by the fact of certain recorded figures on the odometer.

To prove the falsity of the mileage figure, you may need help from a witness. Maybe the prior owner will testify on your behalf, as in the *Schuierer* case, or, perhaps, the mechanic who first clued you in to the odometer tampering.

As we've seen in the *Schuierer* case, the measure of your damages will be determined by subtracting the amount you paid for the car from its fair market retail value given its true mileage. Here, too, a witness—such as an auto mechanic or car dealer—can help to establish the important figures. (Remember, you can wind up winning much more money than you lost, given the law's treble-damage and minimum-statutory-damage provisions. So when you file your suit, be sure to claim the maximum amount of damages that you think you may be entitled to, because you can never win more than you initially claimed—see p. 30.)

Countering the other side. The most common defense in this kind of case is that you failed to prove that the defendant *intended to defraud* you. The easy answer is that it's not necessary for you to prove that the defendant deliberately schemed to cheat you out of your money. It's enough to establish that either (a) the defendant knew about the vehicle's correct mileage but, nevertheless, withheld this information or falsified it; or (b) the defendant should have known the vehicle's correct mileage but recklessly failed to ascertain it or verify it. Prove either of these factors and you're home free.

CHAPTER 33

Brutish Bill Collectors

How 37 Dunning Letters Cost a Creditor $500

Bill collectors perform a legitimate function. They expedite payment of just debts. If you owe money and payment is long overdue, you can't really complain (although you may well be irked) when a bill collector contacts you. You can complain, however, if the "contact" is abusive, threatening, or humiliating. Indeed, you can do more than complain: you can turn the tables on the bill collector and do some collecting yourself—in court.

That's what James Fogarty did in the Nebraska case *LaSalle Extension University* v. *Fogarty*. He signed an application to take some correspondence courses with LaSalle and made a small down payment toward the tuition, but then he dropped the whole idea. The next thing Fogarty knew the school sent him a set of books (for the courses he no longer intended to take) and a letter demanding payment of the remaining tuition. Fogarty responded with a letter explaining that he did not consider that he had made any contract with LaSalle, and therefore no further payment was necessary.

Given Fogarty's explanation, you might expect that LaSalle would have made a few more polite inquiries before dropping the matter altogether as an unfortunate misunderstanding. But no,

LaSalle was made of sterner stuff. In the months that followed, poor Fogarty was bombarded with collection letters—37, to be precise! They varied in content from moderate reminders of the unpaid balance to accusations of dishonesty and moral turpitude. One read: "Honest men pay their debts. Dishonest men do not pay their debts. You owe us $140. Classify yourself."

Some of the letters came in lurid envelopes—for example, bearing an illustration of a lightning bolt about to strike some poor unsuspecting fellow. One of the letters purported to be a "garnishment notice," with the name of Fogarty's employer in the heading of the petition. Another notice was printed on deep red paper and entitled: "Final notice before legal action."

As if this incessant dunning were not enough, LaSalle also wrote to Fogarty's employer, threatening garnishment of his wages. Then the school increased the pressure by writing a collection letter to Fogarty's next-door neighbor, who showed it to him and kidded him about "getting a red letter."

At his wit's end, Fogarty struck back. He sued LaSalle for all the grief it had caused him. Fogarty testified concerning the transaction and the letter of explanation he had sent the school. He related how LaSalle's relentless campaign had humiliated him in his neighbor's eyes, caused him to lose sleep, worry about being fired, and suffer from nervousness and mental anguish. Fogarty called as witnesses his next-door neighbor and his superior at work, both of whom testified about the threatening letters they had received from LaSalle.

The judge concluded that LaSalle had embarked on a deliberate effort to discredit Fogarty and make him suffer. "There was," the judge observed, "no justification for writing the long series of harassing and threatening letters. . . . Certainly the series of thirty-seven letters . . . and the letter written to his employer and the one written to his neighbor, and the adoption of pseudo-legal forms, was wholly unjustified and inexcusable. No reasonable mind could reach any other conclusion than that they were written designedly and for the purpose of harassing Fogarty until he would meet LaSalle's demands, whether the sum claimed was justly due or not."

Even though Fogarty had not suffered any physical injury or monetary loss (e.g., getting fired), he was still entitled to collect money damages based on the mental distress that LaSalle had subjected him to. The court awarded Fogarty $500.

Courtroom Pointers

Legally speaking, there are two different ways to skin a bill collector in court. First, you can sue him for what the common law calls *infliction of mental distress*. This is the theory that James Fogarty relied on when suing LaSalle University; it is appropriate when you're up against a creditor who is doing his own bill collecting—as LaSalle was or as a department store might do—or when you're being hounded by an attorney to whom some creditor has turned over your account.

Second, you can sue under a 1978 federal statute, the Fair Debt Collection Practices Act. (Technically, the act is section 1692 of title 15 of the United States Code.) The act does not apply to either attorneys or to creditors who do their own collecting; it zeroes in on bill collectors (nonlawyers) who are hired by a creditor to chase after you for payment. Thus, for example, if the ABC Department Store (or its attorney) is dunning you directly, look for relief under the first legal theory—infliction of mental distress. But if ABC sics the Acme Collection Agency on your trail, rely on the federal act, which specifically hits bill collectors.

Elements of your case. If, like James Fogarty, you're suing for infliction of mental distress, there are three elements to the case you will present in court:

1. The creditor (or attorney) dunned you mercilessly or went to outrageous extremes in tracking you down and hounding you.

2. The creditor or attorney intended to make you suffer or was oblivious to the likelihood that you would.

3. As a result of the tactics employed by the creditor or attorney, you suffered severe mental pain.

If you're suing a bill collector under the federal act, you'll first have to prove that he violated the act. Therefore, it is important that you know exactly what the act provides. Basically, the act sets forth a laundry list of nasty deeds that bill collectors are prohibited from performing:

• A bill collector can't keep on badgering you, by phone or mail or in person, after you have notified him *in writing* to cease all further communications.

• No bill collector can use profanity or abusive language against you, or threaten you with violence.

• A bill collector must not contact your friends, relatives, or co-workers to spread the word about your financial distress.

• A bill collector is forbidden to use any deceptive techniques designed to make himself look like a government official, a credit rating bureau, a lawyer, and so on.

• Bill collectors must not send you phony legal-looking documents or threaten you with legal action that they don't really intend to take.

• A bill collector can't telephone or visit you at unusual or inconvenient times (e.g., before 8:00 A.M. or after 9:00 P.M.).

Assuming you can prove that a bill collector has violated the act, you will then have to establish that his violation caused you to suffer some actual damage—for example, your credit rating slipped because of false rumors spread by the bill collector.

Proving your side. Whether you're suing under the 1978 act or for mental distress, be prepared to tick off the full sequence of contacts between you and the bill collector (or creditor or attorney). Emphasize those aspects of each encounter that were particularly intimidating or humiliating.

For example, in a Texas case the consumer was besieged by endless phone calls, embarrassing postcards, and telegrams timed so that they would be delivered to his home late at night.

In a Missouri case, the bill collector followed a consumer around at work (while she was waiting on tables in a restaurant) and harangued her in front of customers: "Your day's arrived"; "I think you're a dead beat."

In an Oklahoma case, a bank vice-president inflicted severe mental distress on a woman by telephoning her repeatedly about an overdue loan repayment: "You have a poor attitude," said the irate veep at one point. "I will do everything in my power to make your life miserable and make you pay for this."

A Mississippi bill collector tried to force a mother into paying her son's debts by threatening her over the telephone, "Listen, you goddamned bitch, if you don't pay this bill . . . I am going to send the law down there tonight to put both you and your son in jail."

As evidence of dunning tactics, present in court any intimidating letters you may have received. If the bill collector bothered any of your relatives, friends, or co-workers, ask them to appear as witnesses on your behalf.

Under the federal act, you don't have to prove any particular intent on the part of the bill collector; the very fact that he violated the act is enough to make him liable to you. But if you're suing a creditor or attorney for infliction of mental distress, you must establish that he intended to make you suffer. The longer your catalog of the defendant's dirty tricks is, the more likely the judge is to infer that the defendant acted deliberately, or at least recklessly.

Finally, you will have to show that the defendant's misconduct *caused* your suffering. Any evidence of actual losses—such as getting fired or being denied credit—is appropriate. To underline your mental distress, point out instances when you suffered from nervousness, lack of sleep, humiliation, or other problems.

Countering the other side. The defendant is likely to argue that he has a right to seek payment of a debt. On that point, he is absolutely correct. But that's not why you're suing. Your complaint relates not to his right to seek payment, but to the *methods* he used in pursuing that right. No bill collector (or creditor or attorney) has any right to browbeat you, invade your privacy, subject you to ridicule, or threaten you, even if you do legitimately owe money. It is this excessive behavior that is the crux of your lawsuit and why you should wind up doing a little collecting of your own in court.

CHAPTER

Libel and Slander

The $500 Poison-Pen Letter

"Sticks and stones may break my bones, but words can never hurt me." So goes the nursery rhyme we remember from childhood. As we grow older, however, and build our reputations in the community, we learn that words can do as much, if not more, damage than sticks and stones. When those words are falsehoods uttered about us, we may suffer humiliation, ostracism, loss of a job, or other damage. For legal relief, we must look to the law of *defamation*, which encompasses two closely related wrongs, *libel*—written falsehoods, and *slander*—spoken falsehoods.

A recent New York case, *Bukofsky* v. *Sparer,* shows how an innocent man, Alfred Bukofsky, was mistakenly libeled by, of all people, an attorney, but wound up vindicating himself in court. It seems that on November 12, 1976, Bukofsky's wife was involved in an accident as she was driving his car. (At the time, Bukofsky himself was in the hospital recovering from a heart attack.) Mrs. Bukofsky's car collided with one driven by Lorraine Johnson. The accident was reported to Bukofsky's insurance company, Safeco, which paid the claim under the collision provision of Bukofsky's policy.

So far everything is straightforward enough. But now the cast of characters grows, identities become blurred, and in the confusion, poor Bukofsky gets libeled. It just so happened that the car driven by Lorraine Johnson was not her own, but one borrowed from an attorney named Richard Sparer. Coincidentally, on that same day (November 12, 1976), Sparer was involved in a car accident himself; the car he was driving was not his (Lorraine Johnson having borrowed it) but one he had borrowed from his law partner, Mr. Claybrook. Sparer tried to press a claim against the other driver in his accident, but repeated attempts to track down that driver proved unsuccessful.

Sparer had just about given up hope when what should arrive at his law office but a claim letter from Safeco, Bukofsky's insurer. Sparer erroneously assumed that this letter related to the collision he had had while driving his law partner's car. In fact, the letter concerned the collison between Mrs. Bukofsky and Lorraine Johnson (who, of course, had been driving Sparer's car). The Safeco letter sought reimbursement for the claim that the insurer had paid out to Mrs. Bukofsky.

Since Sparer thought that the Safeco letter had been written on behalf of the elusive driver in his own accident, he wrote a strongly worded letter to Safeco, mistakenly leveling some serious accusations against poor unsuspecting Alfred Bukofsky. Sparer's letter charged that Bukofsky had backed out of a parking lot at a "gin mill" and collided with the car Sparer was driving; according to Sparer, Bukofsky was "completely inebriated" at the time of the accident. Needless to say, Sparer refused to pay anything to Safeco.

When Safeco informed Bukofsky of the charges that had been made against him and sent him a copy of Sparer's letter, Bukofsky was understandably upset and sued attorney Sparer for libel. In court Bukofsky testified as to how the false charges had been made against him. The letter from Sparer was entered in evidence.

"Based on the credible evidence," the court concluded, "the defendant sent a letter to Safeco Insurance Company in which plaintiff was falsely accused of behavior which is criminal in nature, i.e., driving while intoxicated. . . ." A false accusation of criminal behavior is clearly libelous, ruled the court.

Sparer tried to defend himself on two grounds. First, he had coincidentally been involved in another car accident and had honestly, though mistakenly, thought that he was clearing that mess up when he wrote to Safeco—just a case of mistaken identity, without any maliciousness, Sparer claimed. The court rejected this line of defense: Sparer enjoyed no legal privilege to communicate as he had with Safeco; even though he admittedly bore Bukofsky no specific malice, nevertheless it was Bukofsky he had named and accused of a crime in disregard of the truth and without any legal justification. That's libel, plain and simple.

Second, Sparer argued that no real harm had been done. To be sure, Bukofsky had been upset by the defamatory remarks. But he had not experienced any direct dollars-and-cents loss (e.g., a hike in his insurance premiums) as a result of the libelous letter. So why should he win anything in court? Because damage to a man's reputation is automatically *presumed,* reasoned the court, whenever he's falsely accused of committing a crime. There was thus no need for Bukofsky to have proved any specific monetary losses caused by the libel.

To compensate him for damage to his good name, the court awarded Bukofsky a $500 judgment against attorney Sparer.

Courtroom Pointers

Alfred Bukofsky's complaint was based on libel, because Richard Sparer's defamatory remarks had been committed to writing; had Sparer spoken the same remarks, say, in a phone conversation with a Safeco representative, the result would have been slander. The basic distinction between libel and slander is that the former is written, while the latter is oral. This distinction has practical importance, as we'll soon see, because there are different evidentiary burdens when you sue for libel, as opposed to slander.

Elements of your case. Regardless of whether you have been libeled or slandered, you will have to prove three elements in court:

1. The defendant made certain false remarks about you that subjected you to ridicule, the dislike of others, undeserved suspicion, ostracism, and so forth.

2. The falsehood was communicated to someone other than

you. (This element is known technically as *publication*. Without publication of the falsehood to some third party, there can be no libel or slander.)

3. As a result of the falsehood, your reputation suffered, or you were shunned by others.

Proving your side. First, establish that the defendant made certain false statements damaging to your reputation. Over the years, courts have held an endless variety of falsehoods to constitute defamation. For example, it can be defamatory to falsely accuse someone of being a liar, a drunkard, a racketeer, a man who abandoned his wife, an attempted suicide, a kosher butcher who sells bacon, or a rape victim. What makes such a charge defamatory, according to one New York court, is that it "necessarily tends to expose one to public contempt, to induce an unsavory opinion of him in the minds of right-thinking persons, and to deprive him of their friendly intercourse in society. Such a charge tends to cause one to be shunned, avoided or deprived of the friendly association of a considerable number of respectable members of the community."

If you're suing for libel, you will often have a copy of the defendant's defamatory remarks, which you can introduce in evidence—just as Alfred Bukofsky did with Sparer's letter to Safeco. If you were slandered, testify as to precisely the words that the defendant uttered. Here it helps to have a witness who can confirm having heard what the defendant said. (Incidentally, the very fact that the witness heard it will establish the second element of your case, publication to a third party.)

Usually, the defamatory impact of the defendant's words will be readily apparent, e.g., the defendant claims that you beat your wife. Sometimes, however, defamatory meaning is hidden. For example, the defendant said that you set fire to your barn. On its face, this statement might appear to do no damage to your good name. People can, if they choose, burn down their barns. But suppose that within the context of other facts—such as that you had taken out an insurance policy on your barn—the defendant's statement was *understood by others* in a defamatory sense, that is, you defrauded the insurer by deliberately burning your own barn. Then a seemingly innocuous statement suddenly becomes defamatory. Be sure to bring to the judge's attention whatever outside facts must be considered in order to appreciate the defamatory impact of the defendant's statement.

Publication is usually easy to prove. For example, slanderous remarks were made in front of your fellow office workers. You can testify to this fact and, if possible, present one of your colleagues as a witness.

Proving that your reputation has been injured can be easy or hard, depending on the nature of the defamatory remark. Virtually all libelous remarks are presumed to injure a person's good name. That's because libel is usually expressed in some more or less permanent form (e.g., a newspaper), likely to reach a wider audience than slander and remain in circulation for a longer time. Therefore, money damages for injury to reputation can be collected even though no specific dollars-and-cents loss was suffered by the libel victim. Such was Alfred Bukofsky's situation. The mere fact that he had been libeled entitled him to damages ($500), despite the absence of any ascertainable monetary loss on his part.

Slander is a somewhat different story. Unlike libel, which is generally considered more harmful, slander does not always result in the award of money damages to the victim. There are four categories of slander (technically known as *slander per se*) where the law presumes, as in the case of libel, that a person's reputation has been injured. If the slander aimed at you fits into one of these categories, you can collect money damages (the amount of which the judge will estimate) based on injury to your reputation—without having to prove that you suffered any specific monetary loss (e.g., you were fired).

The four categories of slander per se are:

1. Commission of a crime. The defendant falsely accused you of having committed a serious crime. By *serious*, the law means a crime for which you could be indicted or imprisoned or a crime that involves moral disgrace. If the defendant merely says you double-parked, that remark is not slander per se.

2. Incompetence or dishonesty in business. The defendant falsely stated that you are, for example, a dishonest car salesman, or a butcher of a physician, or a maniac of a teacher, or an alcoholic chauffeur. It is slander per se to falsely discredit the

basic skills or characteristics someone needs to carry out his particular line of work.

3. Loathsome disease. It's slander per se to falsely accuse someone of having venereal disease or leprosy.

4. Unchasteness. The defendant falsely charges a *woman* with being a prostitute or committing adultery or simply fornicating. Such a charge is slander per se. What about such a charge against a man? It's not slander per se, because a man's reputation is presumed to be less vulnerable than a woman's when it comes to unchasteness. (Interestingly, though, a New York court held in 1964 that calling a man a "queer" was slander per se.)

Assuming you can show that the slander of your name falls into one of these four categories, the court will *presume* that your reputation has been injured, and you can collect general money damages. But if the slander is not in one of these four types, you must prove what the law calls *special damages*—that is, you have incurred specific dollars-and-cents losses because of the defendant's remarks (for example, someone canceled a business deal with you). The failure to prove any special damages leaves you out in the cold. You can't collect a dime, no matter how much your reputation may have been besmirched or how many of your friends may have deserted you. Once you establish special damages, however, you can collect not only for those monetary losses, but also general damages based on the injury to your reputation. In other words, special damages are the key to the whole pot of gold. (Sounds arbitrary, doesn't it? Well, it is; largely for historical reasons, certain areas of the law of defamation make very little sense, but you have to learn to live within their limits).

Countering the other side. Several different defenses may arise in a defamation suit. One is honest error—essentially the defense that failed Richard Sparer in the *Bukofsky* case. The defendant claims that he didn't intend to harm you; or he honestly believed the truth of what he said about you; or he thought he was referring to someone other than you (the *Bukofsky* situation).

Your response to this is simple: *the purest of motives are no defense in a defamation suit.* Even if the defendant harbored no ill will against you, he's still held strictly accountable for smearing your good name. Richard Sparer paid $500 to learn that harsh lesson.

The defendant may claim that what he said about you was *true.* It's then up to him to prove that his statement was *entirely* true. Complete truth is a good defense, but near-truth or half-truth won't do at all. A Utah defendant called a woman a "whore" but when put to his proof could only show that she had worked as a dance hall girl—a far cry from prostitution. Therefore, the defense of truth fell through.

Under the law of defamation, certain defendants may enjoy special privileges that limit or wipe out any liability they would otherwise have incurred toward you. For example, an *absolute privilege* attaches to communications made during the course of judicial proceedings, legislative proceedings, or by executive officers in the government. In other words, the people who make such communications are completely immune from liability for defamation, regardless of their motivation or the falsity of their statements. (The rationale here is to promote total freedom of expression without fear of legal repercussions.)

Beside absolute privilege, there is also the so-called *qualified privilege.* Under certain circumstances, the defendant may be insulated from liability for defamation, because he was furthering some legitimate interest in a reasonable manner. For example, the defendant may be under the impression that your account at his store is long past due. (In fact, his books are in error and you're all paid up.) If he consults a lawyer and seeks advice on what to do with a deadbeat like you, he has defamed you (by falsely charging that you refuse to pay just debts). But his communication with the lawyer is privileged, because he had a legitimate interest in collecting a debt (which he erroneously thought was due) and acted reasonably in consulting a lawyer.

To carry our example one step further, however, suppose that the defendant telephones your employer and tells him that you're a no good deadbeat who probably shouldn't be trusted on the job. Now he can no longer hide behind his qualified privilege, for he's clearly abused it. Unlike the lawyer, your employer is not someone who should reasonably have been contacted with news of your alleged indebtedness. What's more, even if it were true that you are in debt, that fact has no bearing on your general trustworthiness at work.

Thus, if a qualified privilege is raised in court, be ready to point out that whatever legitimate interest the defendant may have had, he went too far in pushing it. You will then defeat his claim of privilege and render him liable to you for damages. It always helps in such a setting if you can show that the defendant was primarily motivated by ill will toward you (what lawyers call *malice*), rather than any legitimate business or personal interest. No judge is likely to let a purely malicious gossiper get off scot-free when called to account in a defamation suit.

CHAPTER 35

Wrongful Dishonor

When the Bank Bounces Your Check by Mistake

Bouncing a check is something we all do at one time or other. Unfortunately so do banks. They miscalculate the balance in a customer's account or fail to credit the account with a recent deposit or make some erroneous charge against the account. As a result, the funds in the account may be mistakenly considered "insufficient" to cover checks written by the bank customer. The bank declines to pay out on these checks; they bounce and are returned to the payee marked "insufficient funds."

Who's left holding the bag when a bank is to blame for bouncing your checks? The bank is. The law known as the Uniform Commercial Code (UCC), which applies in all fifty states, brands the bank's error as *wrongful dishonor*, and renders the bank liable to you for any actual losses you suffer as a direct result of such wrongful dishonor. (Section 4–402 of the UCC imposes liability on the bank in these terms: "A payor bank is liable to its customer for damages proximately caused by the wrongful dishonor of an item [e.g., a check].")

What kinds of losses can you sue a bank for if you're the victim of a wrongful dishonor? (In legalistic terms, this question would read: Under the UCC, what "damages" will a court consider to have been "proximately caused by the wrongful dishonor?") For one answer, we can look to the 1975 Texas case of *Northshore Bank* v. *Palmer.*

James Palmer had a checking account at the Northshore Bank. The trouble began when a check forger went to Palmer's bank pretending to be he. The forger presented a stolen check made payable to Palmer for $275 and endorsed in Palmer's name by the forger. Northshore Bank cashed the check on the mistaken assumption that the forger was actually Palmer. (The teller did not ascertain the forger's true identity.)

That error came to light several days later; the forged check was rejected by the bank on which it was drawn and returned to Palmer's bank. What did Palmer's bank do? To save itself from a $275 loss, the bank blithely charged Palmer's account for that amount. Then the bank recalled $275 worth of Palmer's checks that had already been paid and returned them to the payees marked "paid in error." By refusing to pay out on these checks, even though the balance in Palmer's account was sufficient (before the unwarranted $275 charge), the bank left itself wide open to a lawsuit for wrongful dishonor.

To add insult to injury, the bank charged Palmer $5 for each of his checks that it had bounced—just as though Palmer had been the bouncer: Unable to clear things up on a friendly basis, Palmer sued the Northshore Bank for wrongful dishonor.

Applying section 4–402 of the UCC, the Texas court decided that Northshore Bank was clearly guilty of wrongful dishonor. (In this particular case, the dishonor had been intentional, rather than merely mistaken.) But what damages had the bank actually caused Palmer as a direct result of the dishonor? Palmer had lost $275 from his checking account, plus $15 in bounced-check charges. Were there any further losses, though? If so, it was up to Palmer to convince the court; under section 4–402, the victim of a wrongful dishonor can collect only those damages that he can prove he actually suffered as a direct result of the dishonor. This evidentiary burden is sometimes a heavy one for victims like Palmer to shoulder.

But Palmer was prepared. In court he testified about the acute embarrassment he had suffered when he was forced to visit the payees of his three bounced checks and explain the mess he was in. Even more humiliating was the fact that after his checks bounced, Palmer was turned down for credit for the first time in his life. He also testified to losing a solid week from his work and schooling in order to deal with the bank foul-up.

Based on this convincing testimony, the jury awarded Palmer $2,000. The size of Palmer's recovery demonstrates an important general point about a bank's liability in wrongful dishonor cases. If, like Palmer, the victim can prove that substantial damages were actually caused by the bank's mistake, then his award may easily exceed the face value of the checks that were wrongfully dishonored.

Courtroom Pointers

Banks may be intimidating to the average customer, but they're not invulnerable. James Palmer proved that much. So can you when your bank makes the mistake of bouncing your checks despite sufficient funds in your account.

Elements of your case. Basically, there are three elements to a wrongful dishonor case:

1. The bank wrongfully dishonored checks that you had issued from your account.

2. Following this bank error, you suffered certain losses—in legalese, you incurred damages.

3. Your losses were the direct result of the bank's dishonor —in legalese, they were "proximately caused" by the dishonor.

Proving your side. Step number one is establishing that there was a wrongful dishonor. Your best evidence here was probably supplied by the bank itself. When the bank bounced your check, it sent you written notification of the dishonor. A record of the bounced check also showed up on your monthly statement. Eventually, the bounced check itself may have been returned to you. Bring all of these documents to court as evidence of the transaction.

To prove that the transaction was a bank error, you will also need to show that sufficient funds were actually in your account at the time the bank bounced your check. Here again, documentary evidence will be necessary: for example, your monthly statement, deposit slips.

Step two is establishing that you were actually damaged following the wrongful dishonor. Under the UCC, no amount of damages will be presumed; it must be proved in court. Just because one of your checks bounced, a judge will not presume, for instance, that your credit standing has been harmed in any way; you must prove it. (Remember, James Palmer proved damage to his creditworthiness by showing that, following the dishonor, he was refused credit for the very first time in his life.)

Step three is proving to the judge's satisfaction that your losses were caused by the wrongful dishonor. A judge will generally view your losses as having been caused by the dishonor if they should have been reasonably foreseeable as the natural and probable result of the dishonor. James Palmer satisfied this standard of legal causation when he established that the bank's error resulted in his loss of time from work and school, decreased creditworthiness, and humiliation. Many other kinds of losses may be caused by a wrongful dishonor. For example:

• Insurance canceled. In one case, the bank bounced a customer's premium check to his insurance company, resulting in cancellation of the customer's policy. The bank was liable for the customer's loss.

• Car repossessed. A bank customer in another case made an installment payment on his car by check; the bank wrongfully dishonored it. As a result, the seller repossessed the car and auctioned it off. "It is difficult to conceive of a situation," said the court, "wherein a loss could be sustained more directly related to the dishonor of a check than that sustained by [the bank customer] here." Therefore, the bank was liable to the customer for the full market value of his car at the time it was repossessed.

• Arrest and prosecution. Passing bad checks is a crime. When the bank bounces your check, you may be suspected of having done something criminal by the disgruntled payee. Suppose he swears out a criminal complaint, and you're arrested. Was your arrest *caused* by the bank's wrongful dishonor?

For years courts said no. They reasoned that the bank's error didn't cause your arrest; the payee caused your arrest by complaining to the police. So the bank was let off the hook. But not anymore. Now section 4–402 of the UCC specifically provides that the amount you win in court for a bank's wrongful dishonor "may include damages for an arrest or prosecution."

In a Connecticut case, a respectable businessman with an unblemished record was arrested for obtaining money by false pretenses. All that he had done was cash a perfectly good check for $3.62, but his bank wrongfully dishonored it. He sued for the humiliation and inconvenience, claiming that the bank's error had caused his arrest. The court agreed and held the bank liable to him for $2,000.

Countering the other side. The bank may try to show that its dishonor wasn't wrongful. If, in fact, your account lacked sufficient funds at the time of the dishonor, the bank will prevail; a bank is under no duty to pay out on your checks when your balance is too low to cover them. Be prepared to establish, through your banking records (including any dated deposit slips), that the balance in your account was high enough to cover the bounced checks.

A more serious hurdle may arise if the bank concedes that there was a wrongful dishonor but argues that your losses weren't caused by it. (In legalese, the issue here is whether the bank's error was the proximate cause of your loss.) We've already seen a number of cause-and-effect examples, where the losses of bank customers were traced directly to the wrongful dishonor.

But sometimes the customer's proof on this point is too weak. In a 1968 Kentucky case, a customer contended that, as a result of the bank dishonoring checks of hers, she suffered hurt feelings and a case of "nerves"; because of this nervousness, she lost two weeks from work. The court concluded that the causal connection between these items of damage and the wrongful dishonor was too nebulous. The customer's nervousness was not accepted as the natural result of the dishonor; it was not something that the bank could have reasonably anticipated.

To avoid the pitfall in the Kentucky case, don't content yourself with merely testifying to your hurt feelings following the dishonor. Such an adverse reaction is too vague, and depending on the judge, may or may not be directly related to the dishonor. Instead, present evidence of any specific consequences that befell you after the dishonor (remember James Palmer was turned down for credit for the first time). It is much easier for a court to discern the causal connection between such consequences and the bank's wrongful dishonor.

In a 1975 California case, *Kendall Yacht Corporation* v. *United California Bank*, the bank customers, Mr. and Mrs. Kendall, won thousands of dollars because of the emotional distress that the bank's wrongful dishonor had caused them. The Kendalls didn't merely recite their feelings of humiliation when people learned about the bounced checks. Instead, the Kendalls testified that they had suffered from acts of vandalism (eggs were thrown at their car), the filing of criminal charges, and marital problems produced by stress.

The Kendalls clearly convinced the court that their suffering was the result of the wrongful dishonor; "The Kendalls did not merely allege a subjective state of discomfort at having their checks dishonored," observed the court; "rather, they gave proof of objectively verifiable events which followed the dishonoring of their checks and which would have induced mental suffering in any reasonable person." You should follow the example set by the Kendalls, as well as James Palmer in the *Northshore Bank* case, when setting about to prove that the bank's error *caused* the harm you suffered.

CHAPTER

Stopping Payment on Checks

When the Bank Disregards Your Instructions

When you write a check, you expect your bank to honor it, but before the check is cashed, you may change your mind. In that case, you will quickly instruct the bank not to honor the check. That instruction is called a *stop payment order;* if properly made, it is legally binding on your bank.

Oversights can and do occur, however. Through some foul-up, the check you stopped payment on slips by undetected and the bank honors it. Your account is debited for the amount of the check. Who's responsible? In all likelihood, the bank is, and you can sue it for any loss you suffer because of its blunder.

Take a typical example of how this problem might arise: On June 1, you hire a contractor to waterproof the basement of your house. His fee is $1,000, half of which is payable in advance, the remainder when the job is completed. The contractor agrees to begin work on June 5, a Monday. You send a check for $500 to the contractor on June 3.

Monday arrives but the contractor doesn't. You telephone him but get only his answering service; the contractor never calls you back, nor does he show up on June 6 or June 7. Becoming a bit insecure about whether he'll ever show up and do the work, you decide to protect yourself from being ripped off.

On the morning of Thursday, June 8, you visit your bank and place a stop payment order on the $500 check made out to the contractor. You never hear from the contractor again, and by July you've forgotten all about the affair. Then your monthly bank statement arrives. You're shocked to discover that on Friday, June 9, the day after you placed your stop payment order, the bank paid the $500 check and debited your account for that amount.

Immediately you call the contractor for a refund. He no longer has an answering service; indeed, he no longer has a telephone. He's left town without a trace.

So you turn to your friendly bank, but it gives you the runaround too. The bank excuses itself because it had had only 24 hours' advance notice, before the contractor showed up to cash the check. "We need more lead time than that," explains the bank officer benignly, "before we can get the stop payment on computer and flag down the check." The bank refuses to recredit your account with the $500.

Are you out of luck? Not at all. The bank is clearly at fault here, but it looks like you're going to have to sue if you hope to collect the $500 you've lost. A perfect case for small-claims court!

Courtroom Pointers

The law you will rely on is the Uniform Commercial Code (UCC), which applies in all fifty states. Specifically, section 4–403 of the UCC gives you, the bank customer, a legal right to order your bank not to pay out on a designated check. If the bank disregards your order and, as a result, you suffer a financial loss, you can hold the bank liable for that loss.

Before you march into court, try to clear up the misunderstanding on your own. (Beside making practical sense, your efforts will strengthen any lawsuit you may have to bring later on.) Visit the bank as soon as you discover that your stop payment has been disregarded. Explain the situation to a bank officer and seek to have your account recredited for the amount the bank mistakenly paid out.

If the bank is uncooperative, contact the payee who cashed your check to see if he will refund to you the money he received at the bank. For example, you bought a vacuum cleaner at the Acme Department Store and paid the purchase price of $189 by check. On first trying the vacuum cleaner, you discovered that it didn't work, so you complained to Acme about the defective product and also placed a stop payment order on your $189 check. Acme managed to cash the check, nonetheless. Since your bank won't cooperate, try to work out a fair exchange with Acme: you'll return the defective cleaner if Acme will refund your $189.

Suppose Acme refuses. Or maybe the store offers not a refund, but a $189 credit, and you're interested only in cash. Make sure you get Acme's position stated in writing, ideally in a letter to you responding to your complaint. You may well need this evidence in court to prove that you have, indeed, suffered a loss because of the bank's mistake.

Elements of your case. There are two basic elements to your lawsuit against the bank:

1. You placed a stop payment order with the bank on one of your checks.

2. Despite the order, the bank honored the check and debited your account accordingly.

Proving your side. You must first establish that you placed a stop payment order with the bank. You can testify to this effect and then present whatever documentation you received from the bank confirming the stop payment (and probably debiting your account with a service charge for the stop payment).

Next you must show that the bank disobeyed your order and honored the check anyway. Here, too, your best evidence was probably supplied by the bank in the form of your canceled check and your monthly statement which records a debit to your account in the amount of the check.

Countering the other side. Don't expect the bank to roll over and play dead. After all, it has already paid out on your stopped check; if it now has to recredit your account, it winds up holding the bag. (The bank may be able to recoup its loss by taking legal action against the person who cashed your check.)

There are five lines of defense that the bank may pursue, so be prepared. First, the bank may claim that your stop payment order was ineffective, because it wasn't in writing. (Say that you just telephoned the bank and told an officer to stop payment.) This defense presents less of a hurdle than might seem possible. Several states do require *written* stop payment orders under their versions of the UCC (California, Nevada, Texas, and Utah). Most states, however, recognize an oral stop payment for 14 days, after which time it expires unless confirmed in writing. (In the District of Columbia, an oral stop payment is good for only 24 hours.)

Second, the bank may argue that you didn't adequately describe the check you wanted stopped. Suppose you gave the bank an inaccurate description or left out certain information. To counter the bank's position, you'll have to show either that your error or omission was trivial or that you were misled by the bank.

In a 1973 small-claims court case, *Rimberg* v. *Union Trust Company*, the bank customer visited her bank to stop payment on a check. She told the teller that she was certain of the date of the check (July 14, 1972) and the name of the payee ("Seconde Wind"), but her husband, who had written the check, was out of town, and she was uncertain as to whether the amount of the check was $235 or $250. The teller gave her a stop payment form, which she filled out with the amount of $235. As it turned out, the true amount of the check was $250, and it was later honored by the bank.

The customer sued the bank in small claims court for $250. The bank defended itself on the grounds that stop payments cannot be honored unless the *amount* of the check is accurately stated. (Under the bank's computerized system, the amount of the check was the factor that triggered the computer into flagging the check.)

But the customer testified that she had not been warned by the teller that her stop payment would not be effective without a precise statement of the amount of the check. She testified that she was given the clear impression that her stop payment would be effective, regardless of whether the check turned out to be for $235 or $250. Had she been cautioned that the precise dollar amount of the stopped check was absolutely necessary, the customer argued, she obviously would have spent an extra dollar and filled out *two* stop payment forms—one for the $235 amount and one for the $250 amount (a sensible solution that the teller had not bothered to suggest).

Based on the customer's testimony, the court decided that the bank, through the conduct (or misconduct) of its teller, had waived its right to object to the inaccuracy of the stop payment order. The customer was awarded $250.

In a 1976 New York case, the customer described a check perfectly in his stop payment order, except for one thing: he gave the number of the check as "22" rather than "221," the true number. Was this error fatal to the customer's lawsuit against the bank? No. The court ruled: "The single digital mistake in describing the check in the stop order is deemed trivial and insignificant. Enough information was supplied to the bank to reasonably provide it with sufficient information to comply with the stop payment order. The bank is therefore held responsible for its act of improperly making payment upon the check."

A third line of defense that the bank may raise is *time:* you failed to give the bank enough advance notice before the stopped check was presented by the payee. There is no hard-and-fast standard that you are supposed to live up to. Here the UCC is flexible; section 4–403 simply says that the stop payment order must have been received far enough in advance to give the bank a "reasonable opportunity" to respond. What's a "reasonable opportunity"? The cases indicate that as little as a *few hours* may be enough time to give the bank a reasonable opportunity to record the stop payment and put its tellers on notice not to honor the check.

In one case, the customer placed a stop payment order at 9:00 A.M., and the bank, nonetheless, honored the check at 10:40 A.M. that morning. In another case, the stop payment was made at 9:05 A.M., but the check was cashed at about 10:15 A.M. Both times, the courts held that the bank had been given a "reasonable opportunity" to obey the stop payment order. Clearly,

when your bank has had several hours or a day's advance notice, you must vigorously maintain that there was a reasonable
opportunity for the bank to carry out your order.

The fourth defense a bank may throw at you is often the
trickiest. The bank will point to the fine print on the stop payment order you signed (already you sense there's trouble afoot).
It says something like you agree to "hold the bank free from all
liability should payment be made contrary to this request, if
such payment occurs through inadvertence or accident only."
This legalese is a *disclaimer of liability;* the bank is putting
words in your mouth to the effect that you'll let the bank off
scot-free if it carelessly disregards your order.

What can you do now? Simply remind the court that such
disclaimers of liability are unenforceable under the UCC. The
key section here is 4–103, which provides that "no agreement
can disclaim a bank's responsibility for its own lack of good
faith or failure to exercise ordinary care or can limit the measure
of damages for such lack or failure." In other words, even
though you apparently swallowed the bank's disclaimer, still
you can stop the bank from using it against you.

The bank's fifth possible defense is one we've alluded to
earlier. The bank readily admits it made a mistake, and ordinarily it should be liable for your loss—*except you suffered no
loss.* Therefore, you have no right to recover anything.

How could this be? Take a simple example. A bank customer
buys some product by check, later stops payment on the check,
yet retains the product. If the bank honors the stopped check,
what has the customer lost? Nothing, because he presumably
got his money's worth in the product he kept.

In such an obvious case, the bank should not be liable for the
value of the product. Reason as well as the UCC dictate such a
result; section 4–403 states, "The burden of establishing the
fact and amount of loss resulting from the payment of [a check]
contrary to a binding stop payment order is on the customer."
Therefore, you must be prepared to prove the "fact and
amount" of any loss you've suffered because of the dishonor.
Here's why it's important, as stated earlier in this chapter, to
contact the payee of your check and get evidence—written, if
possible—that you've been ripped off (for example, by the

home contractor who cashed your $500 check but skipped town without doing the work). If you bought a defective product, by all means point out to the court that although you may still have the product, it's a useless lemon that you're prepared to return as soon as you get your money back. As long as you can show that the bank's mistake cost you money, the bank won't be able to wriggle off the hook.

CHAPTER

Monthly Statement Blues

The $45 Check that Was Cashed for $10,045

True or false: banks are infallible. True might be your first response, given all those sharp-eyed tellers, vigilant bank officers, and high-speed computers at your local bank. But, then, one month your regular statement from the bank contains a glaring error. For example, you wrote a check for $35, which was clumsily altered by someone to read "$350," and the bank sleepily debited your account for the latter amount. Or someone forged your signature on one of your checks, which the bank overlooked when cashing the check. Or maybe the bank just computed a dollar amount incorrectly. Whatever the error, you'll realize that banks *are* fallible, and their mistakes can spell your loss.

Unless you assert your rights. That's just what one Ohio bank customer did in the 1975 case, *State ex rel Gabalac* v. *Firestone Bank*. Although the customer happened to be a local government agency, namely, the Summit County court clerk's office, and the amount of money involved was relatively large—a $10,000 error! —still the case is worth studying, because believe it or not, it could happen to you!

The court clerk of Summit County, Ohio, maintained the county's official "alimony and support account" with the local

228

Firestone Bank. Drawing on this account, the clerk sent a $45 check to a recipient in Virginia, who deposited it in her local bank. By mistake, the Virginia bank, in processing the check, encoded it not for $45, but for $10,045! This erroneous amount was credited to the recipient's account. Then the canceled check made its way back through banking channels to the Firestone Bank, where you might well assume that the Firestone folks would have immediately spotted the difference between the amount clearly *written* on the check ($45) and the *encoded* error ($10,045). No such luck. Checks passing through the clearing process at Firestone were not examined by human beings. Given the volume of checks to be cleared, only mechanical examination was made, and it was geared to the amount *encoded* on the check ($10,045), not the amount *written* on it ($45). Therefore, the Firestone Bank honored the check and deducted $10,045 from the checking account administered by the Summit County court clerk.

About a week later, this colossal debit was listed on a monthly statement sent to the county clerk along with the canceled $45 check. No doubt you would have instantly hit the roof—or fallen to the floor!—had your bank mistakenly deducted an extra $10,000 from your account. But the court clerk's office didn't bother to review its own monthly bank statement (sound familiar?). In fact, it was not until seven and one-half months later that an audit of the court clerk's office uncovered the gigantic *faux pas*.

When notified of its blunder, Firestone Bank didn't exactly jump at the chance to square accounts with the court clerk's office and then be left holding the bag for $10,000. As a result, Summit County had to sue the bank to recover the extra ten grand paid out on a crummy little $45 check.

In court, the case in favor of the bank customer was pretty straightforward and convincing, until the bank played its trump card: bank customers have a duty to examine their monthly statements and report any errors to the bank. Indeed, Firestone Bank pointed to a warning printed on its statement: "Please examine at once. If no error is reported within 10 days, the account will be considered correct and the checks genuine." The $10,000 error had not been reported to the bank for seven and one-half months after the court clerk received his monthly statement. Therefore, argued the bank, the clerk's office should be barred from complaining about the mistake at this late date.

But the court disagreed. Why? Because of the Uniform Commercial Code. Section 4–406 of the UCC gives a bank customer up to *one year* in which to report an altered check to the bank. Judged by that statutory time frame, the court clerk's complaint was not barred, even though it had been seven and one-half months in coming.

What about the 10-day limitation printed on the bank's statement? As between that limitation and the UCC, the court easily decided that the statute must prevail. In passing, the court made known its obvious dislike for the bank's attempt to wipe out a customer's right after only 10 days: "What happens," the court asked rhetorically, "if the customer is out of town, on a trip overseas, or a cruise, or on an automobile vacation around the United States for more than the ten-day bank reconcilement date?"

In conclusion, the court held that the clerk had made a timely complaint and awarded the clerk's office $10,000 because of the bank's admitted blunder.

Courtroom Pointers

Banks have a basic legal obligation to exercise reasonable care when processing checks written by their customers. The *Firestone Bank* case demonstrates that a bank can be held accountable for fouling up your account.

Elements of your case. There are three basic elements to your case:

1. One of your checks was doctored in some way (or simply misread as in *Firestone*).

2. Because of the bank's carelessness, the check was routinely processed and debited to your account.

3. As a result, you suffered a monetary loss.

Proving your side. Bring into court the monthly statement that records the bank's mistaken debit to your account. Also bring in the canceled check that prompted the mistake. Tell the judge what's wrong with the check: for example, your signature was forged or the amount was altered. Despite this doctoring, you will argue, the bank allowed the check to slip by unnoticed and then improperly debited your account. State exactly how much you lost as a result of the bank's error.

Countering the other side. If you were particularly slow in reporting the error in your account to the bank, you can expect the bank to use that tardiness against you. And the bank may have a leg to stand on. You see, section 4–406 of the UCC (cited in the *Firestone* case) imposes some clear duties on bank customers. As a customer, you have an obligation to carefully review your monthly statements and canceled checks. If you discover that someone has forged your signature or altered a check, you "must notify the bank promptly after discovery thereof." The bank will seek to prove that you failed to exercise reasonable care and promptness in examining your statement and reporting any error to the bank.

If, indeed, it appears that you were unreasonably careless and late, you may be cut off from asserting your claim against the bank. For example, one of the canceled checks returned with your statement on April 1 is a forgery. During the next two weeks, you either don't detect the forgery, or if you do, you fail to report it to the bank. On April 15 the bank honors another of your checks forged *by the same culprit*. It's likely you're to blame, at least in part, for letting lightning strike twice; under UCC section 4–406, the bank may be able to bar you from successfully suing it for the *second* forgery—as well as subsequent ones by the *same* forger.

How can you counter the bank's assertion that you ignored your duties as a careful customer? First, you can argue that, in fact, you were reasonably careful and reasonably prompt in reporting any error. Second, you can turn the tables on the bank and focus on its carelessness. Point out, for instance, that the forged signature bears little resemblance to yours or that the alteration of your check (say, by the addition of zeros) was so clumsy as to have been obvious to any reasonably alert person. If you can prove that the bank failed to use ordinary care, you're practically home free. Why? Because UCC section 4–406 specifically provides that even if the bank proves *you* were careless, nevertheless, your claim against the bank won't be barred if you can reverse things and show that *the bank* was careless. It's sort of a legal tit-for-tat that's the perfect counter to the bank's assault on your carefulness.

Don't be surprised if the bank pulls the same rabbit out of its hat that popped up in the *Firestone* case: namely a 10-day or 30-day limitation on how long you have to report errors in your statement. Your response should pretty much follow the reasoning of the *Firestone* court: UCC section 4–406 calls for reasonable care and promptness on the part of bank customers and sets up one year as the outside limit for exercising that care and promptness. A bank should not be allowed to arbitrarily impose a shorter time limitation on customers who have no say in the matter; the abbreviated time period is unfair and unreasonable in light of the circumstances in your case.

CHAPTER

Stale Checks

When the Check You Forgot Comes Back to Haunt You

Everybody knows what to do with stale bread: feed it to the birds. And when coffee goes stale, you brew a fresh pot. But what do you do about a stale bank check? For example, nine months ago you paid the plumber with a check for $137. He claimed he never received it or, perhaps, he lost it. So you contacted your bank and placed a stop payment order on the phantom $137 check (see chapter 36). Then you sent a replacement check for $137 to the plumber, which he cashed.

Thus, the plumber got his money; you protected yourself against potentially having to pay the same amount twice; and the bank debited your account for $137 when the plumber cashed his replacement check. Looks like a happy ending for everyone concerned, right?

Not necessarily. As too many bank customers have discovered to their regret, stop payment orders don't provide long-term insurance against the grim possibility of double payment. In fact, a stop payment order is surprisingly short-lived; it is binding on a bank for only *six months*, after which time it expires. To keep a stop payment order effective, you must return to the bank and renew it—something most customers forget to do.

Even if you do remember, you probably won't bother to

233

renew the stop payment order. Like most people, you will console yourself with the popular maxim: a bank will not pay out on a check that is over six months old. Such conventional wisdom has just enough truth in it to make it dangerous. Legally speaking, a bank has no *obligation* to pay out on a check that's over six months old, because the check is considered too stale. But—and it's an important *but*—the bank *may* pay out on the stale check if it wishes, so long as it acts with what the law calls "good faith."

The law that governs here can be found in section 4–404 of the Uniform Commercial Code (UCC), which applies in all fifty states. It says: "A bank is under no obligation to a customer having a checking account to pay a check, other than a certified check, which is presented more than six months after its date, but it may charge its customer's account for a payment made thereafter in good faith." (Two states, California and Nevada, omit the last phrase "in good faith" from their enactments of the UCC.)

Because of the UCC, a bank may legally pay out on stale checks that its customers have long since forgotten or written off as lost. This lingering possibility brings us back to that phantom $137 check your plumber claims he never received. He may have told you the truth; he may not have. But who knows where that check is now or into whose hands it's fallen? Suppose that check is presented to the bank—either by the plumber or some third party—a year or so after you originally issued it. Whatever stop payment order you may have placed on the check expired months earlier. Without noticing the staleness of the check or making any special inquiry, the bank cashes the check and debits your account for $137. You first learn about this costly oversight when you get your monthly statement.

Because of the bank's failure to balk at an obviously stale check, you're out $137—a sum that you had already paid with your year-old replacement check. Who's responsible for the loss: you or the bank? A judge may have to decide.

Courtroom Pointers

Before dragging the bank into court, try to settle the problem informally. Visit the bank as soon as you discover that a stale check has been paid by the bank and your account debited. See if the bank can be persuaded to acknowledge its oversight and recredit your account.

Elements of your case. If you can't settle matters on a friendly basis, go to court. The case you'll be presenting has three basic elements:

1. You wrote a check that has long since become stale.
2. Despite the obvious staleness of the check, it was, nonetheless, honored by the bank.
3. The bank failed to act in good faith or with due care.

Proving your side. For starters, your best evidence was supplied by the bank itself. Bring to court the monthly bank statement that records the date and amount of the debit to your account that resulted from the bank's honoring your stale check. Of course, you should also bring in the canceled stale check that the bank returned with your monthly statement. By presenting these two pieces of evidence, you will establish the date of the check and just how stale it was when the bank cashed it.

Proving that the bank did not act in "good faith" is critical. As you will recall, the UCC permits a bank to honor a stale check as long as the bank does so in good faith. Rest assured, therefore, that the bank will try to hide behind the cover of good faith: "We just made an honest mistake," the bank will argue, "the sort of unintentional oversight that occurs when you're processing thousands of pieces of paper. We had only the best of intentions."

To overcome this good-faith defense, you must show that the bank was so careless it should not get off the hook merely by claiming that it acted in good faith. *All banks have a basic legal obligation to exercise ordinary care when handling banking transactions.* When a bank fails to act with care, the good-faith escape hatch should be closed to it.

Therefore, your strategy will be to show that your check was so stale it should have caused a red flag to pop up the moment it was presented. Any reasonably prudent teller or bank officer should have been suspicious because of the age of your check. Some precaution should have been taken; for example, getting in touch with you or checking bank records. By not taking any precautions and treating an obviously stale check as a routine transaction, the bank failed to act with care. Thus, the bank should not now be allowed to take refuge in that blessed state of mind, good faith, which ordinarily lets bank personnel honor stale checks with impunity.

Stripped of its good-faith immunity, the bank may be held liable to you for the loss you've incurred. In a 1978 Louisiana case, *Charles A. Ragusa & Son* v. *Community State Bank,* the bank cashed a three-year-old check. (A stop payment order placed on the check had long since expired.) The bank claimed it had only been acting in good faith.

Not so, ruled the court. "When a bank's actions are put at issue," said the court, "it is incumbent upon the bank to show that it exercised the requisite care with regard to its customer. This the bank has failed to do in the instant case. In fact, the bank did not introduce any evidence in support of its actions or to prove its alleged good faith.

"We believe," continued the court, "that the payment of such an obviously stale check, three years old, demonstrates the bank's lack of due care and prevents it from claiming the defense of good faith. . . ."

New York's Chemical Bank lacked good faith when it cashed a stale check in the 1974 case, *New York Flameproofing Co., Inc.* v. *Chemical Bank.* "Here the check was not merely stale," explained the court; "it was ten years stale. It was written on paper of a different color than currently used for the customer's checks. It was written on paper imprinted with an address from which the customer had moved almost seven years prior to payment."

By way of defense, Chemical Bank offered no evidence— merely its conclusion that it had acted in good faith. But the court rejected this defense in light of the compelling evidence marshaled by the bank's customer: "Such circumstances unexplained would and do justify a finding of such reckless lack of due care as to constitute bad faith. . . . Against such circumstances it is not sufficient for Chemical Bank to merely utter the conclusory allegation of good faith. It must lay bare evidentiary support for such allegation." Lacking this evidence, the bank was held liable to the customer for the amount of the stale check.

Countering the other side. Don't be caught offguard if the bank tries to pull a fast one by relying on some tricky *disclaimer of liability* in your agreement with the bank. That disclaimer is legalese that purports to free the bank from any responsibility or liability for its lack of good faith or failure to use ordinary care. "So even if we were careless," the bank will argue, "we're absolved by this disclaimer in our agreement with the customer."

The disclaimer of liability is *void.* The UCC provides in section 4–103: "No agreement can disclaim a bank's responsibility for its own lack of good faith or failure to exercise ordinary care or can limit the measure of damages for such lack or failure." Tell that to a judge if the bank tries to slip through a loophole in the fine print.

Miscellaneous Bank Goofs

The Passbook Shuffle and the Check-Cashing Mix-up

The most common bank-related problems have been highlighted in the preceding four chapters. Of course, myriad other snags may occur in dealings between the bank and you. Although it is impossible to lay down hard-and-fast rules for resolving all these potential hassles, some general pointers are in order. Here are two fairly representative examples of how bank customers have successfully sued their banks over the latter's mistakes.

In the Illinois case of *Tate* v. *Sears Bank & Trust Company,* Willie and Edna Tate had a joint savings account. One day, Willie Tate visited the bank, presented his savings deposit book, and requested withdrawal of the entire balance registered in the book: $465. The bank refused on the grounds that the deposit book did not accurately reflect the balance in the Tates' account.

The Tates were forced to sue the bank to collect the money that was due them. In court, Willie Tate was the sole witness. He entered his deposit book in evidence and testified that he and his wife had made each deposit and withdrawal reflected in the book and that the balance was as stated in the book: $465.

It's hard to see how the Tates could lose. But the bank spotted a way. It argued that Mr. Tate's case, thorough though it may have seemed, was really incomplete. While Mr. Tate admittedly accounted for every withdrawal recorded in the deposit book, he failed to introduce any evidence establishing that all withdrawals had actually been *entered* in the book. In other words, there might have been some withdrawals that went unrecorded. As far as the bank was concerned, therefore, the balance stated in the deposit book did not necessarily prove the *real* balance, which the bank claimed was less than $465.

But the court disagreed. For one thing, the rules printed in the deposit book itself stated: "No withdrawals of deposits or interest shall be made unless the depositor's pass book be produced and the withdrawal entered therein." According to the court, "This would seem to support the Tates' position and to declare pretty clearly the character of the pass book as having at least some evidentiary value as to the status of the account. . . . The entries in the deposit book are in the nature of admissions by the bank and constitute evidence of all the necessary facts giving rise to liability, even though they may not be conclusive. . . . Since the defense in this case is based on the proposition that the deposit book balance does not represent the true state of the account, the bank should be required to come forward with some evidence to that effect." Because the bank presented no such evidence, the Tates were entitled to recover the recorded balance of $465.

The second case is *Jiang* v. *First National City Bank,* a New York City small-claims court case decided in 1970. On September 3, 1970, Steven Jiang visited his branch of First National City Bank and handed the teller his salary check in the amount of $354.49 and a deposit slip for $350. The teller gave him $4.49 in cash (representing the difference between his salary check and the deposit) and a receipted customer's copy of the deposit slip. However, the bank later credited Jiang's account with only *$35*, not $350.

Jiang was forced to sue the bank in New York City Small-Claims Court. Jiang told his side of the story, which seemed perfectly straightforward, and he had a receipted $350 deposit slip to back up his testimony. It looked like an open-and-shut case in his favor;

the bank had apparently miscalculated his deposit as $35 instead of $350.

But then it was the bank's turn. Its witnesses conceded, as they had to, that Jiang's deposit slip was, indeed, for $350. However, the bank introduced in evidence the third (or "teller's") copy of the Jiang deposit slip. It is on this copy, retained by the bank, that the teller notes any details of the transaction. What did this teller's copy reveal? that the teller had treated the transaction as a deposit of *only $35* and had returned to Jiang not $4.49, *but $319.49!*

So, as often happens in small-claims court, a case that seemed one-sided suddenly became complicated. What was the legal significance of Jiang's receipted deposit slip; what did it prove? "Neither the Uniform Commercial Code nor any decision supplies a direct answer," admitted a perplexed Judge Irving Younger. "It appears to me, however, that two considerations suggest what the answer should be.

"*First.* If commerce is to proceed smoothly, a bank's customer must be able to rely upon the accuracy and definitiveness of the bank's record of his transactions, especially where, as here, the record is put in his hands for no other reason than to be the customer's permanent memorandum of the transaction.

"*Second.* The proof adduced by the bank to avoid its receipt is evidence exclusively of the bank's internal bookkeeping entries. There is no suggestion that the teller's copy of Jiang's deposit slip was prepared by Jiang, acknowledged by him, or even seen by him. . . . In sum, Jiang is not chargeable with knowledge of or assent to the details of the transaction which appear on the teller's copy of the deposit slip."

Given these two considerations, what did Judge Younger make of the testimony by the bank's witnesses that Jiang's receipted deposit slip did not accurately reflect the true nature of the transaction? Judge Younger concluded that when a bank, by testimony given in court, seeks to "avoid or vary a customer's receipted deposit slip, the burden should be on the bank to prove not only (1) that in fact the receipt is incorrect, but also (2) that in fact the customer has benefited by the error. The bank's customer should enjoy the repose of finality so long as he is not thereby unjustly enriched. Hence I hold that the second test must be applied along with the first in determining who should bear the consequences of the bank's mistake."

Had the bank proven that Jiang's receipt was incorrect? After weighing all the conflicting testimony, Judge Younger decided yes. Did that mean Jiang lost? No, because in Judge Younger's estimation, the bank failed to satisfy the second part of his test— namely that Jiang had benefited by the bank's miscalculation: "Jiang's testimony and demeanor struck me as truthful," observed Judge Younger; "no witness testified that he saw Jiang given $319.49 as Jiang had testified; and it is as likely as not that the sum in dispute went into the pocket of some person other than Jiang."

As a result, Judge Younger awarded Jiang $300. (Jiang's real loss had been $315—his $350 deposit had been credited as only $35—but at the time he sued, the jurisdictional limit in New York City Small-Claims Court was only $300. So Jiang had to forgo $15 of what he was truly entitled to. Today the limit in New York City is up to $1,500.)

Courtroom Pointers

Based on court decisions like those in *Tate* and *Jiang*, five basic guidelines emerge that may assist you in resolving any dispute that arises between you and your bank:

First, banks are not infallible. So don't let yourself be buffaloed into thinking that you must be the dummy responsible for any error. If you've checked and rechecked your records and still believe the bank has erred, stick to your guns.

Second, hold onto all bank documents that substantiate your position and bring them to court with you: for example, deposit slips, savings books.

Third, insist on the principle, enunciated in both the *Tate* and *Jiang* cases, that a bank customer is entitled to rely on these documents as proof of transactions conducted with the bank.

Fourth, if the bank springs some internal business records on you—as occurred in the *Jiang* case—point out that such records are completely within the bank's control and never received your assent. Reeemphasize that you're relying, as a bank customer must, on the documentation that was given to you by the bank.

Fifth, stick to the truth as you *know* the truth. Steven Jiang knew he'd gotten only $4.49 from the teller—not $319.49 as the bank claimed. So whatever arguments the bank came up with, he clung to the facts as he knew them. The judge was impressed with his veracity as a witness and ruled in his favor.

CHAPTER 40

Caterers

The Case of the Canceled Wedding Reception

The unthinkable can and does happen. Just ask those travelers who held reservations for the return voyage of the Titanic! If they had hired a caterer for their bon voyage party and given him the customary down payment, chances are they would have had another shock coming: no refund.

Caterers know, of course, that ships sometimes sink, weddings may be postponed, bar mitzvahs be canceled, and even an office party isn't recession proof. Bearing such potential mishaps in mind, caterers generally protect themselves—not you —by stating in their standard catering agreements that there will be no refunds in case of cancellation. So if you're forced to cancel—no matter what the cause or how far in advance—the caterer will simply point to the contract you have signed and keep your deposit. (The caterer prefers to have his cake and eat yours too!)

Such greed may make you angry. But a contract is a contract, right? Wrong. There may be a loophole here that will let you get your deposit back, despite what the contract says. The loophole is supplied by the Uniform Commercial Code (UCC), which applies in all fifty states. Specifically, section 2–302 of the UCC empowers a judge to refuse to enforce contract provisions that are grossly unfair and heavyhanded—what the law calls *unconscionable.* Using UCC section 2–302, you can sue for refund of your catering deposit on the grounds that it would be unconscionable to allow the caterer to pocket it.

Milton Bogatz took good advantage of the UCC in a 1976 New York case, *Bogatz* v. *Case Catering Corporation.* Twelve months prior to his daughter's wedding, Milton signed a catering contract with Case; it reserved Case's Royal Room for the wedding reception on January 20, 1974. With regard to possible cancellations, the contract provided: "In the event that this contract is canceled, the undersigned is liable for the full amount due under this contract [$1,550]." After signing, Milton made a deposit of $750 toward the total contract price of $1,550.

Unfortunately, four months before the wedding, Milton's daughter's engagement was broken, and he had to notify the caterer that there would be no wedding and, hence, no catered reception. Sticking to its contract, Case refused to refund Milton's $750 deposit. So Milton sued the caterer.

The case boiled down to a question of "What's fair?" versus "What's in the contract?" Certainly, it didn't seem fair to let the caterer keep the deposit, when it had been given advance notice sufficient to let it rebook use of the Royal Room. On the other hand, the contract didn't provide for refunds; to the contrary, it called for payment of the entire balance in case of a cancellation.

Judge Nat Hentel came down on the side of fairness. The judge was not being Mr. Nice Guy. He had a firm legal peg to hang his sense of justice on—namely, section 2–302 of the UCC. Judge Hentel ruled that under the circumstances, forcing Milton Bogatz to forfeit $750 because of a canceled wedding would be unconscionable.

"With a cancellation so far in advance of the reserved date," reasoned Judge Hentel, "defendant should not be allowed to profit from the misery of plaintiffs. . . . Failure to re-let the Royal Room is just another business hazard to be faced and absorbed in the type of business defendant conducts." Keeping Bogatz's deposit "would be an unconscionable consequence of cancellation." Therefore, the cancellation clause was rendered unenforceable under the UCC. The judge ordered Case Catering to refund Milton Bogatz's $750 deposit.

Courtroom Pointers

If you've lost a catering contract deposit because your affair was canceled, there's no reason why you can't follow in Milton Bogatz's footsteps. There's no guarantee of success, of course; deciding what is unconscionable requires a subjective judgment, which may vary from judge to judge. But if you think losing your deposit was unconscionable, testing that theory in small-claims court is certainly worth a try.

Elements of your case. Under UCC section 2–302, there are four elements to your case:

1. You entered into an agreement with a caterer (reserving his services and perhaps a banquet room) and paid him a deposit.

2. Well in advance of the scheduled affair, you notified the caterer that you were canceling.

3. The caterer refused to refund your deposit (or agreed to a refund only under onerous conditions, which you had to reject).

4. Under the circumstances, it would be unconscionable for you to forfeit your deposit to the caterer.

Proving your side. A threshold question you will have to decide is when to sue the caterer. Should you wait until your scheduled date for catering so you can see if the banquet room was relet or the caterer hired out his services to someone else? Or should you go directly to court? The answer depends, in part, on how far in advance you are canceling. If you are giving the caterer five or six months' notice, you might just as well wait and see if the caterer relets the room and whether he will therefore return your deposit. But if you gave the caterer time to relet the room, there may be no need to wait.

In this context, consider the 1969 small-claims court case from New York, *Lazan* v. *Huntington Town House, Inc.* Sheldon Lazan hired Huntington Town House to cater his son's bar mitzvah. The guest list kept shrinking until it finally "dwindled away to a point where it would be doubtful that there would be anyone (or only a handful) present at the affair." So Sheldon decided to cancel the catering agreement.

He sent Huntington Town House a registered letter a full 19 months prior to the scheduled bar mitzvah, canceling the agreement and requesting a refund of his $220 deposit. Since the catering agreement said nothing about cancellation, Sheldon assumed he would get his deposit back.

But Huntington Town House responded by sending Sheldon a cancellation agreement rather than a refund. This agreement said that Sheldon would get his deposit back only if Huntington Town House could relet the room; all Sheldon had to do was wait 19 months to see if the room would be relet.

Instead of waiting, Sheldon sued in small-claims court for return of his deposit. Here's how the judge decided the case: "The court finds that . . . enforcement of the agreement is unreasonable, unfair and even unconscionable so as to bring it within the purview of Sec. 2–302 of the Uniform Commercial Code. It is entirely unreasonable for the defendant to hold plaintiff's deposit for 19 months after the plaintiff attempts to cancel the contract. Defendant had much more than ample notice of plaintiff's intention to cancel, and defendant can in no way suffer any damages from plaintiff's cancellation. In fact, in view of the almost daily rising cost of everything, the defendant is probably better off cancelling this agreement now, and charging a higher price at a later date to a new customer." So, with almost 15 months still left before the originally scheduled date for the bar mitzvah, the court ordered Huntington Town House to refund Mr. Lazan's $220 deposit without further delay.

When you go to court, be prepared to give a fairly detailed account of exactly what happened when you signed the catering agreement. For example, in the *Bogatz* case, Milton Bogatz said, in essence: "We were there on a happy occasion, and were excited about the coming wedding, and no one even thought about the possibility of cancellation." This kind of evidence serves two purposes. First, it shows that you signed the agreement at a time when you were particularly vulnerable to being taken advantage of. (The unequal bargaining position you, therefore, occupied is an important element in establishing that it would be unconscionable to enforce the contract against you.)

Second, the evidence is likely to arouse some sympathy from the judge.

Bring your copy of the actual catering agreement along with you to court. Even though you may not like what it says, you can be sure that the defendant will bring a copy. You might just as well be forthright and admit that you signed away any right to the deposit.

Now the ball is in the judge's court. You know that under section 2–302 of the Uniform Commercial Code, the judge can disregard the agreement if he thinks it's unconscionable. But don't be too quick to tell him what the law is. The purpose of the unconscionability rule is to protect innocent, simple people like yourself from being victimized by the big guys. If you sound too well informed, your status as a "little guy" may be undermined.

If you get the feeling that the judge doesn't know about section 2–302, you might want to drop hints by explaining how "unconscionable" the contract is. If the judge still thinks his hands are tied because "a contract is a contract," then you might have to volunteer that under the Uniform Commercial Code, the judge has the right to disregard an unconscionable contract.

Countering the other side. The caterer may raise a few different defenses. First, he may claim that you never actually notified him of your desire to cancel. Anticipating such a potential pitfall down the road, be sure that when you cancel, you notify the caterer *in writing*—ideally, via certified mail, return receipt requested; keep a copy of your notification letter. Then you will be able to point to the copy, as well as proof of mailing and its receipt by the caterer.

Second, the caterer may concede that you gave him notification, but it was not far enough in advance to give him a reasonable opportunity to rebook. This defense raises the iffy question of how much advance notice is reasonable (ultimately, the judge will have to decide). Obviously, the more time you gave the caterer to rebook, the stronger your case will be. (It will be recalled that four months provided sufficient advance notice in the *Bogatz* case.)

Third, the caterer is likely to claim that he suffered a loss as a result of your cancellation and that he is entitled to have that loss deducted from your deposit. You can counter this argument in two ways: You can invoke the rationale used by Judge Hentel in the *Bogatz* case: "Failure to re-let the room is just another business hazard to be faced and absorbed in the type of business the defendant conducts." In other words, if a cancellation occurs, the caterer, not the consumer, should bear the loss.

You can also demand that the caterer document precisely what losses he has suffered because of your cancellation. That's exactly what Milton Bogatz did. Case Catering claimed it had suffered the loss of "sales costs" when it had to relet the room. However, Bogatz pressed the point, demanding to know exactly what those "sales costs" were. The only reply was that sales costs included "manager's salary, bookkeeping, and computer costs." The caterer could not, however, prove *how much time* its manager actually spent handling the Bogatz cancellation; nor were the costs of bookeeping and computer time broken down to show *how much of a loss* was attributable to the cancellation.

Judge Hentel decided that Case Catering had not proven what its losses actually were. The evidence presented by the caterer was, in the judge's words, "very flimsy and unconvincing proof indeed!" If the caterer you are suing claims that he has sustained losses because of your cancellation, use the tactic Milton Bogatz employed—demand proof of exactly how the caterer suffered a loss and in what amount(s). Odds are, the caterer won't be able to respond any more convincingly than Case did.

CHAPTER 41

Tax Preparer's Liability

The Day That H & R Block Goofed

There may well be 17 reasons why you should let someone else prepare your income-tax return. But there are at least two reasons why you shouldn't: first, the tax-preparer may know less than you do; second, despite all his guarantees to back you up in case of an IRS audit, the tax-preparer may abandon you when the going gets tough. Then you'll find yourself facing potential IRS penalties, plus interest charges, not to mention fees for an accountant to get you out of the jam that the careless tax-preparer put you in.

It's enough to make you want to sue, which is exactly what Glenn and Grace Testerman did in a recent Maryland case, *Testerman* v. *H & R Block, Inc.* The Testermans owned and ran a gas station from which they earned a comfortable living. In 1967 they went to the local H & R Block office to have their tax return prepared; they had been induced to patronize Block because of advertisements that boasted "they are tax experts." The operator of the Block office, a Mr. Dunn, spent forty-five minutes examinining a cardboard box full of canceled checks, cash register tapes, and bills that the Testermans had brought with them. On completing his review, Dunn announced that the Testermans had "lost money" during 1967. In no mood to disagree with the tax expert, the Testermans accepted his judgment and signed the return, reporting a loss to the IRS.

Understandably satisfied with Block's results, and, of course, mindful of the Block advertisement that "they will pay the penalty and interest if they make a mistake, and . . . they are tax experts," the Testermans returned the following year for the preparation of their 1968 return. This time a Mrs. Weisberg spent an hour inspecting the contents of the Testerman's cardboard box. Her conclusion, like Mr. Dunn's the year before, was that the Testermans had again "lost money."

"By this time," as a Maryland court later recounted, "the Testermans were overcome by curiosity and asked how it was possible for them to have lost money when, in fact, they had made an adequate livelihood and had drawn cash from the business for their personal use. Mrs. Weisberg replied that 'everybody loses money the first couple of years they are in business.'" Yes, but what about the money they had transferred from the gas station business account to their personal checking account? That money, according to the Block tax expert, "was hard-earned money that was not taxable."

In addition to preparing the 1968 return, Mrs. Weisberg amended the 1965 Testerman return; she used the 1968 loss as a "carryback," thereby producing a tax refund for 1965! This bit of financial legerdemain taxed the IRS's patience a bit too much. Soon the Testermans were audited and confronted with the patent illegality of their tax returns. When the befuddled taxpayers turned to H & R Block for assistance, Mr. Dunn suggested they had better hire their own lawyer. Which they did—and an accountant to boot. After a long hassle, the Testermans wound up paying the delinquent taxes that they clearly owed, plus a penalty and interest.

After the IRS account had been settled, the Testermans returned to the Block office to see if they could recoup some of the losses that the Block people had caused them. After all, hadn't Block's ads promised to "pay the penalty and interest if they make a mistake"? But Mr. Dunn *denied,* despite everything that had taken place, that his office had made a mistake; the Block office in Baltimore had instructed him not to pay the penalties and interest. Tempers, as they say, flared; Dunn told the Testermans "to get the hell out" and called them a "bunch of troublemakers."

The next scene in this tragi-comedy took place in the Montgomery County Circuit Court, where the Testermans sued H & R Block to recover the penalty and interest they had been forced to pay, as well as the additional legal and accounting fees they had incurred to straighten out the whole mess.

In court, the Testermans told their tale of woe: why they had been attracted to Block's office by its advertised expertise (actually, it came out in court that Block employees referred to themselves as "tax consultants" and were told never to refer to themselves as "tax experts," but if someone else did, not to worry about it!); how they had relied on Block's advertised promise to pay any penalty or interest caused by mistakes; what the Block representatives had told them in 1967, and again in 1968, after reviewing their cardboard box full of records.

The Testermans called as a witness the accountant who had bailed them out after Block fouled up. He testified, in essence, that the Block personnel who had prepared the returns "were woefully inadequate—in terms of education and experience—for the tasks which they had undertaken. The errors Block had made bordered on the absurd. It had understated income for both years by deducting sums 'off the top' (from gross income), which the Testermans had drawn periodically from the business for their personal use. Also, Block omitted from gross income the amounts paid for expenses from cash receipts at the service station, which, of course, had not been reflected in bank deposits." The records that the Testermans had delivered to Block in cardboard boxes had, however, accurately reflected all of these transactions.

Both Mr. Dunn and Mrs. Weisberg testified on behalf of H & R Block. "Despite the IRS audit and the consequences which had ensued, Mrs. Weisberg and Dunn insisted that the returns, having been based on the information received from the Testermans, were prepared correctly. They acknowledged that pursuant to the instructions issued by Block, fees are not refunded. If errors result in client dissatisfaction, a 'gift certificate' is to be issued for the following year."

The judge was clearly unimpressed with this weak defense. Block's personnel had failed to display the degree of care that is to be expected of any reasonably competent tax preparer. To make matters worse, in its ads, H & R Block had held its people out as "tax experts"; what's more, Block had promised to pay any penalty or interest caused by its mistakes. The evidence showed that Block had not lived up to these representations. The court awarded the Testermans $690.65 to compensate them for the penalty and interest they had been compelled to pay the IRS, plus money damages to cover the legal and accounting costs they had incurred.

Courtroom Pointers

The Testermans' woes were caused by a professional tax service, but yours might stem from tax preparation done by a CPA or an attorney. Whatever the tax-preparer's status, the legal principles governing his liability to you are essentially the same.

Elements of your case. When suing a tax-preparer over mistakes on your return, you will generally have to establish four basic elements:

1. You consulted a tax-preparer who undertook to complete your tax return.

2. The tax-preparer had a duty to employ that level of skill and care ordinarily exhibited by prudent members of his profession in your locality. (Note that, like any other professional, a tax-preparer is not required to be infallible; he must, however, demonstrate a degree of diligence in your behalf that would normally be forthcoming from others in his calling who know their business.)

3. Despite his duty to you, the tax-preparer failed to use due care. (In legalese, he was *negligent.*)

4. As a result of the tax-preparer's negligence, you suffered certain losses.

Proving your side. You should begin by testifying to the basic facts in your case. For example: when you visited the tax-preparer; who served you; what information and materials you supplied; what the tax-preparer said to you (the remarks made in the Testerman case betrayed a total misunderstanding of basic tax principles); how the IRS responded to your tax return (e.g., by auditing you); what mistakes the IRS found in your return; how much extra you had to pay because of these mistakes (e.g., the tax-preparer refused to pay for penalties and interest).

Whenever possible, point out as the Testermans did, the self-laudatory representations made by the tax-preparer that drew you to him in the first place. For instance, he touted himself as a tax expert or as doing "top quality" work, say, in newspaper ads (by all means, bring the ad into court with you as evidence). You relied on that supposed expertise, to your great misfortune.

Countering the other side. A tax-preparer may try to show that, even though he admittedly made a mistake, he was still exercising all the care that could reasonably have been expected of him (remember, that's generally his only duty toward you). Counter this argument, if you can, by pointing out that no other competent tax-preparer in the vicinity would likely have made the same *faux pas* that was committed by your man: "Your Honor," you might contend, "I'm not complaining about some fine point of tax law on which reasonable men could differ. The oversight here goes to the basics of tax law, which no one could mess up and still call himself a reasonably competent tax preparer."

Another counterargument you may be able to use is that the tax preparer really ought to be held to a higher standard than just plain reasonable care. Suppose the tax preparer advertised himself as an "expert" or doing "100% accurate work." Then he should be held to the high level that he's set for himself.

CHAPTER

Bad Food

The Case of the $575 Walnut Shell

Some folks crave Chinese food; others prefer haute cuisine; still others go for fast food. But nobody likes adulterated food. Yet, that's what all too many of us encounter when we dine out or eat store-bought foods at home. What guarantee do you have that the food you're about to bite into or swallow doesn't contain some nasty hidden surprise? Don't bother reading your menu or the label on a package, because you'll rarely find any guarantee there.

You will find a guarantee, however, set down in the Uniform Commercial Code (UCC), which applies in all fifty states. To be precise, section 2–314 of the UCC states that a seller of food or drink (e.g., a restaurant or market) warrants (guarantees) that it is *fit to eat*. So if you eat some bad food, there has been a breach of warranty, and you can sue for the damages that you've suffered.

Marjorie Stark won a breach of warranty claim in the 1974 New York City Small-Claims Court case, *Stark* v. *Chock Full O'Nuts*. When Chock Full O'Nuts, a New York City restaurant, sold Marjorie Stark a "nutted cheese" sandwich, they weren't kidding. The sandwich contained not only walnuts, but also one walnut shell. Marjorie discovered the shell when she bit down on it and broke her tooth.

Marjorie's next stop was a dentist and then to small-claims court. She sued Chock Full O'Nuts for the cost of her dental treatment. She claimed that a "nutted cheese" sandwich isn't supposed to contain walnut shells. Therefore, the restaurant should be held responsible for the damage to her tooth.

After considering the evidence, the court decided that a nutted cheese sandwich containing a walnut shell is not fit to eat. Therefore, Chock Full O'Nuts had breached its warranty of fitness under UCC section 2–314. The court awarded Marjorie $575 to cover the cost of dental treatment for her broken tooth.

Courtroom Pointers

The problem of bad or dangerous food is widespread. Mass production of meals and packaged foods inevitably results in mistakes. If you become the victim of such a mistake, there's no reason why you can't do exactly what Marjorie did.

Elements of your case. There are four elements of your case:

1. A dangerous condition existed in certain food or drink prepared by a restaurant or sold in a store.

2. The dangerous condition was one that a consumer would not reasonably expect to find in the particular food or drink.

3. You ate the food or drink.

4. As a result, you suffered personal injury.

Proving your case. Proving your case will depend upon your ability to convince the judge that the food you ate was not fit to be eaten *under the particular circumstances of your case.* Some foods are normally a bit dangerous. Baked fish is a good example. If you gobble down a baked bluefish and get a bone caught in your throat, don't expect much sympathy or money in court. Baked bluefish is expected to have bones. You are expected to be careful.

But if you ate a fish stick and choked on a bone, you *would* have a case. No consumer would reasonably expect to find a bone in a fish stick; a bluefish, yes, a fish stick, no. Obviously, what creates the expectations in a consumer is not the particular food he is eating—fish—but the way that it was prepared—baked whole versus boned and fileted.

This standard of *reasonable expectation* has now been adopted by most courts. Put simply, the standard is that a consumer is entitled to get in a food what a normal consumer would reasonably expect to get. In many cases, there is no question about what you, or anyone else, would find reasonable or unreasonable. If you get a mouse in your Coke or a waterbug in your ham sandwich, that's clearly unreasonable by anyone's standards. (In fact, you may have such a good case that you should seriously consider consulting a lawyer.)

Problems arise when a case approaches the border line between reasonable and unreasonable expectations. Then, any facts tending to show what your reasonable expectations were become critical. Just how critical is demonstrated by the Washington, D.C., case of *Hochberg v. O'Donnell's Restaurant, Inc.* Philip Hochberg went to O'Donnell's Restaurant and ordered a martini with an olive. When the drink arrived, Philip noticed that there was a hole in the end of the olive. He drank the martini and ate the olive. At least he tried to eat it; unfortunately the olive still had a pit in it, which caused him to break a tooth.

Philip went to court. Was the fact that he had seen a hole in the olive before eating it important? Absolutely, according to the court: "It appears the crucial consideration . . . is that Mr. Hochberg saw the hole in one end of an olive and therefore assumed it had been pitted, chewed the olive and injured his tooth on the pit. He concedes that if he had not seen the hole in the olive his case would be 'extremely tenuous.' " So the fact that Philip saw the hole in the olive was important, because that fact played a role in creating his *reasonable expectations* as to what was (or was not) inside the olive. Had there been no hole in the olive, Philip probably would not have been able to recover a dime.

In order to prove your case, you should look for and present any evidence that you believe helped to create your expectation as to the fitness of the food you ate. For example, did the menu say that the chicken had been boned? Did the can of peaches say the pits had been removed? Did the lobster bisque

come with a spoon—implying that it was to be eaten as a soup
—or was it spread out on a plate so you could see any pieces of
lobster shell? Be prepared to explain to the judge exactly why
you expected that the food you ate would be safe to eat in the
normal manner, without any special precautions.

You may also want to consider bringing in an expert witness.
That's what Miriam Carpenter did in the Texas case *Carpenter*
v. *Jim Dandy Fast Foods, Inc.* She had eaten a fried chicken
breast at the defendant's restaurant. A piece of bone got stuck
in her throat and medical assistance was required to remove it.
When Miriam went to court, Jim Dandy argued that a chicken
bone is exactly what you'd reasonably expect to find in fried
chicken. Consequently, the restaurant shouldn't be responsible
when such a bone turns up.

Miriam Carpenter, however, had a secret weapon! Pete Ober.
He worked in the meat business and was experienced in cutting up chicken for the retail trade. He examined the chicken
bone removed from Miriam's throat and decided that "he had
never seen a chicken bone cut like that before." He concluded
that "if a person is eating a piece of breast and pulls off one
piece of the breast he should not encounter a bone like the one
in question." Bolstered by this favorable expert testimony, Miriam Carpenter was able to fry Jim Dandy in court for $1,500.

When you sue, you'll have to decide what your damages are.
If you broke a tooth, for instance, your damages will include
the cost of dental care and any pain or suffering you underwent.
If you were incapacitated and missed work for a few days, add
on your lost income. Consider any losses you suffered as a result of your injury and include them as part of your claim.

One injury you might not think of is *loss of appetite!* If you
think that losing your appetite isn't a loss worth suing for, just
ask Gary and Brian Martel. Ask them if they like applesauce.
Brian and Gary were aged eight and ten, respectively, when
they encountered a bottle of Mott's applesauce. Here's how the
judge described what happened in the Michigan case, *Martel*
v. *Duffy-Mott Corporation:* "Brian mixed his applesauce with
the rest of his food and consumed a sizeable portion of the
mixture. Gary ate the applesauce separately and after a spoon-
ful or two reported to his mother that the applesauce tasted

funny. She tasted and smelled the applesauce and immediately telephoned the poison control center . . . which, on the basis of her description of the applesauce, instructed her to take the children and remaining applesauce to the nearest hospital. When she arrived the applesauce was examined by hospital personnel who decided to and did pump the childrens' stomachs."

Other than an intense and continuing dislike for applesauce, the children suffered no further problem. The difficult question posed by this case was whether the boys' continuing dislike for applesauce was an *injury* for which they should be compensated. The court weighed the question and decided yes: "It is a close question whether the boys should be permitted to recover . . . damages for past and future loss of enjoyment of applesauce. Applesauce is but one of a large variety of desserts, most of which . . . can, no doubt . . . fill the gastronomical void created when the boys lost their taste for applesauce. . . . However, we think it sounder to permit a plaintiff who can convince a jury that the food product he consumed was inedible and in consequence he no longer enjoys eating it, to recover damages, including damages for loss of enjoyment, *if he can additionally convince the jury that a true loss was suffered and that it should add a dollar amount therefore.* In some cases loss of enjoyment may be real and substantial, an injury not to be made light of."

Thus, the court was prepared to allow a consumer to be compensated for loss of enjoyment of a particular food. If you lose your appetite for the kind of food you ate, you can claim damages for the loss of future enjoyment from that food. The judge you appear before may not place a high value on such a loss, but, on the other hand, he may just have returned from a rotten lunch and prove highly sympathetic.

CHAPTER 43

Invasion of Privacy

A Case of Trespass by Ma Bell

There are times in life when you just want to be left alone. Whether you take refuge in the seclusion of your home or venture out on some private errand, you don't want to be hassled by other people sticking their noses into your business. It's not that you're antisocial; it's simply that you need moments when you can retreat from the world. The law recognizes this need and shields it through something called the *right of privacy*. If someone intrudes on your privacy, he may be held liable for the distress and humiliation that you have suffered.

Ma Bell invaded the privacy of two of its subscribers in the 1977 Texas case, *Gonzales* v. *Southwestern Bell Telephone Company*. A dispute arose between the telephone company and two customers, Abram and Modesta Gonzales. The company wanted an additional $50 deposit on the two telephones in the Gonzales home, but the couple refused to comply with this demand. As a result, the telephone company notified them that their service was being disconnected.

Mike Johnson, a telephone company employee, went to the Gonzaleses' home to remove the phones, but no one was there. That didn't deter Johnson. Without even bothering to ring the bell, he simply opened the door, entered, announced himself and what he was there for, and when he got no response from the empty house, he blithely went about his business: namely, disconnecting the two phones and taking them out with him.

The Gonzaleses were greatly upset when they returned home and discovered that the unauthorized entry had occurred. They sued Southwestern Bell for invasion of privacy. At the trial, the Gonzaleses' daughter, Socorro, testified that when she came home from school, she noticed that the screen door was broken and mud had been tracked onto the carpet in the house. Mike Johnson admitted entering the house and taking the phones; he explained that he did not bother to ring the bell because it was his experience that "door bells were generally not in working order"!

Modesta Gonzales testified how intensely the whole experience had affected her: She became sick to her stomach and could not sleep because of the thought that somebody had broken into her house like a thief. Mrs. Gonzales also said that she felt bad, because her neighbors had been led to believe that she hadn't paid her phone bill. Abram Gonzales testified that the incident had made him feel "like the size of a red ant, as small as that."

The court decided that the telephone company had illegally violated the Gonzaleses' right of privacy. "There is no question," observed the court, "that the telephone company's employee saw whatever there was to see in the Gonzaleses' bedroom and other areas of their home. Whatever there was to see was the private property of the Gonzaleses. This invasion of privacy by the telephone company's employee into the Gonzaleses' home was a willful wrong which constitutes a legal injury." For the mental suffering inflicted on them, each of the Gonzaleses was awarded $1,800.

Courtroom Pointers

The *Gonzales* case dramatizes how the right of privacy protects the ordinary citizen's right to be left alone—free from unwanted intrusions. This right becomes more and more precious and worth upholding, as so-called civilization constantly encroaches on our private worlds.

Elements of the case. If, like the Gonzaleses, you seek to enforce your right to privacy in court, there are four basic elements that you will have to prove:

1. The defendant intruded upon you or pried into your affairs.

2. The area into which the defendant intruded was one entitled to remain private.

3. The intrusion was one that would ordinarily be offensive to a reasonable man.

4. As a result of the intrusion, you suffered mental distress.

Proving your side. You must first establish exactly how the defendant intruded on your privacy. The clearest example is a trespass in your own home (as in the *Gonzales* case) or some other place that you are occupying (e.g., a motel room or hospital room). It's not necessary, however, that the defendant have physically entered your home. Maybe he just peered into it to spy on you; *a peeping Tom violates your right to privacy.* There have even been cases where the invasion of privacy consisted of incessant phone calls being made to someone's home or office.

In a 1978 Utah case, Jean Jeppson was telephoned at her home by the host of a local television program, "Dialing for Dollars." Without Mrs. Jeppson's knowledge or consent, her name and telephone number were announced on the air, and the following telephone conversation was televised:

> HOST: "This is 'Dialing for Dollars,' do you have your TV set on?"
> JEPPSON: "No, I don't."
> HOST: "Oh, that is unfortunate, because you could have won $50.00."
> JEPPSON: "Well, now I'll tell you, I'd rather have peace in my home than all that garbage on television, even for $50.00."

The Supreme Court of Utah held that there had been an invasion of Mrs. Jeppson's privacy.

Make sure that you point out the essentially private nature of the thing pried into. In the case of your home, the degree of privacy involved is obvious; it becomes less apparent, though, the more you move into public areas, such as streets or restaurants. Even when you're out in public, however, you're entitled to expect that some degree of privacy attaches to your person and property. Thus, forcing a supermarket shopper to open up some of her personal belongings for inspection was found to be an invasion of privacy in a West Virginia case.

In a 1964 Alabama case, a housewife walking through a carnival funhouse was photographed without her consent just as some jets of air blew her dress up over her legs. The photograph later appeared in a local newspaper, violating the housewife's right to privacy. The court explained: "To hold that one who is involuntarily and instantaneously enmeshed in an embarrassing pose forfeits her right of privacy merely because she happened at the moment to be part of a public scene would be illogical, wrong, and unjust."

In a 1963 Georgia case, an insurance company hired Pinkerton National Detective Agency to shadow a housewife involved in an accident to ascertain the true extent of her injuries. Because of their incessant snooping, eavesdropping, and tailgating, the detectives violated the housewife's right to privacy.

Let the facts speak for themselves when it comes to proving the offensive nature of the intrusion. Obviously, no reasonable man would cry "invasion of privacy" if the landlord knocked on his door to collect the rent. On the other hand, few would fail to be offended by the kind of invasion that occurred in the *Gonzales* case.

Finally, you must show that the invasion caused you to experience mental distress, humiliation, nervousness, and so on. You can testify to this fact as the Gonzaleses did. Don't be afraid to recite your symptoms: e.g., lack of sleep, anxiety attacks. If, as a result of the invasion, you consulted a physician, by all means present his bill as a further measure of your damages.

Countering the other side. Expect the defendant to belittle the seriousness of his intrusion on your privacy. You can best answer him by sticking to the facts that indicate just how far he went in encroaching on your private sphere of activity.

The defendant may also argue that you *consented* to the invasion. In response, simply tell the truth—that you did not consent, nor did you do or say anything that might have implied any consent.

CHAPTER 44

Dance Studios

The $32,000 Hustle Lesson

Twenty years ago the Federal Trade Commission accused Arthur Murray dance studios of engaging in unfair sales practices. The company agreed to change its ways. In 1980 the FTC was back, claiming that Arthur Murray, Inc., was once more using improper methods to sell its dance lessons. Arthur Murray, Inc., agreed to change its ways—again. It would seem that some dance studios can give lessons but not learn them.

What seems to bother the FTC are the high-pressure sales tactics used by many dance schools. These tactics are particularly distasteful, when the victims tend to be people least able to afford wasting money—widows and widowers. They are often embarrassed by their foolishness and reluctant to register complaints. Besides, they believe there isn't anything a court can do once you sign a contract.

Actually, the courts are extremely sympathetic to dance-school victims. There are literally dozens of cases in which victims have recovered the money they thought had been lost in the purchase of a costly dance-lesson contract. Most of these cases were based on *fraud*, that is, the victims were deliberately misled regarding their capabilities by smooth-talking dance instructors. So if you are a dance-school victim, why not let the law cut in and help get your money back.

Consider the 1973 Texas case, *Bal-Fel, Inc.,* v. *Boyd.* Mrs. Boyd was a 56-year-old widow. A friend suggested she visit the local Fred Astaire Dance Studio, which she did. She took the bait and was sold an introductory course of five dance lessons for $5. The hook was set after only three lessons when her dance instructor told her that she "had the potential to be a great dancer."

Mrs. Boyd's original $5 investment began to grow. She invested in the Amalgamated Program of Dancing, the Supreme Gold Dance Standard, the Gold Cane Club, the Theatre Arts Club, the Executive Competition Club, the Single-Mingle Club, and the Fiesta Dance Club. All in all, Mrs. Boyd was persuaded to buy 2,500 hours of dancing lessons for about $32,000!

Why did she do it? Mrs. Boyd testified candidly in court: "I was lonely. My husband had passed away. I had no social life, and when I went to this studio, they were very friendly and loving, and in an intimate atmosphere, they would tell me, 'You want to be a great dancer? You are going to be the best . . .' and they would flatter me and play upon my emotional status as a lonely widow to induce me to buy more lessons and I kept getting in deeper. . . ."

Each step in Mrs. Boyd's descent into debt was marked by a new dance-lesson contract, obligating her to pay for a fixed number of lessons. In most cases, the contract required payment up front. And in each case, the contract was a perfectly legal document.

Mrs. Boyd got so deep in debt—even going so far as to sell her house to pay for dance lessons—that she was forced to go to a lawyer. This was the smartest step Mrs. Boyd had taken since her first dancing lesson.

Mrs. Boyd discovered that all contracts are not necessarily binding. Even the most formidable-looking legal document is not enforceable if it was obtained through fraud. All Mrs. Boyd had to do was convince the court that her dance instructor had fraudulently induced her to sign her dance contracts.

Obviously, not every dance-school contract is fraudulently induced. As one judge has said: "A contract is not invalid merely because it is the result of high-pressure salesmanship; and one is not entitled to be extricated by the courts when, because of naivete or poor judgment, he has become embogged in a morass of contractual obligation." Clearly, Mrs. Boyd had exercised poor judgment. But was it all her fault? Or did the dance school deliberatley mislead her into signing the dance-lesson contract? In other words, did the dance school commit fraud?

The judge hearing the case decided that "representing to . . . a woman 56 years old that she could complete nearly 2,500 hours of dancing lessons, and thereby become a 'great dancer,' capable of professional performance in international competition, is conduct manifestly deceptive and fraudulent." As a result, the judge ordered that the dance studio return $32,000 to Mrs. Boyd.

Courtroom Pointers

If, like Mrs. Boyd, you've been defrauded out of thousands of dollars by a dance studio, consult a lawyer immediately; you may be able to get out of the contract and recoup your money. But if you've been taken for only a thousand dollars or so, then you can be your own lawyer in small-claims court.

Elements of your case. There are three basic elements to a fraud claim against a dance studio:

1. The dance studio personnel deliberately deceived you by saying that you were, or could become, a great dancer—a veritable Fred Astaire or Ginger Rogers—if you just purchased enough lessons from the studio.

2. You relied on these representations and purchased the dance lessons recommended.

3. As a result of the fraud, you suffered certain losses—that is, you were defrauded out of the value of what you had bargained for.

Proving your case. The key element of your case is your proof that the dance studio somehow misled you. You must testify as to what lies the dance instructor told you that induced you to buy the dance lessons. For example, did the instructor say you were talented enough to become a dance instructor? Did he say you could become a top-flight professional dancer?

Be sure that whatever the instructor told you was said *before* you signed the dance-lesson contract. Only if fraud *induced* you to sign the contract can you ask the court to help you. The court won't be interested in what you were told after you signed the contract.

When you've finished presenting your case, ask the judge to order the dance studio to return to you whatever money you paid for dance lessons. Be prepared to provide evidence of exactly how much you paid. This evidence may be a copy of the contract or your canceled check.

Countering the Other Side. The most likely defense the dance school will raise is that they never told you anything that was a deliberate lie. They will claim they were merely giving you their opinion—what is called "puffing." They never *intended* to deceive you.

In response, you must simply call the judge's attention to all the surrounding circumstances: for example, your age and obvious lack of any professional dance training. Also remind the judge that the studio was aware of your particular vulnerability (e.g., you were recently widowed or divorced) and played upon it with flattery and cajolery. Under such circumstances, the judge will probably conclude that the dance studio's sales pitch went far beyond mere puffing and entered the realm of undue influence, which is typical of most frauds. It simply strains credulity too far to say that the dance school wasn't aware of the deceitful impact of all those lies they fed to you. They must have known exactly what they were up to.

CHAPTER

On Your Own

We've taken you about as far as we can go together. It's been some legal journey. You've been introduced to such technicalities as jurisdictional limits, suing a corporation, filing a claim, and service of process. You've picked up practical tips on how to negotiate an out-of-court settlement as well as how to present your case in court. Perhaps most importantly, you've learned about the central concept of the elements of a case—the legal legs on which a case stands.

No doubt your mind feels crammed full, and you're afraid that something will fall out by the time you get to court. Don't worry. You were not expected to memorize everything you read; nor do you need to. The main objective is not for you to grasp a wooden set of rules, but to absorb a way of thinking about problems. Given all you've read, you should now be in a much better position to think like a lawyer: that is, logically, objectively, and without passion or bias.

Don't be nervous about taking the law into your own hands and going to court. Remember, the small-claims court was designed especially for people like you; everyone there is as nervous as you are—that's par for the course. And despite any misgivings you may have, you're much better prepared than 99 percent of the people who sue. Ironically, your biggest problem may be to act like "just plain folks" when you get to court, instead of showing off your newly acquired skills.

So relax. There's one good reason why you should, which may have occurred to you already: *You've done the best you can.* Unlike so many victimized consumers, you haven't taken things lying down. You've put in the time and effort to learn about the rules of the game and how they were broken in your situation. And now you're going to play by those rules before the ultimate referee in a dignified manner—not in some fruitless shouting match. Win, lose, or draw, you will have the satisfaction of knowing that you didn't let your problem fester unresolved; you chose to stand up for your rights and have your day in court—on your own!

About the Authors

John M. Striker is a New York City attorney. He is a graduate of Cornell University and earned his Doctor of Laws degree from New York University School of Law in 1968. Mr. Striker worked as an Emmy Award-winning reporter for WNBC-TV News in New York City and as a legal adviser to the New York City Police Department.

Andrew O. Shapiro is a New York City attorney. He is a graduate of Harvard College and earned his Doctor of Laws degree at New York University School of Law at the same time as Mr. Striker. Mr. Shapiro has written numerous articles about the law, as well as a column in *New York* magazine on legal developments.

Constantinople: Capital of Byzantium

Constantinople:
Capital of
Byzantium

JONATHAN HARRIS

**hambledon
continuum**

Continuum UK
The Tower Building
11 York Road
London SE1 7NX

Continuum US
80 Maiden Lane
Suite 704
New York, NY 10038

ISBN 9781847251794

Typeset by codeMantra, India
Printed in the U.S.A.
Book Club Edition

For E.L.F.

Contents

Illustrations

Abbreviations

B = Byzantion

BMGS = Byzantine and Modern Greek Studies

BZ = Byzantinische Zeitschrift

DOP = Dumbarton Oaks Papers

JHS = Journal of Hellenic Studies

REB = Revue des Études Byzantines

Maps

BOSPORUS

Oiplokionion

Miles
Kms

GALATA

Kastellion Tower

Chain

Kentarion Tower

GENOESE

• Monastery of St George of Mangana

Droungarios
Gate

AMALFITANS

PISANS

VENETIANS

• Hagia Eirene

• Hagia Sophia

Augousteion

Brazen Gate

Millon

GREAT PALACE

Harbour
of Boukoleon

Forum of Constantine

Hippodrome

Mese

GOLDEN
HORN

• Christ
Pantepoptes

Pantokrator
Monastery

Aqueduct of Valens

Forum of
Theodosius

• Forty Martyrs

Cistern of
Aspar

Holy
Apostles

Column of
Marcian

Myrelaion
Monastery

Mese

• St Polyeuktos

Forum Bovis

Palace of
Blachernae

• Holy Saviour
in Chora

Lips
Monastery

Forum of Arcadius

• Virgin Peribleptos

Mese

Cistern of
Aetios

Gate of
Adrianople
(Charisios)

Cistern of St. Mokios

• Stoudios Monastery

Golden Gate

Lykos River

Land Walls

SEA OF MARMARA

1 The city of Constantinople

2 The Byzantine empire in 1200

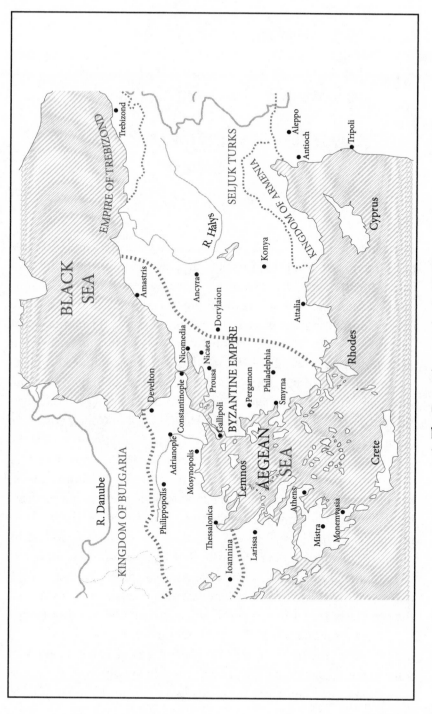

3 The Byzantine empire in 1265

Acknowledgements

I am well aware that the title of this book might cause some eyebrows to be raised. After all, Constantinople and Byzantium are but two names for the same city. The fact is that nowadays the word 'Byzantium' has come to have a dual meaning. It can be used to denote the city of Constantinople before its transformation by Constantine but it can also be a way of referring to the Byzantine empire and civilization as a whole. In a book like this, such double usage could lead to endless misunderstandings. I have therefore used the spelling 'Byzantion' when referring to the ancient, pre-Constantine city and reserved 'Byzantium' for the wider empire. So this is a book about Constantinople's thousand-year reign as the capital of the Byzantine empire.

It is a very wide-ranging theme that also touches on aspects of Constantinople's history both before and after its Byzantine phase, from its first foundation in about 800 BCE to the present day. In treating it I inevitably strayed into all kinds of territory in which I have no expertise whatsoever and was reliant on the scholarly basis laid by others, particularly Gilbert Dagron, Ken Dark, Paul Magdalino and Cyril Mango. I hope that I have done adequate justice to them in the footnotes, but it is worth recording the debt here as well. That said, the same very broad theme inevitably required selectivity, so I hope that other academic colleagues will forgive me if they find their work omitted from the bibliography. Considerations of space meant that not everything could be included. For the same reason, wherever possible I have cited contemporary sources in English translation only, even when these are not necessarily the most accurate or up-to-date editions.

In the course of writing, I received much valued encouragement from many friends and colleagues, especially Judith Herrin, Tony Morris, Nigel Saul, Jonathan Shepard and Martin Sheppard, and I benefited from information passed to me by Robert Hughes, Ian Wadsley and others. Eugenia Russell and Andrew Sargent kindly read an early draft and saved me from many errors, linguistic, factual and stylistic. Those that remain are entirely my fault, not theirs. Eva Osborne, Michael Greenwood, Slav Todorov and Anya Wilson of Continuum ably handled the editorial side. Special mention needs to be made of Michael Heslop and Helen Boss Heslop, under whose hospitable roof the last stages of the book were written, Jan Parkin, with whom I first explored the streets of Istanbul, Emmett Sullivan who advised on computer matters, and Marie-Christine Ockenden without whom I would have sunk without trace beneath my college administrative duties. I am enormously indebted to Karina Cabeza-Boedinghaus who drew the maps. Finally a note of appreciation to the students who have taken my BA and MA options at Royal Holloway over the years. Their healthy scepticism and refreshing irreverence works wonders in getting matters into their true perspective.

As regards the vexed question of the spelling of Byzantine names in the text and footnotes, I have used those versions which seem to me to be most natural and familiar. While, in general, I have tried to transliterate them as closely as possible to the original Greek – Angelos rather than Angelus, and Doukas rather than Ducas – I cannot claim complete consistency. Where there is a recognized English equivalent of a Greek Christian name, I have used it. Hence I have preferred Isaac to Isaakios, Andronicus to Andronikos and Constantine to Konstantinos. Similarly, with surnames, where a Latinized version has become standard, it has been used, most notably Anna Comnena rather than Anna Komnene. When dealing with individuals who lived before 600 CE, I have tended to use the Latinized version: Procopius rather than Prokopios and Eusebius rather than Eusebios or even Evsevios. The reader will still find exceptions, though. For example, Heraclius (610–41) is not called 'Herakleios'.

Introduction

It is worth saying at the outset what this book is not. It is not a survey of the surviving Byzantine buildings of Istanbul. That task has already been carried out superbly by John Freely and Ahmet Çakmak. Nor is it a chronological history of the Byzantine empire. Readers of English who require such an overview will find it in the works of Michael Angold, Timothy Gregory, Donald M. Nicol, George Ostrogorsky, Warren Treadgold and others.

Rather this is a book about power and about how those who have wielded it most successfully and enduringly have hidden its realities beneath a veil of grandeur and myth. Constantinople in Byzantine times was a perfect example. Its ruler, the Byzantine emperor, was surrounded by elaborate and colourful ceremonial and there was scarcely a major building or institution in the city whose origin was not traced back to some kind of divine command or intervention or to some fantastic legend.

This preference for the miraculous and supernatural over the physical and quantifiable presents the historian of Constantinople with a problem. On the one hand, the myths and legends could be seen simply as superstition that obscures the true picture. After all, Constantinople in its heyday was a centre of wealth and power every bit as influential as Washington DC, New York, Tokyo, Paris or London are today. To spend much time examining the tall tales, it could be argued, would perpetuate the idea of Byzantium as some exotic and mysterious wonderland, hovering uneasily on the border of dream and reality. Such a picture might be appropriate to the poems of W. B. Yeats but it hardly does justice to the important political, social and economic realities.[1] Most histories of the Byzantine empire therefore pass over the myths and legends entirely and concentrate on more concrete matters.

On the other hand, these elements cannot be abandoned altogether, since they were clearly extremely important in the minds not only of medieval visitors to Constantinople but also of the Byzantines themselves. Indeed, the rulers of Constantinople assiduously cultivated them and went out of their way to promote a spiritual aura around their city. Thus in 917, the patriarch of Constantinople, who was acting as regent for an underage emperor, wrote to the khan of the Bulgars to warn him not to attack Constantinople. He did not threaten the khan with military force but with the Virgin Mary who, he insisted, was the 'commander in chief' of the city and would not take kindly to any presumptuous assault.[2]

The fact is that far from being completely unrelated to Constantinople's wealth and power, myths, legends and beliefs like this were one of the ways in which the Byzantine emperors bolstered their position, hiding stark everyday reality behind a claim to divine favour. It is this intriguing interaction between the spiritual and the political, the mythical and the actual that forms the main preoccupation of this book. Of the many shibboleths and myths with which the Byzantine emperors surrounded themselves, there are perhaps six which stand out. First and foremost it was an article of faith that Constantinople had been founded by a saintly emperor who had designed it to be the centre of government for the whole Christian world. Secondly, it was believed that the city from the first enjoyed the special protection of God and the Virgin Mary and that it would remain unconquered until the end of the world. Thirdly, there was the political myth that emperors who ruled there were divinely appointed. Fourthly, the city was claimed to be a holy place like Rome or Jerusalem, its church having been founded by an Apostle and its churches filled with relics of the saints. Fifth, its wealth reflected this divine favour and was therefore greater than that of any city anywhere in the world. Finally, the emperor, the source of all benefits for the Christian people, ruled like God, entirely alone. All six myths masked a reality that was greatly at variance with the ideal, but the ideal played a vital role in justifying the reality.

The chapters that follow explore the complex interaction between the mythical and the everyday in the capital city of the Byzantine empire, focusing for convenience on one particular moment in Constantinople's long history: the year 1200 CE. It is not an attempt to debunk myth. For the myth was central to Byzantine power and a major factor in Constantinople's extraordinary success in preserving itself and its empire for over a thousand years. For when the myth died, the power and the wealth perished too.

CHAPTER 1

The City of Wonders

In about the year 1110, according to the sagas of the Norse kings, Sigurd I Magnusson of Norway and a band of followers were sailing back to their distant northern homeland after a pilgrimage to the Holy Land. As they crossed the eastern Mediterranean in their longships, they stopped off for a time to pay a visit to the city of Miklagarth. Their reception was magnificent. The ruler of Miklagarth, whose name was Kirialax, had covered the streets from the harbour to the palace with precious cloth in their honour, and as they rode along these richly adorned thoroughfares the Norwegians were serenaded by choirs and lute players. On reaching Kirialax's palace, the visitors were ushered into a lavish banquet, and purses full of silver and gold coins were handed to them as they took their seats. As if this largesse were not enough, the servants reappeared shortly afterwards bearing great chests filled with gold which were distributed in the same way. Finally they brought in a cloak of costly purple cloth and two gold rings for King Sigurd who stood and made an elegant speech, thanking Kirialax for his generosity. Afterwards, the Norwegians were treated to a display of horsemanship, music and fireworks on a flat plain surrounded by banks of seating. Above the seats were bronze statues that were so skilfully wrought that they looked as if they were alive. When King Sigurd finally left, he presented Kirialax with all of his longships and continued his journey by land. Many of his men, however, chose to remain behind and to enter the service of the ruler of this splendid city.[1]

One might be forgiven for thinking that this entire episode was just another of the fantastic and implausible tales that fill the pages of the Norse sagas. Yet in its essentials the story is probably true. For Miklagarth was a real place. Its proper name was Constantinople and it was the capital city of what is known to history as the Byzantine empire or Byzantium, which in the early twelfth century dominated much of the Balkans and part of what is now Turkey. The inhabitants of the city who welcomed the Norwegians so cordially were the Byzantines, a Greek-speaking Christian people who regarded their empire as a continuation of the old Roman empire. Likewise their ruler, 'Kiria-lax', was a real person, the Byzantine emperor Alexios I Komnenos (1081–1118). His odd name in the saga no doubt arose from his being referred to by his subjects as *Kyr Alexios*, 'the Lord Alexios'.

It is not, however, just the place and its ruler that can be verified from the Saga's account. Its tale of the wonders and wealth of Constantinople is reproduced in a host of travellers' memoirs from the Middle Ages, left behind by pilgrims, soldiers and diplomats, many of them more sober and convincing than the saga yet often breathless with astonishment at what they saw. The almost universal reaction was that recorded by a French visitor of 1203 who noticed that, as his ship drew near to Constantinople, those who had never been there before 'gazed very intently at the city, having never imagined that there could be so fine a place in all the world'. It was 'an excellent and beautiful city', 'rich in renown' and 'the noblest of capitals of the world'.[2] Nor was Constantinople's impact only felt by newcomers. It was also a source of immense pride to its inhabitants. So magnificent a place did they consider it that they seldom even referred to it by name. They preferred to use epithets such as the 'Queen of Cities' (*basileuousa*), the 'Great City' (*megalopolis*) or simply 'the City' (*polis*), there being no possible doubt as to which city was being referred to.[3]

What was it about Constantinople that produced this almost universal admiration and awe? Perhaps the most obvious feature was its size. Visitors coming from the Islamic world would have been familiar with large prosperous cities, notably Baghdad, the seat of the Abbasid Caliphate, and Cordoba in Spain, though even they were impressed by what they saw. Those like Sigurd and his followers, from Scandinavia, western Europe and Russia, on the other hand, would never have seen such a vast urban area. Their world was an undeveloped one where much of the land was still covered in primal forest. Those cities that there were had a population of no more than about 20,000 people at the very most, and the stone churches in villages would have been the largest man-made structures that most people would ever see. By contrast, Constantinople had such a profusion of houses, churches, monasteries and palaces, many built on a colossal scale, 'that no one would have believed it to be true if he had not seen it with his own eyes'. The area enclosed by its walls was almost 30,000 hectares (eleven and a half square miles) and within that area lived a population that must have numbered hundreds of thousands: more, it was asserted, than lived in the whole of England between York and the Thames.[4] Constantinople would therefore have been like nothing that visitors from the west had encountered before, and their reaction was one of open-mouthed astonishment.

There was, however, much more to medieval Constantinople than just its size. Over the centuries, its buildings and monuments had become enmeshed with legends and Christian myths which gave the place a spiritual aura to match its physical grandeur. The potency of this heady mixture is easily missed by a modern observer, so perhaps the best way to appreciate the impact that Constantinople would have had is to follow the path that would have been taken by a visitor who arrived in the city in around 1200 and to consider what they would have seen and, perhaps more importantly, what they would have felt.

There were, and are, two ways to approach Constantinople: by land and by sea. Both offered a striking foretaste of what was to come. King Sigurd and his companions came by sea, and would have been greeted by the sight of the city, its skyline punctuated by tall columns and by domes of churches and surrounded by the defensive Sea Walls. Most visitors, however, came by land, and their first inkling of the city beyond would come when the towers of immense defensive Land Walls that stretched from the Golden Horn to the Sea of Marmara came into view and barred any further progress. These visitors would have to apply for entry through one of the nine gates. There was a tenth, the Golden Gate, an impressive structure topped with two bronze elephants and covered in classical reliefs from an earlier age. That, however, was reserved for emperors returning from victorious campaigns and normally remained closed.[5] Formalities at this stage could be tedious, since the authorities forbade any weapons to be carried inside the walls, and only allowed groups of five or six persons to enter at hourly intervals.[6] Eventually permission would be given and the visitors would probably enter through the Gate of Charisios, also known as the Gate of Adrianople, as this led to the broad Middle Street or *Mese* that ran through the centre of the city.[7]

Gaining access through the Land Walls only brought the visitor into the outlying areas of the city, where much of the land was given over to vineyards, orchards, vegetable plots and cornfields.[8] There were, however, several large monasteries close to the Walls, notably that of the Holy Saviour in Chora which lay near the Gate of Adrianople and that of St John Stoudios, near the Golden Gate. There was also an important imperial residence, the Palace of Blachernae, at the northern extremity of the Land Walls.

It would have taken some time to pass through these less heavily built-up western quarters of the city on foot and to reach the more densely built-up areas, a distance of over four and a half kilometres or some three miles. As they moved along the narrowing promontory on which Constantinople was built, visitors would have soon been aware of the proximity of the sea. They would have smelt the salt in the breeze, heard the cry of seagulls and glimpsed the blue water between the buildings. This was Constantinople's harbour, the Golden Horn, whose southern shore would have been crowded with ships, their masts and rigging standing out against the sky.

Walking east along the Mese, they would have arrived first at one of Constantinople's major monuments. A very large church would have stood on the left-hand side of the street, cruciform in structure and topped by five domes. The Holy Apostles was the second largest church in Constantinople and was dedicated to Christ's Twelve Apostles, excluding Judas but including St Paul. A poem was inscribed over its main door, recounting how each of them met his end:

Mark is put to death by the people of Alexandria.
The great sleep of life Matthew sleeps.
Rome sees Paul die by the sword.
Philip is given what was given Peter.
Bartholomew suffers death on the cross.
Simon too on the cross ends his life.
In Rome vain Nero crucifies Peter.
In life and death John lives.
Luke died peacefully at the end.
The men of Patras brutally crucify Andrew.
A knife severs the life paths of James.
Lances kill Thomas in India.[9]

Through the doorway, the church's cavernous interior was covered in glittering mosaics depicting the life of Christ and the deeds of the Apostles.[10] Visitors who stopped off here would have been shown the Heröon, a round mausoleum, situated to the east of the main church. It housed the tombs of the emperors of Byzantium who had been regularly buried there until 1028 when the mausoleum had become full up. Here in their imposing marble sarcophagi that were made of rare purple or green marble, often overlaid with gold leaf, these imperial personages awaited the last trump. The very magnificence of their resting place was designed to convey to visitors that these were no ordinary rulers, but the heirs of the Caesars, who had occupied an office ordained by God for the benefit of all Christians.[11]

Back on the Mese, the road continued its progress eastwards into the busy and heavily populated quarters. By now, sections of the street were porticoed on either side, providing a sheltered pavement for pedestrians and for shops behind. Tall mansions belonging to Constantinople's great and good fronted onto the thoroughfare.[12] To the left, beyond the Holy Apostles, marched the arches of the Aqueduct of Valens, bearing water into the city from the streams and rivers of Thrace.[13] On the right-hand side stood a basilica, the church of St Polyeuktos, built in the sixth century but now rather dilapidated.[14] The visitors would also have seen nearby a nine-metre-high column of pink granite, protruding above the roof tops. Originally erected in

8

honour of the Emperor Marcian (450–7), it was one of many scattered around the city, bearing the names of long-dead emperors, which one contemporary described as 'looming like massive giants'.[15] Shortly afterwards, the Mese joined up with the other main street, the Triumphal Way, which ran up from the Golden Gate, and the route then led into a large square known as the Forum of Theodosius, also called the Forum of Tauros.

The Forum of Theodosius was the largest public square in Constantinople, with a triumphal arch standing to one side. It would have been very striking to visitors from western Europe where such towns as there possessed no open public space to speak of, the houses being packed in tightly within the walls. In all probability, the Forum would have looked something like Trafalgar Square in London or the Place Vendôme in Paris, because it was dominated by a stone column that stood at its centre, this one bearing the name of the Emperor Theodosius I (379–95). Rather like Trajan's column in Rome, the outside of the column was decorated with spiral reliefs depicting Theodosius's victories. Compared with Trajan's, however, this column was gigantic, standing over forty metres (120 feet) high. There was a doorway in the pedestal and a spiral stairway inside that gave access to the top. It must have towered above the square and there can have been few visitors who did not crane their necks to peer up at it. If they hoped to get a glimpse of the statue of the emperor, they would have been disappointed, for in the year 480 an earthquake had brought it crashing down and it was never replaced. Still intact, however, was the nearby equestrian statue of the Emperor Theodosius, the hoof of his horse crushing a small bound and kneeling man, who no doubt represented some conquered foe. As a memorial to its subject, however, the statue had long since lost its purpose, for by the twelfth century no one could remember who it was supposed to represent.[16]

From the Forum of Theodosius it would have been possible to see its column's twin, that of Theodosius's son, Arcadius (395–408), in another public square over on the Triumphal Way. It was equally tall, with 233 steps inside and fifty-six windows, and it must have been visible over the rooftops even from distant parts of the city.[17] On leaving the Forum of Theodosius, the street led on to another square, the Forum of

Constantine, named for one of the greatest emperors and the founder of the city, Constantine the Great (306–37). The forum was an oval-shaped space with a portico along the length of its periphery, and its centrepiece was another towering column, this one made of reddish Porphyry marble. The column had originally been surmounted with a bronze statue, with seven rays emanating from its head, which was probably a reused image of the pagan god Apollo but was later believed to depict Constantine. Like the statue of Theodosius, this had now vanished, although it had met its end relatively recently. On a spring day in 1106, a particularly strong gust of wind had toppled the statue and sent it plummeting into the forum below where it had killed several unfortunate passers-by. It had since been replaced by a simple cross. The column itself was also showing signs of wear and tear and for some time had had to be held together with stout iron hoops to prevent it from falling down.[18]

As well as the column, the Forum of Constantine possessed another curious feature that would have excited the interest of those passing through it for the first time. All around it, somewhat incongruously in such an overtly Christian city, stood a number of ancient Greek statues of pagan goddesses. There was a nine-metre-high bronze image of Pallas Athena, the goddess of wisdom, helmeted with her hand stretched out towards the south, possibly the work of the Athenian sculptor, Phidias (*c.* 490–*c.* 420 BCE). Nearby was a colossal representation of Hera, the queen of heaven and wife of Zeus, and a depiction of Aphrodite, the goddess of love, being presented with the Apple of Discord by Paris, the episode that was said ultimately to have led to the Trojan War.[19]

These were, in fact, just a few of the many classical statues that were to be found scattered around the highways and squares of Constantinople. Others were to be found in the Forum of the Bull on the Triumphal Way and in the Forum Amastrianon, including a Zeus in a marble chariot, a reclining Hercules and even a winged Priapus, his hallmark feature proudly held in his left hand.[20] Pagan statues such as these appear to have been preserved and cherished by the Byzantines of the twelfth century for their artistic merits alone, but to visitors, unused to realistic portrayals of the human figure they must have been a source of wonder. Hence the remark of the author of the Norse saga that the bronze statues of Constantinople were so skilfully wrought that they looked as if they were alive.

From the Forum of Constantine, the Mese progressed rapidly to the monumental heart of Byzantine Constantinople and opened into the last of the great squares, the Augousteion. Although probably smaller than the Forum of Theodosius, the Augousteion would have been just as impressive, partly because it brought the visitor face-to-face with the towering bulk of the cathedral of Hagia Sophia, also known as St Sophia or the Holy Wisdom. Outside the cathedral, another tall column stood out starkly against the sky, this one with its bronze statue intact. Justinian I (527–65) was depicted seated on a horse, facing east and holding in one hand an orb surmounted by a cross, while his other hand was raised in warning to his enemies. The statue was a favourite with the local herons who regularly built their nests on the emperor's head and along the horse's back, and the wind gusting around the Augousteion would whistle mournfully around it.[21] On the eastern side of the square stood the Brazen Gate, a domed structure that formed the main entrance and vestibule to the Great Palace of the Byzantine emperors.

Apart from the cathedral and the column, the Augousteion was filled with curiosities. There was the Horologion, a mechanical clock, one of whose twenty-four doors flew open at the appropriate hour of the day. There was the *Anemodoulion* or 'the servant of the winds', a four-sided structure that was as tall as many of the city's columns and whose sides were intricately carved with animals and birds but also with a riotous scene of naked women pelting each other with apples. On top of it stood the bronze figure of a woman that served as a kind of weathervane and turned with the direction of the wind. Nearby was the Milion, a triumphal arch, which was surmounted by statues of the Emperor Constantine and his mother Helena, standing on either side of a cross. The arch covered a milestone from which all distances were measured. To one side of the square stood the Senate House, which was decorated with ancient columns and statues.[22]

To the south of the Augousteion stretched the Hippodrome, a long stadium some 400 metres in length which could seat up to 100,000 people. It had originally been designed for the staging of chariot races, and so at the Augousteion end it had twelve gates that could be opened simultaneously at the start of the contest. From there, the chariots raced to the far end of the track, wheeled around the central spine and galloped back to head for the winning post. By the twelfth century, however, the Hippodrome provided the venue for all kinds of public happening, from music and fireworks to displays of tightrope walking, and was by no means reserved for chariot racing. In the year 961, for example, it had been used to display the booty brought back by the successful expedition to reconquer the island of Crete. It was also where executions of prominent people took place and it played a key role in imperial ceremonial, which was why it had a special box, or *Kathisma*, for the emperor that could be reached by a covered walkway from the Great Palace. Evidently the hippodrome was the flat plain with banks of seating described by the author of the Norse saga.[23]

The Hippodrome was decorated with another set of ancient artefacts, which must have been some of the most diverse and whimsical in the entire city. On its central spine stood a granite Egyptian obelisk which was decorated with hieroglyphs and stood on a marble plinth that depicted Theodosius I surrounded by his family and courtiers. Further down the spire was a four-sided, thirty-two-metre-high masonry obelisk. No one could remember who had put it there or why, but some 200 years earlier Emperor Constantine VII Porphyrogenitos (945–59) had decided to improve its appearance by covering it with gilded plates of bronze. It is therefore usually referred to as the column of Constantine Porphyrogenitus.[24]

There was also a profusion of classical statuary scattered around the place, with a plethora of animals complementing the usual gods and goddesses. The gods included a pensive Hercules by Lysippus of Sikyon, the famous sculptor of the fourth century BCE. Among the animals were four gilded copper horses, 'their necks somewhat curved as if they eyed each other as they raced around the last lap', as one contemporary put it, and they stood on a tower above the starting gates. There were also an eagle, a wolf and an elephant. Most celebrated of all was a bronze statue of the Calydonian boar, with realistic bristles down its back, which according to legend was sent to ravage the lands of the king of Calydon after he neglected his sacrifices to Artemis.[25]

Some of the monuments in the Hippodrome had long histories behind them. The Serpent Column, a bronze sculpture of three intertwined serpents whose heads looked out in three directions, had originally been dedicated at Delphi in Greece in 478 BCE to commemorate the resounding defeat of the Persians by the Greeks at the battle of Plataea. A bronze statue of an ass being driven by its keeper had originally been set up by the Roman Emperor Augustus (31 BCE–14 CE), close to the site of his victory over Mark Antony and Cleopatra at Actium in 31 BCE. On the eve of the battle, Augustus had met with a man and his ass and on asking who he was and where he was going received the answer 'I am Eutychus [Prosper], my ass is called Nikon [Victory] and I am going to Caesar's camp.' With hindsight, Augustus decided that this must have been an omen from the gods and commissioned the statue as a thank-offering. Both monuments had adorned the central spine of the Hippodrome for centuries.[26]

Intriguing though the Hippodrome was, for most visitors the most memorable sight of Constantinople was its cathedral of Hagia Sophia. Sheer size was part of it. The building was topped with an enormous dome thirty-two metres across and over fifty-five metres high, which would have been higher even than the columns of Theodosius, Arcadius and Constantine. On the inside, the sense of size and space was even more striking. So high was the roof that a mosaic figure of Christ high up in the dome, which looked to an observer on the pavement below as if it were of normal human size, was in fact so large that its eyes were three palms length apart. So vast was the space enclosed with no apparent means of support, that the dome seemed almost to float in the air, a veritable 'tent of the Heavens'.[27]

The effect was enhanced by the mosaic decoration which covered the entire space of the dome, and the columns of different coloured marble, red, purple and green, which supported the galleries. From the forty small windows around the base of the dome, sunlight suffused the building from different angles at different hours of the day, shining in from the upper windows and illuminating the gold mosaics and marble columns with dazzling light. A 'golden stream of glittering rays', as one poet wrote, shortly after the cathedral's second consecration in 562, 'strikes the eyes of men, so that they can scarcely bear to look'.[28] Emerging into the daylight and the broad space of the Augousteion, many visitors must have concluded, as one Spaniard did, that:

> The church is so immense in size, and so wonderful are the sights to be seen there that, spending many hours of time it were impossible to make a complete examination. Even though the visitor should day by day return seeing all he could, yet always on the morrow there would be new sights to view.[29]

Glancing around the great squares such as the Augousteion, visitors from less favoured regions would have noticed another of Constantinople's claims to fame, its conspicuous prosperity. 'Wealth like that of Constantinople', wrote one, 'is not to be found in the whole world'. What amazed them was the sheer abundance of gold, silver and silks on display in the streets and churches. The market stalls would have been crammed with exotic goods from far-off lands, and on the stalls of the money-changers piles of gold and silver coins and precious stones could be seen. Richly dressed noblemen with flowing beards and tall hats would have passed by on horseback or carried in a litter on their way to or from the emperor's palace. Inside the cathedral of Hagia Sophia, the altar was made of gold and studded with jewels, while the altar rail and pulpit were overlaid with silver. Such riches were not reserved for Constantinople's greatest church. Many others could boast a similar adornment. Even the relatively obscure church of the Forty Martyrs possessed an icon or picture of Christ whose frame was covered in gold and gems.[30]

One of the most visible expressions of Constantinople's wealth was the ability of the Byzantine emperor to offer apparently inexhaustible largesse to foreign dignitaries whom he was attempting to impress. The gifts showered on Sigurd of Norway and his party were by no means unprecedented. The Turkish sultan Kilij Arslan II (1156–92) received 'gold and silver coins, luxuriant raiment, silver beakers, golden Theriklean vessels, linens of the finest weave and other choice ornaments' when he visited Constantinople in 1162. For the Norman prince Bohemond of Taranto, an entire room was filled with gold, silver and silk garments. An envoy from Italy had only to drop a hint to be presented by the emperor at once with a large cloak and a pound of gold coins.[31] As with the size of Constantinople, the source of the amazement was often the contrast with conditions back home. In western Europe especially, economic conditions were primitive. Money did not circulate widely and gold coins were something that most people would never see. The ability of the Byzantine emperor to shower bagfuls of them on his guests must have seemed little short of a miracle.

It would be wrong, however, to believe that visitors to Constantinople were impressed solely by its size, great buildings and wealth. On the contrary, some travellers' accounts scarcely mention these aspects. They were much more interested in something else: Constantinople's reputation as a holy place.

At first sight, it is not immediately obvious why Constantinople should have been accorded any spiritual significance by medieval Christians. After all, the city had played no part in the Gospel story, for it had not even been founded in its present form at the time of Christ. So while pilgrims to Jerusalem could visit the very places where Jesus had walked and taught, and those to Rome could follow in the footsteps of the Apostles Peter and Paul, there was nothing of that kind in Constantinople. On the other hand, it did possess the next best thing, an unrivalled collection of relics, which its rulers had built up over the centuries. Relics could be either mortal remains of saints and holy persons or objects closely associated with them or with the Virgin Mary or even with Christ himself. Such objects were regarded with intense veneration by medieval Christians because they represented a tangible link to the sanctity of the person with whom they were connected. It was believed that prayers made in a place sanctified by the presence of such an object would be all the more efficacious and that in some cases they might even perform miraculous cures.

Constantinople's relic collection was the envy of the Christian world. It has been reckoned that there were some 3,600 of them, representing about 476 different saints. The pick of the collection, which included what was believed to be the Crown of Thorns and other instruments of Christ's passion, was locked away in the chapel of the Holy Virgin of Pharos within the Great Palace and was only shown to high-ranking visitors. There were, however, plenty of others available to public view. In the church of the Holy Apostles, one could see a stone pillar which purported to be that against which Christ had been scourged, along with the tombs of the apostle St Andrew, St Luke the evangelist and St Timothy. The church of the monastery of the Pantokrator boasted the slab of red marble on which Christ had lain after his crucifixion, which still bore the marks of the tears shed by the Virgin Mary.[32] Visitors to Hagia Sophia could gaze upon the stone well cover upon which Christ sat when he conversed with the woman of Samaria, and the table on which the Last Supper had been laid out.[33] The reaction of visitors when confronted with such relics was one of touching enthusiasm, undiluted by any scepticism as to whether these objects were actually what they were supposed to be.

Constantinople's religious aura went far beyond its role of merely providing a setting for numerous relics, however. Such was the antiquity of the city, and so many centuries had passed without it having been captured or sacked by any hostile power, that it had come to acquire a mystical quality in its own right, and a host of myths and legends had become attached to many of its monuments. Even the most everyday objects had become imbued with a spiritual significance. The pillars that supported the galleries of Hagia Sophia, for example, were supposed to have special healing powers when rubbed by afflicted persons, particular columns specializing in certain ailments. Even the bolt on one of the main doors was believed to have the power to cure dropsy when the sufferer placed it in his mouth.[34]

Similar miraculous properties were attributed to other monuments around the city, particularly to the towering columns. The spiral reliefs on the columns of Theodosius and Arcadius, for example, were thought to depict the future events that would befall Constantinople. Unfortunately, they would only become comprehensible once those events had taken place. It was said that there used to be a statue of Aphrodite on a column outside a brothel which had a peculiar power. Whenever an unchaste woman walked past, her skirts would fly up, whereas virtuous women were unaffected. There were no reports of any columns that had a similar effect on men.[35] The classical statues, especially those in the Hippodrome, also attracted their share of strange lore. One of them was appealed to by merchants when they could not agree as to price. Money was placed in its palm and when a fair price was reached it would supposedly close its hand. The statue of the Calydonian boar was regarded with particular awe. One emperor came to believe that it was his alter ego and provided it with new sets of teeth and genitals in the belief that this would have a restorative effect on those parts of his own body.[36]

To medieval visitors to Constantinople these tales and superstitions were every bit as real as the physical grandeur that they saw around them. Indeed in many cases such aspects were more important, for many travellers' accounts are simply lists of the relics that they had seen and miracle stories that they had heard. Many came specifically to see the relics rather than the city itself, and others passed through as part of a pilgrimage to Jerusalem. Inevitably, the locals made sure that they profited from the tourist influx and money changed hands before any relics were put on view. A Russian visitor complained that:

> Entering Constantinople is like entering a great forest;
> it is impossible to get around without a good guide,
> and if you attempt to get around stingily or cheaply
> you will not be able to see or kiss a single saint unless
> it happens to be the holiday of that saint ...[37]

The chances are that by nightfall, visitors who had entered through the Gate of Adrianople at dawn and made their way from there to the Augousteion would have visited several churches on the way and reverently kissed the relics that they were shown there on payment of the usual fee. They would also have been regaled with all kinds of stories about the monuments and statues that they passed. Even so, they had only experienced a fraction of the wonders of Constantinople. It would have taken a lifetime to see them all.

CHAPTER 2

Founding Fathers

No visitor to Constantinople in 1200, or at any time in the Byzantine period for that matter, could have stayed there for long without hearing a great deal about two of its greatest past emperors, Constantine (306–37) and Justinian (527–65). Their magnificent tombs could be seen at the church of the Holy Apostles. Constantine's lay in the Heröon along with those of so many other deceased emperors, his magnificent sarcophagus of purple porphyry marble covered with a sumptuous cloth of gold cover. Justinian was buried in a separate building to the side, his tomb occupying the place of honour at the east end, with some lesser emperors and empresses clustered around.[1] Beyond the church of the Holy Apostles, the names and images of the two great emperors were everywhere. The Forum of Constantine was named for the one, while it was Justinian who was portrayed by the great equestrian statue outside Hagia Sophia in the Augousteion. Across the square, statues of Constantine and his mother frowned down from the Arch of the Milion, and mosaic portraits of Justinian and his wife Theodora gazed from the ceiling of the Brazen Gate to the Great Palace.

Why the memory of these two emperors was revered above that of all others is made manifest in a mosaic panel above the so-called 'beautiful door' in the southwest vestibule of the cathedral of Hagia Sophia. It portrays them standing on either side of the Virgin Mary and the Christ child. Constantine is presenting the Virgin with a model of the city of Constantinople, Justinian with a miniature version of the cathedral of Hagia Sophia. For Constantine was the founder of the city of Constantinople, while Justinian had adorned and beautified the city by providing it with its greatest and most familiar monument. So central were these two figures to the history and ideology of the city that a host of stories and legends had grown up around them and guides were only too happy to recount these to visitors. Although those stories often represented a considerable distortion of events and of the political realities of centuries before, they tell us a great deal about how the Byzantines saw themselves and their city in 1200 and about how they used myth and legend to obscure, distort or justify contemporary reality.

Constantine, as any visitor to Constantinople in 1200 would have been told, was the son of a Roman general named Constantius Chlorus and an innkeeper's daughter called Helena. Constantius had been travelling back to Rome through Asia Minor after conducting some negotiations with the Persians in about 272 BCE and had stopped at Helena's father's inn for the night. Perceiving his important guest to be lonely and far from home, the innkeeper obligingly suggested that Constantius console himself by taking Helena to bed with him. This Constantius willingly did, only to be disconcerted in the middle of the night when a bright light shone around the room. The next day, Constantius presented Helena with an embroidered mantle, dyed in imperial purple and instructed her father to look very carefully after any child that might result from the previous night's exertions, for he had an inkling that the unusual light that had shone over the bed was an omen of future greatness. He then went on to Rome and in the fullness of time became emperor. In the meantime, Helena gave birth to his son, Constantine, but it was only when the boy was in his early teens that his father discovered his existence. Even though he was by now married with several other children, Constantius had his new-found son brought to court.[2]

The Byzantine version of events emphasized the fact that Constantine had been born in pagan times, when the Roman empire had still been given over to the worship of the gods of Mount Olympus. From a very young age, however, Constantine had shown a marked preference for the Christian religion even though it was then regularly being persecuted by the pagan emperors. At the Roman court, so the story went, Constantine was in some danger because the soothsayers and priests in the imperial retinue soon had a foreboding that Constantine would one day achieve supreme power and overthrow the worship of the pagan gods. They therefore plotted to kill him. God, however, forewarned Constantine of the danger and he fled to Britain where his father Constantius was on campaign. When he arrived in the city of York, he discovered that Constantius had been taken ill and was on his deathbed. The dying emperor had by now realized the folly of paganism and had started to believe in Christ. He therefore summoned his son to his side and invested him with the emblems of the imperial office, the sceptre and the purple cloak, and named him as his successor.[3]

Constantine thereby became in the year 306 the first Christian Roman emperor, which was his first and foremost claim to fame. By doing so, he put the Christian Church on course for the dominance which it was later to enjoy, and as a result later generations spoke of him with awe and reverence. The description given of him by one tenth-century hagiographer is typical, blending physical with moral perfection:

> The saintly Constantine was indeed a man distinguished in every way for the courage of his spirit, the keenness of his intelligence, the erudition of his discourse, the uprightness of his sense of justice, the readiness of his benevolence, the propriety of his appearance and the bravery and fortitude he showed in war; he was of great reputation among barbarians and unequalled among those of his own race, firm and unshaken in honesty. Furthermore in looks and elegance of beauty, he was both the most seemly and the most handsome, with a pleasing expression, the height of his body being of good stature, that is to say neither tall nor short; he was rather broad across the shoulders and his neck was thick, and his complexion was ruddy; the hair of his head was not bushy, and he kept his chin quite bare, and he was inclined

not to allow hair to grow on many parts of his face;
his nose was hooked and his countenance was keen-
eyed almost like a lion's; his hair was naturally tawny;
against all his enemies, it was by prayer that he brought
victory within his grasp.[4]

Having accounted for Constantine's accession, the story went on to
describe how he soon found himself at loggerheads with other rulers
of the Roman empire who were by no means as pious and benevolent.
Rome had been seized by a relative of his called Maxentius, a pagan
tyrant who condemned many people to death on account of their
Christian faith and who regularly seduced the wives of the senators.
He was also supposedly given to cutting up babies in order to use their
entrails for the purposes of divination.

Hearing about this state of affairs, in the summer and autumn of
312 Constantine marched east with an army to confront Maxentius.
Having crossed Gaul and marched down through northern Italy,
he encamped with his troops close to the River Tiber in readiness to
make an attack on Rome. The outlook was not bright. Maxentius had
the bigger army and he was entrenched behind formidable fortifications. Constantine retired to his tent to ponder the next move, but at
about midday he suddenly experienced a vision. Looking out at the
sky he saw the noonday sun change into the shape of a cross while
letters beneath it proclaimed the message 'In this, Conquer!' The
emperor was puzzled as to what this might mean, but as he slept that
night, Christ himself appeared to him and commanded that Constantine should make a replica of the device that he had seen in the sky
and place it at the forefront of his army in the battle to come. The very
next day, Constantine did as he was told, replacing the army's pagan
standards with the new Christian device.

Meanwhile in Rome, Maxentius had been busily preparing for a
siege. He stocked up on food supplies and ordered that all the bridges
across the Tiber be cut to impede Constantine's progress. Good pagan
that he was, he sought advice from the priests who guarded the Sibylline
books, a collection of oracles kept in the temple of Apollo. After some
deliberation the priests announced that the books indicated without a

shadow of a doubt that on 28 October Rome's greatest enemy would perish. Maxentius was delighted, for he interpreted the oracle as a clear promise of victory. He decided that rather than wait in Rome, he would march out and confront Constantine in open battle on 28 October. He took his forces to the Milvian Bridge which spanned the Tiber some way upstream from Rome. Since the stone bridge there had been cut on Maxentius's orders, a temporary pontoon replacement was constructed to allow the army to cross.

Once on the other side, battle was joined with Constantine's troops who were sporting their new Christian standards. Maxentius's army outnumbered the opposing forces by up to two to one, but it was no match for Constantine's battle-hardened soldiers. Finding that his troops were being pushed inexorably back towards the river, Maxentius ordered a retreat, no doubt hoping to revert to his original strategy of making a stand in Rome. Unfortunately, the only escape route was across the pontoon bridge and such were the numbers of panicking soldiers who had crowded onto it that it collapsed, spilling the men into the river where the rapid current swept them away. On witnessing this disaster, those left stranded on the northern side gave up the fight and surrendered. Maxentius, knowing that he could expect little mercy if taken alive, tried to reach safety by swimming across the Tiber but he too was carried away and drowned. It never seems to have occurred to him that it was he who was Rome's greatest enemy.

In the aftermath of the victory, which Christian writers could not resist comparing to Pharaoh and his army being drowned in the Red Sea, Constantine entered Rome in triumph and was baptized there by Pope Sylvester.[5] In the years that followed, divine favour continued to bring success and victory to the pious Constantine. He took on various other pagan usurpers who had seized power in the eastern provinces and finally, by 324, he brought the whole of the Roman empire under his own sole rule. Thus the victory of the Christian Church was ensured.

Now that peace was restored, Constantine turned to another project. He wanted to found a new city and to name it after himself. As with everything else that Constantine is supposed to have done, the hand of the Almighty guided him from the beginning. At first he planned to build his city on the site of the ancient city of Troy. God, however, directed him in a dream to choose another spot, the city of Byzantion which lay on the Bosporus to the north. After Constantine had inspected the site and found it well suited to his purpose, an angel appeared and obligingly helped him to sketch out the plan of the walls. On 11 May 330, the city was inaugurated in a colourful ceremony and received a new name in honour of its founder: Constantinople, the city of Constantine.[6]

According to the chroniclers, there were two points about the new city about which Constantine was most particular. In the first place, it was designed from the very beginning to be a Christian city. He was said to have forbidden the presence of pagan temples anywhere in the new city. Those that were there already, he demolished and replaced with churches, such as those of Hagia Sophia and the Holy Apostles.[7] Secondly, from the outset, Constantine was determined that his new foundation was not going to be just any city. He tried to make Constantinople look like the greatest city in the empire, Rome itself. Constantinople was given a palace, a senate house and, in the Hippodrome, an equivalent of Rome's Circus Maximus. As in Rome, there was to be a forum, the Forum of Constantine, and noble Roman families were encouraged to emigrate and settle in the new city.[8] In short, Constantine specifically designed Constantinople to be the new capital city of the empire, a new or second Rome.

The remaining years of Constantine's life were spent establishing Christianity throughout the empire and in combating heresy. In 325, he presided over the First Ecumenical Council held at Nicaea which formulated the definitive statement of Christian belief, the Nicene Creed. He died at Nikomedia in Asia Minor in 337 and his body was carried back to Constantinople for burial in the mausoleum of the church of the Holy Apostles. His tomb was supposed to have miraculously cured a number of sick people, a clear sign of sanctity.[9]

That then was the official version of the life of Constantine and the founding of Constantinople, a Christian city created by a saintly Christian prince to be the new capital city of the Roman empire. It was a version of events which, while by no means entirely fictional, was nevertheless developed largely to bolster Byzantine political ideology. It tended to distort three aspects of the story. First it passed over the fact that Byzantion had existed for nearly a thousand years before Constantine was born and had an important history in its own right before it became Constantinople. Secondly it overplayed Constantine's Christianity as the driving force behind his actions. Finally, and perhaps most significantly, it laid too much stress on the idea that the foundation of Constantinople was designed to replace Rome as the capital of the Roman empire.

Turning first to the history of Byzantion, the Byzantines of later centuries were not unaware that this city had long existed on the site but they were generally confused and uninterested in Constantinople's prehistory. Some claimed that it had been founded by a certain Byzas, others by two men, Byzas and Antes, in whose joint honour the city had been named, though this is probably no more than a fanciful play on the word Byzantion. Another tradition attributed the deed to a certain Zeuxippus.[10]

It is clear from ancient sources that Byzantion must have started life as long ago as the eighth or more probably the seventh century BCE, when it had been founded by a band of colonists from the Greek city of Megara, not far from Athens.[11] Never a major player in its own right, Byzantion had maintained a precarious independence as a city state while great empires contended for power in the region. First there had been the Persians, who captured the city in about 512 BCE. Persian rule came to an end in 478 BCE when a combined Hellenic fleet under the Spartan Pausanias had arrived on the scene. Then there had been Athens, whose maritime empire dominated the region in the fifth century BCE. The Byzantines had fallen in with what seemed to be the predominate power, but in 411, sensing the way the Peloponnesian war was going, they had switched allegiance to Sparta. They acted in much the same way when faced with the growing power of Rome. In about 150 BCE, the Byzantines wisely made a treaty with the Romans, which allowed them to retain their independent status on payment of tribute.[12] The decision turned out to be the right one, for the treaty gave the Byzantines many years of peace and prosperity under the *Pax Romana*. Thus although Byzantion was by no means one of the greatest cities of the ancient world, it had nevertheless been a prosperous and successful one and its history by no means began with Constantine.

Another dubious element of the Byzantine myth was Constantine's Christianity. There is no contemporary evidence that Constantine was a Christian from his earliest youth as his later hagiographers claimed. The coins first issued by Constantine in Britain after his accession in 306 carry effigies of the gods Mars and Apollo. Moreover, the story that Constantius Chlorus bequeathed the empire to Constantine, in spite of having legitimate sons with a better claim, solely because Constantine was a Christian, is very shaky indeed and probably evolved to cover the fact that Constantine's accession was illegal. In the early years of the fourth century, the Emperor Diocletian (284–305) had introduced a system known as the Tetrarchy or rule by four. There would be two emperors, one in the western half of the empire and one in the east. Each emperor would have a junior colleague or Caesar, who would assist the senior emperor and replace him if he died. It also meant that one emperor and one Caesar could be based in the eastern and western halves of the huge empire and so be on hand to deal with crises that arose there. In 306, Constantius Chlorus was the senior emperor in the west and Galerius (305–11) was his counterpart in the east. In theory, when Constantius died he should have been replaced by his Caesar, Severus. By allowing himself to be proclaimed emperor by his father's troops in preference to Severus, Constantine was technically a usurper.[13]

Not until after his victory over Maxentius at the Milvian Bridge in 312 is there any contemporary evidence for Constantine taking any interest in the Christian Church. In 314 he issued an edict of toleration which brought the persecution of Christians to an end, after which he entered into friendly correspondence with Christian bishops and began to subsidize the Church with public funds. Nevertheless, Constantine continued to hedge his bets. The legend that he received baptism from the pope in 312 is demonstrably untrue, as contemporary evidence shows that it was not until he was on his deathbed that he was finally baptized. Moreover, whatever the later legends might have said, he seems to have included at least two pagan temples in Constantinople, one dedicated to Rhea the mother of the Gods and the other to the Fortune of Rome. Constantine is also alleged to have brought to Constantinople the tripod from the shrine of Apollo at Delphi, from which the priestess of Apollo used to pronounce oracles. Christians at the time asserted that Constantine did this to hold the tripod up to public ridicule, but it was a curious action for someone who supposedly wanted to purge his city of pagan associations.[14]

Finally, it was not necessarily the case that Constantine planned Constantinople as a new capital of the Roman empire to replace Rome, as the legend claimed. Those recording these events nearer the time gave other explanations for the decision. One of them, Eunapius of Sardis, claimed that Constantine had shipped people in to populate his new city in order to provide himself with a ready-made claque to applaud him on special occasions:

> For Constantinople, originally called Byzantion, in distant times used to furnish the Athenians with a regular supply of corn, and an enormous quantity was imported thence. But in our times, neither the great fleet of merchant vessels from Egypt and from all Asia, nor the abundance of corn that is contributed from Syria and Phoenicia and the other nations as the payment of tribute, can suffice to satisfy the intoxicated multitude which Constantine transported to Byzantion by emptying other cities, and established near him because he loved to be applauded in the theatres by men so drunk that they could not hold their liquor.[15]

The fifth-century historian Zosimus asserted that Constantine acted out of guilt. Constantine had killed his own son, Crispus, because he suspected him of having slept with his stepmother, Fausta. When Fausta openly grieved over Crispus's death, Constantine decided to get rid of her too. This he accomplished by having her locked in an overheated bath until she died. Suffering pangs of guilt over this double murder, Constantine converted to Christianity, as it was the only religion that promised to absolve him of so heinous a crime. He found, however, that it was impossible to stay in Rome where everyone viewed him reproachfully, and decided to found Constantinople as a new residence for himself. He spent vast sums beautifying his new city, but any of the buildings that he put up were so badly constructed that they soon collapsed.[16]

The remarks of Eunapius and Zosimus should not be taken too seriously. Both were pagans who deeply deplored the favours bestowed by Constantine on the Christian Church and who considered him and his successors to have ruined the Roman empire by abandoning the worship of the Olympian gods. Their views were clearly highly partisan and jaundiced. The later Christian tradition, on the other hand, is equally suspect, for Constantine's actions do not seem to amount to a complete replacement of Rome by Constantinople. True, he laid his new city out on a grandiose scale and provided it with a senate house and other buildings similar to those in Rome. He also built a palace there, and that would certainly suggest that he intended to raise it above the rank of other cities. He seems, however, still to have seen his foundation as second to Rome, for the senators of Constantinople were to be designated only as *clari* (distinguished) unlike those of Rome who were *clarissimi* (most distinguished).[17] Constantine may therefore simply have been following the example of his predecessors and seeking to solve the problem of the empire's long and vulnerable frontiers.

For some time those frontiers had been under severe strain. To the north, the Rhine and Danube frontiers were vulnerable to incursions by Germanic tribes. In the east, a resurgent Persian empire was constantly threatening to invade and attack the wealthy cities of Roman Syria. In this situation, the emperors could no longer reside permanently in Rome, as they had in previous centuries, as the capital was too far away from the threatened frontiers. Instead, by the early fourth century, they were tending to operate from Milan, Ravenna or Trier in the western half of the empire, and from Antioch or Nikomedia in the east. Constantine's new city had certain undeniable strategic advantages. It lay at one of the narrowest crossing points between Europe and Asia, where the Bosporus was only some 500 yards across. It was an advantage that had been well appreciated in ancient times, notably by the Persian King Darius who in the fifth century BCE had built a bridge of boats across the strait close to Byzantion, in order to convey part of his army from Asia to Europe. It also commanded the passage to the Black Sea.[18] Constantine may simply have wanted to have a forward base from which he could march swiftly to both the Danube and eastern frontiers, or sail along the northern coast of Asia Minor to Armenia.

Yet it does not really matter that the version of events cherished by the Byzantines of 1200 was both highly partisan and occasionally fictitious. For even if Constantine was slightly ambivalent in his adhesion to Christianity and even if he did not intend to found a new, Christian capital city, by his actions he had begun a process that was to make Constantinople the world centre that it ultimately became.

It was only in the century after Constantine's death in 337 that Constantinople became an indisputably Christian city, rose to be the seat of government of the eastern half of the Roman empire and began to take on the magnificent appearance that would characterize it ever after. As far as its Christianization went, this development ran in parallel to that of the empire in general. After Constantine, all the emperors with the exception of the short-reigned Julian (361–3) were Christians, and that inevitably encouraged conversions. As the fourth century progressed, Christianity gradually became the official religion of the empire, and by the end of the century most pagan temples had either been forcibly closed down or had fallen into decay.

As far as Constantinople was concerned, the population was overwhelmingly Christian by the mid-fourth century. One visitor complained that it was impossible to buy a loaf of bread in the market there, without the person who sold it to you giving you a lecture about the relationship between the persons of the Trinity. The Christian emperors now felt secure enough to demolish the remaining pagan temples in the city or to convert them for other purposes. At the same time, the city was becoming an important centre of ecclesiastical administration, as the Church recognized its growing political significance. The Second Ecumenical Council of the Church was held there in 381 and it was decided by the assembled prelates that henceforth the bishop of

Constantinople should 'have the primacy of honour' after the pope of Rome, because Constantinople was the New Rome. From about 450 onwards, the bishop of Constantinople bore the title of Patriarch, an honour he shared with the incumbents of only four other sees, Rome, Antioch, Alexandria and Jerusalem.[19]

Nevertheless, Constantinople had a disadvantage when compared with these other patriarchates in that, saintly though Constantine was, his city could not claim any association with one or more of the Apostles. The Churches of Jerusalem and Antioch had been founded by St Peter, and that of Alexandria allegedly by St Mark. Rome could claim two Apostles as its founders, St Peter and St Paul. In later centuries, the Byzantines got round that in typical fashion by developing another legend. The Apostle St Andrew, it was said, had paid a visit to Byzantion and had founded its church, thus putting Constantinople on the same footing as the four other great centres of the Christian Church.[20]

Similarly, whatever his original intentions, the years after Constantine's death saw his city rapidly turn into a capital. During the fourth century, rule of the empire was often divided between two or more emperors, as had been the case under the Tetrarchy. For example Valens (364–78) was co-emperor to his elder brother, Valentinian I (364–75), and ruled the eastern provinces. The same arrangement was reached between Arcadius (395–408) and his brother Honorius (395–423). Those who ruled in the eastern half tended to base themselves and their court permanently in Constantinople, and many of them spent their entire reigns there without feeling the need to travel to any other part of the empire.[21]

The presence of the emperor and court inevitably attracted settlers to the city, eager to take advantage of the opportunities for patronage and trade, and the population grew apace. From the 90,000 who may have been living there in 337, by the second half of the fourth century Constantinople probably had a population of between 200,000 and 300,000. By about 450, it may have had as many as half a million inhabitants.[22] The pagan Zosimus recorded this development in typically acerbic fashion:

The size of Constantinople was increased until it was by far the greatest city, with the result that many of the succeeding emperors chose to live there and attracted an unnecessarily large population which came from all over the world – soldiers and officials, traders and other professions. Therefore they have surrounded it with new walls much more extensive than those of Constantine and allowed the buildings to be so close to each other that the inhabitants, whether at home or in the street, are crowded for room and it is dangerous to walk about because of the great number of men and beasts. And a lot of the sea round about them has been turned into land by sinking piles and building houses on them, which by themselves are enough to fill a large city.[23]

It was not only the presence of the emperor and the size of its population that made Constantinople seem increasingly like a capital city. The emperors who reigned there also went out of their way to make it look like one by adorning it with fine buildings. The city's cathedral of Hagia Sophia, for example, had reputedly been founded by Constantine but it was not completed and consecrated until February 360, under his son and successor, Constantius II (337–61). This first church would probably have been rectangular in shape with a long nave flanked by aisles, the traditional basilica of the later Roman empire. From an early stage it was known as 'the Great Church', indicating that it was built on a grand scale to reflect Constantinople's status. Constantine's successors continued the practice of bringing famous classical statues to the new city, denuding cities across the empire of their cherished artworks. Rome lost the bronze statue of Hercules by Lysippus which had stood on the Capitoline Hill since 209 BCE and which now ended up adorning the Hippodrome. It was presumably during this period that the Athena and Hera in the Forum of Constantine and the statues in the Hippodrome arrived in Constantinople, their purpose being to impart the prestige of antiquity which as a recent foundation it conspicuously lacked.[24]

The unsung hero of Constantinople's beautification was Theodosius I (379–95), often called the Great because he was the last emperor to rule over an empire that stretched from Britain to Syria. Originally from Spain, Theodosius had spent the first part of his career soldiering in the western half of the empire and he had probably never set foot in Constantinople before he arrived there as eastern emperor in November 379. Nevertheless, he recognized the importance of giving the new capital an appearance to match its political role. It was he who laid out the Forum of Theodosius, Constantinople's largest public square, between about 386 and 393, providing it with its tall column, triumphal arch and equestrian statue, and he is credited with setting up another triumphal arch which was later incorporated into the Land Walls as the Golden Gate. A pious Christian, with none of Constantine's ambivalence on religious matters, Theodosius did not neglect to provide Constantinople with a new church, that of St John the Baptist, in the suburb of Hebdomon that lay to the west, just outside the city proper.

Theodosius's most enduring monument was the Egyptian obelisk on the central spine of the Hippodrome. The obelisk had originally been commissioned by the pharaoh Thutmose III (1549–1503 BCE) to commemorate his victories in Syria and had stood for centuries at Deir el Bahri opposite Thebes. The 800-ton monument had been shipped from Egypt on the orders of the Emperor Julian, although it somehow lost about a third of its length on the journey. Theodosius had what was left brought from the southern shore of Constantinople where it had lain for some years, and placed it on a marble plinth carved with figures of himself and family watching the races from the *Kathisma*. Like Cleopatra's Needle in London and the Obelisk of Luxor in Paris, the obelisk was designed to signal that the *arriviste* capital was now of an importance to vie with the great civilizations of the past.[25]

Thus, whatever might have been Constantine's original intentions, by 450 Constantinople was a Christian city and, as Rome became increasingly impoverished and vulnerable, the capital city of the eastern Roman empire. Moreover, it looked the part. As one of Theodosius's courtiers, Themistius, put it:

> Were Constantine to see the capital he had founded
> he would behold a glorious and splendid scene, not a
> bare and empty void; he would find it fair, not with
> apparent but with real beauty ... [the place] is full of
> carpenters, builders, decorators and artisans of every
> description and might fitly be called a workshop
> of magnificence.... Should the zeal of the emperor
> to adorn the city continue, a wider circuit will be
> demanded, and the question will arise whether the
> city added to Constantinople by Theodosius is not
> more splendid than the city that Constantine added
> to Byzantion.[26]

No doubt Themistius was exaggerating to curry favour with his imperial master, but his words clearly demonstrate that Constantine only
began the process by which Constantinople became the greatest city
in the Christian world.

Looking back on these developments, the Byzantines of later
centuries were not unaware of the role played by the successors of
Constantine, such as Theodosius I, in extending, adorning and beautifying Constantinople. Nevertheless, they singled out Justinian as
deserving the credit for giving their city the monumental appearance
that left visitors so awestruck, and considered that his greatest achievement was to have provided Constantinople with 'the mighty church
that was named after the Holy and Ineffable Wisdom', the cathedral of
Hagia Sophia.[27]

Originally from a poor peasant family in Thrace, Justinian reached
the imperial office by a stroke of luck. His uncle Justin, the commander
of the palace guard, had become emperor in 518, but Justin was elderly
and found the challenges of his new role quite overwhelming. Part of
the problem was that Justin was illiterate and had to sign official documents by using a stencil. He therefore sent for his clever nephew to
assist him. When Justin died in 527, it was only natural that Justinian
should step into his shoes, as he had, to all intents and purposes, been
running the empire for some time already.[28]

The young emperor had only been on the throne a few years when he found himself faced with a sudden and terrible crisis, the so-called Nika riot. Constantinople was at that time still suffering from chronic overcrowding, and mob violence was common. It often took the form of pitched battles between the supporters of rival chariot teams that competed in the Hippodrome, the Blues and the Greens. In January 532, matters took a serious turn for the worse when, in protest against the high taxation levied by Justinian's ministers, the Blues and the Greens stopped fighting each other and joined forces to challenge imperial authority. The first sign of trouble came as the emperor took his seat in the *Kathisma* of the Hippodrome before the races. He was greeted by the Green faction not with the usual respectful acclamations but with taunts and catcalls. When an attempt was made to arrest some of the troublemakers, the two factions made a truce and stormed the prison, releasing all the prisoners they found there.

Days of street fighting followed, during which law and order broke down completely. The mob surged through the streets, shouting their watchword 'Nika!' (Victory!) and killing any government officials they could lay their hands on. Amid the confusion, fires broke out and, with no one daring to try to put them out, raged out of control. The night of 14–15 January was particularly disastrous. Flames swept across the Augousteion, engulfing the senate house, the porticoed colonnades, the Brazen Gate of the Great Palace and numerous private houses. The conflagration then reached the cathedral of Hagia Sophia on the far side of the square, which caught fire and, after blazing for some time, collapsed into a smoking ruin.

By now the crowd had decided that they needed a new emperor to replace Justinian and had chosen a nobleman called Hypatius for the purpose. Hypatius himself had no desire whatsoever to don the purple but it did not seem politic to say so in the face of so many determined would-be subjects. As for Justinian, watching developments from his vantage point in the Great Palace, things seemed to have reached the stage where flight was the only option. The emperor gave permission to his courtiers to leave the palace so that they could guard their own houses and sat down to deliberate with his counsellors on what to do next. It was at this point that Justinian's wife, Theodora, intervened in the debate and majestically announced her determination never to leave Constantinople:

> If now it is your wish to save yourself, O Emperor, there is no difficulty. For we have much money, and there is the sea, here the boats. However consider whether it will not come about after you have been saved that you would not gladly exchange that safety for death. For as for myself, I approve a certain ancient saying that royalty is a good burial shroud.

Those words marked the turning point. Justinian and his advisers ceased to contemplate flight and began to discuss ways of fighting back against the factions. The empire's ablest general, Belisarius, who had just returned with his army from the Persian wars, was ordered to bring his troops into the city to restore order. Belisarius waited until a large crowd had gathered in the Hippodrome to acclaim Hypatius as emperor. Having surrounded the place and sealed off all the exits, the soldiers burst in with drawn swords, causing the crowd to stampede in panic over the banks of seating. In the ensuing massacre some 30,000 rioters perished. As for the unfortunate Hypatius, his attempts afterwards to explain that it had all been a ghastly misunderstanding proved unavailing and he was executed.[29]

Normality had been restored on the streets, but the scars left by the upheaval could be seen everywhere. Large swathes of Constantinople's monumental centre lay in charred ruins, particularly the area around the Augousteion and adjoining the Great Palace. In destroying such potent symbols as the Brazen Gate of the palace and the cathedral, the Nika rioters had challenged the very basis of the emperor's authority, with its emphasis on his role as the representative of God on Earth. The damage had to be put right as quickly as possible and it is a measure of Justinian's far-sightedness that he turned the traumatic experience of the riot into an opportunity to rebuild on a grand scale. The obvious priority was to provide a replacement for the ruined cathedral of Hagia Sophia. In place of the old basilica, Justinian chose a new and revolutionary design offered by his architects Anthemius of Tralles and Isidore of Miletus. They proposed to replace the old basilica with a square-domed structure, a radical departure from previous styles. Building went ahead at great speed, and after five years and ten months of work the cathedral was dedicated on 26 December 537. It was, from the first, hailed as a masterpiece:

> For it soars to a height to match the sky, and as if surging up from amongst the other buildings, it stands on high and looks down upon the remainder of the city, adorning it, because it is a part of it, but glorying in its own beauty...[30]

The praise turned out to be premature. Twenty years after its completion the cathedral was severely shaken by an earthquake. One of the four arches that held up the dome was damaged, and six months later, during 558, the entire dome came crashing down. As Anthemius had since died, Isidore the younger, a nephew of Isidore of Miletus, was brought in to repair the damage and he strengthened the dome by making it narrower and slightly higher and by adding buttressing to the exterior. As a result the dome was not quite as breathtaking as it had been before, but considerably more secure.[31]

All these teething troubles had long since been forgotten by 1200. As the years went by and people lived with Hagia Sophia from day to day, they found it increasingly difficult to believe that such a vast and unequalled building and its soaring dome could possibly have been put up by human hands alone. So the inevitable legends grew up. Justinian and the architects must, like Constantine before them, have had divine help, the design being imparted to the emperor by an angel. When during construction there was disagreement between emperor, architects and builders over how many glazed windows there should be, again it was an angel who turned up to resolve the issue.[32]

On one occasion, the workmen had gone off to lunch, leaving the fourteen-year-old son of the foreman to guard the tools. As the boy obediently waited, an angel suddenly descended and asked why work had stopped. On hearing that the workforce was on its lunch break, the impatient visitor told the boy to run and fetch them. This the lad was reluctant to do, because he had promised to guard the tools. The angel therefore made a solemn promise that he would never leave that spot until the boy returned. When the foreman and his men received this message, they at once took the boy to the emperor Justinian, who decreed that he must not return to the cathedral. That way, Hagia Sophia would have its own guardian angel for the rest of time. Guides were fond of pointing out the place, just to the left of the altar, where the angel was still supposed to be mounting his eternal vigil.[33]

After God and his angels, most of the credit was given by the later tradition to Justinian rather than to his architects, one ninth-century account insisting that 'Justinian alone began the church and he alone finished it, with no help from anyone else with regard to building'. Indeed, Justinian himself was supposed to have been so ecstatic when he saw the building going up that he prided himself on having excelled Solomon, builder of the Temple in Jerusalem in Old Testament times.[34] The feat was enough in itself to secure Justinian's reputation and placed him in the esteem of the Byzantines second only to Constantine.

It has to be said, however, that like Constantine, Justinian received mixed reviews from contemporaries as well as from those who lived in the years immediately after his death. He was certainly not the saintly figure of the pious legends. One contemporary, the historian Procopius of Caesarea, described him as:

> insincere, crafty, hypocritical, dissembling his anger, double-dealing, clever, a perfect artist in acting out an opinion he pretended to hold, and even able to produce tears, not from joy or sorrow, but contriving them for the occasion according to the need of the moment ...[35]

Procopius was also particularly hostile to Justinian's wife and empress, Theodora, whom he portrayed as a low-born adventuress who exploited the imperial office shamelessly for her own self-aggrandisement. The most frequent charge made against Justinian and Theodora was that of greed which led them to squeeze their subjects for money using any pretext that they could come up with. They were alleged to have accused wealthy landowners of crimes that they did not commit so that they could seize their property, or to have 'persuaded' them to hand it over as a gift. On one occasion, Justinian appointed a nobleman called Zeno to be governor of Egypt in the hope of helping himself to the absent man's property. Zeno, however, decided to take all his moveable goods with him and loaded a ship with all his gold, silver and precious stones. Not to be outsmarted, Justinian bribed some of his henchmen to unload the cargo and to drop firebrands into the hold. Zeno arrived at the harbour the next day to be told that a fire had broken out and the ship and its cargo had been lost. When Zeno died shortly afterwards, Justinian and Theodora triumphantly produced a will which named them as joint heirs, though many doubted the authenticity of the document.[36]

Many of these stories were probably somewhat exaggerated, but there can be no doubt that Justinian was very eager to get his hands on very large amounts of money, for the policies that he was following were extremely expensive. Not only was he spending vast sums on his building projects, including that of Hagia Sophia, but he had also embarked on the reconquest of the western half of the empire. For things had changed drastically since Constantine's day. During the early years of the fifth century, the western frontiers of the Roman empire had broken down and numerous Germanic tribes had crossed the River Rhine and begun to settle on Roman territory. The Visigoths occupied Spain, the Franks encroached into northern Gaul, the Angles and Saxons invaded Britain, the Ostrogoths took over Italy and the Vandals settled in North Africa. In 476, the last Roman emperor in the west was dethroned by a barbarian general called Odovacar. That left Constantinople as the seat of the only emperor still standing, and so 476 is as good a date as any to mark the transition from a Roman to a Byzantine empire.

Justinian was determined to reverse these events. In 534 a fleet and army sent from Constantinople under Belisarius recaptured North Africa from the Vandals. In 538 Belisarius took Sicily and then invaded Ostrogothic Italy. Another force was sent to occupy part of south-eastern Spain. The reconquest, however, proved to be rather like the dome of Hagia Sophia: initial success was followed by the appearance of ominous cracks. The war with the Ostrogoths dragged on until 554, and while the Byzantine army was enmeshed in Italy the Persians took the opportunity to ravage the eastern province of Syria. At the same time, an outbreak of plague and a series of natural disasters ravaged the empire, depopulating some of its wealthiest provinces. When Justinian died in 565, he bequeathed to his successors an empty treasury, and borders that were becoming impossible to defend. 'Such', concluded the disgruntled Procopius, 'were the calamities which fell upon all mankind during the reign of the demon who had become incarnate in Justinian, while he himself, as having become emperor, provided the causes of them'.[37] While Procopius may have overstated the case, there can be no doubt that Justinian's over-ambitious policy helped to bring about the virtual collapse of the Byzantine empire in the next century when it lost its eastern provinces and Constantinople found itself under siege for the first time.

The Byzantines of 1200 had long since forgotten all the disasters of the later years of Justinian's reign. For them, the legacy of Justinian was what they could see when they walked around Constantinople. It was most obvious in the Augousteion. To the north was Justinian's cathedral of Hagia Sophia, with the statue of the emperor on horseback on the column outside. To the east was the tall, domed Brazen Gate of the Great Palace, rebuilt by Justinian after the Nika riot, its interior decorated with mosaics celebrating Justinian's victories. Some also gave him the credit for building the arch of the Milion.[38]

Justinian had, however, left his mark all over the city, not just in the Augousteion. He was responsible for the appearance of the church of the Holy Apostles as it was by 1200. Founded by Constantine and housing his tomb, the original church had survived the Nika riot unscathed but was starting to show signs of imminent collapse. Justinian demolished the old church and replaced it with a novel five-domed structure that was to endure for nearly a thousand years and was to be visited by generations of pilgrims as they made their way from the Land Walls to the Augousteion.[39] Numerous other churches benefited from Justinian's attention and were still standing in 1200, from Hagia Eirene that stood just behind Hagia Sophia to that of the

Mother of God at Blachernae. Moreover, in his decision to replace the old rectangular basilica with the square-domed design, he had started a trend. All subsequent Byzantine churches were built to this prototype so that the appearance of Constantinople in 1200, with the domes of the churches dominating the skyline, can be indirectly attributed to him.[40] That visible legacy was enough to enshrine Justinian as one of the greatest Byzantine emperors.

There can be no doubt, however, that, of the two, Constantine was considered the greater. As the first Christian emperor, he was regarded both as a model ruler and as a saint, his feast day being celebrated on 21 May.[41] His foundation of Constantinople provided the basis for Byzantine political thought and especially for the doctrine of *Translatio Imperii* or the 'transfer of empire'. The idea was that Constantine, by founding Constantinople, had irrevocably bestowed supreme authority in the Christian world on the emperors who ruled there. As one twelfth-century Byzantine put it, 'power was transferred from Rome to our country and the Queen of Cities, not to mention the senate and the whole administration'.[42] The doctrine was central to the way that the Byzantines perceived Constantinople as essentially the focal point of the Christian world.

Consequently, the Byzantines tended to attribute every aspect of the city to Constantine. Since, by 1200, Constantinople had the greatest collection of relics in the Christian world, it stood to reason that the founder of the city must have been the first to bring such objects there. Hence the legend grew up that when Constantine had laid out the forum that bore his name and set up a column in the centre to carry his statue, he had constructed two vaults at the base of the column. In this he placed a number of sacred objects. These vary between the different accounts, but they were said to have included the axe with which Noah made the Ark, the crosses on which the two thieves were crucified alongside Christ, the twelve baskets of leftovers from the feeding of the 5,000 and a vessel containing the myrrh with which Christ was anointed.[43] Hence the pride with which guides conducted visitors to Constantine's sarcophagus in later centuries and told the stories of his deeds over and over again: he had literally laid the basis for everything that the Byzantines held sacred.

CHAPTER 3

Defence

The deeds of Constantine and Justinian were not the only ingredients in the potent myth of the Queen of Cities. Another boast that the Byzantines of 1200 were proud to make to visitors was that the city had never been taken by a foreign army and that it never would be taken until the end of the world. The 'God-guarded city' was yet another of Constantinople's many epithets. It was not, however, only God himself who was seen as guarding the city. Constantinople was also regarded as enjoying the special protection of the Virgin Mary, or the *Theotokos* as she was known, among many other epithets in Greek. As one contemporary put it:

> About our city you shall know: until the end she will
> fear no nation whatsoever, for no one will entrap or
> capture her, not by any means, for she has been given
> to the Mother of God and no one will snatch her out
> of Her hands. Many nations will break their horns
> against her walls and withdraw with shame ...[1]

Chroniclers recorded how the personal intervention of the Theotokos had often saved the day in times of crisis. She had sometimes been seen on the city walls participating in the defence and was even reported to have grabbed some of the attackers by the hair and thrown them to the ground.[2]

The inhabitants of Constantinople jealously preserved two visible tokens of the Virgin's protection. One was her *Maphorion*, a garment that covered the head and shoulders, which was also sometimes referred to as a veil or as a robe. It had been brought from the Holy Land in the fifth century and was housed in the church of the Virgin in Blachernae, appropriately close to the Land Walls. It was believed that the *Maphorion* had saved Constantinople from an attack by a Russian fleet in 860. The patriarch of Constantinople had brought the precious relic out of the church and had taken it up onto the Sea Walls whereupon the winds rose to scatter the enemy ships. In later years, the emperors used to take it with them when they led their armies out of Constantinople to fight on the frontiers.[3]

The other visible reminder of the Virgin's protection was a picture or icon. This, however, was no ordinary icon. It was popularly believed to have been painted from the life by no less a person than St Luke the Evangelist and it had supposedly been brought from Palestine to Constantinople in the fifth century. The Virgin was depicted holding Christ on her left arm, and gesturing towards him with her right. The icon therefore became known as the *Hodegetria* ('She who Shows the Way'), since the Virgin was pointing out the way of salvation.[4] The *Hodegetria* was usually housed in the monastery of the Hodegoi, which lay close to Hagia Sophia at the very tip of Constantinople's promontory. It was cared for by a special confraternity who organized a procession every week, when twenty men in red outfits carried the icon from its monastery to the church of the Pantokrator. On important feast days, it was processed around the cathedral of Hagia Sophia.[5] Whenever danger threatened, the icon was brought out from its monastery and paraded on the city walls. This had occurred as recently as 1187, when a rebel general, Alexios Branas, had laid siege to Constantinople with his army. It was always the icon that was credited with the subsequent discomfiture of the enemy, so much so that in any victory parade it was the *Hodegetria* that rode at the front in the gilded chariot while the emperor humbly followed along behind.[6]

Quite apart from the *Hodgetria*, Constantinople housed a number of other reportedly miraculous icons, many of which were believed to have the power to protect the city, its emperor and his armies. The church of the Virgin in Blachernae had an ancient depiction of the Mother of God that had been discovered during restoration work in around 1030. There was also the icon of the Virgin known as the *Nikopeia* ('the Bringer of Victory'). Emperors never sallied forth on campaign without taking one or other of these icons with them, 'as a guide and guardian of all the army'.

One of them, probably the *Nikopeia*, accompanied Basil II (976–1025) when he sallied forth into Asia Minor in April 989 to do battle with the rebel Bardas Phokas. When the two armies clashed at Abydos, the emperor stood at the head of his troops with the icon clasped with his left hand and his sword in his right as the enemy charged towards them. In the ensuing mêlée the rebel leader mysteriously dropped dead from his horse, causing his soldiers to lose heart and flee. Clearly, the protectress of the Byzantine emperors had once more come to their aid, and Basil showed his gratitude by having a special silver coin minted to commemorate the victory. The obverse showed the Virgin and Child and the reverse carried the inscription: 'Glorified Mother of God, the one who trusts You does not fail'.[7]

Important though other icons such as the *Nikopeia* were, however, the *Hodegetria* occupied pride of place. It never seems to have been carried on campaign and remained safely within the walls of Constantinople. It was the city's pledge of security from the highest authority.

The boast about Constantinople's invulnerability was not an idle one, since the city did have an extraordinary record of survival. The Roman empire, into which it had been inaugurated in 330, had been a world of cities. One by one they had all suffered the same fate: captured or destroyed by the empire's enemies between the fifth and eighth centuries. Rome itself had been sacked by the Goths in 410 and again by the Vandals in 455: by the twelfth century it was little more than a collection of villages, huddled around the ancient ruins and Christian basilicas. Antioch in Syria had once been one of the most splendid and prosperous cities in the empire. In 540, however, the Persian king, Chosroes I (531–79), captured and largely destroyed it, and it had still not recovered when it was conquered by the Arabs in 636. Jerusalem was sacked by the Persians in 614 and finally lost to the Arabs in 638, as was Alexandria in 642. Some of the empire's outposts in the west held out longer, but Carthage was taken by the Arabs in 697, and Ravenna by the Lombards in 751.

Of all the great cities of the ancient world, Constantinople alone avoided takeover or destruction. That was not for want of anyone willing to try. Over the centuries, a succession of powerful enemies had laid siege to Constantinople. Every time, they had been forced to retire empty-handed. While the Byzantines attributed this invulnerability to the intervention of the Virgin Mary, there were two much more down-to-earth explanations. The first was geography, the physical and material advantages of the city's position. The second was sophisticated military technology which enhanced the advantages of geography and made Constantinople impregnable.

Geography had probably dictated Constantine's choice of Byzantion as the site for his new city. It lay on the crossing point between Europe and Asia, giving relatively swift access to both the vulnerable Danube and eastern frontiers. The site had other advantages, however, when it came to defence. Since it was built on a narrow promontory, almost triangular in shape, there was a natural defence in the sea on two sides of the city. To the north, lay the Golden Horn, itself one of the finest natural harbours in the world, while the Bosporus and the Sea of Marmara bordered to the east and south. A land army would therefore have to approach along the narrow and easily defended promontory.

These strategic advantages had not gone unnoticed in the past. Centuries before Constantine had been born they had been recognized in a legend about the founding of Byzantion. Back in the eighth century BCE, before setting out to colonize new lands and to found the city of Byzantion, the Greek colonists from Megara had piously paid a visit to the oracle of the god Apollo at Delphi to ask where they should found their city. As usual, the god gave an ambiguous answer, advising the colonists to choose a site 'opposite the blind'. Later these words were to become all too clear, for as they sailed north up the Bosporus, they passed the city of Chalcedon. Across the strait, directly opposite, lay the promontory and the Golden Horn, which the Greeks who had founded Chalcedon seventeen years earlier appeared not even to have noticed. The Megarans had therefore founded Byzantion opposite those blind Chalcedonians, taking full advantage of the sheltered anchorage and easily defensible promontory.[8]

It was therefore well known in ancient times that 'the site of Byzantion is, as regards the sea, more favourable to security and prosperity than that of any other city in the world'.[9] Yet it was only at the end of the second century CE that these advantages were seriously put to the test. When, in 192, a contest for the imperial throne broke out between the governor of Syria, Pescennius Niger, and Septimius Severus, governor of Pannonia Superior, the people of Byzantion declared for Pescennius. The contest was decided at the Battle of Issus in Asia Minor when Pescennius was defeated and killed. Severus sent his rival's head to Byzantion in the expectation that the city would now surrender to him. The Byzantines, however, defied him and held out against his armies for three years.

They were able to do this because the city was surrounded by a defensive wall with jutting towers which gave the defenders an excellent field of fire against anyone trying to attack them by land. On the seaward side, a number of harbours were built into the wall and these were closed off against attack by heavy metal chains strung across their mouths. That kept the defenders' ships, of which they had some 500, safe from attack by Severus's fleet and provided a base from which they could sally forth to attack the enemy by sea. Consequently, supplies could still be brought in. Indeed some merchant ships used to sail past Byzantion deliberately, in the hope that the Byzantine ships would come out and 'capture' them. Once inside the Golden Horn, the merchants would then sell their wares at a high price and depart.

Quite apart from the narrow promontory and the excellent harbour, there was another geographical feature that played a part in the city's defence against Severus. The prevailing tide worked to its advantage. The current in the southern Bosporus is very strong as the flow of water pushes down from the Black Sea towards the Sea of Marmara. It runs along the eastern shore at three to four knots, or more when the wind is strong, creating eddies and counter-currents in the inlets and bays. One such counter-current eddies into the Golden Horn at a speed of about half a knot, helping Byzantine ships to reach the safety of their harbours, but tending to force enemy ships onto the rocky outcrops below the city walls. As the contemporary Greek historian Cassius Dio (*c.* 164–*c.* 229) put it:

> The Bosporus is of the greatest advantage to the inhabitants; for it is absolutely inevitable that, once any- one gets into its current, he will be cast up on the land in spite of himself. This is a condition most satisfactory to friends, but most embarrassing to enemies.[10]

The Byzantines could not hold out indefinitely, however, and as food became increasingly scarce much of the population boarded the ships and attempted to sail away. Severus's ships easily intercepted the over- laden Byzantine vessels and sank most of them. The sight of hundreds of corpses floating past was too much for the remaining defenders and in 196 they finally capitulated. Not surprisingly, the now Emperor Septimius Severus (193–211) was in a vengeful mood. He punished the renegade city with the demolition of its defensive walls and the loss of its independent status, handing it over to the citizens of nearby Perinthos.[11]

In spite of Byzantion's final defeat, the lessons of its long defiance did not go unlearned. Cassius Dio, who saw the ruins of the city walls after they had been demolished, was of the opinion that Severus had been most unwise in pulling them down since in doing so he had destroyed 'a strong Roman outpost and a base of operations against the barbarians from Pontus and Asia'.[12] Severus himself does seem to have realized Byzantion's potential. Towards the end of his reign, he relented and rebuilt the city on a larger scale, providing it with exten- sive public baths and even reconstructing its walls. Under Severus's son and successor, Caracalla (211–17), the city's independence was restored.[13] It was much too valuable a site to waste.

The new city of Constantinople possessed all the defensive advantages conferred by nature on the old Byzantion. Its rulers, however, were to utilize the best military technology of their day to turn an easily defended site into an impregnable one. The first step was to provide the city with a new wall which would defend it on the landward side.

When Constantine the Great founded his new city, he constructed a set of walls across the middle of the promontory, enclosing a much wider tract of land in which to expand the built-up area. These proved to be the city's salvation following the catastrophic Roman defeat by the Goths at the Battle of Adrianople in 378. The victorious Goths at once headed for Constantinople since there were no Roman armies to bar their way. When they got there, one look at the strength of the fortifications persuaded them to give up any attempt to capture the place and they withdrew.[14]

By 400 AD, however, the security offered by Constantine's walls was less reassuring. The population had grown to such an extent that much new development had had to go on outside the defences, leaving these areas vulnerable to attack. Early in the reign of Theodosius II (408–50), news arrived of the fate of Rome at the hands of the Goths. It was clear that something would have to be done at once if Constantinople was not to go the same way. Since the emperor was still a minor, in 413 the regent for the young ruler, Anthemius, gave the order for the construction of a new set of walls further west than those of Constantine and covering more than seven kilometres or four miles distance from the top of the Golden Horn to the Sea of Marmara.

These Theodosian or Land Walls were to constitute the main defence of Constantinople for the next thousand years. Constructed of limestone blocks, divided at intervals by layers of bricks, the original or inner wall stood about twelve metres high and was about five and a half metres thick. It was punctuated at intervals by ninety-six towers, providing broad platforms for ballistae and catapults. In front of the wall was a wide, brick-lined ditch, between fifteen and twenty metres across and between five and seven metres deep with a stockade made of brick and wood on the city side. In 447 the defences were made even stronger by the addition of a new wall, between the ditch and the main wall. This outer wall was slightly lower than the inner wall and punctuated by a further ninety-two towers.

Taken together, the inner and outer walls and the ditch provided a three-tier defence that was impossible to penetrate. Any assailant would have first to cross the ditch and stockade while exposed to withering fire from the outer and inner walls. Even if they did get across and managed to capture the outer wall, they would find themselves trapped in the five-metre wide corridor between it and the inner wall.[15]

The fortifications continued along the seaward sides of Constantinople, linking up with the Land Walls, to deter assault by sea. These Sea Walls were not as formidable as their land counterparts but for much of their length they did not need to be because the prevailing current made it impossible for ships to be brought close enough inshore to mount an assault on them. The only area of Constantinople's coast where ships could land was the stretch along the Golden Horn. Any possibility that enemy ships might try to take advantage of that by sailing into the Horn was closed off in times of crisis by a heavy iron chain, 300 metres long, which was strung from a tower within the city, known as the Kentenarion, to another, the Kastellion, in the suburb of Galata on the other side of the water. Wooden floats placed along the length of the chain kept it at the surface of the water, thereby preventing hostile vessels from entering.[16] Thus by the time Justinian became emperor in 527, the defences had been revolutionized and Constantinople had been enclosed in an iron ring.

It was not long before those defences were put to the test, for from the late sixth century on, the Byzantine empire entered a period of crisis. Justinian's effort to reconquer the western provinces had left the empire financially exhausted and vulnerable to attacks on its borders. Within a few years of the great emperor's death, most of Italy was lost to the Lombards, and his successors had to fight an increasingly desperate battle to hold the line elsewhere. Matters came to a head in 602 when the overthrow and assassination of the Emperor Maurice (582–602) signalled a period of internal civil strife of which the empire's enemies quickly took advantage. The Slavs and Avars crossed the Danube and occupied most of the Balkans as far south as the Peloponnese, while in the east the Persians overran Syria, Palestine and Egypt. The empire recovered under the leadership of Heraclius (610–41) and drove the Persians out of the eastern provinces during the 620s. The territory recovered, however, was soon lost again to the Arabs who invaded the empire in 634.

In this situation, it was only a matter of time before Constantinople itself came under threat. The test came in the year 626 when the empire's eastern and western enemies united in an attempt to take its capital. In July of that year, taking advantage of the absence of the Emperor Heraclius on campaign in Armenia, the Persian general, Shahrvaraz, brought his army across Asia Minor and encamped at Chalcedon, opposite Constantinople. Meanwhile, in the Balkans, the Avars and their Slav allies marched south through Thrace to the Land Walls which they bombarded with siege engines.

The Land Walls held firm, however, while geography also put the Persians and Avars at a disadvantage. Their armies were separated by the waters of the Bosporus, making it difficult for them to link up and concert their efforts, for neither possessed a fleet of ships. In desperation, the Avars tried to bridge the gap by launching small boats manned by Slav crews to bring the Persians across to the European side of the Bosporus. The attempt proved to be a disaster. The prevailing tide tended to drive the boats back to the European shore and those that did make it to mid-channel could easily be intercepted by Byzantine warships. With the link between them cut, the two armies were powerless and broke off the siege.[17]

In the later seventh century, a new enemy appeared before the walls of Constantinople. The Arabs had successfully conquered the empire's eastern provinces, and the Ummayyad Caliph, Mu'awiyah I (661–80), was now determined to seize the ultimate prize. In the spring of 674, a large Arab fleet sailed through the Dardanelles, ravaged the coast of Thrace and captured Cyzicus to use as a forward base. There the fleet was joined by a land army under Mu'awiyah's son, Yazid. Unlike in 626, therefore, Constantinople was now threatened by both an army and a fleet.

This time it was technology that saved the city. After enduring the Arab attacks for several years, in 678 the Byzantines counter-attacked by sea. Their ships were equipped with a secret weapon, known as 'Greek fire', the invention of a Syrian architect called Kallinikos and the nearest thing that the Middle Ages had to napalm. It was concocted from a mixture of ingredients which probably included sulphur, pitch and quicklime. It may even have contained some crude oil, specially imported across the Black Sea from Armenia and the Caucasus where surface deposits were still to be found. Whatever its exact composition,

Greek fire was a highly inflammable liquid which, when heated in an airtight bronze container, could be shot onto an enemy ship from a siphon fixed to the prow of the attacking vessel. The liquid was ignited as it emerged from the siphon and once alight would defy all efforts to put it out. It would even burn on the sea and was quite capable of reducing an opposing warship to a blazing wreck in minutes.

It cannot have been an easy task to manoeuvre close enough to score a direct hit, and misses were frequent. That did not really matter, however, for quite apart from the physical damage that it could cause, Greek fire was a demoralizing psychological weapon. It burst from the siphon with a noise like thunder, and was often fired from bronze figureheads in the shape of lions and dragons to heighten the terror that it instilled in the crews of enemy vessels. After one brush with Byzantine vessels armed with Greek fire, enemy ships were likely to make off at the very sight of the dragons' heads, saving the Byzantines from the need to use up precious fuel.[18]

This terrifying weapon, combined with the evident impossibility of breaching the Sea Walls, persuaded the Arabs to withdraw in 678, to the delight of the Byzantines who had enjoyed little success against them thus far. A poet celebrated the victory in verse, asking:

> Where now, O Cursed Ones, are your shining bright
> ranks of arrows; where now the melodious chords of
> bow strings? Where is the glitter of your swords and
> spears, your breastplates and head-borne helmets,
> scimitars and darkened shields ...? And where are the
> ships that were raised on high as if such things were
> unlucky cedar coffins from Lebanon?[19]

The rejoicing was premature, however, for the Arabs were to return and to mount what was perhaps the severest siege yet. In the summer of 717, a powerful army under the command of Maslamah, the brother of the Ummayyad Caliph, marched across Asia Minor to link up with a fleet that had sailed up the Aegean and into the Sea of Marmara. With the fleet to protect his crossing, Maslamah was able to take his troops across the Dardanelles to the European side and march them across Thrace to the Land Walls. There he constructed a series of earthworks parallel to the walls to prevent any help getting through while his fleet set up a blockade by sea. The Arabs clearly hoped to starve Constantinople into submission since there was no hope of breaching the walls.

Before long, however, nature came to the Byzantines' aid. On 1 September, as the Arab fleet moved up to supply the army at the Land Walls, it found itself becalmed in the middle of the current and then slowly blown backwards by the prevailing southerly wind. Seeing their chance, the Byzantine fleet bore down on them. Some twenty Arab vessels were set alight with Greek fire, some running aground under the Sea Walls, some sinking and some being blown burning across the Sea of Marmara. The defeat of the Arab fleet had serious repercussions for the army besieging the Land Walls. On the one hand, it seriously reduced the effectiveness of the blockade and allowed the Byzantines to bring in supplies by sea and to continue to fish in the waters around Constantinople. The Arabs, on the other hand, having destroyed most of the crops of Thrace so as to deny them to the Byzantines, found themselves running short of food as the severe winter of 717–18 set in. Before long they were reduced to eating roots, leaves and even the camels that they had brought with them as beasts of burden. Although Arab reinforcements arrived the following spring, it was by then fast becoming clear that blockade was even less likely to take Constantinople than a direct assault. The siege was lifted on 15 August 718 and the Arabs never returned.[20]

These spectacular victories ensured that Constantinople's reputation for impregnability was established. Nevertheless, the seventh and eighth centuries were a period of severe crisis for the city. The needs of defence took priority over everything else and the building activity that had characterized previous centuries came to a complete halt. The population shrank drastically as repeated outbreaks of plague decimated its inhabitants. During the summer of 745, according to one chronicler, the plague:

> flared up all at once so that entire households were
> completely shut up and there was no one to bury the

50

dead. Because of extreme necessity, a way was devised of placing planks upon animals saddled with four panniers each and so removing the dead or piling them likewise one upon the other in carts. When all the urban and suburban cemeteries had been filled, as well as empty cisterns and ditches, and many vineyards had been dug up and even the orchards within the old walls to make room for the burial of human bodies, only then was the need satisfied.[21]

This was Constantinople's dark age, when it ceased to be the capital of a mighty empire and became instead an embattled fortress, fending off enemies from its very walls. After about 750, however, the empire began to recover and the Byzantines' military fortunes revived. They slowly reconquered the Balkans from the Slavs and halted the Arab advance in the east. In later centuries, the Byzantines were able to go onto the offensive, so that by 1050 the empire incorporated Asia Minor, part of Armenia, Greece and the Balkans south of the Danube, the Aegean and Ionian islands, Cyprus and Crete.

Consequently, Constantinople was no longer threatened as directly as it had been in the seventh and eighth centuries and its population started to recover, reaching about 375,000 by 1050.[22] Nevertheless, there were still attempts to take the city. The Bulgars, on whom the Byzantines waged war on and off throughout the ninth and tenth centuries, mounted several sieges, but, lacking a fleet, there was never a realistic possibility of their succeeding where the Arabs had failed. In 813, their khan, Krum (*c.* 803–14), who had just wiped out an entire Byzantine army along with the emperor, brought his army before the Land Walls. Having got there, he found that there was very little that he could do. So having burned those buildings, villas and palaces that he found outside the walls, Krum rode up and down from the Golden Gate to Blachernae to 'exhibit his forces' and then sued for peace.[23]

Another threat came from the Russians who sailed across the Black Sea against Constantinople on a number of occasions. In 941, their numerically superior fleet was worsted by just fifteen Byzantine vessels armed with Greek fire. Many of the Russian ships were set alight, although most of the casualties resulted when the panic-stricken mariners jumped into the sea and drowned in their heavy armour. The survivors returned with the excuse that the Byzantines 'had in their possession the lightning from heaven, and had set them on fire by pouring it forth, so that the Russians could not conquer them'.[24] By then it must have been clear that there was little hope of capturing Constantinople and those who wanted to make war on the Byzantine emperor generally attacked his outlying provinces or made a show of force before Constantinople to extort concessions.

By 1200, therefore, it had been many years since Constantinople had experienced any direct attack by an external enemy. It had become much more common for the city to be besieged by Byzantine armies led by a general who hoped to usurp the throne from the reigning emperor. This type of warfare was very different from the great sieges of the past. Pitched fighting was seldom entered into and casualties were kept to a minimum, as most of the inhabitants of Constantinople remained neutral and awaited the outcome. What the usurper was hoping for was either to exploit the known weak points in the Land Walls or to persuade someone on the inside to help him to gain entry to the city. The greatest difference of all was that, unlike those mounted by the Arabs, Bulgars and Russians in the past, these attacks sometimes succeeded.

For the impregnable Land Walls did have a few vulnerable points that could be made use of by those in the know. One was the pipes and aqueducts which crossed them to bring in the city's water supply. In emergencies they were generally cut by the defenders and the city could survive on water stored in cisterns, but they still provided a possible bridge over the defences if an attacker had the element of surprise. In the summer of 705, the deposed emperor Justinian II staged a dramatic political comeback when he crept into Constantinople with a band of picked men through the Aqueduct of Valens, causing his rival, Tiberius III Apsimar (698–705), to panic and flee.[25]

Another weakness was to be found at the northern extremity of the Land Walls, as they approached the Golden Horn and linked up with the Sea Walls. The suburb of Blachernae had been left outside the original construction probably because it was of minimal importance in the fifth century. By the seventh century, however, more buildings had been erected there and Blachernae was also home to the *Maphorion* which was housed in the church of the Theotokos there. Following the Avar–Persian siege of 626, therefore, the Land Walls were extended outwards to enclose the Blachernae area, creating a bulge in their otherwise fairly straight line. It was within this outcrop that an important imperial residence was later built, the Palace of Blachernae. It did mean, however, that this area of wall was vulnerable to bombardment from catapults as it protruded out beyond the line of the rest of the Land Walls. Moreover, this section of the wall was only one tier deep, lacking the outer wall and moat which were difficult to construct on the sloping terrain. During the twelfth century, the Blachernae section was completely rebuilt and strengthened. It was made thicker than the existing Theodosian Walls, using larger blocks of stone, and its towers were placed closer together. That went some way towards reducing the danger but the Blachernae section remained a vulnerable point.[26]

While something could be done to counter the danger posed by the aqueducts and the Blachernae 'bulge', there was little that the emperors could do about the so-called *Mesoteichion*. Meaning literally the 'middle of the walls', this was the section of the Land Walls between the Gate of St Romanos and the Gate of Adrianople where the defences had to follow the lie of the land and dip down into the valley of the River Lykos. Consequently it was impossible to construct a deep moat there as the water would drain away while attackers could position themselves on the higher ground further back and use the advantage of height to intimidate the defenders by hurling missiles over the walls. Would-be usurpers knew this point well and always drew up their armies before the Gate of Adrianople to take advantage of the lie of the land.[27]

This was what happened in 1047, when Leo Tornikes led an army to the Land Walls in the hope of unseating the Emperor Constantine IX Monomachos (1042–55). The emperor had recently suffered a bout of illness, and rumours were circulating that he had died, so he judged it prudent to go in person to the Land Walls to encourage the troops that were facing Tornikes's army, taking a seat on the battlements where he was in full view. Unfortunately, he could also be seen by the rebel army, and a mounted archer took the opportunity to loose off an arrow in his direction. Had it struck home, Tornikes would probably have found himself emperor, but Constantine happened to move his head to one side at the last moment. The arrow whistled past his ear and hit one of his young courtiers, who was standing behind, in the ribs.[28]

The weaknesses in the defences, however, seldom delivered victory to a rebel army, and the most likely way for it to take Constantinople was for a sympathizer on the inside to open one of the gates. Tornikes and his followers were clearly relying on this happening in 1047. Rather than make any attempt to assault the walls, they energetically harangued the soldiers on the Land Walls, deriding Constantine IX and his well-known self-indulgent lifestyle and urging the merits of Tornikes. They even staged some comic dances, full of ribald jokes at the emperor's expense. Then they led their prisoners in front of the walls and threatened to put them to death if the gates were not opened. It was all to no avail. The gates remained firmly shut and the defenders unleashed a volley of stones from their catapults, though these all fell short of their targets. Faced with such intransigence, the rebel army eventually gave up and withdrew.[29]

That was not always how things worked out. A similar situation occurred in the summer of 1057 when Isaac Komnenos revolted against Michael VI (1056–7). Isaac was based in Asia Minor and so he led his army towards the Bosporus. His forces easily saw off an army sent against them by Michael VI, but the strait was as formidable a barrier as the Land Walls and Isaac could not cross it as long as the emperor in Constantinople controlled the fleet. Komnenos's army therefore encamped near Nicaea and waited on events. Michael decided to negotiate and sent an embassy to Komnenos's camp offering to adopt him as his heir so that he would succeed as emperor after Michael's death. Komnenos accepted this compromise, but, before it could be carried into effect, news arrived that a popular revolt against Michael had broken out in Constantinople and Komnenos was being invited to sail across and enter the city. Thus on 1 September 1057 he entered Constantinople, effectively having captured the capital without the need for a siege, and mounted the throne as Isaac I (1057–9).[30]

Popular support was only one of the ways to get the gates opened from the inside. Another was to secure the loyalty of the troops guarding a key section of the Land Walls. By 1200 and for a long time before, the bulk of the empire's armed forces were composed of foreign mercenaries, largely from Russia, Scandinavia, Germany, France and England, although African palace guards are also reported.[31] These imported troops included the famous Varangian guard who formed the emperor's personal bodyguard and who were distinguished by the heavy double-edged swords which they carried on their shoulders on ceremonial occasions. Some were exiles from political reverses at home, such as the English Varangians in the service of Alexios I in the later eleventh century who had been forced to leave their homeland by the Norman Conquest of 1066. The Varangians had a reputation for unshakable loyalty to the reigning emperor, a valuable commodity in the murky world of Byzantine politics, which was why they were preferred over native troops. Indeed, most contemporary Byzantines were quite happy to admit that the Varangians and other mercenaries were by far the most faithful and courageous soldiers that the empire had.[32]

One of the most famous Varangians was Harold Sigurtharson or Hardrada. After leaving his native Norway in 1030 following the battle of Sticklestad when his brother, King Olaf Haroldson had been killed, Harold had wandered for some time in Russia, before heading for Constantinople and enrolling with his followers in the Varangian guard. His duties there were not restricted to staying in the palace and guarding the imperial person. Harold took part in Byzantine campaigns in the Aegean, in Bulgaria and in Sicily, during which he acquitted himself more than creditably. In recognition of his martial prowess, he was made leader of the Varangian guard and invested by the emperor with the sonorous title of *Spatharokandidatos*. By the time he left Constantinople in around 1044, he was a rich man from his accumulated salary, imperial gifts and the plunder from the campaigns. Back in his native Norway, Harold succeeded in becoming king, and his twenty years of iron-handed rule earned him the sobriquet of 'Hardrada' or 'the Stern'. He had not, however, lost his taste for overseas adventure. In September 1066, he launched an invasion of England, but on this occasion his military acumen seems to have deserted him. His army was routed and he himself was killed at the battle of Stamford Bridge. As far as the Byzantines were concerned, however, Harold had been an asset who had been worth every bit of the largesse lavished on him by the emperor.[33]

Not all the mercenaries were of the calibre of Harold Hardrada and the Varangians, of course, and would-be usurpers were able to take advantage of that. In the spring of 1081, a young general called Alexios Komnenos, nephew of Isaac, brought his army to the Land Walls to challenge Emperor Nikephoros III Botaneiates (1078–81). The rebels were greeted with the usual whistles and catcalls from the defenders, and to start with there seemed to be no likelihood of a repeat of the popular rising that had given ingress to Alexios's uncle in 1056. The wait therefore began. Inevitably the besieged and the besiegers began to exchange conversation and Alexios thereby discovered which regiments were stationed on which towers along the Land Walls. These included the Varangians and the Immortals, the latter being composed entirely of Byzantine soldiers. Alexios was advised not to try to negotiate with them as they were likely to remain loyal to Nikephoros. Further along, however, was a tower guarded by the Nemitzi, a regiment of foreign, presumably German, mercenaries, and Alexios decided to make contact with them. A man was sent as close as possible to the wall, and the commander of the Nemitzi leant over the battlements to parley. Presumably some kind of financial deal was struck, with Alexios agreeing to better the salary paid by his rival, and it was agreed that the Gate of Adrianople would be opened at a prearranged time. At dawn on 1 April, Komnenos's troops poured into Constantinople, enabling him to ascend the throne as Alexios I (1081–1118) and to place the Komnenian dynasty in power for over a century.[34]

There were, therefore, certain flaws in the stories told by the Byzantines of 1200 about the invulnerability of their God-guarded city. Geography and technology could be given the credit just as well as divine intervention, and, far from being impregnable, the city had in fact been captured on numerous occasions, albeit by usurping generals rather than by a foreign power.

Yet the Byzantines were not blind. They were well aware of the advantages that geography and technology gave them. As recently as 1185, the action of the prevailing current in the Bosporus had been graphically demonstrated. Faced with a popular uprising and a rival candidate for the throne, Emperor Andronicus I had attempted to flee north by ship. In spite of desperate efforts by the crew, the current drove his boat back to the shore, where his executioners were waiting for him.[35] The Byzantines also knew the value of their military technology and especially of the Land and Sea Walls. Their first reaction in any crisis, when was in the offing, was to inspect and repair these fortifications, and to demolish any houses that had been built illegally alongside them. Any earthquake damage was quickly made good, whether there was an immediate threat or not.[36] As for Greek fire, it was an article of faith among the Byzantine ruling classes that the secret was never to be divulged to an outside power.[37]

It was not therefore that the Byzantines denied their material advantages but rather that they saw them as further evidence of divine favour. The walls could be extended and repaired but ultimate security lay in God. Hence the inscription on one of the towers of the Land Walls imploring Christ to 'preserve thy city undisturbed'. When the unpredictable winds of the Bosporus had died down and becalmed the Russian fleet in 941, that was God lulling the breeze and calming the waves.[38] Technology was a gift from God, often transmitted, like so much else, through the founder of the city, Constantine the Great. Greek fire, for example, which had originally been brought to Constantinople by a Syrian refugee in the 670s, was later said to have been revealed to Constantine by an angel and passed down from him to succeeding generations of emperors. It was even said that the use of English mercenaries was something instituted by Constantine. After he had been crowned emperor at York in 306, he allegedly brought 30,000 Britons east with him and they constituted the first inhabitants of his new capital.[39] Even the frequent capture of Constantinople by rebel generals could be subtly twisted to suit the myth. After all, if the usurper succeeded, it was clear that he had had the favour of God in overthrowing a wicked tyrant. If he failed, then it was equally obvious that the Theotokos had once more stepped in to protect the God-guarded city.

It would be wrong, however, to believe that this way of seeing things was the result of cynical calculation. On the contrary, there is every indication that the Byzantines genuinely believed that they were the beneficiaries of special divine protection. So important was that idea that it was even built into imperial protocol. It was laid down that when an emperor set out across the Bosporus by ship to campaign in Asia Minor, he was to leave his capital in God's care:

> When the emperor is a sufficient distance from the imperial harbour, so that he can look upon the city, he rises from his couch and stands looking eastwards with his hands raised to heaven; and making the sign of the cross three times with his hand over the city, he prays to God and says: 'Lord Jesus Christ, my God, I place in Your hands this Your city.'[40]

In this way, military power was given the ultimate justification of divine sanction.

CHAPTER 4

Palaces and Power

The internal politics of the Byzantine empire have long since acquired an unsavoury reputation. 'The most profligate debaucheries', wrote Jean-Jacques Rousseau (1712–78), 'the most abandoned villainies, the most atrocious crimes, plots, murders and assassinations form the warp and woof of the history of Constantinople'.[1] It has to be said that the charge is not without substance. Of the seventy or so emperors who reigned in Constantinople between 330 and 1204, less than half died in their beds at a ripe old age, still in office, and passed the crown to a son or designated successor. Violent changes of ruler litter the pages of Byzantine history, emperors frequently being overthrown by those closest to them. Michael II (820–9) reached the throne by murdering his old comrade-in-arms, Leo V (813–20), who was stabbed to death while praying in church and his body dumped in a cesspit. John I Tzimiskes (969–76) became emperor by sneaking into the bedroom of his uncle, Nikephoros II Phokas (963–9), with a gang of followers who then hacked Nikephoros to pieces with their swords. The emperor's wife, Theophano, was one of the conspirators and had seen to it beforehand that the door of the chamber would be unlocked. When attempts on the throne such as this went wrong, on the other hand, the losers could expect little mercy. When the rebel Bardas Phokas died in the battle of Abydos in 989, his head was paraded on a spear through the streets of Constantinople. One of his associates who was taken alive was put to death by impalement.[2]

59

Deposed emperors or unsuccessful would-be usurpers were not always murdered. Some got away with being forcibly tonsured and made to take monastic vows. They were then immured for the rest of their lives behind the high walls of a monastery. What has made Byzantine politics truly notorious, however, is the regularity with which the losers in the endless round of plots and coups were subjected to a fate which might be considered even worse than death, that of being blinded by having their eyes gouged out with red hot irons. It was a brutal business. The blinding of Romanos IV Diogenes (1068–71), who was ousted by his stepson, Michael Doukas in 1071, was carried out so ineptly by his captors that he died not long afterwards. Most shocking of all, Constantine VI (780–97) was blinded and deposed on the orders of his own mother, Eirene.[3]

Such mutilation was regarded as justified because it provided a 'humane' alternative to killing the victim. Nevertheless, the Byzantines were well aware of what a fearsome punishment it was, and there were examples of individuals being spared at the last moment, merely having their eyelids singed as a warning. In general, however, no emperor could afford such leniency and the deed was usually carried out without mercy. After all, in general it seems to have worked. Mutilation of any kind was deemed to be a disqualification for imperial office and so, in the past, political failures had had their noses split open. Then, in 705, the deposed emperor Justinian II, whose nose had been given the standard treatment, managed to seize back the throne and to reign for a further seven years in spite of this very visible mutilation, earning the sobriquet of *Rhinotmetos* or 'the noseless'. Consequently, blinding became more common as it had the added advantage of physically incapacitating that victim and so ensured that they caused no more trouble. Nikephoros Diogenes, who was blinded in 1094 for plotting against the reigning emperor, retired from Constantinople to his estates and passed his remaining years in the study of classical literature, using secretaries to read the texts to him. Not until 1203 did a blinded former emperor, Isaac II, succeed in regaining the throne.[4]

In view of this long record of plot, counter-plot and mutilation, it is hardly surprising then that the very word 'Byzantine' has acquired in English the pejorative meaning of 'underhand' and 'devious'. That is not entirely fair, since many other societies have displayed a similar propensity for frequent bouts of assassination and intrigue. What was unique to Byzantium was, as always, the way in which theory covered reality. Just as the foundation and survival of Constantinople had been overlaid with myths and pious legends, so had the acquisition and exercise of political power. In spite of the unedifying way in which most Byzantine emperors had reached their position, the office that they held remained imbued with a mystic, sacred aura, with its incumbent regarded as being nothing less than a kind of deputy to Almighty God.

Byzantine political theory had largely been developed and articulated by one man, a certain Eusebius, bishop of Caesarea (*c.* 260–339), a contemporary of Constantine the Great. Eusebius did not know Constantine well and probably only met him two or three times. It is unlikely that Constantine himself even remembered who he was. Nevertheless the good bishop seems to have appointed himself to the task of presenting Constantine as the ideal Christian ruler, a novel undertaking as no Roman emperor of the past had been a Christian. In a speech written in honour of the thirtieth anniversary of Constantine's accession in 336, Eusebius argued that a Christian emperor did not just accede to the throne, but was appointed there by God. He was a sort of lesser image of the Almighty, governing on Earth while God ruled in Heaven:

> The sovereign dear to God, in imitation of the Higher
> Power, directs the helm and sets straight all things on
> earth ... Thus outfitted in the likeness of the kingdom
> of heaven, he pilots affairs below with an upward
> gaze, to steer by the archetypal form.[5]

Whether Eusebius's motive in this was to ingratiate himself with Constantine or to attach the somewhat ambivalent emperor more closely to the camp of the Christians is impossible to tell, but there can be no doubt that he set the pattern of Byzantine political thought for the rest of the empire's existence. The idea that the emperor was God's representative or vicegerent on earth stuck and was repeated by generations of court orators ever afterwards.

It is important to remember, however, that the idea of 'imitation' or *mimesis* of God could, in the opinion of the Byzantines, only be applied to the emperor in Constantinople. No other worldly ruler, be he ever so powerful in worldly terms, could claim to have such a close relationship with the deity. The Byzantine emperors were different because they were, according to their official title, 'Emperor and Autocrat of the Romans'. The subjects they ruled over were the Romans, the name 'Byzantines' that is now given to them being a modern invention to distinguish them from the ancient Romans. The basis of this claim was the doctrine of *Translatio Imperii*, the idea that Constantine had transferred the seat of the Roman empire from Rome to Constantinople.

The Byzantines took the Roman claim extremely seriously. Some envoys who arrived in Constantinople in August 968 bearing a letter addressed to the 'emperor of the Greeks' were thrown into prison for their 'sinful audacity'.[6] It is again Eusebius who makes it clear why it was so important for the Byzantine emperors to be called Roman. The first Roman emperor was Augustus (31 BCE–14 CE) who, Eusebius pointed out, had reigned at the same time that Jesus Christ had been born into the world.[7] Clearly God had united much of the known world under one ruler with a purpose and when Constantine became a Christian that purpose had become plain. God desired all Christians to be ruled by one pious Christian ruler, the Roman emperor.[8]

By 1200, of course, the authority of the Roman emperor in Constantinople had shrunk considerably from what it had been in Constantine's day, and only a very small part of the Christian world was under his rule. That made no difference to the theory. As late as 1398, when the emperor ruled little more than his capital city, the patriarch of Constantinople wrote that:

> The emperor has still to this day the same appointment and support from the Church; he has the same position and prayers: he is anointed with the solemn myrrh, and appointed emperor and autocrat of the

Romans – to wit of all Christians ... No other rulers or
governors of provinces have such a position.[9]

No visitor to Constantinople in 1200 could have gone far without
encountering that theory in visible form. In churches and public spaces
the imperial image was everywhere, whether carved in stone, founded
in bronze or depicted in paint or mosaic. The successors of Constantine were often portrayed standing next to Christ or the Virgin Mary
who were placing their hands upon their crowned heads in token of
blessing and as an indication of the origin of the imperial power. All
emperors and empresses, not only the sainted Constantine and his
equally saintly mother, Helena, were shown with halos. That did not
necessarily denote personal holiness but that of the office they held.
To make the matter absolutely clear, such portraits were often accompanied by an inscription naming the emperor and describing him as
'faithful in Christ emperor and autocrat of the Romans'.[10]

It was only right that the holder of so august a position should be
housed in such a way as to reflect his status. By 1200 the Byzantine
emperor had not one magnificent palace in Constantinople, but two.
These were the Great Palace (sometimes known as Boukoleon) and
the Palace of Blachernae. The Great Palace was the older and more
extensive of the two, situated next to the Hippodrome and Hagia
Sophia in the heart of the city, where Constantine the Great had built
his first residence. Justinian had rebuilt its main entrance, the Brazen
Gate, and remodelled much of the interior.[11] Subsequent emperors
had added new buildings and demolished others.[12] By 1200, therefore,
the Great Palace was not so much a palace as a complex that sprawled
over an extensive site of some five square kilometres. Consequently, it
is rather difficult to envisage what the ground plan of the Great Palace
would have been like at any one time.[13]

On the other hand, there are descriptions of some of the individual
buildings that made up the complex. One, which overlooked the sea
on the south side of the city, was known as the Porphyra. It contained
one room whose walls were lined with purple marble and purple silk
hangings. Since the eighth century it had been reserved for the lying-
in of Byzantine empresses, so that it could be said that the heir of a

reigning emperor was 'Porphyrogenitos' or 'born in the purple' and so earmarked to succeed his father.[14]

Another building frequently referred to was the Boukoleon which overlooked the Sea of Marmara at the southern end of the complex. The Boukoleon had its own harbour with a flight of marble steps leading down to the water where a vessel for the emperor's use was moored. The name derived from a statue of an ox (*bous*) being attacked by a lion (*leôn*) which stood on the harbour wall. The lion was depicted with its left foot on the ox's horn and it was clearly twisting round its victim's head to make a bite at its throat.[15] Then there was the Dekanneakubita or 'the hall of the nineteen couches'. It was the emperor's custom to entertain eighteen guests to dinner there every Christmas day, the diners reclining on couches and being served on vessels of gold. The hall known as the Magnavra contained the emperor's throne room. The interiors of buildings such as these, floors, walls and ceiling, were usually decorated with sumptuous mosaics.[16]

This apparently random collection of buildings had a serious purpose behind it, that of providing a fitting setting for the office of emperor of the Romans and of impressing on subjects and visitors the power and majesty of the current incumbent and his unique relationship with Almighty God. As in other parts of the city, therefore, the imperial image was everywhere. Inside the Brazen Gate, Justinian and Theodora stared down at new arrivals. In the building known as the Kainourgion, Basil I (867–86) and his family covered the ceiling, the children shown carrying Bibles to show how they were being instructed in divine law. John II Komnenos (1118–43) decorated the so-called Golden Chamber with images of his father, Alexios I.[17]

The Great Palace contained something that was far more important in establishing the link between God and his vicegerent, for it was home to a special chapel, dedicated to the Holy Virgin of Pharos. The chapel was so-called because of its proximity to the lighthouse or Pharos that formed the last link in a chain of hilltop beacons which had, in more troubled times, stretched across Asia Minor to give prior warning of Arab raids. Inside, the dome and ceiling were decorated with the usual mosaics depicting Christ and the Virgin, but the chapel also boasted a jewel-encrusted altar, and even the hinges of its doors were made of silver.[18] There was a very good reason for the lavish decoration, for the Pharos chapel housed a number of relics closely associated with Jesus Christ himself.

Foremost among them were two sections of the cross on which Christ had hung during the crucifixion on Mount Calvary, known as the True Cross to distinguish it from the many imitations.[19] According to legend, the True Cross had been discovered by Helena, the mother of Constantine the Great, while she was on pilgrimage in Jerusalem. With the help of the Archbishop of Jerusalem, Macarius, she had organized an archaeological excavation at Calvary, and after having demolished the pagan temple of Aphrodite which stood on the site had duly unearthed three crosses. To discern which was the True Cross from those on which the two thieves had hung, Archbishop Macarius brought them one after another to the bedside of a sick woman. When the shadow of the True Cross fell across her, the woman was immediately healed. The precious relic was then placed in a silver casket and kept in a church that was erected on the site, although Helena took part of the cross back with her to Constantinople.[20]

In the course of time, more of the True Cross was to end up in Constantinople. In June 614 a Persian army captured Jerusalem after a three-week siege, and much of the city was burned. The True Cross was carried off with the rest of the booty to Ctesiphon, the capital of Sassanid Persia, where it only survived because the wife of the Persian king was a Christian and so took good care of it. Fourteen years later, the Byzantine emperor Heraclius led his army into Persia to take revenge and, having virtually wiped out the Persian army at Nineveh, forced the king to accept peace and to hand back the True Cross. The relic was brought back to Jerusalem, amidst great rejoicing in March 630.[21] When the Arabs invaded Byzantine Syria in 634 and Jerusalem was once more threatened, Heraclius took the True Cross with him back to Constantinople to reunite it with the section taken there by Helena.[22] There it had remained ever since.

Another famed relic preserved in the Pharos chapel was the Mandylion of Edessa, a small cloth on which was imprinted what was held to be a miraculous image of the face of Christ. Numerous legends abounded about how the Mandylion had come into being, but the most commonly believed was this. During the lifetime of Christ, Abgar, the ruler of the town of Edessa (now Urfa in eastern Turkey), had sent an emissary to Jesus begging him to come and heal him from arthritis and leprosy. Jesus had declined but instead washed his face in water and then dried it on a piece of cloth. The image of Christ's face was left on the cloth and he gave it to Abgar's emissary to take back to Edessa. On receiving the cloth, Abgar was healed of all his illnesses and, along with the entire population of Edessa, was converted to Christianity. The cloth or Mandylion was credited with saving the city from a Persian attack in 544. It was then reverently preserved in Edessa until 944 when a Byzantine army laid siege to Edessa. The city's Muslim rulers decided to buy security by giving up the Mandylion. The precious relic was then carried back to Constantinople in triumph, which was only fitting, according to the Byzantine emperor of the day, because the Queen of Cities had 'the undoubted right to rule all'. The Byzantines later acquired the autograph letter supposedly written by Christ to Abgar, though sadly this was lost or destroyed in a riot in 1185.[23]

Also in the chapel were a number of other relics associated with Christ, such as his sandals, the tunic which he had worn at the time of his passion, the Crown of Thorns, the lance which pierced his side, and a small phial containing what purported to be some of his blood. Oddest of all, perhaps, was the *Keramion* or Holy Tile, a ceramic tile on which the face of Christ had been miraculously imprinted. There were also relics of major saints such as the right arm of John the Baptist and the head of St Paul.[24] The possession of these objects added enormously to the prestige of the Byzantine emperor. Visiting kings were unfailingly taken to visit the chapel so that they could see for themselves these 'signs of divine protection' and draw the appropriate conclusion.[25]

The Great Palace was also the setting for elaborate ceremonial which had exactly the same end in view: to 'evoke the admiration both of strangers and of our own subjects'.[26] All foreign dignitaries and ambassadors were to be received in a splendid audience chamber inside the Magnavra hall. They were led in to the strains of organ music by an official holding a golden staff and were expected to prostrate themselves three times on the floor before the throne. While this was happening, two bronze lions that stood next to the throne would suddenly start to roar and the birds in a gilded tree would burst into song, no doubt to the astonishment of the envoys, while the emperor's throne could be mechanically lifted up so that he could gaze down on his grovelling visitors on the floor below. He was a sight to behold:

> The emperor himself was seated on a couch decorated with two head rests. The couch was raised on a high platform and overlaid with gold. Under his feet was a stool. A magnificent robe gave him an air of great distinction. Very proudly he held up his head and puffed out his chest (an effort that caused his cheeks to take on a deep red tinge), while his eyes with their faraway gaze, showed plainly that he was thinking profoundly and wholly given up to his own meditations.

The whole set-up was designed to present the emperor as almost superhuman by virtue of his office. The only concession was made to visiting monarchs, who were not expected to grovel on the floor. They were, however, given a seat that was deliberately placed lower down than the throne of their host, to emphasize his superior position as emperor of the Romans.[27]

The same applied to the endless round of ceremonies which took up much of the emperor's time while he was resident in the Great Palace. Every year on Holy Saturday, for example, the emperor would process from the Great Palace to the Cathedral of Hagia Sophia. Inside the church the procession would pass the cover of the Holy Well, where Christ spoke to the Samaritan woman, and enter the sanctuary followed by a eunuch carrying a bag containing 100 pounds of gold. An official would then take the bag from the eunuch and hand it to the emperor who would then lay it on the altar and cense it with incense. So it went on throughout the ceremony, with ritual actions and greetings prescribed for particular locations throughout the city. Tedious and occasionally rather silly as such rituals might seem, they were carefully adapted for their purpose, being designed, as one emperor put it, to make the imperial power 'more admirable to foreigners and to our own people'.[28]

In general, they seem to have worked. An Arab visitor to Constantinople who witnessed an imperial procession as it wound from the Brazen Gate to the cathedral of Hagia Sophia was clearly impressed:

> [The emperor] is preceded by ten thousand elders wearing clothes of red brocade; their hair reaches their shoulders, and they wear no upper cloak. Then behind them come ten thousand young men wearing clothes of white brocade. All go on foot. Then come ten thousand boys dressed in clothes of green brocade. Then come ten thousand servants wearing clothes of brocade the colour of the blue sky; in their hands they hold axes covered with gold. Behind them follow five thousand chosen eunuchs wearing white Khorasian clothes of half silk; in their hands they hold golden crosses. Then after them come ten thousand Turkish and Khorasian pages wearing striped breastplates; in their hands they hold spears and shields wholly covered with gold. Then come a hundred most dignified patricians wearing clothes of coloured brocade; in their hands they have gold censers perfumed with aloes. Then come twelve chief patricians with clothes woven with gold; each of them holds a golden rod.[29]

The numbers are clearly exaggerated but the effect is clear: even a potentially hostile observer was impressed by the spectacle and pageantry. This was not always the case. An ambassador from Italy who witnessed a similar ceremony in 968 recorded it with a much more jaundiced eye:

> A numerous company of tradesmen and low born persons, collected on this solemn occasion to welcome and honour [the Emperor] Nikephoros

68

[II Phokas], lined the sides of the road, like walls, from the palace to Hagia Sophia, tricked out with thin little shields and cheap spears ... His nobles for their part, who with their master passed through the plebeian and barefoot multitude, were dressed in tunics that were too large for them and were also because of their extreme age full of holes. They would have looked better if they had worn their ordinary clothes.[30]

Individual reactions, however, make no difference to the main point of all this pageantry. The Byzantines were constantly exerting themselves to promote the special status of their city and their emperor, whether through imperial portraits in mosaic, grandiose palaces or by ostentatious public display.

The everyday reality of Byzantine politics was, of course, much less impressive than the theory and the ceremony. In 1200 the heir of Constantine the Great who ruled the Byzantine empire was Alexios III (1195–1203), a monarch about whom posterity has had little good to say. His contemporary, the historian Niketas Choniates, presents him as a far cry from the ideal emperor, a spendthrift who neglected the interests of the empire while busying himself with trivial pursuits, such as building new bath houses and planting vineyards at a time when he should have been attending to the defences of Constantinople.[31] Most unedifying of all was the way in which Alexios III had come to the throne.

Alexios was not a *Porphyrogenitos*. He had not been born in the Purple Chamber in the Great Palace and his father had not been a reigning emperor. He was a scion of a wealthy Constantinopolitan family, one of six sons of veteran soldier Andronicus Angelos and his wife Euphrosyne. These were, however, troubled times. On 24 September 1180, after a reign of thirty-eight years, the redoubtable emperor Manuel I Komnenos had died, leaving as his heir an eleven-year-old boy, his son Alexios II (1180–3). A council of regency therefore had to be formed under the child's mother, Maria of Antioch, with real power in the hands of a nephew of the late emperor, Alexios Komnenos, who held the title of *protosebastos*. The regency of Maria and Alexios soon proved unpopular in Constantinople, and in 1182 another of Manuel I's kinsmen, Andronicus Komnenos, staged a revolt and led an army across Asia Minor towards Constantinople.

As a prominent nobleman, Angelos could not avoid becoming involved in these events. He was sent by the regency with a force to crush the rebel but he ended up switching sides and fleeing with his family to the opposing camp. The Angelos family were to regret that move. Once Andronicus Komnenos had captured Constantinople and installed himself as the new regent to the young emperor, he instituted a reign of terror in which prominent aristocrats were his main victims. Realizing that he might be the next target, Andronicus Angelos entered into a conspiracy against the regent. When it was betrayed, most of the plotters were rounded up and executed, but Angelos and his sons, including Alexios, escaped their pursuers when they reached the coast and found a boat full of empty wine jars. Heaving the jars into the sea, they crowded aboard and succeeded in eluding Andronicus's forces. Having reached a safe distance, father and sons scattered to maximize their chances. Alexios went to Syria where he was given asylum at the court of the Ayyubid Sultan, the famous Saladin.[32]

Not all the brothers went so far. Theodore and Isaac Angelos ended up in Bithynia in Asia Minor where they found refuge in the cities of Nicaea and Prousa whose inhabitants had refused to accede to Andronicus Komnenos's coup. Determined to crush all opposition, Andronicus set out to besiege these towns. Nicaea held out at first and the regent was forced to bring up siege engines to attack the walls. He even had Isaac Angelos's mother, Euphrosyne, brought from Constantinople and used the frail old lady as a human shield by placing her in front of a battering ram as it was hauled towards the walls. The stratagem failed. The Nicaeans carefully shot their arrows around Euphrosyne, killing the soldiers who were guarding her, and then sallied forth to rescue her. When the leader of the rebellion, Theodore Kantakouzenos, was killed in a skirmish, however, the spirit of the defenders flagged. Isaac Angelos negotiated peace with Andronicus. The town opened its gates and Isaac was sent back to Constantinople to live peacefully in the family mansion there, though several other prominent men among the defenders were executed.

This latter action prompted the people of Prousa to put up stiffer resistance. The city had to be taken by storm and large numbers of its inhabitants were massacred. Theodore Angelos was taken prisoner and Andronicus gave orders that he should be blinded. Clearly, already Andronicus feared that some member of the Angelos family might be planning to replace him. The unfortunate Theodore was then placed on an ass which was then sent trotting off to wander where it would. Theodore would doubtless have starved had not some Turks from the neighbouring sultanate of Konya found him and taken pity on him.[33]

Back in Constantinople, Andronicus Komnenos had by now had himself crowned emperor as Andronicus I (1183–5) and had disposed of the young Alexios by having the unfortunate lad strangled with a bow string. His corpse was brought to Andronicus so that he could kick it before it was dumped in the Bosporus.[34] Donning the imperial purple did not set Andronicus's mind at rest, however. He saw conspiracies everywhere and scarcely a day went by without some unfortunate wretch being arraigned and executed. Inevitably, his suspicion fell on Isaac, the only member of the Angelos family within his reach. On the evening of 11 September 1185, a number of armed men led by Stephen Hagiochristophorites arrived at the Angelos mansion bearing orders to arrest him. As they pounded on the doors, Isaac cowered inside, but then, reasoning that he was likely to die anyway, he crept to the stables and saddled a horse. His pursuers were taken completely by surprise as Isaac charged out sword in hand and had no time to react before he killed Hagiochristophorites with a single blow to the head and cut off the ear of one of the others. Isaac then galloped down the Mese towards Hagia Sophia to take sanctuary.

News of these dramatic events soon spread and popular demonstrations broke out against the by now universally detested Andronicus. Sensing that all was lost, Andronicus left Constantinople by ship in the hope of sailing across the Black Sea to Russia. Unfortunately, the current carried the ship back to shore before it could make much headway. Andronicus was taken prisoner, dragged back to Constantinople and lynched in the Hippodrome by the furious crowd.[35] Isaac Angelos now found himself emperor as Isaac II (1185–95).

Naturally, one of Isaac's first moves was to recall the scattered members of his family to the capital. His father, Andronicus Angelos, seems by this time to have died, but Alexios was brought back from Syria and given the prestigious title of *sebastokrator*. Isaac had a particular affection for Alexios because he was the only one of the six brothers who had escaped completely unscathed during Andronicus's reign of terror.[36]

Alexios seems to have had little gratitude for his brother's kindness. By the spring of 1195, he was plotting to seize the throne and had gathered a group of supporters. These seem to have included an individual called Alexios Doukas Mourtzouphlos. Mourtzouphlos, whose last name was a nickname meaning 'blackened and blind', because his dark, bushy eyebrows met over his nose and hung over his eyes, was to play an important part in Constantinople's political life over the next few years.[37] In April 1195, Alexios accompanied Isaac II on a military expedition against insurgents in Thrace. The campaign was a leisurely one, and while based near the town of Kypsella, Isaac had time to go hunting. He invited his brother, the *sebastokrator*, to join him, but Alexios complained of feeling unwell so the emperor went off without him. Left behind in the camp, Alexios and his fellow conspirators seized the imperial regalia which had been left behind in a tent, and Isaac returned to discover that his brother had been proclaimed emperor in his place. Isaac's first reaction was to try a repeat of his tactic against his tormentors ten years before, and he spurred his horse to make a charge against the conspirators in the camp. He lost heart, however, when he saw that none of his servants would follow him. He then fled west to a small port called Makre, doubtless hoping to escape by sea, but he was apprehended and taken to a nearby monastery. There, like his brother Theodore before him, Isaac was blinded before being taken back to Constantinople to be imprisoned first in the dungeons beneath the Palace of Boukoleon, and then at Diplokionion on the Bosporus.[38]

It might be thought that after having perpetrated such a crime against his own brother, Alexios would never have been accepted in

Constantinople as emperor. While outsiders might find such regular bloodletting disturbing, a German monk noting with distaste the tendency of the Byzantines to 'butcher or blind their own kings',[39] the Byzantines seem to have accepted it as the way in which God appointed his vicegerent on Earth. Consequently, even before Alexios arrived back in the capital, the great and the good were quick to throw in their lot with the new regime. They hastened to find Alexios's wife Euphrosyne and 'placed their heads under her feet as foot stools, nuzzled their noses against her felt slipper like fawning puppies and stood timidly at her side, bringing their feet together and joining their hands'. Within days, Alexios had been crowned by the patriarch in the cathedral of Hagia Sophia. The only objector appears to have been the horse that was led forward to bear him away from the ceremony. It bucked and reared so violently when the new emperor tried to mount, that his jewelled crown was knocked off his head and damaged. Another, more placid steed had to be found.[40] Perhaps the readiness of the court and people of Constantinople to accept the coup of 1195 is not really surprising but it still fits very uneasily with Eusebius's portrait of the emperor as the imitation of God.

Given the dangers attendant on being the emperor of Byzantium, one might initially wonder why there were so many individuals who, like Alexios III, were prepared to go to such extraordinary lengths and to risk everything to reach the throne. The fact was that being emperor gave access to almost limitless wealth which provided certain compensations for the burden of being God's deputy on Earth. Eusebius had painted an austere portrait of Constantine, spending hours on his knees at prayer in the Great Palace,[41] but for those who had a taste for the high life the possibilities were endless. Alexios III, according to Choniates, believed that he had been given the throne 'not to exercise lawful dominion over men but to supply himself with lavish luxury and pleasures'.[42]

He was by no means alone in that assumption and it would appear that while some parts of the Great Palace were designed to parade the majesty of the imperial office, there were other, more private sections. Here the mosaics displayed not pious emperors but humorous scenes of cavorting animals and playful children. In one surviving set of floor mosaics, a man tumbles backwards off a donkey, which seems to be giving him a kick for good measure. Another shows two boys riding on a camel. Hunting scenes were a favourite subject.[43] On the outside, because it was a collection of buildings rather than a single edifice, the Great Palace had room for extensive gardens. There were shady porticoes, a courtyard for playing ball games and numerous fountains.[44]

Moreover, by 1200 the Byzantine emperors were not confined to the Great Palace. They used to spend much of their time in the rather less formal surroundings of their second palace in Constantinople, that of Blachernae. Situated close to the Land Walls and overlooking the Golden Horn, it had come into use much more recently. It was the favoured residence of the emperors of the Komnenos family, one of whom, Manuel I Komnenos (1143–80), had extended it, installed long galleries and commissioned new mosaics.[45] The result was a rather more compact and practical residence than the Great Palace, though no less impressive to visitors. One observer, writing in the mid-twelfth century, commented that:

> The Palace of Blachernae, although having founda-
> tions laid on low ground, achieves eminence through
> excellent construction and elegance and, because of
> its surroundings on three sides, affords its inhabit-
> ants the triple pleasure of looking out upon sea, fields
> and city. Its exterior is of almost matchless beauty, but
> its interior surpasses anything that I can say about it.
> Throughout it is decorated elaborately with gold and
> a great variety of colours, and the floor is marble,
> paved with cunning workmanship; and I do not know
> whether the exquisite art or the exceedingly valuable
> stuffs endows it with the more beauty or value.[46]

The emperor also had the use of a number of smaller palaces outside the city walls. Among them were Philopation, just outside the Golden Gate in the Land Walls, and Skoutarion close to Chrysopolis on the Asian side of the Bosporus.[47]

These were the places where the emperors could relax and enjoy the sweets of power to the full. Hunting was probably the commonest imperial pastime. Emperors would either sally forth into the countryside from the Palace of Blachernae or spend a few days in the extensive stretch of parkland that surrounded the Philopation, which was well stocked with game, particularly boar and wild asses.[48] Some emperors seem to have derived immeasurable delight from the chase and pursued their quarry with reckless abandon. Basil I is credited with bringing down a deer and a wolf by throwing his club at them and breaking their back legs. When confronted on one occasion by a large lion-like creature, most of Manuel I's retinue ran away. The emperor, however, stood his ground and despatched the animal with his sword.[49] Isaac I Komnenos particularly enjoyed bringing down crane with a bow and arrow:

> He would shoot them down from the sky, and truly his pleasure in this was not unmixed with wonder. The wonder was that a bird so exceptionally big, with feet and legs like lances, hiding itself behind the clouds, should in the twinkling of an eye be caught by an object so much smaller than itself. The pleasure he derived was from the bird's fall, for the crane, as it fell, danced the dance of death, turning over and over, now on its back, now on its belly.[50]

There were other pleasures opened up by the imperial office. Many Byzantines loved chariot races, but the imperial incumbent had no need to watch them with the common herd in the Hippodrome. He could stage his own in the privacy of one of his palaces, as Alexios III did at Blachernae in 1199 to celebrate the marriages of his daughters. Then there were the pleasures of the table with many emperors earning themselves reputations as gourmets and gluttons. Emperors also had plenty of scope for indulging their sexual tastes. One discovered that there was no one to gainsay him if he wished to sleep with his niece, and another used to take parties of prostitutes out into the countryside during the summer months for open-air orgies.[51]

Even when out on campaign with their armies, Byzantine emperors were not inclined to rough it. A tenth-century military treatise lays down that the equipment to be taken into the field should include thick tufted rugs for reclining on, a bath with a hide cistern of red leather, flax-blue cushions, silver coolers for scented wine and rose-water, two gilded chairs concealing chamber pots, silken sheets, linen towels, assorted ointments and perfumes and the imperial silver table service. For the transport of this last item alone some eighty pack animals were required.[52]

Such were the material benefits of the imperial office. One emperor who had enjoyed them all to the full during his ten-year reign had been Alexios III's brother, Isaac II:

> Daily he fared sumptuously and served up a sybaritic table, tasting the most delectable sauces, heaping up the bread, and feasting on a lair of wild beasts, a sea of fish, and an ocean of deep-red wine. On alternate days, when he took pleasure in the baths, he smelled of sweet unguents and was sprinkled with oils of myrrh ... The dandy strutted about like a peacock and never wore the same garment twice, coming forth daily from the palace like a bridegroom out of his bridal chamber or the sun rising out of a beauteous mere.[53]

By 1200, of course, Isaac's circumstances were rather different. He was blind and a prisoner while his brother Alexios enjoyed the lifestyle that he had lost. No wonder that Isaac plotted and schemed, hoping against hope one day to be restored to his rightful place on the throne and to all the perquisites that came with it.[54]

In view of what has been said so far, it might be wondered how the Byzantine empire survived for so many centuries, when the main elements in its political structure were high-sounding theory masking endless political intrigue and personal gratification. Had that been the case, then the empire probably would not have survived. The fact is that just as Byzantine political theory covered over the seamier side of life at the top, it also obscured one of the greatest strengths of Byzantine government: that the responsibility for running the empire did not in actual fact rest with only one man.

The theory was clear on this point. When it came to affairs of state, it was frequently said, the Byzantine emperor was like a helmsman, standing alone at the tiller, guiding the ship through the buffeting waves. Or else, he was like the sun, shining alone in the firmament.[55] Yet the emperor could rely on a number of sources of support. He stood at the summit of a ruling class who provided many of his generals and advisers. He had the use of a sophisticated bureaucracy based in the Great Palace. Last, and by no means least, he had the often formidable assistance of his wife and female relatives.

By the year 1200, the Byzantine ruling class was a very visible group in Constantinople. Their mansions and palaces lined the Mese, the Triumphal Way and the other principal thoroughfares and were clustered in the area known as Sphorakion to the north of the Forum of Constantine. Some were miniature versions of the Great Palace, consisting not of just one building but of a complex of them, including bathhouses and private chapels, their interiors decorated with expensive mosaics. The names of these great families, Komnenos, Palaiologos, Bryennios, Botaneiates, Doukas, Kamateros, Kantakouzenos and, of course, Angelos, crop up again and again. For by the late twelfth century, their members monopolized many of the highest positions in the army and in the Church and bore sonorous honorific titles such as *Patrikios*, *Magistros* and *Protostrator*. Many were linked to the imperial family by marriage or descent.[56]

The same people surrounded the emperor at court and constituted the membership of the Senate, which was by now a purely honorific body. They followed him from the Great Palace to Blachernae and, when the heat of the city became unbearable in the summer, out into the countryside to one of the suburban palaces. Here they would discuss affairs of state with the emperor and help him to decide policy. Anna Comnena recalled that her father, Alexios I, used to talk over such matters with her uncle, George Palaiologos.[57]

Yet although the great families of Constantinople were the constant companions of the emperor and provided many of his most important generals and officers, they also presented the greatest threat. It was, after all, from their ranks that usurpers were most likely to arise, for they had the resources and personal authority to gather an army and lead it against Constantinople. This was the fear that had prompted Andronicus I to embark on his reign of terror in 1183–5, for he reasoned that if he got rid of the giants, there would only be pygmies to rule over. His fears proved to be justified when he was toppled by Isaac Angelos.[58]

The emperors must therefore have been grateful for their second source of support, bureaucrats of the Great Palace who filled the higher offices in the administration. They too bore grandiloquent titles such as *Megas Logothetes* (Chief Minister) and *Epi tou Kanikleiou* (literally 'He who holds the Inkstand'). Their main duties were to draft letters, laws, decrees and treaties, to oversee the treasury and postal services, and to organize the collection of taxes. In many cases, however, they were far more influential than that. Prominent individuals often advised the emperor on policy and tactics. The lowlier individuals carried out the vital task of publicizing and explaining that policy in public, by means of formal speeches on special occasions, praising the reigning emperor and his achievements.

Entry into this elite cadre was dependent not on birth but on education. Entrants had to have completed the traditional course of higher education in the Greek classics. This did not in itself provide much in the way of vocational qualification for the task of administering an empire, but it did give the opportunity to those of relatively modest backgrounds to get a foot on the ladder. Michael Psellos (*c.* 1022–*c.* 1080), who rose to become the most important adviser to successive emperors during the eleventh century, had no link to any of the great families of Constantinople, but he could recite Homer by heart and that was enough to obtain him his first post as a secretary at court. With that kind of example in mind, an ambitious father counselled his son:

> Learn your letters as much as you are able. See that
> man over there, my child: he used to walk on foot, and
> now he has a fat mule with a fine harness. This one,
> when he was a student, used to go barefoot, and see

him now in his pointed boots! This other one, when he was a student, never combed his hair, and now he is well combed and proud of his locks. That one in his student days never saw a bath door from afar, and now he bathes three times a week. That one was full of lice as big as almonds and now his purse is full of gold pieces with the emperor Manuel's effigy.[59]

As the author of this passage went on to say, education did not necessarily guarantee a place at court, and Constantinople was full of highly educated but impecunious men. Those who did make it by virtue of their educational accomplishments alone, like Psellos, would have had a vested interest in supporting the reigning emperor on whose patronage they depended. After all, new emperors tended to rid themselves of the counsellors of the old regime and bring in creatures of their own,[60] although Psellos himself was remarkable for his ability to survive changes of ruler. They could therefore generally be counted on to remain loyal, at least until things had reached such a pass that they realized that the time had come to sink or swim.

There was another reason why members of the bureaucracy were more trustworthy than the aristocracy. Many of them were eunuchs, and as such they were specifically prohibited by virtue of their physical mutilation from occupying the imperial throne. Emperors could entrust them with the highest powers of state without fear that they might make a bid for the throne. Some eunuchs had arrived in Constantinople as slaves, either captives in war or even as gifts from foreign ambassadors, but many were of Byzantine origin. It was not uncommon for parents to castrate one of their sons as a baby, a practice that was particularly common in Paphlagonia in northern Asia Minor. That might appear cruel, but it did give the boy an opportunity for a glittering career at court in later life. No less than ten of the most important posts at court that involved close contact with the emperor were specifically reserved for eunuchs, including that of *Parakoimomenos* or chamberlain, whose splendid title meant 'He who keeps watch alongside' the imperial person. Childhood castration certainly worked well for a certain John who came from humble origins in Paphlagonia to hold the office of *Orphanotrophos* at the Byzantine court.[61]

Some members of the imperial bureaucracy rose to positions of extraordinary power and influence. A notable example is Basil Lekapenos. An illegitimate son of an emperor, Romanos I Lekapenos (920–44), Basil had been castrated in infancy to preclude any attempt on the throne in later life and was given a job in the palace administration. He rose to become *Parakoimomenos*, a post he was to hold during the reigns of four emperors and from which he commanded extraordinary influence. Not only did Basil dominate the administration of the empire, he also commanded armies in the field and played an important role in bringing new emperors to power in 963 and 969. For many years, therefore, he was the most powerful individual in the Great Palace.[62] He was by no means unique in wielding such power. During the eleventh century, Michael Psellos, who was not a eunuch, could boast that the emperor was ready to follow whatever course of action he advised. This was still the case in Alexios III's day, for the chief *Parakoimomenos* George Oinaiotes was an extremely influential voice at court. In 1197, he succeeded in persuading Alexios to make an attack on the Vlach leader, Chrysos, in the town of Prosakon, although the assault proved a humiliating failure.[63]

Apart from the aristocracy and the bureaucrats, there was a third group at court which exerted a powerful influence on the emperor and on the way he ruled: the emperor's mother, sisters and other female relatives, and his wife the empress. For them a special section of the Great Palace and the Palace of Blachernae was set aside, the so-called *gynaikonitis* or women's quarters. Never were theory and practice more at odds in Byzantium than when it came to their role in government. The theory was that women could play no role in public life. They could not act as judges or bankers, were generally veiled in public and their frequently cited role model was Penelope in the *Odyssey* who patiently waited at home and wove a tapestry until her husband returned from the Trojan War. Consequently, as Michael Psellos pointed out, it would be improper for the Roman empire to be governed by a woman, rather than by a man.[64]

Yet in spite of all that, a succession of powerful women had moulded Byzantine history and culture, starting with Helena, the mother of Constantine. Theodora, the consort of the great Justinian, was so deeply involved in affairs of state that a male contemporary exclaimed in horror that 'she claimed the right to administer the whole Roman empire!' Eirene, the widow of Leo IV (775–80) even ruled the empire alone between 797 and 802, though she had to describe herself as an emperor, rather than as an empress, in legal documents in order to preserve decorum.[65]

A more recent example had been the extraordinary position occupied by Anna Dalassena, the mother of Alexios I Komnenos. Alexios had seized power in a coup in 1081, but for the first years of his reign there was no doubt where real power lay:

> In all matters, however ordinary, he did nothing without [his mother's] advice: she gradually became his confidante and co-partner in government. Gradually and surreptitiously he involved her more and more in state affairs; on occasions he even declared openly that without her brains and good judgement the Empire would not survive.[66]

When, a few months after his accession, Alexios was compelled to lead his army against the Normans who had invaded the Balkan provinces, it was Anna Dalassena whom he appointed to rule in the capital in his absence. A special gold-sealed document or *chrysobull* was issued proclaiming that any decrees made by Anna would have the same validity as those of the emperor himself.[67]

Anna Dalassena certainly seems to have been a formidable individual. Courtiers quailed before her very glance, and her arrival in the Great Palace was the signal for sweeping moral reforms. She insisted that everyone participate in communal hymn-singing and expected that they keep to strict breakfast times. She was also a noted patron of monks and hermits and left a monument in the church and monastery of Christ the All-Seeing (*Pantepoptes*) which she founded and endowed.[68]

In 1200, women still played an important role in the politics of the Byzantine court, with the empress Euphrosyne standing at the centre of much of the intrigue. She had played an important part in Alexios III's coup in 1195 by persuading the court and the patriarch to accept the downfall of Isaac II and to proclaim Alexios as emperor when he returned to Constantinople from Thrace.[69] A member of one of the great families of Constantinople, the Kamateroi, Euphrosyne seems to have ensured that the elevation of her husband to the purple therefore brought benefits for the whole clan. Her brother, Basil Kamateros, became prominent at court while her brother-in-law, Michael Stryphnos was appointed admiral of the fleet.[70] She also involved herself with the everyday business of government, which inevitably brought down on her the fury of the contemporary historian Niketas Choniates:

> Because the empress had overstepped the bounds and held in contempt the conventions of former Roman empresses, the empire was divided into two dominions. It was not the emperor alone who issued commands as he chose; she gave orders with equal authority and often nullified the emperor's decrees, altering them to her liking.[71]

Euphrosyne's interference in government may not have been as unhelpful as Choniates implies. Alexios had not been emperor long before Euphrosyne became alarmed at the way that he was frittering away the revenues. She therefore secured the appointment as her minister of a certain Constantine Mesopotamites, who had held office under the previous regime. The idea seems to have been that Mesopotamites would bring some order into the empire's currently rather chaotic financial affairs.

This well-meant move had serious repercussions. The appointment of Mesopotamites enraged Basil Kamateros and other of Euphrosyne's relatives who had been doing rather well under the old system where nobody asked too many questions. There was little that they could do to remove the hated minister, so they decided to strike at Euphrosyne instead. In the summer of 1196, they secured an audience with Alexios and accused the empress of adultery with a young general called Vatatzes. The emperor, who seems to have suffered from extraordinary gullibility, had Vatatzes murdered without further question and had some of the palace eunuchs and chambermaids tortured to extort evidence. After vacillating for a time and even dining cosily with Euphrosyne at Blachernae as if nothing had happened, Alexios suddenly acted and banished her to a nunnery on the Black Sea.

She was only in disgrace for six months, however. During that time her relatives relented, realizing that they had brought shame on their family and never having dreamt that the normally emollient Alexios would act so drastically. Meanwhile Constantine Mesopotamites lobbied tirelessly for the empress's recall. Alexios gave way, and in the spring of 1197 Euphrosyne returned. Before long she was more powerful than ever.[72]

Byzantine political theory had nothing to say about bureaucrats, eunuchs or women. Yet it was they who made the whole system workable. However self-indulgent, bloodthirsty or simply mediocre the imperial incumbent was, there was always a body of older, wiser heads to advise and restrain him. Moreover, when, as often happened, the emperor was toppled and replaced, there was an element of continuity. In spite of the inevitable purges, there would always be some bureaucrats left to carry on with business as usual in the Great Palace, and in some cases the new emperor would even marry his predecessor's wife. While the panegyrists regurgitated the theory and soldiers and aristocrats schemed and jockeyed for position in the corridors of the Great Palace and the Palace of Blachernae, the task of government went on.

CHAPTER 5

Churches and Monasteries

The Byzantines regarded Constantinople not just as a ruling city, but also as a holy one. A number of ingredients made up this claim. They included the supposed foundation of the city's church by the Apostle Andrew, its acquisition of an unrivalled collection of relics, its divine protection against capture, and the clear mark of God's favour in prompting Constantine to move his capital there. Constantinople was one of five cities whose bishops were honoured with the title of patriarch, the others being Rome, Alexandria, Antioch and Jerusalem. Moreover, by 1200 the Byzantines had come to see themselves as the guardians of correct Christian belief, or Orthodoxy, which had been defined by the seven Ecumenical Councils of the Church, starting with that of Nicaea in 325, a council that had been presided over by Constantine the Great.

Hence we find 'New Jerusalem', 'Leader of Faith' and the 'Guide of Orthodoxy' among Constantinople's many epithets.[1] There was, however, a particularly strong tension between myth and reality here, for it was difficult for Constantinople to be a holy place while also being a centre of political power and wealth.

The most striking and obvious aspect of Constantinople's claim to holiness, was the sheer number of churches and monasteries contained within its walls, described by one visitor as being 'infinite in number'.[2] Whereas in a western European medieval city the skyline would have been dominated by towers or spires, in Constantinople it was the wide domes with their surmounting crosses that would have spread across

84

the cityscape and which would have been one of the most striking features of the place when viewed for the first time.

This abundance of ecclesiastical buildings was partly the legacy of the great Justinian, who had built the two largest and most prominent, the cathedral of Hagia Sophia and the five-domed church of the Holy Apostles, as well as numerous smaller churches. It was also the result of a spate of church building and restoration that had begun in the ninth century, when the Byzantine empire recovered from its time of troubles. That process of construction and renovation had continued ever since, as each new emperor sought to leave his mark with some magnificent church or monastery. His successors in their turn exerted themselves to outdo him. Michael III (842–67) began the trend in a modest way when he reconstructed and redecorated the chapel of the Holy Virgin of Pharos, where the imperial collection of relics was kept.[3] Basil I (867–86) went further and ordered the building of a completely new church, the five-domed Nea Ekklesia within the precincts of the Great Palace which was inaugurated in 881. Its interior, in the words of a contemporary, gleamed 'with gold and is resplendent with beautiful images as with stars'.[4] Romanos I Lekapenos (920–44) built the monastery of the Myrelaion as the burial place for himself and his family, probably because as a usurper who had sidelined the legitimate emperor he deemed it impolitic to assign himself a place in the mausoleum of the Holy Apostles. John I Tzimiskes (969–76) rebuilt the church of Christ the Saviour at the Brazen Gate of the Great Palace because he disliked the original cramped and inconvenient building.[5]

A further impetus for new building came in 1028 when, with the burial of Constantine VIII, there was no more room in the Heröon or anywhere else at the Holy Apostles for further deceased rulers.[6] The emperors thereafter vied with each other to build ever more magnificent and lavishly decorated churches and to establish new monasteries which would ultimately serve as their final resting place. Romanos III Argyros (1028–34) constructed the splendid church and monastery of the Virgin Peribleptos in the south of Constantinople, sparing no expense and 'pouring rivers of gold' into the project in an attempt to rival Hagia Sophia. He also took care to preserve his own memory by having it decorated with a mosaic depicting himself, and ultimately

85

he was buried there in a sarcophagus made of red jasper.[7] John II Komnenos (1118–43) founded the monastery of the Pantokrator, whose church was noted for its elaborate mosaic pavement and painted glass. His son, Manuel I, added to its prestige by securing a relic for it: the slab of red marble on which Christ had lain after his crucifixion. He had it shipped to Constantinople from Ephesus and, when it arrived at the harbour of Boukoleon, carried it up to the palace on his own back. After Manuel's death in 1180, the slab was used to surmount his tomb.[8] This tradition of imperial church building continued right up to 1200. Alexios III, not wanting the Angelos dynasty to lag behind in the competition, was probably responsible for the construction of the church of the Virgin Kyriotissa, close to the final section of the Aqueduct of Valens.[9]

It is very noticeable in the surviving descriptions of churches like the Nea Ekklesia, the Peribleptos and the Pantokrator that little of the expense in building them was lavished on their exteriors. Byzantine churches were, like those in medieval western Europe, constructed in the shape of a cross, but they had a square plan and lacked the long nave of Romanesque and Gothic architecture. They tended to be built of brick rather than stone and lacked the elaborate carving and tracery which graces the façades of western cathedrals.

Their most striking and costly feature was to be found on the inside, in the mosaic decoration which covered their walls and ceiling. The idea behind the decoration of Byzantine churches was that the moment that worshippers crossed the threshold, they left behind the material, everyday world and entered the Kingdom of Heaven. The square design of the church meant that they were at once surrounded and enfolded by the space: there was no long vista to a distant altar. Within that intimate space, the decorative scheme of mosaics was designed to act as a window onto the divine, conveying the people's veneration towards heaven and involving them in the metaphysical world. The effect was enhanced by following a strict pattern of iconography which divided the church into three levels. The lowest level depicted the saints, facing forward and gazing directly at the visitor, often at eyelevel. Above the saints, on the second level, on the higher walls and ceilings, were depicted selected incidents from the lives of

Christ and the Virgin Mary, particularly the Nativity, the baptism of Christ, the betrayal in the garden of Gethsemane, the crucifixion, and the death of the Virgin.

It was, however, at the third and highest level of the church that the two most important images were to be found. One was the Virgin and Child, which was always placed in the apse at the far end of the church, behind the altar, so that when the congregation were facing the priest and the altar screen or iconostasis they would also be facing the image of the Virgin and Child. The other, high up in the top of the dome, was the image of Christ Pantokrator. The word 'pantokrator' has two meanings in Greek. It can mean 'All-ruling', signifying that Christ was the ruler of all creation, but it can also mean 'All-holding'. The dome and its image stood directly over the place where the congregation were gathered. Their eyes would inevitably be drawn up to the figure in the dome, while Christ looked down, literally holding or enfolding his people, his hand lifted in blessing.[10]

To those who entered Byzantine churches, the effect of the glittering mosaics, whether viewed by flickering candlelight or lit up by the sun pouring in through the upper windows, must have been stunning. Some Russians reported that when they entered the churches of Constantinople 'we knew not whether we were in Heaven or on earth. For on earth there is no such splendour or such beauty'.[11] Visual grandeur was a major ingredient in Constantinople's credentials as a holy city.

So universal and standardized was the scheme of decoration in Byzantine churches by the year 1200 that most Byzantines probably thought that it had always been that way. After all, Christ himself had made it clear that he wanted his image to be venerated and displayed. If he had not done so, he would never have sent the image of his face, imprinted on the Mandylion, to the ruler of Edessa. The Virgin Mary likewise had sat for her portrait by St Luke, who had thus created the famous Hodgetria icon. It was therefore believed that images such as these had been venerated from the earliest days of the Christian Church.[12]

As was so often the case in Byzantium, however, such beliefs were later formulations designed to justify the current situation. The use of religious imagery in this way was, in fact, of much more recent date.

Centuries before, the empire had been split asunder by a bitter dispute over whether it was even legitimate to depict Christ and the saints at all, let alone venerate those images in churches. The dispute lasted for over a century and a half, a period remembered as that of Iconoclasm, or the breaking of the icons.

The crisis had its origin in the later seventh century, when Byzantine armies were being repeatedly defeated in the field by the Muslim Arabs. So successful had the Muslims been that they had conquered the empire's eastern provinces of Syria, Palestine and Egypt, extinguished the last Byzantine toehold in North Africa and had even started to threaten Constantinople itself. As disaster followed disaster, many Byzantines began to ask why it was that Christians were being worsted by infidels. Fearful that they were being punished for some heinous sin, these doubters sought to discover what it was that the Christians were doing wrong. At first they were very poorly informed about the new religion of Islam, but they soon came to realize that Muslims were very particular about the matter of idolatry. Images of living beings were not generally permitted in mosques, in case the worshippers were tempted to misdirect their prayers away from God alone. In Byzantium, by contrast, it had become the practice to pray to icons, or pictures of Christ, the Virgin or one of the saints. The answer seemed clear. The Byzantines had fallen into the sin of idolatry, a practice sternly outlawed by the Second Commandment.

In 717 one of these opponents of icon veneration became emperor as Leo III (717–41). After fighting off the Arab threat to Constantinople, Leo fired the first shot in the conflict to come. In the year 726 a troop of soldiers was dispatched to the Brazen Gate of the Great Palace to remove the icon of Christ that was fixed there. News of what was happening soon spread and a hostile crowd, composed mainly of women and led by a certain Theodosia, surged across the Augousteion to the rescue. They rushed for the ladder on which one of the soldiers had perched himself in order to prise off the icon and pushed it away from the wall, sending the unfortunate man hurtling to his death. Theodosia was shortly afterwards despatched by the soldier's comrades who cut her throat with a ram's horn, or so at least the later tales would have it.[13]

The violence of the reaction may have prompted Leo to move more cautiously for the rest of his reign, but under his son and successor, Constantine V (741–75), all restraint was thrown aside. A church council was convened in February 754 in the Palace of Hieria on the Asian side of the Bosporus where it was solemnly decreed that all icons were to be destroyed and the decoration of churches was to be changed so that only inanimate objects like the cross were depicted. It was not just churches that were affected by the decree. At the Milion, Constantine V ordered the removal of a series of depictions of the Ecumenical Councils of the Church and replaced them with one showing his favourite charioteer winning a race in the Hippodrome, although lionizing a sportsman might well be regarded as just another form of idolatry.[14]

Inevitably there was opposition, especially from monks, but Constantine V was not a man to be trifled with. One monk was flogged to death just for reproving the emperor, another was dragged through the streets and lynched.[15] When the protests continued, Constantine V went beyond attacking individual monks. He is supposed to have made a group of obdurate monks parade around the Hippodrome holding women by the hand, in front of a jeering crowd, and to have turned monasteries into barracks for soldiers.[16]

Yet in spite of all these measures, in the end the defenders of icon veneration, the so-called iconodules or iconophiles, won the argument and they did so by developing a sophisticated theology to justify their case. Foremost among them was John of Damascus (*c.* 665–749), a Greek who had held high office in the court of the Caliph in Damascus and later became a monk in a monastery near Jerusalem. As he lived in Arab territory, he was safe from iconoclast persecution and could write and say anything that he liked. In his three works in defence of icons, John justified their veneration on the basis of two ideas. The first was derived from Plato and the Neoplatonists: the image was a symbol and mediator. He drew a distinction between the icon itself and the person depicted on it. When you venerated an icon, that veneration was directed not to the wood of which the icon was made but to the saint who lay beyond it. The act of veneration of an icon was not, therefore, idolatry but a legitimate and praiseworthy act of worship.

In the second place, John went further and linked icon veneration to the incarnation, so that it was not just legitimate, but essential to orthodox Christian belief. Only by accepting icons could one accept the truth of the incarnation of Christ. If you denied that Christ could be depicted in wood and paint, you denied that he could be present in flesh and bone. John pointed to the transfiguration on Mount Tabor, when divine glory had shone around Jesus, and his disciples had bowed down and worshipped him. They were not worshipping the flesh and bone of which the human Christ was composed, but the Godhead which lay beyond it, and so it was with icons.[17]

These ideas ultimately won the day, and by the 780s iconoclasm was on the wane. At the Seventh Ecumenical Council at Nicaea in 787 the decrees of the Council of Hieria were reversed and the veneration of icons was declared to be legitimate and orthodox. Iconoclasm had a brief revival between 815 and 842 but thereafter died out altogether. By the year 1200, the ideas of John of Damascus were encapsulated in every church in Constantinople. Each one acted as icon, its decoration providing a conduit through which the veneration of the worshippers passed from this material world to the ultimate spiritual reality that lay beyond. It was therefore not just the beauty of the decoration of Byzantine churches that enhanced Constantinople's aura of holiness but also the theological significance attached to the depiction of Christ and the saints.

There was yet another element in Constantinople's reputation as a holy city. It was also a centre for the monastic life, possessing around 300 monasteries and convents by the year 1200.[18] One of the largest and best-known monasteries in Constantinople in 1200 was that of St John Stoudios. Dedicated to St John the Baptist, the monastery took its name from the influential senator called Stoudios who had founded it in the fifth century. It was sequestered in the extreme south-west of the city, not far from the Golden Gate, its walls enclosing a complex of buildings, orchards and fountains. As one of its monks wrote, it provided an idyllic haven of calm amidst the bustle and temptations of the city:

No barbarian looks upon my face, no woman hears my voice. For a thousand years no useless man has entered the monastery, none of the female sex has trodden its court. I dwell in a cell that is like a palace; a garden, an olive grove and a vineyard surround me. On one hand is the great city with its market places and on the other the mother of churches and the empire of the world.[19]

It was not only prayer and contemplation that went on at the Stoudite monastery. It had been a hotbed of opposition to iconoclasm under its formidable abbot Theodore of Stoudios (759–826), and during the ninth century it became a centre both of monastic reform and of manuscript production. It also had a social function, providing a hospice for the sick and for travellers.[20]

Monks and nuns played an important role in all medieval societies. Most Christians were painfully aware that they themselves fell woefully short of the standards of life laid down in the Gospels. They therefore placed their hopes for salvation in the spiritual elite of men and women who had given up the good things of this world and who had dedicated themselves to the service of God. By their virtues and prayers, it was hoped, they would act as intercessors with God for the rest of humanity. Consequently, monks were revered by all classes of society. The very wealthy and prominent established and endowed new monasteries, leaving precise instructions to the monks to pray for their souls. The less affluent made gifts of money or food, again in the hope that the monks would remember them in their prayers.

While monks and monasteries were to be found throughout the Christian world, the monastic life was practised rather differently in Constantinople and the Byzantine empire. There were no monastic orders, along the lines of the Benedictines, Dominicans or Cistercians in western Europe, all Byzantine monks following instead the rule of St Basil. Byzantine monks wore a different type of habit from the familiar western one, covering their heads with a close-fitting black cowl. Perhaps most important of all, there was not quite the same emphasis on community and enclosure as was the case in the west. Byzantine monasteries were marked by a strong streak of individualism and a tendency for monks to wander from place to place.

In many respects, a typical Byzantine monk was Symeon the New Theologian (949–1022). Born into a wealthy provincial family, Symeon lived a dissolute life in Constantinople as a young man before deciding to seek a life of holiness and entering the monastery of St John Stoudios. There he embarked on a regime of abstinence and self-denial so rigorous that it disturbed the rather self-satisfied calm of the place and caused resentment among the other monks. He was finally summoned before the abbot who demanded that Symeon tone down his ascetic lifestyle so as to fit in better with the community as a whole. In the end, Symeon lost patience with his less rigorous brethren. He quit the Stoudite monastery and went to the neighbouring house of St Mamas of Xerokerkos, a rather run down and dilapidated establishment, of which, at the age of thirty-one, he became abbot.[21]

That was not the end of his adventures. Symeon was clearly not an easy man to live with, and opposition and controversy followed him to his new home. He made it clear from the outset that he intended to be 'an abbot of most untameable zeal' and he was determined to reform St Mamas which, he said, had become a meeting place for worldly men. He got his way to start with, but he pushed his flock too far. His excessive zeal led to crisis as a group of thirty monks burst into the chapel and angrily barracked him while he was giving a sermon during matins. The strict regime that he had imposed on them had just become too much. In the face of determined opposition, Symeon resigned as abbot in 1005 and became an ordinary monk again. That did not end the controversy which seemed to follow Symeon wherever he went. He soon got involved in a theological dispute with an influential clergyman, Stephen, former Metropolitan of Nikomedia. The patriarchal synod took Stephen's side and, in January 1009, Symeon was exiled to a village on the Asian side of the Bosporus. Even there the cantankerous monk managed to get into disputes with the local peasants and he was still living outside Constantinople when he died in March 1022.[22]

Had that been all there was to Symeon's life, then he certainly would never have been regarded as a saint. He was certainly not noted for kindliness or works of charity. Indeed he rejected charity as a means of salvation and claimed that any kind of friendship or family ties were unsuitable for monks, whose only obedience should be to God, their spiritual mentor and the emperor, in that order. What marked him out were the ideas that he put forward about the role of monks as mystics. As a youth, he had been particularly struck by a passage in the mystical writer, John Klimakos, which talks of a vision of non-material light which shines beyond all fire. Inspired by Klimakos's work, Symeon urged constant prayer and contemplation which would lead to a vision of that light as a step towards the ultimate goal of 'deification' (*theosis*): a kind of sharing in the essence of God, through grace.[23] He himself experienced this vision of light, as his biographer records:

> One night, as he was praying ... he saw a light coming from above, radiating its beams from heaven upon him: a pure and immense light illuminating every-thing, creating a brilliance equal to the light of day. He too was illumined by it, and it seemed to him that the entire building, including the cell which he inhab-ited, had disappeared, passing into nothingness in the twinkling of an eye. He found himself carried up into the air, completely forgetful of his body. In this state – as he told and wrote to his intimates – he was both filled with a great happiness and overcome with hot tears.[24]

Symeon's ideas were to prove immensely influential, especially after his biography was written by his disciple Niketas Stethatos (*c*. 1005–*c*. 1090), abbot of St John Stoudios. In 1052 Symeon's body was brought back to Constantinople and re-interred in the church of the monastery of St Mamas. His tomb became famous for its ability to heal the sick, a sure sign of sanctity. A home-grown saint was yet another addition to Constantinople's credentials for holiness.[25]

Greatly as the Byzantines admired monks, they had always con-sidered that the highest spiritual calling was not that of living a com-munal life in a monastery but of the solitary hermit. Such individuals were seen as particularly holy because they went far beyond the kind of renunciation of the world that was required for entry into a monastery. Many of them performed extraordinary feats of self-denial and even self-harm which were considered to be a mark of profound sanctity. St Theodore of Sykeon (d. 613), for example, prevailed upon a local blacksmith to build him an iron cage. In this the hermit would stand in all weathers, going without food for several days at a time and wearing a heavy corselet of iron which weighed over twenty kilograms (some fifty pounds). Such self-destructive asceticism was seen as praiseworthy because it was in essence a form of martyrdom, of laying down one's life for Christ. In subsequent generations there were many who followed Theodore of Sykeon's example, such as Theodore of Koloneia, patriarch of Antioch (970–6) who wore an iron corselet beneath a hair shirt.[26]

Even the trials of St Theodore of Sykeon, however, pale into insignificance compared to those of the hermits known as stylites. These rigorous ascetics lived out their lives not in monasteries but standing on the tops of the ancient columns that were to be found in Constantinople and all over the empire. They took their inspiration from St Symeon Stylites (*c.* 386–459), a Syrian monk who spent the last forty-seven years of his life standing on a pillar near Antioch. What moved Symeon to pursue this particular method of mortifying the flesh is not entirely clear, though it may have been a way of escaping from the crowds of people who came to seek his advice and prayers, such was his reputation for holiness. If so, he did not succeed, for on one occasion more than 1,000 visitors were counted at the foot of his column. His reputation was only enhanced by the hardships he endured, exposed to the elements day and night, summer and winter. Whatever spiritual benefit it may have conferred, the prolonged standing did not do him much physical good, a malignant ulcer developing on his left foot. He must have had an iron constitution, though, as he ultimately lived to over eighty. On the night he did finally die, his body had been in an upright position for so long that it remained like that and it took some time for his acolytes to realize next morning that the great man had passed away.[27]

Symeon's fame spread throughout the empire and it was not long before someone decided to follow his example in Constantinople. Daniel the Stylite (409–93) moved from Syria to the imperial capital and stood almost continuously for thirty-three years on a column at Anaplous on the Asian side of the Bosporus. Daniel, however, faced an even greater challenge, as the climate of Constantinople was not nearly so amenable as that of Syria. On one occasion, the column very nearly blew down in a gale. During one particularly severe winter an icy wind blew down from the Black Sea with such violence that it ripped off the holy man's tunic and left him frozen stiff, his face 'hidden by ice as though it were covered by glass'. Fearing the worst, his team of disciples brought buckets of warm water with which to thaw him out. To their immense relief, Daniel opened his eyes and recounted the beautiful dreams that he had experienced. Thereafter the emperor insisted that a small shelter be erected on top of the column, overruling the hermit's protest that Symeon the Stylite had had no shelter.[28]

Stylites continued to be part of the Constantinopolitan scene in subsequent centuries. Luke the Stylite (*c.* 900–79), for example, stood for over forty years on the column of Eutropios in Chalcedon. On his death, another took his place but his vigil came to an abrupt end in 989 when a freak wave dashed the column to the ground and drowned him.[29] These ascetics continued to command the devotion of rich and poor alike. When faced with a dangerous rebellion in 1187, Emperor Isaac II Angelos summoned some stylites to the palace to pray for his survival. Maria Skleraina, mistress of Constantine IX, sent a gift of 700 gold pieces to a stylite named Lazaros (*c.* 996–1053), whose pillar was at Mount Galesion near Ephesus. Even the fishermen of Constantinople gave a tenth of their catch to Luke the Stylite in return for his blessing on their labours.[30]

Another peculiar Byzantine religious phenomenon was that of the holy fool. Perhaps as a conscious reaction to the celebrity status enjoyed by some stylites and hermits, this group sought to evade any admiration for their sanctity and hence any temptation to the sin of pride by behaving so outrageously as to attract only disgust and opprobrium. Their role model was Andrew *Salos* (the fool) who is thought to have died in about 474, although he may have been legendary and never have existed at all. Originally from the area north of the Danube, Andrew was supposedly brought to Constantinople as a slave when he was a young boy. Although his master treated him kindly, Andrew yearned to be free and so pretended that he was mad. He was therefore locked up in the church of St Anastasia which acted as a kind of lunatic asylum. During the night, Andrew was visited in a dream by St Anastasia herself who encouraged him to continue in his madness. When it was clear that no cure was forthcoming, Andrew was released after four months.

The rest of Andrew's life was spent wandering the streets of Constantinople getting into all kinds of trouble, and the surviving record reads like an uproarious slapstick farce. On one occasion Andrew relieved himself behind a tavern, provoking its owner to rush out and rain blows on him while a passer-by, who was carrying a shepherd's crook, laid into him with that as well. The hapless Andrew staggered into the middle of the road and passed out, whereupon he was run over by an ox cart. By a miracle, he got up afterwards completely unhurt. There was, of course, method in Andrew's madness, calculated as it was to highlight the vanity of this passing world. Thus when Andrew went into one of the main squares of Constantinople and saw women selling jewellery he began shouting loudly 'Chaff and dust!' He had reckoned without a local wit, however, who quipped as he passed, 'If you have chaff to sell, take it to the Anemodoulion', meaning that the wind vane was the place where all the chaff would be blown away.[31] Fool though he was, however, Andrew was recognized as a saint. His prophecies were regarded as divinely inspired and were carefully recorded.[32]

With its myriad churches and monasteries, with its hermits and saints, therefore, Constantinople was able to present itself as a holy as well as a capital city. Those two roles, however, did not sit easily together and by 1200 there was a healthy scepticism among some of the population of Constantinople. A popular saying of the time ran 'A large church and little grace', suggesting that some people at least felt that the grandiose imperial foundations and those who serviced them did not necessarily provide a window onto the divine.[33] One problem was that many of Constantinople's churches and monasteries were built and endowed by the emperor and so were intimately bound up with his wealth and power. Take, for example, one of the largest and most beautiful, the church and monastery of St George of Mangana. Its story is inseparable from that of its founder, the emperor Constantine IX Monomachos (1042–55).

Monomachos was not a Porphyrogenitos but a member of a noble Constantinopolitan family. He was lucky enough to possess both good looks and considerable wealth, but in one respect the former proved to be a disadvantage. During the 1030s Monomachos was a frequent visitor to the palace, where he charmed the empress Zoe with his conversation and wit. Zoe's second husband, Emperor Michael IV (1034–41), was less impressed and decided to rid himself of a potential threat to the throne which, after all, Michael only held by virtue of his marriage to Zoe. Constantine was arrested on a trumped-up charge and sentenced to exile on the Aegean island of Lesbos.[34]

Given the nature of Byzantine politics, one might consider Monomachos to have been lucky to escape murder or blinding. Yet to a noble Byzantine, exile from Constantinople was a fate very close to death. Well might Monomachos have uttered the words of another Byzantine noble who was forced to leave Constantinople on a diplomatic mission:

> O thrice-happy city, eye of the universe, ornament of
> the world, star shining afar, beacon of this lower world,
> would that I were within you, enjoying you to the full!
> Do not part me from your maternal bosom![35]

There was, however, one consolation for Monomachos in his dreary exile. He had been married twice but, after the death of his second wife, he was prevented from marrying again by Byzantine church law which did not permit a third marriage. He therefore took Maria Skleraina, the niece of his late wife, as a mistress, and the couple were, by all accounts, completely devoted to one another. So when Monomachos departed for Lesbos, Maria went too and used her money and possessions to ameliorate her lover's situation as much as possible.[36]

One day in the early summer of 1042, a messenger arrived from Constantinople with momentous news. Michael IV had died and his nephew and briefly reigning successor, Michael V (1041–2), had been overthrown in a popular uprising. The Empress Zoe and her sister Theodora were now in control of the Great Palace. With the news came a summons to return to Constantinople immediately. Zoe had decided that her old favourite was to become her husband, and when he reached the capital a splendid reception awaited him. A guard of honour was waiting to escort him on the final leg of his journey, and an ecstatic crowd cheered him as he rode up to the Brazen Gate of the Great Palace. The patriarch of Constantinople was soon prevailed upon to make an exception to the rule on third marriages in this particular case, and on 11 June 1042 Monomachos married Zoe and was crowned emperor as Constantine IX.[37]

After all his trials and tribulations, therefore, Constantine had finally arrived at the summit of power, the dark days of Lesbos left far behind. The moment is captured in a mosaic portrait of the imperial couple on the wall of the cathedral of Hagia Sophia. Kneeling one on either side of a seated Christ, Constantine and Zoe both wear elaborate crowns and both have halos to denote the sanctity of the office they held. Some alteration is noticeable around the heads of the figures. It is possible that Constantine's head had been substituted for that of one of his predecessors in power, Romanos III or Michael IV.[38]

Many men in this situation would simply have forgotten about Maria Skleraina who had been left behind on Lesbos. After all, the need for her was past, and even to admit to her existence could jeopardize all that had been won. Not so Constantine, as his friend and biographer, Michael Psellos, recalled:

> The emperor did not forget his beloved, even after his accession. With his physical eyes he beheld Zoe, but in his mind's eye was the image of his mistress; while he enfolded the empress in his arms, it was the other woman he clasped in the imagination of his heart.[39]

Against the urgent advice of his friends and relatives, Constantine decided to ask Zoe to recall Maria, presenting her simply as a victim of unjust punishment. Somewhat surprisingly, Zoe readily agreed. Maria was brought back to Constantinople and lodged in a modest house not far from the palace. There Constantine visited her secretly but it soon became clear that there was little need for concealment. The fact was that Zoe, now aged over sixty, considered herself much too old to be jealous. It was therefore agreed that Maria should be allowed to come and live inside the Great Palace. Nor was that all. Maria became, in effect, Constantine's second consort, taking part in official processions alongside the emperor and empress and being given a say in affairs of state. A special title was created for her, that of *Sebaste*.[40]

The cosy *ménage à trois* lasted for about two years. Then Maria fell ill, complaining of chest pains and difficulty in breathing. The doctors brought in by the emperor proved unable to help her and she died in 1044. Constantine was inconsolable and resolved to build for her a tomb that reflected the depths of his feeling for his lost love. The setting was to be the church of St George of Mangana which stood to the northern extremity of the precincts of the Great Palace and which was already renowned for possessing an important relic, the head of St George. Constantine had the existing building pulled down to make way for a magnificent new church, along with a complex of monastic buildings, including a hospital and a bath house, and extensive gardens. The cost was astronomical but the result spectacular:

> Its every detail excited the greatest admiration.
> People marvelled at the size of the church, its beauti-
> ful symmetry, the harmony of its parts, the variety
> and rhythm of its loveliness, the streams of water, the
> encircling wall, the lawns covered with flowers, the
> dewy grass always sprinkled with moisture, the shade
> under the trees ... It was as if a pilgrimage had ended,
> and here was the vision perfect and unparalleled.[41]

Inside, Constantine's church was equally striking, as a Spanish envoy who visited it some three centuries later recorded:

The main building of the church is very lofty, and it is everywhere adorned with mosaic work. There is seen here the figure of our Lord Jesus Christ as he appeared ascending into Heaven. The flooring of the church is a wonder of workmanship being flagged with slabs of porphyry and jasper in many colours, with scroll work very deftly accomplished.[42]

It was in this setting that Maria Skleraina was laid to rest. Zoe died in 1050, at an advanced age, and Constantine's last years were clouded by illness, as he suffered appallingly from gout. Michael Psellos recorded the ravages that it wrought on Constantine's once fine physique:

I myself saw his fingers, once so beautifully formed, completely altered from their natural shape, warped and twisted with hollows here and projections there, so that they were incapable of grasping anything at all. His feet were bent and his knees, crooked like the point of a man's elbow, were swollen, making it impossible for him to walk steadily or to stand upright for any length of time.[43]

He used often to go to the hospital attached to the church he had built, to seek relief.[44] Constantine died on 11 January 1055 and was buried in the church of St George of Mangana: not beside Zoe, who had made him emperor, but next to Maria Skleraina, the woman who had risked everything for him and for whom he had risked everything in return.

Thus it was that one of Constantinople's greatest and most famous churches had come into being not so much as a result of pious devotion but as a memorial to a relationship that the Church would have considered adulterous and immoral. Yet that was in many ways typical of the way things worked in Constantinople, because the Church and everyday life were so closely intertwined that the latter was bound to invade the former.

Inevitably, the Byzantine Church and its clergy, like the emperors, did not live up to the ideal. The senior ecclesiastic in Constantinople was the patriarch, an office that was held in 1200 by John X Kamateros (1198–1206). He was certainly no saint. It was an open secret that he held his position largely because he was a close relative of the empress Euphrosyne. Yet John was by no means an unworthy patriarch and seems to have taken his duties seriously enough. His main failing seems to have been an inordinate fondness for doctrinal disputation. A year before he became patriarch he had caused a furore by using the occasion of a party at a friend's house loudly to advertise his opinions on the theology of the Eucharist and by accusing anyone who disagreed with him of heresy.[45]

There had been both better and worse patriarchs than John X in the past. The nadir must have been Theophylact (933–56) who was enthroned at the age of sixteen on the insistence of his father, Emperor Romanos I Lekapenos. Not surprisingly, the young patriarch did not always have his mind on the job, being much more interested in horse breeding. He was alleged to have possessed a stable of over 2,000 horses and on one occasion broke off a church service in Hagia Sophia halfway through on receiving news that his favourite mare was giving birth.[46] At the other end of the scale was the courageous and principled Nicholas Mystikos (901–7 and 912–25) who once dared to have the doors of Hagia Sophia closed in the face of Emperor Leo VI (886–912), in protest at the emperor's marrying for a fourth time.[47]

The patriarch of Constantinople, however, was not really expected to be a saint. The job was an administrative one and involved its incumbent in the mire of Byzantine politics too much for him to rise above the things of this world. It was to the monasteries and to the hermits that the Byzantines looked for holiness. Sadly they were often disappointed.

There was one great disadvantage of attempting to pursue a pure monastic life in a great capital city. The world and its politics had the habit of breaking in, not least because monasteries were regularly used as dumping grounds for the losers in the endless power games of the Byzantine court. In 1059, for example, the monastery of St John Stoudios received a novice in the person of Emperor Isaac I Komnenos.

Isaac had just abdicated in the face of vociferous opposition to his rule and took refuge in the monastic life and spent the remainder of his life in writing and contemplation. Michael VII Doukas ended up in the same place in the spring of 1078. The emperor who dethroned Michael VII, Nikephoros III Botaneiates, was himself toppled three years later, though at least his conqueror had the goodness to send him to a different monastery, that of the Virgin Peribleptos. When asked later whether he found the sudden change in lifestyle tolerable, Nikephoros replied that he could cope with it for the most part but that he found it difficult to do without eating meat.[48]

Monasteries in the area just outside Constantinople frequently received such political prisoners. In 944, Romanos I Lekapenos was sent to a monastery on Prote, one of the Princes' Islands in the Sea of Marmara, after having been ousted from the Great Palace by his rebellious sons Stephen and Constantine. He had the satisfaction the following year of being joined by his sons, who by then had themselves become the victims of yet another palace coup. The ex-emperor is said to have met the disconsolate pair at the door with withering sarcasm:

> O happy hour that has compelled your majesties to visit my humble estate ... Here is boiled water for you, colder than the Gothic snows: here are soft beans, greenstuff and fresh cut leeks. There are no fishmongers' delicacies to cause illness; that is rather brought about by our frequent fasts. Our modest abode has no room for a large and extravagant company; but it is just large enough for your majesties who have refused to desert your father in his old age.[49]

The forcible insertion of political undesirables can hardly have been helpful to spiritual life in the monasteries. True, some of these enforced monks and nuns accepted their lot and even displayed some vocation for the monastic life. Romanos Lekapenos happily turned to hoeing the beans until his death in 948, and Michael VII went on to become bishop of Ephesus. Others, however, harboured hopes of returning to political life and in some cases they succeeded in doing just that. Empress Euphrosyne, who was banished by her husband Alexios III to the convent of Nematarea at the Black Sea end of the Bosporus in 1196, returned to Constantinople only six months later. Michael Psellos fell out of favour at court in about 1054 and took the monastic habit, a step he attributed 'partly to an innate desire which I had experienced from my earliest years ... and partly to the complete metamorphosis in political affairs'. No sooner had the emperor died, however, than he was back in the Great Palace and enjoying the favour of the new incumbent, the monastery having served its purpose as a temporary asylum.[50]

Even those who did stay put often made it clear that they had no intention of renouncing the things of this world. When Eirene, wife of Alexios I Komnenos, founded and endowed the convent of the Virgin Full of Grace (Kecharitomene), she made provision in the foundation charter that female members of her family should be allowed to join the community, perhaps as an asylum from any political reverses they might suffer. She was careful to stipulate, however, that:

> if perhaps as a result of her customary very luxurious way of life, she were not able to change to one too harsh ... she will follow the diet and the singing of psalms as far as she is able in the cell that will be given to her ... together with its lavatory and the rest of the necessary attendance that goes with this room. She will live on her own and eat more food than the usual diet of the other nuns ... and she will be permitted to have also two free women or even slaves as her servants and they must be maintained by the convent.[51]

It would seem that Eirene's daughter, Anna Comnena, was later to take advantage of this opportunity when she fell into disgrace as a result of her opposition to her brother John II. She probably made little contribution to the spiritual life of the community, railing against the solitude and devoting herself to the study of the works of Aristotle and to writing a biography of her father. Only on her deathbed did she actually become a nun.[52]

It was not just that politics invaded monastic life in Constantinople: the world of the monastery also invaded politics. Believing, as did all Byzantines, in the efficacy of the prayers of saintly monks, many emperors brought them into the palace to act as spiritual advisers or took them with them on campaign to pray for the success of the venture.[53] Their position was much the same as that of Rasputin at the court of the last Russian tsar, and like Rasputin these palace monks soon attracted an unenviable reputation. After all, even the most saintly would have been hard put to maintain quite the same standards of self-denial on being catapulted from the austerity of a monastery into the sybaritic environment of the court. They were lampooned for their luxurious lifestyle, for gorging themselves at magnificent banquets and for making free with the imperial wine cellars.[54] More seriously, they were accused of giving dubious advice to the emperor on matters about which, with their limited experience, they knew nothing, and they were widely blamed for unpopular policies and failures. Isaac II Angelos was criticized for taking too much notice of the prophecies of the Stoudite monk, Dositheos, whom he appointed as patriarch of Constantinople. On the basis of Dositheos's prophecies, in 1189 Isaac adopted an aggressive stance towards the German emperor, Frederick Barbarossa, with disastrous consequences. The Germans easily overcame the Byzantine army that was sent against them, and Isaac had to make a humiliating climbdown. Michael Psellos accused the monks who advised the empress Theodora in 1055–6 of having 'brought ruin on the whole empire'.[55]

The problem was not confined to monks in the palace, for they were everywhere in Constantinople. Not only were there large numbers of them, thanks to the proliferation of monasteries, but Byzantine abbots were never as strict as those in the west about insisting that monks remain cloistered behind high walls. Monks could be found pushing and shoving in crowds, swearing in the market, riding on horses and having affairs with women.[56] The original idea of monasticism, that monks would give up the things of this world by fleeing from cities to desert places, seemed to have been lost. No wonder that by 1200 the most prestigious monasteries had become those which were situated far away from the capital, such as those on Mount Athos in Macedonia or Mount St Auxentios in Asia Minor, remote from the temptations that abounded in Constantinople.

Disappointed in monks and monasteries, Byzantines in search of holiness might have turned to the individual hermits and holy men such as the stylites. The stylites of 1200, however, were not made of the same stern stuff as St Symeon Stylites, as one contemporary complained:

> A few great Stylites are recorded among the saints of old, sky-climbers who reached heaven by using pillars for ladders. But this generation sprouts the Stylite kind like trees in a forest, and these are not trees of life or trees of knowledge but very mean little trees indeed ...[57]

The columns used by stylites now usually had shelters on top and stairways inside by which to ascend and descend.[58] It would seem that they could not resist making use of the latter to get involved with the latest political upheaval. This was all in good tradition. The first Constantinopolitan stylite, Daniel, had come down from his column in 475 to oppose the usurper Basiliscus, but his successors seem to have made a habit of it. When Isaac I Komnenos entered Constantinople in triumph in 1057, the stylites were among the crowd that thronged the streets to cheer him.[59] Clearly by 1200, the authority of hermits had greatly waned since the days of St Symeon Stylites: they had become just another aspect of the everyday world.

There were still holy fools on the model of Andrew Salos in Constantinople in 1200, but here too there was some wariness and scepticism as to their credentials for holiness. One nobleman gave this advice in dealing with those who pretended to be fools:

> I recommend you to have pity on them and to be generous, but you should not play and laugh with them. This is no use. I have seen people laugh and play with such a person until they killed him with their pranks. No, you should neither outrage nor beat

a fool, whoever it is. Listen to him, whatever he says;
do not despise him, he may be trying to outwit you
with his folly.[60]

Such wariness no doubt stemmed from the fact that apparently extreme
forms of asceticism were often a cloak for fraudulent extortion of
money from gullible admirers. Hermits used to come into Constantinople from the countryside bearing baskets of fruit and vegetables to
'sell' in the streets. What they were really looking for was donations
and they would persuade the pious but credulous to part with two or
three gold coins for a single apple or pear. Others dealt in relics, such
as the monk Andrew, whose offerings included no less than ten hands
of St Prokopios, fifteen jaws of St Theodore, eight legs of St Nestor,
twelve arms of St Demetrius and even the beards of the babies killed
in the Massacre of the Innocents.[61] Then there were those who faked
their ascetic sufferings. One individual was reported to have walked
around Constantinople wearing, in imitation of Theodore of Sykeon,
an iron harness that apparently bit into his flesh and caused him to
bleed profusely. Naturally such mortification of the flesh attracted a
horde of admirers who showered gifts on the holy man. It turned out,
however, that this particular hermit was not suffering at all, for he had
simulated the bleeding by smearing himself with ox liver beforehand.

It was incidents like this which prompted the scholar and teacher
John Tzetzes to write sarcastically to his former servant, Demetrius
Gobinos. Gobinos had run away to the nearby city of Philippopolis
in Thrace to start a new life as a sausage maker, but Tzetzes scornfully
advised him to return to Constantinople since he would be able to
make a much better living there:

> For now, every disgusting and thrice-accursed wretch
> like you has only to put on a monastic habit, or
> hang bells from his penis or wrap fetters or chains
> round his feet, or a rope or chain round his neck – in
> short to dress himself up to look self-effacing in an
> ostentatious and highly theatrical way, and put on
> an artificial and highly calculated air of artless sim-

106

plicity. Immediately the city of Constantine showers him with honours, and the rogue is publicly feted as a saint above the Apostles, above the martyrs, and above whatever is pleasing to God. Why describe in detail the sweetmeats and delicacies and titbits, the bags of money and the privileges with which the city regales this monster? Leading ladies, and not a few men, of the highest birth, consider it a great thing to fit out their private chapels, not with icons of saintly men by the hand of some first-rate artist, but with the leg irons and fetters and chains of these accursed villains, which they obtain from them after much supplication, and then replace with others.[62]

Harsh words indeed, and a good indication that the Byzantines were not as blinkered to reality by their own myth-making as might at first be thought.

CHAPTER 6

'Two Thirds of the Wealth of this World'

Conspicuous prosperity was very much part of the Byzantine myth. Visitors to Constantinople were regularly informed by their hosts that the city was the richest in the world and that just as its inhabitants surpassed other people in wisdom, so they excelled them in wealth.[1] While some may have resented the arrogance with which this was no doubt stated, the evidence was undeniable. Foreigners were astonished by the opulence that they saw around them in Constantinople, especially the abundance of precious metals, jewels and silk.[2] The availability of such moveable wealth played an important part in Byzantine diplomacy, gold coins and costly silk garments being routinely lavished on kings, rulers and dignitaries on whom the Byzantines wanted to make an impression. Yet while the wealth of Constantinople was undeniable, what was much less apparent was where it all came from. The Byzantine attitude seems to have been that riches were simply a corollary of Constantinople's importance and holiness, something only to be expected in a city so favoured by God. There was, of course, rather more to the question than that, and a number of more down-to-earth factors seem to have lain behind the prosperity of medieval Constantinople: good organization inherited from the past, geography, wide circulation of money and, above all, trade.

Perhaps the most surprising thing about Constantinople is not so much that it flourished but that it survived at all. By medieval standards it was a huge city, with something around 375,000 inhabitants in 1200.[3] No other city in the Christian world could match it in size, but

Constantinople consequently faced a severe challenge in finding the means of feeding and watering its population. The immediate resources for doing so were not plentiful. Constantinople had only one natural source of fresh water, the small River Lykos, which entered the city by passing under the Land Walls between the Gate of St Romanos and the Gate of Adrianople. It was hardly adequate to supply all the inhabitants of such a large centre of population, and besides it tended to dry up for six months of the year. When it came to food supplies and particularly to the all-important staple, bread, up to the mid-seventh century the Byzantine emperors had been able to rely on imported corn from the province of Egypt. In 642, however, Egypt was lost to the Arabs and with it Constantinople's main source of grain. In the dark days of the later seventh century, therefore, it was probably more likely that the Byzantine capital would have been brought to its knees by starvation, rather than being taken by storm.

That the city survived was partly due to the superb infrastructure which it had inherited from the emperors of the fourth, fifth and sixth centuries. In response to the rapid growth of Constantinople's population, they had taken steps to secure the water supply by creating a network of aqueducts to carry water in from the streams and rivers of Thrace. In 368, for example, Emperor Valens (364–78) had ordered the restoration and enlargement of an aqueduct which entered through subterranean pipes near the Gate of Adrianople and then marched majestically over the rooftops to deliver water to a reservoir near the Forum of Theodosius.[4] Aware that this source could easily dry up during a drought or be physically cut during a siege, as indeed the Aqueduct of Valens was by the Avars in 626, the emperors also constructed a series of underground cisterns beneath the streets, their vaulted roofs supported by hundreds of columns to store the precious water for when it was most needed. One was the Basilika cistern, built by Justinian close to Hagia Sophia, a masterpiece of architecture covering some 9,800 square metres. Another, the cistern of Aspar, built in 459, was large enough to contain a modern football pitch.[5] Later emperors were careful to keep the aqueducts and cisterns in good repair as they knew that the survival of the city depended on them.[6]

As far as the grain supply was concerned, with the loss of Egypt the rulers of Byzantium sought out new sources of supply. All of Constantinople's hinterland of Thrace, Bulgaria, the Crimea and the lands around the Aegean was tapped and its produce shipped to the capital.[7] As in the case of water, the emperors knew the importance of ensuring that the capital was well supplied with bread, and they exempted bakers from all public service so as to ensure that nothing interrupted their vital work. They also stockpiled corn in special depots whenever an enemy army looked likely to mount a siege.[8]

Getting it wrong could be dangerous. In the late 1070s, the food supplies came under severe pressure as refugees flooded into Constantinople from Asia Minor which was rapidly being overrun by the Seljuk Turks. The chief minister, Nikephoritzes, attempted to stave off the crisis by extending state control over the corn trade, stockpiling grain in the Thracian port of Rhaidestos on the Sea of Marmara. The policy backfired when farmers proved unwilling to sell to the government at the fixed price it was offering and the shortages in Constantinople worsened. An open revolt broke out in Thrace in 1077 and the hated warehouses were burned to the ground. Nikephoritzes perished in a coup d'état the following year.[9]

Fortunately, Constantinople was not entirely dependent on corn and other foodstuffs brought in from Thrace or further afield. There were other sources of food closer to hand, notably an abundance of fish. Entire shoals of mackerel, bonito and tuna were brought to its very walls by the same currents that made Constantinople so difficult to attack by sea.[10] A large fishing fleet of over 1,000 boats was ready at all times to intercept the shoals as they migrated south from the Black Sea in winter and back north again in summer, and the fish could also be caught in fixed nets into which the current would obligingly sweep them. The owners of the boats and nets were obliged by law to land their catch on piers and beaches by the city walls and to sell directly to fishmongers who in turn sold the fish to the public at one of several markets. The price was fixed by the authorities, and the fishmongers were forbidden to sell their wares to outsiders for conveyance beyond the city walls. Only if there was a surplus which might otherwise go bad was any export permitted. The needs of the city came before all other considerations.[11]

Meat was provided by livestock that was driven into Constantinople from the surrounding area and marketed to butchers and pork merchants in the Forum of Theodosius.[12] Fruit and vegetables could be brought in from outside or grown inside the city itself. The area closest to the Land Walls was by no means entirely covered in buildings and was largely given over to orchards and market gardens. Once harvested, the crops could be preserved in hot weather by hanging them in baskets suspended over the cool waters of the underground cisterns until they were needed.[13]

Wine was imported into Constantinople in vast quantities, for it was by no means a drink reserved for the rich and was sold at officially fixed prices in taverns throughout the city. Innkeepers were obliged by law to serve full measure in vessels bearing the regulation stamp or risk having their hair and beard shaved off and being expelled from the innkeepers' guild. They were also supposed to close their premises at eight o'clock in the evening because

> if, in fact, the frequenters of these inns had a right
> of access thereto at night time after spending the day
> there, it might end that, under the influence of drink,
> they would be able to indulge in violence and rioting
> with impunity.[14]

In spite of this prohibition, disdainful observers from among the palace bureaucrats were quick to blame any disturbance on the effects of over-indulgence by the masses.[15]

Not that the courtiers or clergy themselves were averse to a good vintage. Surviving letters contain long passages praising or excoriating the wines of different regions. Michael Choniates, bishop of Athens from 1182 to 1204, poured scorn on the rough Retsina that was all he could get in his see and longed for the delicate wines of Euboea, Chios and Rhodes.[16] Among the courtiers, drinking sessions at the palace could be testing occasions and the ability to hold one's drink was an essential skill for the ambitious. Michael Psellos discerned this quality in John the Orphanotrophos, chief minister to Michael IV (1034–41):

It has often been a cause of surprise to me, when I have sat with him at banquets, to observe how a man, a slave to drink and given to ribaldry as he was, could bear the burden of power. In his cups he would carefully watch how each of his fellows behaved. Afterwards, as if he had caught them red-handed, he would submit them to questioning and examine what they had said and done in their drunken moments. They came to fear him more, therefore, when he was tipsy than when he was sober.[17]

In general, therefore, apart from brief crises such as that of the 1070s, Constantinople remained not only sufficiently well fed and watered but well enough supplied with luxury items such as wine to provide a cup for a workman in his local tavern and to satisfy the appetites of the likes of John the Orphanotrophos. All in all, it was a wonder of organization in a world where subsistence farming was the norm.

Just to say that Constantinople succeeded in feeding itself, however, does not explain its extraordinary prosperity or why it throve to the extent that it was a source of wonder and envy to neighbouring peoples. Part of the answer lies in another important factor in Constantinople's economic life which set it apart from much of the rest of the world. The Byzantine empire had the mechanism for being wealthy, that is to say it boasted a money economy where coins of all values circulated freely.

As in all medieval societies, copper coins were used in twelfth-century Constantinople for everyday transactions such as the purchase of food. One would buy ten or eleven mackerel, depending on the honesty of the vendor, while two would purchase a meal of soup and greens from a street vendor in Blachernae.[18] What marked Byzantium out from western Europe in particular, however, was the wide circulation of higher value coins, especially gold. This was another area in which the Byzantines were genuinely indebted to Constantine the Great. He had introduced a new gold coin, the *solidus* or *nomisma*, which became the standard means of exchange not only in Byzantium but in the entire Mediterranean world. By 1200, the *nomisma* had been replaced by the *hyperpyron* (plural: *hyperpyra*) which contained 20.5 carats and had been introduced by Alexios I in 1092, along with lesser denominations in electrum, billon and copper.[19]

Part of the reason for the wide circulation of these gold coins was taxation. In the Byzantine provinces, households without land paid a hearth tax, while those with land paid a combined hearth and land tax, all rendered in gold or silver, although the emperor also levied various exactions payable in kind, usually food and wine.[20] This was something that distinguished the Byzantine emperor from his counterparts elsewhere in the Christian world. In France, for example, the king drew not money from his subjects but feudal services and payments in kind. Attempts to impose a money tax in France, the 'Saladin tithe' of 1188, proved a failure because it was impossible to collect the payments in the face of entrenched opposition.[21] In Byzantium, the absolute position of the emperor meant that there was never any question of his right to tax his subjects.

It was not that taxes were any more popular in Constantinople than they have ever been anywhere else. Niketas Choniates no doubt voiced a widespread opinion in his unflattering description of the hardhearted tax collector, John of Poutze:

> He was by nature more inexorable and relentless than any man. It would have been easier to make a stone smile or laugh than to change his mind against his wishes. Even more remarkable than this, not only was he unmoved by tears, unbending before the pleas of supplicants, impervious to the lure of silver and unaffected by the enchantments of gold, but he was also inhumanly unapproachable. That which was distressing and insufferable to the men of those days was the fact that there was no clear response forthcoming from him to a petitioner's request, but he took great satisfaction in remaining silent; sometimes he would dismiss a supplicant without ever speaking to him.[22]

Unpopular and burdensome as taxes must have been, however, the necessity of paying them did ensure that everyone handled money and that high value coins like the *hyperpyron* must have circulated freely and were by no means only ever seen by the wealthy. Fishermen, for example, were allegedly able to pay one *hyperpyron* every fourteen days to the government as a tax on their boat and its catch.[23] That, and the large number of Byzantine coins which have survived from this period, suggests that a significant proportion of the population had money and so would have been able to use it as an everyday means of exchange and as a means of storing wealth.

For the Byzantine empire did have a banking system, provided by the money changers, whose stalls could be seen lining the Mese and the great squares. They would exchange gold coins for the silver and bronze ones that were needed for every day expenses, or take the silver and bronze accumulated by the shopkeepers in exchange for gold so that taxes could be paid. They also exchanged the coins brought by foreign visitors for Byzantine ones.[24] Although strictly regulated, it was a lucrative trade. One of the money changers, Kalomodios, was so wealthy that he attracted the notice of Emperor Alexios III who had him arrested on a trumped-up charge in the hope of relieving him of his money. Yet wealthy though Kalomodios was, he was not, apparently, unpopular. When news of his arrest spread, a crowd of his supporters invaded Hagia Sophia and threatened to do violence to the patriarch unless he interceded for the money changer. Knowing the power of the Constantinopolitan mob, Alexios III wisely backed down and Kalomodios was released unharmed.[25] Such spontaneous popular support for Kalomodios is suggestive. He and other money changers and bankers may well have been appreciated for the service that they provided, possibly enabling even those of relatively modest means to store what money they made in good times as a reserve against times of dearth, although specific evidence for this is lacking.

The existence of a money economy and taxation, however, were symptoms of Constantinople's wealth, rather than causes of it. There had to be other factors to ensure that money circulated widely. It is tempting to take a modern view and to assume that the Byzantines must have grown rich by making something and selling it. There is some evidence to support that view, for twelfth-century Constantinople was a centre of production. Its main products were expensive luxury goods such as soap, perfume, candles and, above all, work in precious metal and garments of silk.[26]

Yet although Constantinople produced luxury goods, that was not the source of its wealth. The fact was that the prevailing ideology meant that the Byzantines were not prepared to sell their wares to whoever produced the purchase price. To take the example of the silk industry, its manufacture and sale was a tightly controlled imperial monopoly. The export of raw silk was forbidden and that of finished goods was strictly regulated. Certain types of silk garment were simply not for sale. Foremost among them were the cloaks of deep purple whose colour came from the shells of the rare Murex mollusc, found in the waters off the Peloponnese and nearby islands. Since it took up to 12,000 shells to dye just one garment, such silks were astronomically expensive and were reserved for the use of the emperor alone. For anyone else to don such finery was tantamount to declaring their candidature for the throne and was therefore high treason. Private citizens were forbidden to manufacture purple cloth. Only officially licensed guilds had that privilege.

The restrictions did not stop there. The Byzantine authorities had drawn up a long list of types of finished garment that were reserved either for certain classes of society or for the Byzantines alone, with their export strictly forbidden. Anyone found selling them to foreigners was liable to be flogged and to have their hair shaved off. As with everything else in Byzantium, the origin of this prohibition was traced back to Constantine the Great. He had been visited, as he so frequently was, by an angel who had presented him with these particular vestments but had warned him that they should never be given to non-Romans.[27]

Behind the legend, there was a clear objective to the policy: to maintain the rarity of silk garments in neighbouring countries and thereby retain exclusive possession of a potent symbol of authority and power. That objective emerges from an incident that took place in 968. Bishop Liudprand of Cremona, the envoy of the German emperor Otto I, was about to leave Constantinople when some Byzantine officials demanded that he produce any silk garments that he had purchased during his stay:

> Those that are fit for you shall be marked with a leaden seal and left in your possession; those which are prohibited to all nations, except to us Romans, shall be taken away and their price returned ... As we surpass all other nations in wealth and wisdom, so it is right that we should surpass them in dress. Those who are unique in the grace of their virtue should also be unique in the virtue of their raiment.[28]

The rule was not completely inflexible. The harassment of Liudprand was no doubt partly motivated by annoyance at his master's attacks on Byzantine territories in Italy. He had been allowed to take out similar items on another visit to Constantinople some twenty years earlier. Other visitors to whom there was no particular objection were treated more leniently. William of Mandeville, earl of Essex who passed through Constantinople in the autumn of 1176 on his way back from a pilgrimage to Jerusalem, took away with him a number of silk cloths which he distributed among local churches when he got home. Bishop Gunther of Bamberg, who visited in 1065, seems to have acquired during his stay a fine silk tapestry depicting a mounted emperor.[29] One gets the impression, however, that the Byzantines viewed such transactions as a favour bestowed rather than as a straightforward commercial sale.

These are not the actions of a society that lived by making goods and exporting them. There were, of course, Byzantine merchants who travelled overseas to trade, particularly to Egypt. A party of them sailed to Alexandria in 1192 and returned with goods to the value of 39,000 *hyperpyra*.[30] Commercial enterprise was not, however, greatly valued in a city where service at court was regarded as the highest calling. Niketas Choniates looked disdainfully on his fellow bureaucrat Constantine Mesopotamites because of his 'aptitude for trade and his insatiable gathering in of unjust gain'. Emperor Theophilos (829–42) was horrified when he discovered that his wife had been making money by shipping goods. He ordered that both ship and cargo be burned, an action that earned him high praise from an otherwise hostile chronicler.[31] One suspects too that the Byzantines might not have been very good at commerce. A Jewish merchant was scathing about the lack of commercial acumen among some of his Byzantine counterparts that he encountered in Cairo because 'they do not distinguish between first-class and inferior goods; for every quality they pay the same price!'[32]

There was another factor that diverted the energies of the Byzantines away from commerce: the reluctance most of them felt to travel beyond the walls of the Queen of Cities. The lands beyond, even the provinces of the Byzantine empire, they regarded as hostile and barbaric. Most intimidating of all was that fearsome and uncertain element, the sea. The dangers were, of course, very real. During the 1030s, a Byzantine merchant ship on its way back from Syria was sent crashing onto the rocky coast of Asia Minor when the shank of its anchor sheared off, and it went down with its entire cargo of glass. Even a short voyage across the Sea of Marmara, like that taken by Alexios III and his retinue in late 1200, could suddenly become fraught with peril:

> At this time, a violent storm blew up suddenly, swelling the waves. The ship was lifted upright, bow over stern, and all but sank as water poured in from both sides. The sailors, thrown into confusion, dripped with sweat, and the passengers shouted for help and invoked God, and there was the sound of wailing and piercing screams.

The ship succeeded in taking shelter behind one of the Princes' Islands and then in reaching Chalcedon. From there it made the crossing to the Boukoleon harbour of the Great Palace, those on board 'recovering from their vertigo and spitting out the brine'.[33]

While anyone who ventured forth on the sea in frail wooden ships had to face these dangers, the Byzantines seem to have been particularly aware of them. Their literature abounds with sea metaphors. The emperor, for example, was always being likened to a helmsman, guiding his ship through the tempestuous swell, facing seas of troubles and waves of enemies. Such images reflected only too well the wariness and apprehension with which the Byzantines viewed the surrounding waters, as well as the reluctance they felt in venturing forth from the centre of sophistication and civilization that was their capital city.[34] Commercial enterprise on the high seas was not for them.

So the problem of Constantinople's wealth remains. Yet although the Byzantines were not a commercial people, the ultimate source of Constantinople's wealth did lie in trade. The difference was that it was a trade that was carried on by others. Once again, Constantinople's great advantage was its geographical position. Situated at the crossing point between Europe and Asia, it was an obvious entrepôt where goods from one part of the world could be exchanged for those of another. In the words of a contemporary:

> All sorts of merchants come here from the land of Babylon, from the land of Shinar, from Persia, Media, and all the sovereignty of the land of Egypt, from the land of Canaan, and from the empire of Russia, from Hungaria, Patzinakia, Khazaria, and the land of Lombardy and Sepharad. It is a busy city, and merchants come to it from every country by sea or land, and there is none like it in the world except Baghdad, the great city of Islam.[35]

These merchants gathered in the commercial sector, along the Golden Horn, the place where ships could safely be moored. Arab, Turkish and, occasionally, Jewish traders brought spices, perfume, carpets, porcelain and jewels, as well as glassware.[36] Italians, from the mercantile cities of Amalfi, Ancona, Genoa, Pisa and Venice, brought timber, gold and wool.[37] Russians, who had journeyed down the River Dnieper and across the Black Sea, brought wax, honey, amber, swords and fur, and the Bulgarians came laden with linen and honey.[38] These products were then sold at various markets throughout the city. Perfume, for example, was marketed from stalls that were set up in the Augousteion between the Milion and the Brazen Gate of the Great Palace.[39]

Having disposed of their goods, the merchants could then load up their ships with products that were in high demand in their home countries, both those brought by other foreign merchants and those produced in Constantinople itself. Silk garments were a favourite export for the Italians, who sold what they brought back from the east at two annual fairs in Pavia.[40] The rarity value placed on such products in western Europe, where there was little or no silk industry before the twelfth century, can be gauged from the fact that they were often used to adorn the tombs of major saints and rulers. When the grave of St Cuthbert (d. 687) in Durham Cathedral was opened in May 1827, the skeleton was found to be wrapped in silk vestments. Embroidered with designs of fish, birds and fruit, they are believed to be of Byzantine manufacture, placed in the coffin in homage to one of England's greatest saints. Similar precious Byzantine silks were acquired for the burial places of St Dunstan at Canterbury and St Siviard at Sens, and that of the great Frankish emperor, Charlemagne (768–814) at Aachen.[41] Byzantine silks were also highly prized in the Islamic world, which did have a silk industry of its own, suggesting not only that they were of premium quality and craftsmanship but perhaps also that the export restrictions imposed by the Byzantines had the effect of driving the price up.[42]

Silk was by no means the only commodity brought back by Italian merchants from Constantinople. It was presumably in a Venetian ship that the golden altarpiece known as the Pala d'Oro in St Mark's church reached Venice in around 1105. Manufactured in Constantinople, it is one of the supreme examples of the craft of Byzantine goldsmiths. The bronze doors of Constantinopolitan manufacture which are to be found in Rome, Amalfi, Trani and Salerno presumably arrived in the same way. Italian merchants were, however, happy to buy up all kinds of goods for export, even on one occasion a stolen icon.[43]

Given that most of this trade was conducted by foreign merchants, it might be asked how the Byzantines themselves benefited from it. They did benefit from it, and benefited very greatly. The principal way of doing so was by charging a customs duty, known as the *Kommerkion*. Unlike a modern government, the Byzantine authorities had no interest in using taxation to discourage imports and encourage exports. The

Kommerkion was levied at the rate of 10 per cent on all goods coming into or going out of the city and on all transactions in between.[44] So lucrative was the Constantinople trade that merchants could still turn a profit, in spite of such a prohibitive level of duty.

The *Kommerkion*, along with the taxation of their own subjects, was a major source of the fantastic wealth of the Byzantine emperors. It was not the only one. Basil II (976–1025), for example, is reputed to have built up a surplus of 200,000 gold pieces in the imperial treasury from the booty brought back from his successful wars against the Arabs and Bulgars.[45] Unlike conquest, however, the *Kommerkion* was regular and dependable and its proceeds must have lain behind much of the ostentatious display for which Constantinople was famous. It proba-bly funded the generous diplomatic gifts such as the purses full of gold and silver coins handed to Sigurd of Norway and his companions, and the lavish rebuilding and redecorating of Constantinople's churches and palaces. It also promoted a kind of trickle-down effect. Some of the proceeds were passed on to the courtiers and aristocrats whom the emperors invested with grandiose titles such as *Protospatharios* and *Kouropalatios*. With the title came a generous yearly stipend, pay-able in gold during Holy Week.[46] The courtiers and aristocrats in their turn provided the market for Constantinople's industries producing luxury goods, to clothe their persons in silk and adorn their houses in mosaic. Finally, the rest of the population, from money changers to innkeepers, benefited both from the presence of affluent custom-ers and from the influx of merchants as providing a ready market for their wares. There was no need to leave the great city and brave the cruel and unpredictable sea. The Byzantines could just wait at home for others to come to them.

These were the hard commercial facts that made Constantinople the wealthiest city in Christendom. Profiting from trade in this way was not just a matter of sitting back and collecting the *Kommerkion*, however. So lucrative was Constantinople's commerce that it could lead to conflict since foreign powers were often tempted to use mili-tary muscle to improve the position of their merchants. Among the first to do so were the Russians. In 907, according to one account, the prince of Kiev, Oleg, sailed down the Bosporus with a powerful fleet, destroying churches, monasteries and suburban settlements as he went. Taken by surprise, the Byzantines came to terms and on 2 September 911 concluded a commercial treaty with the Russians. In view of the success of the Russian fleet, the Byzantines were compelled to offer extremely generous terms. Russian merchants were exempted from paying the *Kommerkion* and were allotted a special lodging place in the suburban quarter of St Mamas, situated on the European shore of the Bosporus to the north of the Golden Horn. There they were to be supplied with six months' free lodging and, the treaty stipulated, baths whenever they wanted them. The wariness with which the Byzantines viewed their trading partners is reflected in another clause. The Russians were not permitted to enter Constantinople itself, except by one gate only, unarmed, and never in groups of more than fifty at a time, accompanied by an imperial officer.[47]

The 911 treaty gave the Russians far-reaching privileges that no other foreign merchant group enjoyed, but the Byzantines had no intention of letting it remain the last word on the matter. In 941, when the Russians attacked Constantinople again, they were met by a Byzantine fleet armed with Greek fire and their ships were virtually annihilated. In the aftermath, a new treaty was concluded in 944 that restored the status quo. The exemption from the *Kommerkion* was withdrawn and the Russians were specifically forbidden to buy silk fabrics that cost more than fifty gold pieces.[48] Nevertheless, it is worth noting that the Russians were not excluded altogether, in spite of their misdemeanours, for the Byzantines were only too well aware of how much they profited from the presence of foreign merchants on the Golden Horn. Another treaty made in 971 specifically provided that Russians who journeyed to Constantinople to trade should be regarded as friends, and at the end of the twelfth century they still had distinct presence in Constantinople, in an area close to the church of the Forty Martyrs.[49]

Conflict could also arise as a result of aggression from the Byzantine side, especially when the emperors tried to squeeze more profit out of Constantinople's trade than was brought in by the *Kommerkion*. When the Byzantine authorities tried to change the terms on which the Bulgars traded in Constantinople in 894 they sparked off a war which lasted for thirty-four years. In 1200, Alexios III hit on a novel way of supplementing his income. He dispatched a fleet of six ships commanded by Constantine Phrangopoulos to the Black Sea, ostensibly to salvage a shipwreck. Phrangopoulos was, in fact, a pirate who cruised the Black Sea and preyed on merchant shipping on its way to and from Constantinople. Both Byzantine and Turkish merchants fell victim to his attacks and once they got back to Constantinople they appealed to Alexios for redress. By this time, however, the emperor had already sold his cut of the loot from their vessels, so the Turkish merchants went to Konya and appealed to the Seljuk sultan, Rukn al-Din. Faced with the threat of war, Alexios backed down, distanced himself from Phrangopoulos's depredations and compensated the Turkish merchants.[50]

In spite of such conflicts, Constantinople's trade continued to flourish and by 1200 the most important group of foreign merchants was neither the Russians nor the Turks, but those from the Italian city states. They had been trading with Constantinople for centuries, making annual voyages there to sell their cargoes and then loading up with the products of the east. As the years went by they had gradually been able to improve their position and extract important concessions from the emperor, initially not by making war on him but by allying themselves with him. The first to do so were the Amalfitans who seem to have been accorded a privileged status for supporting the Byzantines in southern Italy. By the mid-tenth century they had their own commercial quarter, not in a suburban outpost as the Russians had had, but a stretch of land along the southern bank of the Golden Horn inside the walls of Constantinople. Within the quarter were shops, houses, bakeries, churches, warehouses and landing stages all for the exclusive use of this group of merchants.[51] Some decades later, the Venetians too were able to improve their position by negotiating a treaty in 992 that reduced the toll they had to pay when their ships entered the Dardanelles at Abydos, profiting perhaps by their reputation for loyalty to the Byzantine cause in Italy or from the need of the Byzantines for allies in their long struggle with the Bulgars.[52]

During the eleventh and twelfth centuries, these modest gains were greatly extended, especially in the case of the Venetians, who were able to improve their trading position by doing the Byzantines a great service. In 1081, Robert Guiscard, Norman duke of southern Italy, had launched an attack across the Adriatic against the Byzantine provinces in the Balkans and had inflicted a serious reverse on the imperial army at the battle of Dyrrachion. Desperate to stop the victorious Normans from marching on to Thessalonica and Constantinople, the Byzantine emperor, Alexios I Komnenos, sought an ally who would close the Adriatic to Norman ships and so prevent reinforcements from reaching his adversary. Venice was the obvious choice, situated as it was at the top of the Adriatic and having a strong fleet at its disposal. The Venetians were happy to help, as they probably had no desire to see both sides of the Adriatic in Norman hands. Although their fleet was badly mauled by the Normans off Corfu in the spring of 1084, they played a significant part in the campaign as Alexios first wore down the Norman army and then expelled it from the Balkans altogether.

In seeking to draw the Venetians into the conflict, Alexios had promised that 'all their desires would be satisfied'. Once the war was over, he proved as good as his word and issued a *chrysobull*, an imperial document with a gold seal, in their favour, granting them far-reaching concessions in the maritime trade with Constantinople. They were given the right to trade in nearly all ports of the empire, including the capital, free of the *Kommerkion* and other dues. They were also granted their own commercial quarter, known as the Embolo, close to that occupied by the Amalfitans in the district of Perama alongside the Golden Horn. By the mid-twelfth century, the Venetian Embolo was the largest of the Italian commercial quarters, measuring approximately half a kilometre in length and containing three landing stages and four churches where services were conducted in Latin, rather than Greek. There were also shops, taverns, warehouses and mills.[53]

Some years later, the needs of foreign policy dictated that similar concessions should be made to other Italian city states. In 1111 a treaty was made with Pisa, giving a reduction in the *Kommerkion* from 10 to 4 per cent, and a commercial quarter and a landing stage on the Golden Horn, concessions that may have been a response to an attempt by a Pisan fleet to force its way through the Dardanelles. In 1155, Manuel I Komnenos, needing support for his ambitious plans to destabilize the

Norman position in Italy, negotiated a similar agreement with Genoa, which received the same reduction in the *Kommerkion* along with a commercial compound and a wharf. Like that granted to the Pisans, it lay to the east of the Venetian Embolo, closer to the entrance to the Golden Horn.[54]

These treaties left the Italians and, particularly the Venetians, pre-eminent players in Constantinople's trade and enabled them to dominate the flow of goods in a triangle between the Byzantine capital, western Europe and Egypt. Spices, particularly pepper, cinnamon and saffron, almonds, raisins and cochineal, were shipped out of the empire while timber, iron, copper and textiles were brought in.[55]

It might be thought that for so much of the empire's trade to have been in the hands of foreigners who were not paying the full *Kommerkion* could hardly have been beneficial in the long run, since the Byzantine emperors had granted away one of their major sources of income. The loss was probably not as drastic as it might at first sound. The Byzantine government took care to recoup any shortfall by making sure that the full *Kommerkion* was charged on any Byzantines or foreigners who traded with the Venetians in Constantinople. Moreover, it would seem that some of the more generous provisions of these treaties were not always implemented in practice.[56]

Nevertheless, it is clear that the Byzantine government regarded all these concessions as temporary measures, which could be withdrawn once the empire was in a stronger position and no longer had any need of these Italian allies, in much the same way as the treaty with the Russians had been renegotiated from a position of strength. The moment seemed to have arrived when John II Komnenos succeeded Alexios I in 1118. The Venetians, who had the most far-reaching privileges, were the obvious target and so when a Venetian embassy arrived to request a renewal of the treaty of 1082, John refused outright. Venice, however, was not prepared to sit back and accept the loss of its privileged status and showed itself as ready to resort to force as the Russians had. In August 1122, a fleet of more than 100 ships set out down the Adriatic, attacking the Byzantine island of Corfu on the way. After spending some time off the Syrian coast fighting the Egyptian navy, the fleet returned to Byzantine waters in 1125, ravaging the islands of Rhodes, Chios, Kos, Lesbos, Samos and Andros before sailing back to Venice. Clearly, the Venetians were a power to be reckoned with, and John II, in the face of this display of naval might, had no option but to give way and to restore the original commercial privileges in a treaty of 1126.[57]

Another attempt to rein in Venetian privileges was made in March 1171, when Manuel I Komnenos secretly brought troops into Constantinople and suddenly ordered the arrest of all Venetians in the city and the confiscation of their goods. The same fate was visited on those Venetians in provincial towns, it having been arranged beforehand that the authorities there were to strike simultaneously so that no warning arrived from elsewhere. In the small port of Almyros, however, the coup was bungled and some twenty ships which had been in the harbour were able to escape the net. Sailing back to their own city, they raised the alarm, prompting a near-riot as the people of Venice clamoured for revenge. A fleet of 140 vessels was hastily constructed in less than four months and set out for Constantinople. This time, however, the Byzantines were lucky. The Venetians reached as far as the island of Chios, but while they were there plague broke out on board their ships. Over 1,000 people died within the first few days of the epidemic and attempts to shake it off by sailing from island to island were unsuccessful. The Venetians had no option but to turn back. Manuel I's gamble had paid off and the privileges enjoyed by the Venetians since 1082, to the detriment of the Byzantine exchequer, had been brought to an end.[58]

Curiously, only a few years after the death of Manuel I in 1180, negotiations began to bring the Venetians back to Constantinople. Towards the end of 1183, the Venetians reoccupied their Embolo by the Golden Horn, and the following year a new treaty was concluded with Andronicus I, promising 1,500 gold pieces in compensation for the losses incurred in 1171. Andronicus was overthrown in 1185, but his successor, Isaac II Angelos, confirmed the agreement and specifically reissued the treaty made with Alexios I in 1082 along with all the trading privileges it contained. Similar *rapprochements* were made with the Genoese and the Pisans after their merchants were expelled from Constantinople in 1182.[59]

There were probably a number of reasons for this readiness to reinstate the Italian merchants. By 1185, the Byzantines were once more at war with the Normans of southern Italy and so were once more in need of naval support and of allies in the Italian peninsula. It is also likely that the Italians were invited back because they helped to maintain the economic prosperity of Constantinople through investment and stimulation of demand. The drain that their privileges made on the tax revenue was probably negligible by comparison.[60] There is a third possible reason, which may well have been the most important of all. By the mid-twelfth century Venetian, Pisan and Genoese merchants had come to dominate trade not only with western Europe and Egypt but also within the empire itself. They were to be found established in provincial towns such as Corinth, Dyrrachion, Thebes, Raidestos, Sparta and Almyros, from where they organized the shipping of agricultural produce such as corn, wine, cheese and oil both to Italy and to Constantinople.[61] They were therefore now playing a leading role in providing the Byzantine capital with items of everyday diet.

This was the situation inherited by Alexios III when he became emperor in 1195 and there is no indication that he planned to abandon the policy of his predecessors. As was customary, his accession to the throne brought a Venetian delegation hurrying to Constantinople, and a new treaty was signed in November 1198 which was in effect a restatement of those issued by the previous emperor. Venice received complete freedom from the *Kommerkion* whether importing or exporting goods, along with a good deal of judicial autonomy within the Embolo. In return the Venetians agreed to help the Byzantines if an attack was made on them by the ruler of southern Italy or by the emperor of the Germans.[62]

At the same time, Alexios was concerned to increase his revenues and so he could not resist testing the water every now and then. He often imposed duties on Venetians ships and cargoes in spite of the provisions of the treaty and dragged his feet in paying the outstanding compensation for the seizures of 1171. He also ostentatiously favoured one of Venice's main trading rivals, Pisa.[63] That does not mean that Alexios wanted to break with the Venetians altogether, however. For better or worse, they were part of Constantinople's economy. It was they, rather than divine favour, that kept the city a byword for wealth and luxury and kept its citizens well fed and contented. It was, perhaps, the last that was the most important consideration, for what could happen when the people of Constantinople became angry and discontented was something that no emperor wished, or dared, to contemplate.

CHAPTER 7

Democracy

The breathless accounts by visitors of the wealth and splendour of Constantinople were based, of course, on what they saw of the lives of the rich and powerful. Inevitably, it was only a tiny proportion of Constantinople's citizens that lived in such style and there was a huge gulf between them and the rest of the population. For the educated aesthetes of the palace, these people had no right to any say in how the empire should be run and were described disdainfully by the wealthy courtier Niketas Choniates as

> the stupid and ignorant inhabitants of Constantinople ...
> the sausage sellers and tanners, as well as those who
> pass the days in taverns and eke out a niggardly exis-
> tence from cobbling and with difficulty earn their
> bread from sewing.[1]

After all, they lacked the requisite education in the classics and spoke a vulgar and homely Greek that was a source of wry amusement and pained condescension to the likes of Choniates. Princess Anna Comnena, in her biography of her father, felt compelled to offer a translation of a popular song into a more archaic and 'proper' form for the benefit of her readers: everyday Byzantine Greek, the idiom that was rapidly developing into the demotic Greek heard today in Greece and Cyprus, was simply not acceptable in ruling circles.[2] That anyone who spoke like that should have any entry into the corridors of power was unthinkable. Yet once again, theory and reality were at odds. The people of Constantinople were by no means silent and downtrodden proles, helpless before the monolithic weight of imperial authority. They had a voice, and even if it did not express itself in elegant Greek it certainly made itself heard.

It is sometimes difficult to escape from the influence of the bureaucrats of the palace, who wrote the histories and letters from which most of our information about Byzantine Constantinople comes, and to catch a glimpse of the city's ordinary folk. Nevertheless, they were there. As well as the butchers, tanners, innkeepers, shoemakers and tailors mentioned by Choniates, there would also have been shopkeepers, bakers, fishermen, shipbuilders and those who lived by the myriad other trades that flourished in the great city. Then there were also the women who played an active part in the city's economy and owned the market stalls that sold everything from pies to jewellery.[3] Given the advantages of flourishing trade and a money economy, their lot in general was probably much better than that of their counterparts elsewhere in the medieval world. Those advantages should not be exaggerated, however, for Constantinople had plenty of social problems.

Perhaps first and foremost was the overcrowded state of some parts of the city, quarters that were by no means as glamorous and awe-inspiring as the Augousteion and the great forums and which were hidden away behind the façades of the magnificent palaces and churches. The most populous districts lay to the north of the Mese, between the church of the Holy Apostles and the Forum of Constantine, before they gave way to the more fashionable district of Sphorakion which occupied the area between the Forum and the Arch of the Milion. At least one visitor looked beyond the main tourist sites and noticed that

> The city itself is squalid and fetid and in many places
> harmed by permanent darkness, for the wealthy
> overshadow the streets with buildings and leave these
> dirty, dark places to the poor and to travellers ...[4]

Typical of the dwellings in Constantinople's back streets were the 'miserable and disgusting quarters' given to one visiting dignitary, who complained that they 'neither kept out the cold nor afforded shelter from the heat' and had no supply of water. Some streets and squares were covered in mud and roamed by stray dogs.[5] Here people lived in three-, four- or even five-storey tenement blocks. The scholar John Tzetzes, who lived on the first floor of such a building, complained bitterly of his sufferings in a letter. The priest and his family who lived above had numerous children and kept pigs up there with them. Quite apart from the noise, urine from the pigs and the children used to seep down into Tzetzes's room. Underneath, there was a farmer who used his rooms to store hay. Another three-storey house had a donkey mill in the basement.[6]

The authorities were aware of the problems likely to arise from houses and apartments being packed so tightly together, and had introduced building regulations to lay down the minimum space between buildings. There was supposed, for example, to be at least ten feet between houses before either householder could construct a balcony, otherwise it would ruin the other's view and cut out the sunlight.[7]

Nevertheless disputes between neighbours were common. One curious case has been recorded because it involved one of the architects of the cathedral of Hagia Sophia, Anthemius of Tralles, back in the sixth century. His neighbour, a lawyer called Zeno, constructed a balcony that spoiled the view from Anthemius's window. When the subsequent court case went against him, Anthemius plotted revenge. He took advantage of the fact that Zeno's elegant salon was built over one of Anthemius's ground floor rooms. The architect filled a number of kettles with water and ran leather pipes from them to beams of the ceiling. He then boiled the water in the kettles, causing the steam to rise up the pipes. With nowhere to escape, the steam pressed against the beams and caused them to shake violently overturning the furniture in the room above and causing Zeno and his guests to run out into the street in panic thinking that a major earthquake had struck.[8]

The overcrowding of the city had another unfortunate result. Accidents frequently occurred when crowds of people were gathered. During the 960s, panic broke out among the spectators at the Hippodrome who thought that they were about to be attacked by imperial troops. In the ensuing stampede, many people were trampled to death.[9] Apart from overcrowding, the inhabitants of Constantinople suffered from all the other problems of large cities. Crime was rife, especially in the dark and crowded quarters.[10] Prostitution flourished, one visitor primly asserting that just as Constantinople exceeded other cities in wealth, so it excelled them in vice. Various attempts had been made by the authorities to stamp it out, including the creation of a sanctuary for those who wanted to escape exploitation. It was much more common, however, for emperors to be numbered among the clients than among the rescuers of prostitutes.[11] Inevitably, even in a city renowned for its wealth, there was poverty. One well-educated but impoverished supplicant addressed repeated appeals to the emperor, begging for help in his impoverished old age:

> Send a spark from your golden rays ... so that I may be able to warm myself from the cold throughout the year ... because I am undergoing a double frost ... [T]he one that keeps blowing upon me is the bitter wind of poverty ... the other is the cold that I endure from adversity.[12]

There were physical dangers too. Fires were a regular hazard. On 25 July 1197, for example, a major conflagration broke out in the grain and oil warehouses around the Droungarios Gate in the Sea Walls, close to the Venetian quarter. It burned all night and well into the next day, creating such heat that the lead on the roofs melted and poured down like rainwater. A large swathe of the harbour area was gutted, with mansions, churches and monasteries reduced to ruins.[13] Another peril was earthquakes, such as that which occurred in the spring of 1162, causing a number of buildings to collapse. More severe was that of 25 October 989 which turned houses 'into tombs for the inhabitants' and even brought down part of the dome of Hagia Sophia.[14] All these disasters would have left many people homeless and destitute.

Some protection was afforded to better-off tradesmen and manual workers by joining a guild. At least nineteen of these are known to have existed and they covered trades from leather cutters and candle makers to bakers and innkeepers. Membership was expensive but it

131

probably brought some kind of financial protection in the event of ill fortune. Guild members were also entitled to participate in certain imperial ceremonies and processions. Indeed, they were expected to do so and could be fined for not turning up.[15]

For the many who could not afford guild membership, the hardness of everyday life would have been mitigated by some opportunity for leisure and an escape from the everyday grind. As in medieval western Europe, most holidays were religious festivals and saints' days. The great feasts of the church such as Easter Sunday and the Assumption of the Virgin (15 August) were occasions for grand imperial processions. Lesser feasts were celebrated in more homely fashion, the Ascension of the Prophet Elijah on 20 July being marked by the staging of a miracle play.[16] There was also a host of festivals that were specific to certain localities or groups, such as the guilds who staged annual processions in honour of their patron saint. The guild of notaries, for example, had its special holiday on 25 November, the feast of the Holy Notaries, Marcian and Martyrius, two obscure individuals who were martyred by a heretical patriarch in 351.[17]

The festivals were no doubt the excuse for a great deal of fun that had no connection whatsoever with the religious ceremonies. Moreover, curious though it may seem in such an overtly Christian society, there were many festivals that had no link whatsoever with the Church and which probably had their origins in pagan times. There was, for example, the feast of Agatha, which was celebrated only by female weavers with singing, dancing and processions.[18] Another festival took place around midsummer, when a series of curious rituals were enacted. People would gather privately in their homes with friends and dress the eldest daughter of the house in a wedding dress. Objects would be thrown into a vase containing sea water. The girl would then draw out some of the objects at random and predict the fate of their owners. Drinking and dancing would follow and the revellers would spill out into the summer night to jump over lighted bonfires. The Church took a dim view of this kind of thing and banned it in the 1170s, though evidently without much success, for elements of the custom still survive in Greece and the southern Balkans.[19]

The very persistence of such traditions in Byzantine Constantinople is a good indication that its people had minds of their own and did not blindly accept everything that was handed down from higher authority. On the contrary, the Constantinopolitan mob was a fearsome and dangerous phenomenon which regularly made its feelings known. With such a large population concentrated so tightly in an urban setting, news, ideas and resentments could spread very quickly and a large crowd be gathered in no time at all. The dangers of popular unrest were ever present and the tiniest spark could ignite a serious conflagration.

One recurring source of tension during the twelfth century arose from Constantinople's rich ethnic mix. Thanks to its political and commercial importance, Constantinople was thronged with pilgrims, traders and immigrants from all over the world. Apart from the Italian merchants who lived in their special compounds by the Golden Horn, there were other westerners who served as mercenary soldiers in the imperial armies, particularly Normans, English, French and Scandinavians, as well as passing pilgrims. The Byzantines tended to refer to all these western European immigrants indiscriminately as 'Latins'. There were Turkic people such as Pechenegs and Cumans who also served in the imperial armies, and a small Arab community mostly composed of merchants. There were even some Christian Africans, probably from Nubia, who came as pilgrims or served as guards in the palace.[20] Constantinople also had a significant Jewish presence, not inside the city itself but in the suburb of Galata on the other side of the Golden Horn where a community of some 2,500 souls could be found.[21]

These groups were all allowed to have their own places of worship. The westerners had their special churches in which the mass was said in Latin rather than Greek, and the Slavs had theirs where the liturgy was in Old Church Slavonic. The English had a church dedicated to St Nicholas and St Augustine of Canterbury, the Scandinavians one to St Olaf, and the Russians had their church of St Boris and St Gleb.[22] More surprisingly in this overwhelmingly Christian city there were mosques for the Arabs, one of which, known as the Mitaton, stood just outside the Sea Walls on the Golden Horn.[23] Part of the reason for the existence of the mosques was, of course, that the Byzantines had treaties with several Muslim powers, but the same concession was also accorded to the Jews, who had no outside government to protect them. There were synagogues in Galata and it was enshrined in Byzantine law that Jews were to be afforded the same protection of the law as everyone else.[24]

For the most part these different groups lived alongside each other without tension. Indeed John Tzetzes prided himself on his ability to speak to the people he met in the streets in their own languages:

> One finds me a Scythian (Pecheneg) among Scythians, Latin among Latins, and among any other tribe a member of that folk. When I embrace a Scythian I accost him in such a way: 'Good day, my lady, good day my lord: *salamalek alti, salamalek altugep*' ... To a Latin I speak in the Latin language: 'Welcome, my lord, welcome, my brother: *Bene venesti, domine, bene venesti frater*' ... So I talk with all of them in a proper and befitting way; I know the skill of the best management.[25]

There is no evidence that the populace of Constantinople resented the presence of Muslims, for example. The burning down of a mosque is recorded on one occasion but there is no sign that the Muslims were specifically being targeted, for a church was ransacked on the same occasion.[26] Perhaps the relatively small number of Arab and Turkish merchants meant that their presence went largely unnoticed.

As in other parts of the Christian world, Jews were sometimes singled out for scorn and denunciation because they were seen as enemies of Christianity and the descendants of the crucifiers of Christ. Numerous stories circulated in Byzantine literature of their supposed machinations against the true faith. There was, for example, the tale of the Jew who attacked an icon of Christ in Hagia Sophia with a knife: the icon at once spurted blood all over its assailant who was then arrested on suspicion of murder. Only when he allegedly showed his accusers the icon with the knife still in it was he believed and he subsequently converted to Christianity, along with his whole family.[27]

Consequently, the Jews in Galata often faced petty restrictions, such as not being allowed to ride on horseback, and occasional harassment from their neighbours:

> For their condition is very low and there is much hatred against them, which is fostered by the tanners, who throw out their dirty water in the streets before the doors of the Jewish houses and defile the Jews' quarter. So the Greeks hate the Jews, good and bad alike, and subject them to great oppression, and beat them in the streets and in every way treat them with rigour.[28]

There were even some examples of officially sanctioned persecution, as under Romanos I Lekapenos (920–44). There was, however, never anything in Byzantium along the lines of the savage pogroms perpetrated against the Jews in England, Germany and elsewhere in western Europe at the time of the Crusades. There even survives a letter from a Jew living in Thessalonica, the second city of the Byzantine empire, which contrasts conditions for Jews there favourably with the situation he had left behind in Egypt.[29]

When it comes to the Italian mercantile communities, particularly the Venetians, Pisans and Genoese, however, the picture is much darker. As their share of Constantinople's maritime trade had increased during the twelfth century, thanks to the treaties that their home cities had negotiated with the Byzantine emperor, so had their numbers. One contemporary estimated there to be 60,000 of them in Constantinople by 1182, an evident exaggeration but one which betrays how the Byzantines felt that the Italians were coming to proliferate in their city.[30]

There were other causes of resentment. Thanks to their treaties, the Italians enjoyed a privileged position in Constantinople's trade, and a certain amount of judicial immunity within their own commercial quarters along the Golden Horn. For example, the treaty agreed between Venice and Alexios III in 1198 allowed Venetians in Constantinople to have their case heard by Venetian judges in all cases apart from murder and riot.[31] Had the Italians been concentrated, like the Jews, in a distant suburb such as Galata these privileges might have gone unnoticed, but their enclaves were all sited along the most crowded area of Constantinople, right under the noses of the most volatile section of the city's population. Before long, dislike of the Venetians in particular was becoming widespread for reasons that were voiced by the historian John Kinnamos:

> The nation is corrupt in character, jesting and rude more than any other because it is filled with sailors' vulgarity. As they formerly offered an allied force to Emperor Alexios [I Komnenos] when that Robert [Guiscard] crossed from Italy to Dyrrachion and besieged the place, they received various recompense, and in particular a confined space in Constantinople was assigned to them ... Also on this account they alone of all the rest pay tithes on commerce to none of the Romans from it. Their immoderate enrichment from that source quickly elevated them to boastfulness. They used to treat the citizen like a slave, not merely one of the general commonality, but even one who took pride in the rank of *sebastos* ...[32]

It would be wrong, however, to see the people of Constantinople simply as narrow-minded xenophobes who were roused to fury by the wealth and success of the Italians. The situation was much more complicated than that. A major contributing factor to the volatility was the deep antagonisms that existed between the Italians themselves. All were deadly commercial rivals who were frequently at war with each other and who often carried on their battles in and around Constantinople. The Pisans and Venetians used regularly to fight in the street and their ships clashed in the Bosporus within sight of the Sea Walls.[33]

The stage was set for some very ugly intercommunal violence along the shores of the Golden Horn as the Byzantine population became involved in the fighting. The first outbreak seems to have occurred in 1162. The Pisans and Venetians had temporarily patched up their differences and banded together to mount an attack on the Genoese quarter. In this enterprise they were joined by a mob of local

Byzantines. Outnumbered and caught off-guard, the Genoese were driven out of Constantinople.[34] Only in 1170 did the Genoese return, with the blessing of the Emperor Manuel I, but almost at once the Venetians attacked them again, demolishing many of the houses within their compound. This time Manuel I took drastic action, and the recurring incidents of communal violence were probably one of the reasons behind his decision to have all the Venetian residents of Constantinople arrested in March 1171.[35]

In later decades, however, the Constantinopolitan mob ceased to participate in the quarrels of the Italians and attacked them on their own account. The worst incident took place in May 1182. Taking advantage of the political upheaval that was then going on as Andronicus Komnenos seized power, and spurred on by rumours that the Italians were planning to take over the city, a large crowd invaded the Genoese and Pisan quarters on the Golden Horn. The casualties were less than they might have been because many of the Italians had heard about what was going to happen beforehand and had fled in ships. Those left behind, however, mainly the old and the sick, were killed without mercy and there were reports of pregnant women being among the victims. Even a hospital was attacked and the patients murdered in their beds.[36]

After the Venetians, Genoese and Pisans had been compensated for their losses and brought back into the city, the emperors still had great difficulty in restraining their own citizens. In 1187 when another outbreak occurred, the emperor sent officials to defuse the situation, but an incident was averted not thanks to their efforts but to a ruse on the part of the Italians. Collecting up the bodies of some Byzantines who had been killed in a skirmish the night before, they cut their hair and dressed them in western clothes to look like Latin victims of the mob. This had a sobering effect on the crowd who decided that they had done enough damage and dispersed.[37] Nevertheless, the people of Constantinople remained an unpredictable and dangerous force that had to be handled with extreme care.

Although the unjust punishment of a thief or hatred of the Italians might push the people of Constantinople to violence, the most common cause of upheaval was resentment against the emperor or the policies that he was pursuing. For once again, theory and practice were widely at odds when it came to the role of the voiceless majority in Byzantine political life. The theory was that the emperor, God's vice-gerent, was an absolute ruler, answerable to God alone. Democracy had no part to play in this scheme of things, as Eusebius of Caesarea had made clear:

> Monarchy excels all other kinds of constitution and government. For rather do anarchy and civil war result from the alternative, a polyarchy based on equality. For which reason there is one God, not two or three or even more.[38]

In practice, the emperors knew that their power could be seriously challenged by the Constantinopolitan mob. As Choniates disapprovingly observed:

> Their indifference to the authorities was preserved as though it were an innate evil; him whom today they extol as an upright and just ruler, tomorrow they will disparage as a malefactor, thus displaying in both instances their lack of judgement and inflammable temperament.[39]

Consequently, opposition to a reigning emperor was frequently voiced. Among the courtiers, scurrilous songs and pasquinades lampooning the ruler and his consort circulated freely. Alexios I Komnenos even found some, directed at himself, scrawled on a piece of paper left in his tent while he was on campaign in the Balkans. But such activity was risky. The chances of keeping one's identity and authorship secret were slim in that closed world and discovery meant instant dismissal and exile to some wretched town far from the capital.[40]

Those outside the charmed circle of the court, on the other hand, had much less to lose and consequently nothing to fear. If a large group of people decided to vent their feeling there was, in practice, very little that the emperor could do about it. To take one example, Nikephoros II Phokas (969–76), although a successful general, was never popular in Constantinople, largely because of the heavy taxes that he levied to pay his army. On one occasion, as he rode through the streets of the city he was greeted with a chorus of yells, boos and insults. No retribution followed. Nikephoros rode on looking neither to left nor to right and put the incident down to drunken high spirits. He was not the only butt of popular resentment. The Empress Euphrosyne, wife of Alexios III Angelos, was also greeted with catcalls and jeers whenever she appeared in public, and people even taught their pet parrots to mock and mimic her. There were limits. When one woman and her daughter went so far as to hurl stones at the emperor from the roof of their house, soldiers were sent in and both were executed. In general, however, the emperors took a conciliatory line towards such behaviour, preferring to allow their subjects to get their anger off their chests. Nevertheless, Nikephoros II took the precaution of building a strong wall around the Great Palace.[41]

Nikephoros was right to take precautions, for the people of Constantinople did not restrict themselves to words in their opposition to unpopular rulers. If the emperor miscalculated and pushed his luck too far, the result could be a popular uprising. His advisers would have been able to remind him of the so-called Nika riot of January 532 when the Hippodrome factions had united in their opposition to the Emperor Justinian and had very nearly brought about his overthrow. Nothing had changed by the twelfth century, for mob violence could be sparked off by the slightest pretext. In around 1200 a riot began over the arrest and flogging of a thief. The crowd were incensed because they knew that the man had been acting on the orders of a corrupt prison governor, John Lagos, who set his charges free by night to steal and then took a cut of the proceeds. A pitched battle with fully armoured troops ensued, some rioters clambering onto the roofs and hurling down stones and tiles. The next day, all was quiet, the episode apparently having been completely forgotten, but it was another reminder of how volatile and dangerous the emperor's subjects could be.[42]

One of the most dramatic of such incidents occurred in 1042. The background to the affair was this. The emperor Constantine

VIII (1025–8) had died leaving only three daughters. The eldest, Zoe, had then married a prominent nobleman, and her husband became emperor as Romanos III Argyros (1028–34). When he accidentally drowned in the bath (an accident that some said had been engineered by his wife), Zoe married again, this time to Michael IV (1034–41). When it looked as if he too would shortly pass away, Zoe, rather than looking for a third husband, instead adopted Michael's young nephew Michael Kalaphates. On the emperor's death, Zoe's adopted son became Michael V (1041–2), the idea being that he would rule alongside, and in deference to, the legitimate empress. This was considered to be only right, given Michael V's humble origins: His father had earned his living by caulking the hulls of ships before they were launched into the Golden Horn.[43]

Within a few months, however, the headstrong Michael V had grown tired of Zoe's presence and decided to free himself of her tutelage. Aided and abetted by his uncle Constantine who held the office of Nobilissimos, he laid careful plans. Both the emperor and the Nobilissimos were well aware that their action might not go down well with all sections of Constantinople's population. There was a strong sense of loyalty to the Macedonian dynasty, from which Zoe was descended, and her sidelining might be resented. Michael therefore first tested the prevailing mood by processing publicly to Hagia Sophia on Easter Sunday. He was pleased to note a favourable reaction. Cheers greeted his appearance and silk carpets were strewn in his path. A procession to the church of the Holy Apostles the following Sunday brought forth a similar response.[44]

Convinced now of the populace's personal loyalty to him, Michael acted swiftly. Guards were sent to Zoe's room in the Great Palace. She was shorn of her hair and shipped off to a convent on the island of Prinkipo in the Sea of Marmara. The eparch or governor of the city of Constantinople, Anastasius, was despatched to the Forum of Constantine to read out a proclamation announcing the coup and promising that the people would reap great benefits from the change of regime. The announcement was greeted with stunned silence by the assembled crowd, until a single voice cried out:

> We do not want a blasphemer of the cross and a
> caulker as our emperor, but the original heir, our
> mother Zoe![45]

The cry was taken up by the whole throng and Anastasius judged it
prudent to retire from the scene with some alacrity. Michael and his
uncle had seriously miscalculated and could only look on in horror
as rioting broke out across the city. The culmination of the popular reaction is described in detail by an eyewitness, the statesman and courtier
Michael Psellos, who on 20 April 1042 was working in the Great Palace:

> I was in the outer porch, dictating some of the more
> confidential dispatches, when suddenly there assailed
> our ears a hubbub like the sound of horses' hooves
> and the hearts of most of us trembled at the sound.
> Then there came a messenger with the news that all
> the people were roused against the emperor ...

From his vantage point, Psellos had a good view of the oncoming
mob:

> Every man was armed; one clasped in his hands an axe,
> another brandished a heavy iron broadsword, another
> handled a bow, and another a spear, but the bulk of
> the mob, with some of the biggest stones in the folds
> of their clothing and holding others ready in their
> hands, ran in general disorder ... And the women –
> but how can I explain this to people who do not know
> them? I myself saw some of them, whom nobody till
> then had seen outside the women's quarters, appear-
> ing in public and shouting and beating their breasts
> and lamenting terribly at the empress's misfortune ...
> 'Where can she be', they cried, 'she who alone is noble
> of heart and alone is beautiful? Where can she be, she
> who alone of all women is free, the mistress of all the
> imperial family, the rightful heir to the empire, whose

141

father was emperor, whose grandfather was monarch
before him – yes and great-grandfather too? How was
it this low-born fellow dared to raise a hand against a
woman of such lineage?'[46]

The first target of the crowd was the mansions owned by members
of the emperor's family, all of which were reduced to rubble within
a few hours. In the palace, the emperor had realized his mistake and
had had Zoe hastily shipped back from the convent. She was taken
to the *Kathisma*, the emperor's own viewing box that overlooked the
Hippodrome, to reassure the crowd that she was unharmed, but the
stratagem did nothing to abate their fury. Instead they marched off to
find another of Constantine VIII's daughters, Theodora, and took her
off to Hagia Sophia where she was proclaimed empress.

Michael and his uncle Constantine now panicked and hurried
down to the harbour of Boukoleon where they boarded a ship. After
sailing along by the southern Sea Walls, they landed at the monastery
of St John Stoudios and took sanctuary in its church. The building was
soon surrounded by an angry crowd who threatened to pull it down
over the heads of the fugitives. At this point, however, a detachment of
soldiers arrived, accompanied by Psellos, to take control of the situation. Forcing their way through the crowd, they gained admission to
the church. Until then, wrote Psellos:

> I too had gone along with the mob, having no mod-
> erate feeling about [the Emperor Michael]. I was not
> indifferent to his treatment of the empress [Zoe], and
> a certain mild resentment against the man stirred me
> on my own account. But when I reached the sacred altar
> where he was, and saw both the refugees, one, who had
> been emperor, clinging to the Holy Table of the Word,
> and the other, the Nobilissimos, standing on the right
> of the altar, both with their clothes changed, their spirit
> gone and utterly put to shame, then there was no trace
> whatever of anger left in my heart.[47]

1. Mosaic of Constantine and Justinian, Hagia Sophia (Wayne Boucher, Cambridge2000.com)

2. Remains of the Arch of Theodosius on the site of the Forum of Theodosius
(Author's photograph)

3. The Aqueduct of Valens (Author's photograph)

4. The Basilika cistern (Author's photograph)

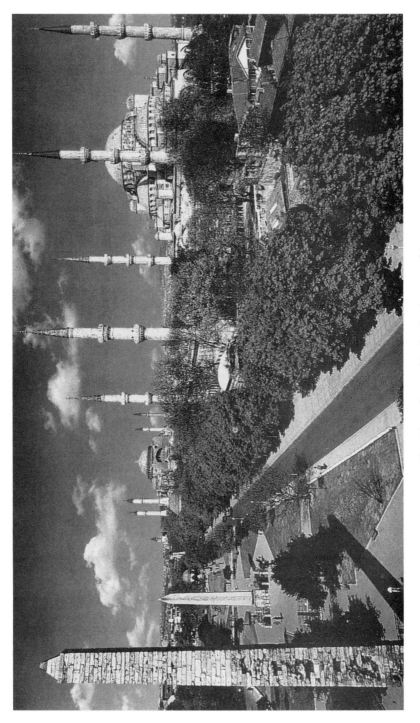

5. The Hippodrome (Author's photograph)

6. Mosaic of Constantine IX and the Empress Zoe, Hagia Sophia (Author's photograph)

7. Marble roundel of a Byzantine Emperor, Campello de Ca'angaran, Venice
(Author's photograph)

8. Gold Hyperpyron of Alexios III Angelos (A.H. Baldwin and Sons Ltd)

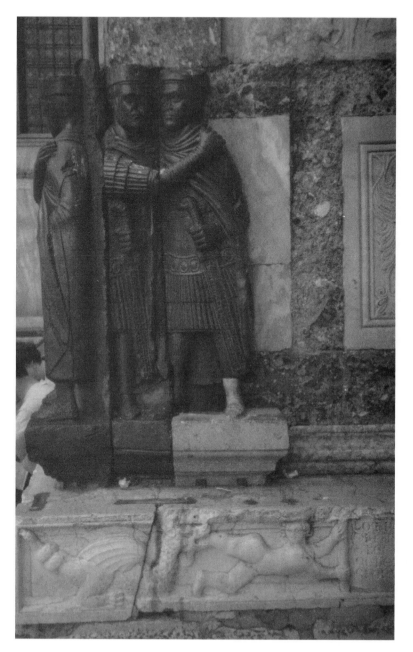

9. Porphyry sculpture of the Tetrachs, Venice (Author's photograph)

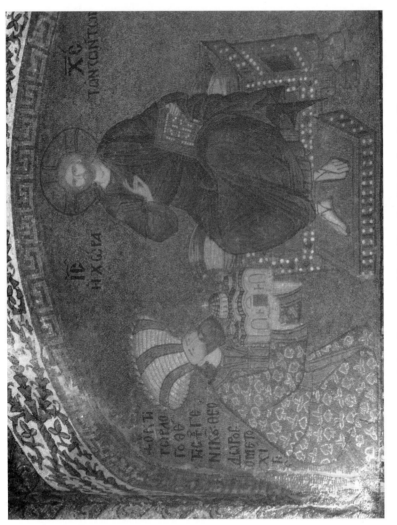

10. Mosaic of Theodore Metochites, Church of St Saviour in Chora
(Wayne Boucher, Cambridge2000.com)

By now it was getting dark and another official arrived to ask Michael and Constantine to leave the church, promising them that they would not be harmed. When they refused and clung even more tightly to the altar, the mob could be restrained no longer and burst in to drag the two men from their sanctuary. Once they were off consecrated ground, they in all probability would have been lynched had not yet another official arrived bearing a branding iron and instructions from Theodora that they were to be blinded. Psellos describes how the two men reacted when they learned their fate. Constantine, realizing that there was no escape, offered himself as the first victim, lying down on the ground with the crowd jostling for a better view. Michael, on the other hand, was overcome with terror and had to be forced to the ground and held down so that the deed could be done, possibly by the chief Varangian, Harold Hardrada. So ended Michael's five-month reign. He was despatched to a monastery to live out the rest of his life as a monk. In the battle to unthrone him, some 3,000 citizens of Constantinople had been killed.[48]

The events of 1042 were particularly dramatic but they were by no means unique. In 945 the people of Constantinople had protested vociferously to prevent the legitimate emperor of the Macedonian dynasty, Constantine VII Porphyrogenitos, great-grandfather of Zoe and Theodora, from being sidelined by the Lekapenos family.[49] Nor did the crowd always act in favour of legitimacy. In 1057, Michael VI was replaced by Isaac Komnenos when a popular revolt in Constantinople forced him to flee.[50] Such support from the people could be fickle. Andronicus I, who was welcomed into Constantinople in 1182, was lynched by a mob in the Hippodrome just three years later.[51]

In view of such salutary lessons, the emperors were well aware of the need to consider public opinion and to present themselves in a way likely to secure popular approval. One way in which they did this was by ensuring that the high claims that they made for their office and the visible symbols by which that was made manifest should be viewed by as wide an audience as possible. In spite of the wall built by Nikephoros Phokas, the Great Palace, far from being an enclosed fortress where the emperor secluded himself from his subjects, was open to the public from soon after daybreak until nine o'clock and again after three in the afternoon. There was, moreover, a covered walkway which connected the Great Palace to the *Kathisma*. Here and at other locations, he would show himself and his family to the crowd on high days and holidays, the occasion often accompanied by music. The great imperial ceremonies, such as the processions to Hagia Sophia on important feast days, were specifically designed to evoke the admiration and awe of the emperor's subjects.[52]

Placating public opinion, however, went far beyond lordly displays of imperial dignity and frequently descended to shameless bribery. One way of doing this was to distribute honorific titles, such as membership of the Senate, more widely. So, soon after his accession, Constantine X Doukas (1059–67), according to Michael Psellos, conferred senatorial status on manual workers and abolished previous distinctions of ranks. Alexios III Angelos was therefore following a well-established precedent when he bestowed prestigious titles and offices on 'the baseborn, the vulgar, the money changers and the linen merchants'. The most visual expression of an emperor trying to appeal to the mass of the population was a painted panel commissioned by Andronicus I on the gates of the church of the Forty Martyrs. The emperor was depicted, wearing not the usual imperial vestments but the costume of a labourer, and holding a sickle in his hand. Andronicus was about to launch his purge of the court aristocracy and this was perhaps a way of appealing for popular support.[53]

Titles could only be used to buy the allegiance of a small section of the populace, so for the rest, the emperors of Byzantium resorted to much the same policy as that of their Roman predecessors, that of 'bread and circuses'. Lavish entertainments were laid on during public holidays to keep the Constantinopolitans contented and occupied. The fountains in the palace courtyard were made to gush wine and gold coins were scattered to the crowd.[54]

Most effective of all were the spectacular shows organized in the Hippodrome. During the fifth and sixth centuries, the main event in the Hippodrome had been chariot races, with much of the population being divided between two supporters' clubs, the Blues and the Greens. By the twelfth century, chariot races were still being run but they took place much less frequently, about three times a year, and were much more firmly under official control, no doubt with a view to restraining the crowd trouble that had been endemic in the past.[55] Nevertheless, race days were spectacular and impressive occasions, as emerges from an account left by an Arab visitor:

> One day before the day of the assembly, a proclamation is made in the town that the emperor intends to visit the Hippodrome. The people hasten thither for the spectacle and jostle in throngs and in the morning the emperor comes with his intimates and servants, all of them dressed in red ...[56]

The whole city would be gripped by feverish excitement, a provincial visitor complaining about the noise and mayhem that broke loose as the crowd surged towards the Hippodrome. The emperor would take his seat in the *Kathisma* and the show would begin with various entertainments and displays, including wrestling contests and displays of juggling. Emperors varied the diet according to their own fancy. Nikephoros II Phokas and Constantine VIII introduced gladiatorial contests, though these bouts were not, it would seem, to the death. Andronicus I laid on tightrope walking and acrobatics. Constantine IX Monomachos, who loved nothing more than a good show, had a giraffe and an elephant paraded around the arena to the delight of the crowd.[57] When these preliminaries were over, the main business of the day began:

> The last entertainment is the horse races. Beforehand they prepare agile and trained horses, and eight horses are brought forward. They also have in readiness two big vehicles embellished with gold. To each of them four horses are harnessed, and in them two men take their places, dressed in clothes woven of gold. Then they let the horses go, urging them on until they reach the two gates, and outside this gate there is a place with idols and statues and the drivers have to wheel around

them three times in competition with one another.
Whoever wins is laden with gifts.[58]

Some of the entertainments provided in the Hippodrome were less
concerned with display or competition and more with pitiless cru-
elty. Before the chariot racing began, various species of wild animals
would sometimes be set on each other, in ascending order of fierce-
ness: dogs upon foxes, cheetahs upon antelopes, and finally lions on
bulls.[59] Animals were not the only victims, for the Hippodrome was
often the venue for high-profile public executions. In about 1104, for
example, the leader of the heretical Bogomil sect was publicly burned
there. This was a relatively rare occurrence in Byzantium, which never
reacted to heresy with the same ferocity as did western Europe in the
later Middle Ages and the Reformation. Nevertheless, the reaction of
the crowd to the spectacle was to demand that all the members of the
sect be consigned to the flames, something that the emperor declined
to do. On another occasion, the crowd took matters into their own
hands and burned a suspected sorcerer in the Hippodrome without
bothering with the formality of a trial.[60]

Not surprisingly, in view of some of these activities, the Hippodrome was not entirely approved of by the Church. St John Chrysostom, who was bishop of Constantinople between 398 and 404,
denounced the place as a 'Satanodrome' and it was considered to be an
unsuitable place for monks, clergy and women. According to a pious
fable, a monk who crept off to watch the races there was struck down
by divine wrath. Byzantine law stipulated that a woman should not go
there without the permission of her husband and for her to do so was
grounds for divorce.[61] Yet there was never any question of the emperors suspending the entertainments in the Hippodrome. They played
a vital role in providing a safety valve for the often violent passions of
one section of the population.

There was another way in which the emperors placated the people
of Constantinople that was less controversial and fitted in much better with the theory of the role of the Byzantine emperor in the world.
Basil I, we are told, 'was a generous benefactor of the poor, spending
lavish amounts of money on charity'.[62] He was not in the least unusual

146

in this, for most Byzantine emperors, if they reigned long enough, took care to undertake conspicuous works of charity. The emperor also played the leading role in any response to disasters, such as fires or earthquakes. When a fire devastated part of the northern area of Constantinople in the early 1190s, Isaac II Angelos was quick to pay out money to compensate those left homeless.[63]

There was, however, much more to this than just remedial alms-giving. The emperors were responsible for providing a series of charitable institutions which were unequalled elsewhere in the medieval Christian world and which provided social services of one kind or another to a significant proportion of the population. Alexios I Komnenos, for example, built a refuge for orphans, the disabled and former soldiers on the acropolis, one of the city's hills near the mouth of the Golden Horn, where several thousand people were fed and housed at the state's expense. There were so many beneficiaries in fact that Alexios's daughter, Anna Comnena, reckoned that if you wanted to visit every inmate it would have taken you all day from morning to evening:

> I myself saw an old woman being assisted by a young
> girl, a blind person being led by the hand by another
> man who had his sight, a man without feet making
> use of others' feet, a man who had no hands being
> aided by the hands of his friends, babies being nursed
> by foster-mothers and the paralysed being waited on
> by strong, healthy men.[64]

Alexios's son, John II, established a hospital of fifty beds attached to the monastery of the Pantokrator in 1136. The remarkable thing about this foundation was that it was not a mere hospice where the sick were made comfortable but were not actually treated. The Pantokrator hospital was specifically organized to treat and cure specific conditions such as fractures, ophthalmia, and stomach disorders. Treatment at the hospital was free to those who could not afford to pay a doctor, and the doctors that staffed it were paid by the state. It was even laid down that a certain number of female doctors were to be employed to tend women patients.[65]

Other similar institutions were scattered across the city. Isaac II attached a hospital to the church of the Forty Martyrs, while the older Hospital of St Sampson stood between the church of St Eirene and the cathedral of Hagia Sophia. The Myrelaion of Romanos I and Constantine IX's splendid monastic complex of St George in Mangana also had hospitals attached.[66] There were institutions to house the insane, the elderly and the poor, such as the *Ptochotropheion* or Hospice for Beggars, founded by Michael IV, and a hospital for lepers sequestered on the opposite side of the Golden Horn.[67]

In all this the emperors were ostensibly acting in accordance with Byzantine political theory which identified *philanthropeia* or love of mankind as one of the prime duties of the Emperor of the Romans. It was something that they had to be seen to do and hence the special rituals such as that on Maundy Thursday when the reigning emperor would visit every home for the aged in Constantinople and distribute gifts to the occupants.[68] Nevertheless, it should never be forgotten that simple self-preservation was also an element in imperial philanthropy. The fate of Michael V was a constant reminder of what could happen if the views and needs of the people of Constantinople were taken too lightly.

CHAPTER 8

The Beginning of the End

According to legend, shortly after Constantinople had been inaugurated in 330, Constantine the Great consulted a famous astrologer, Vettius Valens, to discover how long the city would last. The answer was very precise: 696 years exactly. When the year 1026 came and went with nothing untoward taking place, such was the deep streak of pessimism in the Byzantine character, like that of their ancient Greek forebears, that it seemed impossible that the wealth and strength of the great city could last for ever. A succession of prophets of doom arose to predict when it would finally cease to be and when, as a consequence, the world would come to an end, since it was impossible to conceive the latter without the former.[1]

Nevertheless, in the early years of the thirteenth century, Constantinople seemed as prosperous and secure as ever. On the wharfs and jetties along the Golden Horn, goods were unloaded and loaded, merchants bought and sold and visitors stared in wonder at the profusion of moveable wealth on display. In the domed churches the performance of the liturgical round went on serenely, watched by the silent host of mosaic saints and angels. Out on the periphery, the unconquered Land Walls stood sentinel as they had always done.

True, Alexios III Angelos had a long list of external problems to face. There could be no doubt that the power and prestige of the empire had diminished somewhat since the death of Manuel I in 1180. On the eastern frontier, the empire faced a resurgent Seljuk Turkish sultanate, based at Konya and ruled by Rukn al-Din (1196–1204), while in the west there was the perennial threat that southern Italy might be used as a launch pad for an invasion of the Byzantine Balkans. There were internal dangers too, for two outlying Byzantine provinces had broken away from the centre. Cyprus had been seized by the king of England, Richard the Lionheart, while he was on his way to crusade in the Holy Land. Although Alexios had complained bitterly to the pope, there was still no sign that he was going to get the island back. In 1186 Bulgaria had revolted and by 1200 was an independent kingdom under its formidable tsar, Kalojan (1197–1207). Much of Alexios's reign was spent fighting the Bulgars and their Vlach allies in the Balkans, and while it cannot be said that he enjoyed great success in this undertaking, none of these enemies posed any direct threat to Constantinople itself. Few can have imagined at the time that this was the city's Indian summer.

The real weakness lay elsewhere. Behind the appearance of continued strength and prosperity lay a fatal flaw. It was nothing new. On the contrary, it had been a feature of the life of the city virtually since its foundation. The weakness was that, in spite of the exalted claims made for the person and office of emperor and in spite of all attempts to establish the hereditary principle, in practice the throne was within the reach of anyone who could muster sufficient force to seize it. As a result, in the previous two centuries, Constantinople had frequently been attacked not by the armies of a foreign power but by those gathered by an ambitious general or nobleman who hoped to unseat the reigning emperor. Moreover, unlike the sieges mounted by foreign powers, these attacks sometimes succeeded, especially when there was someone on the inside to assist the rebels. It was one such twist in the interminable saga of the struggles for the Byzantine throne that was to have catastrophic repercussions and was to begin the long process by which Byzantine Constantinople was almost completely to disappear.

Even by Byzantine standards, Alexios III's reign was particularly notable for plots and conspiracies. As a usurper who had reached the throne by overthrowing and blinding his brother Isaac, Alexios had little moral authority to cow those who were considering doing the same to him. Moreover, since he came to the throne relatively late in life, he did not have a son who was a *Porphyrogenitos*, born to the wife of a reigning emperor in the purple chamber of the Great Palace, who would have been an obvious successor. That presented further incentive for rebellion as it meant that Alexios and his family seemed to have no better title to the throne than anyone else.

Alexios and his wife Euphrosyne did have three children who had been born before his accession but they were all daughters, Eirene, Eudokia and Anna. The best policy in these circumstances was to marry them off to prominent noblemen and so provide a wealthy and able successor. In the case of Eudokia, that did not prove to be an easy task. She had been married, back in the 1180s before her father's accession. Her uncle, the unfortunate Isaac II, had negotiated a diplomatic match with Stefan, one of the sons of Stefan Nemanja, the ruler of Serbia (1166–96). Stefan was later to succeed his father as Stefan the First Crowned (1196–1228), but Eudokia was not destined to reign beside him for long, for the couple fell out disastrously. Eudokia complained about her husband's amorous affairs, his gluttony and excessive drinking, while Stefan declared that his wife was scabious. He finally got rid of her in 1198 by the tried and tested means of trumping up a charge of adultery. He had Eudokia seized and deprived her of most of her clothes, and she was sent back to Constantinople dressed only in her undergarments.[2]

In spite of this disgrace, as the daughter of a reigning emperor, Eudokia should have had no difficulty in finding another husband. Unfortunately, once back in Constantinople she entered into a passionate liaison with Alexios Doukas Mourtzouphlos, one of the conspirators who had helped her father to the throne in 1195. Mourtzouphlos was said to have loved Eudokia 'since the first appearance of hair on his cheek' but he was already a married man.[3]

Alexios had more success with his other daughters, both of whom were provided with their second husbands during 1199. The eldest, Eirene, married Alexios Palaiologos, a member of an old and distinguished family, while Anna was given to the rather more obscure Theodore Laskaris. As it turned out, Anna had the better match. The aristocratic Palaiologos died only a few years after the wedding, but Theodore soon carved out a high reputation as a soldier. Shortly after his marriage, he took part in the expedition against the rebel forces of Ivanko in Philippopolis and proved himself to be able and enthusiastic.[4] In all probability, after Palaiologos's death, Alexios III would have regarded Laskaris as his likely successor.

There were plenty of people, however, who thought that they had a better claim to the throne than the upstart Laskaris did. One of these was John Komnenos Axouchos, a great-grandson of Emperor John II Komnenos, who formed a plot against Alexios III in the summer of 1200. Among his co-conspirators was the emperor's former supporter Alexios Doukas Mourtzouphlos. It is possible that Mourtzouphlos hoped that he would one day be free to marry Eudokia, in which case he too would have a claim to the throne.

On 31 July the rebels broke into Hagia Sophia where an obliging monk crowned John Komnenos as emperor. They then marched across the Hippodrome and forced their way into the Great Palace through a doorway below the *Kathisma*, the imperial box. Reaching the audience chamber, John, whose nickname was 'the Fat', sat himself down on the throne there, but it proved unequal to the burden of his weight and collapsed, sending the would-be emperor sprawling on the floor. A crowd of looters had managed to gain entry to the palace at the same time and made a spirited attempt to force entry to the chapel of the Holy Virgin of Pharos with its valuable collection of relics and its silver door hinges. While this was going on, however, Alexios III had been preparing a counter-strike from the Palace of Blachernae. A force was sent in boats along the Golden Horn, to disembark just to the north of the Great Palace. Joining up with the Varangian guard, it drove John Komnenos's supporters from the Hippodrome and then entered the palace to hunt down the usurper. Pursued through the corridors, John Komnenos was overtaken and decapitated. His supporters were soon rounded up. Mourtzouphlos was thrown into prison where he was to remain for the next three years. For the time being, any hopes on Eudokia's part that she might be allowed to marry him were dashed.[5]

Alexios III's triumph over John the Fat did not put an end to the threat to his position. There remained plenty of other candidates with a claim to the throne, not least Alexios's predecessor and brother Isaac II, who was still alive. Alexios, however, seems to have regarded Isaac as presenting little danger. The former emperor was, after all, completely blind and was securely held as a prisoner at Diplokionion on the Bosporus to the north of Constantinople. Consequently, Alexios allowed him a comfortable existence and permitted visitors to come and go. The emperor also released Isaac's son, who was also named Alexios, and allowed him to move freely around the city. Perhaps he thought that young Alexios could do no harm since he was not a *Porphyrogenitos*, having been born before Isaac became emperor.[6]

Whatever motivated Alexios's leniency, he had underestimated his brother. Among the visitors to Diplokionion were numerous western Europeans, possibly men who had found favour at court during Isaac's reign. Isaac secretly entrusted them with letters to be delivered to his daughter Eirene when they returned home. Eirene was married to Philip, duke of Swabia, the claimant to the German imperial crown, and from her distant home she established contact with her father and brother, promising them help in restoring Isaac to the throne.

In September 1201, Alexios III unwittingly provided an opportunity for them to take advantage of this offer. Another potential usurper was giving trouble in Thrace, and the emperor led his army out to deal with the threat. For some reason, he took his nephew with him and that proved to be a great mistake. Young Alexios succeeded in escaping from the army and making his way to the small port of Athyra on the Sea of Marmara where a boat was waiting to ferry him out to a Pisan merchant vessel at anchor just offshore. His disappearance was soon noticed in Alexios III's camp, but although orders were given to search ships in the Sea of Marmara, the fugitive was not apprehended. It was said that he could not be found by the officials who boarded his vessel because he had cut his hair, donned Italian clothes and so become indistinguishable from the rest of the crew. The ship was allowed to proceed and it delivered its passenger safely to the Italian port of Ancona.[7]

Young Alexios had a clear purpose in his flight to the West. He was hoping to acquire that essential prerequisite for any attempt on the Byzantine throne, an army. The best kind of army to have was one composed of western European mercenaries, the type of men whom Niketas Choniates described as 'wrought of bronze and delighting in blood'. It was with an army composed of such soldiers that Alexios

I Komnenos had seized Constantinople back in 1081, and young Alexios no doubt had such precedents in mind as he headed north from Ancona with a few followers, bound for his brother-in-law's court in Germany.[8]

He had only got as far as Verona, however, when he received news that must have seemed like an answer to his prayers. In the nearby port of Venice a huge army of French and Flemish knights was gathering waiting to embark on a fleet of Venetian ships. The leaders of this expedition, which later came to be known as the Fourth Crusade, planned to sail to Egypt to fight against the Saracens there and ultimately to recover Jerusalem. Unfortunately, their plans were being hampered by shortage of money. They were in dispute with the Venetians over the price of their passage to Egypt and were unable to raise the sum demanded. Thus Alexios was able to contact the leaders and offer to solve their difficulties. If they would first accompany him to Constantinople and help him to overthrow his uncle and restore the imprisoned Isaac II to the throne, he would provide them in return with generous financial assistance from the Byzantine treasury for their enterprise in Egypt and the Holy Land.[9] It seemed to be the perfect arrangement for both sides.

When, in June 1203, young Alexios returned to Constantinople accompanied by a Venetian fleet of some 200 ships, under the command of the doge, Enrico Dandolo, along with thousands of formidably armed western knights and foot soldiers, many Byzantines probably expected just another routine stand-off between two claimants to the Byzantine throne. To start with events lived up to that expectation.

It was usual in these cases for the rebel claimant to make some kind of appeal to the people of Constantinople in the hope that they would take his side and open the gates of the city. It had happened on occasion before and there was good reason to hope that it might work this time. After all, Alexios III was not popular and his nephew was representing the aggrieved party. Young Alexios therefore boarded a galley, was rowed across from the fleet's anchorage at Chalcedon and stood prominently on deck as the vessel was rowed up and down before the Sea Walls to show himself to the crowds that had gathered there. He was not greeted by the catcalls and jeers that were often hurled at rebel leaders but neither did he receive any encouragement. Most of the onlookers responded with stony silence, while a few shouted that they had no idea who the young man was.[10] It was a sensible reaction. At this stage of the game Alexios III, secure behind the defences of Constantinople, seemed to hold all the advantages. It did not matter who prevailed in the end, provided that one avoided being associated with the losing side.

When an appeal to the people failed, as it often did, the next step for a would-be usurper was some kind of demonstration of military might which usually fell short of an all-out assault on the city. This is what young Alexios's western allies attempted on 5 July 1203. The Venetian fleet sailed across from Chalcedon and allowed the army to make a landing close to the suburb of Galata. Once ashore, they were much more successful than they had probably hoped, capturing the Kastellion tower that secured the chain across the Golden Horn on the Galata side. The Latins were therefore able to lower the chain and bring their fleet into the Golden Horn. From there, over the next few weeks, they were able to make assaults on the Sea Walls at their weakest point, where it was possible to bring ships armed with scaling ladders close inshore. What had started as just a demonstration of resolve had delivered to the besieging army an advantage which very few of their predecessors had enjoyed.[11]

In spite of these menacing developments, the Byzantine response suggests that they still saw the episode in terms of competition for the throne and not as an assault on their city by a foreign power. The resistance that was offered to the crusaders and Venetians was at best half-hearted. One French knight who participated in the day's fighting noted that as the crusaders sailed across from Chalcedon the Byzantine army on the other side of the strait did not wait for them to arrive or contest their landing but 'fell back and did not dare wait for them'. Similarly when on 17 July Alexios III led a large army out of the Land Walls to confront the crusaders who had set up camp there, it only needed the outnumbered Frenchmen to show willing to fight for the Byzantine army to beat an ignominious retreat. Clearly, few Byzantines were willing to risk their lives in a conflict between two members of the

Angelos family, neither of whom promised to be a much better emperor than the other. The strongest resistance to the attackers, therefore, came from English and Danish mercenaries and from the Pisan traders in Constantinople who were always happy to strike at their Venetian rivals.[12]

Alexios III was only too well aware of this and as the days went by he seems to have become increasingly anxious that, now that he no longer looked the firm bet that he had done a few weeks previously, the population might turn against him and he would suffer the same fate as Michael V or Andronicus I. He may have been further depressed by his humiliation outside the Land Walls on 17 July and by the fire which broke out close to the Sea Walls on the same day. This was deliberately started by some of the attacking troops to prevent the defenders from using the houses close to the walls as hiding places, and devastated a large area by the Sea Walls towards the Palace of Blachernae.[13] Alexios now took counsel with his eldest daughter and some of the female domestics in the palace. He gathered about 1,000 pounds of gold and a collection of imperial diadems and stole out of the Palace of Blachernae by night. He rode out of Constantinople to the town of Develton on the Thracian coast of the Black Sea, where he had already made arrangements for his reception.

Since Alexios had entrusted almost no one with his plans, the discovery of his absence from Blachernae on the morning of 18 July came as a surprise and a shock not only to the courtiers, but also to most members of his own family. After the initial consternation had died down, a eunuch called Constantine Philoxenites seized the initiative. He and his supporters assumed, wrongly, that the Empress Euphrosyne and other close associates of Alexios III must be party to some kind of plot and promptly ordered the Varangian guard to arrest them. Deeming the emperor to have forfeited his throne by his flight, Philoxenites had Alexios's blinded and imprisoned brother, Isaac II, brought up from the dungeons and placed once more on the imperial throne. Isaac immediately sent word to his son Alexios, who was still with the crusade fleet on the other side of the Golden Horn, inviting him to come into the city. In August 1203, Alexios was crowned as Alexios IV, to rule as co-emperor alongside his father.

That should have been the end of the matter. Another round of contention for the imperial throne had taken place and this time Isaac II and his son Alexios IV had emerged victorious. There followed the inevitable purges. Those who had abetted Alexios III in the coup of 1195 were hunted down and hanged. Known close associates of the runaway emperor among the courtiers and bureaucrats lost their jobs. Those who had been out of favour before 18 July now found that their fortunes had dramatically reversed. Among them was Alexios Doukas Mourtzouphlos who seems to have been released from prison, his part in the events of 1195 apparently forgotten in the light of his later break with Alexios III. It was probably now that Mourtzouplos was able at last to marry Alexios III's daughter Eudokia. The new regime was not without its tensions. It soon became clear that Alexios IV was the real ruler of the empire and that Isaac II was being sidelined. Isaac resented his relegation but, blind and increasingly feeble as he was, there was little he could do. He contented himself with passing his days defaming his son to anyone who would listen and indulging in crude horseplay with some of the courtiers.[14] None of this was unusual, however. It was all part of the rhythm of Byzantine politics as they had been carried on for centuries.

Unfortunately, there was one outstanding piece of business that ensured that this particular dynastic struggle was to have tragic consequences for Constantinople. In order to secure the help of the crusaders in restoring his father to the throne, Alexios IV had rashly promised to pay them the sum of 200,000 silver marks as well as to supply provisions for every man in the army. Now that his allies had fulfilled their side of the bargain, he discovered that he would have some difficulty discharging his. The promised sum could not be raised immediately from the imperial treasury. Alexios handed over what he could and then sought to make up the shortfall by appropriating church goods, particularly the gold and silver frames of icons which he had melted down into coin.[15]

One could hardly imagine an action which would endear Alexios less to Byzantine public opinion. As word spread, resentment flared during the hot summer nights of July and August 1203 and the ever volatile Constantinopolitan mob took to the streets. It was not, however, against

Alexios IV himself that they vented their outrage but against Latins, regardless of whether they were associated with the crusading fleet or not, since they were blamed as the primary cause of Alexios's exactions. Those closest to hand were the Pisan and Amalfitan merchants who lived along the Golden Horn. Their houses and warehouses were attacked and burned to the ground and their occupants had to flee the city. The fury of the mob was even turned on inanimate objects. In one rampage the colossal bronze statue of Athena which stood at the edge of the Forum of Constantine was smashed because it was believed that the goddess's outstretched arm was beckoning the crusaders to attack the city.[16]

Further devastation was wreaked on the night of 19 August. A group of Pisans, Venetians and Frenchmen decided to make a raid across the Golden Horn on the mosque of the Mitaton, which stood just outside the Sea Walls, in the belief that the Arab merchants there had secret hoards of treasure. When the Arabs defended themselves against the onslaught, a crowd of local Byzantines came to their rescue. In the ensuing pitched battle the Latins were driven off, but they took revenge by setting alight some of the buildings round about. Fanned by a north wind, the fire spread quickly south into the city:

> The flames divided, took many different directions and then came together again, meandering like a river of fire. Porticoes collapsed, the elegant structures of the market places toppled and huge columns went up in smoke like so much brushwood. Nothing could stand before those flames. Even more extraordinary was the fact that burning embers detached themselves from this roaring and raging fire and consumed buildings at a great distance. Shooting out at intervals, the embers darted through the sky, leaving a region untouched by the blaze, then destroying it when they turned back and fell upon it.[17]

Perama and the Venetian Embolo were quickly engulfed and the fire moved south at terrifying speed, passing quite close to Hagia Sophia and crossing the Mese and the Forum of Constantine. The southern end of the

Hippodrome was severely damaged and the flames reached the far side of the city where the Sea Walls overlooked the Sea of Marmara. Only after raging unchecked for a week did the fire finally die down.[18]

Faced with such anarchy, Alexios IV became increasingly concerned for his safety, warning his western allies that his people 'hate me because of you; if you leave me, I shall lose my empire, and they will put me to death'.[19] He was right to be worried. By January 1204 the resentment of the people had reached fever pitch and they were openly criticizing the emperors Isaac II and Alexios IV in the streets. Opposition crystallized around two possible claimants to the throne. One was Nicholas Kannavos, a young man of no experience who was decidedly unwilling to don the purple. The other was Alexios Doukas Mourtzouphlos who had recently endeared himself to the people by daring to take on the crusaders in a skirmish just outside the Land Walls. It all worked itself out in typically Byzantine fashion. On the night of 27–28 January, Mourtzouphlos had Alexios IV seized and imprisoned, with Kannavos suffering the same fate shortly afterwards. Some weeks later, Alexios was strangled, after attempts to poison him proved unsuccessful. So shocking was the news of his son's overthrow that Isaac II died too, leaving Mourtzouphlos sole emperor as Alexios V.[20]

Mourtzouphlos was not destined to enjoy supreme power for long. The crusaders were not prepared to accept the overthrow of the emperor that they had placed in power, especially as they knew that the new emperor had no intention of handing over the balance of the money promised by the previous incumbent. Their fleet was still anchored menacingly in the Golden Horn and their armies ranged unopposed outside the Land Walls. Mourtzouphlos, who was popular in Constantinople precisely because he was seen as a strong man who would stand up to the Latins, had to make a show of challenging them. Shortly after seizing power, Mourtzouphlos led a sally against the foraging force led by Henry of Flanders. The attack ended in disaster when the emperor found himself deserted by his troops and was forced to flee. The Latin troops even captured an icon of the Mother of God that Mourtzouphlos's army had carried with it, a disaster which seemed to symbolize the withdrawal of the Virgin's centuries-old protection of Constantinople.[21]

With hindsight, contemporaries were forced to conclude that that was exactly what had happened, for in April 1204 the army of the Fourth Crusade was to achieve what nobody else had to date and succeeded in taking Constantinople by storm. They were able to do so because they had already obtained a crucial advantage, that of bringing their fleet into the Golden Horn. From there, they could bring their ships close inshore and attack the Sea Walls which, unlike the Land Walls, were only one layer thick: there was no moat or outer wall to provide a first line of defence. The Venetians had equipped their ships very well for the task. They had constructed bridges that were lashed to the masts of their ships and projected forwards. These provided high platforms from which troops could jump between the battlements of the Sea Walls once the vessels were beached on the fore-shore of the Golden Horn directly in front of them.

After one failed attempt, the crusaders were assisted by a strong breeze which drove their vessels onto the shore. Two of them, the *Pilgrim* and the *Paradise*, were beached directly in front of a tower, allowing a number of men to leap onto it. A number of other towers were taken in the same way, while down at beach level the French knights were able to break open several of the gates and enter the city by that route.[22]

Even at this stage, the defenders might have beaten off the attack. A determined assault on the foothold gained by the crusaders might well have driven them back into the sea. Yet the people of Constantinople seem still to have believed that all that was happening was another change of ruler. Once the crusaders had gained a foothold on the Sea Walls, resistance appears to have petered out. Mourtzouphlos rode around the city streets, desperately urging the populace to rise up to repel the attack but he met only with apathy and indifference. Those who met the Latin troops as they cautiously advanced into the city tended to welcome them. Some shouted the name of Boniface, marquis of Montferrat, one of the leaders of the army, in the belief that he was to be the next emperor; others even formed processions with icons and crosses to welcome the conquerors who were, after all, their fellow Christians. Mourtzouphlos, realizing that he no longer had any support in the struggle, followed in the footsteps of Alexios III and fled through the Golden Gate out into the Thracian countryside, taking the ex-empress Euphrosyne and his wife Eudokia with him.[23]

Only once the city was captured did it become clear what had actually happened: that Constantinople, after remaining inviolate for centuries, had finally been delivered into the hands of a hostile and ruthless foreign power. Following its capture on 12 April 1204, it was subjected to several days of pillage by the victorious troops on a scale never experienced before. Naturally the palaces of the wealthy were an obvious target and were stripped of any gold and silver objects, furniture, furs and silks.[24] More controversially, the victors, in spite of being crusaders under oath to fight for the Christian faith, treated many of Constantinople's churches in the same way. A crowd of them entered Hagia Sophia to remove the gold and silver candlesticks and ecclesiastical vessels, including a huge ciborium that weighed thousands of pounds. So numerous and heavy were these objects that they had to bring donkeys and mules into the cathedral to carry them all away. Another group went to the church of the Holy Apostles and burst into the Heroön, the mausoleum where the emperors of the past lay buried. They opened the tomb of the Emperor Justinian and found that his corpse was miraculously uncorrupted after over 600 years. Consequently, they left it alone, but they stripped off anything of value from the sarcophagus. The tomb of Romanos III in the church of the Virgin Peribleptos suffered a similar fate, as did the church of the monastery of Christ Pantokrator, the burial place of Manuel I and John II. Eyewitnesses were astonished at the sheer amount of booty that was seized, estimated by one of them to be greater than anything that had ever been taken from any city since the creation of the world.[25]

Much of what was seized in Constantinople in April 1204 was carted back to the West by returning soldiers and some of it still survives today. Some returning crusaders piously presented various precious objects that they had stolen to their local churches. When the German crusader Heinrich von Ülmen got back to Hesse in 1207 he presented the nunnery of Stuben with a silver-gilt, enamelled reliquary, designed to hold a portion of the True Cross. Made in about 964 or 965 at the command of the eunuch Basil Lekapenos the *Parakoimomenos*, it must almost certainly have come from either Hagia Sophia or the Great Palace. It is now housed in the cathedral of Limburg-an-der-Lahn. A crystal cross reliquary presented by Robert of Clari to the monastery of Corbie in Picardy was possibly taken from the chapel of the Holy Virgin of Pharos. Many similar objects found their way back to Flanders, sent back by the Flemish emperors who were to rule Constantinople after 1204.[26] The greatest haul of looted objects, however, ended up in Venice. The treasury of the church of St Mark there boasts jewelled chalices, reliquaries, enamelled book covers, gold-framed icons and silver patens, magnificent examples of Byzantine ecclesiastical gold and silverware.[27]

It was not, however, just the sack and looting of April 1204 which caused lasting damage to Byzantine Constantinople. The tragedy in this case was that the regime which now came to power in Constantinople and which ruled there for fifty-seven years, had neither the wherewithal nor the desire to repair the damage done in 1204. This was the so-called Latin Empire of Constantinople.

A peculiar hybrid of western feudalism and Byzantine political thought, the Latin empire came into being when, with the looting over, the conquerors moved to legitimize their position. They implemented a pact which had been made between the Venetians and the crusaders in March 1204, shortly before the final attack, which provided for the replacement of the Byzantine ruling hierarchy with a Latin one. An electoral council of six Venetians and six Frenchmen was to elect a new emperor from among the crusader leadership. The choice fell on Baldwin, count of Flanders, who was crowned in Hagia Sophia by Bishop Nivelon of Soissons on 16 May 1204.[28]

Baldwin I initiated a series of rulers whose hold on power was precarious even compared to their Byzantine predecessors'. The first Latin emperor reigned less than a year before being captured by Kalojan's Bulgarians in a skirmish near Adrianople in April 1205. Dragged off to a dungeon in Trnovo, according to Niketas Choniates, he suffered the indignity of having his arms and legs lopped off and being thrown into a ravine where he lingered for three days. Whether this was true or merely wishful thinking, Baldwin was never seen again by his comrades in Constantinople.[29]

When it was clear that Baldwin was not coming back, his brother Henry, who had been acting as regent, was elected emperor. His reign (1206–16) proved to be the only period during which the Latin empire enjoyed effective government, with external enemies being driven back and much being done to reconcile the population of Constantinople to Latin rule. Even a Byzantine was prepared to admit that Henry 'behaved quite graciously' to the inhabitants of the city.[30] After Henry's death, however, matters reverted to the previous chaos. His successor, his brother-in-law Peter of Courtenay, was crowned in Rome in April 1217. He then sailed across the Adriatic with the intention of marching overland to Constantinople. On the way, his army was surrounded and forced to surrender by the Greek ruler of Epiros, Theodore Angelos. Peter, like Baldwin, disappeared into captivity and was never seen again.

For the next two years, Peter's wife Yolanda held the fort as regent in Constantinople until a new emperor finally arrived in the person of her son Robert of Courtenay (1221–8). The elder son, Philip of Namur, had very wisely declined this dubious honour. The new emperor soon succeeded in undoing all the achievements of Henry I, alienating his Byzantine subjects and, thanks to inept diplomacy, uniting his external enemies. He even fell out with his own French knights, who were so outraged by his marrying a woman of humble origins that they invaded his bedchamber in the Great Palace one night and dragged her from his bed. Robert fled to Rome and although the pope persuaded him to return to Constantinople, he died on the way back. The last Latin emperor was Baldwin II (1228–61) who was only eleven years old when he succeeded so that a succession of regents ran the empire until 1237. Even when he was old enough to rule, Baldwin spent little time in Constantinople, preferring to travel west to seek favours from his relatives in France, Flanders and England.[31]

Instability and incompetence at the top, however, was only part of the problem with the Latin empire. The seeds of its weakness had been sown at the time of its inception, when the Venetians and the crusaders had made a pact dividing up the Byzantine empire between them. The treaty had only assigned to the Latin emperor a fraction of the territories that his Byzantine predecessor had enjoyed, and he had not succeeded even in subduing all of these. The rest went to the Venetians, or else was parcelled out as fiefs among western knights. As a result, the Latin emperor was unable to bring in the substantial receipts from the Land Tax that his Byzantine predecessors had enjoyed.[32]

The Byzantine emperors had had another source of income in the *Kommerkion*, the 10 per cent levy on all imports and exports into the city. That too was denied to the Latin emperors, for the city's trade was now largely, though not entirely, in the hands of the Venetians whose Embolo on the Golden Horn had been hugely expanded and who enjoyed complete immunity from the *Kommerkion*. One might have thought that the Latin emperors would nevertheless still be able to profit from Constantinople's burgeoning trade, perhaps by taxing markets in the city where imported goods were sold. Unfortunately it would seem that, as the thirteenth century progressed, Constantinople's trade went into steep decline. This may have been partly because the disappearance of the Byzantine court and bureaucracy robbed merchants of a lucrative market for luxury goods. It might also have been the result of the devastation of the area to the north of the Black Sea – which had once been a source of furs, wax and amber and a market for exported goods – when the Mongol armies of Genghis Khan swept in during 1221 and 1222. Whatever the precise reason, by 1250 Constantinople was no longer the thriving commercial metropolis that it had once been and Venetian merchants seem to have been losing interest in acquiring property there. Consequently, its rulers could no longer use the trade to fill their coffers.[33]

To make ends meet, the Latin emperors resorted to a variety of methods. Baldwin II toured the West begging for money from his relatives and mortgaging his family's ancestral lands there. When he was particularly hard up in 1248, he even pledged his son, Philip, to some Venetian merchants as security on a loan of 24,000 hyperpera. The luckless Philip had to remain in Venice as a virtual hostage for some thirteen years.[34]

There was, however, another way for the Latin emperors to raise cash which did not require a trip to western Europe and that was to milk their main asset, Constantinople, of anything of value. One of Constantinople's prime assets was relics of the saints. Several thousand of them are known to have existed, scattered throughout the numerous churches of the city. To the newly arrived Latin conquerors, especially the priests among them, these relics were the object of avid desire. Quite apart from their intrinsic spiritual value, the possession of a major relic by a church, monastery or cathedral in western Europe would bring pilgrims, and their money, flooding in. Consequently, there was no shortage of individuals ready to go to any lengths to secure such a relic in Constantinople for their home church. An English priest allegedly stole a piece of the True Cross and took it back to the priory of Bromholm in Norfolk. Bishop Garnier of Troyes sent the head of St Philip back to his home diocese, to be followed shortly after by the relics of St Helen the Virgin. Abbot Martin of Pairis purloined 'a not inconsiderable piece of St John' in addition to a number of other items.[35]

No doubt many of these relics were of dubious provenance and passed off on gullible clerics, over-eager to enhance the reputation of their home church. The Latin emperors, however, had an unrivalled source to exploit, the collection housed in the chapel of the Holy Virgin of Pharos within the Great Palace. This had remained largely intact after the city fell, although Nivelon, bishop of Soissons, one of the most senior clerics to accompany the Venetian fleet to Constantinople, helped himself to a thorn from the Crown of Thorns, a fragment of the robe of the Virgin Mary and other items which he sent back as a gift to his own diocese.[36]

It was the defeat of the Latin emperor Baldwin I at Adrianople in April 1205 which provided the catalyst for the wholesale exploitation of the Pharos relic collection. Hoping to bring help to the now beleaguered Latin regime, Nivelon of Soissons left Constantinople for the West, taking with him a number of important relics from the Pharos chapel, including the head of John the Baptist. They were probably taken either to give authority to his appeal or to be sold to raise money for troops and supplies. In the end they provided neither, nor did they ever return to Constantinople. Nivelon died when he had only got as far as Apulia in southern Italy, and in his deathbed will he arranged for the relics to be distributed among a number of churches in France. The elbow of St Stephen went to Châlons-sur-Marne, while the Baptist's head ended up in the cathedral of Soissons.[37]

The pattern was set for the future. In 1208, Henry I sent a collection of relics to western Europe to be sold. In 1237, Baldwin II pawned the Crown of Thorns and other relics of the Passion to a Venetian merchant for 13,134 hyperpera. The True Cross suffered the indignity of having bits broken off it to be sold separately, though parts of it remained in Constantinople long after the end of the Latin empire. The other famous relic from the chapel, however, the Mandylion of Edessa, seems to have disappeared without trace.[38] In this way, one of the pillars of Constantinople's reputation as a holy city and pilgrimage site was broken up and lost for ever.

The pilfering of relics and other treasures, damaging though it was to Constantinople's prestige, made little impact on the physical appearance of the city. Moreover, not everything was taken. The famous icon of the Hodegetria, which one might have expected to have been sold off with everything else, remained in Constantinople throughout the period of the Latin empire, housed in the church of the monastery of the Pantokrator.[39] More damaging as far as appearances were concerned was another of the money-making activities of the Latins. Ever since its foundation, a prominent feature of the city had been the antique bronze statues that Constantine and his successors had brought from all over the empire to beautify the new foundation. Their aesthetic qualities were, however, lost on those whom Niketas Choniates labelled 'these barbarians, haters of the beautiful'. Rather they saw them as a source of metal to be made into coins. One by one the statues were dismantled and melted down in furnaces. One of the first to go, no doubt because it was one of the largest, was the colossal statue of the goddess Hera in the Forum of Constantine, which was pulled down and broken up, a team of eight oxen being called in to drag away the enormous head. The Anemodoulion, the rather eccentric weathervane which stood in the Augousteion, suffered the same fate. The statues that lined the Hippodrome were also removed. Lysippos of Sicyon's Hercules, the Calydonian boar, statues of victorious charioteers of the past and countless other priceless masterpieces all went into the furnace.[40]

Some were spared destruction to be taken away as trophies. The four bronze horses, symbols of the chariot races that had taken place in the

Hippodrome over the centuries, were appropriated by the Venetians and shipped off to become ornaments on the façade of Saint Mark's church. A few were left in place. The serpent column from Delphi was one of them, perhaps because it served a more practical purpose as a drinking fountain, and there were some others that survived and which are attested in later centuries.[41] Nevertheless, the conquerors of 1204 largely annihilated one of the curious and striking aspects of the city within a few short years.

The ransacking of Constantinople did not end with the bronze statues. In their ceaseless search for something to sell, the Latin emperors went so far as to have the copper and lead stripped from the roofs of buildings, including those of their own residence, the Great Palace, and then to sell it for scrap. The emperors were not the only culprits here. The Latin patriarch of Constantinople, Matthew of Jesolo (1221–6), did much the same, targeting the roofs of the churches of Constantinople.[42] With their roofs gone, the churches inevitably fell into ruin. Sometimes the damage done to the churches was for liturgical rather than financial reasons. The western Church used a different liturgy and ceremonial from the Orthodox Church of the Byzantine empire, so changes were made in those churches and monasteries that were taken over by Latin clergy. In the chapel of the St Sampson Hospital the iconostasis, the screen which stood between the altar and the congregation, was taken out and according to one report used as a latrine cover for the patients.[43]

The greatest damage, however, did not come about through Latin greed or vandalism but simply as a consequence of there no longer being the resources available to maintain the enormous heritage of fine buildings. Many of them just fell into ruin through lack of routine repairs. The church of St John the Theologian in Hebdomon was in such a bad condition by 1260 that it was being used as a stable. Even the Great Palace, the residence of the Latin emperors, was in a state of decay. It had been damaged by stones hurled over the walls by Latin catapults during the sieges of 1203 and 1204 and the damage had never been made good. Inside, the mosaic decoration on the ceilings and walls became blackened with soot from the smoky lamps and fires used to light and warm the place. Even the figures on the pediments of columns somehow got smashed.[44]

By contrast, there is virtually no evidence of anything being created or built under the Latin regime. There are some surviving frescoes depicting the life of St Francis of Assisi in the church of the Virgin Kyriotissa and it would seem that Emperor Henry I ordered the building of a church in honour of an Icelandic saint, Thorlac. Some work may have been done to buttress the walls of Hagia Sophia.[45] That, however, was as far as it went.

Consequently by 1261, Constantinople was in a sorry state, 'a plain of desolation', as one later observer put it, 'full of ruins ... with houses razed to the ground and a few buildings which had survived the great fire'. The damage caused by the three fires which had raged in the city during 1203 and 1204 had largely been left. One contemporary reckoned that more houses had burned down as a result of these fires than existed in the whole of France, and even a sober modern commentator has estimated that between one-third and one-sixth of the city was burned down. Hence the remark of Niketas Choniates that Constantinople had been 'laid waste by fire and blackened by soot, taken and emptied of all wealth' was still the case over fifty years after the sack.[46] Yet the city had known war, fire and depopulation in the past, particularly in the dark days of the seventh and eighth centuries, and it had recovered. Even the immense damage caused by the Nika Riot of 532 had been repaired within fifty years. There was every reason to expect that it would once more rise from the ashes.

CHAPTER 9

The Ruin of Byzantine Constantinople

While the Latins had been busy stripping Constantinople of all its moveable assets, its two runaway former rulers had had little success in staging a political comeback. Mourtzouphlos, the short-reigned Alexios V, having escaped from the stricken city with the ex-empress Euphrosyne and his wife Eudokia in April 1204, travelled through Thrace until he reached Mosynopolis. He had heard that the other refugee emperor, Alexios III Angelos, was residing in the town and hoped that he might be received favourably. After all, although the two men had had their differences in the past, Mourtzouphlos was delivering Alexios's wife and daughter safe and sound and, having married Eudokia, he could now present himself as Alexios's son-in-law.

Eudokia's father certainly extended an affable welcome to the new arrivals, but family ties stood for little in the world of Byzantine politics. Constantinople may have fallen, but the business of making and unmaking emperors went on as usual. Alexios III had no intention of allowing a rival to remain at large, and so he artfully invited Mourtzouphlos and Eudokia to refresh themselves after their long journey and take a bath. On Alexios's orders, armed men then burst into the bath house, seized Mourtzouphlos and blinded him there and then, while Eudokia cowered in one of the window bays, screaming hysterically. Since he no longer presented a threat, the now sightless Mourtzouphlos was turned out of Mosynopolis and left to wander across Thrace as best he could. Before long he was picked up by some French knights led by Thierry of Loos who took him back to Constantinople.

After some debate among Emperor Baldwin and other leaders of the Fourth Crusade as to a fitting punishment for the man who had defied them and murdered their protégé, Alexios IV, they decided to dispose of him in spectacular fashion. In October 1204, he was taken to the top of one of the highest columns in the city, that of Theodosius, and, in front of a huge crowd of onlookers, was then hurled to his death on the flagstones below.[1]

Alexios III profited little from his treachery. When he heard that a Latin army was approaching, he left Mosynopolis with Euphrosyne and Eudokia and began a series of wanderings around the former territories of his empire. Arriving in Thessalonica, the fugitives were welcomed by Margaret of Hungary, the widow of Isaac II who does not seem to have borne a grudge for Alexios's treatment of her husband. Alexios, however, was incapable of refraining from intrigue and when his plots were uncovered he and his family were told to leave Thessalonica. They moved on to Corinth where Alexios disposed of Eudokia by marrying her to Leo Sgouros, a local magnate who had set himself up as ruler of the town. From there, Alexios and Euphrosyne tried to travel to Ioannina in Epiros where a cousin of Alexios, Michael Angelos, was holding power. They very nearly did not make it. Some Latin soldiers took them prisoner on the way and they were only released when Michael Angelos paid a substantial ransom demand.

Alexios did not stay in Ioannina for long. He seems to have developed a restless urge to keep travelling in the vague hope that one day he would be restored to the Great Palace in Constantinople. He and Euphrosyne seem at one point to have travelled to Germany, perhaps in the hope of enlisting help in the way their nephew had. Finally, Alexios left Euphrosyne behind in Epiros and set off alone. The couple were never to meet again, Euphrosyne dying in the town of Arta a few years later. By that time Alexios was far away, in Konya in Asia Minor, the capital of the Seljuk Turks and residence of their sultan, Kaikosru I (1192–6, 1204–11). Alexios clearly intended to call in a favour. In the later 1190s, when Kaikosru had been ousted from power by his brother Rukn al-Din, the sultan had fled to Constantinople and had been hospitably enough received by Alexios III, though the help that he hoped to receive in toppling Rukn al-Din was not forthcoming.

Now the roles were reversed, for Kaikosru was once more settled in power in Konya and it was Alexios who was the homeless refugee.[2]

If Alexios hoped for assistance in recovering Constantinople from the Latins, he was disappointed. Kaikosru was far too cautious to strike out across the disputed lands of north-western Asia Minor to take on a foe as formidable as Henry of Flanders. Instead, he prepared to mount an attack on Alexios's son-in-law, Theodore Laskaris, whose lands bordered the sultanate of Konya to the south-west. Following the sack of Constantinople, Laskaris had escaped to Nicaea where he had set up a kind of Byzantine government in exile. In 1208, Laskaris had himself crowned emperor, thus staking his claim to the lost capital city and, by implication, negating Alexios III's title to the throne. In 1211 Alexios accompanied a Turkish army as it invaded Laskaris's territory. For a time, it looked as if the invaders were likely to prevail in a battle fought around Antioch on the Meander. At the height of the battle, however, Theodore Laskaris came face to face with Kaikosru and killed him in single combat. The Turks retreated, leaving the hapless Alexios behind. Taken prisoner, he was sent by Laskaris to a monastery at Nicaea. One can almost picture him there, forgotten and unloved, passing the long days in reflection on his own chequered career, from his stay as a refugee from the tyranny of Andronicus Komnenos at the court of Saladin, through his seizure of power and eight years as emperor to the time when he was a wanderer once more. Perhaps he even paused to consider the part he had played in bringing Constantinople to the sad situation it was now in.

Of all the Constantinopolitan elite of the period before 1204, therefore, it was Theodore Laskaris who prospered. His son-in-law and successor, John III Vatatzes (1222–54) went on to defeat the forces of the Latin empire of Constantinople at Poimamenon in 1225 and reoccupy lost imperial territories in Asia Minor and the Balkans. In the event, however, it was not the Laskaris family who were to have the honour of regaining Constantinople from the increasingly fragile Latin regime there. In 1258, a child of seven, John IV Laskaris, inherited the throne in Nicaea, a situation always fraught with danger in Byzantine politics. Within a short time, power was seized by one of the ablest and most ruthless generals, Michael Palaiologos, who was appointed as regent after probably having had the previous regent murdered during a church service. Once he was secure in power, the regent had himself crowned emperor as Michael VIII (1259–82) and had his young charge sidelined and later imprisoned. His dynasty was destined to rule Byzantine Constantinople for the rest of its existence as a Christian city.

Michael could, however, claim little credit for the recovery of the capital which took place almost by accident. In July 1261 one of his generals, Alexios Strategopoulos, was in Thrace with his army, close to the Land Walls. Information was conveyed to him from inside the city that it was virtually undefended, much of the Latin garrison having gone off to attack a nearby island. News also came that one of the small gates in the walls had been left open. On the night of 25 July some fifteen men crept in through this opening and after pitching the sentry over the walls, opened one of the main gates to Strategopoulos's troops. Their appearance in the street came as a complete surprise. Men rushed to the monasteries to take sanctuary and women hid in doorways and alleyways as the soldiers rushed past. In the Venetian quarter, houses were set on fire, but there was no wholesale massacre of Latins as might have been expected. The few who were still in the city, including Emperor Baldwin II, realized that the situation was hopeless and made for the nearest ship. By dawn, Constantinople was once more in Byzantine hands.[3]

Michael VIII was on the Asian side of the Bosporus with another part of the army when the news of the capture of Constantinople arrived. It was very early in the morning and the emperor was still asleep in his tent. The news was given to Michael's sister Eulogia, who went into the emperor's tent to pass it on. The emperor proved to be a very heavy sleeper and only by pulling his big toe and tickling his feet with a feather did Eulogia succeed in waking him and telling him what had happened. At first Michael did not believe it, but then a messenger arrived bringing the crown and sceptre of the Latin emperor, which Baldwin II had left behind in his rush to escape.[4]

On 15 August, the Feast of the Dormition of the Virgin, the patron and protector of Constantinople, Michael VIII made his ceremonial entry into the city, processing through the Golden Gate. According to custom, the emperor followed behind a chariot at the front of the procession. In the chariot was placed the famous icon of the Hodegetria which had been found safe and sound in the church of the Pantokrator. It was an acknowledgement that the triumph, like the preservation of Constantinople in the past, was the result of the Virgin's intervention, and hence the choice of day for Michael's entry. At the monastery of Stoudios, the icon was reverently placed in the church and the emperor then mounted his horse and rode along the Triumphal Way and the Mese towards the Augousteion, to the cheers of the crowds that lined the road, to take up residence in the Great Palace.[5]

Shrewd political operator that he was, Michael VIII was well aware of how hugely beneficial this spectacular coup was for his own position. He now felt strong enough to order the blinding of the young John Laskaris, who was still only a child, and to have him immured in a castle on the Sea of Marmara. Even by the standards of Byzantine political life, this was an atrocious crime, and Michael was swiftly excommunicated for it by the Patriarch of Constantinople, Arsenios. Typically, Michael responded by dethroning Arsenios and replacing him with someone more pliant who promptly lifted the excommunication. Still, the emperor was not unaware of the damage that his actions had done to his public image. He may have remembered the fate of his predecessor Michael V when he had tried to thrust aside the legitimate empress Zoe.[6]

Michael had therefore to try even harder to prove himself a worthy Roman emperor, and one way to do that was to restore the city of Constantinople to its former glory. In doing so, Michael could claim to be following in the footsteps of the greatest emperor of them all, Constantine, who had founded the city in the first place. Indeed, it would seem that he liked to think of himself as a new Constantine, because he had restored what Constantine had created. Almost as soon as he was in control of the city, Michael began an intensive series of building works. First and foremost, the Sea Walls along the Golden Horn were raised to prevent a repetition of the tactics used by the Latins in April 1204. The Blachernae palace was refurbished and decorated not with the traditional mosaics but with frescoes, painted onto plaster, celebrating Michael's many victories. This may well have been an economy measure as fresco is considerably cheaper than mosaic and Michael could not afford to be too lavish in view of all that remained to be done. Streets and porticoes were repaired and schools and hospitals founded. To make the point clear, Michael went so far as to set up a column outside the church of the Holy Apostles. On top of the column was a statue of Saint Michael and before him knelt the figure of an emperor, presenting the Archangel with a model of the city. The emperor depicted could, of course, have been either Constantine or Michael himself.[7]

Michael was also assiduous in that other imperial duty, the founding and beautification of churches and monasteries. Hagia Sophia received new communion vessels and altar cloths and probably a new mosaic of the *Deesis*, a figure of Christ between the Virgin Mary and St John the Baptist. Other churches received new roofs of tiles or lead and new furnishings to replace those stolen by the Latins. The monastery of St Demetrius, which had been founded by a member of the Palaiologos family in the past, was refounded and restored.[8]

All this restoration activity seems to have paid off. Michael VIII was able to persuade the people of Constantinople to accept him and his family as the legitimate imperial dynasty and to forgive the murky path he had followed to reach the throne. A measure of his success was that when he died in 1282 he was succeeded by his twenty-four-year-old son Andronicus II (1282–1328) without any upheaval or bloodshed. No one was murdered, no one was blinded and Andronicus was even safe enough to make a visit to John Laskaris in his castle and to try to assuage his conscience by providing for the comfort of the prisoner. It would even appear that when Laskaris died his body was brought to Constantinople for burial in the Palaiologos family's favourite monastery, St Demetrius.[9] A very different man from his father, Andronicus was renowned for his piety and for his patronage of learning and scholarship. He liked to preside over gatherings where literary and philosophical subjects were discussed, and contemporaries likened his court to the Stoa of ancient Athens.

The process of restoration that had begun under Michael continued under Andronicus. The monastery of Virgin Tou Libos which had originally been founded in the tenth century was refurbished and became the next burial place for members of the imperial family.[10] It was also a time when not only the emperor but also his wealthier magnates were happy to spend their money in restoring a decayed church or building a new one. The church of the All-Blessed Virgin (Pammakaristos) was refurbished by a successful general named Michael Glabas, and after his death in 1304 his widow converted the south aisle into a side chapel in his memory.[11]

The most prominent of the patrons at this time was Theodore Metochites (1270–1332), chief minister of Andronicus II in the latter part of his reign. Metochites was both a statesman and a scholar, a prominent member of the emperor's literary circle as well as a powerful personality who dominated the court. His pupil Nikephoros Gregoras gives this description of him:

> By the size of his body, the harmony of its limbs and other features, and by the brightness of his eyes he drew all eyes upon himself. In his natural ability as a speaker, his capacity for work, strength of memory and clear understanding of all branches of knowledge he achieved great heights. He was so fluent in replying to all questions, whether about antiquity or the present day, as if his tongue were a book, that his friends had little or no need of books. For he was a living library and a ready store of information, far excelling all previous men of learning ... The most remarkable fact about him was that, while public affairs were in such a state of confusion, with the impending storm and a whole series of responsibilities continually flooding into his mind, nothing ever prevented him from reading and writing. So skilled was he in both spheres of activity that he could work from early morning until evening in the palace, entirely devoted to the administration of public business and dispatching it with great enthusiasm, as if he had no literary interests at all. Leaving the palace late he would then devote himself completely to reading, as if he were a scholar entirely detached from public life.[12]

Metochites amassed a considerable fortune through his tenure of office, though some said, probably rightly, that much of it was achieved through selling of offices and pocketing of bribes. He expended a good deal of his wealth on a magnificent new palace for himself and his family, complete with marble floors, gardens, piped water, baths and porticoed courtyard.[13] He was, however, also the patron and protector of the monastery and church of Holy Saviour in Chora, which lay close to the Land Walls and the Palace of Blachernae. He provided the monastery with a library which became the largest in Constantinople, while its church was rebuilt between 1316 and 1321 and given lavish new mosaic decoration depicting the lives of Christ and the Virgin. Metochites also built a side chapel to house his own tomb and decorated it most appropriately with frescoes depicting the Last Judgement.[14]

So it was that, thanks to the efforts of Michael VIII, Andronicus II, Metochites, Glabas and others, much had been done to restore Constantinople to its pre-1204 state. The city was once more a place of wonder and pilgrimage. The Byzantines had even succeeded in putting together another collection of relics of the passion to replace those taken by the Latins, including the sponge soaked in vinegar that was offered to Christ and the reed that he was forced to hold, as well as part of the by-now much divided True Cross. These were now normally kept in the monastery of St George of Mangana but they were publicly displayed in Hagia Sophia during holy week. Western travellers were surprised to see the Crown of Thorns among them as that was supposedly in the Sainte Chapelle in Paris after having been acquired by the king of France who had paid off the debt to the Venetians when it had been pawned by Baldwin II. Most, however, asked no questions and were content to accept the mystique, one fourteenth-century Russian visitor exclaiming that 'There is much that amazes one there, which the human mind cannot express'.[15] It was almost as if nothing had changed, which is certainly what the Byzantines wanted outsiders to think. Unfortunately, things were by no means what they had been.

The root of the problem was that the empire that Michael VIII had reconstituted in 1261 was a great deal smaller than that ruled over by Alexios III Angelos in 1200. It consisted only of about a third of Asia

Minor, a strip of territory across the Balkans, part of the Peloponnese and some of the Aegean islands, and this shrinkage of territory meant that the Palaiologan emperors received only a fraction of the tax receipts that their predecessors had enjoyed. The other source of revenue, customs duties, was also in decline, as much of Constantinople's trade was now firmly in the hands of the Venetians and Genoese, who did not pay the *Kommerkion*. It was estimated that by the mid-fourteenth century the Genoese earned 200,000 gold pieces in duties a year, by diverting trade through their new commercial quarter in Galata across the Golden Horn, while the Byzantine treasury received a mere 30,000. By contrast, in the sixth century, when Justinian had built so many of Constantinople's great buildings, the empire had enjoyed an annual revenue of about five or six million gold pieces a year, but that had now shrunk to one million hyperpyra, and these coins were of lower value because they had a much smaller gold content than the old solidus of Justinian's day.[16] All this meant that the emperors no longer had the means to lavish large sums on beautifying their capital city and it explains why private individuals such as Theodore Metochites and Michael Glabas were now more prominent as patrons.

Things got worse from the 1280s on, as the empire shrank still further. Conscious of the threat of an expedition from western Europe to reconquer Constantinople after 1261, Michael VIII had concentrated most of the imperial forces in the western part of the empire. The eastern frontier appeared to be less vulnerable, as the emperor had a long-standing peace treaty with the Seljuk sultan in Konya. This took no account, however, of the semi-independent bands of nomadic Turks who owed little allegiance to the increasingly feeble sultanate and who therefore felt themselves bound by no treaty. They began to raid over the border into Byzantine territory and, when they encountered almost no opposition, began to settle there. Andronicus II saw the danger and led an army into Asia Minor in 1290, but following two serious reverses at Magnesia and Bapheon in 1302, the Byzantine armies withdrew, leaving the Turks to conquer the area unmolested. By 1330, the whole of Asia Minor was lost, apart from a few towns which still held out.[17] The extent of the disaster could hardly be concealed from the people of Constantinople. As a passing Catalan mercenary observed:

> The Turks had, in truth, conquered so much terri-
> tory, that their armies arrived in battle array before
> Constantinople; and only an arm of sea, less than two
> miles wide separated them from the city as they bran-
> dished their swords and threatened the emperor, who
> could see it all. Imagine the torment he must have
> felt, for they would have seized Constantinople itself
> had they possessed the means by which to cross that
> arm of sea.

Nor could they ignore the crowds of refugees that daily arrived in Constantinople from the conquered provinces. Many were completely destitute and were forced to live in squalor on the city's rubbish dumps.[18]

In the face of the disaster, opposition to the rule of the ageing Andronicus II and his chief minister Metochites grew ever more stri-dent, and gathered around the person of his youthful grandson, also named Andronicus. In May 1328, young Andronicus and his sup-porters forced their way into Constantinople and compelled the old emperor to abdicate. With his patron gone, Metochites too fell from power. A mob attacked his mansion near the Chora monastery and, having stripped it of anything of value, razed it to the ground. Even the marble pavement was prised up and sent off as a gift to a foreign ruler.[19] Metochites himself was banished to the town of Didymotei-chon in Thrace where he was forced to endure harsh conditions, in contrast to the wealth and luxury that he had once enjoyed, and, worst of all, absence from the centre of civilization, the Great City. He was therefore profoundly grateful when a charitable monk took pity on him and sent him a case of wine:

> The fact is that nothing pleasant or useful comes to
> me from here, either in illness or in health, either
> when it comes to drinks or comestibles. This is espe-
> cially true whenever, following the Christian way of
> life, I abstain from meat and am obliged to turn to
> a fish diet ... As you know, local inhabitants are very

far removed from the sea and whatever is caught in
the local rivers is utterly useless, unpleasant and taste-
less to me ... For it is clear how difficult my present
circumstances are, how hard my present experience
is, and how different from all my former way of life;
and you showed yourself both as a noble and useful
person, when I was precisely in most urgent need to
have the indispensable use of wine.[20]

After two years in Thrace, Metochites was allowed to return to
Constantinople and to take up residence in his monastery of the
Chora. His last days were sad, troubled by illness and by the view from
his window which looked out on the spot where his house had once
stood. He died on 13 March 1332, one month after his former master,
Andronicus II.

The accession of the young and vigorous Andronicus III (1328–41)
seemed to open a new era and promise recovery from the depressing decline under his predecessor. Realizing that there was no hope
of recovering Asia Minor for the time being, the new emperor made
peace with the Turks but he was successful in recovering a swathe of
lost territory in the western half of the empire. The recovery was to
be short-lived, however, for in June 1341 Andronicus died, aged only
forty-five. His son and heir, John, was only nine years old and the
inevitable result was civil war as Andronicus's right-hand man John
Kantakouzenos fought for power with the empress-mother Anna of
Savoy and the patriarch of Constantinople who were acting as regents
for the young emperor. Civil wars such as this were not uncommon
in Byzantium, and indeed in the whole medieval world, but this one
was particularly destructive. It raged for six years and effectively bank-
rupted the empire. Even the crown jewels had to be pawned by Anna
of Savoy to pay for troops, and when Kantakouzenos finally won and
had himself crowned as John VI (1347–54) he discovered that there
was no gold or silver plate for the coronation banquet, as it had all
long since been sold.[21] Perhaps realizing the damage that his ambi-
tions had done to the empire, the new emperor refrained from taking

bloody reprisals against his defeated enemies. After seven years in power, he abdicated and handed power back to John V Palaiologos. The former emperor changed his name to Joseph and took monastic vows, spending the rest of his life writing theological tracts and his own political memoirs.

As well as ruining the empire financially, the civil war of 1341–7 also led to the loss of most of its territory. Neighbouring rulers took advantage of the Byzantines' preoccupation with fighting each other to take over large tracts of imperial territory, the king of Serbia, Stefan Dushan (1331–55), helping himself to most of Thessaly and Macedonia. More serious in the long term, however, were the actions of a group of Turks known as the Osmanlis or Ottomans, who ruled the north-western section of Asia Minor. After having fought alongside John Kantakouzenos in the civil war, the Ottomans seized first Tzympe, on the European side of the Bosporus, and then in 1354 the town of Gallipoli. From this bridgehead, the Turks began the systematic conquest of Thrace, taking Adrianople in about 1369 and laying the foundations of the future Ottoman empire. By 1400, Constantinople was reduced to an isolated outpost in the midst of territory dominated by the Ottomans.[22]

The dramatic decline in the fortunes of the Byzantine empire was reflected in the appearance of Constantinople. With the emperor bankrupt, the restoration programme that had begun during the reigns of the first two emperors of the Palaiologos family ground to a halt. Many of the great buildings of the city could no longer be maintained, something that was only too apparent to visitors. Ruy Gonzalez Clavijo, a Spanish diplomat who passed through in 1403, commented that:

> Everywhere throughout the city, there are many great palaces, churches and monasteries but most of them are now in ruin. It is plain, however, that in former times, when Constantinople was in its pristine state, it was one of the noblest capitals in the world.[23]

Even the Great Palace was in a ramshackle state, according to another visitor:

180

> The emperor's palace must have been very magnif-
> icent, but now it is in such a state that both it and
> the city show well the evils which the people have
> suffered and still endure ... Inside, the house is badly
> kept, except for certain parts where the emperor, the
> empress, and attendants can live, although cramped
> for space. The emperor's state is as splendid as ever, for
> nothing is omitted from the ancient ceremonies, but,
> properly regarded, he is like a bishop without a see.[24]

The cathedral of Hagia Sophia remained as splendid as ever, though many of its doors were permanently blocked up due to lack of money, and when repairs were needed the Byzantine government had to petition the ruler of Novgorod to send donations.[25] Even the orb had fallen from the hand of the great statue of Justinian that stood outside the cathedral, to which one visitor attached heavy significance:

> And it is said there that the fall of the apple is a token
> that the emperor has lost a great part of his lordship.
> For he used to be emperor of Romania, of Greece, of
> Asia Minor, of Syria, of the land of Judaea, in which is
> Jerusalem, of the land of Egypt, of Persia and Arabia;
> but he has lost all, except Greece ...[26]

Even within the shrunken Byzantine empire, Constantinople ceased to hold a pre-eminent position. Other Byzantine cities, particularly Mistra and Thessalonica, had become rival centres of commerce and government. Trebizond on the Black Sea was now the capital of a breakaway empire, independent of the emperor in Constantinople, with its own palace and hierarchy. Constantinople was no longer a great imperial capital and certainly no longer looked like one.

Given the city's isolation in the midst of Turkish territory, it was inevitable that sooner or later the Ottoman sultans would attempt to capture it and so remove what had become an anomalous enclave within their domains. Yet that was easier said than done, for Constantinople's defences remained intact and as formidable as ever. To start with, the Ottomans had no fleet and so could not make an assault by sea as the Fourth Crusade had done. On the landward side the Theodosian Walls still presented an impenetrable barrier. Sultan Yildirim Bayezid besieged Constantinople for nearly eight years between 1394 and 1402 without success, and an attempt to breach the Land Walls by storm in 1422 was driven off.

Also still intact was the Byzantine belief that Constantinople enjoyed the special protection of God and the Virgin Mary. Soldiers who had fought in the siege of 1422 reported seeing her on the Land Walls in the midst of the fighting and she was generally credited with saving the city on that occasion. Even if the enemy did ever succeed in breaching the Land Walls, it was said, they would only advance as far as the Forum of Constantine. Then an angel would descend from heaven and would present a sword to an unknown man standing by the column. He would lead the counter-attack and drive the invaders from the city. Great store was set on the weekly processions with the icon of the Hodegetria, the visible token that the popular myths were divine promises.[27]

Such pious hopes were overtaken by events. In February 1451, the Ottoman Sultan Murad II suffered an apoplectic fit and died. Some in Constantinople were inclined to rejoice, for Murad had made no secret of his ambition to capture the city and it was he who had launched the attack of 1422. He was succeeded by his young and inexperienced son, Mehmed II (1451–81), who might have been expected to adopt a less aggressive policy, at least until he was more securely settled on the throne. Such naïve hopes were soon disabused. Young Mehmed discerned from the moment of his accession that the only way to make himself secure from overthrow was to pull off a spectacular victory, the capture of Constantinople. Secretive and obsessive, he was consumed day and night with the project he had set himself. Once he summoned his vizier to him in the small hours and complained:

> See this pillow? I have passed the whole night dragging it about from one corner of the bedchamber to the other, reclining and rising without sleep. Therefore I say to you, let neither silver nor gold entice you to

cast aside the resolution you have now given me. Let
us struggle steadfastly against the Romans. By placing
our trust in the assent of God and in the prayer of the
Prophet, we will take the city.

Mehmed went about planning his attack with painstaking thorough-
ness. He pondered endlessly over various strategies, pored over lists
of reserve troops, tax revenues, supplies and weapons and traced out
the line of the Land Walls with pen and paper.[28] By the spring of 1452
he was ready to move, but he did not march against Constantinople
at once. Instead, he concentrated on building a castle, the so-called
Rumeli Hisar, on the European side of the Bosporus, where the strait
was at its narrowest, some way to the north of Constantinople. When
it was completed in August, cannon were mounted on the battlements
with a view to closing the passage to ships and supplies coming from
the Black Sea. Slowly but surely, the sultan was drawing the noose
tighter, and in April 1453 he began the siege in earnest, drawing up an
Ottoman army of some 80,000 before the Land Walls and bringing a
powerful fleet into the Sea of Marmara and the Bosporus to maintain
the blockade by sea.

Constantinople was now in greater peril than it had ever been
before. Invested by land and sea, the Byzantines and their Venetian
and Genoese allies were heavily outnumbered. The courtier and statesman George Sphantzes was entrusted by the emperor Constantine
XI (1449–53) with assessing the number of able-bodied men available for the defence. Worryingly, he came up with the paltry figure of
4,973.[29] Nevertheless, Mehmed's army still had to face the formidable
defences that had foiled so many attackers in the past, including his
father Murad in 1422. The Land Walls had never before been breached
and Mehmed may well have considered the best strategy to be to aim
for a repeat of the success of the Fourth Crusade by storming the Sea
Walls along the Golden Horn. This was probably what he had in mind
when he manoeuvred his fleet into the Golden Horn by means of a
clever stratagem. The ships were beached at Diplokionion and then
hauled overland to be relaunched into the Golden Horn. The tactic
was not new and had allegedly been tried by some Russian attackers

in the tenth century, but Mehmed's use of it with impunity in 1453 indicates how powerless the Byzantines now were to influence what was happening outside the walls of Constantinople.[30]

In the event, however, the breakthrough was not to occur in the Sea Walls that guarded the Golden Horn but at the Land Walls where no one had ever succeeded before. In the epic sieges of the seventh and eighth centuries, the Byzantines had had a technological advantage over their attackers. Now it was the other way round, as the Ottomans had been able to take advantage of technical advances and equip themselves with cannon. These were by no means new weapons in 1453. They had been used as early as 1347 by the English during their siege of Calais although they were very small devices that had little effect on the town's walls. What was new was the size of the cannon available to Mehmed. The largest of them, constructed by a Hungarian engineer, had a barrel that measured over eight metres long. It was a fairly crude device and so difficult to load that it could only be fired seven times a day, but the cannon balls it fired weighed over 650 kilograms. It was therefore able to have a considerable impact on masonry, even that as mighty as the Land Walls.

Mehmed had this monster gun dragged down from Adrianople by a team of sixty oxen and set up along with a number of others opposite the most vulnerable section of the Land Walls, the *Mesoteichion*, where the fortifications dipped into the valley of the River Lykos. The Greek historian Michael Kritoboulos described the devastating effect that it was to have:

> They set fire to it through the short hole behind, igniting the powder. And when this took fire, quicker than it takes to say it, there was a fearful roar first, and a shaking of the earth beneath and for a long way off, and a noise such as was never heard before. Then, with an astounding thunder and a frightful crashing and a flame that lit up all the surroundings and then left them black, the rod, forced out from within by a dry hot blast of air, violently set in motion the stone as it came out. And the stone, borne with tremendous

184

force and velocity, hit the wall, which it immediately shook and knocked down, and was itself broken into many fragments and scattered, hurling the pieces everywhere and killing those who happened to be nearby. Sometimes it demolished a whole section, and sometimes a half-section, and sometimes a larger or smaller section of a tower, or turret, or battlement. And there was no part of the wall strong enough or resistant enough or thick enough to be able to withstand it ...[31]

Although the defenders were able to make good some of the damage caused by this and other cannon under cover of darkness, as the weeks went by the gaps in the outer wall became more and more apparent. The cannon also took their toll on morale, and the faith of the Byzantines in the certainty of divine protection began to waver. Some remembered a prophecy that Constantinople would fall in 1492, the year 7000 since the creation of the world, and wondered if perhaps the sums had been a few years out. There were ominous signs of divine displeasure. When the icon of the Hodegetria was being processed through the city, it suddenly slipped from the hands of the bearers and fell to the ground from where it proved extremely difficult to raise it. When the procession resumed, it was caught in a violent downpour of rain and hail, which threatened to sweep away the small children and against which it was impossible to go on. The next day, a dense fog covered the whole city, and some said that this was a token of the divine presence wrapping itself in cloud as it abandoned Constantinople to its fate.[32]

So in the event it proved. After six weeks of bombardment, the gaps in the wall to the south of the Gate of Adrianople were large enough for Mehmed to decide on a full-scale attack. On the night of 28–29 May 1453, his elite Janissary troops broke through after heavy fighting. The last Byzantine emperor, Constantine XI, was killed in the ensuing struggle, and by morning the Ottomans were in control of the city.[33] As in 1204, there followed the inevitable sack of the city as its churches and private houses were ransacked for anything of value:

> Costly apparel, silver, gold, copper and tin vessels, and
> books beyond number ... Innumerable books were
> loaded onto the wagons and hauled in all directions;
> they were dispersed throughout East and West. For a
> single gold coin, ten books were sold – the works of
> Aristotle and Plato, books of theological content and
> on every subject. Gold and silver were pulled from the
> evangelisteries which were adorned with many differ-
> ent jewels; some were sold and the rest were thrown
> away. All the icons were thrown to the flames ...[34]

Among the icons to perish was the Hodegetria. In the days before the
final assault, it had been brought from the Great Palace to Metochites's
church of the Chora to be close to the walls at the time of crisis. Turkish troops reached the church very shortly after the first breakthrough
had occurred, and the icon was grabbed and hacked with its precious
golden frame into four pieces which were then shared among the looters. The commodity that was most in demand, however, was people
since captives could command a high price as slaves. Indeed, many of
the victors later expressed annoyance that so many of the inhabitants
had been killed, thus robbing them of the chance of profit.[35] Thousands of the city's inhabitants were rounded up and sold into slavery
from which their only hope of redemption was if their relatives were
able to buy them back with a huge ransom.

As in the case of the sack of 1204, however, it was not the pillage itself
that did the damage but what came after. Indeed Mehmed was at pains
to limit the ravages committed by his troops in the aftermath of victory. When the sultan entered Constantinople in the early afternoon
of 29 May, he was allegedly taken aback at the destruction that had
been wrought:

> [He] looked about to see its great size, its situation, its
> grandeur and beauty, its teeming population, its love-
> liness, and the costliness of its churches and public
> buildings, and of the private houses and community

houses and those of the officials ... When he saw what a large number had been killed, and the ruin of the buildings, and the wholesale ruin and destruction of the city, he was filled with compassion and repented not a little at the destruction and plundering. Tears fell from his eyes as he groaned deeply and passionately: 'What a city we have given over to plundering and destruction!'[36]

Arriving at the cathedral of Hagia Sophia, Mehmed was quick to announce its conversion to a mosque, and on his orders one of his attendants climbed into the pulpit and proclaimed that there was no God but God. When Mehmed discovered one of his soldiers smashing the marble pavement of the floor, he struck him with his sword and announced that while the troops could take the captives and the booty, the buildings were his.[37] Wholesale destruction was not Mehmed's intention by any means.

Yet the sad truth, as Mehmed soon discovered, was that he had conquered 'a city of ruins', with many of the great palaces, churches and monasteries already in an advanced state of dilapidation.[38] There was clearly much to be done if the city was to become the impressive new capital of his empire, and that meant that many of the old Byzantine buildings had to go. One of the first victims was the great church of the Holy Apostles, which had long been in a poor state of repair. Mehmed decided to use its site for a new mosque and a splendid tomb for himself. The church was duly demolished and the magnificent Mosque of the Conqueror was erected in its place between 1462 and 1470.[39] Other churches and monasteries were taken over for other uses. The monastery of the Pantokrator was handed over to some fullers, St Eirene became an armoury and St George of Mangana became the abode of Dervishes. Others provided living space for newly arrived Turkish families.[40]

Some churches did remain in the hands of the conquered Byzantine population, but in the long run these too tended to be turned into mosques. The Virgin Pammakaristos became the seat of the patriarch of Constantinople after 1462, but by 1588 that too had become a mosque.[41] By the early years of the eighteenth century, only three of the Byzantine churches of Constantinople were still used for Christian worship. One of them was the little thirteenth-century church of the Virgin of the Mongols (Mouchliotissa) which survived because it could prove that Mehmed II had granted the church in perpetuity to the Byzantine architect who had built the Mosque of the Conqueror.[42]

The other Byzantine monuments were either destroyed or slowly decayed as the years went by. The palaces of the Byzantine emperors, already in an advanced state of disrepair before the conquest, did not long survive it. Mehmed II at once ordered the construction of a new palace, and the Great Palace site was abandoned. In 1609 any traces of it were removed to make way for the construction of the Mosque of Sultan Ahmed, better known as the Blue Mosque. The Palace of Blachernae, out on the edge of the city, survived longer but only as ruins, and most of those had gone by the 1540s.[43] The column of Theodosius, from which Mourtzouphlos had plummeted to his death, was demolished in about 1500 to make way for some new bath houses. The huge statue of Justinian which stood in the Augousteion outside Hagia Sophia was taken down in the 1540s so that its metal could be used in casting cannon. The column of Arcadius lasted longer, though in the end it became decidedly unsafe and it too was demolished. Many churches, such as the Virgin Peribleptos and St George of Mangana, simply crumbled and disappeared as the years went by, their marble columns and pavements carted away for use in new buildings.[44]

The conversion of a church into a mosque meant at least that the building survived, but the change of use was often followed by the mutilation or destruction of its mosaic decoration since pictorial representations of the human figure were incompatible with strict Islamic views on idolatry. The Turkish writer Khoja (1539–99) exulted that 'the churches that were within the city were emptied of their vile idols and cleansed of their filthy and idolatrous impurities', but there does not seem to have been a systematic policy of destroying the mosaics. Often they were just whitewashed over or left to decay gradually over the years. Those in the dome of Hagia Sophia could be seen in 1597, although they were rather the worse for wear and had in some cases been defaced. Some were still visible as late as 1718.[45]

Along with the churches, the columns and the palaces, other features of the Byzantine city disappeared one by one. The classical statues that remained in the city had little chance of survival, for the Turks had much less tolerance of them and their pagan associations than the Byzantines had had. One sixteenth-century visitor recorded that some workmen had accidentally dug up a statue of an armed soldier but almost at once they smashed it to pieces with hammers.

> When we showed our annoyance, the workmen laughed at us and asked whether we wished, in accordance with our custom, to worship and pray to it.[46]

Not everyone was blind to the beauties of the works of the ancients. One Turkish pasha brought back a bronze statue of Hercules as part of the booty from a campaign in Hungary and had it set up in the Hippodrome. After his death, however, it was almost immediately pulled down and sent to the furnace. The ox and lion at the harbour of Boukoleon was still there in 1532 but it too disappeared in the years that followed. Only the serpent column in the centre of the Hippodrome survived.[47]

Alongside the destruction of the Byzantine legacy, a new city had arisen, no less splendid, in which the columns were replaced by minarets, and the crosses on the domes of the churches by crescents. Like their Byzantine predecessors, Ottoman sultans of the sixteenth and seventeenth centuries vied with each other to display their piety and wealth by building at least one *külliye*, a complex of religious, educational and charitable buildings, of which a mosque was the central feature. One of the most striking of these is the vast Süleymaniye, built between 1550 and 1557 for Süleyman the Magnificent (1520–66). The huge dome of the central mosque is surrounded by no less than 400 smaller domes that cover a hospital, an orphanage, a soup kitchen, an insane asylum, a library, baths, a hospice for travellers, and Süleyman's own tomb. Between the buildings are colonnaded courtyards with fountains. Constantinople had once more become a grandiose imperial capital, albeit of a different empire.

There were still curious visitors to Constantinople who searched behind the façade of the new for lingering traces of the Byzantine past. Among them was an Englishman, George Sandys (1578–1644), who was finding refuge in travel from an unhappy, arranged marriage and a pending lawsuit brought by his wife's relatives. As his ship sailed into the Golden Horn in the autumn of 1610, Sandys was delighted with the view from the deck:

> There is hardly in nature a more delicate object, if beheld from the sea or adjoyning mountains: the loftie and beautifull cypresse trees so entermixed with the buildings that it seemeth to present a city in a wood to the pleased beholders. Whose seven aspiring heads (for on so many hils and no more, they say it is seated) are most of them crowned with magnificent mosques, all of white marble, round in forme ....[48]

Sandys lodged in Galata, in the house of the English ambassador, Sir Thomas Glover, and from there began his explorations of the city. It is clear from his account that his interest was in Constantinople's Byzantine past rather than its Ottoman present. He considered that Hagia Sophia 'exceedeth all not onely the rest' of the mosques but even 'all other fabricks whatsoever throughout the whole universe'. On his visit to the building, he experienced something of what a medieval visitor would have seen, for the dome was still 'adorned with mosaike painting' of 'inexpressable statelinesse'. He found too that many of the old Byzantine superstitions lived on. The Turks were accustomed to wipe their handkerchiefs on one of the columns of the former cathedral as they believed that the condensation that it exuded had curative powers.

When he had finished in Hagia Sophia, Sandys ambled over to the Hippodrome. The banks of seating had by now disappeared under the houses which ringed the open space, leading Sandys to compare the Hippodrome to Smithfield Market in London. Still there, however, were the column with its three serpent heads, the Egyptian obelisk of the emperor Theodosius and the column of Constantine Porphyrogenitos which Sandys described as a 'colossus built of sun dry stone'.

Elsewhere he remarked the column of Arcadius, 'farre surpassing both Trajan's and that of Antonius, which I have seene in Rome', and within the gateway of the Topkapi palace he visited a church, probably that of St Eirene, which still contained many of the weapons taken from the defeated Byzantines in 1453. He even found some remnants of the Great Palace, though they had now been converted into 'a stable for wilde beasts'.

In spite of all these discoveries, Sandys was disappointed with Constantinople, concluding as he departed in January 1611 aboard the *Trinity* of London that 'there is not in the world an object that promiseth so much a far off to the beholders, and entred so deceiveth expectations'. What saddened him most was that the Byzantine monuments that he had seen were 'all the remains that are left ... of so many goodly buildings, and from all parts congested antiquities, wherewith this sovereign city was in past times so adorned'. Along with the buildings, he discovered, had perished all memory of the society that had constructed them so that even the local Greeks were completely ignorant of the history of their forebears.[49]

A more positive assessment was made by the Frenchman Pierre Gilles (1490–1555) who spent several years in Constantinople during the 1540s. He was certainly distressed that 'the inhabitants are daily demolishing, effacing and utterly destroying the small remains of Antiquity'. He did have a stroke of luck, though, in rediscovering a Byzantine monument that had been lost and forgotten for generations. Wandering in the area behind the mosque of Hagia Sophia, he noticed that the local people were able to draw up freshwater fish from their wells. It so happened that Gilles met a man whose house had a secret passage that led down to a subterranean world in which a vast lake stretched away into the darkness beyond the flickering light cast by a flaming torch. The owner of the house produced a small skiff and rowed Gilles through a forest of columns that held up a towering vaulted roof while the shadowy shapes of large carp moved in the waters beneath. The Frenchman realized that he had stumbled upon nothing less than the Basilika cistern which had been built by Justinian to keep Byzantine Constantinople supplied with water and whose very existence was now unsuspected by the people living above.

Perhaps it was the thrill of this discovery that prompted Gilles to end his account on a rather more positive note than Sandys. For him, the loss of Constantinople's ancient and Byzantine past was deeply saddening but it was balanced by an element of continuity:

> I shall end with this reflection; that though all other cities have their periods of government, and are subject to the decay of time, Constantinople alone seems to claim to herself a kind of immortality and will continue a city, as long as the race of mankind shall live either to inhabit or rebuild her.[50]

That thought still holds good today.

CHAPTER 10

Epilogue: Byzantine Constantinople Today

The proof of Gilles's words is apparent to any visitor to Constantinople in the early twenty-first century. The city has moved on once more and is now officially known as Istanbul, the largest city, but not the capital, of the Turkish republic. It is a huge and sprawling metropolis of some sixteen million people, whose suburbs extend far beyond the limits of the narrow promontory alongside the Golden Horn. They stretch up both sides of the Bosporus towards the Black Sea, westwards out towards the airport, and on the Asian side along the Sea of Marmara almost as far as Izmit, or Nikomedia as it once was. Beyond Galata, tall, gleaming towers provide office space for banks and multinational companies. Within this metropolitan area, traffic congestion frequently reaches gridlock, particularly in the old city and on the approaches to the two mighty bridges which now link Europe with Asia across the Bosporus.

Given that so much of Byzantine Constantinople had vanished even when Pierre Gilles visited during the sixteenth century, it might be supposed that no traces at all would be left to see now that the developers and financiers have moved in. It is true that, within the old city, many of the great monuments of the Byzantine era have disappeared completely. Gone forever are St George of Mangana with its towering church, hospital and extensive gardens, the Milion Arch, the Brazen Gate, and the breathtaking audience chamber in the Magnavra hall of the Great Palace. No traces at all remain above ground of the great mansions and palaces of grandees like Niketas Choniates and

193

Theodore Metochites, and the columns of Theodosius and Arcadius no longer tower over the rooftops.

Yet in spite of all that has been lost and all that has since been built to cover over the traces, echoes of the past still linger, even in the city's new name. The change to Istanbul was instituted by the founder of the Turkish republic, Kemal Atatürk (1871–1938) in a conscious attempt to distance the city from its Byzantine and Ottoman past. Ironically Istanbul is not a Turkish word at all but of Greek origin and was already in use in Byzantine times as one of Constantinople's many epithets. It is derived from the Greek words '*eis tin polin*', meaning 'to the city'.[1] For all its modernity, Istanbul has a Byzantine name.

Moreover, thanks to the constant expansion of Istanbul, more traces of the past are coming to light all the time. As new buildings are constructed, the bulldozers often turn up features that have been covered up for centuries. The reconstruction of the Palace of Justice near the Hippodrome during the 1960s revealed the stone base of one of the statues that had once adorned the stadium. Of the statue itself, however, there was no sign. It may have been one of those melted down during the period of Latin rule. In the Balat area, close to where the Palace of Blachernae once stood, the remains of an impressive mansion have been found, no doubt the house of some high official like Theodore Metochites. It had its own bath house, complete with hypocaust heating. The demolition of a building in 1998 revealed the brick substructure of what had once been the church and monastery of the Virgin Peribleptos in the south of the city, the foundation of Romanos III (1028–34) who thought that 'nothing in the whole world was good enough for this church'.[2]

Even more sensational is an unwitting discovery made during construction of a tunnel under the Bosporus designed to carry 75,000 passengers an hour on fast metro trains. On the plot of land marked out for a huge interchange station at Yenikapı on the southern side of the old city, archaeologists are racing against time to investigate what appears to be one of the small harbours that stood along Constantinople's southern shore, similar to that at Boukoleon where the imperial galley was moored. Seven sunken ships have been found buried in the mud, along with mosaics, ceramics, coins and thousand-year-old shipping ropes and anchors all preserved in almost perfect condition. There is also a subterranean stone tunnel, nearly two metres across, leading from the harbour. What it was for and where it leads remains an intriguing mystery.[3]

Quite apart from new discoveries, echoes of Byzantium can also be found just by walking the streets of Istanbul. For the visitor can still enter the old city through the opening in the Land Walls known as the Gate of Adrianople, just as the visitors of 1200 did.[4] These days the area is known as Edirne Kapısı, but it means the same, *Edirne* being the Turkish name for Adrianople and *kapı* the word for 'gate'. The gate itself is gone, and is replaced by a large gap in the walls that lets in two lanes of thunderous traffic. On either side of the Gate of Adrianople, the Land Walls still stretch from the Golden Horn to the Sea of Marmara, although inevitably they bear the scars of the years. While the tall towers and the inner wall are mostly intact, the outer wall is in much worse condition and the moat, stockade and outworks have largely disappeared. The section between the Gate of Adrianople and the Gate of St Romanos still bears the marks of Mehmed's cannon, and the Land Walls suffered further damage in the earthquake of 17 August 1999. Somewhat controversially, parts of the walls have been rebuilt in recent years, though this may be the only way to preserve them. Whatever view one takes of that, the Land Walls remain one of the great sights of Byzantine Constantinople, their towers standing sentinel as far as the eye can see as they have done for centuries.[5]

It is still possible to go from the Gate of Adrianople to the Hippodrome on foot, for Fevzi Paşa Caddesi more or less follows the route of the old Mese. It is not a particularly congenial walk, passing through some very busy and congested streets, but the route does pass a number of important Byzantine sites. To the north of the Adrianople Gate, there are some traces of that other residence of the Byzantine emperors, the Palace of Blachernae. Much of what remains is underground, a series of chambers which may have served as storerooms or dungeons. All that can be seen above ground are some towers. One is named after Isaac II Angelos because it bears an inscription recording that he had it repaired in 1188. Isaac is also reputed to have spent part of his time of imprisonment in the tower before he was restored to power in 1203, though there is no contemporary evidence to support that. Nearby is another Byzantine building, known now as Tefkur Sarayı, which may have been a later addition to the palace, and the site of the church of the Virgin in Blachernae where the robe or *maphorion* of the Virgin Mary was kept. The church and the robe have long gone, but the spring that flows there is still a place of pilgrimage. The whole area is still surrounded by the walls that were rebuilt during the twelfth century to reduce the vulnerability of the Blachernae 'bulge'.[6]

Heading east from the Edirne Kapı, the road passes just to the south of a former mosque known as Kariye Camii. This was originally the church of Holy Saviour in Chora, all that remains of the monastery that once surrounded it. The building houses some of the best surviving Byzantine art in Istanbul, mostly dating from the early fourteenth century when the church was refurbished by Theodore Metochites. The church was thoroughly looted on the morning of 29 May and the icon of the Hodegetria which was housed there was hacked to pieces, but its mosaics and frescoes were spared and some of them remained visible throughout its time as a mosque. During the seventeenth and eighteenth centuries, much of the fresco decoration was whitewashed over and this had the effect of preserving it until 1948 when the building became a museum and the surviving artwork was restored to its former glory.[7]

On entering the church, the visitor is confronted with a mosaic portrait of Metochites himself, bearded in the Byzantine fashion, wearing an elaborate robe and sporting a flamboyant hat. The chief minister is shown kneeling before Christ, offering him the church that he had restored at such great expense. The ceilings of the narthaxes or entrance halls are covered with mosaics depicting the life of Christ and of the Virgin Mary. To the right of the entrance is the side chapel where Metochites's tomb can still be seen, along with the fresco depictions of the Resurrection and Last Judgement whose figures, far from the stiff poses of mosaics, seem almost to move. Most impressive of all is the Harrowing of Hell in the apse of the chapel, showing the risen Christ dragging Adam and Eve out of Hades while Satan lies bound at his feet. It is a sobering thought, however, that magnificent though these mosaics and frescoes are, they are only chance survivals.

In its heyday, Constantinople possessed a score of churches far more magnificent than this. Such is the extent of our loss.

Returning to Fevzi Paşa Caddesi, the road heads east and passes the site of the church of the Holy Apostles. There is almost nothing now remaining of the church, although an archaeological survey in 2001 did unearth what may be the base of some of its walls.[8] Gone too are the tombs of the Byzantine emperors in the mausoleum attached to the church. Some of their marble sarcophagi may have survived the demolition of the church, however, for they can still be seen outside the Istanbul Archaeological Museum, though which emperors originally occupied them is anyone's guess.[9] The site is now occupied by the mosque of the Conqueror (Fatih Camii), not, unfortunately, that built by Mehmed II but a replacement constructed in 1771 after the original had been flattened by an earthquake.

Beyond Fatih Camii, the road passes what remains of the Aqueduct of Valens on the left and on the right the ruins of the church of St Polyeuktos, a sixth-century basilica. Hidden away in a nearby side street is a survivor of the many columns that once used to dot the skyline, that of Marcian (Kız taşı) that once supported an equestrian statue of the emperor of that name. From here, the road eventually links up with Ordu Caddesi in the approximate area of the Forum of Theodosius. Although the column of Theodosius no longer stands, some fragments of the triumphal arch that stood in the forum do survive and lie piled up on the right-hand side of the road, close to the busy Aksaray bus station. Ordu Caddesi leads on to the column of Constantine (Çemberlitaş) marking the site of the Forum of Constantine. The column is held together by iron hoops as it has been since the sixteenth century.[10]

After Constantine's column, the road descends to Sultanahmet square which is the site of the Augousteion and is still an open space dividing Hagia Sophia from the Hippodrome (At Meydanı). The latter can be traced rather than seen. The banks of seating have all gone but it is easy enough to see where the racetrack would have been. The central spine can also be discerned, for it is still marked by three monuments that were there in Byzantine times, the Egyptian Obelisk of Theodosius, the serpent column of Delphi and the column of

Constantine Porphyrogenitos. The last two, however, are no longer at their best. The Serpent column has been reduced to just a stump. The serpent heads have disappeared, apart from the upper jaw of one serpent which is in the Archaeological Museum.[11] The column of Constantine Porphyrogenitos has lost the bronze cladding which once covered it and is now just a rather enigmatic white pyramid.

The Great Palace which stood next to the Hippodrome is no longer there and its site is covered by the Blue Mosque. There are, however, two small fragments of it remaining. The nearby mosaic museum houses parts of a mosaic pavement from the Great Palace that was unearthed during an archaeological excavation in 1935. The pavement depicts scenes of mischievous boys, animals and hunts. It may possibly have formed the walkway from the palace to the Kathisma, the imperial box overlooking the Hippodrome. Another fragment of the palace can be found down the hill from the Hippodrome, a section of wall punctuated by three large marble-framed windows and a gateway. This probably formed part of the complex known as the Palace of Boukoleon and would have been situated close to or on the waterfront, giving access via a marble staircase to the harbour where the imperial galley was moored. In 1959, however, the shallow waters at this point were filled in to permit the building of a new road, Kennedy Caddesi, along the shoreline so that the palace wall now stands back some way from the Sea of Marmara.[12]

The best-known Byzantine monument was and is the cathedral of Hagia Sophia (Aya Sofya) which still stands across the Augousteion from the Hippodrome. Outwardly it is little changed, although minarets and a number of small buildings were erected close to it during the period when it was a mosque. It is now a museum, and its interior is a far gloomier and darker place than it ever was in Byzantine times. Most of the mosaic decoration that was once its glory has disappeared although a few isolated examples survive, including the portraits of Constantine IX Monomachos and Zoe and of John II Komnenos and his wife Eirene. Even without its mosaics, however, Hagia Sophia can still impress by its sheer size and by the way the dome seems to hover over the nave with no visible means of support.

Other Byzantine buildings can be seen scattered throughout the city. A significant number of churches survive, though some are in poor condition. The church of the monastery of St John Stoudios (Imrahor Camii), where Michael V met his fate in 1042 and Symeon the New Theologian was excessively pious, still stands. During the nineteenth century it was in good enough condition to be recommended as an essential stop for visitors, but in 1894 it was seriously damaged by an earthquake which left it little more than a roofless shell. One striking feature does remain: the church's marble pavement which depicts animals and, curiously enough, scenes from classical mythology.[13] The church of Christ Pantokrator (Zeyrek Camii) which was founded by John II Komnenos in the 1130s as the centrepiece for his monastery and hospital, and as a place of burial for members of his family, was once one of the best-known and most magnificent churches of Constantinople. These days it is rather dilapidated and nothing remains of the tombs of the Komnenian emperors or of the mosaic decoration that once must have covered the walls. The church has, however, retained its wonderful inlaid mosaic floor, a carved doorway and traces of its stained glass, and a programme of restoration and research on the building has now begun.[14]

Others are in better repair, often because they are still working mosques. Among these is the Küçük Ayasofya mosque which was once the church of St Sergius and St Bacchus. Built by Justinian in around 536, it stands to the south of Hagia Sophia and has a distinctive pumpkin-shaped dome. Inside, there is everything one would expect to find in a mosque, from the mimbar or pulpit to the mihrab indicating the direction of Mecca. Rather incongruously, however, a carved inscription in Greek runs the length of the gallery, praising 'our sceptred Justinian' who 'honours with a splendid abode the servant of Christ, Creator of all things, Sergius'.[15] The Gül mosque which stands close to the Golden Horn has been tentatively identified as the church of St Theodosia, dedicated to the lady who had her throat cut with a ram's horn after rushing to the aid of the icon on the Brazen Gate. The Kalenderhane mosque was once the church of the Virgin Kyriotissa that was probably built by Alexios III, and the Fenari Isa mosque is probably the Virgin Tou Libos. Eski Imaret mosque was the church of Christ the All-Seeing or Pantepoptes, which was built by Anna Dalassena, the formidable mother of Emperor Alexios I Komnenos, sometime before 1087. It lies tucked away in the streets behind the mosque of the Conqueror and it was close to this church that Alexios V Mourtzouphlos stationed himself in April 1204 when preparing to do battle with the attacking fleet of the Fourth Crusade. Although converted into a mosque very shortly after the Turkish conquest, the building still preserves its gallery which would have been reserved for the Empress Anna and her entourage.[16]

In churches discussed so far, there survives little or any of what would have been one of their most striking features: their mosaic and fresco decoration. A relatively complete cycle of mosaics does still exist, however, in the Virgin All-Blessed or Pammakaristos (Fethiye Camii), perhaps because the church did not become a mosque until the late sixteenth century. The mosaics date from the early fourteenth century, when the building was refurbished by the Byzantine general Michael Glabas, and so are contemporary with those in the Chora church. The Pammakaristos has, however, been closed up for several years now and it is very difficult to gain admission.[17]

Not all the Byzantine churches of Istanbul are now mosques. While St Saviour in Chora and Hagia Sophia became museums after a period as mosques, Justinian's church of St Eirene (Aya Irini), the largest surviving Byzantine church in Istanbul after Hagia Sophia, has never been either. After the Turkish conquest it served as an arsenal for the elite Janissaries until they were disbanded in 1826. Nowadays it is used as an exhibition and concert venue. Then there is the tiny Virgin of the Mongols or Mouchliotissa which has the distinction of being the only Byzantine church in Istanbul which is still used for its original purpose. Built in the late thirteenth century, during the reign of Andronicus II, it provides the setting for the celebration of the Greek Orthodox liturgy, a rite almost unchanged since Byzantine times.[18]

Apart from churches, two of the cisterns that stored water and made Constantinople independent of outside supplies are still in existence. One, the cistern of a thousand and one columns (Binbirdirek), misnamed as there are only 244, has recently been restored and reopened as a shopping arcade. The other, the Basilika cistern (Yerebatan Sarnıcı), that extraordinary vaulted structure of 336 columns, has been restored and opened to the public. A visit these days can hardly hope to reproduce the thrill of discovery experienced by Pierre Gilles when he first beheld the forest of columns by torchlight. Nevertheless the sheer size of this subterranean space cannot fail to amaze and the cistern preserves two of the few survivors of the hundreds of classical statues and sculptures that once adorned Byzantine Constantinople. In the far left-hand corner are two square slabs of marble carved as Gorgons' heads. Probably originally from some dismantled pagan temple, they were reused during Justinian's reign to provide bases for two of the columns in the cistern and have remained there ever since.[19]

While the Land Walls, churches and cisterns provide the most obvious reminders of Byzantium, there are all kinds of other fragments scattered throughout Istanbul. Though not as impressive as the Land Walls, some stretches of the Sea Walls survive. The longest stretch is to be found along Kennedy Caddesi, and one of the towers still stands intact some 200 metres above the Galata bridge over the Golden Horn. Other fragments can be seen along the Golden Horn and the southern shoreline. Many of these fragments still carry Greek inscriptions recording the restoration of the wall by Theophilos (829–42), such as this one:

> Possessing Thee, O Christ, a Wall that cannot be broken, Theophilos, emperor and pious autocrat, erected this wall upon new foundations: which, Lord of All, guard with Thy might, and display to the end of time standing unshaken and unmoved.[20]

There are many other structures that are clearly Byzantine in origin scattered around Istanbul, such as the crumbling monumental base of the column of Arcadius which lies covered in ivy in Haseki Kadın Sokak. In the case of many other remains, their identity and even the precise function is a complete mystery. In Cemal Nadır Sokak, a street that lies in an area to the north of the Forum of Constantine that was known in Byzantine times as Sphorakion, there is an intriguing Byzantine substructure. It comprises twelve rooms and passages of various shapes and sizes. There is a substantial central hall, some six metres high, whose roof is supported by two rows of six columns. Clearly, these are the remains of a very impressive building indeed, but at the present time there is no clue as to what it was.[21]

Byzantine traces can also be seen in the great Ottoman buildings of the city. In the mosque complex of the Süleymaniye, the columns of porphyry marble that hold up the porticoes were reused from an earlier Byzantine building, possibly some part of the Great Palace. Many of those which line the inner courtyard of the Blue Mosque can be traced back to the Hippodrome. Other broken bits and pieces have found their way to the city's museums. The Military Museum, for example, preserves some links from the chain that was stretched across the Golden Horn during the last siege of 1453. The Archaeological Museum houses, among other artefacts from the period, the St Francis frescoes from the church of the Virgin Kyriotissa that probably date from the Latin occupation of 1204–61 and two fifth-century marble pedestals honouring the popular charioteer Porphyrius that were found in the Hippodrome. Perhaps most poignant of all are the two stone lions which flank one of the museum's staircases. They used to stand on some remnants of the Palace of Boukoleon which overlooked the harbour of the same name. These ruins were demolished in 1871 but the lions were preserved. Dating from the sixth century, they must once have looked down on the marble steps that led to the mooring for the imperial galley and watched the emperors as they came and went.[22]

While something of Byzantine Constantinople can still be found in modern Istanbul, the problem remains that many of the Byzantine monuments stand isolated among the intensive urban development that has taken place around them. The tenth-century church of the Myrelaion (Bodrum Camii), for example, is now closely hemmed in on all sides by buildings, such is the pressure on space for housing. As a result, it is by no means easy to find the church that Romanos I Lekapenos built as his own burial place, and the same applies to many of the other Byzantine churches. With the possible exception of the Hippodrome and Sultanahmet square, Istanbul has no Byzantine equivalent of the Acropolis in Athens or the Forum in Rome, a dedicated space set aside from the everyday life of the city to preserve an important aspect of its past.

There is, however, another way to form an idea of Byzantine Constantinople and that is to visit Venice. The two cities had been closely intertwined for centuries, from the time when Venice was an outpost of Byzantine rule in Italy, through the years when Venice dominated Constantinople's overseas trade, to the last days of Byzantium in 1453 when Venetian volunteers fought on the walls alongside the Byzantines against the Ottomans. This long association was bound to leave its mark on Venice. Furthermore while Constantinople experienced two catastrophic sacks in 1204 and 1453, followed by intense urban development in the twentieth century, all of which effaced much of the legacy of the past, Venice has been largely left as it was. Venice may lack the youthful vibrancy of the streets of Istanbul but its medieval buildings are still intact.

Part of the visible Byzantine influence in Venice can be seen in those buildings. In the days when Byzantium was the superpower and Venice the client state, it was only natural that Byzantine styles in art and architecture should be followed by those who wanted to make an impression. The rulers of Venice even brought in artists from Constantinople to work on the mosaic decoration of their churches. The most prominent surviving monument to this period is the church of St Mark itself. Completed in 1064, its interior mosaic decoration is clearly influenced by Byzantine styles, and may even have been the work of Byzantine artists. Byzantine influence is visible on the outside too. The church has five domes, arranged in the form of a cross, and may therefore reflect the architecture of the now vanished church of the Holy Apostles.[23] Venice may also provide a clue to the appearance of secular buildings in Constantinople, particularly the houses of great magnates such as Niketas Choniates and Theodore Metochites. Several of the palaces along the Grand Canal in Venice, such as Enrico Dandolo's Palazzo Farsetti, were built in the medieval period, and with their loggias and the rounded arches of their windows probably reflect Byzantine models.

As well as reflecting Byzantine architectural and artistic influence, Venice is full of objects brought from Constantinople in the wake of the Fourth Crusade. Many are housed in the treasury of St Mark's but others are visible outside. The most famous are the four bronze horses that stand on the façade of St Mark's but were originally sited in the Hippodrome. These days, thanks to the pollution drifting across the lagoon from the chemical plants at Mestre, the horses on the façade are replicas and the originals are kept inside the church. Below the façade, close to the entrance to the Palace of the Doges in St Mark's Square, stand four enigmatic figures made of porphyry marble, clasping each other around the shoulders. For a long time in the later Middle Ages it was said that these were four impious Saracens who had been turned to stone for trying to rob the treasury of St Mark's. Later art historians suspected that the group was of Constantinopolitan manufacture and depicted a group of imperial rulers, possibly either the Tetrarchs who divided the empire between them under Diocletian or else the sons of Constantine. Their origin in Constantinople was confirmed in 1965, when an excavation at the Myrelaion monastery in Istanbul unearthed a porphyry foot which exactly matched that missing from one of the figures in Venice. The four figures, like the horses above, were probably carted back in triumph in 1204.[24]

Some of these plundered objects have poignancy all of their own. One is the icon of the Virgin Mary that sits above the altar in a side chapel of St Mark's. This is reputedly the icon known as the Bringer of Victory (*Nikopeia*) that had for centuries been carried by the Byzantine emperors into battle and was credited with Basil II's victory at Abydos in April 989. It may even have been that which was lost by Alexios V Mourtzouphlos early in 1204 when he unsuccessfully clashed with a party of crusaders led by Henry of Flanders. Whether this is true or not can never now be known, but the icon is clearly Byzantine and highly enough prized to be enclosed in a jewelled and enamelled frame.[25]

Another relic of Byzantium is hidden away, far from busy St Mark's Square, in the quiet Campiello de Ca'Angaran close to the church of San Pantalon. On a wall above two doorways is a large marble roundel bearing the sculpted image of a bearded Byzantine emperor. In his right hand he holds a sceptre and in his left, like the statue of Justinian in the Augousteion, a crowned orb. Behind him a sunburst pattern suggests his radiance and glory. How it came to be in this obscure corner of Venice will never now be known. Some returning mariner, perhaps, carried it home and fixed it onto the wall of his house to let posterity know that he was there when Constantinople was conquered in 1204. Nor is their any certainty as to who the emperor depicted on it might be. The roundel gives no clue to his name, but since it dates from the twelfth century it might well be Alexios I Komnenos or Isaac II or even Alexios III Angelos whose adventures have been traced in this book.[26] Whoever he is, the emperor stands in that secluded spot summer and winter, keeping his lonely vigil, a perpetual exile from the Queen of Cities.

Notes

Introduction

1   See the arguments of Averil Cameron, 'The exotic mirage', *The Times Higher Education Supplement,* 21 September 1990, pp. 13–15.

2   Nicholas I, Patriarch of Constantinople, *Letters,* ed. and trans. R. J. H. Jenkins and L. G. Westerink (Washington, DC, 1973), pp. 70–1.

Chapter 1

1   Snorri Sturluson, *Heimskringla: Sagas of the Norse Kings,* trans. Samuel Laing (3rd edn, London, 1961), pp. 284–7.

2   Geoffrey of Villehardouin, *The Conquest of Constantinople,* in *Chronicles of the Crusades,* trans. M. R. B. Shaw (Harmondsworth, 1963), pp. 29–160, at 59; Fulcher of Chartres, *Chronicle,* trans. M. E. McGinty, in *The First Crusade: The Chronicle of Fulcher of Chartres and Other Source Materials,* ed. E. Peters (2nd edn, Philadelphia, 1998), pp. 47–101, at 62; Odo of Deuil, *De profectione Ludovici VII in orientem,* ed. and trans. V. G. Berry (New York, 1948), pp. 62–3; Ruy Gonzalez Clavijo, *Embassy to Tamerlane,* trans. G. Le Strange (London, 1928), p. 88. On reactions to Constantinople, see Ruth J. Macrides, 'Constantinople: the crusaders' gaze', in *Travel in the Byzantine World,* ed. R. J. Macrides (Aldershot, 2002), pp. 193–212.

3   Niketas Choniates, *O City of Byzantium: Annals of Niketas Choniates,* trans. H. J. Magoulias (Detroit, 1984), p. 317; Michael Psellos, *Fourteen Byzantine Rulers,* trans. E. R. A. Sewter (2nd edn, Harmondsworth, 1966), p. 114; Anna Comnena, *The Alexiad,* trans. E. R. A.

Sewter (Harmondsworth, 1969), p. 63; Demetrius John Georgacas, 'The Names of Constantinople', *Transactions and Proceedings of the American Philological Society*, 78 (1947), pp. 347–67, at 358–66.

4   Villehardouin, p. 59; Ralph Coggeshall, *Chronicon Anglicanum*, ed. J. Stevenson (London, 1875), p. 150; Gilbert Dagron, 'The urban economy, seventh-twelfth centuries', in *The Economic History of Byzantium: From the Seventh through the Fifteenth Century*, ed. Angeliki E. Laiou, 3 vols (Washington, DC, 2002), ii, pp. 393–461, at 394–5.

5   Robert of Clari, *The Conquest of Constantinople*, trans. E. H. McNeal (Toronto, 1996), pp. 108–9; A. A. Vasiliev, 'Harun-Ibn-Yahya and his description of Constantinople', *Annales de l'Institut Kondakov*, 5 (1932), pp. 149–63 at 155; Alexander van Millingen, *Byzantine Constantinople: The Walls of the City and Adjoining Historical Sites* (London, 1899), pp. 59, 73; Theodore Macridy and Stanley Casson, 'Excavations at the Golden Gate, Constantinople', *Archaeologia*, 81 (1931), pp. 63–84; Cyril Mango, 'The Triumphal Way of Constantinople and the Golden Gate', *DOP*, 54 (2000), pp. 173–88; Sarah Bassett, *The Urban Image of Late Antique Constantinople* (Cambridge, 2004), p. 212.

6   Fulcher of Chartres, p. 62; Krijnie N. Ciggaar, *Western Travellers to Constantinople: The West and Byzantium, 962–1204. Cultural and Political Relations* (Leiden, 1996), p. 46; R. Janin, *Constantinople Byzantine* (2nd edn, Paris, 1964), pp. 269–70.

7   Millingen, *Byzantine Constantinople: The Walls*, pp. 85–9; Janin, *Constantinople*, pp. 281–2.

8   Odo of Deuil, p. 65; Clavijo, pp. 87–8.

9   From Mount Athos, Codex Lavra, K. 34, translation at http://www.patriarchate.org/ecumenical_patriarchate/chapter_4/html/holy_apostles.html

10 Nicholas Mesarites, *Description of the Church of the Holy Apostles at Constantinople*, ed. and trans. Glanville Downey, *Transactions of the American Philosophical Society*, 47 (1957), pp. 855–924, at 867–89; Emile Legrand, 'Description des œuvres d'art et de l'église des Saints Apôtres de Constantinople: poème en vers iambiques par Constantin le Rhodien', *Revue des Études Grecques*, 9 (1896), pp. 32–65 at 58–65; Procopius of Caesarea, *The Buildings*, trans.

H. B. Dewing (London and Cambridge, MA, 1940), pp. 48–55; Cyril Mango, *The Art of the Byzantine Empire, 312–1453: Sources and Documents* (Englewood Cliffs, NJ, 1972), pp. 232–3; Ann Wharton Epstein, 'The rebuilding and decoration of the Holy Apostles in Constantinople: a reconsideration', *Greek, Roman and Byzantine Studies*, 23 (1982), pp. 79–92; Ken Dark and Ferudun Özgümüş, 'New evidence for the Byzantine church of the Holy Apostles from Fatih Camii, Istanbul', *Oxford Journal of Archaeology*, 21 (2002), 393–413; R. Janin, *La géographie ecclésiastique de l'empire byzantin: première partie: le siège de Constantinople et le patriarchat oecumenique. Tome III: les églises et les monastères* (2nd edn, Paris, 1969), pp. 41–9.

[11] Mesarites, *Description*, pp. 891–3; Legrand, 'Description', p. 38; John Skylitzes, *Synopsis historiarum*, ed. J. Thurn (Berlin, 1973), p. 48; A. A. Vasiliev, 'Imperial porphyry sarcophagi in Constantinople', *DOP*, 4 (1948), pp. 1–26; Glanville Downey, 'The tombs of the Byzantine Emperors in the church of the Holy Apostles in Constantinople', *JHS*, 79 (1959), pp. 27–51; Philip Grierson, 'The tombs and obits of the Byzantine emperors (337–1042)', *DOP*, 16 (1962), pp. 3–60; Janin, *Géographie*, p. 49.

[12] Marlia Mundell Mango, 'The porticoed street at Constantinople', in *Byzantine Constantinople: Monuments, Topography and Everyday Life*, ed. Nevra Necipoğlu (Leiden, 2001), pp. 29–51; Ken Dark, 'Houses, streets and shops in Byzantine Constantinople from the fifth to the twelfth centuries', *Journal of Medieval History*, 30 (2004), pp. 83–107.

[13] Janin, *Constantinople*, p. 200

[14] Martin Harrison, *A Temple for Byzantium: The Discovery and Excavation of Anicia Juliana's Palace-Church in Istanbul* (London, 1989); Janin, *Géographie*, pp. 405–6.

[15] Legrand, 'Description', p. 46; Pierre Gilles (Gyllius), *The Antiquities of Constantinople*, trans. John Ball (London, 1729), p. 256; Janin, *Constantinople*, pp. 84–6.

[16] Theophanes Confessor, *The Chronicle of Theophanes Confessor. Byzantine and Near Eastern History AD 284–813*, trans. C. Mango and R. Scott (Oxford, 1997), pp. 107, 193; Marcellinus Comes,

The Chronicle of Marcellinus, trans. B. Croke (Sydney, 1995), p. 27; Robert of Clari, pp. 110–11; Legrand, 'Description', pp. 42–3; Gilles, pp. 193–4; Janin, *Constantinople*, pp. 81–2; Bassett, *Urban Image*, pp. 208–12.

[17] Legrand, 'Description', pp. 43–4; Gilles, pp. 250–4; E. H. Freshfield, 'Notes on a vellum album containing some original sketches of public buildings and monuments, drawn by a German artist who visited Constantinople in 1574', *Archaeologia*, 72 (1921–2), 87–104; J. H. W. G. Liebeschuetz, *Barbarians and Bishops: Army, Church and State in the Age of Arcadius and John Chrysostom* (Oxford, 1990), pp. 273–8; Janin, *Constantinople*, pp. 82–4.

[18] John Malalas, *The Chronicle*, trans. Elizabeth Jeffreys, Michael Jeffreys and Roger Scott (Melbourne, 1986), p. 174; Comnena, p. 380; Michael Glykys, *Annales*, ed. I. Bekker (Bonn, 1836), p. 617; Legrand, 'Description', pp. 37–9; John Zonaras, *Annales*, ed. M. Pinder and T. Büttner-Wobst, 3 vols (Bonn, 1841–97), ii, p. 18; Janin, *Constantinople*, pp. 77–80; Garth Fowden, 'Constantine's porphyry column: the earliest literary allusion', *Journal of Roman Studies*, 81 (1991), pp. 119–31; Bassett, *Urban Image*, pp. 192–204.

[19] Choniates, pp. 305–6, 357; R. J. H. Jenkins, 'The bronze Athena at Byzantium', *JHS*, 67 (1947), pp. 31–3; Janin, *Constantinople*, pp. 62–4; Bassett, *Urban Image*, pp. 188–92, 204–8.

[20] Choniates, pp. 353, 358; Averil Cameron and Judith Herrin (eds), *Constantinople in the Early Eighth Century: The Parastasis Syntomoi Chronikai* (Leiden, 1984), pp. 114–17; Janin, *Constantinople*, pp. 68–70; Bassett, *Urban Image*, pp. 248–9.

[21] Procopius, *Buildings*, pp. 32–7; Robert of Clari, p. 107; Legrand, 'Description', pp. 37, 47; Pero Tafur, *Travels and Adventures, 1435–1439*, trans. Malcolm Letts (London, 1926), pp. 140–1; Cyril Mango and John Parker, 'A twelfth-century description of St Sophia', *DOP*, 14 (1960), pp. 233–45, at 236; Cyril Mango, 'The columns of Justinian and his successors', *Art Bulletin*, 41 (1959), pp. 1–16; P. W. Lehmann, 'Theodosius or Justinian? A Renaissance Drawing of a Byzantine Rider', *Art Bulletin*, 41 (1959), pp. 39–57; Stella Papadaki-Oekland, 'The representation of Justinian's column in a Byzantine miniature of the twelfth century', *BZ*, 83 (1990), pp. 63–71.

22   Vasiliev, 'Harun-ibn-Yahya', p. 160; Choniates, pp. 183, 358; Cameron and Herrin, *Constantinople*, pp. 100–3; Legrand, 'Description', pp. 39–42; Janin, *Constantinople*, pp. 59–62; Bassett, *Urban Image*, pp. 238–40.

23   Constantine VII, *De ceremoniis aulae Byzantinae*, ed. J. Reisky, 2 vols (Bonn, 1829–30), i, pp. 364–9; V. Minorsky, 'Marvazi on the Byzantines', *Annuaire de l'Institut de Philologie et d'Histoire Orientales et Slaves*, 10 (1950), pp. 455–69 at 462; Leo the Deacon, *The History of Leo the Deacon: Byzantine Military Expansion in the Tenth Century*, trans. Alice-Mary Talbot and Denis F. Sullivan (Washington, DC, 2005), pp. 80–1; Sturluson, pp. 286–7; Comnena, pp. 502–4; Choniates, pp. 160, 172, 192–4.

24   Linda Safran, 'Points of view: the Theodosian obelisk base in context', *Greek, Roman and Byzantine Studies*, 34 (1993), pp. 409–35; Bassett, *Urban Image*, pp. 219–22; Janin, *Constantinople*, pp. 192–3.

25   Choniates, pp. 67–8, 285, 305, 358–62; Alan Cameron, *Porphyrius the Charioteer* (Oxford, 1973), pp. 4–12; L. Vlad Borelli and A. Guidi Toniato, 'The origins and documentary sources of the horses of San Marco', in *The Horses of San Marco*, ed. Guido Perocco, trans. J. and V. Wilton-Ely (London, 1979), pp. 127–36, at 127–8; Janin, *Constantinople*, pp. 183–94; Bassett, *Urban Image*, pp. 214, 222–3.

26   Herodotus, *The Histories*, trans. A. D. Godley, 4 vols (Cambridge, MA, and London, 1920–5), iv, pp. 254–5; Pausanias, *Description of Greece*, trans. W. H. S. Jones, 5 vols (Cambridge, MA, and London, 1918–35), iv, p. 443; Thomas F. Madden, 'The Serpent Column of Delphi in Constantinople: placement, purposes and mutilations', *BMGS*, 16 (1992), pp. 111–45; Bassett, *Urban Image*, pp. 152–4, 213, 224–7.

27   Clavijo, p. 74; Procopius, *Buildings*, pp. 16–17; Mango and Parker, 'Twelfth-century description', pp. 237–8.

28   Paul the Silentiary in W. R. Lethaby and Harold Swainson, *The Church of Sancta Sophia, Constantinople: A Study of a Byzantine Building* (London and New York, 1894), p. 46. See also Tafur, p. 139; Anthony, Archbishop of Novgorod, *Description des lieux-saints de*

Constantinople, in *Itinéraires russes en orient,* ed. B. de Khitrowo (Geneva, 1889), pp. 85–111, at 97; Janin, *Géographie,* pp. 455–70.

[29] Clavijo, p. 76.

[30] Benjamin of Tudela, *The Itinerary,* trans. M. N. Adler (London, 1907), p. 13; Choniates, pp. 183, 315; Robert of Clari, p. 110.

[31] Choniates, p. 68; Comnena, p. 328; Liudprand of Cremona, *The Embassy to Constantinople and Other Writings,* trans. F. A. Wright (London, 1993), p. 156.

[32] Robert of Clari, pp. 108, 112–13; Choniates, p. 125, Anthony of Novgorod, pp. 101–2; K. N. Ciggaar, 'Une description de Constantinople dans le Tarragonensis 55', *REB,* 53 (1995), pp. 117–40 at 121; Ioli Kalavrezou, 'Helping hands for the empire: imperial ceremonies and the cult of relics at the Byzantine court', in *Byzantine Court Culture from 829 to 1204,* ed. Henry Maguire (Washington, DC, 1997), pp. 53–79, at 53; Janin, *Géographie,* pp. 232–6.

[33] *The Letter of the Three Patriarchs to the Emperor Theophilos and Related Texts,* ed. J. A. Munitiz, J. Chrysostomides, E. Harvalia-Crook and Ch. Dendrinos (Camberley, 1997), pp. lx-lxi; Anthony of Novgorod, p. 88; George P. Majeska, *Russian Travelers to Constantinople in the Fourteenth and Fifteenth Centuries* (Washington, DC, 1984), pp. 224–5.

[34] Robert of Clari, pp. 106–7; Anthony of Novgorod, p. 90.

[35] Robert of Clari, pp. 110–11; Gunther of Pairis, *The Capture of Constantinople,* trans. A. J. Andrea (Philadelphia, 1997), pp. 116–17. In general on the legends, see Gilbert Dagron, *Constantinople imaginaire: études sur le recueil des 'Patria'* (Paris, 1984); J. Chrysostomides, *Byzantine Women* (Camberley, 1994), pp. 5–6.

[36] Tafur, p. 143; Theophanes Continuatus, *Chronographia,* ed. I. Bekker (Bonn, 1838), p. 379; Cyril Mango, 'Antique Statuary and the Byzantine Beholder', *DOP,* 17 (1963), pp. 55–75 at 62; Liz James, '"Pray not to fall into temptation and be on your guard": pagan statues and Christian Constantinople', *Gesta,* 35 (1996), pp. 12–20.

[37] Majeska, *Russian Travelers,* pp. 44–7.

Chapter 2

[1] Mesarites, Nicholas, *Description of the Church of the Holy Apostles at Constantinople*, ed. and trans. Glanville Downey, in *Transactions of the American Philosophical Society*, 47 (1957), pp. 855–924, at 891–93; Niketas Choniates, *O City of Byzantium: Annals of Niketas Choniates*, trans. H. J. Magoulias (Detroit, 1984), pp. 263, 357; K. N. Ciggaar, 'Une description de Constantinople dans le Tarragonensis 55', *REB* 53 (1995), pp. 117–40, at 121; Glanville Downey, 'The tombs of the Byzantine emperors in the Church of the Holy Apostles in Constantinople', *JHS*, 79 (1959), pp. 27–51, at 44.

[2] Anonymous, *Life of Constantine*, trans. Frank Beetham, in Samuel N. C. Lieu and Dominic Montserrat, *From Constantine to Julian: Pagan and Byzantine Views* (London and New York, 1996), pp. 97–146, at 107–11.

[3] Anonymous, *Life of Constantine*, pp. 97–146, at 111–13; Alexander P. Kazhdan, '"Constantin imaginaire": Byzantine legends of the ninth century about Constantine the Great', *B*, 57 (1987), pp. 196–250, at 212–15.

[4] Anonymous, *Life of Constantine*, p. 115.

[5] Ibid., pp. 115–23; Theophanes Confessor, *The Chronicle of Theophanes Confessor. Byzantine and Near Eastern History AD 284–813*, trans C. Mango and R. Scott (Oxford, 1997), p. 23; Eusebius, *Life of Constantine*, trans. Averil Cameron and Stuart Hall (Oxford, 1999), pp. 80–2; John Malalas, *The Chronicle*, trans. Elizabeth Jeffreys, Michael Jeffreys and Roger Scott (Melbourne, 1986), p. 172; Kazhdan, '"Constantin imaginaire"', pp. 219–22; Timothy D. Barnes, *Constantine and Eusebius* (Cambridge, MA, and London, 1981), pp. 42–5.

[6] Philostorgius, *Kirchengeschichte*, ed. Joseph Bidez and Friedhelm Winkelmann (3rd edn, Berlin, 1981), pp. 20–2; *Chronicon paschale, 284–628 AD*, trans. Michael Whitby and Mary Whitby (Liverpool, 1989), p. 17; Anonymous, *Life of Constantine*, pp. 127–8; Theophanes Confessor, p. 46; Kazhdan, '"Constantin imaginaire"', pp. 235–9.

[7] Theophanes Confessor, p. 47; Socrates Scholasticus, *Ecclesiastical History*, trans. E. Walford (London, 1844), pp. 62–3; Sozomen, *Ecclesiastical History*, trans. E. Walford (London, 1846), pp. 48–9;

Eusebius, *Life of Constantine*, p. 140; Demetrius John Georgacas, 'The names of Constantinople', *Transactions and Proceedings of the American Philological Society*, 78 (1947), pp. 347–67, at 354–8.

8   *Chronicon paschale*, pp. 15–16; Anonymous, *Life of Constantine*, p. 128.

9   Anonymous, *Life of Constantine*, p. 141–2.

10   John Lydus, *On Powers or the Magistracies of the Roman State*, ed. and trans. A. C. Bandy (Philadelphia, 1983), p. 245; Averil Cameron and Judith Herrin (eds), *Constantinople in the Early Eighth Century: The Parastasis Syntomoi Chronikai* (Leiden, 1984), pp. 101, 115; Anonymous, *Life of Constantine*, p. 126; Procopius, *The Buildings*, trans. H. B. Dewing (London and Cambridge, MA, 1940), pp. 56–7; Nikephoros Gregoras, *Byzantina Historia*, ed. L. Schopen and I. Bekker, 3 vols (Bonn, 1829–55), i, p. 305; Georgacas, 'Names of Constantinople', pp. 348–53; Gilbert Dagron, *Constantinople imaginaire: études sur le recueil des 'Patria'* (Paris, 1984), pp. 62–3, 79–80.

11   Strabo, *Geography*, trans. H. L. Jones, 8 vols (Cambridge, MA, and London, 1917–32), iii, pp. 280–5.

12   Herodotus, *The Histories*, trans. A. D. Godley, 4 vols (Cambridge, MA, and London, 1920–5), iii, pp. 26–7, 153, 173; Thucydides, *The Peloponnesian War*, trans. Charles Forster Smith, 4 vols (Cambridge, MA, and London, 1928–35), i, pp. 160–1, iv, pp. 330–1; Tacitus, *The Annals*, trans. John Jackson, 3 vols (Cambridge, MA, and London, 1931–7), ii, pp. 406–7.

13   Zosimus, *New History*, trans. R. T. Riley (Canberra, 1982), pp. 28–9. On Constantine's accession and the Tetrarchy, see Averil Cameron, *The Later Roman Empire* (London, 1993), pp. 47–52; Barnes, *Constantine and Eusebius*, pp. 28–43; A. H. M. Jones, *Constantine and the Conversion of Europe* (2nd edn, London, 1962), pp. 65–73.

14   Zosimus, p. 38; Eusebius, *Life of Constantine*, p. 143; Socrates Scholasticus, p. 63; Richard Krautheimer, *Three Christian Capitals: Topography and Politics* (Berkeley, Los Angeles and London, 1983), pp. 60–1.

15   Eunapius of Sardis, *Lives of the Philosophers*, in Philostratus and Eunapius, The *Lives of the Sophists*, trans. Wilmer Cave Wright (Cambridge, MA, and London, 1952), pp. 317–563, at 383.

16   Zosimus, pp. 36–7.

17   Anonymous Valesianus, in Ammianus Marcellinus, *History*, trans. John C. Rolfe, 3 vols (Cambridge, MA, and London, 1935–9), iii, pp. 526–7.

18   Herodotus, ii, pp. 289–91; Pliny the Elder, *The Natural History*, trans. H. Rackham, W. H. S. Jones and D. E. Eicholz, 10 vols (Cambridge, MA, and London, 1938–62), ii, pp. 174–5; Ovid, *Tristia*, trans. A. L. Wheeler (Cambridge, MA, and London, 1937), pp. 50–1; Gilbert Dagron, *Naissance d'une capitale: Constantinople et ses institutions de 330 à 451* (Paris, 1974), pp. 43–7; Krautheimer, *Three Christian Capitals*, p. 45; Jones, *Constantine*, p. 219.

19   Gregory of Nyssa, *De deitate Filii et Spiritus Sancti*, in *Patrologiae Cursus Completus, Ser: Graeco-Latina*, ed. J.-P. Migne, 161 vols (Paris, 1857–66), xlvi, cols 553–76, at 557; Malalas, p. 187; J. Stevenson, *Creeds, Councils and Controversies: Documents Illustrating the History of the Church, AD 337–461* (2nd edn, London, 1989), pp. 117, 362; Dagron, *Naissance*, pp. 46, 54, 458, 480.

20   Francis Dvornik, *The Idea of Apostolicity in Byzantium and the Legend of the Apostle Andrew* (Cambridge, MA, 1958), pp. 138–80.

21   Dagron, *Naissance*, pp. 55–60.

22   David Jacoby, 'La population de Constantinople à l'époque byzantine: un problème de démographie urbaine', *B*, 31 (1961), pp. 81–109; Pauline Allen, 'The Justinianic Plague', B, 49 (1979), pp. 5–20, at 10; Dagron, *Naissance*, pp. 524–5.

23   Zosimus, p. 39.

24   St Jerome, *Chronicon*, ed. Rudolf Helm, Eusebius Werke 8 (Berlin, 1956), p. 232; Pliny the Elder, *Natural History*, ix, pp. 156–9; Strabo, iii, p. 107; *Chronicon paschale*, p. 34; Cyril Mango, *The Art of the Byzantine Empire, 312–1453: Sources and Documents* (Englewood Cliffs, NJ, 1972), p. 26; Krautheimer, *Three Christian Capitals*, pp. 50–5; Sarah Bassett, *The Urban Image of Late Antique Constantinople* (Cambridge, 2004), pp. 219–22.

25   *Chronicon Paschale*, pp. 49–50, 54; Bassett, *Urban Image*, pp. 152–4; John Freely and Ahmet S. Çakmak, *The Byzantine Monuments of Istanbul* (Cambridge, 2004), pp. 42–7; Alexander van Millingen, *Byzantine Constantinople: The Walls of the City and Adjoining Historical Sites* (London, 1899), pp. 63, 338–9.

26   Cited in van Millingen, *Byzantine Constantinople: The Walls*, p. 42.

27   Michael Psellos, *Fourteen Byzantine Rulers*, trans. E. R. A. Sewter (2nd edn, Harmondsworth, 1966), p. 72; idem, *Historia Syntomos*, p. 55.

28   Procopius of Caesarea, *The Secret History*, trans. H. B. Dewing (Cambridge, MA, and London, 1935), pp. 70–5.

29   Procopius of Caesarea, *History of the Wars*, trans. H. B. Dewing and Glanville Downey, 5 vols (Cambridge, MA, and London, 1914–28), i, pp. 219–39; *Chronicon paschale*, pp. 114–27; Geoffrey Greatrex, 'The Nika Riot: a reappraisal', *JHS*, 117 (1997), pp. 60–86.

30   Procopius, *Buildings*, p. 13.

31   Malalas, pp. 297, 303; Agathias of Myrina, *The Histories*, trans. J. D. Frendo (Berlin and New York, 1975), pp. 143–4; William Emerson and Robert L. van Nice, 'Hagia Sophia: the collapse of the first dome', *Archaeology*, 4 (1951), pp. 94–103.

32   Mango, *Art of Byzantium*, pp. 96–8; Dagron, *Constantinople imaginaire*, p. 200.

33   Michael Glykys, *Annales*, ed. I. Bekker (Bonn, 1836), pp. 497–8; Pero Tafur, *Travels and Adventures*, 1435–1439, trans. Malcolm Letts (London, 1926), pp. 144–5; W. R. Lethaby and Harold Swainson, *The Church of Sancta Sophia, Constantinople: A Study of a Byzantine Building* (London and New York, 1894), pp. 132–3; Ciggaar, 'Une description', p. 126; Dagron, *Constantinople imaginaire*, pp. 200–1.

34   Mango, *Art of the Byzantine Empire*, p. 101; Glykys, pp. 497–8; Lethaby and Swainson, *Church of Sancta Sophia*, p. 141; Dagron, *Constantinople imaginaire*, pp. 207–8, 303–4.

35   Procopius, *Secret History*, pp. 98–9.

36   Ibid., pp. 92–3, 142–5; Evagrius Scholasticus, *The Ecclesiastical History*, trans. Michael Whitby (Liverpool, 2000), pp. 232–3.

37 Procopius, *Secret History*, pp. 222–3.

38 Procopius, *Buildings*, pp. 86–9; Theophanes Confessor, p. 314. Malalas p. 285 says that Justinian only moved the Milion.

39 Procopius, *Buildings*, pp. 48–53.

40 Ibid., pp. 36–9. For a description of Constantinople at the end of Justinian's reign, see Brian Croke, 'Justinian's Constantinople', in *The Cambridge Companion to the Reign of Justinian*, ed. Michael Maas (Cambridge, 2005), pp. 60–86.

41 Choniates, p. 244; Donald M. Nicol, 'Byzantine political thought', in *The Cambridge History of Medieval Political Thought c. 350 – c. 1450*, ed. J. H. Burns (Cambridge, 1988), pp. 51–79, at 55.

42 Anna Comnena, *The Alexiad*, trans. E. R. A. Sewter (Harmondsworth, 1969), p. 62; Liudprand of Cremona, *The Embassy to Constantinople and Other Writings*, trans. F. A. Wright (London, 1993), p. 201; Michael Psellos, *Historia Syntomos*, ed. and trans. W. J. Aerts (Berlin and New York, 1990), pp. 36–7; John Kinnamos, *The Deeds of John and Manuel Comnenus*, trans. C. M. Brand (New York, 1976), pp. 165–6; Nicol, 'Byzantine political thought', pp. 59–60.

43 Cameron and Herrin, *Constantinople*, p. 85; Anonymous, *Life of Constantine*, p. 128; Dagron, *Constantinople imaginaire*, pp. 85–97.

Chapter 3

1 Lennart Rydén, 'The Andreas Salos Apocalypse: Greek text, translation, and commentary', *DOP* 28 (1974), pp. 199–261, at 215.

2 *Chronicon paschale, 284–628 AD*, trans. Michael Whitby and Mary Whitby (Liverpool, 1989), pp. 169, 178, 180; V. Grumel, 'Homélie de Saint Germain sur la délivrance de Constantinople', *REB*, 16 (1958), pp. 183–205, at 194, 201; N. H. Baynes, 'The supernatural defenders of Constantinople', in N. H. Baynes, *Byzantine Studies and Other Essays* (London, 1955), pp. 248–60; Averil Cameron, 'Images of authority: elites and icons in late sixth-century Byzantium', *Past and Present*, 84 (1979), pp. 1–35, at 5–6, 18–24; Hans Belting, *Likeness and Presence: A History of the Image before the Era of Art*, trans. Edmund Jephcott (Chicago, 1994), pp. 495–8; Paul J. Alexander, 'The strength of empire and capital as seen through Byzantine eyes',

Speculum, 37 (1962), pp. 339–57, at 339–40; Jonathan Shepard, 'The uses of "history" in Byzantine diplomacy', in *Porphyrogenita: Essays on the History and Literature of Byzantium and the Latin East in Honour of Julian Chrysostomides*, ed. Charalambos Dendrinos, Jonathan Harris, Eirene Harvalia-Crook and Judith Herrin (Aldershot, 2003), pp. 91–115, at 92–4.

3   Pseudo-Symeon Magister in Theophanes Continuatus, *Chronographia*, ed. I. Bekker (Bonn, 1838), pp. 674–5; John Skylitzes, *Synopsis historiarum*, ed. J. Thurn (Berlin, 1973), p. 34; Anna Comnena, *The Alexiad*, trans. E. R. A. Sewter (Harmondsworth, 1969), p. 225; Norman H. Baynes, 'The finding of the Virgin's robe', in Norman H. Baynes, *Byzantine Studies and other Essays* (London, 1955), pp. 240–7; R. Janin, *La géographie ecclésiastique de l'empire byzantin: première partie: le siège de Constantinople et le patriarchat oecuménique. Tome III: les églises et les monastères* (2nd edn, Paris, 1969), pp. 161–70.

4   Cyril Mango, *The Art of the Byzantine Empire, 312–1453: Sources and Documents* (Englewood Cliffs, NJ, 1972), p. 40; *The Letter of the Three Patriarchs to the Emperor Theophilos and Related Texts*, ed. J. A. Munitiz, J. Chrysostomides, E. Harvalia-Crook and Ch. Dendrinos (Camberley, 1997), pp. 38–9, 148–9; Thomas F. Mathews, *The Art of Byzantium* (London, 1998), pp. 65–7; Janin, *Géographie*, pp. 199–207.

5   Anthony, Archbishop of Novgorod, *Description des lieux-saints de Constantinople*, in *Itinéraires russes en orient*, ed. B. de Khitrowo (Geneva, 1889), pp. 85–111, p. 99; Pero Tafur, *Travels and Adventures, 1435–1439*, trans. Malcolm Letts (London, 1926), pp. 141–2; J. P. Thomas and A. C. Hero, *Byzantine Monastic Foundation Documents: A Complete Translation of the Surviving Founders' Typika and Testaments*, 5 vols (Washington, DC, 2000), ii, p. 756; Ruy Gonzalez Clavijo, *Embassy to Tamerlane*, trans. G. Le Strange (London, 1928), pp. 84–5; N. Krijnie, 'Une description de Constantinople dans le Tarragonensis 55', *REB*, 53 (1995), pp. 117–40, at 127–8.

6   Niketas Choniates, *O City of Byzantium: Annals of Niketas Choniates*, trans. H. J. Magoulias (Detroit, 1984), pp. 90, 209–10; Leo the Deacon, *The History of Leo the Deacon: Byzantine Military*

Expansion in the Tenth Century, trans. Alice-Mary Talbot and Denis F. Sullivan (Washington, DC, 2005), pp. 200–1; Bissera V. Pentcheva, 'The supernatural protector of Constantinople: the Virgin and her icons in the tradition of the Avar siege', *BMGS*, 26 (2002), pp. 2–41; Robert Lee Wolff, 'Footnote to an incident of the Latin occupation of Constantinople: the church and the icon of the Hodegetria', *Speculum*, 6 (1948), pp. 319–28.

7   Skylitzes, p. 384; Michael Psellos, *Fourteen Byzantine Rulers*, trans. E. R. A. Sewter (2nd edn, Harmondsworth, 1966), pp. 36–7, 69–70; Wolff, 'Footnote', p. 326; Warren Treadgold, *A History of the Byzantine State and Society* (Stanford, CA, 1997), pp. 518–19.

8   Herodotus, *The Histories*, trans. A. D. Godley, 4 vols (Cambridge, MA, and London, 1920–5), ii, pp. 344–5; Tacitus, *The Annals*, trans. John Jackson, 3 vols (Cambridge, MA, and London, 1931–7), ii, pp. 406–9; Strabo, iii, pp. 280–5.

9   Polybius, *The Histories*, trans. W. R. Paton, 6 vols (Cambridge, MA, and London, 1922–7), ii, pp. 392–3.

10 Cassius Dio, *Roman History*, trans. E. Cary, 9 vols (Cambridge, MA, and London, 1914–27), ix, pp. 185–7. Cf. Polybius, ii, pp. 396–9.

11 Cassius Dio, ix, pp. 183–95; Zosimus, *New History*, trans. R. T. Riley (Canberra, 1982), p. 37.

12 Cassius Dio, ix, p. 195.

13 John Malalas, *The Chronicle*, trans. Elizabeth Jeffreys, Michael Jeffreys and Roger Scott (Melbourne, 1986), p. 155; *The Scriptores Historiae Augustae*, trans. David Magie, 3 vols (Cambridge, MA, and London, 1930–2), ii, p. 5.

14 Malalas, p. 173; *Chronicon paschale*, p. 16; Ammianus Marcellinus, *History*, trans. John C. Rolfe, 3 vols (Cambridge, MA, and London, 1935–9), iii, pp. 502–3; R. Janin, *Constantinople Byzantine* (2nd edn, Paris, 1964), pp. 263–5.

15 On the Land Walls, see Alexander van Millingen, *Byzantine Constantinople: The Walls of the City and Adjoining Historical Sites* (London, 1899); Byron C. P. Tsangadas, *The Fortifications and Defense of Constantinople* (New York, 1980), pp. 7–21; Clive Foss and David Winfield, *Byzantine Fortifications: An Introduction* (Pretoria, 1986), pp. 41–77; Janin, *Constantinople*, pp. 265–83.

[16] Leo the Deacon, pp. 129–30; Choniates p. 117; Geoffrey of Villehardouin, *The Conquest of Constantinople*, in *Chronicles of the Crusades*, trans. M. R. B. Shaw (Harmondsworth, 1963), pp. 29–160, at 66; Robert of Clari, *The Conquest of Constantinople*, trans. E. H. McNeal (Toronto, 1996), p. 69; van Millingen, *Byzantine Constantinople: The Walls*, p. 229; Tsangadas, *Fortifications*, pp. 33–59; Janin, *Constantinople*, pp. 287–300. The chain is first mentioned as being used in Byzantine times in 626: Theophanes Confessor, *The Chronicle of Theophanes Confessor. Byzantine and Near Eastern History AD 284–813*, trans C. Mango and R. Scott (Oxford, 1997), p. 545.

[17] *Chronicon paschale*, pp. 170–81; Theophanes Confessor, p. 447; Nikephoros, *Short History*, ed. and trans. C. Mango (Washington DC, 1990), pp. 59–61; Tsangadas, *Fortifications*, pp. 80–106; J. D. Howard-Johnston, 'The siege of Constantinople in 626', in *Constantinople and its Hinterland. Papers from the Twenty-seventh Spring Symposium of Byzantine Studies, Oxford, April 1993*, ed. Cyril Mango and Gilbert Dagron (Aldershot, 1995), pp. 131–42.

[18] Theophanes Confessor, pp. 493–4; Nikephoros, *Short History*, pp. 84–7; Leo VI, *Tactica sive de re militari liber*, in *Patrologia Graeca*, vol. 107, cols 669–1120, at 992; Comnena, pp. 360–1; Leo the Deacon, pp. 188, 198; J. R. Partington, *A History of Greek Fire and Gunpowder* (Cambridge, 1960), pp. 10–21, 28–32; John Haldon and M. Byrne, 'A possible solution to the problem of Greek Fire', *BZ*, 70 (1977), pp. 91–9, at 92; Tsangadas, *Fortifications*, pp. 107–33.

[19] David Olster, 'Theodore Grammaticus and the Arab siege of 674–8', *Byzantinoslavica*, 56 (1995), pp. 23–8, at 23–4.

[20] Theophanes Confessor, pp. 545–50; Nikephoros, *Short History*, pp. 123–5; E. W. Brooks, 'The campaign of 716–718, from Arabic sources', *JHS*, 19 (1899), pp. 19–33, at 23, 28; Tsangadas, *Fortifications*, pp. 134–52.

[21] Theophanes Confessor, pp. 585–6; Pauline Allen, 'The Justinianic plague', B, 49 (1979), pp. 5–20, at 18–19.

[22] Gilbert Dagron, 'The urban economy, seventh–twelfth centuries', in *The Economic History of Byzantium: From the Seventh through the Fifteenth Century*, ed. Angeliki E. Laiou, 3 vols (Washington,

DC, 2002), ii, pp. 393–461, at 394–5; David Jacoby, 'La population de Constantinople à l'époque byzantine: un problème de démographie urbaine', *B*, 31 (1961), pp. 81–109, at 109.

23 Theophanes Confessor, p. 686.

24 Liudprand of Cremona, *The Embassy to Constantinople and Other Writings*, trans. F. A. Wright (London, 1993), pp. 135–6; *The Russian Primary Chronicle: The Laurentian Text*, ed. and trans. S. H. Cross and O. P. Sherbowitz-Wetzor (Cambridge, MA, 1953), p. 72.

25 Theophanes Confessor, p. 522; Nikephoros, *Short History*, p. 103. In general on the mechanics of revolts in Byzantium, see Jean-Claude Cheynet, *Pouvoir et contestations à Byzance (963–1210)* (Paris, 1990), pp. 157–73.

26 *Chronicon paschale*, p. 181; Choniates, pp. 211, 298; van Millingen, *Byzantine Constantinople: The Walls*, pp. 122–4; Janin, *Constantinople*, p. 283.

27 Comnena, pp. 95, 98; Choniates, p. 208; van Millingen, *Byzantine Constantinople: The Walls*, pp. 85–6; Tsangadas, *Fortifications*, p. 19.

28 Psellos, *Fourteen Byzantine Rulers*, p. 217.

29 Ibid., pp. 212–13, 216–17; Michael Attaleiates, *Historia*, ed. W. Brunet de Presle and I. Bekker (Bonn, 1853), pp. 27–8.

30 Psellos, *Fourteen Byzantine Rulers*, pp. 297–8; Attaleiates, pp. 56–60; Skylitzes, pp. 498–500.

31 A. A. Vasiliev, 'Harun-ibn-Yahya and his description of Constantinople', *Annales de l'Institut Kondakov*, 5 (1932), pp. 149–63, at 156.

32 Comnena, pp. 95–6; A. A. Vasiliev, 'The opening stages of the Anglo-Saxon immigration into Byzantium in the eleventh century', *Annales de l'Institut Kondakov*, 9 (1937), pp. 39–70; Sigfús Blöndal, *The Varangians of Byzantium* (Cambridge, 1978), pp. 103–21.

33 Snorri Sturlson, *Heimskringla: Sagas of the Norse Kings*, trans. Samuel Laing (London, 1961), pp. 160–72.

34 Comnena, pp. 95–7.

35 Choniates, p. 192.

36 Theophanes Confessor, p. 534; Genesios, *On the Reigns of the Emperors*, trans. Anthony Kaldellis (Canberra, 1998), p. 69; Choniates, pp. 36, 176, 222; Kinnamos, pp. 205–6; van Millingen, *Byzantine Constantinople: The Walls*, p. 101.

37 Constantine VII Porphyrogenitos, *De administrando imperio*, ed. G. Moravcsik, trans. R. J. H. Jenkins (Washington, DC, 1967), pp. 68–71.

38 Liudprand, p. 136; van Millingen, *Byzantine Constantinople: The Walls*, p. 100.

39 Theophanes Confessor, p. 494; Constantine VII Porphyrogenitos, *De administrando imperio*, pp. 66–7, 227; Partington, *History of Greek Fire*, pp. 12–14; Shepard, 'The uses of "history"', p. 115.

40 Constantine VII Porphyrogenitos, *Three Treatises on Imperial Military Expeditions*, ed. and trans. John F. Haldon (Vienna, 1990), pp. 114–15.

Chapter 4

1 Jean-Jacques Rousseau, 'A discourse on the moral effects of the arts and sciences', in *The Social Contract and Discourses*, trans. G. D. H. Cole (3rd edn, London, 1993), p. 9.

2 Genesios, *On the Reigns of the Emperors*, trans. Anthony Kaldellis (Canberra, 1998), pp. 22–3; Leo the Deacon, *The History of Leo the Deacon: Byzantine Military Expansion in the Tenth Century*, trans. Alice-Mary Talbot and Denis F. Sullivan (Washington, DC, 2005), pp. 137–41, 216–17.

3 Theophanes Confessor, *The Chronicle of Theophanes Confessor. Byzantine and Near Eastern History AD 284–813*, trans. C. Mango and R. Scott (Oxford, 1997), pp. 648–9; Michael Psellos, *Fourteen Byzantine Rulers*, trans. E. R. A. Sewter (2nd edn, Harmondsworth, 1966), pp. 365–6.

4 Anna Comnena, *The Alexiad*, trans. E. R. A. Sewter (Harmondsworth, 1969), pp. 36–7, 289–91; Leo the Deacon, pp. 189–90. On the practice of blinding, see Judith Herrin, 'Blinding in Byzantium', in *Polypleuros Nous: Miscellanea für Peter Schreiner zu seinem 60 Geburtstag*, ed. Cordula Scholz and Georgios Makris (Munich and Leipzig, 2000), pp. 56–68.

5 Eusebius of Caesarea, *Tricennial Oration*, in H. A. Drake, *In Praise of Constantine: A Historical Study and New Translation of Eusebius's Tricennial Orations* (Berkeley and Los Angeles, 1976), pp. 83–127, at 85

and 87; Timothy D. Barnes, *Constantine and Eusebius* (Cambridge, MA, and London, 1981), pp. 253–5.

6   Liudprand of Cremona, *The Embassy to Constantinople and Other Writings*, trans. F. A. Wright (London, 1993), pp. 199–200.

7   Eusebius, *Tricennial Oration*, p. 120.

8   Paul J. Alexander, 'The strength of empire and capital as seen through Byzantine eyes', *Speculum*, 37 (1962), pp. 339–57, at 348–54; Donald M. Nicol, 'Byzantine political thought', in *The Cambridge History of Medieval Political Thought c. 350 – c. 1450*, ed. J. H. Burns (Cambridge, 1988), pp. 51–79, at 52–5.

9   Ernest Barker, *Social and Political Thought in Byzantium from Justinian I to the Last Palaeologus* (Oxford, 1957), p. 194.

10 See, e.g., Thomas F. Mathews, *The Art of Byzantium* (London, 1998), pp. 35–9; Cyril Mango, *The Art of the Byzantine Empire, 312–1453: Sources and Documents* (Englewood Cliffs, NJ, 1972), pp. 225–8; Robin Cormack, *Writing in Gold: Byzantine Society and its Icons* (London, 1985), pp. 163–5.

11 Procopius of Caesarea, *The Buildings*, trans. H. B. Dewing (Cambridge, MA, and London, 1940), pp. 82–7.

12 Mango, *Art of the Byzantine Empire*, p. 199; Niketas Choniates, *O City of Byzantium: Annals of Niketas Choniates*, trans. H. J. Magoulias (Detroit, 1984), p. 243.

13 Two early attempts to reconstruct the layout of the palace were A. G. Paspates, *The Great Palace of Constantinople*, trans. William Metcalfe (London, 1893), and Jean Ebersolt, *Le Grand Palais de Constantinople et le Livre des Cérémonies* (Paris, 1910), both of which were strongly criticised by J. B. Bury, 'The Great Palace', *BZ*, 21 (1912), 210–25. For more recent assessments, see Cyril Mango, *The Brazen House: A Study of the Vestibule of the Imperial Palace* (Copenhagen, 1959), pp. 12–13; S. Miranda, 'Études sur le palais sacré de Constantinople. Le Walker Trust et le Palais de Daphnè', *Byzantinoslavica*, 44 (1983), pp. 41–9, 196–204; R. Janin, *Constantinople Byzantine* (2nd edn, Paris, 1964), pp. 121–2; Paul Magdalino, 'Manuel Komnenos and the Great Palace', *BMGS*, 4 (1978), pp. 101–14.

[14]   Liudprand of Cremona, pp. 10–11, 83; Comnena, p. 219; Choniates, p. 96; Janin, *Constantinople*, pp. 121–2; Judith Herrin, *Women in Purple: Rulers of Medieval Byzantium* (London, 2001), p. 65.

[15]   Comnena, p. 105; Leo the Deacon, p. 137; William of Tyre, *A History of Deeds Done Beyond the Sea*, trans. E. A. Babcock and A. C. Krey, 2 vols (New York, 1943), ii, p. 379; Janin, *Constantinople*, pp. 120–1; Alexander van Millingen, *Byzantine Constantinople: The Walls of the City and Adjoining Historical Sites* (London, 1899), pp. 269–87.

[16]   Liudprand of Cremona, pp. 153–5; Theophanes Confessor, pp. 339, 554, 565, 612, 621; Constantine VII Porphyrogenitos, *De ceremoniis aulae Byzantinae*, ed. J. Reisky, 2 vols (Bonn, 1829–30), i, p. 222; Janin, *Constantinople*, pp. 117–18.

[17]   Procopius, *Buildings*, pp. 86–7; Mango, *Art of the Byzantine Empire*, pp. 197–8; Paul Magdalino and Robert Nelson, 'The emperor in Byzantine art of the twelfth century', *Byzantinische Forschungen*, 8 (1982), pp. 123–83.

[18]   Robert of Clari, *The Conquest of Constantinople*, trans. E. H. McNeal (Toronto, 1996), p. 103; Romilly J. H. Jenkins and Cyril A. Mango, 'The date and significance of the Tenth Homily of Photios', *DOP*, 9/10 (1956), pp. 125–40, at 134–9; Ioli Kalavrezou, 'Helping hands for the empire: imperial ceremonies and the cult of relics at the Byzantine court', in *Byzantine Court Culture from 829 to 1204*, ed. Henry Maguire (Washington, DC, 1997), pp. 53–79, at 55–7; R. Janin, *La géographie ecclésiastique de l'empire byzantin: première partie: le siège de Constantinople et le patriarchat oecumenique. Tome III: les églises et les monastères* (2nd edn, Paris, 1969), pp. 232–6. On the beacons, see Constantine VII Porphyrogenitos, *Three Treatises on Imperial Military Expeditions*, ed. and trans. John F. Haldon (Vienna, 1990), pp. 132–5; P. Pattenden, 'The Byzantine early warning system', *B*, 53 (1983), pp. 258–99.

[19]   Robert of Clari, p. 103; Anthony, Archbishop of Novgorod, *Description des lieux-saints de Constantinople*, in *Itinéraires russes en orient*, ed. B. de Khitrowo (Geneva, 1889), pp. 85–111 at 97.

[20]   Anonymous, *Life of Constantine*, trans. Frank Beetham, in Samuel N. C. Lieu and Dominic Montserrat, *From Constantine to*

Julian: Pagan and Byzantine Views (London and New York, 1996), pp. 97–146, at 133–5; Theophanes Confessor, pp. 41–2.

21   *Chronicon paschale, 284–628 AD*, trans. Michael Whitby and Mary Whitby (Liverpool, 1989), p. 156; Theophanes Confessor, pp. 431, 455, 458–9.

22   Theophanes Confessor, p. 468.

23   Constantine VII Porphyrogenitos, 'Story of the Image of Edessa', trans. Bernard Slater and John Jackson, in Ian Wilson, *The Turin Shroud* (London, 1978), pp. 235–51; *The Letter of the Three Patriarchs to the Emperor Theophilos and Related Texts*, ed. J. A. Munitiz, J. Chrysostomides, E. Harvalia-Crook and Ch. Dendrinos (Camberley, 1997), pp. 32–7; Evagrius Scholasticus, *The Ecclesiastical History*, trans. Michael Whitby (Liverpool, 2000), pp. 225–8; Robert of Clari, p. 104; Choniates, p. 191.

24   Leo the Deacon, pp. 121, 207–8; Anthony of Novgorod, pp. 97–8; Robert of Clari, pp. 102–5; Krijnie N. Ciggaar, 'Une description de Constantinople dans le Tarragonensis 55', *REB* 53 (1995), pp. 117–40, at 120–1; eadem, *Western Travellers to Constantinople: The West and Byzantium, 962–1204. Cultural and Political Relations* (Leiden, 1996), pp. 47–9; J. Durand, *Le Trésor de la Sainte Chapelle* (Paris, 2001), p. 35; Hans Belting, *Likeness and Presence: A History of the Image before the Era of Art*, trans. Edmund Jephcott (Chicago, 1994), pp. 526–7; Kalavrezou, 'Helping hands', pp. 67–70.

25   John Kinnamos, *The Deeds of John and Manuel Comnenus*, trans. C. M. Brand (New York, 1976), p. 69; William of Tyre, ii, p. 381.

26   Constantine VII, *De ceremoniis*, i, pp. 4–5.

27   Psellos, *Fourteen Byzantine Rulers*, pp. 288–9; Constantine VII, *De ceremoniis*, i, 566–70; Liudprand of Cremona, p. 153; Kinnamos, p. 69; Gerard Brett, 'The Automata in the Byzantine "Throne of Solomon"', *Speculum*, 29 (1954), pp. 477–87; Titos Papamastorakis, 'Tampering with history from Michael III to Michael VIII', *BZ*, 96 (2003), pp. 193–209, at 197–8; Janin, *Constantinople*, pp. 117–19.

28   Constantine VII, *De ceremoniis*, i, pp. 1, 33–4.

29   A. A. Vasiliev, 'Harun-Ibn-Yahya and his description of Constantinople', *Annales de l'Institut Kondakov*, 5 (1932), pp. 149–63,

at 158; Nadia Maria El Cheikh, *Byzantium Viewed by the Arabs* (Cambridge, MA, 2004), pp. 155–7.

30 Liudprand of Cremona, p. 181.

31 Choniates, pp. 249–50, 296.

32 Ibid., pp. 138, 148, 291; Robert of Clari, p. 56; Eustathios of Thessalonica, *The Capture of Thessaloniki*, trans. J. R. Melville-Jones (Canberra, 1988), pp. 32–3, 38–9, 40–1.

33 Choniates, pp. 150, 155–60; C. M. Brand, *Byzantium Confronts the West, 1180–1204* (Cambridge, MA, 1968), pp. 52–3.

34 Choniates, pp. 151–2.

35 Ibid., pp. 187–95; Robert of Clari, pp. 50–6.

36 Choniates, pp. 232, 236, 246; Robert of Clari, pp. 56–7.

37 Alberic of Trois Fontaines, *Chronica*, ed. Paul Scheffer-Boichorst, *Monumenta Germaniae Historica. Scriptores*, 23 (Hannover, 1874), pp. 631–950, at 870; Gunther of Pairis, *The Capture of Constantinople*, trans. A. J. Andrea (Philadelphia, 1997), p. 82; Choniates, pp. 247, 307; Brand, *Byzantium Confronts*, p. 111.

38 Choniates, pp. 247–8; Brand, *Byzantium Confronts*, pp. 112–13.

39 Gunther of Pairis, p. 90.

40 Choniates, pp. 250–1.

41 Eusebius of Caesarea, *Life of Constantine*, trans. Averil Cameron and Stuart Hall (Oxford, 1999), p. 160.

42 Choniates, p. 252.

43 James Trilling, 'The soul of the empire: style and meaning in the mosaic pavement in the Byzantine imperial palace in Constantinople', *DOP*, 43 (1989), pp. 27–72, and plates 19 and 35.

44 Mango, *Art of the Byzantine Empire*, p. 195; Vasiliev, 'Harun-Ibn-Yahya', pp. 156–7; Genesios, p. 111; A. R. Littlewood, 'Gardens of the palaces', in *Byzantine Court Culture from 829 to 1204*, ed. Henry Maguire (Washington, DC, 1997), pp. 13–38.

45 Choniates, p. 117; Kinnamos, pp. 131–2; Robert of Clari, p. 105; Benjamin of Tudela, *The Itinerary*, trans. M. N. Adler (London, 1907), p. 13; Steven Runciman, 'Blachernae Palace and its decoration', *Studies in Memory of David Talbot Rice*, ed. Giles Robertson and George Henderson (Edinburgh, 1975), pp. 277–83; Janin, *Constantinople*, pp. 123–8.

46   Odo of Deuil, *De profectione Ludovici VII in orientem*, ed. and trans. V. G. Berry (New York, 1948), pp. 64–5.

47   Steven Runciman, 'The country and suburban palaces of the emperors', in *Charanis Studies: Essays in Honor of Peter Charanis*, ed. Angeliki E. Laiou-Thomadakis (New Brunswick, NJ, 1980), pp. 219–28, at 223–4; Janin, *Constantinople*, pp. 143–5, 152–3.

48   Liudprand of Cremona, p. 194; Odo of Deuil, p. 49; Kinnamos, pp. 63, 69; Choniates p. 8.

49   Genesios, p. 111; Kinnamos, p. 200.

50   Psellos, *Fourteen Byzantine Rulers*, p. 321.

51   Choniates, pp. 32, 59, 117, 177, 280–1; Psellos, *Fourteen Byzantine Rulers*, p. 57. Cf. Genesios, pp. 90–1.

52   Constantine VII, *Three Treatises*, pp. 102–9.

53   Choniates, p. 242.

54   Ibid., p. 294.

55   Constantine VII Porphyrogenitos, *De administrando imperio*, ed. G. Moravcsik, trans. R. J. H. Jenkins (Washington, DC, 1967), p. 49; Barker, *Social and Political Thought*, p. 55; Comnena, p. 295; Alexander P. Kazhdan and Ann Wharton Epstein, *Change in Byzantine Culture in the Eleventh and Twelfth Centuries* (Berkeley, CA, 1985), p. 250.

56   Choniates, p. 323; Leo the Deacon, pp. 50, 190; Michael Angold, 'Inventory of the so-called Palace of Botaneiates', *The Byzantine Aristocracy, IX–XIII Centuries*, ed. Michael Angold (Oxford, 1984), pp. 254–66; Odo of Deuil, pp. 54–7; Jean-Claude Cheynet, *Pouvoir et contestations à Byzance (963–1210)* (Paris, 1990), pp. 199–202.

57   Comnena, p. 460.

58   Eustathios of Thessalonica, pp. 54–5.

59   Ptochoprodromos, trans. Cyril Mango, *Byzantium: The Empire of the New Rome* (London, 1980), pp. 82–3; Psellos, *Fourteen Byzantine Rulers*, pp. 178–9, 334; Jonathan Harris, *Byzantium and the Crusades* (London, 2003), pp. 16–22.

60   Leo the Deacon, pp. 144–5.

61   Masudi, *The Meadows of Gold. The Abbasids*, trans. Paul Lunde and Caroline Stone (London and New York, 1989), p. 345; Psellos, *Fourteen Byzantine Rulers*, p. 75; Shaun Tougher, 'Byzantine

eunuchs: an overview, with special reference to their creation and origin', in *Women, Men and Eunuchs: Gender in Byzantium*, ed. Liz James (London, 1997), pp. 168–84, at 170–2; Herrin, *Women in Purple*, pp. 186–7.

62 Psellos, *Fourteen Byzantine Rulers*, p. 28; W. G. Brokkaar, 'Basil Lecapenus: Byzantium in the Tenth Century', in *Studia Byzantina et Neohellenica Neerlandica*, ed. W. F. Bakker, A. F. van Gemert and W. J. Aerts (Leiden, 1972), pp. 199–234.

63 Psellos, *Fourteen Byzantine Rulers*, p. 336; Choniates, pp. 277–8; Brand, *Byzantium Confronts*, pp. 128–9, 143.

64 Psellos, *Fourteen Byzantine Rulers*, p. 262; J. Chrysostomides, *Byzantine Women* (Camberley, 1994), p. 6; Barbara Hill, *Imperial Women in Byzantium* (Harlow, 1999), pp. 14–18.

65 Procopius, *The Secret History*, trans. H. B. Dewing (Cambridge, MA, and London, 1935), pp. 178–9; Herrin, *Women in Purple*, pp. 100–1.

66 Comnena, p. 116.

67 Ibid., pp. 117–18.

68 Comnena, p. 121; John Zonaras, *Annales*, ed. M. Pinder and T. Büttner-Wobst, 3 vols (Bonn, 1841–97), iii, p. 764; Hill, *Imperial Women*, pp. 78–83, 161–5.

69 Choniates, pp. 250–1.

70 Brand, *Byzantium Confronts*, p. 142; Demetrios I. Polemis, *The Doukai: A Contribution to Byzantine Prosopography* (London, 1968), p. 131.

71 Choniates, p. 252.

72 Ibid., pp. 265–9; Brand, *Byzantium Confronts*, pp. 144–6; Hill, *Imperial Women*, pp. 204–7.

Chapter 5

1 Niketas Choniates, *O City of Byzantium: Annals of Niketas Choniates*, trans. H. J. Magoulias (Detroit, 1984), p. 317; Alexander P. Kazhdan and Ann Wharton Epstein, *Change in Byzantine Culture in the Eleventh and Twelfth Centuries* (Berkeley, CA, 1985), p. 255.

2 William of Tyre, *A History of Deeds Done Beyond the Sea*, trans. E. A. Babcock and A. C. Krey, 2 vols (New York, 1943), ii, p. 382.

3   R. J. H. Jenkins and Cyril A. Mango, 'The date and significance of the Tenth Homily of Photios', *DOP*, 9/10 (1956), pp. 125–40, at 135; R. Janin, *La géographie ecclésiastique de l'empire byzantin: première partie: le siège de Constantinople et le patriarchat oecuménique. Tome III: les églises et les monastères* (2nd edn, Paris, 1969), pp. 232–6.

4   Cyril Mango, *The Art of the Byzantine Empire, 312–1453: Sources and Documents* (Englewood Cliffs, NJ, 1972), p. 194; A. A. Vasiliev, 'Harun-Ibn-Yahya and his description of Constantinople', *Annales de l'Institut Kondakov*, 5 (1932), pp. 149–63, at 156; Paul Magdalino, 'Observations on the Nea Ekklesia of Basil I', *Jahrbuch der Österreichischen Byzantinistik*, 37 (1987), pp. 51–64; Janin, *Géographie*, pp. 361–4.

5   Leo the Deacon, *The History of Leo the Deacon: Byzantine Military Expansion in the Tenth Century*, trans. Alice-Mary Talbot and Denis F. Sullivan (Washington, DC, 2005), p. 175; C. L. Striker, *The Myrelaion (Bodrum Camii) in Istanbul* (Princeton, NJ, 1981), pp. 6–10; Rosemary Morris, *Monks and Laymen in Byzantium, 843–1118* (Cambridge, 1995), pp. 18–19; Janin, *Géographie*, pp. 351–4.

6   Glanville Downey, 'The tombs of the Byzantine emperors in the church of the Holy Apostles in Constantinople', *JHS*, 79 (1959), pp. 27–51, at 27.

7   Michael Psellos, *Fourteen Byzantine Rulers*, trans. E. R. A. Sewter (2nd edn, Harmondsworth, 1966), pp. 71–2; Ruy Gonzalez Clavijo, *Embassy to Tamerlane*, trans. G. Le Strange (London, 1928), pp. 64–5; Ken Dark, 'The Byzantine church and monastery of St Mary Peribleptos in Istanbul', *Burlington Magazine*, 141 (1999), pp. 656–64; Janin, *Géographie*, pp. 218–22.

8   Robert of Clari, *The Conquest of Constantinople*, trans. E. H. McNeal (Toronto, 1996), pp. 112–13; Choniates, p. 125; John Kinnamos, *The Deeds of John and Manuel Comnenus*, trans. C. M. Brand (New York, 1976), pp. 207–8; Anthony, Archbishop of Novgorod, *Description des lieux-saints de Constantinople*, in *Itinéraires russes en orient*, ed. B. de Khitrowo (Geneva, 1889), pp. 85–111, at 105–6; Robert Ousterhout, 'Architecture, art and Komnenian ideology at the Pantokrator Monastery', in *Byzantine Constantinople: Monuments, Topography*

and Everyday Life, ed. Nevra Necipoğlu (Leiden, 2001), pp. 133–50; A. H. S. Megaw, 'Notes on recent work of the Byzantine Institute in Istanbul', *DOP*, 17 (1963), pp. 333–71, at 335–64; Janin, *Géographie*, pp. 515–23; Robin Cormack, *Writing in Gold: Byzantine Society and its Icons* (London, 1985), pp. 200–11.

9 John Freely and Ahmet S. Çakmak, *The Byzantine Monuments of Istanbul* (Cambridge, 2004), pp. 235–44; C. L. Striker and Y. D. Kuban, *Kalenderhane in Istanbul: The Buildings, their History, Architecture and Decoration* (Mainz, 1997).

10 Thomas F. Mathews, *The Art of Byzantium* (London, 1998), pp. 111–35; Cormack, *Writing in Gold*, pp. 151–8.

11 *The Russian Primary Chronicle: The Laurentian Text*, ed. and trans. S. H. Cross and O. P. Sherbowitz-Wetzor (Cambridge, MA, 1953), p. 111.

12 *The Letter of the Three Patriarchs to the Emperor Theophilos and Related Texts*, ed. J. A. Munitiz, J. Chrysostomides, E. Harvalia-Crook and Ch. Dendrinos (Camberley, 1997), pp. 32–5, 38–9.

13 Theophanes Confessor, *The Chronicle of Theophanes Confessor. Byzantine and Near Eastern History AD 284–813*, trans C. Mango and R. Scott (Oxford, 1997), p. 559; 'Life of St Theodosia of Constantinople', trans. Nicholas Constas in *Byzantine Defenders of Images: Eight Saints' Lives in Translation*, ed. Alice-Mary Talbot (Washington, DC, 1998), pp. 1–7.

14 Stephen the Deacon, *La vie de Étienne le jeune*, trans. M.-F. Auzépy (Aldershot, 1997), pp. 166, 264–5.

15 Theophanes Confessor, p. 598; Stephen the Deacon, pp. 169–71, 269–72.

16 Theophanes Confessor, pp. 605, 611–12; *Letter of the Three Patriarchs*, pp. 166–8.

17 John of Damascus, *On Holy Images*, trans. Mary H. Allies (London, 1898), pp. 3–13, 17–22.

18 Peter Charanis, 'The monk as an element of Byzantine society', *DOP*, 25 (1971), 63–84, at 64.

19 Freely and Çakmak, p. 71.

[20] Clavijo, pp. 68–9; Morris, *Monks and Laymen*, pp. 16–18; N. G. Wilson, *Scholars of Byzantium* (2nd edn, London, 1996), p. 66; Janin, *Géographie*, pp. 430–44.

[21] Niketas Stethatos, *Un grand mystique Byzantin: vie de Syméon le Nouveau Théologien*, ed. I. Hausherr and G. Horn (Rome, 1928), pp. 7, 19, 26–7, 33, 41–5. On St Mamas, see Janin, *Géographie*, pp. 314–15.

[22] Stethatos, pp. 47, 79, 101–9, 131–3.

[23] Ibid., p. 13; John Klimakos, *The Ladder of Divine Ascent*, trans. C. Luibheid and N. Russell (London, 1982), p.137; Basil Krivochéine, *In the Light of Christ. St Symeon the New Theologian: Life – Spirituality – Doctrine* (Crestwood, NY, 1986), pp. 163–238.

[24] Stethatos, p. 8, translated by D. J. Geanakoplos, *Byzantium: Church, Society and Civilisation Seen through Contemporary Eyes* (Chicago, 1984), p. 182.

[25] Stethatos, pp. 184–5; Krivochéine, pp. 61–3.

[26] Elizabeth Dawes and Norman H. Baynes, *Three Byzantine Saints* (2nd edn, Crestwood, NY, 1977), pp. 106–8; Leo the Deacon, p. 150.

[27] Robert Doran, *The Lives of Symeon Stylites* (Kalamazoo, MI, 1992), pp. 81–2.

[28] Dawes and Baynes, *Three Byzantine Saints*, pp. 21–2, 34–5, 37–8.

[29] Leo the Deacon, p. 218; Germaine da Costa-Louillet, 'Saints de Constantinople aux VIIIe, IXe et Xe siècles', *B*, 25–7 (1955–7), pp. 783–852, at 839–52; Morris, *Monks and Laymen*, pp. 60–1.

[30] Choniates, p. 210; Gregory the Cellarer, *The Life of Lazaros of Mt. Galesion: An Eleventh-Century Pillar Saint*, trans. Richard Greenfield (Washington, DC, 2000), p. 347; Gilbert Dagron, 'The urban economy, seventh–twelfth centuries', in *The Economic History of Byzantium: From the Seventh through the Fifteenth Century*, ed. Angeliki E. Laiou, 3 vols (Washington, DC, 2002), ii, pp. 393–461, at 458.

[31] Costa-Louillet, 'Saints de Constantinople', pp. 179–214; Lennart Rydén, 'A note on some references to the church of St Anastasia in the tenth century', *B*, 44 (1974), pp. 198–201, at 198–9; idem, 'The date of the Life of St Andrew *Salos*', *DOP*, 32 (1978), pp. 129–55; idem, 'The holy fool', in *The Byzantine Saint*, ed. Sergei Hackel (London, 1981), pp. 106–13.

32　Lennart Rydén, 'The Andreas Salos Apocalypse: Greek text, translation, and commentary', *DOP*, 28 (1974), pp. 199–261.

33　Michael Angold, *Church and Society in Byzantium under the Comneni, 1081–1261* (Cambridge, 1995), p. 461.

34　Psellos, *Fourteen Byzantine Rulers*, pp. 162–4.

35　Constantine Manasses, cited in Cyril Mango, *Byzantium: The Empire of the New Rome* (London, 1980), p. 74. Cf Ihor Ševenko, 'Constantinople viewed from the eastern provinces in the middle Byzantine period', *Harvard Ukrainian Studies*, 3–4 (1979–80), pp. 712–47, at 717.

36　Psellos, *Fourteen Byzantine Rulers*, p. 181.

37　Ibid., pp. 164–5.

38　Cormack, *Writing in Gold*, pp. 184–9; John Beckwith, *Early Christian and Byzantine Art* (2nd edn, Harmondsworth, 1979), pp. 232–3.

39　Psellos, *Fourteen Byzantine Rulers*, p. 181.

40　Ibid., p. 182–6.

41　Ibid., p. 252; Michael Attaleiates, *Historia*, ed. W. Brunet de Presle and I. Bekker (Bonn, 1853), p. 48.

42　Clavijo, p. 77; Anthony of Novgorod, p. 100; Nicolas Oikonomides, 'St George of Mangana, Maria Skleraina, and the "Malyjsion" of Novgorod', *DOP*, 34–5 (1980–1), pp. 239–46; Janin, *Géographie*, pp. 70–6.

43　Psellos, *Fourteen Byzantine Rulers*, p. 222.

44　John Skylitzes, *Synopsis historiarum*, ed. J. Thurn (Berlin, 1973), p. 477. On the hospital of St George in Mangana, see Timothy Miller, *The Birth of the Hospital in the Byzantine Empire* (2nd edn, Baltimore and London, 1997), pp. 116, 149.

45　Angold, *Church and Society*, pp. 129–30.

46　Skylitzes, pp. 242–3.

47　Theophanes Continuatus, *Chronographia*, ed. I. Bekker (Bonn, 1838), p. 370.

48　Attaleiates, p. 69; John Zonaras, *Annales*, ed. M. Pinder and T. Büttner-Wobst, 3 vols (Bonn, 1841–97), iii, pp. 673–4; Anna Comnena, *The Alexiad*, trans. E. R. A. Sewter (Harmondsworth,

1969), p. 103; Demetrios I. Polemis, *The Doukai: A Contribution to Byzantine Prosopography* (London, 1968), p. 44.

49 Liudprand of Cremona, *The Embassy to Constantinople and Other Writings*, trans. F. A. Wright (London, 1993), pp. 139–42; Theophanes Continuatus, pp. 433–5.

50 Choniates, pp. 268–9; Psellos, *Fourteen Byzantine Rulers*, pp. 254–8, 267.

51 John Thomas and Angela C. Hero, *Byzantine Monastic Foundation Documents*, 5 vols (Washington, DC, 2000), ii, p. 670. On the Kecharitomene, see Janin, *Géographie*, pp. 188–91.

52 Choniates, pp. 5–9; Comnena, pp. 460–1; Robert Browning, 'An unpublished funeral oration on Anna Comnena', *Proceedings of the Cambridge Philological Society*, 188 (1962), pp. 1–12, at 4.

53 Psellos, *Fourteen Byzantine Rulers*, p. 106; Comnena, p. 49; Thomas and Hero, *Byzantine Monastic Foundation Documents*, i, p. 251.

54 Choniates, p. 305; Psellos, *Fourteen Byzantine Rulers*, p. 270.

55 Choniates, p. 222; Psellos, *Fourteen Byzantine Rulers*, p. 270.

56 Alexander P. Kazhdan, 'Eustathius of Thessalonica: the life and opinions of a twelfth century Byzantine rhetor', in *Studies on Byzantine Literature of the Eleventh and Twelfth Centuries*, ed. Alexander P. Kazhdan and Simon Franklin (Cambridge, 1984), pp. 115–95, at 151.

57 Eustathius of Thessalonica, in Paul Magdalino, 'The Byzantine Holy Man in the Twelfth Century', in *The Byzantine Saint*, ed. Sergei Hackel (London, 1981), pp. 51–66, at 60.

58 Robert of Clari, p. 110.

59 Dawes and Baynes, *Three Byzantine Saints*, pp. 50–1; Psellos, *Fourteen Byzantine Rulers*, p. 301.

60 Rydén, 'Holy Fool', pp. 111–12; Morris, *Monks and Laymen*, pp. 61–3.

61 Christopher of Mitylene, *Die Gedichte*, ed. Eduard Kurtz (Leipzig, 1903), pp. 76–7; A. Karpozelos, 'Realia in Byzantine Epistolography, X–XII Centuries', *BZ*, 77 (1984), 20–37, at 23.

62 John Tzetzes, *Epistulae*, ed. P. A. Leone (Leipzig, 1972), pp. 150–2, trans. Magdalino, 'Byzantine holy man', pp. 54–5.

Chapter 6

[1] Liudprand of Cremona, *The Embassy to Constantinople and Other Writings*, trans. F. A. Wright (London, 1993), pp. 12, 203.

[2] Robert of Clari, *The Conquest of Constantinople*, trans. E. H. McNeal (Toronto, 1996), p. 101; Fulcher of Chartres, *Chronicle*, trans. M. E. McGinty, in *The First Crusade: The Chronicle of Fulcher of Chartres and Other Source Materials*, ed. E. Peters (2nd edn, Philadelphia, 1998), pp. 47–101, at 62; Benjamin of Tudela, *The Itinerary*, trans. M. N. Adler (London, 1907), p. 13; Nadia Maria El Cheikh, *Byzantium Viewed by the Arabs* (Cambridge, MA, 2004), p. 205.

[3] Gilbert Dagron, 'The urban economy, seventh-twelfth centuries', in *The Economic History of Byzantium: From the Seventh through the Fifteenth Century*, ed. Angeliki E. Laiou, 3 vols (Washington, DC, 2002), ii, pp. 393–461, at 394–5; David Jacoby, 'La population de Constantinople à l'époque byzantine: un problème de demographie urbaine', *B*, 31 (1961), pp. 81–109, at 109.

[4] Averil Cameron and Judith Herrin (eds), *Constantinople in the Early Eighth Century: The Parastasis Syntomoi Chronikai* (Leiden, 1984), p. 153; P. Bono, J. Crow and R. Bayliss, 'The water supply of Constantinople: archaeology and hydrology of an early medieval city', *Environmental Geology*, 40 (2001), pp. 1325–33; Cyril Mango, 'The water supply of Constantinople', in *Constantinople and its Hinterland: Papers from the Twenty-seventh Spring Symposium of Byzantine Studies, Oxford, April 1993*, ed. Cyril Mango and Gilbert Dagron (Aldershot, 1993), pp. 9–18, at 10–13; John L. Teall, 'The grain supply of the Byzantine empire, 330–1025', *DOP*, 13 (1959), pp. 87–139, at 102–4.

[5] Procopius of Caesarea, *The Buildings*, trans. H. B. Dewing (Cambridge, MA, and London, 1940), pp. 90–3; *Chronicon paschale, 284–628 AD*, trans. Michael Whitby and Mary Whitby (Liverpool, 1989), p. 127; Mango, 'Water supply', pp. 16–17.

[6] Theophanes, *The Chronicle of Theophanes Confessor. Byzantine and Near Eastern History AD 284–813*, trans C. Mango and R. Scott (Oxford, 1997), p. 608; John Skylitzes, *Synopsis historiarum*, ed. J. Thurn (Berlin, 1973), p. 366; Niketas Choniates, *O City of Byzantium: Annals of Niketas Choniates*, trans. H. J. Magoulias

(Detroit, 1984), p. 182; Odo of Deuil, *De profectione Ludovici VII in orientem*, ed. and trans. V. G. Berry (New York, 1948), p. 65; V. Minorsky, 'Marvazi on the Byzantines', *Annuaire de l'Institut de Philologie et d'Histoire Orientales et Slaves*, 10 (1950), pp. 455–69, at 463; John Kinnamos, *The Deeds of John and Manuel Comnenus*, trans. C. M. Brand (New York, 1976), pp. 205–6; Ruy Gonzalez Clavijo, *Embassy to Tamerlane*, trans. G. Le Strange (London, 1928), p. 76.

7 Teall, 'Grain supply', pp. 117–32; Paul Magdalino, 'The grain supply of Constantinople, ninth to twelfth centuries', in *Constantinople and its Hinterland: Papers from the Twenty-seventh Spring Symposium of Byzantine Studies, Oxford, April 1993*, ed. Cyril Mango and Gilbert Dagron (Aldershot, 1993), pp. 35–47, at 36; Angeliki E. Laiou, 'Exchange and trade, seventh-twelfth centuries', in *The Economic History of Byzantium: From the Seventh through the Fifteenth Century*, ed. Angeliki E. Laiou, 3 vols (Washington, DC, 2002), ii, pp. 697–770, at 741.

8 *Book of the Eparch*, in E. H. Freshfield, *Roman Law in the Later Roman Empire* (Cambridge, 1938), pp. 3–50, at 41–2; Theophanes Confessor, p. 534; Dagron, 'Urban economy', pp. 453–6.

9 Michael Attaleiates, *Historia*, ed. W. Brunet de Presle and I. Bekker (Bonn, 1853), pp. 201–4; Magdalino, 'Grain supply', pp. 39–42; Dagron, 'Urban economy', p. 453.

10 Tacitus, *The Annals*, trans. John Jackson, 3 vols (Cambridge, MA, and London, 1931–7), iii, p. 407; Fynes Moryson, *An Itinerary*, 4 vols (Glasgow, 1907–8), ii, p. 97.

11 *Book of the Eparch*, pp. 40–1; Gunther of Pairis, *The Capture of Constantinople*, trans. A. J. Andrea (Philadelphia, 1997), p. 84; Dagron, 'Urban economy', pp. 447, 457–9; Andrew Dalby, *Flavours of Byzantium* (Totnes, 2003), p. 65; George C. Maniatis, 'The organizational setup and functioning of the fish market in tenth-century Constantinople', *DOP*, 54 (2000), pp. 13–42.

12 *Book of the Eparch*, pp. 39–40; Dagron, 'Urban economy', pp. 456–7.

13 Odo of Deuil, p. 65; Anthony, Archbishop of Novgorod, *Description des lieux-saints de Constantinople*, in *Itinéraires russes en orient*, ed. B. de Khitrowo (Geneva, 1889), pp. 85–111, at 101; J. Koder, 'Fresh vegetables for the capital', in *Constantinople and its*

Hinterland. Papers from the Twenty-seventh Spring Symposium of Byzantine Studies, Oxford, April 1993, ed. Cyril Mango and Gilbert Dagron (Aldershot, 1995), pp. 49–56.

14 *Book of the Eparch*, pp. 43–4; Dagron, 'Urban economy', pp. 459–60.

15 Choniates pp. 215–16, 305.

16 A. Karpozelos, 'Realia in Byzantine epistolography, X–XII centuries', *BZ*, 77 (1984), pp. 20–37, at 26.

17 Michael Psellos, *Fourteen Byzantine Rulers*, trans. E. R. A. Sewter (2nd edn, Harmondsworth, 1966), p. 94.

18 Choniates, pp. 33–4; Dagron, 'Urban economy', p. 459.

19 M. F. Hendy, *Studies in the Byzantine Monetary Economy, c. 300–1450* (Cambridge, 1985), pp. 513–17; M. F. Hendy, 'Byzantium, 1081–1204: an economic reappraisal', *Transactions of the Royal Historical Society* 5th series, 20 (1970), pp. 31–52, at 43–5; Cécile Morrisson, 'Byzantine money: its supply and circulation', in *The Economic History of Byzantium: From the Seventh through the Fifteenth Century*, ed. Angeliki E. Laiou, 3 vols (Washington, DC, 2002), iii, pp. 909–66, at 932–3; Alexander Kazhdan and Giles Constable, *People and Power in Byzantium: An Introduction to Modern Byzantine Studies* (Washington, DC, 1982), pp. 43–4.

20 Hendy, *Studies*, pp. 237–42; Alan Harvey, *Economic Expansion in the Byzantine Empire, 900–1200* (Cambridge, 1989), pp. 91–6, 103–5.

21 Christopher Tyerman, *England and the Crusades* (Cambridge, 1988), pp. 75–8.

22 Choniates, p. 32.

23 Gunther of Pairis, p. 84.

24 *Book of the Eparch*, p. 14; Robert of Clari, p. 110; Odo of Deuil, *De profectione Ludovici VII in orientem*, ed. and trans. V. G. Berry (New York, 1948), p. 67; Dagron, 'Urban economy', pp. 432–5; Morrisson, 'Byzantine money', pp. 952–3.

25 Choniates, pp. 287–8.

26 *Book of the Eparch*, pp. 21–7, 29–35; R. S. Lopez, 'Silk industry in the Byzantine Empire', *Speculum*, 20 (1945), pp. 1–42, at 6–7; George C. Maniatis, 'Organization, market structure and modus operandi

of the private silk industry in tenth century Byzantium', *DOP*, 53 (1999), pp. 263–332; Dagron, 'Urban economy', pp. 438–44, 461.

27   Constantine VII Porphyrogenitos, *De administrando imperio*, ed. G. Moravcsik, trans. R. J. H. Jenkins (Washington, DC, 1967), pp. 66–9; *Book of the Eparch*, pp. 17, 23; Lopez, 'Silk industry', pp. 1–3, 14.

28   Liudprand, pp. 202–3.

29   Ralph de Diceto, *Opera Historica*, ed. William Stubbs, 2 vols (London, 1876), i, p. 428; John Beckwith, *Early Christian and Byzantine Art* (2nd edn, Harmondsworth, 1979), pp. 218–19.

30   S. D. Goitein, *A Mediterranean Society: The Jewish Communities of the World as Portrayed in the Documents of the Cairo Geniza*, 6 vols (Berkeley, CA, 1967–93), i, p. 44, iv, p. 168; Laiou, 'Exchange and trade', p. 750.

31   Choniates, p. 242; Genesios, *On the Reigns of the Emperors*, trans. Anthony Kaldellis (Canberra, 1998), p. 69; Theophanes Continuatus, *Chronographia*, ed. I. Bekker (Bonn, 1838), pp. 8–9; Skylitzes, p. 51.

32   Goitein, i, pp. 45–6.

33   Choniates, p. 291; Frederick van Doorninck, 'The Byzantine ship at Serçe Limani: an example of small-scale maritime commerce with Fatimid Syria in the early eleventh century', in *Travel in the Byzantine World*, ed. Ruth Macrides (Aldershot, 2002), pp. 137–48.

34   See, e.g., Anna Comnena, *The Alexiad*, trans. E. R. A. Sewter (Harmondsworth, 1969), p. 295; Psellos, *Fourteen Byzantine Rulers*, p. 169; Kazhdan and Constable, *People and Power*, pp. 42–3; Mango, *Byzantium*, pp. 82–7; George T. Dennis, 'The Perils of the deep', *Novum Millennium: Studies on Byzantine History and Culture Dedicated to Paul Speck*, ed. Claudia Sode and Sarolta Takács (Aldershot, 2001), pp. 81–8.

35   Benjamin of Tudela, p. 12. Cf. Fulcher of Chartres, p. 62.

36   Minorsky, 'Marvazi on the Byzantines', pp. 462–3; *Book of the Eparch*, pp. 19–20; Masudi, *The Meadows of Gold. The Abbasids*, trans. Paul Lunde and Caroline Stone (London and New York, 1989), pp. 320–4; Goitein, i, pp. 42–59, 211; Doorninck, 'Byzantine ship at Serçe Limanı', pp. 140–1; Stephen W. Reinert, 'The Muslim presence in Constantinople, 9th–15th centuries: some

preliminary observations', *Studies on the Internal Diaspora of the Byzantine Empire*, ed. H. Ahrweiler and A. E. Laiou (Washington, DC, 1998), pp. 125–50, at 130–43.

[37] Charles M. Brand, *Byzantium Confronts the West, 1180–1204* (Cambridge, MA, 1968), p. 204.

[38] *Book of the Eparch*, p. 28; Constantine VII, *De administrando imperio*, pp. 56–63; Dimitri Obolensky, *The Byzantine Commonwealth: Eastern Europe, 500–1453* (London, 1971), p. 245; Jonathan Shepard, 'Constantinople – gateway to the north: the Russians', in *Constantinople and its Hinterland: Papers from the Twenty-seventh Spring Symposium of Byzantine Studies, Oxford, April 1993*, ed. Cyril Mango and Gilbert Dagron (Aldershot, 1993), pp. 243–60, at 244–5.

[39] *Book of the Eparch*, p. 30; Marlia M. Mango, 'The commercial map of Constantinople', *DOP*, 54 (2000), pp. 189–207, at 198–205.

[40] Liudprand, p. 203; Shepard, 'Constantinople – gateway to the north', pp. 250–3; Lopez, 'Silk industry', p. 37; Laiou, 'Exchange and trade', p. 740; M. E. Martin, 'The Venetians in the Byzantine empire before 1204', *Byzantinische Forschungen*, 13 (1988), pp. 201–14, at 204.

[41] Eadmer, *Liber Miraculorum S. Dunstani, Memorials of St Dunstan*, ed. William Stubbs (London, 1874), pp. 245–6; C. F. Battiscombe, *The Relics of St Cuthbert* (Oxford, 1956), pp. 9–13, 505–25; Beckwith, *Early Christian and Byzantine Art*, pp. 172–3; 216–19.

[42] El Cheikh, *Byzantium Viewed by the Arabs*, p. 60; Goitein, i, pp. 103, 417.

[43] Niketas Stethatos, *Un grand mystique Byzantin: vie de Syméon le NouveauThéologien*, ed. I. Hausherr and G. Horn (Rome, 1928), pp. 226–7; Beckwith, *Early Christian and Byzantine Art*, pp. 248–50; Margaret E. Frazer, 'Church doors and the gates of paradise: Byzantine bronze doors in Italy', *DOP*, 27 (1973), pp. 147–62.

[44] Benjamin of Tudela, p. 13; H. Antoniadis-Bibicou, *Recherches sur les douanes à Byzance: l'Octava, le Kommerkion et les commerciaires* (Paris, 1963), pp. 97–155.

[45] Psellos, *Fourteen Byzantine Rulers*, p. 45.

46   Liudprand of Cremona, pp. 155–6; Harris, *Byzantium and the Crusades*, pp. 16–19.

47   *The Russian Primary Chronicle: The Laurentian Text*, ed. and trans. S. H. Cross and O. P. Sherbowitz-Wetzor (Cambridge, MA, 1953), pp. 65–8; Obolensky, *Byzantine Commonwealth*, pp. 243–5.

48   *Russian Primary Chronicle*, pp. 71–7; Obolensky, *Byzantine Commonwealth*, pp. 246–7.

49   Leo the Deacon, *The History of Leo the Deacon: Byzantine Military Expansion in the Tenth Century*, trans. Alice-Mary Talbot and Denis F. Sullivan (Washington, DC, 2005), pp. 198–9; Anthony of Novgorod, p. 105; Lopez, 'Silk industry', pp. 34–5.

50   Choniates, p. 290; Lopez, 'Silk industry', p. 32; Brand, *Byzantium Confronts*, pp. 138–9.

51   Michel Balard, 'Amalfi et Byzance (Xe–XIIe siècles)', *Travaux et Mémoires*, 6 (1976), pp. 85–95, at 87–9.

52   G. Tafel and G. Thomas, *Urkunden zur älteren Handels- und Staatsgeschichte der Republik Venedig*, 3 vols (Vienna, 1856–7), i, pp. 36–9; Constantine VII, *De administrando imperio*, pp. 118–21; D. M. Nicol, *Byzantium and Venice: A Study in Diplomatic and Cultural Relations* (Cambridge, 1988), pp. 39–44; Martin, 'Venetians in the Byzantine Empire', pp. 204–6.

53   Tafel and Thomas, *Urkunden*, i, pp. 51–3; Comnena, pp. 137, 191; Nicol, *Byzantium and Venice*, pp. 57–8, 60–3; David Jacoby, 'Italian privileges and trade in Byzantium before the Fourth Crusade: a reconsideration', *Anuario de Estudios Medievales*, 24 (1994), pp. 349–69, at 350–1; idem, 'The Venetian quarter of Constantinople from 1082 to 1261: topographical considerations', *Novum Millennium: Studies on Byzantine History and Culture Dedicated to Paul Speck*, ed. Claudia Sode and Sarolta Takács (Aldershot, 2001), pp. 153–70; Thomas F. Madden, *Enrico Dandolo and the Rise of Venice* (Baltimore and London, 2003), pp. 8–9; Louise B. Robbert, 'Rialto businessmen and Constantinople, 1204–1261', *DOP*, 49 (1995), pp. 43–58, at 47 and 49.

54   Comnena, pp. 445–6; Catherine Otten-Froux, 'Documents inédits sur les Pisans en Romanie aux XIIIe–XIVe siècles', in *Les Italiens à Byzance*, ed. Michael Balard, Angeliki E. Laiou and Catherine

Otten-Froux (Paris, 1987), pp. 153–95, at 155; Gerald W. Day, *Genoa's Response to Byzantium, 1155–1204* (Urbana, IL, and Chicago, 1988), pp. 8, 24–7; Nicol, *Byzantium and Venice*, pp. 75–6; Jacoby, 'Italian privileges', pp. 357–61.

55 Martin, 'Venetians in the Byzantine Empire', p. 212.

56 Jacoby, 'Italian privileges', pp. 354, 363–4.

57 Kinnamos, p. 210; Nicol, *Byzantium and Venice*, pp. 77–81.

58 Kinnamos, pp. 211–14; Choniates, pp. 97–8; Brand, *Byzantium Confronts*, p. 67; Nicol, *Byzantium and Venice*, pp. 97–103; Martin, 'Venetians in the Byzantine empire', pp. 212–13; Madden, *Enrico Dandolo*, 52–6.

59 Nicol, *Byzantium and Venice*, pp. 108–114; Day, *Genoa's Response*, pp. 28–30; Brand, *Byzantium Confronts*, pp. 195–206.

60 Harvey, *Economic Expansion*, pp. 223–4; Hendy, *Studies*, pp. 590–602; Hendy, 'Byzantium, 1081–1204: an Economic Reappraisal', pp. 40–1; Laiou, 'Exchange and trade', pp. 751–2; Alexander P. Kazhdan and Ann Wharton Epstein, *Change in Byzantine Culture in the Eleventh and Twelfth Centuries* (Berkeley, California, 1985), pp. 176–7.

61 Harvey, *Economic Expansion*, pp. 214–24; Nicol, *Byzantium and Venice*, pp. 91–2; Martin, 'Venetians in the Byzantine Empire', pp. 211–12; Jacoby, 'Italian Privileges', p. 365.

62 Brand, *Byzantium Confronts*, pp. 200–6; Madden, *Enrico Dandolo*, pp. 113–16.

63 Choniates, p. 295.

Chapter 7

1 Niketas Choniates, *O City of Byzantium: Annals of Niketas Choniates*, trans. H. J. Magoulias (Detroit, 1984), p. 193.

2 Anna Comnena, *The Alexiad*, trans. E. R. A. Sewter (Harmondsworth, 1969), pp. 82–3, 461.

3 Choniates, pp. 33–4; Angeliki E. Laiou, 'Women in the marketplace of Constantinople (10th–14th centuries)', in *Byzantine Constantinople: Monuments, Topography and Everyday Life*, ed. Nevra Necipoğlu (Leiden, 2001), pp. 261–73.

4   Odo of Deuil, *De profectione Ludovici VII in orientem*, ed. and trans. V. G. Berry (New York, 1948), p. 65.

5   Liudprand of Cremona, *The Embassy to Constantinople and Other Writings*, trans. F. A. Wright (London, 1993), p. 177; Paul Magdalino, 'Medieval Constantinople: built environment and urban development', in *The Economic History of Byzantium: from the Seventh through the Fifteenth Century*, ed. Angeliki E. Laiou, 3 vols (Washington, DC, 2002), ii, pp. 529–37, at 533–5.

6   John Tzetzes, *Epistulae*, ed. P. A. Leone (Leipzig, 1972), p. 33; Alexander Kazhdan and Giles Constable, *People and Power in Byzantium: An Introduction to Modern Byzantine Studies* (Washington, DC, 1982), p. 50; John P. Thomas and A. C. Hero, *Byzantine Monastic Foundation Documents: A Complete Translation of the Surviving Founders' Typika and Testaments*, 5 vols (Washington, DC, 2000), i, p. 336.

7   Leo VI, *Les Nouvelles de Léon le sage*, ed. P. Noailles and A. Dain (Paris, 1944), pp. 372–5.

8   Agathias of Myrina, *The Histories*, trans. J. D. Frendo (Berlin and New York, 1975), pp. 141–3.

9   Leo the Deacon, *The History of Leo the Deacon: Byzantine Military Expansion in the Tenth Century*, trans. Alice-Mary Talbot and Denis F. Sullivan (Washington, DC, 2005), p. 112.

10 Odo of Deuil, p. 65; Choniates, p. 288.

11 Odo of Deuil, p. 65; Michael Psellos, *Fourteen Byzantine Rulers*, trans. E. R. A. Sewter (2nd edn, Harmondsworth, 1966), p. 108; Choniates p.177; J. Chrysostomides, *Byzantine Women* (Camberley, 1994), p. 9.

12 Michael J. Kyriakis, 'Poor poets and starving literati in twelfth-century Byzantium', *B*, 44 (1974), pp. 290–309, at 296.

13 Paul Magdalino, 'Constantinopolitana', in *Aetos: Studies in Honour of Cyril Mango*, ed. Ihor Ševčenko and Irmgard Hutter (Stuttgart and Leipzig, 1998), pp. 220–32 at 227–30.

14 Leo the Deacon, pp. 217–18; Choniates, p. 67; John Kinnamos, *The Deeds of John and Manuel Comnenus*, trans. C. M. Brand (New York, 1976), p. 157; Glanville Downey, 'Earthquakes at Constantinople and vicinity, AD 342–1454', *Speculum*, 30 (1955), pp. 596–600.

[15] *Book of the Eparch*, in E. H. Freshfield, *Roman Law in the Later Roman Empire* (Cambridge, 1938), pp. 3–50, at 5; Speros Vryonis, 'Byzantine *Demokratia* and the guilds in the eleventh century', *DOP*, 17 (1963), pp. 289–314, at 296–9; George C. Maniatis, 'The domain of private guilds in the Byzantine economy', *DOP*, 55 (2001), pp. 339–69.

[16] Liudprand of Cremona, p. 191.

[17] Michael Angold, *Church and Society in Byzantium under the Comneni, 1081–1261* (Cambridge, 1995), pp. 388, 458.

[18] Ibid., pp. 457–8.

[19] Ibid., pp. 466–7; Kazhdan and Constable, pp. 67–8.

[20] V. Minorsky, 'Marvazi on the Byzantines', *Annuaire de l'Institut de Philologie et d'Histoire Orientales et Slaves*, 10 (1950), pp. 455–69 at 462; Robert of Clari, *The Conquest of Constantinople*, trans. E. H. McNeal (Toronto, 1996), pp. 79–80; A. A. Vasiliev, 'Harun-Ibn-Yahya and his description of Constantinople', *Annales de l'Institut Kondakov*, 5 (1932), pp. 149–63, at 156; Stephen W. Reinert, 'The Muslim presence in Constantinople, 9th–15th centuries: some preliminary observations', in *Studies on the Internal Diaspora of the Byzantine Empire*, ed. H. Ahrweiler and A. E. Laiou (Washington, DC, 1998), pp. 125–50.

[21] Benjamin of Tudela, *The Itinerary*, trans. M. N. Adler (London, 1907), p. 14; Andrew Scharf, *Byzantine Jewry from Justinian to the Fourth Crusade* (London, 1971), p. 117; David Jacoby, 'The Jews of Constantinople and their demographic hinterland', in *Constantinople and its Hinterland: Papers from the Twenty-seventh Spring Symposium of Byzantine Studies, Oxford, April 1993*, ed. Cyril Mango and Gilbert Dagron (Aldershot, 1993), pp. 221–32.

[22] Snorri Sturluson, *Heimskringla: Sagas of the Norse Kings*, trans. Samuel Laing (3rd edn, London, 1961), p. 170; A. A. Vasiliev, 'The opening stages of the Anglo-Saxon immigration into Byzantium in the eleventh century', *Annales de l'Institut Kondakov*, 9 (1937), pp. 39–70, at 60–2; Andrea Arkel-de Leeuwvan Weenen and K. N. Ciggaar, 'St Thorlac's in Constantinople, built by a Flemish emperor', *B*, 49 (1979), pp. 428–46, at 428, 430; S. Blöndal, *The Varangians of Byzantium* (Cambridge, 1978), pp. 185–8.

23   Choniates, p. 303; Reinert, 'Muslim presence', pp. 137–43.

24   *The Theodosian Code*, trans. C. Pharr (Princeton, NJ, 1952), pp. 469–70.

25   Alexander Kazhdan and Ann Wharton Epstein, *Change in Byzantine Culture in the Eleventh and Twelfth Centuries* (Berkeley, CA, 1985), pp. 259–60.

26   Choniates, p. 288.

27   *The Letter of the Three Patriarchs to the Emperor Theophilos and Related Texts*, ed. J. A. Munitiz, J. Chrysostomides, E. Harvalia-Crook and Ch. Dendrinos (Camberley, 1997), p. 46.

28   Benjamin of Tudela, p. 14.

29   S. D. Goitein, *A Mediterranean Society: The Jewish Communities of the World as Portrayed in the Documents of the Cairo Geniza*, 6 vols (Berkeley, CA, 1967–93), i, p. 58; Nicolas de Lange, 'Byzantium in the Cairo Geniza', *BMGS*, 16 (1992), pp. 34–47, at 41, 44.

30   Eustathios of Thessalonica, *The Capture of Thessaloniki*, trans. J. R. Melville-Jones (Canberra, 1988), pp. 34–5.

31   Thomas F. Madden, *Enrico Dandolo and the Rise of Venice* (Baltimore and London, 2003), p. 116; Donald M. Nicol, *Byzantium and Venice: A Study in Diplomatic and Cultural Relations* (Cambridge, 1988), pp. 120–3; Charles M. Brand, *Byzantium Confronts the West, 1180–1204* (Cambridge, MA, 1968), pp. 202–3.

32   Kinnamos, p. 210. Cf Choniates, p. 97.

33   Choniates, p. 295.

34   Caffaro *et al.*, *Annali genovesi*, ed. Luigi T. Belgrano and Cesare Imperiale di Sant'Angelo, 5 vols (Rome, 1890–1929), i, p. 68; Gerald W. Day, *Genoa's Response to Byzantium, 1155–1204* (Urbana, IL, and Chicago, 1988), pp. 26–8.

35   Kinnamos, p. 211; Choniates, pp. 97–8; Brand, *Byzantium Confronts*, p. 67; Nicol, *Byzantium and Venice*, pp. 97–103; M. E. Martin, 'The Venetians in the Byzantine empire before 1204', *Byzantinische Forschungen*, 13 (1988), pp. 201–14, at 212–13; Madden, *Enrico Dandolo*, 52–6.

36   William of Tyre, *A History of Deeds Done beyond the Sea*, trans. E. A. Babcock and A. C. Krey, 2 vols (New York, 1943), ii, pp. 464–7;

Eustathios of Thessalonica, pp. 33–5; Choniates, pp. 140–1; Brand, *Byzantium Confronts*, pp. 41–3.

37 Choniates, pp. 215–16.

38 Eusebius of Caesarea, *Tricennial Oration*, in H. A. Drake, *In Praise of Constantine: A Historical Study and New Translation of Eusebius's Tricennial Orations* (Berkeley, CA, and Los Angeles, 1976), pp. 83–127, at 87.

39 Choniates, p. 132; Vryonis, 'Byzantine *Demokratia*', pp. 291–2.

40 Comnena, pp. 396–7; Morgan, 'A Byzantine satirical song', *BZ*, 47 (1954), pp. 292–7; Margaret Alexiou, 'Literary subversion and the aristocracy in twelfth century Byzantium: a stylistic analysis of Timarion (ch. 6–10)', *BMGS*, 8 (1982–3), pp. 29–45.

41 Leo the Deacon, pp. 113–15; Choniates, pp. 252, 285.

42 Procopius of Caesarea, *History of the Wars*, trans. H. B. Dewing and G. Downey, 5 vols (Cambridge, MA, and London, 1914–28), i, pp. 218–21; Choniates, pp. 288–9; Jean-Claude Cheynet, *Pouvoir et contestations à Byzance (963–1210)* (Paris, 1990), pp. 202–5.

43 Psellos, *Fourteen Byzantine Rulers*, pp. 102–3.

44 Michael Attaleiates, *Historia*, ed. W. Brunet de Presle and I. Bekker (Bonn, 1853), p. 12; John Skylitzes, *Synopsis historiarum*, ed. J. Thurn (Berlin, 1973), p. 417; Psellos, *Fourteen Byzantine Rulers*, pp. 131–2; Vryonis, 'Byzantine *Demokratia*', pp. 303–5.

45 Skylitzes, p. 418; Vryonis, 'Byzantine *Demokratia*', pp. 305–6.

46 Psellos, *Fourteen Byzantine Rulers*, pp. 138–9.

47 Ibid., pp. 145–6.

48 Skylitzes, p. 419; Sturluson, *Heimskringla*, p. 171.

49 Liudprand, pp. 140–1.

50 Psellos, *Fourteen Byzantine Rulers*, pp. 297–8; Attaleiates, pp. 56–60; Skylitzes, pp. 499–500.

51 Choniates, pp. 192–3.

52 Constantine VII Porphyrogenitos, *De ceremoniis aulae Byzantinae*, ed. J. Reisky, 2 vols (Bonn, 1829–30), pp. 4–5; Liudprand of Cremona, p. 139; Michael Jeffreys, 'The Comnenian Proskypsis', *Parergon*, 5 (1987), pp. 38–53.

53 Psellos, *Fourteen Byzantine Rulers*, p. 338; Choniates, pp. 183, 265; Vryonis, 'Byzantine *Demokratia*', pp. 309–13.

54 Vasiliev, 'Harun-Ibn-Yahya', pp. 156–7; Mango, *Art of the Byzantine Empire*, p. 195; Leo the Deacon, p. 144.

55 Alan Cameron, *Porphyrius the Charioteer* (Oxford, 1973), pp. 252–8; Cyril Mango, 'Daily life in Byzantium', *Jahrbuch der Österreichischen Byzantinistik*, 31 (1981), pp. 337–53, at 346–7.

56 Minorsky, 'Marvazi on the Byzantines', p. 461.

57 Leo the Deacon, p. 112; Psellos, *Fourteen Byzantine Rulers*, p. 57; Choniates, p. 160; Timotheus of Gaza, *On Animals*, trans. F. S. Bodenheimer and A. Rabinowitz (Paris and Leiden, 1949), p. 31; Attaleiates, pp. 48–50; Giovanni Mercati, 'Gli aneddoti d'un codice bolognese', *BZ*, 6 (1897), pp. 126–43, at 141.

58 Minorsky, 'Marvazi on the Byzantines', p. 462. Cf. Vasiliev, 'Harun-Ibn-Yahya', p. 155.

59 Minorsky, 'Marvazi on the Byzantines', p. 462; Benjamin of Tudela, pp. 12–13.

60 Choniates, p. 143; Comnena, pp. 502–4; Angold, *Church and Society*, pp. 485–7.

61 Justinian, *The Civil Law*, trans. S. P. Scott, 17 vols (Cincinnati, 1932), xvii, p. 55; Gregory the Cellarer, *The Life of Lazaros of Mt. Galesion: An Eleventh-Century Pillar Saint*, trans. Richard Greenfield (Washington, DC, 2000), pp. 331–2; Kazhdan and Constable, *People and Power*, pp. 66–7.

62 Genesios, *On the Reigns of the Emperors*, trans. Anthony Kaldellis (Canberra, 1998), p. 112.

63 Choniates, p. 244.

64 Comnena, pp. 492–4; Demetrios Constantelos, *Byzantine Philanthropy and Social Welfare* (New Brunswick, NJ, 1968), pp. 241–56.

65 Thomas and Hero, *Byzantine Monastic Foundation Documents*, ii, pp. 726–81, at 757, 760; Timothy Miller, *The Birth of the Hospital in the Byzantine Empire* (2nd edn, Baltimore and London, 1997), pp. 12–29; Constantelos, *Byzantine Philanthropy*, pp. 171–9.

66 Choniates, p. 244; Procopius of Caesarea, *The Buildings*, trans. H. B. Dewing (Cambridge, MA, and London, 1940), pp. 36–7; Attaleiates, p. 48; Miller, *Birth of the Hospital*, pp. 113–17.

67 Theophanes Continuatus, *Chronographia*, ed. I. Bekker (Bonn, 1838), pp. 449, 458–9; Psellos, *Fourteen Byzantine Rulers*, p. 107;

Leo the Deacon, p. 149; Rydén, Lennart, 'A note on some references to the church of St Anastasia in the tenth century', *B*, 44 (1974), pp. 198–201, at 198–9; Alice-Mary Talbot, 'Old age in Byzantium', *BZ*, 77 (1984), pp. 267–78, at 278; Constantelos, *Byzantine Philanthropy*, pp. 222–40, 257–69.

[68] Constantine VII, *De ceremoniis*, i, pp. 177–80; Eusebius of Caesarea, *Life of Constantine*, trans. Averil Cameron and Stuart Hall (Oxford, 1999), pp. 153–4; Ernest Barker, *Social and Political Thought in Byzantium from Justinian I to the Last Palaeologus* (Oxford, 1957), pp. 55–6; Constantelos, *Byzantine Philanthropy*, pp. 43–61.

Chapter 8

[1] John Zonaras, *Annales*, ed. M. Pinder and T. Büttner-Wobst, 3 vols (Bonn, 1841–97), iii, pp. 14–15; Michael Glykys, *Annales*, ed. I. Bekker (Bonn, 1836), p. 463; A. A. Vasiliev, 'Medieval ideas of the end of the world: west and east', *B*, 16 (1942–3), pp. 462–502, at 489–90.

[2] Niketas Choniates, *O City of Byzantium: Annals of Niketas Choniates*, trans. H. J. Magoulias (Detroit, 1984), pp. 291–2.

[3] Choniates, p. 314; George Akropolites, *Historia*, ed. A. Heisenberg and P. Wirth (Stuttgart, 1978), pp. 8–9; C. M. Brand, *Byzantium Confronts the West, 1180–1204* (Cambridge, MA, 1968), p. 120.

[4] Choniates, pp. 280–2.

[5] Ibid., pp. 289–90; Brand, *Byzantium Confronts*, pp. 122–4.

[6] Choniates, p. 294.

[7] Ibid., pp. 294–5; Brand, *Byzantium Confronts*, pp. 275–6.

[8] Choniates, p. 140; Anna Comnena, *The Alexiad*, trans. E. R. A. Sewter (Harmondsworth, 1969), pp. 97–8.

[9] Geoffrey of Villehardouin, *The Conquest of Constantinople*, in *Chronicles of the Crusades*, trans. M. R. B. Shaw (Harmondsworth, 1963), pp. 44–5; Jonathan Harris, *Byzantium and the Crusades* (London, 2003), pp. 151–5; Michael Angold, *The Fourth Crusade* (Harlow, 2003), pp. 79–92; Jonathan Phillips, *The Fourth Crusade and the Sack of Constantinople* (London, 2004), pp. 127–41.

10 Villehardouin, pp. 63–4; Robert of Clari, *The Conquest of Constantinople*, trans. E. H. McNeal (Toronto, 1996), pp. 67–8.

11 Phillips, *Fourth Crusade*, pp. 168–70. In 821 the rebel Thomas the Slav succeeded in penetrating the Golden Horn with his fleet but he was ultimately unable to take Constantinople: John Skylitzes, *Synopsis historiarum*, ed. J. Thurn (Berlin, 1973), pp. 33–4.

12 Choniates, p. 298; Robert of Clari, pp. 68, 95; Villehardouin, pp. 72–3; Phillips, *Fourth Crusade*, pp. 176–81.

13 Choniates, p. 298; Villehardouin, p. 71; Thomas F. Madden, 'The fires of the Fourth Crusade in Constantinople, 1203–1204: a damage assessment', *BZ*, 84–5 (1991–2), pp. 72–3, at 73–4.

14 Choniates, pp. 299, 301–4, 333–4.

15 Ibid., p. 302; Villehardouin, pp. 50, 75–6.

16 Choniates, pp. 302, 305–6.

17 Ibid., p. 303.

18 Villehardouin, p. 79; Madden, 'Fires', pp. 74–84.

19 Villehardouin, p. 77.

20 Choniates, pp. 307–9; Villehardouin, p. 84.

21 Robert of Clari, pp. 88–91; Choniates, p. 312; Villehardouin, pp. 85–6; Robert Lee Wolff, 'Footnote to an incident of the Latin occupation of Constantinople: the church and the icon of the Hodegetria', *Traditio*, 6 (1948), pp. 319–28.

22 Villehardouin, pp. 90–1; Robert of Clari, pp. 70–1, 95–100. For a detailed account of the siege of April 1204, see Phillips, *Fourth Crusade*, pp. 235–57.

23 Choniates, pp. 313–14; Villehardouin, p. 91; Gunther of Pairis, *The Capture of Constantinople*, trans. A. J. Andrea (Philadelphia, 1997), pp. 107–8.

24 Choniates, p. 322; Villehardouin, pp. 92–3; Phillips, *Fourth Crusade*, pp. 258–80.

25 Choniates, pp. 315, 357; Ruy Gonzalez Clavijo, *Embassy to Tamerlane*, trans. G. Le Strange (London, 1928), p. 65; Gunther of Pairis, pp. 109–12; Villehardouin, p. 92; Christopher G. Ferrard, 'The amount of Constantinopolitan booty in 1204', *Studi Veneziani*, 13 (1971), pp. 95–104, at 104.

[26] Angold, *Fourth Crusade*, p. 236; W. G. Brokkaar, 'Basil Lecapenus: Byzantium in the tenth century', in *Studia Byzantina et Neohellenica Neerlandica*, ed. W. F. Bakker, A. F. van Gemert and W. J. Aerts (Leiden, 1972), pp. 199–234, at 219; Jacqueline Lafontaine-Dosogne, 'L'art byzantin en Belgique en relation avec les croisades', *Revue Belge d'Archéologie et d'Histoire de l'Art*, 56 (1987), pp. 13–47.

[27] John Beckwith, *Early Christian and Byzantine Art* (2nd edn, Harmondsworth, 1979), pp. 210–13; Thomas F. Mathews, *The Art of Byzantium* (London, 1998), pp. 68–9, 130; Rodolfo Gallo, *Il Tesoro di San Marco e la sua storia* (Venice and Rome, 1967), pp. 9–13, 133–55 and plates 28, 32, 35, 37 and 39.

[28] G. L. Tafel and G. M. Thomas, *Urkunden zur älteren Handels- und Staatsgeschichte der Republik Venedig*, 3 vols (Vienna, 1856–7), i, pp. 444–52; Villehardouin, pp. 88, 94–7; Robert of Clari, pp. 91–2, 116–18; Choniates, p. 329.

[29] Choniates, p. 353; Robert L. Wolff, 'The Latin Empire of Constantinople, 1204–61', in *A History of the Crusades*, ed. K. M. Setton, 6 vols (Madison, WI, 1969–89), ii, pp. 187–233, at 203–4.

[30] Akropolites, p. 28.

[31] Wolff, 'Latin Empire', pp. 212–17.

[32] Ibid., pp. 190–2.

[33] Louise B. Robbert, 'Rialto businessmen and Constantinople, 1204–1261', *DOP*, 49 (1995), pp. 43–58, at 44, 56. The case for Venetian merchants still reaping rich profits from the Constantinople trade is made by David Jacoby, 'Venetian settlers in Latin Constantinople: rich or poor?', in David Jacoby, *Byzantium, Latin Romania and the Mediterranean* (Aldershot, 2001), No. VII; idem, 'The economy of Latin Constantinople, 1204–1261', in *Urbs Capta: The Fourth Crusade and its Consequences*, ed. A. E. Laiou (Paris, 2005), pp. 195–214. Even if Jacoby is right, however, one thing is clear: very little of the proceeds of Constantinople's trade was being invested in the infrastructure of the city under Latin rule.

[34] Wolff, 'Latin Empire', pp. 220–6; Robert L. Wolff, 'Mortgage and redemption of an emperor's son: Castile and the Latin Empire of Constantinople', *Speculum*, 29 (1954), pp. 45–84.

35 Alberic of Trois Fontaines, *Chronica*, ed. Paul Scheffer-Boichorst, *Monumenta Germaniae Historica. Scriptores*, 23 (Hannover, 1874), pp. 631–950, at 886; Gunther of Pairis, pp. 125–7; Francis Wormald, 'The rood of Bromholm', *Journal of the Warburg and Courtauld Institutes*, 1 (1937–8), pp. 31–45; Giles Constable, 'Troyes, Constantinople and the relics of St Helen in the thirteenth century', *Mélanges offerts à René Crozet* (Poitiers, 1966), pp. 1035–42.

36 Anonymous of Soissons, *Concerning the Land of Jerusalem and the Means by which Relics were Carried to this Church from the City of Constantinople*, in Andrea, *Contemporary Sources*, pp. 223–38, at 235.

37 Alberic of Trois Fontaines, p. 886; Anonymous of Soissons, p. 236; Angold, *Fourth Crusade*, p. 233.

38 Henry of Valenciennes, *Histoire de l'Empereur Henri de Constantinople*, ed. Jean Longnon (Paris, 1948), pp. 106–7; Robert of Clari, p. 112; Wolff, 'Mortgage and redemption', pp. 52–3; Angold, *Fourth Crusade*, pp. 236–40; George P. Majeska, *Russian Travelers to Constantinople in the Fourteenth and Fifteenth Centuries* (Washington, DC, 1984), pp. 34, 130, 222.

39 Robert of Clari, p. 126; Wolff, 'Footnote', pp. 320–1.

40 Choniates, pp. 357–62. In general, see Anthony Cutler, 'The *De Signis* of Nicetas Choniates: a reappraisal', *American Journal of Archaeology*, 72 (1968), pp. 113–18.

41 L. Vlad Borelli and A. Guidi Toniato, 'The origins and documentary sources of the horses of San Marco', in *The Horses of San Marco*, ed. Guido Perocco, trans. J. and V. Wilton-Ely (London, 1979), pp. 127–36; Thomas F. Madden, 'The Serpent Column of Delphi in Constantinople: placement, purposes and mutilations', *BMGS*, 16 (1992), pp. 111–45, at 120–2; Pero Tafur, *Travels and Adventures, 1435–1439* (London, 1926), p. 143.

42 Robert L. Wolff, 'Hopf's so-called "fragmentum" of Marino Sanudo Torsello', *The Joshua Starr Memorial Volume* (New York, 1953), pp. 149–59, at 150–1; Robert L. Wolff, 'Politics in the Latin Patriarchate of Constantinople, 1204–1261', *DOP*, 8 (1954), pp. 228–303, at 278.

43 Alice-Mary Talbot, 'The restoration of Constantinople under Michael VIII', *DOP*, 49 (1993), pp. 243–61, at 247.

44 George Pachymeres, *Relations historiques*, ed. A. Failler, 5 vols (Paris, 1984–2000), i, pp. 174–7, 218–19; Majeska, *Russian Travelers*, pp. 142, 242–3; Talbot, 'Restoration', pp. 248, 250.

45 C. L. Striker and Y. D. Kuban, *Kalenderhane in Istanbul: The Buildings, their History, Architecture and Decoration* (Mainz, 1997), pp. 128–42; Andrea Arkel-de Leeuwvan Weenen and K. N. Ciggaar, 'St Thorlac's in Constantinople, built by a Flemish Emperor', *B*, 49 (1979), pp. 428–46 at 440; Talbot, 'Restoration', p. 247.

46 Gregoras, Nikephoros, *Byzantina Historia*, ed. L. Schopen and I. Bekker, 3 vols (Bonn, 1829–55), i, p. 8788; Choniates, pp. 313, 322; Villehardouin, pp. 91–2; Gunther of Pairis, p. 105; Madden, 'Fires', pp. 84–5, 88–9; Talbot, 'Restoration', p. 249.

Chapter 9

1 Niketas Choniates, *O City of Byzantium: Annals of Niketas Choniates*, trans. H. J. Magoulias (Detroit, 1984), pp. 333–4; George Akropolites, *Historia*, ed. A. Heisenberg and P. Wirth (Stuttgart, 1978), pp. 8–10; Gunther of Pairis, *The Capture of Constantinople*, trans. A. J. Andrea (Philadelphia, 1997), pp. 114–16; Geoffrey of Villehardouin, *The Conquest of Constantinople*, in *Chronicles of the Crusades*, trans. M. R. B. Shaw (Harmondsworth, 1963), pp. 29–160, at 98–9, 108–9.

2 Akropolites, pp. 12–16; Choniates, pp. 286–7, 339.

3 Akropolites, pp. 181–6.

4 Ibid., pp. 186–7; George Pachymeres, *Relations historiques*, ed. A. Failler, 5 vols (Paris, 1984–2000), i, pp. 194–206.

5 Akropolites, pp. 187–9; Pachymeres, i, pp. 216–18.

6 Pachymeres, i, pp. 254–8, 266–70, ii, pp. 332–55; Donald M. Nicol, *The Last Centuries of Byzantium, 1261–1453* (2nd edn, Cambridge, 1993), pp. 44–5.

7 Pachymeres, i, pp. 250–3; Cyril Mango, *The Art of the Byzantine Empire, 312–1453: Sources and Documents* (Englewood Cliffs, NJ, 1972), pp. 245–6; Alice-Mary Talbot, 'The restoration of Constantinople under Michael VIII', *DOP*, 49 (1993), pp. 243–61, at 249–51, 253, 258–60.

8 Talbot, 'Restoration', 251–5; Thomas F. Mathews, *The Art of Byzantium* (London, 1998), p. 159.

9 Pachymeres, iii, pp. 118–20; Majeska, *Russian Travelers*, pp. 39, 267–8.

10 Theodore Macridy, 'The Monastery of Lips and the burials of the Palaeologi', *DOP*, 18 (1964), pp. 253–77; Alice-Mary Talbot, 'Building activity in Constantinople under Andronikos II: the role of women patrons in the construction and restoration of monasteries', in *Byzantine Constantinople: Monuments, Topography and Everyday Life*, ed. Nevra Necipoğlu (Leiden, 2001), pp. 329–43, at 336–7.

11 Hans Belting, Cyril Mango and Doula Mouriki, *The Mosaics and Frescoes of St Mary Pammakaristos (Fethiye Camii) at Istanbul* (Washington, DC, 1978), pp. 11–22; Mathews, *Art of Byzantium*, p. 153.

12 Translation from N. G. Wilson, *Scholars of Byzantium* (2nd edn, London, 1996), pp. 256–7.

13 Mango, *Art of the Byzantine Empire*, pp. 246–7; Ihor Ševčenko, 'Theodore Metochites, the Chora, and the intellectual trends of his time', in *The Kariye Djami*, ed. Paul A. Underwood, 4 vols (Princeton, NJ, 1968–75), iv, pp. 19–91, at 31.

14 John Beckwith, *Early Christian and Byzantine Art* (2nd edn, Harmondsworth, 1979), pp. 315–19; Robert Ousterhout, *The Art of the Kariye Camii* (London, 2002), pp. 70–80.

15 George P. Majeska, *Russian Travelers to Constantinople in the Fourteenth and Fifteenth Centuries* (Washington, DC, 1984), pp. 28, 30, 216–20; Sir John Mandeville, *The Travels*, trans. C. W. R. D. Moseley (Harmondsworth, 1983), pp. 46–9.

16 Nikephoros Gregoras, *Byzantina Historia*, ed. L. Schopen and I. Bekker, 3 vols (Bonn, 1829–55), iii, pp. 841–2; Michael F. Hendy, *Studies in the Byzantine Monetary Economy, c. 300–1450* (Cambridge, 1985), pp. 161–4, 172, 513–36.

17 Nicol, *Last Centuries*, pp. 80–9, 122–47.

18 Ramon Muntaner, *The Catalan Expedition to the East: From the Chronicle of Ramon Muntaner*, trans. Robert D. Hughes (Woodbridge and Barcelona, 2006), pp. 46, 49.

19 Ševčenko, 'Metochites', pp. 30, 36.

20 Ibid., p. 89; Nicol, *Last Centuries*, pp. 160–1.

21   Gregoras, ii, p. 788.

22   Nicol, *Last Centuries*, pp. 241–6.

23   Ruy Gonzalez Clavijo, *Embassy to Tamerlane*, trans. G. Le Strange (London, 1928), p. 88.

24   Pero Tafur, *Travels and Adventures, 1435–1439* (London, 1926), p. 145.

25   Majeska, *Russian Travelers*, pp. 32–4.

26   Mandeville, *Travels*, p. 46.

27   John Kananos, *De Constantinopoli anno 1422 oppugnata narratio*, ed. I. Bekker (Bonn, 1838), pp. 472–8; Doukas, *Decline and Fall of Byzantium to the Ottoman Turks*, trans. H. J. Magoulias (Detroit, 1975), p. 226; Tafur, pp. 141–2; Clavijo, pp. 84–5; Nicol, *Last Centuries*, pp. 302, 333.

28   Doukas, pp. 201–2; Michael Kritoboulos, *History of Mehmed the Conqueror*, trans. C. T. Rigg (Princeton, NJ, 1954), pp. 14–15.

29   George Sphrantzes, *The Fall of the Byzantine Empire*, trans. M. Philippides (Amherst, MA, 1980), p. 69.

30   *The Russian Primary Chronicle: The Laurentian Text*, ed. and trans. S. H. Cross and O. P. Sherbowitz-Wetzor (Cambridge, MA, 1953), p. 64.

31   Kritoboulos, p. 45.

32   Ibid., pp. 58–60; A. A. Vasiliev, 'Medieval ideas of the end of the world: west and east', *B*, 16 (1942–3), pp. 462–502, at 497–8.

33   Kritoboulos, pp. 72–4. The classic account of the siege remains Steven Runciman, *The Fall of Constantinople, 1453* (Cambridge, 1965).

34   Doukas, p. 240.

35   Ibid., pp. 215, 224–5.

36   Kritoboulos, p. 77.

37   Doukas, p. 231; H. Inalcik, 'The policy of Mehmed II towards the Greek population of Istanbul and the Byzantine buildings of the city', *DOP*, 23–4 (1969–70), pp. 231–49.

38   Kritoboulos, p. 27.

39   Ibid., p. 140; Ken Dark and Ferudun Özgümüs, 'New evidence for the Byzantine church of the Holy Apostles from Fatih Camii, Istanbul', *Oxford Journal of Archaeology*, 21 (2002), pp. 393–413, at 394–5.

40 Doukas, p. 244; Steven Runciman, *The Great Church in Captivity* (Cambridge, 1968), pp. 187–9.

41 Belting, Mango and Mouriki, *Mosaics and Frescoes of St Mary Pammakaristos*, p. 36; Runciman, *Great Church*, pp. 184–5, 190.

42 Demetrius Cantemir, *History of the Growth and Decay of the Othman Empire*, trans. N. Tindal (London, 1734), p. 105; Runciman, *Great Church*, p. 191.

43 Kritoboulos, pp. 140, 149; Pierre Gilles, *The Antiquities of Constantinople*, trans. John Ball (London, 1729), pp. 245–6.

44 Gilles, pp. 129–30, 193–4, 250–4; E. H. Freshfield, 'Notes on a vellum album containing some original sketches of public buildings and monuments, drawn by a German artist who visited Constantinople in 1574', *Archaeologia* 72 (1921–2), 87–104; *Preliminary Report of the Excavations Carried Out in the Hippodrome of Constantinople in 1927 on Behalf of the British Academy* (London, 1928), pp. 19–20.

45 Khoja Sa'd-Ud-Din, *The Capture of Constantinople from the Taj-Ut-Tevarikh*, trans. E. J. W. Gibb (Glasgow, 1879), p. 33; Fynes Moryson, *An Itinerary*, 4 vols (Glasgow, 1907–8), ii, p. 94; Lady Mary Wortley Montagu, *The Complete Letters*, ed. Robert Halsband, 3 vols (Oxford, 1965–7), i, pp. 398–9; Runciman, *Great Church*, p. 188.

46 Ogier Ghiselin de Busbecq, *The Turkish Letters*, trans. E. S. Forster (Oxford, 1977), p. 45.

47 Gilles, pp. 110–12; Alexander van Millingen, *Byzantine Constantinople: The Walls of the City and Adjoining Historical Sites* (London, 1899), pp. 270–3. I have been unable to substantiate the claim that the Hercules of Lysippus was still in Constantinople in the sixteenth century: Anthony Cutler, 'The *De Signis* of Nicetas Choniates: A Reappraisal', *American Journal of Archaeology*, 72 (1968), pp. 113–18, at 117.

48 George Sandys, *A Relation of a Journey Begun in An. Dom. 1610* (London, 1632), p. 31.

49 Ibid., pp. 31–6.

50 Gilles, pp. 12, 283.

Chapter 10

[1] Ruy Gonzalez Clavijo, *Embassy to Tamerlane*, trans. G. Le Strange (London, 1928), p. 89; Demetrius John Georgacas, 'The names of Constantinople', *Transactions and Proceedings of the American Philological Society*, 78 (1947), pp. 347–67, at 336–67.

[2] Michael Psellos, *Fourteen Byzantine Rulers*, trans. E. R. A. Sewter (2nd edn, Harmondsworth, 1966), p. 72; Louis Robert, 'Théophane de Mytilène à Constantinople', *Comptes Rendus de l'Académie des Inscriptions et Belles Lettres* (1969), pp. 42–64, at 52, 56; Ken Dark and Ferudun Özgümüş, 'The last Roman imperial palace? Rescue archaeology in Istanbul', *Minerva*, 12.4 (2001), pp. 52–5, at 53; Ken Dark, 'The Byzantine church and monastery of St Mary Peribleptos in Istanbul', *Burlington Magazine*, 141 (1999), pp. 656–64.

[3] See The Guardian Unlimited: http://www.guardian.co.uk/international/story/o,,1694106,00.html

[4] There is also an excellent website that reconstructs the monuments of Constantinople as they would have appeared in 1200: www.byzantium1200.com

[5] John Freely and Ahmet S. Çakmak, *The Byzantine Monuments of Istanbul* (Cambridge, 2004), pp. 49–54.

[6] Freely and Çakmak, pp. 63, 73–4, 253–5; Alexander van Millingen, *Byzantine Constantinople: The Walls of the City and Adjoining Historical Sites* (London, 1899), pp. 131–53.

[7] Robert Ousterhout, *The Art of the Kariye Camii* (London, 2002), pp. 15–16; Freely and Çakmak, pp. 269–77.

[8] Ken Dark and Ferudun Özgümüş, 'New evidence for the Byzantine church of the Holy Apostles from Fatih Camii, Istanbul', *Oxford Journal of Archaeology*, 21 (2002), pp. 393–413, at 394–5.

[9] A. A. Vasiliev, 'Imperial porphyry sarcophagi in Constantinople', *DOP*, 4 (1948), pp. 1–26.

[10] Pierre Gilles, *The Antiquities of Constantinople*, trans. John Ball (London, 1729), p. 175.

[11] Apparently, it was still intact in 1718: Lady Mary Wortley Montagu, *The Complete Letters*, ed. Robert Halsband, 3 vols (Oxford, 1965–7), i, p. 400.

[12] Freely and Çakmak, pp. 151–2.

13   *Murray's Hand-Book for Travellers in Constantinople, Brûsa and the Troad* (London, 1893), pp. 52–3; Freely and Çakmak, pp. 65–72.

14   A. H. S. Megaw, 'Notes on recent work of the Byzantine Institute in Istanbul', *DOP*, 17 (1963), pp. 333–71, at 335–64; Freely and Çakmak, pp. 211–20.

15   Freely and Çakmak, pp. 129–36.

16   Niketas Choniates, *O City of Byzantium: Annals of Niketas Choniates*, trans. H. J. Magoulias (Detroit, 1984), pp. 312–13; Freely and Çakmak, pp. 204–7.

17   Freely and Çakmak, pp. 264–9.

18   Ibid., pp. 136–44, 256–8.

19   Ibid., pp. 59–60, 146–51.

20   Ibid., pp. 164–7.

21   John Freely, *Blue Guide: Istanbul* (3rd edn, London, 1991), p. 176.

22   Van Millingen, *Byzantine Constantinople: The Walls*, pp. 273–4; *Preliminary Report of the Excavations Carried Out in the Hippodrome of Constantinople in 1927 on Behalf of the British Academy* (London, 1928), p. 19.

23   Thomas F. Mathews, *The Art of Byzantium* (London, 1998), pp. 148–50; John Beckwith, *Early Christian and Byzantine Art* (2nd edn, Harmondsworth, 1979), pp. 278–9.

24   Mathews, *Art of Byzantium*, p. 23; Sarah Bassett, *The Urban Image of Late Antique Constantinople* (Cambridge, 2004), p. 242.

25   Mathews, *Art of Byzantium*, p. 68; Robert Lee Wolff, 'Footnote to an incident of the Latin occupation of Constantinople: the church and the icon of the Hodegetria', *Traditio*, 6 (1948), pp. 319–28, at 326; Rodolfo Gallo, *Il Tesoro di San Marco e la sua storia* (Venice and Rome, 1967), pp. 133–55.

26   Hayford Pierce and Royall Tyler, 'A marble emperor roundel of the twelfth century', *DOP*, 2 (1941), pp. 3–9. A similar roundel in the collection of Dumbarton Oaks in Washington DC is thought to depict John II Komnenos: Mathews, *Art of Byzantium*, pp. 38–9.

Select Bibliography

Primary Sources

Agathias of Myrina, *The Histories*, trans. J. D. Frendo (Berlin and New York, 1975)

Akropolites, George, *Historia*, ed. A. Heisenberg and P. Wirth (Stuttgart, 1978)

Alberic of Trois Fontaines, *Chronica*, ed. Paul Scheffer-Boichorst, *Monumenta Germaniae Historica. Scriptores*, 23 (Hannover, 1874), pp. 631–950

Ammianus Marcellinus, *History*, trans. John C. Rolfe, 3 vols (Cambridge, MA, and London, 1935–9)

Anonymous, *Life of Constantine*, trans. Frank Beetham, in Samuel N. C. Lieu and Dominic Montserrat, *From Constantine to Julian: Pagan and Byzantine Views* (London and New York, 1996), pp. 97–146

Anonymous of Soissons, *Concerning the Land of Jerusalem and the Means by which Relics were Carried to this Church from the City of Constantinople*, in Alfred J. Andrea, *Contemporary Sources for the Fourth Crusade* (Leiden, 2000), pp. 223–38

Anthony, Archbishop of Novgorod, *Description des lieux-saints de Constantinople*, in *Itinéraires russes en orient*, ed. B. de Khitrowo (Geneva, 1889), pp. 85–111

Attaleiates, Michael, *Historia*, ed. W. Brunet de Presle and I. Bekker (Bonn, 1853)

Barker, Ernest, *Social and Political Thought in Byzantium from Justinian I to the Last Palaeologus* (Oxford, 1957)

Benjamin of Tudela, *The Itinerary*, trans. M. N. Adler (London, 1907)

Book of the Eparch, in E. H. Freshfield, *Roman Law in the Later Roman Empire* (Cambridge, 1938), pp. 3–50

Busbecq, Ogier Ghiselin de, *The Turkish Letters*, trans. E. S. Forster (Oxford, 1977)

Cameron, Averil and Herrin, Judith (ed.), *Constantinople in the Early Eighth Century: The Parastasis Syntomoi Chronikai* (Leiden, 1984)

Cantemir, Demetrius, *History of the Growth and Decay of the Othman Empire*, trans. N. Tindal (London, 1734)

Cassius Dio, *Roman History*, trans. E. Cary, 9 vols (Cambridge, MA, and London, 1914–27)

Choniates, Niketas, *O City of Byzantium: Annals of Niketas Choniates*, trans. H. J. Magoulias (Detroit, 1984)

Christopher of Mitylene, *Die Gedichte*, ed. Eduard Kurtz (Leipzig, 1903)

Chronicon paschale, 284–628 AD, trans. Michael Whitby and Mary Whitby (Liverpool, 1989)

Ciggaar, Krijnie N., 'Une description de Constantinople dans le Tarragonensis 55', *REB*, 53 (1995), pp. 117–40

Clavijo, Ruy Gonzalez, *Embassy to Tamerlane*, trans. G. Le Strange (London, 1928)

Comnena, Anna, *The Alexiad*, trans. E. R. A. Sewter (Harmondsworth, 1969)

Constantine VII Porphyrogenitos, *De ceremoniis aulae Byzantinae*, ed. J. Reisky, 2 vols (Bonn, 1829–30)

—, *De administrando imperio*, ed. G. Moravcsik, trans. R. J. H. Jenkins (Washington, DC, 1967)

—, 'Story of the Image of Edessa', trans. Bernard Slater and John Jackson, in Ian Wilson, *The Turin Shroud* (London, 1978), pp. 235–51

—, *Three Treatises on Imperial Military Expeditions*, ed. and trans. John F. Haldon (Vienna, 1990)

Dawes, Elizabeth and Baynes, Norman H., *Three Byzantine Saints* (2nd edn, Crestwood, NY, 1977)

Doran, Robert, *The Lives of Symeon Stylites* (Kalamazoo, MI, 1992)

Doukas, *Decline and Fall of Byzantium to the Ottoman Turks*, trans. H. J. Magoulias (Detroit, 1975)

Eadmer, *Liber Miraculorum S. Dunstani, Memorials of St Dunstan*, ed. William Stubbs (London, 1874)

Eunapius of Sardis, *Lives of the Philosophers, in* Philostratus and Eunapius, *The Lives of the Sophists*, trans. Wilmer Cave Wright (Cambridge, MA, and London, 1952), pp. 317–563

Eusebius of Caesarea,*Tricennial Oration*, in H. A. Drake, *In Praise of Constantine: A Historical Study and New Translation of Eusebius's Tricennial Orations* (Berkeley, CA, and Los Angeles, 1976), pp. 83–127

—, *Life of Constantine*, trans. Averil Cameron and Stuart Hall (Oxford, 1999)

Eustathios of Thessalonica, *The Capture of Thessaloniki*, trans. J. R. Melville-Jones (Canberra, 1988)

Evagrius Scholasticus, *The Ecclesiastical History*, trans. Michael Whitby (Liverpool, 2000)

Freshfield, E. H., 'Notes on a vellum album containing some original sketches of public buildings and monuments, drawn by a German artist who visited Constantinople in 1574', *Archaeologia* 72 (1921–2), 87–104

Fulcher of Chartres, *Chronicle*, trans. M. E. McGinty, in *The First Crusade: The Chronicle of Fulcher of Chartres and Other Source Materials*, ed. E. Peters (2nd edn, Philadelphia, 1998), pp. 47–101

Genesios, *On the Reigns of the Emperors*, trans. Anthony Kaldellis (Canberra, 1998)

Gilles (Gyllius), Pierre, *The Antiquities of Constantinople*, trans. John Ball (London, 1729)

Glykys, Michael, *Annales*, ed. I. Bekker (Bonn, 1836)

Gregoras, Nikephoros, *Byzantina Historia*, ed. L. Schopen and I. Bekker, 3 vols (Bonn, 1829–55)

Gregory the Cellarer, *The Life of Lazaros of Mt. Galesion: An Eleventh-Century Pillar Saint*, trans. Richard Greenfield (Washington, DC, 2000)

Grumel, V., 'Homélie de Saint Germain sur la délivrance de Constantinople', *REB*, 16 (1958), pp. 183–205

Gunther of Pairis, *The Capture of Constantinople*, trans. A. J. Andrea (Philadelphia, 1997)

Henry of Valenciennes, *Histoire de l'Empereur Henri de Constantinople*, ed. Jean Longnon (Paris, 1948)

Herodotus, *The Histories*, trans. A. D. Godley, 4 vols (Cambridge, MA, and London, 1920–5)

Jerome, *Chronicon*, ed. Rudolf Helm, Eusebius Werke 8 (Berlin, 1956)

John Lydus, *On Powers or the Magistracies of the Roman State*, ed. and trans. A. C. Bandy (Philadelphia, 1983)

John of Damascus, *On Holy Images*, trans. Mary H. Allies (London, 1898)

Justinian, *The Civil Law*, trans. S. P. Scott, 17 vols (Cincinnati, 1932)

Kananos, John, *De Constantinopoli anno 1422 oppugnata narratio*, ed. I. Bekker (Bonn, 1838)

Khoja Sa'd-Ud-Din, *The Capture of Constantinople from the Taj-Ut-Tevarikh*, trans. E. J. W. Gibb (Glasgow, 1879)

Kinnamos, John, *The Deeds of John and Manuel Comnenus*, trans. C. M. Brand (New York, 1976)

Kritoboulos, Michael, *History of Mehmed the Conqueror*, trans. C. T. Rigg (Princeton, NJ, 1954)

Legrand, Emile, 'Description des œuvres d'art et de l'église des Saints Apôtres de Constantinople: poème en vers iambiques par Constantin le Rhodien', *Revue des Etudes Grecques*, 9 (1896), pp. 32–65

Leo VI, *Les Nouvelles de Léon le sage*, ed. P. Noailles and A. Dain (Paris, 1944)

—, *Tactica sive de re militari liber*, in *Patrologia Graeca*, vol. 107, cols 669–1120

Leo the Deacon, *The History of Leo the Deacon: Byzantine Military Expansion in the Tenth Century*, trans. Alice-Mary Talbot and Denis F. Sullivan (Washington, DC, 2005)

The Letter of the Three Patriarchs to the Emperor Theophilos and Related Texts, ed. J. A. Munitiz, J. Chrysostomides, E. Harvalia-Crook and Ch. Dendrinos (Camberley, 1997)

'Life of St Theodosia of Constantinople', trans. Nicholas Constas, in *Byzantine Defenders of Images: Eight Saints' Lives in Translation*, ed. Alice-Mary Talbot (Washington, DC, 1998), pp. 1–7

Liudprand of Cremona, *The Embassy to Constantinople and Other Writings*, trans. F. A. Wright (London, 1993)

Majeska, George P., *Russian Travelers to Constantinople in the Four-teenth and Fifteenth Centuries* (Washington, DC, 1984)

Malalas, John, *The Chronicle*, trans. Elizabeth Jeffreys, Michael Jeffreys and Roger Scott (Melbourne, 1986)

Mandeville, Sir John, *The Travels*, trans. C. W. R. D. Moseley (Harmondsworth, 1983)

Mango, Cyril, *The Art of the Byzantine Empire, 312–1453: Sources and Documents* (Englewood Cliffs, NJ, 1972)

Marcellinus Comes, *The Chronicle of Marcellinus*, trans. B. Croke (Sydney, 1995)

Masudi, *The Meadows of Gold. The Abbasids*, trans. Paul Lunde and Caroline Stone (London and New York, 1989)

Mesarites, Nicholas, *Description of the Church of the Holy Apostles at Constantinople*, ed. and trans. Glanville Downey, in *Transactions of the American Philosophical Society*, 47 (1957), pp. 855–924

Minorsky, V., 'Marvazi on the Byzantines', *Annuaire de l'Institut de Philologie et d'Histoire Orientales et Slaves*, 10 (1950), pp. 455–69

Moryson, Fynes, *An Itinerary*, 4 vols (Glasgow, 1907–8)

Muntaner, Ramon, *The Catalan Expedition to the East: From the Chronicle of Ramon Muntaner*, trans. Robert D. Hughes (Wood-bridge and Barcelona, 2006)

Nicholas I, Patriarch of Constantinople, *Letters*, ed. and trans. R. J. H. Jenkins and L. G. Westerink (Washington, DC, 1973)

Nikephoros, *Short History*, ed. and trans. C. Mango (Washington, DC, 1990)

Odo of Deuil, *De profectione Ludovici VII in orientem*, ed. and trans. V. G. Berry (New York, 1948)

Pachymeres, George, *Relations historiques*, ed. A. Failler, 5 vols (Paris, 1984–2000)

Pausanias, *Description of Greece*, trans. W. H. S. Jones, 5 vols (Cambridge, MA, and London, 1918–35)

Philostorgius, *Kirchengeschichte*, ed. Joseph Bidez and Friedhelm Winkelmann (3rd edn, Berlin, 1981)

Pliny the Elder, *The Natural History*, trans. H. Rackham, W. H. S. Jones and D. E. Eicholz, 10 vols (Cambridge, MA, and London, 1938–62)

Polybius, *The Histories*, trans. W. R. Paton, 6 vols (Cambridge, MA, and London, 1922–7)

Procopius of Caesarea, *History of the Wars*, trans. H. B. Dewing and Glanville Downey, 5 vols (Cambridge, MA, and London, 1914–28)

—, *The Secret History*, trans. H. B. Dewing (Cambridge, MA, and London, 1935)

—, *The Buildings*, trans. H. B. Dewing (Cambridge, MA, and London, 1940)

Psellos, Michael, *Fourteen Byzantine Rulers*, trans. E. R. A. Sewter (2nd edn, Harmondsworth, 1966)

—, *Historia Syntomos*, ed. and trans. W. J. Aerts (Berlin and New York, 1990)

Ralph Coggeshall, *Chronicon Anglicanum*, ed. J. Stevenson (London, 1875)

Ralph de Diceto, *Opera Historica*, ed. William Stubbs, 2 vols (London, 1876)

Robert of Clari, *The Conquest of Constantinople*, trans. E. H. McNeal (Toronto, 1996)

The Russian Primary Chronicle: The Laurentian Text, ed. and trans. S. H. Cross and O. P. Sherbowitz-Wetzor (Cambridge, MA, 1953)

Rydén, Lennart, 'The Andreas Salos Apocalypse: Greek text, translation, and commentary', *DOP*, 28 (1974), pp. 199–261

Sandys, George, *A Relation of a Journey Begun in An. Dom. 1610* (London, 1632)

The Scriptores Historiae Augustae, trans. David Magie, 3 vols (Cambridge, MA, and London, 1930–2)

Skylitzes, John, *Synopsis historiarum*, ed. J. Thurn (Berlin, 1973)

Socrates Scholasticus, *Ecclesiastical History*, trans. E. Walford (London, 1844)

Sozomen, *Ecclesiastical History*, trans. E. Walford (London, 1846)

Sphrantzes, George, *The Fall of the Byzantine Empire*, trans. M. Philippides (Amherst, MA, 1980)

Stephen the Deacon, *La vie de Étienne le jeune*, trans. M.-F. Auzépy (Aldershot, 1997)

Stethatos, Niketas, *Un grand mystique Byzantin: vie de Syméon le Nouveau Théologien*, ed. I. Hausherr and G. Horn (Rome, 1928)

Stevenson, J., *Creeds, Councils and Controversies: Documents Illustrating the History of the Church, AD 337–461* (2nd edn, London, 1989)

Strabo, *Geography*, trans. H. L. Jones, 8 vols (Cambridge, MA, and London, 1917–32)

Sturluson, Snorri, *Heimskringla: Sagas of the Norse Kings*, trans. Samuel Laing (3rd edn, London, 1961)

Tacitus, *The Annals*, trans. John Jackson, 3 vols (Cambridge, MA, and London, 1931–7)

Tafel, G. and Thomas, G., *Urkunden zur älteren Handels- und Staatsgeschichte der Republik Venedig*, 3 vols (Vienna, 1856–7)

Tafur, Pero, *Travels and Adventures, 1435–1439*, trans. Malcolm Letts (London, 1926)

The Theodosian Code, trans. C. Pharr (Princeton, NJ, 1952)

Theophanes Confessor, *The Chronicle of Theophanes Confessor. Byzantine and Near Eastern History AD 284–813*, trans. C. Mango and R. Scott (Oxford, 1997)

Theophanes Continuatus, *Chronographia*, ed. I. Bekker (Bonn, 1838)

Thomas, J. P. and Hero, A. C., *Byzantine Monastic Foundation Documents: A Complete Translation of the Surviving Founders' Typika and Testaments*, 5 vols (Washington, DC, 2000)

Thucydides, *The Peloponnesian War*, trans. Charles Forster Smith, 4 vols (Cambridge, MA, and London, 1928–35)

Timotheus of Gaza, *On Animals*, trans. F. S. Bodenheimer and A. Rabinowitz (Paris and Leiden, 1949)

Tzetzes, John, *Epistulae*, ed. P. A. Leone (Leipzig, 1972)

Villehardouin, Geoffrey of, *The Conquest of Constantinople*, in *Chronicles of the Crusades*, trans. M. R. B. Shaw (Harmondsworth, 1963), pp. 29–160

William of Tyre, *A History of Deeds Done beyond the Sea*, trans. E. A. Babcock and A. C. Krey, 2 vols (New York, 1943)

Wortley Montagu, Lady Mary, *The Complete Letters*, ed. Robert Halsband, 3 vols (Oxford, 1965–7)

Zonaras, John, *Annales*, ed. M. Pinder and T. Büttner-Wobst, 3 vols (Bonn, 1841–97)

Zosimus, *New History*, trans. R. T. Riley (Canberra, 1982)

Secondary Works

Alexander, Paul J., 'The strength of empire and capital as seen through Byzantine eyes', *Speculum*, 37 (1962), pp. 339–57

Alexiou, Margaret, 'Literary subversion and the aristocracy in twelfth century Byzantium: a stylistic analysis of Timarion (ch. 6–10)', *BMGS*, 8 (1982–3), pp. 29–45

Allen, Pauline, 'The Justinianic plague', *B*, 49 (1979), pp. 5–20

Angold, Michael, 'Inventory of the so-called Palace of Botaneiates', in *The Byzantine Aristocracy, IX–XIII Centuries*, ed. Michael Angold (Oxford, 1984), pp. 254–66

—, *Church and Society in Byzantium under the Comneni, 1081–1261* (Cambridge, 1995)

—, *The Fourth Crusade* (Harlow, 2003)

Antoniadis-Bibicou, H., *Recherches sur les douanes à Byzance: l'Octava, le Kommerkion et les commerciaires* (Paris, 1963)

Arkel-de Leeuwvan Weenen, Andrea, and Ciggaar, K. N., 'St Thorlac's in Constantinople, built by a Flemish emperor', *B*, 49 (1979), pp. 428–46

Balard, Michel, 'Amalfi et Byzance (Xe–XIIe siècles)', *Travaux et Mémoires*, 6 (1976), pp. 85–95

Barnes, Timothy D., *Constantine and Eusebius* (Cambridge, MA, and London, 1981)

Bassett, Sarah, *The Urban Image of Late Antique Constantinople* (Cambridge, 2004)

Battiscombe, C. F., *The Relics of St Cuthbert* (Oxford, 1956)

Baynes, Norman H., 'The finding of the Virgin's robe', in Norman H. Baynes, *Byzantine Studies and other Essays* (London, 1955), pp. 240–7

—, 'The supernatural defenders of Constantinople', in N. H. Baynes, *Byzantine Studies and Other Essays* (London, 1955), pp. 248–60

Beckwith, John, *Early Christian and Byzantine Art* (2nd edn, Harmondsworth, 1979)

Belting, Hans, *Likeness and Presence: A History of the Image before the Era of Art*, trans. Edmund Jephcott (Chicago, 1994)

Belting, Hans, Mango, Cyril and Mouriki, Doula, *The Mosaics and Frescoes of St Mary Pammakaristos (Fethiye Camii) at Istanbul* (Washington, DC, 1978)

Blöndal, Sigfús, *The Varangians of Byzantium* (Cambridge, 1978)

Bono, P., Crow, J. and Bayliss, R., 'The water supply of Constantinople: archaeology and hydrology of an early medieval city', *Environmental Geology*, 40 (2001), pp. 1325–33

Borelli, L. Vlad and Toniato, A. Guido, 'The origins and documentary sources of the horses of San Marco', in *The Horses of San Marco*, ed. Guido Perocco, trans. J. and V. Wilton-Ely (London, 1979), pp. 127–36

Brand, Charles M., *Byzantium Confronts the West, 1180–1204* (Cambridge, MA, 1968)

Brett, Gerard, 'The automata in the Byzantine "Throne of Solomon"', *Speculum*, 29 (1954), pp. 477–87

Brokkaar, W. G., 'Basil Lecapenus: Byzantium in the tenth century', in *Studia Byzantina et Neohellenica Neerlandica*, ed. W. F. Bakker, A. F. van Gemert and W. J. Aerts (Leiden, 1972), pp. 199–234

Brooks, E. W., 'The campaign of 716–718, from Arabic sources', *JHS*, 19 (1899), pp. 19–33

Browning, Robert, 'An unpublished funeral oration on Anna Comnena', *Proceedings of the Cambridge Philological Society*, 188 (1962), pp. 1–12

Bury, J. B., 'The Great Palace', *BZ*, 21 (1912), 210–25

Cameron, Alan, *Porphyrius the Charioteer* (Oxford, 1973)

Cameron, Averil, 'Images of authority: elites and icons in late sixth-century Byzantium', *Past and Present* 84 (1979), pp. 1–35

—, 'The exotic mirage', *The Times Higher Education Supplement*, 21 September 1990, pp. 13–15

—, *The Later Roman Empire* (London, 1993)

Charanis, Peter, 'The monk as an element of Byzantine society', *DOP*, 25 (1971), 63–84

Cheynet, Jean-Claude, *Pouvoir et contestations à Byzance (963–1210)* (Paris, 1990)

Chrysostomides, J., *Byzantine Women* (Camberley, 1994)

Ciggaar, Krijnie N., *Western Travellers to Constantinople: The West and Byzantium, 962–1204. Cultural and Political Relations* (Leiden, 1996)

Constable, Giles, 'Troyes, Constantinople and the relics of St Helen in the thirteenth century', *Mélanges offerts à René Crozet* (Poitiers, 1966), pp. 1035–42

Constantelos, Demetrios, *Byzantine Philanthropy and Social Welfare* (New Brunswick, NJ, 1968)

Cormack, Robin, *Writing in Gold: Byzantine Society and its Icons* (London, 1985)

Costa-Louillet, Germaine da, 'Saints de Constantinople aux VIIIe, IXe et Xe siècles', *B*, 24 (1954), pp. 179–264 and 25–7 (1955–7), pp. 783–852

Croke, Brian, 'Justinian's Constantinople', *in The Cambridge Companion to the Reign of Justinian*, ed. Michael Maas (Cambridge, 2005), pp. 60–86

Cutler, Anthony, 'The De Signis of Nicetas Choniates: a reappraisal', *American Journal of Archaeology*, 72 (1968), pp. 113–18

Dagron, Gilbert, *Naissance d'une capitale: Constantinople et ses institutions de 330 à 451* (Paris, 1974)

—, *Constantinople imaginaire: études sur le recueil des 'Patria'* (Paris, 1984)

—, 'The urban economy, seventh–twelfth centuries', in *The Economic History of Byzantium: From the Seventh through the Fifteenth Century*, ed. Angeliki E. Laiou, 3 vols (Washington, DC, 2002), ii, pp. 393–461

Dark, Ken, 'The Byzantine church and monastery of St Mary Peribleptos in Istanbul', *Burlington Magazine*, 141 (1999), pp. 656–64

—, 'Houses, streets and shops in Byzantine Constantinople from the fifth to the twelfth centuries', *Journal of Medieval History*, 30 (2004), pp. 83–107

—, and Özgümüş, Ferudun, 'The last Roman imperial palace? Rescue archaeology in Istanbul', *Minerva*, 12.4 (2001), pp. 52–5

—, 'New evidence for the Byzantine church of the Holy Apostles from Fatih Camii, Istanbul', *Oxford Journal of Archaeology*, 21 (2002), pp. 393–413

Day, Gerald W., *Genoa's Response to Byzantium, 1155–1204* (Urbana, IL, and Chicago, 1988)

Dennis, George T., 'The perils of the deep', *Novum Millennium: Studies on Byzantine History and Culture Dedicated to Paul Speck*, ed. Claudia Sode and Sarolta Takács (Aldershot, 2001), pp. 81–8

Doorninck, Frederick van, 'The Byzantine ship at Serçe Limanı: an example of small-scale maritime commerce with Fatimid Syria in the early eleventh century', in *Travel in the Byzantine World*, ed. Ruth Macrides (Aldershot, 2002), pp. 137–48

Downey, Glanville, 'Earthquakes at Constantinople and vicinity, AD 342–1454', *Speculum*, 30 (1955), pp. 596–600

—, 'The tombs of the Byzantine emperors in the church of the Holy Apostles in Constantinople', *JHS*, 79 (1959), pp. 27–51

Durand, J., *Le trésor de la Sainte Chapelle* (Paris, 2001)

Dvornik, Francis, *The Idea of Apostolicity in Byzantium and the Legend of the Apostle Andrew* (Cambridge, MA, 1958)

Ebersolt, Jean, *Le Grand Palais de Constantinople et le Livre des Cérémonies* (Paris, 1910)

El Cheikh, Nadia Maria, *Byzantium Viewed by the Arabs* (Cambridge, MA, 2004)

Emerson, William and van Nice, Robert L., 'Hagia Sophia: the collapse of the first dome', *Archaeology*, 4 (1951), pp. 94–103

Ferrard, Christopher G., 'The amount of Constantinopolitan booty in 1204', *Studi Veneziani*, 13 (1971), pp. 95–104

Foss, Clive and Winfield, David, *Byzantine Fortifications: An Introduction* (Pretoria, 1986)

Fowden, Garth, 'Constantine's porphyry column: the earliest literary allusion', *Journal of Roman Studies*, 81 (1991), pp. 119–31

Frazer, Margaret E., 'Church doors and the gates of paradise: Byzantine bronze doors in Italy', *DOP*, 27 (1973), pp. 147–62

Freely, John, *Blue Guide: Istanbul* (3rd edn, London, 1991)

— and Çakmak, Ahmet S., *The Byzantine Monuments of Istanbul* (Cambridge, 2004)

Gallo, Rodolfo, *Il Tesoro di San Marco e la sua storia* (Venice and Rome, 1967)

Georgacas, Demetrius John, 'The names of Constantinople', *Transactions and Proceedings of the American Philological Society*, 78 (1947), pp. 347–67

Goitein, S. D., *A Mediterranean Society: The Jewish Communities of the World as Portrayed in the Documents of the Cairo Geniza*, 6 vols (Berkeley, CA, 1967–93)

Greatrex, Geoffrey, 'The Nika riot: a reappraisal', *JHS*, 117 (1997), pp. 60–86

Grierson, Philip, 'The tombs and obits of the Byzantine emperors (337–1042)', *DOP*, 16 (1962), pp. 3–60

Haldon, John and Byrne, M., '*A possible solution to the problem of Greek Fire*', *BZ*, 70 (1977), pp. 91–9

Harris, Jonathan, *Byzantium and the Crusades* (London, 2003)

Harrison, Martin, *A Temple for Byzantium: The Discovery and Excavation of Anicia Juliana's Palace-Church in Istanbul* (London, 1989)

Harvey, Alan, *Economic Expansion in the Byzantine Empire, 900–1200* (Cambridge, 1989)

Hendy, M. F., 'Byzantium, 1081–1204: an economic reappraisal', *Transactions of the Royal Historical Society*, 5th series, 20 (1970), pp. 31–52

—, *Studies in the Byzantine Monetary Economy, c. 300–1450* (Cambridge, 1985)

Herrin, Judith, 'Blinding in Byzantium', *in Polypleuros Nous: Miscellanea für Peter Schreiner zu seinem 60 Geburtstag*, ed. Cordula Scholz and Georgios Makris (Munich and Leipzig, 2000), pp. 56–68

—, *Women in Purple: Rulers of Medieval Byzantium* (London, 2001)

Hill, Barbara, *Imperial Women in Byzantium* (Harlow, 1999)

Howard-Johnston, J. D., 'The siege of Constantinople in 626', in *Constantinople and its Hinterland: Papers from the Twenty-seventh Spring Symposium of Byzantine Studies, Oxford, April 1993*, ed. Cyril Mango and Gilbert Dagron (Aldershot, 1995), pp. 131–42

Inalcik, H., 'The policy of Mehmed II towards the Greek population of Istanbul and the Byzantine buildings of the city', *DOP*, 23–4 (1969–70), pp. 231–49

Jacoby, David, 'La population de Constantinople à l'époque byzantine: un problème de démographie urbaine', *B*, 31 (1961), pp. 81–109

—, 'The Jews of Constantinople and their demographic hinterland', in *Constantinople and its Hinterland: Papers from the Twenty-seventh Spring Symposium of Byzantine Studies, Oxford, April 1993*, ed. Cyril Mango and Gilbert Dagron (Aldershot, 1993), pp. 221–32

—, 'Italian privileges and trade in Byzantium before the Fourth Crusade: a reconsideration', *Anuario de Estudios Medievales*, 24 (1994), pp. 349–69

—, 'The Venetian quarter of Constantinople from 1082 to 1261: topographical considerations', *Novum Millennium: Studies on Byzantine History and Culture Dedicated to Paul Speck*, ed. Claudia Sode and Sarolta Takács (Aldershot, 2001), pp. 153–70

—, 'Venetian settlers in Latin Constantinople: rich or poor?', in David Jacoby, *Byzantium, Latin Romania and the Mediterranean* (Aldershot, 2001), No. VII

—, 'The economy of Latin Constantinople, 1204–1261', in *Urbs Capta: The Fourth Crusade and its Consequences*, ed. A. E. Laiou (Paris, 2005), pp. 195–214

James, Liz, '"Pray not to fall into temptation and be on your guard": pagan statues and Christian Constantinople', *Gesta*, 35 (1996), pp. 12–20

Janin, R., *Constantinople Byzantine* (2nd edn, Paris, 1964)

—, *La géographie ecclésiastique de l'empire byzantin: première partie: le siège de Constantinople et le patriarchat oecuménique. Tome III: les églises et les monastères* (2nd edn, Paris, 1969)

Jeffreys, Michael, 'The Comnenian Proskypsis', *Parergon*, 5 (1987), pp. 38–53

Jenkins, R. J. H., 'The bronze Athena at Byzantium', *JHS*, 67 (1947), pp. 31–3

—, and Mango, Cyril, 'The date and significance of the Tenth Homily of Photios', *DOP*, 9/10 (1956), pp. 125–40

Jones, A. H. M., *Constantine and the Conversion of Europe* (2nd edn, London, 1962)

Kalavrezou, Ioli, 'Helping hands for the empire: imperial ceremonies and the cult of relics at the Byzantine Court', in *Byzantine Court*

Culture from 829 to 1204, ed. Henry Maguire (Washington, DC, 1997), pp. 53–79

Karpozelos, A., 'Realia in Byzantine epistolography, X–XII Centuries', *BZ*, 77 (1984), pp. 20–37

Kazhdan, Alexander P., 'Eustathius of Thessalonica: the life and opinions of a twelfth century Byzantine rhetor', in *Studies on Byzantine Literature of the Eleventh and Twelfth Centuries*, ed. Alexander P. Kazhdan and Simon Franklin (Cambridge, 1984), pp. 115–95

—, '"Constantin imaginaire": Byzantine legends of the ninth century about Constantine the Great', *B*, 57 (1987), pp. 196–250

—, and Constable, Giles, *People and Power in Byzantium: An Introduction to Modern Byzantine Studies* (Washington, DC, 1982)

—, and Wharton Epstein, Ann, *Change in Byzantine Culture in the Eleventh and Twelfth Centuries* (Berkeley, CA, 1985)

Koder, J., 'Fresh vegetables for the capital', in *Constantinople and its Hinterland. Papers from the Twenty-seventh Spring Symposium of Byzantine Studies, Oxford, April 1993*, ed. Cyril Mango and Gilbert Dagron (Aldershot, 1995), pp. 49–56

Krautheimer, Richard, *Three Christian Capitals: Topography and Politics* (Berkeley, CA, Los Angeles and London, 1983)

Krivochéine, Basil, *In the Light of Christ. St Symeon the New Theologian: Life – Spirituality – Doctrine* (Crestwood, NY, 1986)

Kyriakis, Michael J., 'Poor poets and starving literati in twelfth-century Byzantium', *B*, 44 (1974), pp. 290–309

Lafontaine-Dosogne, Jacqueline, 'L'art byzantin en Belgique en relation avec les croisades', *Revue Belge d'Archéologie et d'Histoire de l'Art*, 56 (1987), pp. 13–47

Laiou, Angeliki E., 'Women in the marketplace of Constantinople (10th–14th centuries)', in *Byzantine Constantinople: Monuments, Topography and Everyday Life*, ed. Nevra Necipoğlu (Leiden, 2001), pp. 261–73

—, 'Exchange and trade, seventh–twelfth centuries', in *The Economic History of Byzantium: From the Seventh through the Fifteenth Century*, ed. Angeliki E. Laiou, 3 vols (Washington, DC, 2002), ii, pp. 697–770

Lange, Nicolas de, 'Byzantium in the Cairo Geniza', *BMGS*, 16 (1992), pp. 34–47

Lehmann, P. W., 'Theodosius or Justinian? A Renaissance drawing of a Byzantine rider', *Art Bulletin* 41 (1959), pp. 39–57

Lethaby, W. R. and Swainson, Harold, *The Church of Sancta Sophia, Constantinople: A Study of a Byzantine Building* (London and New York, 1894)

Liebeschuetz, J. H. W. G., *Barbarians and Bishops: Army, Church and State in the Age of Arcadius and John Chrysostom* (Oxford, 1990)

Littlewood, A. R., 'Gardens of the palaces', in *Byzantine Court Culture from 829 to 1204*, ed. Henry Maguire (Washington, DC, 1997), pp. 13–38

Lopez, R. S., 'Silk industry in the Byzantine Empire', *Speculum*, 20 (1945), pp. 1–42

Macrides, Ruth J., 'Constantinople: the Crusaders' gaze', in *Travel in the Byzantine World*, ed. Ruth Macrides (Aldershot, 2002), pp. 193–212

Macridy, Theodore, 'The Monastery of Lips and the burials of the Palaeologi', *DOP*, 18 (1964), pp. 253–77

—, and Casson, Stanley, '*Excavations at the Golden Gate, Constantinople*', *Archaeologia*, 81 (1931), pp. 63–84

Madden, Thomas F., 'The fires of the Fourth Crusade in Constantinople, 1203–1204: a damage assessment', *BZ*, 84–5 (1991–2), pp. 72–93

'The Serpent Column of Delphi in Constantinople: placement, purposes and mutilations', *BMGS*, 16 (1992), pp. 111–45

—, *Enrico Dandolo and the Rise of Venice* (Baltimore and London, 2003)

Magdalino, Paul, 'Manuel Komnenos and the Great Palace', *BMGS*, 4 (1978), pp. 101–14

—, 'The Byzantine holy man in the twelfth century', in *The Byzantine Saint*, ed. Sergei Hackel (London, 1981), pp. 51–66

—, 'Observations on the Nea Ekklesia of Basil I', *Jahrbuch der Österreichischen Byzantinistik*, 37 (1987), pp. 51–64

—, 'The grain supply of Constantinople, ninth to twelfth centuries', in *Constantinople and its Hinterland: Papers from the Twenty-seventh*

Spring Symposium of Byzantine Studies, Oxford, April 1993, ed. Cyril Mango and Gilbert Dagron (Aldershot, 1993), pp. 35–47

—, 'Constantinopolitana', in *Aetos: Studies in Honour of Cyril Mango*, ed. Ihor Ševčenko and Irmgard Hutter (Stuttgart and Leipzig, 1998), pp. 220–32

—, 'Medieval Constantinople: built environment and urban development', in *The Economic History of Byzantium: From the Seventh through the Fifteenth Century*, ed. Angeliki E. Laiou, 3 vols (Washington, DC, 2002), ii, pp. 529–37

Magdalino, Paul and Nelson, Robert, 'The emperor in Byzantine art of the twelfth century', *Byzantinische Forschungen*, 8 (1982), pp. 123–83

Mango, Cyril, *The Brazen House: A Study of the Vestibule of the Imperial Palace* (Copenhagen, 1959)

—, 'The Columns of Justinian and his successors', *Art Bulletin*, 41 (1959), pp. 1–16

—, 'Antique statuary and the Byzantine beholder', *DOP*, 17 (1963), pp. 55–75

—, *Byzantium: The Empire of the New Rome* (London, 1980)

—, 'Daily life in Byzantium', *Jahrbuch der Österreichischen Byzantinistik*, 31 (1981), pp. 337–53

—, *Le développement urbain de Constantinople (IVe–VIIe siècles)* (Paris, 1985)

—, 'The water supply of Constantinople', in *Constantinople and its Hinterland: Papers from the Twenty-seventh Spring Symposium of Byzantine Studies, Oxford, April 1993*, ed. Cyril Mango and Gilbert Dagron (Aldershot, 1993), pp. 9–18

—, 'The Triumphal Way of Constantinople and the Golden Gate', *DOP*, 54 (2000), pp. 173–88

—, and Parker, John, 'A twelfth-century description of St Sophia', *DOP*, 14 (1960), pp. 233–45

Mango, Marlia M., 'The commercial map of Constantinople', *DOP*, 54 (2000), pp. 189–207

—, 'The porticoed street at Constantinople', in *Byzantine Constantinople: Monuments, Topography and Everyday Life*, ed. Nevra Necipoğlou (Leiden, 2001), pp. 29–51

Maniatis, George C., 'Organization, market structure and modus operandi of the private silk industry in tenth century Byzantium', *DOP*, 53 (1999), pp. 263–332

—, 'The organizational setup and functioning of the fish market in tenth-century Constantinople', *DOP*, 54 (2000), pp. 13–42

—, 'The domain of private guilds in the Byzantine economy', *DOP*, 55 (2001), pp. 339–69

Martin, M. E., 'The Venetians in the Byzantine Empire before 1204', *Byzantinische Forschungen*, 13 (1988), pp. 201–14

Mathews, Thomas F., *The Art of Byzantium* (London, 1998)

Megaw, A. H. S., 'Notes on recent work of the Byzantine Institute in Istanbul', *DOP*, 17 (1963), pp. 333–71

Mercati, Giovanni, 'Gli aneddoti d'un codice bolognese', *BZ*, 6 (1897), pp. 126–43

Miller, Timothy, *The Birth of the Hospital in the Byzantine Empire* (2nd edn, Baltimore and London, 1997)

Millingen, Alexander van, *Byzantine Constantinople: The Walls of the City and Adjoining Historical Sites* (London, 1899)

Miranda, S., 'Études sur le palais sacré de Constantinople. Le Walker Trust et le Palais de Daphnè', *Byzantinoslavica*, 44 (1983), pp. 41–9, 196–204

Morgan, G., 'A Byzantine satirical song', *BZ*, 47 (1954), pp. 292–7

Morris, Rosemary, *Monks and Laymen in Byzantium, 843–1118* (Cambridge, 1995)

Morrisson, Cécile, 'Byzantine money: its supply and circulation', in *The Economic History of Byzantium: From the Seventh through the Fifteenth Century*, ed. Angeliki E. Laiou, 3 vols (Washington, DC, 2002), iii, pp. 909–66

Murray's Hand-Book for Travellers in Constantinople, Brûsa and the Troad (London, 1893)

Nicol, Donald M., 'Byzantine political thought', in *The Cambridge History of Medieval Political Thought c. 350 – c. 1450*, ed. J. H. Burns (Cambridge, 1988), pp. 51–79

—, *Byzantium and Venice: A Study in Diplomatic and Cultural Relations* (Cambridge, 1988)

—, *The Last Centuries of Byzantium, 1261–1453* (2nd edn, Cambridge, 1993)

Obolensky, Dimitri, *The Byzantine Commonwealth: Eastern Europe, 500–1453* (London, 1971)

Oikonomides, Nicolas, 'St George of Mangana, Maria Skleraina, and the "Malyjsion" of Novgorod', *DOP*, 34–5 (1980–1), pp. 239–46

Olster, David, 'Theodore Grammaticus and the Arab siege of 674–8', *Byzantinoslavica*, 56 (1995), pp. 23–8

Otten-Froux, Catherine, 'Documents inédits sur les Pisans en Romanie aux XIIIe–XIVe siècles', *in Les Italiens à Byzance*, ed. Michael Balard, Angeliki E. Laiou and Catherine Otten-Froux (Paris, 1987), pp. 153–95

Ousterhout, Robert, 'Architecture, art and Komnenian ideology at the Pantokrator Monastery', in *Byzantine Constantinople: Monuments, Topography and Everyday Life*, ed. Nevra Necipoğlu (Leiden, 2001), pp. 133–50

—, *The Art of the Kariye Camii* (London, 2002)

Papadaki-Oekland, Stella, 'The representation of Justinian's column in a Byzantine miniature of the twelfth century', *BZ*, 83 (1990), pp. 63–71

Papamastorakis, Titos, 'Tampering with history from Michael III to Michael VIII', *BZ*, 96 (2003), pp. 193–209

Partington, J. R., *A History of Greek Fire and Gunpowder* (Cambridge, 1960)

Paspates, A. G., *The Great Palace of Constantinople*, trans. William Metcalfe (London, 1893)

Pattenden, P., 'The Byzantine early warning system', *B*, 53 (1983), pp. 258–99

Pentcheva, Bissera V., 'The supernatural protector of Constantinople: the Virgin and her icons in the tradition of the Avar siege', *BMGS* 26 (2002), pp. 2–41

Phillips, Jonathan, *The Fourth Crusade and the Sack of Constantinople* (London, 2004)

Pierce, Hayford and Tyler, Royall, 'A marble emperor roundel of the twelfth century', *DOP*, 2 (1941), pp. 3–9

Polemis, Demetrios I., *The Doukai: A Contribution to Byzantine Prosopography* (London, 1968)

Preliminary Report of the Excavations Carried Out in the Hippodrome of Constantinople in 1927 on Behalf of the British Academy (London, 1928)

Reinert, Stephen W., 'The Muslim presence in Constantinople, 9th-15th centuries: some preliminary observations', *Studies on the Internal Diaspora of the Byzantine Empire*, ed. H. Ahrweiler and A. E. Laiou (Washington, DC, 1998), pp. 125–50

Robbert, Louise B., 'Rialto businessmen and Constantinople, 1204–1261', *DOP*, 49 (1995), pp. 43–58

Robert, Louis, 'Théophane de Mytilène à Constantinople', *Comptes Rendus de l'Académie des Inscriptions et Belles Lettres* (1969), pp. 42–64

Runciman, Steven, *The Fall of Constantinople, 1453* (Cambridge, 1965)

—, *The Great Church in Captivity* (Cambridge, 1968)

—, 'Blachernae Palace and its decoration', in *Studies in Memory of David Talbot Rice*, ed. Giles Robertson and George Henderson (Edinburgh, 1975), pp. 277–83

—, 'The country and suburban palaces of the emperors', in *Charanis Studies: Essays in Honor of Peter Charanis*, ed. Angeliki E. Laiou-Thomadakis (New Brunswick, NJ, 1980)

Rydén, Lennart, 'A note on some references to the church of St Anastasia in the tenth century', *B*, 44 (1974), pp. 198–201

—, 'The date of the Life of St Andrew Salos', *DOP*, 32 (1978), pp. 129–55

—, 'The holy fool', in *The Byzantine Saint*, ed. Sergei Hackel (London, 1981), pp. 106–13

Safran, Linda, 'Points of view: the Theodosian obelisk base in context', *Greek, Roman and Byzantine Studies*, 34 (1993), pp. 409–35

Scharf, Andrew, *Byzantine Jewry from Justinian to the Fourth Crusade* (London, 1971)

Ševčenko, Ihor, 'Theodore Metochites, the Chora, and the intellectual trends of his time', in *The Kariye Djami*, ed. Paul A. Underwood, 4 vols (Princeton, NJ, 1968–75), iv, pp. 19–91

—, 'Constantinople viewed from the Eastern Provinces in the middle Byzantine period', *Harvard Ukrainian Studies*, 3–4 (1979–80), pp. 712–47

Shepard, Jonathan, 'Constantinople – gateway to the north: the Russians', in *Constantinople and its Hinterland: Papers from the Twenty-seventh Spring Symposium of Byzantine Studies, Oxford, April 1993*, ed. Cyril Mango and Gilbert Dagron (Aldershot, 1993), pp. 243–60

Striker, C. L., *The Myrelaion (Bodrum Camii) in Istanbul* (Princeton, NJ, 1981)

—, and Kuban, Y. D., *Kalenderhane in Istanbul: The Buildings, their History, Architecture and Decoration* (Mainz, 1997)

Talbot, Alice-Mary, 'Old age in Byzantium', *BZ*, 77 (1984), pp. 267–78

—, 'The restoration of Constantinople under Michael VIII', *DOP*, 49 (1993), pp. 243–61

—, 'Building activity in Constantinople under Andronikos II: the role of women patrons in the construction and restoration of monasteries', in *Byzantine Constantinople: Monuments, Topography and Everyday Life*, ed. Nevra Necipoğlu (Leiden, 2001), pp. 329–43

Teall, John L., 'The grain supply of the Byzantine Empire, 330–1025', *DOP*, 13 (1959), pp. 87–139

Tougher, Shaun, 'Byzantine eunuchs: an overview, with special reference to their creation and origin', in *Women, Men and Eunuchs: Gender in Byzantium*, ed. Liz James (London, 1997), pp. 168–84

Treadgold, Warren, *A History of the Byzantine State and Society* (Stanford, CA, 1997)

Trilling, James, 'The soul of the empire: style and meaning in the mosaic pavement in the Byzantine imperial palace in Constantinople', *DOP*, 43 (1989), pp. 27–72

Tsangadas, Byron C. P., *The Fortifications and Defense of Constantinople* (New York, 1980)

Vasiliev, A. A., 'Harun-Ibn-Yahya and his description of Constantinople', *Annales de l'Institut Kondakov*, 5 (1932), pp. 149–63

—, 'The opening stages of the Anglo-Saxon immigration into Byzantium in the eleventh century', *Annales de l'Institut Kondakov*, 9 (1937), pp. 39–70

—, 'Medieval ideas of the end of the world: west and east', *B*, 16 (1942–3), pp. 462–502

—, 'Imperial porphyry sarcophagi in Constantinople', *DOP*, 4 (1948), pp. 1–26

Vryonis, Speros, 'Byzantine *Demokratia* and the guilds in the eleventh century', *DOP*, 17 (1963), pp. 289–314

Wharton Epstein, Ann, 'The rebuilding and decoration of the Holy Apostles in Constantinople: a reconsideration', *Greek, Roman and Byzantine Studies*, 23 (1982), pp. 79–92

Wilson, N. G., *Scholars of Byzantium* (2nd edn, London, 1996)

Wolff, Robert Lee, 'Footnote to an incident of the Latin occupation of Constantinople: the church and the icon of the Hodegetria', *Traditio*, 6 (1948), pp. 319–28

—, 'Hopf's so-called "fragmentum" of Marino Sanudo Torsello', in *The Joshua Starr Memorial Volume* (New York, 1953), pp. 149–59

—, 'Mortgage and redemption of an emperor's son: Castile and the Latin Empire of Constantinople', *Speculum*, 29 (1954), pp. 45–84

—, 'Politics in the Latin Patriarchate of Constantinople, 1204–1261', *DOP*, 8 (1954), pp. 228–303

—, 'The Latin Empire of Constantinople, 1204–61', in *A History of the Crusades*, ed. K. M. Setton, 6 vols (Madison, WI, 1969–89), ii, pp. 187–233

Wormald, Francis, 'The rood of Bromholm', *Journal of the Warburg and Courtauld Institutes*, 1 (1937–8), pp. 31–45

Websites

Byzantium 1200: www.byzantium1200.com

The Ecumenical Patriarchate of Constantinople: http://www. patriarchate.org/ecumenical_patriarchate/chapter_4/html/ holy_apostles.html

The Guardian Unlimited: http://www.guardian.co.uk/international/ story/o,,1694106,00.html

Index